THE NEW OXFORD HISTORY
OF ENGLAND

General Editor · J. M. ROBERTS

A Land of Liberty?

ENGLAND

1689–1727

JULIAN HOPPIT

OXFORD
UNIVERSITY PRESS

OXFORD
UNIVERSITY PRESS

Great Clarendon Street, Oxford OX2 6DP

Oxford University Press is a department of the University of Oxford.
It furthers the University's objective of excellence in research, scholarship,
and education by publishing worldwide in

Oxford New York

Auckland Bangkok Buenos Aires Cape Town Chennai
Dar es Salaam Delhi Florence Hong Kong Istanbul Karachi Kolkata
Kuala Lumpur Madrid Melbourne Mexico City Mumbai Nairobi
São Paulo Shanghai Singapore Taipei Tokyo Toronto

and associated companies in Berlin

Oxford is a registered trade mark of Oxford University Press
in the UK and in certain other countries

Published in the United States
by Oxford University Press Inc., New York

British Library Cataloguing in Publication Data

Data available

Library of Congress Cataloging-in-Publication Data

Hoppit, Julian.
England, 1689–1727 / Julian Hoppit.
p. cm. — (The new Oxford history of England)
Includes bibliographical references (p.   ) and index.
1. Great Britain—History—William and Mary, 1689–1702. 2. Great
Britain—History—Anne, 1702–1714. 3. Great Britain—History—George I, 1714–1727. 4.
England—Civilization—18th century. 5. England—Civilization—17th century. I. Title. II.
Series.
DA460 .H66 2000   941.06′8′092—dc21   00–026511

ISBN 0–19–822842–2 (hbk)
ISBN 0–19–925100–2 (pbk)

1 3 5 7 9 10 8 6 4 2

Typeset by Graphicraft Limited, Hong Kong
Printed in Great Britain
on acid-free paper by
T.J. International Ltd,
Padstow, Cornwall

TO MY PARENTS

General Editor's Preface

The first volume of Sir George Clark's *Oxford History of England* was published in 1934. Undertaking the General Editorship of a *New Oxford History of England* forty-five years later it was hard not to feel overshadowed by its powerful influence and well-deserved status. Some of Clark's volumes (his own among them) were brilliant individual achievements, hard to rival and impossible to match. Of course, he and his readers shared a broad sense of the purpose and direction of such books. His successor can no longer be sure of doing that. The building-blocks of the story, its reasonable and meaningful demarcations and divisions, the continuities and discontinuities, the priorities of different varieties of history, the place of narrative—all these things are now much harder to agree upon. We now know much more about many things, and think about what we know in different ways. It is not surprising that historians now sometimes seem unsure about the audience to which their scholarship and writing are addressed.

In the end, authors should be left to write their own books. None the less, the *New Oxford History of England* is intended to be more than a collection of discrete or idiosyncratic histories in chronological order. Its aim is to give an account of the development of our country in time. It is hard to treat that development as just the history which unfolds within the precise boundaries of England, and a mistake to suggest that this implies a neglect of the histories of the Scots, Irish, and Welsh. Yet the institutional core of the story which runs from Anglo-Saxon times to our own is the story of a state-structure built round the English monarchy and its effective successor, the Crown in Parliament, and that provides the only continuous articulation of the history of peoples we today call British. It follows that there must be uneven and sometimes discontinuous treatment of much of the history of those peoples. The state story remains, nevertheless, an intelligible thread and to me appears still to justify the title both of this series and that of its predecessor.

If the attention given to the other kingdoms and the principality of Wales must reflect in this series their changing relationship to that central theme, this is not the only way in which the emphasis of individual volumes will be different. Each author has been asked to bring forward what he or she sees as the most important topics explaining the history under study, taking account of the present state of historical knowledge, drawing attention to areas of dispute and to matters on which final judgement is at present difficult (or, perhaps, impossible) and not merely recapitulating what has recently been the fashionable centre of professional debate. But each volume, allowing for its special approach and proportions, must also provide a comprehensive account, in which politics is always likely to be prominent. Volumes have to be demarcated chronologically but continuities must not be obscured; vestigially or not, copyhold survived into the 1920s and the Anglo-Saxon shires until the 1970s (some of which were to be resurrected in the 1990s, too). Any single volume should be an entry-point to the understanding of processes only slowly unfolding, sometimes across centuries. My hope is that in the end we shall have, as the outcome, a set of standard and authoritative histories, embodying the scholarship of a generation, and not mere compendia in which the determinants are lost to sight among the detail.

J. M. ROBERTS

Preface

This history of England in the period between the Glorious Revolution and the accession of George II has been written for 'general' readers, a protean and chimerical audience to be sure. To whet and sate its appetite I have written an overview from many perspectives, aiming to depict the period's main events and structures, continuities and changes, vitality and variety, peculiarities and familiarities. That said, though the book contains plenty of information it has been conceived neither as a comprehensive textbook (they are usually mythical) nor, because it has been written to be read, as a work of reference. Above all else it attempts to evoke the spirit of the age, conforming to the view that 'English textbook writers are really essayists, interpreters, and commentators.'[1]

I have outlined in Chapter 1 many of the main features of this extraordinary period of England's history and of how I have come to understand and write about them. But if this book is a very personal view it is of course much more than mine alone, resting as it does on the labours and generosity of many others. That dependence has been all the greater because this is certainly not the distillation of a lifetime's study of England between 1689 and 1727. My background as a historian of England's economy and legislature between 1660 and 1800 may have given me a sense of broad developments within this period, but it left me poorly prepared in other ways. It has been my good fortune, therefore, to have been helped into the intricacies of late seventeenth and early eighteenth-century England by many friends and colleagues, among them Tony Claydon, Tim Hitchcock, Henry Horwitz, Clyve Jones, and Jonathan Scott. Others have helped very directly. Stuart Handley and Andrew Hanham of the 1690–1715 House of Commons section of the History of Parliament kindly made available valuable unpublished material. I owe a particular debt to John Morrill who helped me get going and whose friendship encouraged me to keep going. Paul Langford, the author of the succeeding volume in this series, was generous with good advice at an early stage and later Joanna Innes and Jon Parry were always available to talk through issues. Not the least of my debts is to the General Editor of the series, John Roberts, who has been constantly supportive and judiciously critical even as I assaulted him with my first drafts. Finally, I have been saved from many slips by comments on drafts by several friends—David Hayton, with extraordinary generosity and insight, considered

---

[1] B. Bailyn, *On the Teaching and Writing of History*, ed. E. C. Lathem (Hanover, New Hampshire, 1994), p. 21.

the complete manuscript and John Beattie, John Morrill, and Stephen Taylor particular chapters. Without their considerable efforts this book would have been worse still.

This book was largely researched at Cambridge University Library, perhaps the best library with extensive holdings on open access in the English-speaking world. I tried the patience of its staff sorely, especially in the Rare Books room, and never found it wanting. That the book was written at all was due in no small measure to the kindness of University College London and the British Academy/Humanities Research Board in providing me with two terms of research leave. I am also grateful to the History department at University College for making available a grant to cover the cost of some of the illustrations.

Many authors are consumed by their books and retain a sense of proportion only through the love, friendship, and kindness of others. No one has done more here than Karin Horowitz; my younger brother, his family, and Jon Parry also shine in this respect; and Martin Daunton, Ros Davies, Richard Fisher, Joanna Innes, and Peter Salt deserve special mention. Sadly Donald Coleman did not live to see this book, but his memory was often inspiring. Finally, but of course also first, are my parents.

July 1999   JULIAN HOPPIT

In this paperback edition I have taken the opportunity to correct minor errors. I am grateful to my father, friends and colleagues for pointing out many of these.

Contents

Plates

Figures, Maps, and Tables

Acknowledgements to the Illustrations

Plates 3, 4, 5, 8, 10, 18, 20, and 21 are copyright British Museum; plate 2 by permission The Pepys Library, Magdalene College, Cambridge; plate 11 by courtesy of the Royal Astronomical Society Archives; plate 13 by permission of The Provost and Fellows, Worcester College, Oxford; plates 7, 16, and 17 by permission of Cambridge University Library; plates 1, 6, 9, 12, 14, 15, and 19 by permission of the Guildhall Library, Corporation of London.

Note on the text

In this period England employed the 'old style' Julian calendar, which before 1700 was 10 days and from 1700 11 days behind the Gregorian calendar usually used in Europe. Dates are given in old style unless otherwise stated, though the new year is taken to begin on 1 January not, as was common contemporary practice, on 25 March. I have reproduced quotations exactly as in the sources cited, allowing all the peculiarities of capitalization, italicization, spelling, and grammar to shine through. Footnotes mainly provide references to quotations or brief biographical summaries; place of publication is London unless indicated otherwise. The Bibliography provides a guide to some of the secondary literature behind the book.

CHAPTER I

England after the Glorious Revolution

A general history of any nation for a specific period involves particular artifice, for a pair of terminal dates are unlikely to serve all of its parts equally well. Historians have indeed long recognized the benefits of thinking of a period's many histories unfolding at different speeds, with their continuities and changes often being only loosely connected. So, for example, the histories of government, war, work, and consumption may interlock, but they also have their own trends and turning points, rhythms and melodies. Yet though this means that the chronological limits of this book must be porous, they are not equally so, for the period's histories are urged on by the unfolding implications of the Glorious Revolution of 1688–9 much more than they are lured to a close by the death of George I in 1727.

If many aspects of England's history in the late seventeenth and early eighteenth century were untroubled by either the accession as joint monarchs of William III and Mary II in 1689 (the culmination of the Glorious Revolution) or the death of George I, it is also true that the monarchical succession in this period influenced society at large to an unusual degree. At heart this was because in December 1688 James II (Mary's father), his Queen, and infant Prince fled to France in the face of a massive foreign army headed by William, the Dutch Stadholder. The invasion and the flight were dramatic enough, but they reverberated and resonated down to the middle of the eighteenth century because of the complex nature of the Glorious Revolution and because neither James II nor his legitimate heirs renounced their claim to the throne. Far from the Glorious Revolution solving England's problems and ushering in a period of calm assurance and inexorable progress, it provoked many anxieties and insecurities, divisions and disorders. Only slowly did England come to terms with what had happened. But a second less apparent, yet no less significant source of change, was also unsettling people's lives— slow if erratic economic growth. In agriculture, industry, and trade (internal and overseas) output and productivity inched ahead. If such progress was often overlooked by contemporaries, they were vividly aware of some of its manifestations: England's increasing dependence upon an expanding and frequently predatory commercial empire; marked social and geographical mobility; the growing pursuit of pleasure; and, pre-eminently, urbanization. But like the Glorious Revolution contemporaries were struck not only by the positive aspects of these changes, but by the challenges they posed, more than anything bemoaning the uncertainties that surrounded them.

AN ANXIOUS AGE

In 1689 England was well used to times of troubles. 'This Fire of Contention, for at least an hundred Years, hath sometimes been kept smothering in, and sometimes *Vesuvius* like hath burst out into such Flames, as have endanger'd the whole Country round about.'[1] Many well remembered the nation being torn apart in the 1640s by civil war and regicide and in the 1650s by Oliver Cromwell's republican experiment. The Restoration of Charles II in 1660 failed to settle matters, for after a brief honeymoon terrible tensions reappeared between the Crown, Church, Parliament, and people. Nor did the Glorious Revolution—the Dutch invasion, James's flight, and the accession of William and Mary—ease matters. If anything it made them worse. Old stresses between the King and Parliament, Church and Dissent, appeared to be undiminished and were joined by bitter divisions over the succession (involving rebellion and war in Ireland and Scotland, Union between England and Scotland, and plots, riots, and insurrection in England) and two protracted, costly, and bloody wars on the continent. So when in 1703 the Bishop of Salisbury wrote to Sophia Electress of Hanover, Queen Anne's designated successor, even he, an enthusiast for the Glorious Revolution, felt duty bound to warn that "Tis now a full hundred years that we have been fluctuating *from one expedient to another*'.[2]

Central to the anxieties of this period was the difficulty of establishing a generally agreed relationship between politics and religion. James II had been widely resented because he was a Roman Catholic King to an overwhelmingly Protestant nation, which many likened to a free people being subject to an enslaver. That such resentment was felt even by those who were politically highly conservative meant that after James's flight many saw no need to alter constitutional fundamentals. Yet such fundamentals did change. In particular in 1689 a limited toleration was granted to Protestant Dissenters from the established Church of England, finally shattering the façade of orthodoxy's

---

[1] 'The Unprejudic'd Laymens Free Thoughts on the Subject the Convocation are Upon' [1690], in *A Collection of State Tracts, Publish'd on Occasion of the Late Revolution in 1688. And During the Reign of King William III*, 3 vols. (1705–7), vol. 1, p. 666.

[2] G. Burnet, *A Memorial Offered to Her Royal Highness the Princess Sophia, Electoress and Duchess Dowager of Hanover. Containing a Deliniation of the Constitution and Policy of England* (1815), p. 39.

hegemony and provoking concerns that the Church was in danger, concerns which, heightened by William III's Calvinism and George I's Lutheranism, lasted for a full generation.[3] Outside the Church scholarship was increasingly questioning traditional landmarks, from Newton's work on gravity to detailed textual criticism of the Bible. Even within the Church the increasing willingness of some to challenge traditional theology eroded old certainties. For many this was all too much and, drawing on the lessons of the rule of the saints in the 1650s, such heterodoxy was often damned as the handmaiden of disunity, chaos, and atheism. Through the period there were frequent and vociferous complaints that immorality and irreligion was sweeping the nation: drunks and Dissenters, prostitutes and pamphleteers, actors and activists might all be censured. Anxiety bred censoriousness, uncertainty a vivid paranoia.

The question of the succession was the second major source of uncertainty in this period. Though many were relieved to see William and Mary replace James some saw it as a catastrophe. Critics of the Glorious Revolution decried it for meddling in God's order or for threatening their fundamental interests. Domestically many retained their allegiance to James and his son, with some actively working for a restoration. Scheming, secrecy, and sedition were pervasive, Jacobite plots and risings ever threatening. Moreover, the succession question was much more than a purely national issue. Within the British Isles it led England to impose her will on both Ireland and Scotland, the legacy of which is still felt. In Ireland a Roman Catholic majority saw James as a potential saviour from Protestant dictators; but he was defeated in battle and the Roman Catholic majority subjected to the Protestant ascendancy's so-called 'Penal laws' (even if in practice they might be circumvented). In Scotland James had fewer supporters, but as a descendant of her own Stewart royal family he was vital to national identity, leading to an attempt to break away from English thinking on the succession after the question was revived in 1700. The breakaway made little progress. The Union of 1707 involved the abolition of the Edinburgh Parliament and after the failure of the Jacobite rising of 1715–16 parts of the Highlands were militarized.

Jacobitism was in fact also a powerful pawn in the European balance of power, helping to draw Britain into war against France and Spain, and into periodic breakdowns in her relations with a number of other nations. Indeed, one of the most important consequences of the Dutch invasion of 1688 was that it decisively involved England in European affairs, especially in the Nine Years War (1689–97) and the War of the Spanish Succession (1702–13). War is always full of uncertainty and these two, largely waged against France, the

[3] The Church of England is conveniently often referred to as the 'Anglican Church', though this label was not used in this period.

greatest power of the day, were particularly so. It was not merely that battles were won and lost, but that at times the burden upon domestic resources produced a chaos that many found hard to bear. A crisis in the domestic coinage in 1696, the ravages of privateers upon overseas trade, and unprecedented levels of taxation and mobilization were felt by all. Not the least challenge was that to pay for huge armies and navies a permanent national debt was erected on the security of heightened parliamentary taxation. England may have hoped that the flight of James II had rid it of the threat of kingly absolutism, but because of this 'financial revolution' it found itself governed by an increasingly powerful State. But it was also an experimental State, capable of both great achievements and enormous blunders, notably the catastrophe that enveloped public and private credit with the bursting of the South Sea Bubble in 1720.

If few doubted that the great wars against France were just, many questioned the treaties, strategies, and sacrifices they entailed. The most enduring anxiety was whether the wars were producing domestic changes threatening the very society the nation had gone to war to defend. Some worried that the financial revolution entailed moving wealth from countryside to town and from landowner to businessman, profoundly unsettling the traditional order and threatening a new distribution of power. In this view, bankers, stockjobbers, and contractors had succeeded in achieving a social revolution where James II had failed. But such disquiet was, in practice, partly consequent upon longer term changes associated with broadly based economic growth. England in 1700 was at the centre of the long transition from the early modern to the modern world. If its population was stagnant, agriculture, industry, and commerce were all enjoying some slow growth. Though this aided employment and income, growth was very slow, easily allowing pessimists to seize upon the supposed costs involved: dislocation of the customary economy, erosion of hospitality, growing idleness, increasing luxuriousness, heightened social mobility, and greater social disorder in towns. Moreover, if the economy was growing stronger it was still liable to profound dislocations. In the 1690s many harvests failed, leading to widespread hardship; war dislocated trade, heightened taxes, and removed the main breadwinner from many families; and with the economy becoming increasingly involved in international trade it was further prey to the uncertainties of pirates, rocks, trade winds, and distant correspondents. All told, it is hardly surprising that some wondered 'what is human Life but a Scene of Trouble and Sorrow, where is a Succession of Evils and Miseries, like the restless Waves of the Sea, rolling on the neck of one another?'[4]

---

[4] J. Filkes, *A Funeral Sermon Preach'd upon the Death of Samuel Wright of Daventry, Gent.* (1712), p. 6.

And so, even a generation after the Glorious Revolution, some believed that uncertainties and insecurities abounded because the nation had been unable to solve old problems and had been entrapped by new ones. Even if some of these anxieties were imagined rather than real, self-interested rather than general, because they were felt in so many different ways they had a pervasive influence. In particular, pessimism was a breeding ground for the fractious and factious. In town and countryside social tension sometimes boiled over, in politics the contest for power was at fever pitch—party politics became the norm and society at large highly politicized. It was little wonder that the age produced great satires, that irony was a common weapon, or that the jeremiad was one of the era's characteristic voices:

a Nation which hath stood its ground, and kept its privileges and freedoms for Hundreds of Years, is in less than a Third of a Century, quite undone; hath lavishly spent above 160 Millions in that time, made Hecatombs of *British* Lives, stockjobb'd (*or canonaded*) away its Trade, perverted, and then jested away its Honour, Law, and Justice; burlesqu'd its Religion; disavow'd the Divinity of its Author, then banish'd it, and in the Room thereof, offer'd Sacrifice to an *Idol* of the *People's* setting up, which has produced Swarms of others of Monstrous Shapes, and Forms; compounded of the Dregs of all former Heresies, Sects, Schisms, and Rebellions; hatch'd from Incest, Whoredom, and Adultery; and all centring in Atheism, Anarchy, and Confusion.[5]

AN AGE OF PROSPECTS

Foreigners tended to take a far less gloomy view. Famously when Tsar Peter the Great undertook his 'western embassy' its focal point was the four months spent at Deptford in 1698, acquiring a familiarity of England's maritime abilities that led him to reckon 'it a much happier Life to be an Admiral in *England*, than *Czar* in *Russia*.'[6] He took back with him to Russia not just skills and gifts, but experts with which to reform his government and armed forces. Even twenty years later, Russian apprentices were being sent to the banks of the Thames to be trained. What was important here was not simply that England was judged a leading power worth emulating, but that initially at least she had the confidence to allow another country to exploit this expertise. Amidst the jeremiads there were, in fact, many who saw England as a favoured nation, moving out of its times of troubles into a brighter world of opportunities.

Few doubted that England had enormous natural potential. 'God hath planted us in a Serene, a Temperate and a Healthy Climate, free from the

[5] *A Computation of the Increase of London, and Parts Adjacent* (1719), p. 19. 'Hecatombs' was a great public sacrifice among the ancient Greeks and Romans.

[6] J. Perry, *The State of Russia, under the Present Czar* (1716), p. 164.

Terrors and Desolations of Earthquakes and *Volcano*'s; free from the frequent Annoyances of Plagues and Pestilences; in a rich and fertile Land, that plentifully yields all we can desire, not only for the Support, but for the Comforts and Delights of Life; and that in such Abundance, as affords Supplies, not only for its Nation, but for many Foreign Countries, and for a beneficial Commerce with the remotest Nations.'[7] England's fruitfulness and island situation made her, by such views, peculiarly able to exploit those commercial opportunities which, in a society unused to continuous technological development, provided the main hope of leaving hardship and want behind. 'Our *Foreign Trade* is now become the Strength and Riches of the Kingdom . . . and is the living Fountain from whence we draw all our Nourishment: It disperses that Blood and Spirits throughout all the Members, by which the Body Politick subsists'.[8] Though such mercantile capitalism had its exploitative side, notoriously in the expanding slave trade, real benefits were brought back to England. Favourable comparisons were often drawn between English prosperity and foreign poverty—foreigners were often struck by the ability of the poor to afford shoes and white bread. Moreover, it meant that England's horizons were growing. After a century of soul searching and looking inwards, the advantages of an expansiveness of spirit were now being seen. Colonial adventures in the West Indies and North America provided a safety valve for some of the tensions within England, extended the world of political obligations enormously, and brought home a dazzling array of new experiences. The order of things could not but change.

It was one thing to be blessed by God, another to reap the harvest. In so far as contemporaries explained this they put it down to the belief that the English enjoyed unparalleled liberty, allowing them to think innovatively and to exploit opportunities that came their way: '*England* is a Country of Liberty, every one lives there as he wishes'.[9] Freedom of speech, of worship, and of the press were all celebrated as never before, and the capacity for social mobility frequently observed. Such freedoms, even if overdrawn, were real enough. But the social flexibility they allowed was not only of economic significance, for it meant that there was a wider pluralism and heterodoxy. Toleration, accommodation, and compromise, even if reluctantly given, was central to everyday life. Whereas the jeremiads were erected on a false memory of national solidarity and mono-culturalism, there were many who enjoyed the variety of English life, from Protestant refugees escaping the intolerance of Louis XIV to alehouse pranksters

---

[7] E. Saunders, *A Discourse of the Dangers of Abusing the Divine Blessings . . . a Sermon Preach'd before the Honourable House of Commons . . . December the 8th, 1721* ([1721?]), p. 10.

[8] W. Wood, *A Survey of Trade* (1718), p. 4.

[9] B.-L. de Muralt, *Letters Describing the Character and Customs of the English and French Nations* (2nd edn., 1726), p. 2.

mocking their social superiors. In every sense England in this period was a medley, and one that many enjoyed. It was possible, therefore, to emphasize not social divisions, but rich diversity wedded to common identities and mutual interests. 'So far is it from being true, which Mr. *Hobbes* asserts . . . *That Men are naturally in a State of War and Enmity with one another*; that the Contrary *Principle*, laid down by . . . *Aristotle*, is most certainly true, *That Men are naturally akin and Friends to each other.*'[10]

The guarantee of England's freedoms was the rule of law and a balanced constitution that supposedly prevented particular interests from becoming over powerful. To its champions the Glorious Revolution had decisively established that achievement. Voltaire, in exile in London from 1726–9 (and who reckoned England 'the land of liberty'), thought she was the only nation 'on earth which has succeeded in controlling the power of kings by resisting them' and had established a 'wise system of government in which the prince . . . has his hands tied for doing evil, in which the aristocrats are great without arrogance and vassals, and in which the people share in the government without confusion.'[11] Much of this was puff, though even a Roman Catholic could declare that England's constitution 'undoubtedly is the best in the world', but there had been a decisive change in 1689 through the institutionalization of Parliament.[12] In the 1670s and 1680s both Charles II and James II had seen Parliament as an opponent rather than an ally or resource, and strove to rule without it: from 1679 to 1688 it met just five times, with the Commons conducting business for a total of only 171 days. After the Glorious Revolution all monarchs governed through it, if not always enthusiastically: from 1689 to 1698 it met eleven times and the Commons did business on nearly 1,300 days. Interests did not now fester, they were aired, debated, and weighed; even if bills and elections might be battlegrounds, Parliament was ultimately an arena of compromise. Nor were the effects of this merely felt in the conduct of 'high politics', for the availability of Parliament provided the nation at large with the legislative means of tackling particular problems. In that way stronger relations between centre and locality were forged and new political communities established that sometimes crossed traditional fault lines, even if only briefly. Such links were the more important because frequent parliaments were joined to frequent elections, encouraging and not closing off debate and the expression of alternative views of the public good. Parties may

[10] *The Works of the Most Reverend Dr John Tillotson, Lord Archbishop of Canterbury*, ed. T. Birch, 3 vols. (1752), vol. 1, p. 305.

[11] *Voltaire's Correspondence*, ed. T. Besterman, 107 vols. (Geneva, 1953–65), vol. 2, p. 37; Voltaire, *Letters on England*, trans. L. Tancock (Harmondsworth, 1980), p. 45.

[12] M. W. Farr, 'Correspondence between Sir Robert Throckmorton and Nathaniel Pigott 1706–7', *University of Birmingham Historical Journal*, 8 (1961), p. 91.

have been at one another's throat in all of this, but they worked within a system that could cope with the strain; factionalism was becoming institutionalized.

There is no question that by the middle of the 1720s the divisions and heats which had beset seventeenth-century England, and which had provided the opportunity for the Glorious Revolution, were now less potent and threatening. It was not so much that divergent views had gone away, but that many of them had been brought within the system. A series of compromises had proved that heterodoxy did not necessarily mean anarchy, taking the sting out of many anxieties. The mere passage of time also helped. Perhaps there was some sense of exhaustion. Few were now alive who as adults had endured the strains of the Restoration world. And even those who had reluctantly embraced the accession of William and Mary never forgot that it had given them what they most prized, a Protestant establishment wedded to an active mixed constitution. Moreover, the gains won at the peace treaties in 1697 and 1713, the latter on the back of the Duke of Marlborough's famous victories in battle, not only guaranteed that achievement but also established England (more accurately 'Britain' and, from 1707, the 'United Kingdom of Great Britain') as a European great power capable of exercising its authority across the Atlantic and into the Mediterranean.

Changes within the political system and in England's international fortunes were central to the history of this period, but they rested upon the vitality of her economy and society. The provision of the material wherewithal for this was undoubtedly impressive, but it bespoke other changes. As her economy expanded so the costs of political instability mounted. More important, as none seriously denied the importance of prosperity, and because this often rested on the efforts of new interests, so a more complex society had to be tolerated. Few doubted the value of merchants, many marvelled at dockyards and ironworks, and the burgeoning service sector with its expanding professions (doctors, attorneys, and surveyors) was widely utilized. One of the most striking features of the period, indeed, is the way these most vibrant parts of society were embraced by old England. Town and countryside were closely interwoven, not so much by new wealth flowing into landed estates as by old wealth embracing the London season, urban professionals, and the diversions of spas and county towns (such as assembly rooms, races, and fairs).

Urbanization beyond London was, indeed, one of the most important features of the evolution of English society from the late seventeenth century. It rested upon heightened specialization in and interdependence between her economic regions, greater agricultural productivity, and the willingness of people to abandon traditional ways of life. Many did so only because they were driven by want, but some were lured by the vivacity and novelty towns offered—from strolling players and ballad singers to coffee-houses and clubs.

A critical feature of this was the function towns played in setting new stand-ards, not only in fashion and leisure, but in sociability. This was especially the case amongst the more prosperous, who developed ideas of politeness that contrasted with older traditions of hospitality. That such ideas were avowedly socially exclusive was vital to their function as a new ideology that many within polite society embraced, providing a common ground even to those of very different religious or political views. Undoubtedly this found its most remark-able expression in the outpourings of a liberated press—from newspapers to periodicals, plays, novels, pamphlets, translations, sermons, and books. Certainly an age studded with writers of the stature of Addison, Congreve, Defoe, Gay, Pope, Steele, and Swift was distinctive, but they were only part of a wider pursuit of pleasure which if originating after 1660 was only now really bearing fruit.

It may have been, as one Scot remarked in 1726, that 'The English People are not a little vain of Themselves, and their Country', but by then there were some good reasons for it.[13] For the most part disunity had been overcome by establishing a political and religious compromise which most could live with; England's international fortunes had been dramatically transformed; and her economy and society were evidently more productive and vibrant than ever. To that extent therefore the pessimists were right, England was abandoning old values and old ways.

SCALE AND SCOPE, SOURCES AND METHODS

This book is organized around the two main structures underpinning English history just outlined: the uncertainties and insecurities consequent upon the Glorious Revolution and the challenge to many social norms by the halting experience of economic progress. That English society did not unravel in the face of these disruptions was due both to their substantial perceived bene-fits and because of an increasing (if still incomplete) willingness towards accommodation and compromise that allowed rival views to coexist. In 1689 it had still been hoped that the old chimera of social solidarity, an ancient constitution, and religious orthodoxy could be 'restored'; by 1727 pluralism and heterodoxy in many walks of life were accepted, however reluctantly.

This complex history can only be told by unpacking its constituent parts. But there are many ways that might be done. Here there has been a desire to avoid over compartmentalization, so that links can be made between constituent parts of England's history that are often kept apart, even at the risk of occasional repetition, the separation of some topics usually kept together,

---

[13] *James Thomson (1700–1748) Letters and Documents*, ed. A. D. McKillop (Lawrence, 1958), p. 48.

and employing different methodologies between chapters. A single narrative is also eschewed, for that would be too exclusive. Rather at the outset some foundation stones are put in place, on top of which are then laid a number of different histories, all related but all different. The bedrock of the book is laid in Chapters 2, 3, and 4, which explore the broad features of England's polity, economy, and society, and her experience of two major wars. Of the remaining ten chapters, three discuss political developments at the centre, which relate particularly closely to the chapters exploring religious history and England's imperial endeavours. The economic history of the period is mainly told in Chapters 10 and 11, though those chapters also explore aspects of the social, cultural, and intellectual history of the period. Intellectual history, a sub-discipline too narrowly defined by some of its practitioners, is dealt with in many places through the book (ideas really mattered to these two generations) but is discussed in concerted fashion in Chapter 6. The final two chapters explore different aspects of the social history of the period, the impact of new patterns of urban life and leisure and the authorities' struggles to maintain order in the midst of so much political, religious, economic, and social change.

If the structure of this book is central to its identity and aspirations, it has also been written within other important limits. First and foremost, no part of England's history has been excluded from consideration, though the book is necessarily selective. This book provides an overview which emphasizes certain features because they had a particular importance in the period, either in terms of continuity or change—though of course defining and weighing importance is a very personal thing. A second significant constraint is that this is a history of England, though one attempting to pay due regard both to the way that history is composed of local and regional experiences and also of how it must be placed in its wider contexts, both within and beyond the British Isles. Forays outside England are only made when it aids the understanding of her history—though given the union of the English and Scottish Crowns since 1603 particularly in the realm of foreign relations 'Britain' not 'England' must be used. Similarly, if there is a constant concern to locate the history of England between 1689 and 1727 in both its immediate and longer term chronological context, the focus is very much upon this particular period. A fourth self-imposed constraint has been to avoid engaging explicitly with the arguments of the hundreds of historians who have also worked on this period. As the discussion of further reading near the end of the book makes clear, a rich and rapidly expanding historiography underpins this book, both in terms of detail and structure, but methodological or evidential debates are kept in the background. Sides are taken, as they must be, but usually it is done silently. Nor, indeed, is this merely a work of synthesis. Much primary research has been undertaken into the nooks and crannies of the period, not just because it aids understanding but also because it adds depth and colour in ways that a dependence upon secondary literature alone cannot. To maximize the efficiency of this, however, attention has been concentrated on printed sources. Many of these are editions of manuscript sources, from diaries and correspondence to debates and court records, but many are contemporary printed works—somewhat reflecting the enormous explosion of publishing in this period, with slightly more works published in these thirty-eight years than in the previous one hundred. Finally, the book was written with a constant eye on the word limit of the series. Rarely does any piece of historical writing have a 'natural' length, for so much depends on an author's perceptions of his or her readership and the choices then made between narrative and analysis, generalization and specialization. This book could have been half or twice as long, but either way England's history in this remarkable period would have looked and felt rather different.

CONCLUSION

The death of George I at Osnabrück in the summer of 1727 was no milestone in England's history. There was no question of shipping his body to London for a State funeral and he was buried in the family vault in the Leineschloss church in Hanover. Life in England went on much as before. If George was not unloved by his people, he was personally unendearing, had lived intermittently in England for less than thirteen years, and aside from his Protestantism represented too little that was dear to them. So in so far as the death of one person can mark the end of the era we must look elsewhere. One particular man, an 84-year-old, stands out. He had lived through the civil wars, the disinterment of Oliver Cromwell's body for posthumous execution as a traitor, the commercial, Glorious, and financial revolutions, two major and a handful of minor wars, the Union of England and Scotland, imperial expansion, and a Jacobite rising. He had witnessed the last visitation of the plague in England, the building of Wren's St Paul's, the development of a coffee-house culture, and in old age the vogue for Handel's operas. He had been born into a land of hardship and occasional want and died with it well able to feed itself even though large amounts of corn were exported overseas or distilled into gin. Yet in itself to have seen so much was not so unusual. But unlike George I this man was buried in Westminster Abbey, with the Lord Chancellor, the Dukes of Montrose and Roxburgh, and the Earls of Pembroke, Sussex, and Macclesfield as his pall-bearers. 'He lived honoured by his compatriots and was buried like a king who had done well by his subjects.'[14]

---

[14] Voltaire, *Letters on England*, p. 69.

Few doubted that the achievements of Sir Isaac Newton, who died in March 1727, warranted such majestic comparisons.

> All-piercing Sage! Who sat not down and dreamt
> Romantic Schemes, defended by the Din
> Of specious Words, and Tyranny of Names,
> But bidding his amazing Mind attend,
> And with heroick Patience Years on Years
> Deep-searching, saw at last the SYSTEM dawn,
> And shine, of all his Race, on Him alone.[15]

Newton's work on gravity had transformed not merely the common world-view, but that of the solar system. His developments in optics and calculus only underscored his genius as the climax of the Scientific Revolution. But the advance of important new ways of thinking and the abandonment of error and superstition was not so straightforward. Newton was much more complex. He had spent much of his life as a public servant, vigorously pursuing coiners to the gallows, and delved long and deep into alchemy and biblical chronology. He was moreover vain, argumentative, and high-handed. This was no saint or unregenerate modernist who had died, but a man who neatly encapsulates the Janus-like complexity of late seventeenth and early eighteenth-century England—its mixture of old and new, fear and confidence, despair and hope, aggression and poise. With its anxieties and prospects it was indeed an era on the cusp.

[15] J. Thomson, *A Poem Sacred to the Memory of Sir Isaac Newton* (3rd edn., 1727), p. 6.

CHAPTER 2

The Glorious Revolution and the Revolution Constitution

In 1751 Henry Fielding, the writer and Justice of the Peace, bemoaned that

There is nothing so much talked of, and so little understood in this Country, as the *Constitution*. It is a Word in the Mouth of every Man; and yet when we come to discourse of the Matter, there is no Subject on which our Ideas are more confused and perplexed. Some, when they speak of the Constitution, confine their Notions to the Law; others to the Legislature; others, again, to the governing or executive Part; and many there are, who jumble all these together in one Idea. One Error, however, is common to them all: for all seem to have the Conception of something uniform and permanent, as if the Constitution of *England* partook rather of the Nature of the Soil than of the Climate, and was as fixed and constant as the former, not as changing and variable as the latter.[1]

The root explanation of this telling analysis is that, for better and for worse, England has never had a comprehensive written constitution, enabling her political structures to be remarkably responsive to the twists and turns of altered circumstances. Indeed, changes have taken place virtually unnoticed, even unintended, as well as before the full gaze of the public, to the extent that even to this day what constitutes the constitution is unfixed, confused, and occasionally contentious. If precedent has provided a guide, so have the vagaries of custom, tradition, and idealism, allowing one man's interpretation to be another's poison. Above all else England's constitution has been mutable and its principles riddled by compromise.

The Glorious Revolution of 1688–9 forced contemporaries to think hard about England's constitution and the sort of polity and society they wished to inhabit. Few periods in the nation's history have seen as much speculation on this score as the early months of 1689. Yet the debates and resolutions made then failed to settle the matter for too many questions went unresolved and too

---

[1] *An Enquiry into the Causes of the Late Increase of Robbers and Related Writings*, ed. M. R. Zirker (Oxford, 1988), p. 65.

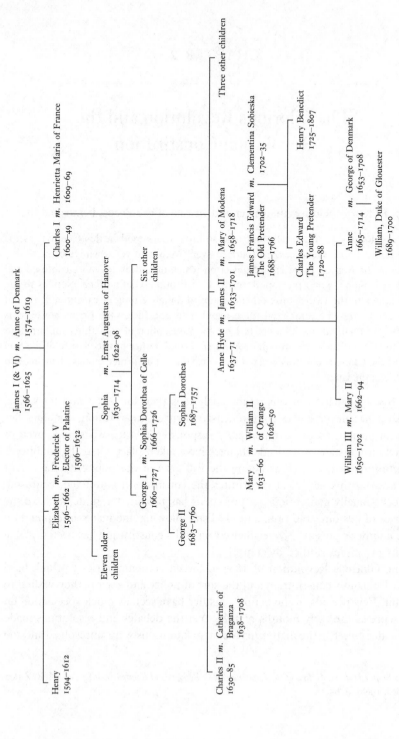

FIG. 1 The succession to the Crowns of England and Scotland, 1603–1727

many questions gained answers only generally acceptable during a relatively short-lived crisis. Finally, many answers had unforeseen consequences, taking a generation to work through both the theory and practice of politics. Constitutionally, the Glorious Revolution had obvious short-term dimensions and hardly less profound long-term consequences. Yet if the full ramifications of the events of late 1688 and the decisions of early 1689 must be appreciated there was nothing pre-ordained or inevitable about the path taken. England's constitutional development after 1688 was fractured, disputed, and frequently unclear. No grand plan was being followed and uncertainty was ubiquitous.

THE DUTCH INVASION AND THE GLORIOUS REVOLUTION

James II succeeded his brother Charles II as King of England in 1685. Though the prospect of this moment had divided many, when it happened it was generally and forcefully acclaimed. For the moment Protestant suspicions of having a Catholic King were put to one side. Yet only three years later, just before Christmas 1688, in the face of a foreign army sweeping over southern England, James fled to France with his wife and infant son. Though he soon made an attempt to reclaim Ireland he never returned to England and spent the rest of his days in an exile reeking of pathos. With little delay Convention assembly—effectively a Parliament elected via a summons from William rather than the king—interpreted his flight as a renunciation of the throne and offered it to William, the Dutch Stadholder and Prince of Orange, and his wife Mary, daughter of James. It was gratefully accepted. At core, therefore, the Glorious Revolution was dynastic, a breaking of the hereditary succession. Though it was much more than that, examining the transfer of the Crown must be the starting-point.

On 5 November 1688 William and his army had landed at Torbay in Devon. The date was already celebrated as marking two key moments of England's deliverance from Catholic threats, of the failure of the Spanish armada in 1588 and of the Gunpowder Plot on 5 November 1605. Consequently William's landing only heightened providentialist explanations of national events. The Prince of Orange, however, left nothing to such higher considerations. He came at the head of a massive, well-trained, and seasoned force. Some 500 ships, four times the number of the catastrophic Spanish armada, brought 5,000 horses and over 20,000 men, most of them Dutch. William came prepared for the worst and for some time he anticipated it, expecting James II to meet force with force. Worse, in England suspicions of the Dutch abounded. Within living memory Britain and Holland had waged war against each other and they continued to be bitter trading rivals. In English eyes, moreover, the Dutch were associated with the dangers of republican government and Calvinism in religion. From the outset, therefore, William's Dutch origins were an issue to be confronted. Whatever else it was worth, therefore, the invitation sent to him on 30 June from seven of the great and the good of England, calling upon him to help the nation in its hour of need, failed to do that. Shrewd politician that he was, William knew that he had to make a 'Declaration' that at the very least gave the English no cause for alarm at his invasion. In this document the injustices of the previous three years were skilfully illustrated and laid at the door not of James but of 'evil Counsellors'. Their policies had challenged 'the established Laws, Liberties and Customs, and, above all, the Religion . . . that is established among them'. At the core of the crisis, it was said, lay attempts to subvert the Protestant establishment in Church and State by reviving Roman Catholicism. Consequently, arbitrary government had been introduced: laws were being dispensed with; local government personnel were being purged; institutions as various as corporations and Oxford colleges were being reconstituted and manipulated; and ancient rights were being denied. In short, for three years a revolution in the socio-political order had been taking place. William came, according to this version, as a conservator and restorer, not as an invader or radical. Indeed, he made no claim on the throne at this stage, nor any plea to topple James. In fact, 'this our Expedition is intended for no other design, but to have a free and lawful Parliament assembled as soon as is possible'.[2] On this last point, and many others, William was as good as his word.

As a piece of propaganda William's Declaration passed comment only upon the British causes of the Glorious Revolution, not the equally important international ones. Here William was driven by Dutch foreign policy objectives, especially the desire to ensure that England did not ally with Louis XIV in the forthcoming war between the Republic and France. For years the Dutch had felt the pressure of French expansionism: in 1672 William had personally led Dutch resistance to a French invasion; in 1685 the Sun King's revocation of the Edict of Nantes, depriving Gallic Protestants of a measure of protection, looked like initiating a renewed attempt to impose Catholicism across Europe; and in 1687 serious economic warfare between the Dutch republic and France broke out, largely instigated by Louis. From the Dutch perspective, therefore, in 1688 full-scale military conflict appeared to be imminent and if England joined with France then the republic would be caught in a massive pincer movement. It was to prevent this possibility that the Dutch committed huge resources to the invasion of England.

[2] E. N. Williams (ed.), *The Eighteenth-Century Constitution, 1688–1815* (Cambridge, 1960), pp. 10–16.

Having disembarked, William led his army to Exeter, 'a genteel and rich city and a considerable port', to take stock.[3] For day after day the overwhelming response to the invasion among the English was inaction. William hoped to attract Englishmen to his side, but his Declaration had no immediately visible effect and few made the move. All the while James was gathering together his army and with his standard now raised the battle for English hearts and minds was joined on both sides. With bloody civil war and war between the three kingdoms threatening, memories of the 1640s were much to the fore. Yet remarkably James's natural supporters, the landed gentry and Anglican clergy, also stayed at home, sheltering behind drawn curtains and closed shutters. As King he reasonably expected more and such passive disobedience was crucial in influencing subsequent events. For once the silence was deafening, showing the profound and widespread distrust people had of their King and of the overriding desire to avoid repeating the horrors of the 1640s. To William the absence of active expressions of loyalty to James was interpreted as leaving unlocked a door to be pushed open. It was characteristic of him that he decisively seized the opportunity, discovering that in the event it opened with little effort.

On 21 November the invaders began their march across England which was to end in London only four weeks later. There was no battle en route and, aside from a skirmish or two, no bloodshed. This was all the more remarkable given William's rather ordinary military skills and resulted from a complete collapse of support for James, especially desertions and intrigues within the army. On 22 November, only three days after the King had joined his army at Salisbury, two of his closest advisers and most important officers, Churchill[4] and Grafton,[5] his nephew, abandoned their master and threw in their lot with William, contributing to a collapse of morale and will across the body of the army. At the same time James was deserted in the nation at large. For many the issue was uncomplicated. As Lord Delamere put it, 'No man can love fighting for its own sake, nor find any pleasure in dangers . . . but when I see all lies at stake, I am not to choose whether I will be a slave and a Papist, or a

---

[3] H. M. C., *Report on the Manuscripts of the Earl of Egmont*, vol. 2 (Dublin, 1909), p. 194.

[4] John Churchill, 1650–1722, from a Devonshire family, active against Monmouth's rebellion in 1685, corresponded with William before his invasion and with James long after his flight. Privy Councillor and Earl of Marlborough 1689, dismissed in 1692, restored to favour 1698, his wife was long Anne's confidante helping to secure his dukedom in 1702, led Britain's continental armies to many victories 1702–12, rewarded in 1705 with land and money to build Blenheim Palace, lost authority as his wife's star waned and that of the Tories waxed; voluntary exile 1712–14, initially buried at Westminster Abbey.

[5] Henry Fitzroy, 1663–1690, the illegitimate son of Charles II by Barbara Villiers, Countess of Caslemaine, made Duke of Grafton, in 1689 committed himself to William's kingship, killed at the siege of Cork.

Protestant and a free man'.[6] At Nottingham members of the northern nobility and gentry issued a declaration in favour of William, cataloguing their reasons for abandoning James: he was dispensing with laws as he pleased; he put papists into offices; he sacked honest judges; he discouraged and discountenanced Protestants; he declared that the use of law against arbitrary proceedings was rebellion; he used a standing army to enforce policies; and he denied subjects the right to petition. Consequently, 'We count it rebellion to resist a king that governs by law, but he was always counted a tyrant that made his will the law; to resist such a one we justly esteem it no rebellion, but a necessary defence'.[7]

James literally broke down, faced as he was by a massive enemy army, intrigue and desertions in both army and navy, the almost total neutralism of those who should have been his natural allies, violent anti-Catholicism in the capital, and the rejection of his own daughters, especially Anne. As his authority crumbled, his body and mind collapsed. He was twice bled and had to resort to opium to get any sleep. The King of England was humbled and the emptiness of his majesty dramatically exposed. Whatever the rhetoric of divine ordination, events now clearly showed that all power, even monarchical power, was fundamentally consensual at base. By mid-November 1688 it appears that the silent majority viewed James as a threat to the fundamental national interests. More generally, the collapse of James's authority demonstrated once and for all that a line could be drawn between what was and what was not acceptable kingly behaviour. Even though there was much debate over just where to make the distinction, its key features—that the monarch must be Protestant, employ the prerogative sparingly, and govern through Parliament—were generally understood and all subsequent monarchs appreciated the practical necessity of ruling with the agreement of the majority of the political nation.

Indecision and repeated nosebleeds marked James's last days in England. With his confidence in tatters he was unable accurately to assess his position. He returned quickly to London (William lagged well behind taking nearly a month to move from Salisbury to the capital) in the hope of reviving his position. But by now his attempts at conciliation, especially the calling of a new Parliament, were seen for what they were, the stratagems of desperation and won few over. At the last this foolish King determined on one final foolish act, he fled. On 8 December 1688 he took the Great Seal, the pre-eminent emblem of monarchical rule and technically required for the conduct of much government, from the Lord Chancellor, Judge Jeffreys, and demanded back those

---

[6] H. M. C., *Calendar of the Manuscripts of the Marquis of Ormonde, K. P.*, new series, vol. 8 (1920), p. 9.

[7] H. M. C., *Ormonde*, p. 13.

writs which had not yet been sent out calling a new Parliament.[8] The writs were burnt. Three days later, in the dead of night, the King slipped out of Whitehall Palace and as he was rowed from Westminster to Vauxhall he cast the Great Seal into the Thames. Hoping to escape to France he was stopped by suspicious fishermen at Rochester. But that he initially failed hardly mattered for he had shown an unwillingness to stay, to lead, to be King. But his pique and disgust with his people, not to mention his stupidity, were all evidenced by the fate of those charred writs and that lost seal. By making no provision for his absence he had tried to leave his country without a government or the means of a legal government so that any other, aside from his restoration, would have to be 'illegal'. As ever, he had failed to realize that 'legality' alone could not save him, for his monarchy was no longer credible. When James made his second, and this time successful flight (he was allowed to escape by William), he had in many respects already denied the very possibility of his own restoration or, indeed, that of his son, the infant 'Old Pretender'.

THE ACCESSION OF WILLIAM AND MARY

On the 18th of December, and soaked by driving rain, William entered London and the capital was put under an army of occupation—all the English troops in and about London were sent at least twenty miles away and the Dutch army was brought into the capital. Still William made no claim to the throne and many options remained. But they were dramatically reduced by the successful flight of James to France two days before Christmas. Recalling James was improbable, establishing a regency or offering the throne to William and Mary (from the Convention assembly, which was only retrospectively declared to be a Parliament) much more likely. Difficult choices had to be made and major scruples and hurdles had first to be overcome. In the first place, to offer the throne to Mary was to break the hereditary succession. Even if James was taken, by his flight, to have abdicated, then the next in line to the throne was his young son. Second, as Mary had a much more immediate hereditary claim than her husband, to offer the throne jointly to them was to step still further away from the rules of princely inheritance. Finally, the Crown was offered to William and Mary by the Convention assembly, convened on 22 January, which, strictly speaking, had no authority to do so. Given these difficulties, it was hardly surprising that debate raged not only in the Convention, but in coffee houses and on street corners. Alternative assumptions and opinions vied

---

[8] George Jeffreys, 1644–1689, the leading legal supporter of Charles II and James II, becoming Baron Jeffreys of Wem, most famous for conducting the 'bloody assize' in western England after Monmouth's rebellion of 1685, arrested attempting to flee abroad in 1688, died in the Tower.

with one another as biblical precept, history, and parliamentary precedent were ransacked for exemplars. Yet though such ideas and information were like quicksand, the profound difficulties and irregularities were all overcome, demonstrating both the limited options available and the extent of common thinking about the way forward among the majority of political leaders of the country. It was the urgency and agreement within the Convention that is striking, not sloth and dissension.

There is no doubt that by January 1689 William wanted to be King and would not be a Prince Regent to his wife as Queen: 'he could not think of holding any thing by apron-strings'.[9] Equally, Mary soon demonstrated that she would not be Queen alone and would only rule jointly with her husband. Significantly, Princess Anne also stepped aside for her brother-in-law. With these three closing ranks so decisively and with London under the watchful gaze of Dutch troops, the Peers and Commons of the Convention had little choice in deciding the succession. Indeed, a solitary, realizable option remained. So the succession of William and Mary was ultimately determined not by 'Parliament' but by princes. But if the assembly ultimately had only a minor role in deciding the succession it was vital in underwriting and legitimating it. For the sake of unity, legality, and future good government, the Convention had to come to some sort of quasi-formal version of events.

Not the least of the difficulties was that in January 1689 James, though now in France, still claimed to be King. So, given that most no longer wished him to be King, his flight had to be described as a renunciation of the throne and the rights of his son had to be negated. This was the pressing task facing members of the Convention when it first met. It is notable that it was the Commons which first adopted the firm position that James had abdicated and that the throne was vacant, and that the Lords, despite considerable opposition to such a wording, eventually agreed to this. But in justifying this, fiction and fact melded. William's invasion was called an expedition. James, the majority said, did not abscond in fear of his life but fled because of a base cowardice that conclusively affirmed his culpability and evilness. In English eyes this was evidenced above all else by his aggressive Catholicism—his promotion of Catholics to places of power in the universities, the courts, the armed forces, and government were seen as a prelude to the imposition of popery upon the country. To the Protestant majority Catholicism was indeed commonly seen as the handmaiden of arbitrary government and Protestantism alone was compatible with freedom. Time and again 'Popery and Slavery' were lumped together. So in the debates in the Convention, the story was that the people, threatened by tyranny, passively resisted James and he renounced them. Many agreed

    [9] G. Burnet, *History of his Own Time*, 6 vols. (Oxford, 1823), vol. 3, p. 374.

with the great Whig lawyer Somers that 'the King's going to a foreign Power, and casting himself into his hands, absolves the People from their Allegiance.'[10] James 'has quitted the government . . . and here is an apparent end of the Government' thought Sir Richard Temple.[11]

There was never any question that the Crown would be filled. The experience, memories, and myths of the Cromwellian interregnum convinced the vast majority that a republican commonwealth was closer to purgatory than Zion. Commons and Lords alike, deeply committed as they were to ideas of hierarchy and patriarchy, rigidly held to the need for monarchy—for a single fount of authority and a parental figure to lead, educate, order, and protect. Yet though these were conservative revolutionaries there was no realistic chance of restoring James. As the Whig Wharton put it, James 'is not our King. 'Tis not for mine, nor the interest of most here, that he should come again.' Consequently, Wharton believed that 'Abdication and Direliction are hard words to me, but I would have no loop-hole to let in the King.'[12] This was a vital issue for, if the throne was empty, the choice (in so far as there was one) of a successor depended in part upon the way it was deemed to have been vacated. Was James's flight to be interpreted as desertion, 'death', or abdication? More important, by what authority was the vacant throne to be filled: by right of conquest, by right of succession, or by right of Parliament? At this stage there was a determination to avoid seeing the Revolution as treasonous rebellion and few discussed events in terms of invasion and conquest. But if the Crown was to be filled by hereditary right, then to exclude the claim of the infant Prince but to allow that of Mary was also highly problematic (this was one function of the absurd warming-pan myth—that a healthy baby had been smuggled into the bed of James's allegedly barren wife, Mary of Modena). Yet, equally, there was a great reluctance among parliamentarians to admit that the Crown might pass to William and Mary through a vote at Westminster. As the former Solicitor General Heneage Finch put it, 'No man will say the Monarchy is elective, let the Administration be ever so ill'.[13] To most a

---

[10] A. Grey, *Debates of the House of Commons, from the Year 1667 to the Year 1694*, 10 vols. (1763), vol. 9, p. 17. John Somers, 1651–1716, educated Trinity College, Oxford, defended the seven Bishops in 1688, MP 1689, member of the Whig Kit-Cat club, created Baron Somers 1697, Lord Chancellor 1697–1700, Lord President of the Council 1708–10, a noted bibliophile.

[11] Grey, *Debates*, vol. 9, p. 10.

[12] Grey, *Debates*, vol. 9, p. 11. Thomas Wharton, 1648–1715, MP from 1673, joined William 1688, Comptroller of the Household 1689–1702, succeeded to barony 1696, dismissed at Queen Anne's accession, leading Whig magnate of her reign, created 1st Earl 1706 and Marquis of Wharton 1715, Lord Lieutenant of Ireland 1708–10, loved horse racing and rakishness.

[13] Grey, *Debates*, vol. 9, p. 18. Heneage Finch, 1647?–1719, educated Christ Church, Oxford, Solicitor General 1679–86, one of counsel for the seven Bishops in 1688, created Baron Guernsey and Privy Councillor 1703, created Earl of Aylesford 1714.

monarch was God's earthly representative, chosen by Him for the benefit of His people. For men to meddle in that choice was to tamper with the divine order, the inevitable price of which was chaos.

As is clear, there could be no logical or universally acceptable way out of the position in which the Convention found itself in late January 1689. It effectively had to assign priorities to its preferences and then paper over the cracks. For the majority, the main priority was to offer the Crown to William and Mary to prevent a restoration and to provide reliable, much-needed kingship. The Commons decided that this could be best achieved by adopting a ragbag resolution on 28 January that James 'having endeavoured to subvert the Constitution . . . by breaking the Original Contract between King and People; and, by the Advice of Jesuits, and other wicked Persons, having violated the fundamental Laws; and having with-drawn himself out of the Kingdom; hath abdicated the Government; and that the Throne is thereby vacant.'[14] At first the assertion that James had abdicated went too far for the Lords to agree to, not least because James denied it. They were also more tender on the issues of an original contract, hereditary rights, rebellion, and any hint that the monarchy might be elective. Consequently, they preferred 'deserted' to 'abdicated' and wanted to exclude from the resolution that the throne was vacant. Some believed James still to be King, though it seems clear that many Lords did not want him back given the unanimous agreement of both Houses on 29 January to a resolution that it was 'inconsistent with the Safety and Welfare of the Protestant Religion, to be governed by a Popish Prince', a position at loggerheads with a belief in strict hereditary succession.[15] By a majority of 52 to 47 the Lords voted on 31 January against offering the throne to William and Mary. But gradually they were forced by circumstances (the positions taken by William, Mary, and Anne), internal divisions, and self-interest reluctantly to accept the Commons' position. William and Mary were offered the throne on 13 February.

On 11 April William and Mary were crowned at Westminster by Compton, the Bishop of London. The absence of the Archbishop of Canterbury, some other bishops, and a number of judges demonstrated the magnitude of the revolution that had taken place and that serious divisions still existed. Crowning the Prince and Princess of Orange by parliamentary authority was the consequence of a conquest. The line of male primogeniture was broken and the new monarch's authority rested briefly upon military might and more permanently upon the wishes of the majority of the political elite expressed through a legislature with a dubious claim to legitimacy. To that extent the Crown had indeed

[14] *Journals of the House of Commons*, 10 (1688–93), p. 14.
[15] *Journals of the House of Lords*, 14 (1685–91), p. 110.

been made elective. But this also shows just how determined Lords and Commons were quickly to establish a new monarchy which enjoyed reasonably widespread consent. Parliament fell in behind William and Mary in 1689 because they wanted a Protestant monarch, because James had so alienated opinion that he lacked significant support, because the English government depended upon a supreme monarch to direct the nation, and because there was a largely unspoken determination to avoid civil war. Contemporaries marvelled at it all. Tillotson, the future Archbishop of Canterbury, thought 'It was a wonderful *Deliverance* indeed, if we consider all the Circumstances of it: The *Greatness* of it; and the *Strangeness* of the *Means* whereby it was brought about; and the *Suddenness* and *Easiness* of it.'[16] But, as was soon discovered, it was one thing to establish the new regime, quite another to secure it. That was to be a long and painful process, full of doubt and rich in anxiety.

THE REVOLUTION IN PARLIAMENT

To crown William and Mary was a dynastic revolution with important but not necessarily revolutionary implications for the constitution. In England it was a strikingly limited affair, more akin to a palace coup than a popular uprising. That it was part of a wider and prolonged constitutional revolution was due to William's original reasons for invading England, his steadfast adherence to those Dutch motives, and his dependence upon Parliament for satisfying them. Such has not always been the view. It was a commonplace through much of the eighteenth and nineteenth centuries to view the offer of the Crown to William and Mary as conditional, as dependent upon their acceptance of a new coronation oath and, especially, the Declaration of Rights. Here, it was said, was a contract, perhaps informed by Lockean ideas of sovereignty. Writing in 1790 Burke believed that 'If the *principles* of the Revolution of 1688 are any where to be found, it is in the statute called the *Declaration of Right* . . . This Declaration . . . is the cornerstone of our constitution'.[17] By specifying the wrongs of James and the rights of the people, it is often claimed that the Declaration heralded a fundamental shift of beliefs and power towards Parliament and away from the executive.

The Declaration of Rights was drafted largely in the Commons and was presented to William and Mary immediately before they were formally offered the Crown on 13 February. Though at that stage William studiously ignored it, later that year it was translated into a statute. It began by detailing twelve evils

[16] *The Works of the Most Reverend Dr John Tillotson, Lord Archbishop of Canterbury*, ed. T. Birch, 3 vols. (1752), vol. 1, p. 300.

[17] E. Burke, *Reflections on the Revolution in France*, ed. C. C. O'Brien (Harmondsworth, 1976), p. 100.

committed by James—by implication no monarch should behave in any of these ways—including keeping an army during peacetime (the standing army controversy), interfering in parliamentary elections and suspending laws without the consent of Parliament. Thirteen 'undoubted rights and liberties' in opposition to these and other evils were then listed. These say so much about political perceptions among the elite that they are worth detailing.[18]

. . . the said lords spiritual and temporal, and commons . . . for the vindicating and asserting their ancient rights and liberties, declare;

1. That the pretended power of suspending of laws, or the execution of laws, by regal authority, without consent of Parliament, is illegal.

2. That the pretended power of dispensing with laws, or the execution of laws, by regal authority, as it hath been assumed and exercised of late, is illegal.

3. That the commission for erecting the late court of commissioners for ecclesiastical causes, and all other commissions and courts of like nature are illegal and pernicious.

4. That levying money for or to the use of the crown, by pretence of prerogative, without grant of Parliament, for longer time, or in other manner than the same is or shall be granted, is illegal.

5. That it is the right of the subjects to petition the King, and all commitments and prosecutions for such petitioning are illegal.

6. That the raising or keeping a standing army within the kingdom in time of peace, unless it be with consent of Parliament, is against law.

7. That the subjects which are protestants, may have arms for their defence suitable to their conditions, and as allowed by law.

8. That election of members of Parliament ought to be free.

9. That the freedom of speech, and debates or proceedings in parliament, ought not to be impeached or questioned in any court or place out of parliament.

10. That excessive bail ought not to be required, nor excessive fines imposed; nor cruel and unusual punishments inflicted.

11. That jurors ought to be duly impanelled and returned, and jurors which pass upon men in trials for high treason ought to be freeholders.

12. That all grants and promises of fines and forfeitures of particular persons before conviction, are illegal and void.

13. And that for redress of all grievances, and for amending, strengthening and preserving of the laws, parliaments ought to be held frequently.

The Declaration stressed that these were 'the true, ancient, and indubitable rights and liberties of the people', though in fact they were mostly inspired by concerns over the ways Charles II and James II had ruled. Certainly the Declaration reiterated old rights rather than invented new ones, laying more weight, by implication, upon precedence than abstract reasoning—this was a triumph of history not of Lockean contractarianism. Many of these thirteen

---

[18] Williams (ed.), *The Eighteenth-Century Constitution*, pp. 28–9.

points were, moreover, vague, allowing plenty of scope for varied interpretation, just as others were soon ignored by William. Nor did the Declaration require a fundamental change in the constitutional balance between executive and legislature. Nevertheless, by specifying via statute what had previously been frequently unwritten expectations, by being part of the offer of the Crown, and by being a thoroughly worked out compromise, the Declaration was a fundamental document of what contemporaries called not the 'Glorious Revolution' but the 'happy Revolution'. Indeed, that both the House of Lords and William accepted it tardily suggests that they at least saw it as challenging their authority.

After 1688 no monarch however popular could rule as Charles II had ruled or as James II had tried to rule. Yet this was not because princely wings had been clipped by the Declaration of Rights. Indeed, all monarchs after 1688 had more power at their disposal than had James because they were Protestants, had at least the passive support of the bulk of the nation, and because they were prepared to rule through Parliament. This last aspect was especially important, for whereas James had rightly seen Parliament as a potential check to his authority, after 1688 the legislature was a vital means of exercising the royal will (albeit frequently through ministerial intermediaries). Neither Parliament nor monarch were supine after 1688, nor were they always in harmony, but they did develop a way of working together that stood in dramatic contrast to the pre-Revolution order. Though both monarchical and legislative authority was strengthened as a consequence of the Revolution, Parliament benefited disproportionately. In three dramatic ways its position within English life was transformed and a new political morphology developed: it met more frequently and conducted a much greater volume of business; much politics was party based and rested upon carefully articulated ideologies; and finally because of the Triennial Act of 1694 this was an era of remarkable electoral activity, helping to forge important links between central and local politics.

William came to England primarily to assist Dutch foreign policy and once crowned his objectives were to secure his authority within Britain (by subduing Scotland and Ireland) and make England contribute to his continental war effort. For both he needed men and money which only Parliament could provide. The old medieval hope that the King should 'live of his own', from the income of his own lands and certain other revenues, had been wishful thinking since Henry VIII's vain expeditions to France in the early sixteenth century. The House of Commons, which held sole responsibility for framing measures dealing with public finance, was well aware of the strength of its hand here, well remembering its foolish generosity to James in 1685 in granting him revenues for life. As one MP put it to the Commons, 'You have an infallible security for the administration of the Government: All the Revenue is in your hands . . . and you may keep that back.'[19] For Parliament met at the behest of the monarch; elections were called by the Crown (though limited by the Triennial Act) and sessions begun and ended at their whim. Yet a parsimonious Parliament could ensure that they were called and courted with some predictability. Initially William was not given a civil list and was granted revenues sufficient to cover only a year's expenditure, forcing him to call Parliament annually, thereby making it a much more significant feature of the government of England.

Between the Restoration of Charles II in 1660 and the Revolution in 1688 six Parliaments were elected and they met for twenty-two sessions. But the majority of these sessions lasted less than ten weeks, far too little time decisively to resolve contentious political issues or to pass a considerable body of legislation, incapacities that were especially marked in the decade before the Glorious Revolution when conflict between monarch and legislature was frequently intense. A dramatic change followed 1688. Annual parliamentary sessions averaging twenty weeks became the norm, producing a major impact upon the volume of legislation. From 1660 to 1688 Parliament passed 564 statutes; between 1689 and the accession of George II 2,510—a rise from an average of just 19 per year before 1688 to 66 thereafter. Parliament as a legislature had come of age and whereas previously it had been an occasional event it was now a permanent institution. This transformation rested far less on general or public acts than might be imagined. Measures to tax, raise armies, and the like were of course passed and of considerable significance. And certainly between 1689 and the passage of the Septennial Act in 1716 a series of major public and constitutional statutes were enacted that laid much of the framework for the conduct of political and the religious society until the constitutional changes of the second quarter of the nineteenth century. But most legislation, about two-thirds, was local or even personal in scope, such as that allowing landed estates to be reordered, workhouses to be built, and bridges to be constructed. Such particularism, however, had important general consequences. Not least the Commons became a means available to MPs, local communities, and specific interests to air grievances, great and small, national and parochial, and attempt their legislative solution. In that way, the centre and locality and the general and specific became much better connected one to another after 1688, easing some of the sources of friction which had existed through the seventeenth century between central executive authority and local powerbrokers.

Such legislative fertility was not, however, without its problems for it might erode some of the bases of the commonplace reverence for the rule of law. If

[19] Grey, *Debates*, vol. 9, p. 36.

some saw the law as an ass—inconsistent, incomplete, and unjust—most saw the common law as a sacred inheritance and the courts a vital safeguard of liberty and property. This did not change after 1688, but the proliferation of statute law raised questions about Parliament and the permanence of the law. Some bemoaned encroachments upon the common law and worried that the ancient inheritance of fundamental law was being subverted. Certainly contemporaries were inclined to view Parliament's jurisdiction as vast. As Defoe put it in 1705, Parliament has 'an Unbounded Unlimited Reach, a kind of Infinite attends their Power'.[20] Whigs enthusiastically embraced such a position, though many Tories remained attached to the supremacy of regal authority. Celebrating Parliament, Addison, echoing Locke, argued that 'Every one knows, who has consider'd the Nature of Government, that there must be in each particular Form of it an absolute and unlimited Power; and that this Power is lodg'd in the Hands of those who have the making of its Laws'.[21]

The dramatic increase in the frequency and length of parliamentary sessions, and of the volume of legislation considered, was one of the main aspects of the revolution in Parliament in these years. A second arose in connection to the responsibilities heaped on the shoulders of parliamentarians. After 1688 membership of the Commons came to be viewed differently. Previously the work of an MP was intermittent and usually light; the duties of representation were not considerable. After the accession of William, the business of the House demanded that a significant proportion of the 513 MPs (558 after the Union with Scotland in 1707) were active, while the greater frequency of elections and the incidence of contests also changed the nature (and the expense) of the unsalaried job. Parliamentarians now had to spend up to half the year in London, keeping a second house there. While there, moreover, they were withdrawn from direct involvement in their local affairs and responsibility there devolved or shifted to others. In that way the growth of parliamentary government after the Revolution contributed to something of a decline of elite involvement in local government, formal or informal, with their place being partly taken by others, often of a lesser social rank.

AN AGE OF ELECTORAL POLITICS

In 1689 England's political elite were sure that both frequent meetings of and frequent elections to Parliament were vital safeguards of good government—though quite what was meant by 'frequent' was a matter of some dispute. In 1716 one MP, looking back over a generation used to annual sessions and

---

[20] *Defoe's Review*, facsimile edn., 22 vols. (New York, 1938), vol. 5, p. 388.
[21] J. Addison, *The Freeholder*, ed. J. Leheny (Oxford, 1979), p. 107.

triennial Parliaments, believed that 'We are guarded by our representatives in parliament, against any arbitrary encroachments of the supreme executive power; and by frequent and new parliaments, against the weakness, folly, and corruption of our representatives'.[22] Only frequent elections purified the House of Commons, acting as a check on the invidious disease of court corruption —by education, manners, and wealth the Lords were supposedly already immune. Electors could be trusted to oust those MPs who, dependent on the Crown, gave priority to personal preferment. (Certainly there was some considerable turnover of MPs, only a quarter of those in William's last Parliament had sat in his first.) Furthermore, only through frequent meetings could Parliament scrutinize the workings and policies of the executive, attention that was felt to be doubly necessary when the nation was engaged in expensive foreign war. Parliament did not, it must be stressed, want to direct the war effort—initially at least, all matters of foreign affairs and the making of war and peace it recognized as prerogatives of the Crown—but it did want to audit levels of expenditure.

In such a climate the passage of the Triennial Act in 1694, limiting the length of each Parliament to three years, was of less significance than the raising of the limit to seven years with the passage of the Septennial Act in 1716. But the reality of frequent, short-lived Parliaments was a novelty in 1694, just as the absence of so-called place measures to keep Crown office holders out of the Commons left it liable to executive influence. That the Triennial Act was necessary is some indication of the uncertainty then felt by the political nation about the role of the legislature and the will of the monarch. In 1694 minds were being cast forward to the prospect of peace, when William would have reduced financial requirements and less need of Parliament. In fact the Act was a sign of Parliament's conviction that it ought to regulate its own constitutional position, not least because William was not entirely to be trusted. It was never forgotten that he was a foreigner with European commitments, preferring to surround himself with familiar Dutch faces rather than the cream of English society. Certainly William unsuccessfully opposed the Triennial Act, though it is unlikely that he would ever have eschewed annual sessions.

Frequent elections, however, were time-consuming, expensive, and divisive, providing the ideal climate for the gestation of party conflicts and stylized political instability—and similarly frequent local municipal elections heightened such pressures in many towns. Party politics was certainly not invented in the England of William and Anne, but it did assume a significance that worried many. Paraphrasing the Whig argument in 1716 in favour of the Septennial Bill, Walter Moyle told Horace Walpole 'that the Triennial Act

---

[22] W. Cobbett (ed.), *The Parliamentary History of England*, 36 vols. (1806–20), vol. 7, p. 330.

never answer'd the ends at first propos'd by it; that it serv'd for no other end, but to keep alive our animosities, which by the short intervals between elections had not time to cool; and that it debauch'd the common people's morals and principles, and made them capable of the worst impressions, and ruin'd the gentry, who by the frequent returns of elections were put to great expences, and become slaves to the populace'. For their part the Tories 'harrangued on the topicks of liberty, and said that frequent elections were the safety of the kingdom, by placing proper checks on the crown, minister, and even the House of Commons itself; that to repeal this bill, was in effect to own the king could not trust his people'.[23]

Between the Glorious Revolution and the Septennial Act, general elections took place on average every two years, giving a very distinctive hue to the political and constitutional histories of these years. Moreover, frequent elections were joined by more frequent contests, amending but by no means overturning earlier practice whereby MPs were usually selected by the machinations of local bigwigs than elected by voters. Even so, in the fifteen general elections between 1689 and 1727 an average of just 37 per cent of constituencies were contested at the polls, ranging from a low of 23 per cent in 1689 to a high of 53 per cent in 1722—even when there were contests, moreover, the turnout of voters was often low. Yet if in most cases electors had no opportunity to cast their votes (each voter had two) they could influence the choice of their representatives in other ways and the absence of a contest does not mean that there was not frequently fierce political debate. A distinction should be drawn between political divisions within constituencies and contested elections because, before the nineteenth century, constituencies returned two members and Whigs and Tories might agree to take one seat each, obviating the need of a contest with all of its costs. It was also often the case that in counties electors often gathered well before polling day to express their preferences, at which point candidates who appeared to have insufficient support might retire gracefully from the fray, saving face as well as money. But if a democratic element might exist even when there were no contests, sometimes the democratic element was non-existent, especially because of the influence of members of the House of Lords upon the composition of the Commons. By the end of Anne's reign, for example, nearly 60 borough MPs were nominated to their seats by peers and some 32 MPs were from families of the English peerage (there was some overlap between these two groups). Peers, moreover, often attempted to

[23] W. Coxe, *Memoirs of the Life and Administration of Sir Robert Walpole*, 3 vols. (1798), vol. 2, p. 63. Moyle, 1672–1721, MP for Saltash 1695–98, a noted political theorist. Walpole, 1678–1757, younger brother of Robert Walpole, Fellow, King's College, Cambridge, 1702, MP from 1702, Ambassador to The Hague 1722 and Paris 1723–30, Privy Councillor 1730, created Baron Walpole 1756.

influence the electorate in both boroughs and counties. Small boroughs were especially liable to such manipulation, though even they could be difficult to control, prompting some to call for the abolition or reform of such constituencies, others to stamp out bribery at elections.

The right to vote was strictly limited and generally available only to the upper reaches of society. Men aged 21 and over could vote in the fifty-two county constituencies of England and Wales if they held freehold property worth forty shillings per annum; in the 217 borough constituencies a patchwork of voting rights existed, based variously upon property, residence, membership of the corporation, and freemen. Only in some boroughs did artisans, craftsmen, and shopkeepers have votes. All told for England in 1701 there were perhaps 118,000 county electors and 70,000 borough electors, though even where there were contests many of those eligible to vote did not do so. The right to vote reflected neither the distribution of population nor that of income and wealth, just as the map of constituencies was unevenly spread. Borough seats were especially common in south-west England and very sparse in parts of the north. Each county, whatever its size or population, returned two members. Consequently, the counties of Wales had one MP per 875 voters, whereas in England the ratio was one per 2,000 voters. The addition of Scottish members in 1707 brought a further anomaly, with a ratio there of one MP per 60 voters.[24] However, to the late seventeenth-century mind disproportional representation was natural and needed little justification. This was an age which only infrequently heard the call for the redistribution of seats or of the franchise.

TOLERATION AND THE RELIGIOUS SETTLEMENT

The domestic causes of the Glorious Revolution centred on the religious basis of political society. Changing monarchs entailed the conclusive rejection of the principle that a nation followed the faith of its ruler, not vice versa. Deep anxiety about that relationship had been commonplace in the century and a half since the Henrician reformation but a *modus vivendi* had usually been found. Under James, however, it was not, largely because his religion was not that of the overwhelming majority of his people. His Catholicism and his favouring of Roman Catholicism engendered much hostility and met substantial passive resistance. By the summer of 1688 an impasse had been reached which only evolved into crisis with the birth of his son on the 10th of June.

---

[24] As Scotland had 45 MPs and a population of 1.2m, and England and Wales 513 MPs and a combined population of *c.*5.3m, the ratio of voters to MPs north of the border is explained by so few men being able to vote there.

Until then English hopes were kept alive by the prospect that at his death James would be succeeded by his Anglican daughter, Mary. But now, with a Catholic heir (the young Prince's godfathers were the Pope and Louis XIV), a permanent disjunction between the faith of monarch and people looked inevitable. It was this environment which William gambled upon when he made his descent, though his accession failed to settle the religious issues conclusively.

In the second half of the seventeenth century Anglicanism, the established Church adhered to by the majority of people, co-existed far from easily with a number of fairly small religious groups, of which the most important were Roman Catholics, Presbyterians, Congregationalists, Baptists, and Quakers. Such pluralism existed despite widespread distrust of heterodoxy. Memories of the abolition of episcopacy, the rule of the Saints, and the proliferation of sects during the interregnum, were still strong and to many religious orthodoxy was seen as an essential buttress to an orderly civil society. Certainly the Church of England provided, through its parochial structure, an important conduit of ideas and policies from the centre. Before 1689 pulpits resounded to acclamations of monarchy, hierarchy, order, and obligation, a potent ideology few could fail to hear. Furthermore, the close association of Church and State re-established after the Restoration was reconfirmed by subsequent statutes, particularly the Test and Corporation Acts. Office in civil and military government was reserved for communicants of the Church of England, thereby pushing many Dissenters and all Catholics to the margins of society (some Dissenters swallowed both pride and principles, occasionally conforming in order to hold office).

Though the Glorious Revolution was viewed by many as enabling the restoration of the supremacy of the established Church they were soon disappointed. Vital to this was William's own religious predilections as an unenthusiastic Calvinist. Moreover, for him the issue was not merely English, but also British and European. Not least, nervous about the security of the regime, he wished to tie closely to it as many as possible. All Protestants in Scotland and Ireland needed wedding to the new regime, and allies in Europe, actual and potential, needed to be assured that the new Anglo-Dutch connection was not merely insular Anglicanism writ large. In England William initially flowed with the tide of extreme anti-Catholicism, reconfirming in the middle of January 1689 an order banishing Catholics not normally resident in London at least ten miles from the capital. Behind the scenes, however, he adopted a far more conciliatory stance, promising to make concessions to English Catholics in order to secure recognition by and strengthen his alliance with Austria and Spain. With regard to Dissenters he also shifted ground. His Declaration stated that he hoped the free Parliament he aimed to institute would make 'such other laws . . . as may establish a good agreement between the Church of

England and all Protestant Dissenters; as also for the covering and securing of all such, who would live peaceably under the government, as becomes good subjects, from all persecution on account of their Religion, even Papists themselves not excepted'. But by March 1689 he urged Parliament to consider the 'Admission [to public office] of *all* Protestants that are willing and able to serve.'[25] This shift was partly produced by William's personal inclinations, partly by his reactions to expressions of loyalty from Dissenters to the new regime, partly by the ways Dissenters and moderate Anglicans, looking for a mutual accommodation, attempted to redraw the legal bases of Protestantism as a whole in the first half of 1689. To them the dynastic revolution and the role of the Convention therein meant that any part of the constitution might be reconsidered, especially what they saw as the excessively narrow Restoration religious settlement.

Early in 1689 three overlapping options for redrawing the statutory basis of the Church of England's supremacy were considered in Parliament: the abolition of the requirement that office holders take the sacramental test; the redrawing of the boundaries of that Church to incorporate moderate Dissenters (so-called 'Comprehension'); and allowing other Dissenters freedom of worship. All of these touched a very raw nerve, offering as they did a head-on challenge to the Anglican supremacy. Moreover, to Churchmen and their supporters they appeared to be the very negation of the basis of the Glorious Revolution which had so tested their fundamental beliefs and assumptions. To them protecting the pre-1685 basis of the establishment in Church and State had been the main reason for their abandonment of James in November and December 1688. In their eyes the new regime was to restore the *status quo ante*, not to reform in favour of some broader Protestant hegemony. Consequently, battle was joined in Parliament over the three options for change. As Anglicans in favour of the *status quo ante* just held a majority there it was to be expected that resistance would be stiff. Repeal of the Corporation Act and an attempt to enlarge the Church to incorporate moderate Dissenters both failed, but Toleration was enacted. Comprehension would have rendered repeal unnecessary and so its failure was especially important. More significant still, Comprehension and Toleration were conceived as twin pillars of a new establishment in Church and State. As originally envisaged Toleration aimed only to deal with those few Dissenters who would be left outside the Church after Comprehension. The failure of the latter, however, now meant that Toleration had to apply to large groups within society and was burdened with an importance it was ill-designed for.

[25] Williams (ed.), *The Eighteenth-Century Constitution*, p. 16; *Journals of the House of Lords*, 14 (1685–91), p. 150 (emphasis added).

Almost unintentionally the Toleration Act, which obtained the royal assent in late May 1689, was one of the most important parts of the Revolution settlement. At first blush, its terms appear modest, allowing those Protestants outside the established Church who had taken the oaths of Allegiance and Supremacy and who formally rejected transubstantiation the freedom to worship in their own meeting-houses. Their ministers had to subscribe to most of the Thirty-nine Articles and the meeting-houses had to be registered. Crucially, Toleration offered nothing to non-Christians (such as Jews, Socinians, and Deists) or to Quakers and Catholics. Yet such simple and limited allowances masked great significance. First, the failure to enact Comprehension showed that William could be markedly naive in English affairs. By adopting a pan-European perspective he frequently underestimated the parochialism and intensity of assumptions governing England's political nation. Second, the death of Comprehension was a significant victory for Parliament over prerogative. It vividly demonstrated that the Glorious Revolution was much more than a dynastic affair alone and made fully apparent that it had a vital statutory basis which monarchs could control only to a limited degree. Third, it soon became clear that the passage of Toleration had broken the Anglican hegemony. As John Locke put it, 'Toleration has now at last been established by law in our country. Not perhaps so wide in scope as might be wished for . . . Still, it is something to have progressed so far.'[26] The exclusive relationship between citizenship and Anglicanism was severed. Further, Toleration was associated with liberalization in the religious basis of political society, as in those Dissenters who bypassed the Test and Corporation Acts by resorting to occasional conformity. In practice, moreover, Catholics did gain some benefits from the Act—though other legislation attacked them financially and professionally. According to Burnet 'the papists have enjoyed the real effects of the toleration, though they were not comprehended within the statute that enacted it.'[27] Finally, institutionally the Church was challenged by the proliferation of meeting-houses which followed Toleration. In the first year of the Act's operation 796 temporary and 143 permanent meeting-houses were licensed. By 1710 over 2,500 places were licensed—there were about 9,500 Anglican parish churches. No longer could Anglicanism plausibly claim sole responsibility for the care of souls.

Anglicanism felt constantly threatened and in crisis for many years after 1689, with its champions railing against the Toleration and aiming to turn the clock back to the Restoration religious settlement in place in the 1670s.

---

[26] *The Correspondence of John Locke*, ed. E. S. de Beer, 8 vols. (Oxford, 1976–89), vol. 3, p. 633.
[27] *History of his Own Time*, vol. 4, p. 22.

Religious issues loomed large in political affairs from Anne's succession until Walpole's ministry in the early 1720s. The lower house of Convocation, though it generally met only briefly, frequently took issue with anything tending towards religious pluralism, often bringing them into conflict with their bishops. From the 1690s moreover the Tories strove to re-establish the Anglican hegemony, particularly by outlawing occasional conformity, which was done by Act in 1711, and attempting to reduce the influence of Dissenters in many aspects of public life. For example, by the Schism Act of 1714 educational provision was largely brought under Anglican control in the hope that Dissent, if unable to reproduce itself, would tend towards extinction.

FORGING LOYALTY

When William invaded England he knew that the overwhelming majority of the political nation had originally sworn allegiance to James II. The importance of this is difficult to exaggerate, for oath taking was a solemn and sacred engagement, ended only by death and thus capable of providing 'the strongest ligaments of human societies'.[28] William had, therefore, to hope that the political nation would break their vows and though in the winter of 1688–9 most disloyalty to James took the form of passive disobedience, this is effectively what happened. Individuals sitting at home watching events unfold as they agonized over their obligations were in fact participating in the crisis. Sadly for them matters were not settled by the offer of the Crown to William and Mary. Because the new monarchs in turn required oaths of allegiance this entailed going beyond earlier passive disobedience to an effective rejection of the prior oaths to James. If some believed that by his flight James had dissolved such oaths, others were less clear. As one cleric worried, 'For a prince, that makes his way to a throne by ye sword, to make ye people swear to his title seems to me a very strange imposition'.[29] The gravity of the tens of thousands of personal crises this created was easily foreseen by the new regime and framing the new oaths was an essential and very delicate task. It was not imagined by William and his advisers that oaths could produce loyalty, but oaths established some of the fundamental boundaries of political society, including some and excluding others. No less significantly, oaths also functioned as interpretations of the Revolution, for their terms reverberated with implications and innuendo.

---

[28] M. Goldie, 'Thomas Erle's Instructions for the Revolution Parliament, December 1688', *Parliamentary History*, 14 (1995), p. 347.

[29] *Letters of Humphrey Prideaux Sometime Dean of Norwich to John Ellis Sometime Under-Secretary of State 1674–1722*, ed. E. M. Thompson, Camden Society, New Series, 15 (1875), p. 158.

It is notable that the oaths of allegiance and supremacy to William and Mary began their life in the Declaration of Rights. Vitally, the form laid down, '*I . . . do sincerely promise and swear, That I will be faithful, and bear true allegiance, to their Majesties King William and Queen Mary: So help me God*', avoided the issue of legitimacy, failing to require either a recognition of the right or legality of William and Mary to be monarchs or a rejection of James's claims.[30] That is, the oath was part and parcel of the Convention's interpretation of the dynastic revolution that sought to accommodate as wide a range of views as possible. This was a highest common denominator oath, drawn up in a spirit of accommodation which demanded as little as possible. By expressing loyalty in *de facto* rather than *de jure* terms, and by simply ignoring James, many tender consciences were salved. Though it was required to be taken by all civil and military office holders and Anglican clerics, the vast majority went along with it, though often only after much mental torture. Thousands upon thousands marched before JPs to take the new oath, even most fellows of Oxford colleges. Many, however, did not, feeling they had to argue through the full consequences. To them, as James still claimed to be King and the oaths made to him could only be broken by his death, to swear to William and Mary as monarchs was impossible. The Earl of Arran put the matter clearly: 'I cannot violate my duty to the King [James], my master. I must distinguish between his popery and his person: I dislike the one; but have sworn and do owe allegiance to the other.'[31]

The most significant body unwilling to take the new oath was about four hundred Anglican clerics. Almost by definition this was a phalanx of men rich in principle and fidelity. Ideals meant more to them than pragmatism. Many were eminent divines, not least Sancroft, the Archbishop of Canterbury, and seven other bishops, some of whom had previously championed the Church in the face of James II's policy of extending toleration. Clerics who refused to take the oath, the so-called non-jurors, were eventually deprived of their benefices and seceded from the Church, sometimes establishing their own alternative congregations.[32] Numerically the non-jurors were insignificant, accounting for perhaps 4 per cent of the Anglican clergy, but they symbolized the trials, tribulations, and shattered hegemony of Anglicanism more generally in the generation after 1688, and their continued presence constantly recalled the fudge at the heart of the Revolution settlement. Moreover, some became active opponents of the new regime, though far from all of these were Jacobites desiring

[30] Williams (ed.), *The Eighteenth-Century Constitution*, p. 29.
[31] J. Dalrymple, *Memoirs of Great Britain and Ireland from the Dissolution of the Last Parliament of Charles II until the Sea-Battle of La Hogue*, 2 vols. (4th edn., Dublin, 1773–88), vol. 1, p. 286.
[32] The non-juring schism is discussed in more detail below, see pp. 216–17.

James's restoration, though only with the death of James in September 1701 did the oaths to which they were committed expire, leaving the way free for some to acknowledge the Revolution regime.

Taking the new oath was a test but it was not much of one and the more enthusiastic supporters of the new order soon pressed for something stiffer, either by recognizing William and Mary by right and/or by abjuring James. If eventually new oaths on these lines were adopted, between 1690 and 1696 a succession of Bills to establish them all failed in the face of considerable opposition. This was not so surprising, for they threatened to open up old wounds and challenge the passive obedience that had hitherto sustained the monarchy reasonably well. But all this changed in 1696 when a plan to assassinate William was uncovered. In this moment of crisis an Association document declaring William 'rightful and lawful' King was drawn up as an act of loyalty (Mary had died in 1694). Subscription to this Association was voluntary, but it was undeniably a test and many in the Commons signed. In the following year the new oath reached the statute book and was to be taken by all new (but not current) office holders, civil and military, and all future members of the Commons. This was a decisive step towards establishing William as a King deserving the same loyalty as previous monarchs and more clearly challenged the prior oaths to James. Yet still there was no requirement to renounce James before he died in 1701 and the requirement to renounce his son only came in 1702, barely two weeks before William's unexpected death, in the face of imminent war with France over the Spanish and British successions following the deaths of the Duke of Gloucester, Charles II of Spain, and James II. At that juncture the irreversibility of the Glorious Revolution was clear enough to most and the triumph of pragmatism over principle sufficiently advanced for traditional commitments of loyalty to the Crown to be demanded. However, the significance of this was much more than a question of loyalty; its implications were profound. It was tantamount to the assertion of the right of Parliament to depose a King and place the Crown on the head of whomsoever they chose. As such it marked a vital step in the transformation of the way the Glorious Revolution was comprehended—that kingship was no unfettered freehold, that there was an elective element in the monarchical succession, and that there had been some resistance in 1688 (passive or active). Finally, after 1688 the currency of oaths was inevitably devalued and the sanctity of political society and obligation eroded. Oaths demonstrated the politics of pleasure as well as principle. 'Our Fathers of old took Oaths, as their Wives, To Have and to Hold, for the Term of their Lives; But we take the Oaths, like a Whore, for our Ease, And a Whore and a Rogue may part when they please.'[33]

---

[33] *The Weekly Journal, or British Gazetteer*, 21 January 1716, p. 313.

THE PROTESTANT SUCCESSION

By the Declaration of Rights the monarchical succession was settled in William and Mary for their lives, then the children of Mary, then Anne and her children, and finally upon the children of William should he outlive Mary and have children by another wife. This was clear enough perhaps, but very perilous for in 1689 the joint-monarchs were childless and there was little prospect that this would change. The early death of Mary in 1694 meant that William would be succeeded by his sister-in-law. Anne, who had married George Prince of Denmark in 1683, had given birth to a son and heir, William Duke of Gloucester, in 1689. None of the Princess's six previous pregnancies had been successful, but in 1694 the child was still alive and Anglican hopes were heaped on his narrow shoulders. He was a potential saviour, '*the most hopeful prince*', providentially conceived in the very midst of the crisis of late 1688, a Stuart with some hereditary right to the throne.[34] If he lived then except for Jacobite challenges the succession was pretty well a closed book.

On 24 January 1700 Princess Anne suffered a miscarriage. It was her seventeenth and last pregnancy of which only the Duke of Gloucester survived infancy. Six months later, however, he died, struck down by smallpox at Windsor. The end of the Protestant branch of the Stuart dynasty was now clearly in view; the King and his heir were childless. The succession question was revived and was once again given added urgency by the storm clouds gathering in Europe. As William's health and inclination was against remarriage the two options available were to resort to the strict hereditary succession cast aside in 1689 or, as had been decided with the accession of William and Mary, to favour a Protestant successor. That the latter course was adopted should not mask the fact that some gave serious thought to restoring not James II but his son the Prince of Wales, providing he could be raised in the Anglican faith. Anne herself appears to have been in contact with her father over such a possibility, though probably as a means of keeping clear the path to her own accession. More important, William was committed to settling the succession question before war with France broke out again. He had long been clear that if Anne died childless then the succession should pass to the next Protestant along the line of hereditary succession, to Sophia, dowager Electress of Brunswick-Lüneburg, that is to say to the House of Hanover. He had indeed unsuccessfully attempted to insert a clause to that effect in the Declaration of Rights. Sophia's credentials and pedigree were excellent. Born in 1630 she was the granddaughter of James I of England, a Lutheran, and in 1701 had alive four sons, one daughter, one grandson, and one granddaughter. To pass the

---

[34] From the Act of Settlement in Williams (ed.), *The Eighteenth-Century Constitution*, p. 57.

succession to her and her heirs was to confirm the link between monarchy and Protestantism, establish a clear future line of descent through three generations, and add weight to England's position on the anti-French side of the European balance of power. Sophia herself did not live to inherit the throne, but her son, George I, did.

William's solution to the succession question was adopted in the Act of Settlement passed in June 1701. Despite the hopes of Jacobites and republicans, settling the succession upon the House of Hanover encountered remarkably little public opposition; indeed in the Commons only one MP spoke against it. Further, Catholics were once again explicitly debarred from the throne. The Bill passed both Houses without division and as in 1689 urgency was again the order of the day. Nothing could more clearly show the continued commitment of parliamentarians to the Protestant succession and of their willingness to break with strict hereditary right. As in 1689 a foreign, Protestant King was deemed preferable to a Catholic one: 'it is better to have a Prince from Germany, than one from France.'[35] It was not, however, altogether such plain sailing. The Act of Settlement was passed by a Parliament which had jurisdiction over England, Ireland, and Wales but not Scotland, which had its own independent legislature at Edinburgh. Furthermore, as the Stuart dynasty was of Scottish origin (James VI of Scotland had become James I of England in 1603) the Act of Settlement was interpreted north of the border as yet another example of English presumption, arrogance, indeed imperialism. The call of Scottish independence was soon heard loud and clear. A separate succession was mooted and prevented only by the Union of the two countries in 1707, a Union based upon the loss of Scottish political independence. This was a decisive moment in the creation of a unitary State in Britain. Though the majority of Scottish institutions and customs remained untouched the legislature in Edinburgh was abolished. After 1707 Westminster, where Scottish peers and MPs were in a small minority, provided Scotland with laws and set its taxes. Edinburgh's importance as a capital was thereby reduced and the focal point of Scottish political society moved south. Little wonder that re-establishing Scottish independence became a priority for many north of the border.

It was beyond the capability of the Act of Settlement and Act of Union to end speculation on the question of the succession, not least because of the continued hopes and machinations of Jacobites, most especially in the four years before Anne died. The existence of Jacobitism was, indeed, a defining

---

[35] *Letters Illustrative of the Reign of William III. From 1696 to 1708. Addressed to the Duke of Shrewsbury by James Vernon, Esq. Secretary of State*, ed. G. P. R. James, 3 vols. (1841), vol. 3, p. 129.

characteristic of the whole of post-Revolution era to the extent that there was nothing inevitable about the monarchical succession which transpired. At almost any point a different path might have been taken. All monarchs on the English throne were faced by a rival claimant who frequently received considerable domestic and international support. Whatever the scale of that support, whatever the chances of reinstating James or crowning his son, the mere possibility of a restoration dramatically influenced the political world. For both Jacobites and their opponents it was a world of gossip, suspicion, and secrecy, a world where reality and invention melded completely. Politics was haunted by spies and plots, risings and rebellions, rioting and disorder. Even those committed to the new regime often made contact with the exiled court, realizing the importance of taking out insurance policies should a restoration eventuate—Marlborough, Harley, and Bolingbroke were prominent among them. Treason and treachery was commonplace, loyalty and probity at a premium. Nor, indeed, was Jacobitism always hidden in the dark. In 1696, 1716, and 1723 the dismembered bodies of executed traitors were put atop Temple Bar in London. Such an environment is far removed from order and the reasoned pursuit of politics. Consequently, though foundation stones were being laid from 1689 onwards, it was not until after the failure of the Jacobite rising and invasion of 1715–16 and the exposure of the Jacobite Atterbury plot in 1722 that high politics took on its distinctively eighteenth-century appearance. Even then, the birth of the 'Young Pretender', Charles, in 1720 and the rising in 1745 kept old issues alive.

MONARCHICAL AUTHORITY AND PARLIAMENTARY POLITICS

More than the line of succession was determined in 1701 and as the full title of the Act of Settlement suggests, 'An Act for the further limitation of the Crown, and better securing the rights and liberties of the subject', William was the butt of serious criticism.[36] Without embarrassment Parliament introduced clauses into the body of the Act which forcefully pointed up perceived inadequacies in his kingship and worries about the accession of the Hanoverians. Restrictions on future monarchs were imposed that went well beyond those contained in the Declaration of Rights. It was now decided that monarchs had to be Anglicans, not merely Protestants, and that they could only leave their realm with parliamentary consent. This was an implied rebuke of the Calvinist William who spent nearly 40 per cent of his reign abroad, mostly waging war in Flanders

[36] 12 and 13 William III, c. 2.

against France. Allied to this it was further enacted that foreign-born monarchs could not engage the nation in wars in defence of their homeland. English interests were further to be protected by preventing foreigners from being Privy Councillors, members of the Commons or Lords, or civil or military office holders. The independence of the legislature from monarchical interference was additionally strengthened by banning placemen and pensioners from the Commons. The sanctity of the rule of law and independence of the judiciary was also underlined: '*the laws of* England *are the birthright of the people*' and to minimize political manipulation judges were to be well paid and have tenure during good behaviour rather than at the whim of the monarch.[37] Parliament, ever wary that the Crown might attempt to restore its power to dispense with laws, only allowed habeas corpus to be suspended in extreme situations, and then only temporarily (three Acts were required to achieve this for a period of only seven months in 1689). Finally, executive accountability was provided for by forbidding royal pardons to impeached ministers and by trying to ensure that the Privy Council took a more prominent role in policy formation. In framing these clauses one of William's advisers rightly noted that 'the parties strive to outdo one another . . . [in] weakening the crown', for the clauses signified a dramatic and important diminution of monarchical autonomy.[38]

The anti-monarchical elements of the Act of Settlement marked a significant shift in opinion since the Glorious Revolution. In the early months of 1689 few seriously considered the possibility of establishing a republic. Monarchy was revered, though increasingly more often in theory than reality. William III certainly provoked resentment and distrust, albeit on nothing like the same scale as James II. In part this was personal. English insularity had little enthusiasm for foreign kings and their foreign ways and this made it that much easier to question or challenge kingly power. Further, William was often absent abroad and even when in England preferred to keep himself at a distance from polite society. To many Englishmen, this was not the sort of committed kingship they desired. As a man, moreover, William was unappealing. He lacked warmth and was notoriously quiet and withdrawn, a virtue born of reasoned contemplation but interpreted as sullen disdain. Though he could make an effort to be more sociable and ebullient, as Burnet observed 'his cold silent way was too deeply rooted in him to be changed'.[39] By contrast, Anne struck a chord

---

[37] Williams (ed.), *The Eighteenth-Century Constitution*, p. 59.
[38] Quoted in H. Horwitz, *Parliament, Policy and Politics in the Reign of William III* (Manchester, 1977), p. 283.
[39] *A Supplement to Burnet's History of My Own Time*, ed. H. C. Foxcroft (Oxford, 1902), p. 312.

with the people. To her very marrow she was English, Anglican, Stuart. She made the most of it, declaring to her first Parliament that 'I know my own Heart to be entirely *English*', a statement which echoed Elizabeth I's famous speech at Tilbury and reflected poorly upon William, as well as upon the Pretender and his mother living in Paris as dependants of Louis XIV.[40] Anne made desperate efforts to maintain the image and power of monarchy, though tellingly she 'took exception to the expression that "her right was Divine" '.[41] Yet despite being fêted by the majority of the political nation, even she could not stop the rot of kingship. Symbolically she was the last to use the royal veto against legislation which had passed through both the Commons and Lords. She was also the last monarch to attempt to cure victims of scrofula by the 'royal touch'—both William III and George I refused to do so. The first Hanoverian had indeed a far less elevated conception of monarchy than any of the Stuarts. Under William, Anne, and George the institutional authority of the throne was evolving and weakening. Little wonder then that one foreign observer of the English scene in the 1720s noted that 'The English do not consider their King to be so very much above them'.[42]

Personal factors only partly explain the weakening of monarchy after 1688. Stronger institutional and ideological factors were at work. In the first place, except by resort to contorted theories of providentialism, the breaking of the hereditary succession in 1689 and 1701 killed once and for all the belief that monarchs were transcendentally descended from God and that complete loyalty was their due. Moreover, the role of legislation in legitimating the succession in 1689 and actually providing for it in 1701 dramatically displayed the importance of statutory authority. More generally, as has been shown, the quarter century following the Glorious Revolution was one of unexampled growth in the passage of Acts of Parliament, great and small. Beyond any previous experience, Parliament became a regular and important part of the government of the nation in its widest sense and frequently provided an alternative to seeking redress by litigating in the central courts or by petitioning the Privy Council or departments of State.

The rise of Parliament necessarily raised questions about its relationship with executive government. For one, were the component parts of the triumvirate of King, Lords, and Commons in Parliament of equal weight, and who was to provide the lead in framing legislation? The infrequency of parliamentary politics for much of the latter part of the Restoration era, and the

[40] *Journals of the House of Commons*, 13 (1699–1702), p. 788.

[41] H. M. C., *Calendar of the Manuscripts of the Marquis of Bath*, vol. 1 (1904), p. 199.

[42] *A Foreign View of England in the Reigns of George I and George II. The Letters of Monsieur César de Saussure to his Family*, trans. and ed. Madame van Muyden (1902), p. 40.

failure then of Danby's schemes of parliamentary management, meant that answers to such questions had to be worked out in the cauldron of practice under William and Anne. More than that, vital though the questions were, some hesitated to ask them, for they explicitly challenged important assumptions about government and sovereignty. William himself was in no doubt that the Glorious Revolution had left monarchical authority entirely intact. Incisive and bold, a natural leader, he kept a firm grip on the reins of government, for example by refusing to appoint a Lord Treasurer. He assumed that Parliament's function was mainly enabling, largely through providing the wherewithal to fulfil his objectives. Like James II he had a well developed sense of kingly prerogative. Indeed, he used the royal veto to prevent legislation reaching the statute book far more frequently than either of his two predecessors. Unlike James, however, the objectives he was most committed to were European rather than domestic and his disinterested view of many internal matters provided something of a safety valve in dealings with Parliament. Furthermore, his frequent absences necessitated the evolution of the executive's administrative machinery, effectively weakening the Crown's independence. Nevertheless, William encountered much opposition because of his insistence that forming foreign policy was solely his responsibility and because his energetic pursuit of war consumed English resources voraciously. This was felt somewhat from 1692 to 1694, but it is significant that it was only at the conclusion of the war in 1697 that relations with Parliament effectively broke down. William's failure then to maintain a large peacetime army as a guard against Jacobite threats vividly demonstrated the willingness of Parliament to clip the monarch's wings. William himself knew it, complaining of the 'mass of impertinences' Parliament had inflicted upon him.[43] Parliament now not only had an established, permanent presence in the government of the nation, it was also far from coy in exercising its power in pursuit of its (far from unchanging) version of the nation's interest.

Despite the expansion of parliamentary government after 1688, most members of the political nation recognized the need for strong executive action and did not yet envisage a limited monarchy. Rather they wanted to ensure that executive policy was well formed and subject to a degree of parliamentary accountability. One hope was that the Crown would make full use of a revived Privy Council, where policy would be worked out collectively and semi-publicly among the nation's elite. But this hope was out-of-date, for the role of the Council had been changing for some time as government grew too considerable and complex to be transacted within a single body. By the 1690s the

---

[43] *Letters of William III and Louis XIV, and their Ministers*, ed. P. Grimblot, 2 vols. (1848), vol. 2, p. 324.

Council 'now acts with absolute Power only upon very urgent or unexpected Occasions'.[44] Sub-committees had proliferated and gradually a new form of cabinet government was emerging—as was noted 'Cabinet Councils in England are Modern, and Excentrick'.[45] To that extent, the clauses in the Act of Settlement aimed at enhancing the role of the Privy Council were romantic nostalgia, demonstrating how poorly the legislature understood the changes taking place in the workings of the executive. This was also witnessed by Parliament's attempts to make Crown ministers toe the line. For many decades it had kept an eye on the executive not only by taking issue with particular policies, but more generally by attempting to impeach those of the Crown's leading ministers deemed to have formed and implemented bad government. The impeachment of Strafford and Laud had indeed been milestones on the road to civil war just as that of Danby was emblematic of the fractured nature of Restoration politics. But though in 1692 Somers, then Attorney General, claimed that impeachments and money 'are the two only things that make this House considerable' both before and after 1688 impeachments gradually became less significant.[46] Two changes deserve highlighting. First, from 1679 it became much more possible for ministers whose advice had been rejected by the Crown to resign. This had the effect of redirecting and focusing responsibility upon those ministers who remained in office and also signalled that the Crown could offer only partial protection to its ministers. Furthermore, it meant that, whatever the rhetoric, the King could do wrong. Second, the move after 1688 to implement much more central policy by statutory authority meant that the legislature was not only involved in but in a very real sense responsible for that policy. The expansion of the scope and jurisdiction of genuinely public policy, even into such sanctuaries of the prerogative as foreign policy, was crucial. Acts were passed after debate and due consideration. Thus when Robert Harley, the Earl of Oxford, was vindictively impeached in 1715 the question rightly asked by one of his supporters was 'If then the command of the Sovereign, after mature deliberation in Council . . . followed by the approbation of two Parliaments, be not sufficient justification for ministers employed in a treaty, acting against no known law, nor charged with any corruption, whose life, whose property is safe in Great Britain?'[47] The release of Oxford from the Tower in 1717 on the collapse of his impeachment marked, with Walpole's resignation from office just three months earlier, the end of an

[44] H. Misson, *Memoirs and Observations in his Travels over England* (1719), p. 225.

[45] *The Letters of Daniel Defoe*, ed. G. H. Healey (Oxford, 1955), p. 35.

[46] *The Parliamentary Diary of Narcissus Luttrell, 1691–1693*, ed. H. Horwitz (Oxford, 1972), p. 236.

[47] Quoted in C. Roberts, *The Growth of Responsible Government in Stuart England* (Cambridge, 1966), p. 405.

era, an era which had seen the slow and frequently fraught development of a working relationship between Crown, ministers, and Parliament.

From the Crown's point of view, management of Parliament might be considered in terms of patronage or policy, or some mix of the two. That is to say, at one extreme Parliamentary compliance might be purchased through the establishment of what opponents called a Court party that held a majority in both Houses, at the other all would be gambled on the innate quality of proposals effectively communicated by ministerial intermediaries. Especially under William and Anne many feared that the former was being attempted. Votes in the Commons and Lords might be guaranteed by creating peerages, packing the episcopal bench with friends, buying or fixing boroughs, and providing parliamentarians with places and pensions. Certainly this was attempted up to a point. In 1711–12, for example, Anne created twelve peers to ease the passage of the Peace negotiated by her ministers through Parliament. And parliamentarians certainly held office. The Crown had an indirect interest in or influence upon some boroughs, though these could not all be depended upon to toe the line and the numbers liable to such patronage were never sufficient to ensure a majority, nor might the rewards be sufficient to ensure compliance. In the 1690s, for example, there were about 120–60 MPs who were placemen, around a quarter or a third of the total. Moreover, because the incumbents of those offices held for life could not be sacked their support for the executive was far from certain. Consequently, though the opposition and independents in Parliament frequently railed against patronage this had as much to do with political posturing as ensuring good government. Indeed, the wide-ranging place clauses in the Act of Settlement were redrawn in more moderate terms only five years later in the Regency Act.

The key lesson gradually and somewhat reluctantly learned by both William and Anne was that it was only possible to exert some measure of control over the legislature by employing ministers who had the confidence of Parliament. That in turn depended upon finding both men and policies acceptable to St James's and Westminster alike—though the Crown also discovered that the electorate paid close attention to who was in and out of office, often favouring the former. To William and Anne this involved compromise and concession. Both had initially wanted to establish mixed ministries, composed of all shades of political opinion. By turns, however, in order to secure working majorities in the Commons, both were forced to establish ministries much more closely tied to party fortunes. Hence, electoral politics could not be ignored by the Court and disjunctions between the alignment of ministries and the composition of the Commons became difficult to sustain. Whereas once the Crown had a virtually free hand in its choice of ministers, by the late 1690s that choice was somewhat circumscribed. Consequently, a minister who oversaw the counsels of the King, exerted significant influence over available Court patronage, and who had the support of majorities in the Commons and Lords would indeed be a 'Prime Minister'—though the title was only a recent and unofficial invention. If Godolphin, Somers, and Harley all nearly fulfilled such criteria, it was not until Robert Walpole established his regime in the early 1720s that the nation truly had a Prime Minister. He himself denied it, partly in self-defence, partly out of respect for monarchical self-esteem, partly because of the traditional leading role played by the Lord Chancellor. What was undeniable is that under George I the mainspring of government was ministerial not monarchical. Monarchy was not emasculated by 1727, but George I was a pale shadow of previous kings.

AN OVERBEARING PARLIAMENT?

After 1688 monarchical authority waned, albeit relatively rather than absolutely, because William, Anne, and George failed to immerse themselves in English affairs to anything like the extent of their predecessors, because they were financially absolutely dependent upon Parliament, and because parliamentarians were increasingly willing to interfere in areas of government which had once been out of bounds. Such willingness was partly the product of Parliament being more self-confident of its power and importance, but much also arose as an unintended consequence of contrasting alignments at Westminster seeking to influence national policy. At times, these two features helped to stimulate Parliament to act with the same sort of cavalier haughtiness for which James had been criticized.

Party politics as an integral and persistent feature of government was established for the first time in this era, the fundamental divide being between Whigs and Tories. In 1689 Whigs were keen critics of the monarchy of Charles II and James II, unhappy with the anti-Dissenting nature of the Anglican establishment and enthusiastic supporters of the Glorious Revolution. For their part the Tories took a contrary stance, placing much faith in a strong monarchy joined to an Anglican hegemony. For them the Glorious Revolution was a challenging and unsettling experience. Yet under William and Anne party alignments were often unclear and sometimes ephemeral, not least because both parties had their own separate reasons to criticize the post-Revolution regime, the Whigs because they were keen to establish a legislative counterbalance to monarchy while still supporting the new regime, the Tories because coming to terms with their betrayal of James II was painful and prolonged. Furthermore, the underlying ideologies of the parties evolved, especially that of the Whigs. Their greater commitment to the Protestant succession meant that under Anne they were staunch supporters of the Hanoverians.

Consequently, with her death they were rightly seen as the keenest supporters of monarchy, a position diametrically opposed to that which they had occupied in the years leading up to the Glorious Revolution. As Lord Cowper put it, by the Hanoverian accession 'It is an old scandal now almost worn out, thrown out by their adversaries on the Whigs, that they are against the prerogative of the crown'.[48] Despite these changes, party battles were central to parliamentary politics in this era and that this led to bad as well as good government is undeniable. Among the plethora of examples that might be cited, the Whig impeachment of Henry Sacheverell in 1710 for preaching fire and brimstone Toryism stands out. Less spectacular, but of equal consequence, was the party basis upon which contested elections were determined. The frequency of elections in this period, the intensity of party strife, the peculiarities of the franchise, and the public nature of voting provided plentiful opportunities for malpractice at the polls. Such malpractice could be challenged via a petition to the Commons seeking a review. However, the outcome of such reviews almost always depended not upon the merits of the case but upon the balance of party forces among undisputed MPs. Whigs and Tories found in favour of their candidates. By such means, for example, in 1715 a Whig majority of 65 at the original polls was within a short period raised to 115. Such partisanship inevitably threw doubt upon the judgement of MPs and seriously diminished the importance of the ballot box and, hence, the democratic element in the constitutional medley. By encroaching upon the rights of electors the Commons made itself liable to censure and condemnation. It could appear to be 'the most corrupt Court in Xtendom, nay in the world.'[49]

The high-handed nature of the Commons became absolutely clear in the case of the 'Aylesbury men' (*Ashby* v. *White*) which ran between 1701 and 1705. Though not strictly speaking a controverted election, this case centred on whether the determination of the right to vote lay with the Commons or courts. Early in 1701, prompted by the local bigwig Wharton, Matthew Ashby, a poor cobbler in Aylesbury, brought an action at the county assizes against the constables of Aylesbury who had supervised the recent election for depriving him of his vote. He won and was awarded £5 damages. White and the other constables appealed and the case eventually reached the highest court in the land, the House of Lords. They decided for Ashby, declaring that the right to vote was a piece of property, the exercise of which could only be determined in a court of law, not the House of Commons. This asserted the ultimate primacy of the Lords in many areas which, along with the fact that the judgement

[48] 'An Impartial History of Parties', in John, Lord Campbell, *The Lives of the Lord Chancellors and Keepers of the Great Seal of England*, 8 vols. (1845–69), vol. 4, p. 428.

[49] *The Parliamentary Diary of Sir Richard Cocks 1698–1702*, ed. D. W. Hayton (Oxford, 1996), p. 225.

ran in the face of custom, provoked a fierce reaction from the Commons. Only the Commons could decide who had the vote it was said. Both Houses rushed to justify their positions in the press and there the matter might have rested except that five other inhabitants of Aylesbury (three of them illiterate) decided to emulate Ashby and brought a case against the constables at the assizes. Here the Commons bared its teeth and jailed them for contempt. Later, in an action of great arbitrariness, in the dead of night they were whisked from Newgate to the custody of the Commons' Serjeant-at-Arms to avoid the possibility of a grant of habeas corpus. Stalemate resulted, ended only by the prorogation of Parliament and the release of the Aylesbury men. The Commons had suffered three blows however. Its capacity for arrogance had been made brutally public, a brake was put upon the invention of traditions of parliamentary privilege, and standards of legal accountability had been tried upon Parliament. Parliament, powerful though it was, was no free agent for it too was bound by tradition, by law, and, crucially, by expectation. If it behaved unreasonably its authority was liable to be weakened. Thus in 1701 when an indignant Commons jailed five of the nearly three hundred Whiggish signatories to a petition from Kent urging support for William's foreign policy they overstepped the mark and suffered a backlash. As one ditty noted 'Nature has left this tincture in the blood, That all men wou'd by tyrants if they cou'd, Not kings alone, not ecclesiastic pride, But parliaments, and all mankind beside.'[50] Many MPs received instructions from constituents urging what the Kentish petition had urged, constraining the independence of the representatives. Similarly, Whig vindictiveness in impeaching Sacheverell in 1710 contributed significantly to the conclusive Tory victory at the polls soon after.

THE MAKING OF OLIGARCHICAL POLITICS

On 1 August 1714 Queen Anne died. It was not unexpected. For much of her adult life she had been grossly overweight and infirm, frequently unable to walk. The previous December she had been close to death but recovered. Her precarious health naturally provided plentiful opportunities for Jacobite intrigue and the months before the Queen's death were rich in subterfuge, even within the ministry. Rumour and suspicion abounded, not least that Anne intended to prepare the way for the succession of her half-brother at her death. With the succession uncertain and consequently the Anglican supremacy in Church and State potentially vulnerable, on the face of it the conduct of politics

---

[50] 'The History of the Kentish Petition', reprinted in W. Scott (ed.), *A Collection of Scarce and Valuable Tracts, on the Most Interesting and Entertaining Subjects*, 13 vols. (2nd edn., 1809–15), vol. 11, p. 253.

was remarkably similar to that of most of the second half of the seventeenth century. And though George I succeeded peacefully to the throne, in the following year he was faced by a major Jacobite rising. That this failed catastrophically should not obscure the fact that much politics after 1688 was based on fear and uncertainty. Yet within a decade all this had changed. By the mid-1720s Jacobitism seemed a fairly remote threat; ministerial stability was the order of the day; the division of responsibility between legislature and executive was generally agreed; elections were now occasional; and the power of the Church of England was still considerable. It would be wrong, however, to ascribe such stability only to changes after 1714 for many developments had their origins not only under William and Anne, but under their predecessors. Altered circumstances as much as new advances were critical.

George I was himself partly responsible for the new climate. Unlike William and Anne he happily countenanced one-party government and looked pre-dominantly to the Whigs for support. In his eyes the Tories, who for so long had carped at the prospect of the Hanoverian succession, were tainted by Jacobitical tendencies and the desertion of Britain's allies when making peace with France in 1713. It was also put to him that the clauses in the Act of Settlement restricting monarchical independence had been largely Tory meas-ures. Secondly, like William he spent much time abroad (about 20 per cent) and happily allowed the development of government machinery that operated without his oversight. His disengagement with government went further how-ever, for he was relatively unconcerned with domestic considerations, rarely got in the way of his ministers, and after 1717 was a largely silent or occasional attender of the Privy Council. Even in foreign policy, though he was much more active than is generally realized, his was the only reign in this period devoid of major (though not of minor) warfare. This alleviated the nation of much pressure, especially financial and economic, enabling a calmer political climate to prevail. In this sense the death of Louis XIV in August 1715 did mark the end of an era, the passing of the threat of Catholic imperialism and universal monarchy. Finally, the weakness of the Jacobite threat was made very clear, both in 1714 when absolute tranquility followed Anne's death (surely Jacobitism's golden opportunity), and in the following year when pitifully few gathered beneath the Old Pretender's standard in England despite, or perhaps because of, considerable Scottish support for the Stuart cause.

Altered circumstances alone would not have made for political stability. In 1715 the Riot Act made available great power to maintain order—the con-tinued assembly of twelve or more people together, after having been ordered to disperse by a JP, could be broken up by unrestrained deadly force. The passage of the Septennial Act in 1716, though opposed by many, instantan-eously took much of the sting out of electoral politics, though it encountered considerable opposition both then and subsequently. With elections now due every seven rather than every three years the opportunities for frequent competition in the constituencies were much reduced. Religious issues also moved out of the political mainstream following the repeal of the Tory Schism and Occasional Conformity Acts in 1719. This in turn took place on the back of the decision made in 1717 by the Whigs and George I to re-consign Convocation, the Church's own representative assembly, to oblivion. But the failure of the University and Peerage Bills in 1719, both of which aimed to enhance central political control, show that there were limits to the construction of oligarchy. The former, claiming that Oxford and Cambridge were 'infected with Principles of Sedition', sought to give the Crown enhanced powers to appoint heads and Fellows of colleges, as well as to other university posts, and the latter to fix the composition of the House of Lords.[51] Both failed with the Peerage Bill meeting virulent opposition. As one critic put it, by stopping new creations the House of Lords 'may in time become corrupt and offensive, like a stagnated Pool, which hitherto has been preserv'd wholesom and pure by the fresh Streams that pass continually into it.'[52] Had either Bill passed, the political history of eighteenth-century England would have taken a rather different course.

CONCLUSION

To many Englishmen James II's policies had appeared to aim at introducing virulently monarchical government by emulating the absolutism of the universal monarch, Louis XIV. England's ancient constitution in Church and State was thereby threatened and a condition of slavery was imminent. In such a situation William, the Dutch invader, could be styled a deliverer. As one correspondent wrote to John Locke at the very close of December 1688 'I know you can be no stranger to the wonderfull successe which God Almighty hath given to the prince of Orange in his late undertaking to deliver our miserable and distressed kingdoms from popery and slavery, which mercy we in England esteem no lesse then the Israelites deliverance from Ægypt by the hand of Moses'.[53]

Truly the Glorious Revolution was miraculous. The reigning monarch was ousted, his crown placed upon the head of a foreigner and his wife, and in England all with virtually no bloodshed (though in Ireland and Scotland the toll was much heavier).[54] An army of occupation met, for the most part, with

[51] From the draft Bill reproduced in B. Williams, *Stanhope: A Study in Eighteenth-Century War and Diplomacy* (Oxford, 1932), p. 456.

[52] *The Plebian* (1719), no. 1, p. 4.   [53] *Locke Correspondence*, vol. 3, p. 530.

[54] See below, pp. 93–7 and 249.

passive acceptance. For many this invasion and dynastic revolution was the price of restoring a vague and generally idealized 'ancient constitution'. In truth, however, the constitution which emerged after 1688 was new, not old. The permanent place of Parliament within the government of the nation, the willingness of all monarchs to rule through it, the decline in monarchical power, and the challenge to the Anglican establishment eventually created, whatever the stresses and strains, a workable mode of government the nation had sought for over a century. To contemporaries this was essentially an Anglican, mixed, and balanced government, with monarchy, aristocracy, and democracy all present, and executive, legislature, and judiciary both inter-dependent and independent from one another. As Sir John Lowther remarked, 'The true interest of England is to preserve the government in all its parts in an equal balance and not to set one part above the other. It is agreed by most that this is a good government.'[55] A balanced government meant, of course, that all parts, not only the monarchical, were limited. Even so, it was agreed that every political society had to have a final arbiter. Few dissented that in the English case absolute authority resided only in legislative action, that is the agreed deliberations of Crown, Peers (which included the twenty-two English and four Welsh members of the episcopal bench), and Commons. Law, long revered, now had an established pre-eminence. 'A main and fundamental point of this constitution is, That the subjects ought to be governed by laws enacted in parliament, and not by the mere pleasure of the king.'[56] Parliament in its widest sense was pre-eminent by 1727 in ways that had been unimagin-able in 1688.

[55] *Parliamentary Diary of Luttrell*, p. 129.

[56] 'A Memorial Drawn by King William's Special Direction, Intended to be Given in at the Treaty of Ryswick, Justifying the Revolution, and the Course of his Government', in Scott (ed.), *A Collection of Scarce and Valuable Tracts*, vol. 11, p. 110.

CHAPTER 3

The Facts of Life

Though the Dutch invasion in 1688 cost little English blood, few were under any illusion that for a time the country teetered on the brink of civil war. It took little effort to recall the anarchy, chaos, death, and destruction this threatened. And though military conflict was avoided in England, for a time it seemed that the nightmare of a world turned upside down had returned. A powerful rumour quickly spread that thousands of Irish, the remnants of James's army, were ravaging the country. 'This rumour begun in the south, and went northward so effectually that most people believed it . . . Now it was that the whole nation was in such a ferment that they sweat for fear! Now all was up in arms, yet nobody knew where they were to fight!'[1] Disturbances soon occurred. A London crowd 'assembled in a tumultuous manner at St John's Clerkenwell, the popish monastery there, on a report of gridirons, spits, great cauldrans, & c. to destroy protestants: they began some outrageous acts, till the horse and foot guards were sent to suppresse them.'[2] Even so, 'The rabble people demolish all Papist Chapells & severall popish Lords & Gent: houses, especialy that of the Spanish Ambassador' along with Roman Catholic chapels in other parts of the country.[3]

To the elite, social disorder was all too latent within English society in this period and political discord was only one of its many catalysts. For the majority life was inherently unpredictable and uncertain. Most people occasionally experienced poverty. The economy was prone to the disruptions of bad weather, war, and monetary chaos. Disease and death were constant spectres. For both society as a whole and the individual the uncertainties of life were fundamental and almost endless. Contemporaries were sure that society ought to be stable, ordered, and predictable, yet equally certain that it was rarely so.

---

[1] 'The Diary of Abraham de la Pryme, the Yorkshire Antiquary', *Publications of the Surtees Society*, 54 (1870), p. 15.

[2] N. Luttrell, *A Brief Historical Relation of the State Affairs from September 1678 to April 1714*, 6 vols. (Oxford, 1857), vol. 1, p. 474.

[3] *The Diary of John Evelyn*, ed. E. S. de Beer, 6 vols. (Oxford, 1955), vol. 4, p. 610.

The nightmare scenario had been comprehensively set out by Hobbes a generation earlier. Where

men live without other security, than what their own strength, and their own invention shall furnish them . . . there is no place for Industry; because the fruit thereof is uncertain: and consequently no Culture of the Earth; no Navigation, nor use of the commodities that may be imported by Sea; no commodious Building; no Instruments of moving, and removing such things as require much force; no Knowledge of the face of the Earth; no account of Time; no Arts; no Letters; no Society; and which is worst of all, continuall feare, and danger of violent death; And the life of man, solitary, poore, nasty, brutish, and short.[4]

Happily, Hobbes's worst fears were unfulfilled in late seventeenth and early eighteenth-century England. Political discord was contained and then undermined. Warfare was endured and survived. Britain's empire was extended and its value increased. Population began slowly to grow. Many towns flourished. Agriculture, industry, and commerce all showed signs of expansion. Consequently, society was not static and stagnant, it was on the move, beginning to challenge or render irrelevant old assumptions. Thus by 1727 jeremiads against social disorder reflected not fundamental flaws in the capacity of society to endure but rather its ability to evolve and uncertainty as to the true value of changes that were unexpected, often glimpsed only indirectly, and somewhat unusual.

DEMOGRAPHIC DIMENSIONS

It was a commonplace of perceptions of national well-being in this era that 'People are the real strength and riches of a country'.[5] Labour rather than capital was the primary determinant of prosperity. 'People are . . . the chiefest, most fundamental, and pretious commodity, out of which may be derived all sorts of Manufactures, Navigation, Riches, Conquests, and solid Dominion'.[6] Yet despite this, no formal census was taken (though something approaching one was attempted in 1694 for tax purposes) and few attempts were made to enumerate the people. The historical demography of this period is, therefore, necessarily speculative. There is no doubt that in 1689 England was thinly inhabited compared with today, having around 4.93 million people, about a tenth of today's figure. Further, if England was large in relation to Scotland

[4] T. Hobbes, *Leviathan*, ed. R. Tuck (Cambridge, 1991), p. 89. Thomas Hobbes, 1588–1679, political philosopher.

[5] *The Political and Commercial Works of that Celebrated Writer Charles D'Avenant*, ed. C. Whitworth, 5 vols. (1771), vol. 1, p. 73.

[6] [W. Petyt], *Britannia Languens, or a Discourse of Trade* (1680), reprinted in J. R. McCulloch (ed.), *A Selection of Early English Tracts on Commerce* (Cambridge, 1970), p. 458.

(around 1.2 million), Ireland (some 2 million), and Wales (about 300,000), in contemporary European terms it was small, accounting for only about 4 per cent of the continent's inhabitants. France had nearly 22 million people, Spain about 8.5 million, and the areas now constituting Italy and Germany some 12 million each. In an era of intense international rivalry the smallness of England's population was viewed by many as a significant weakness.

There had in fact been a thinning of England's population in the generation before 1689, easing pressure upon resources. From the 1650s to the 1680s the contraction was of the order of 8 per cent, from 5.28 million to 4.86 million, mainly because of a great wave of emigration to North America as people sought to escape religious persecution, political turmoil, grinding poverty, and social tensions. But this outflow slowed in the 1680s and the Glorious Revolution coincided with a small increase in numbers, such that by 1726 England's population totalled 5.44 million, a 10 per cent rise from the low point of the 1680s. If this increase was sufficiently slow to prevent major social problems emerging it was marked and, aside from temporary setbacks, not subsequently reversed. Indeed, the growth established in the early eighteenth century was to be followed for nearly two hundred years, albeit at accelerated rates. Demographically, a corner was starting to be turned in this period.

The geographical distribution of people in 1700 is impossible to pin down with any precision, though undeniably the majority, probably 80 per cent, lived in hamlets and villages scattered across the nation. With agriculture bulking so large and much of the best land to be found in lowland England, there was a concentration of people in the south and east, that is south of a line from the Humber to the Severn. Slowly, however, that was already changing. The expansion of the textile industries of the West Riding and Lancashire, the metal trades of Birmingham and Sheffield, and coal mining around Newcastle upon Tyne, to cite only the most notable examples, were drawing more and more people northward, a movement that was to reach its apogee in the early nineteenth century.

The lives of most people were tied, directly or indirectly, to the land and an economy in which the forces of nature were too powerful ever to be gainsaid. Not that it is helpful to describe the economy as 'pre-industrial' or its agricultural sector as 'peasant'. Private property dominated and, except in those relatively few places where manorial institutions remained vibrant, individualism was a powerful force. This was not some pre-lapsarian paradise awaiting the destructive passions of the imminent industrial revolution. No economic transformation was envisaged though the economy was already heavily monetized and much production was for the market rather than subsistence. Exchange, and thus some local or regional specialization, was central. Yet specialization was often due as much to natural circumstances as to market forces. Farmers worked with patterns of soil, relief, and climate such that England, as much as France, was a land of *pays* and *terroirs*. So, for example, sheep dominated the landscape of wold and downland in Dorset, Wiltshire, Sussex, and Kent; cattle grazed the pastoral vales of Cheshire and the Welsh marches; Suffolk and Norfolk were famous for their turkeys; and the recently drained fenlands sent barges full of corn down the river Great Ouse. What was true of agriculture was no less true of industry. Manufacturers frequently favoured agrarian settings, not least because they were able to exploit the power of fast flowing rivers and idle hands made available by farming's familial division of labour (much production took place in workers' homes), the seasonal swings of farmwork, or the spread of mixed husbandry and pastoralism. Thus if 83 per cent of the population were country dwellers about 28 per cent were part of the rural non-agricultural economy. In many areas a fruitful symbiosis between agriculture and industry existed, linked not only in their workforces, but by capital, credit, raw materials, and market networks. This was especially true of the dominant woollen industry, whose various branches were concentrated in particular locales, such as serges in Devon, stuffs and stockings in and around Norwich, bays and says on the Suffolk-Essex border, stockings in Nottinghamshire, kerseys and dozens in the West Riding, and fustians in Lancashire.

Most people lived in the 8,800 or so villages and hamlets scattered across the country, but towns and cities exerted a strong, pervasive, and growing influence on English life. Everybody came into regular contact with urban centres —to trade, marry, play, or escape. Most frequently these were the market towns without which regional and local specialization would have been impossible. At the start of our period England had about 750 such towns, reduced by the 1720s to a little over 600 through improved communications and the success of some at the expense of smaller neighbours. If such towns were often small (few had a population of more than two or three thousand) most provided the fulcrums about which a region's agriculture and industry rotated, helping to define its culture and identity. One such was Richmond in North Yorkshire where 'there is a very large space for the Markets which are divided for the fish market flesh market and corn' and which acted as a focal point for what contemporaries called 'Richmondshire'.[7] Yet if market towns helped to identify locales, confirming their natural distinction, they also served as the vital conduits of new ideas (oral and literary) and goods (decencies and luxuries) from outside by which the face of society was slowly changed.

England was more urbanized than most European States. Perhaps one in five people were urban dwellers, a proportion which had roughly doubled through the course of the seventeenth century. In particular, the great growth of

---

[7] *The Journeys of Celia Fiennes*, introduced by J. Hillaby (1983), p. 247.

London had further developed a vital dynamic of the nation's demographic regime, accounting for about three-quarters of all urbanization in the seventeenth century. London was far and away the largest and most influential city, its 500,000 people making up a half of all people living in English towns, and was at that moment overtaking Paris as Christendom's largest city. Only six other English urban centres had more than 10,000 people: Norwich (30,000), Bristol (21,000), Newcastle (16,000), Exeter (14,000), York (12,000), and Great Yarmouth (10,000). Yet London's share of national population, which had risen so substantially in the seventeenth century, now entered a century or so of relative stagnation, hovering between 10 and 12 per cent until the advent of the railway age in the mid-nineteenth century. Consequently, the continued urbanization of the England after 1700 took place elsewhere, a development that was propagated in the Restoration era but flourished vigorously after 1688. One prominent source was in the expansion of those manufacturing centres generally associated with the economic advances of the second half of the eighteenth century—Birmingham, Leeds, Manchester, and Sheffield. In fact, by 1700 they had already emerged as important centres of industry and trade. Defoe, for example, memorably described Manchester as 'one of the greatest, if not really the greatest mere village in England' because it was not only an industrial centre in its own right but also an entrepôt for manufacturing within a much wider region spreading out into Lancashire, Cheshire, and Derbyshire, where 'The number of the poor that are employed in the manufactures of Manchester, by a modest computation, are above fourtie thousand.'[8] Urbanization was also associated with the development of England's overseas trade, especially with the Caribbean and North America fuelling the growth of Bristol, Liverpool, and Whitehaven. In 1698 Celia Fiennes found Liverpool 'grown to a large fine town . . . its a very rich trading town . . . there are abundance of persons you see very well dress'd and of good fashion; the streets are faire and long, its London in miniature as much as ever I saw any thing'.[9] European trade and the fisheries supported the prosperity of Exeter, Hull, King's Lynn, and Great Yarmouth. Alongside such vibrancy, old regional centres, such as Norwich, Worcester, and York, might appear stagnant and in decay, but they too were growing and changing. Their populations rose slowly, often because of changes in the elite's culture of leisure such as the development of spas, assembly rooms, theatres, and clubs.

[8] D. Defoe, *A Tour Through the Whole Island of Great Britain*, ed. P. Rogers (Harmondsworth, 1978), p. 544. Daniel Defoe, 1661?–1731, from a Dissenting background, a supporter of the Glorious Revolution, perhaps the most prolific writer of his day, famous for novels such as *Robinson Crusoe* (1719) and the political periodical *Review* (1704–13), he was also a failed businessman and a government spy. H. M. C., *The Manuscripts of Lord Kenyon* (1894), p. 410.

[9] *The Journeys of Celia Fiennes*, p. 213.

DEATH, DISEASE, AND DOCTORS

As a starting point three variables—fertility, mortality, and migration—need to be explored to account for the changes in the size and distribution of England's population. Traditionally, most weight has been put on the second of these because, assuming fertility levels were at their biological maximum and migration was negligible, population growth could only result from a declining death rate. With the eye caught by the ravages of epidemics, supposedly pre-modern societies were periodically so wasted by disease and death that significant shifts in overall population size resulted. Only through such catastrophes, it is argued, would pressure on resources be eased sufficiently to allow for a period of subsequent population growth.

Certainly death was a much more present experience in late Stuart England than it is today. Queen Anne for example became pregnant seventeen times, yet only one child, the Duke of Gloucester, lived beyond infancy, and even he died aged 11. Less exceptional was the unhappy experience of Claver Morris, a physician in Wells in Somerset, who buried three wives and a daughter before his own death. In fact, mortality in England worsened markedly in the generation before the Glorious Revolution, life expectancy at birth falling to a nadir of around 30 in the decade 1680–9. Thereafter it usually improved, rising to over 37 by the start of the eighteenth century and 42 by 1750–9. The improvement was not only partial but discontinuous, for recovery was occasionally interrupted by severe setbacks, especially in the late 1720s when the nation was plunged into the pitch black of severe crisis mortality. Even so, the improvement of mortality from the late seventeenth century was clear, obviously contributing to the rise of population after 1689. Moreover, England's mortality regime was by the end of the period at the mild end of the European scale, for in France in the 1740s life expectancy at birth was only 25.

Only tentative explanations of the rise in life expectancy and the easing of mortality can be advanced. To contemporaries epidemics held the key, the last significant visitation of the plague in 1666 retrospectively marking the end of an era. However, fear of the plague was still considerable and quarantine orders to prevent its importation were issued against vessels from the West Indies in 1692, the Baltic in 1709 and 1713, and Marseilles and the Levant between 1720 and 1722. Banishing the plague was the most potent symbol of England's more general avoidance of crisis mortality in this era. In fact, in only one year, 1719/20, did the death rate rise to more than 10 per cent above trend. Indeed, the 1690s and 1700s, when war stretched resources to the limit, were remarkably free from demographic crisis in England. Shorter-lived crises occurred, but again infrequently—in February 1692, November 1693, June 1705, August and September 1719, and September 1720—and only a small minority of parishes were affected. The remarkably low incidence of crisis mortality in this era kills two related myths: that the population was periodically decimated by diseases that were then incurable; and that harvest failures and the collapse of food provision pushed the nutritional status of many to such low levels that they were easy pickings for what were otherwise non-fatal diseases. In this, England was somewhat unusual. In 1709, for example, when wheat prices doubled in northern France the death rate there soon doubled, 'many died in the extremities of cold and hunger; and there were great disorders in many parts of that oppressed kingdom'; but in England at the same time a similar price rise had no effect on the death rate.[10] There were food shortages in England, but they were never sufficiently frequent, severe, or widespread to push significant numbers of people below the breadline for long enough to produce starvation —not least because of the effectiveness of England's inter-regional and inter-national trade links. Gradual improvement in agricultural productivity may moreover have allowed some small general increase in food provision in the period, helping modestly to improve people's diet and health.

As a contributor to total population size the significance of crisis mortality is easily exaggerated, the effects tending to be ephemeral rather than structural and enduring. In this era, endemic or background mortality was much more significant than it had been a century earlier. Most marked in this regard were the high levels of infant mortality. At the start of the eighteenth century only about 80 per cent of babies lived to enjoy their first birthday and only 67 per cent saw their fifteenth—levels lower than for early Stuart and late Hanoverian England. Parents frequently, though not usually, lost some of their children. This was most likely in towns. In London, which had exceptionally high levels of mortality among most age groups, nearly half of all deaths at the end of our period were of children under the age of 10. So concerned did contem-poraries become with high levels of infant mortality that statistics collected in London of the numbers and causes of death (the so-called 'Bills of mortality') started to record age of death at the end of our period. Yet parents were nei-ther desensitized by the loss of so many children, nor unwilling to form close loving bonds with their offspring. Contemporary diaries are full of depictions of affection and respect between parent and child, of powerful emotional ties and familial responsibilities shattered by death at great personal cost. Typically some thought mothers were especially affected by the death of their children: 'The Affections of Women are laid deep in their Natures, so that the common Afflictions of Life . . . from the Loss of Children, or of their Husbands, go far-ther into their Minds, and sink, and shake them more violently'.[11]

[10] *A Supplement to Burnet's History of My Own Time*, ed. H. C. Foxcroft (Oxford, 1902), p. 420.
[11] G. Burnet, 'A Sermon Preached at the Funeral of the Right Honourable Anne, Lady-Dowager Brook', in *A Third Collection of Several Tracts and Discourses Written in the Years 1690, to 1703* (1703), p. 11.

People who lived to adulthood had no guarantee of enjoying a ripe old age, for even their life expectancy averaged only about 60. Consequently, though England's population had a relatively large proportion of older people in these years, old age in modern terms was a fairly infrequent experience—the exceptions, such as the death at 106 of Elizabeth Lock of Covent Garden in 1711, proving the rule. If mortality crises were rare, death was bewilderingly random and ever threatening. If not sufficiently virulent to cause epidemics, other diseases such as smallpox, chicken pox, influenza, dysentery, and whooping cough were all commonplace scourges. Smallpox was especially prevalent in the late seventeenth and early eighteenth centuries, particularly in towns. Without respect for social bounds, carrying off Queen Mary in 1694, the Duke of Gloucester in 1701, and the Duke of Rutland in 1721, its threat was potent and feared. In 1706 it 'struck so great a terror upon the country people round us that the trade in general is incredibly diminished'.[12] Such diseases had almost certainly become more important through the seventeenth century. In part this was because heightened international trade, especially extra-European trade, confronted the nation with unwelcome imports of new scourges—malaria, for example, became a significant hazard in and around the Essex marshes in this period. Hardly less important, internal migration and trade, especially to and from London, provided efficient communication routes for diseases. In fact London played a very significant role in keeping nationwide levels of births and deaths close to parity in this period because, with deaths exceeding births there, its rapid growth depended upon high levels of migration.

A further insight into the nature of mortality in this period can be gained by looking at its seasonal incidence. Here a very clear pattern existed, with the four months from January to April typically seeing considerable numbers of deaths, the five months from May to October relatively few and the other months being about average. Evidently, climate played its part in this, the colder winter months leading to death through, or associated with, hypothermia for the very young and old (many infants also lacked immunity or antibodies) and respiratory infections for all. Yet if what might be called the social world of death was age related, to contemporaries ill health threatened all.

Naturally contemporaries tried hard to avoid pain and ill health, and to attempt cures if they failed. Medical advice, effective and not, was part of the very fabric of common culture, passed down through word of mouth and mutual aid. In 1700 the common view was that illness was often caused by upsetting the body's constitutional balance (of the sanguine, choleric, melancholy, and phlegmatic 'humours') and that external signs were very significant:

[12] H. M. C., *The Manuscripts of his Grace the Duke of Portland*, vol. 4 (1897), p. 282.

the body had become too hot or too cold, too wet or too dry. Remedies, most notably herbal ones, sought to restore a state of equilibrium. All might share in this knowledge, and housewives from all backgrounds would have their medical recipes to turn to in an hour of need. When these failed, most communities would have their particular 'expert' who could be called upon, frequently a nurse or a wise woman. Female midwives, for example, were to be found everywhere, skilled from experience rather than formal training. Outside help was also available from itinerant healers selling potions and cures and the literate bought popular medical works, especially Culpeper's *The English Physician Enlarged*. Most people had little recourse to 'professional' medical expertise, being confident in the skills of self-diagnosis or the efficacy of local amateurs. The power of such 'ignorance' and 'faith' should not be underestimated, for modern medicine is well used to the important benefits of placebos upon the mind and, thereby, upon the body.

More formalized medical knowledge was increasingly available as the medical profession expanded and evolved. Male apothecaries, surgeons, barbersurgeons, and physicians received instruction (sometimes abroad, between 1713 and 1730 there were nearly 400 English-speaking students of medicine at the University of Leiden) and were, to a degree, regulated. Such medical practitioners had proliferated through the seventeenth century—in towns such as Chester and Nottingham by tenfold—and the surgeon-apothecary was beginning to play the part of a general practitioner. Even so medical expertise was much more available in towns than the countryside, and even the gentry might have to travel far and wide to find one in an emergency. Moreover, the profession was in a state of flux as rival groups contested knowledge and skill while distancing themselves from more popular medicine. Yet the instruction available to them was limited. Diagnosis was usually based on external manifestations; few drugs were available to prescribe; operations were rare because so crude and dangerous; and bleeding, sweating, clysters, purging, and emetics were the stock in trade. Rich patients were just starting to be packed off in great numbers to Bath and other spas to take the waters. Hospitals were few and far between, the capital being the best provided: St Thomas', St Bartholomew's, and 'Bedlam' (Bethlem), a hospital for the insane, were joined by the Westminster in 1720 and Guy's in 1724.[13] Yet it is indicative that the very term 'hospital' was applied with equal frequency to places for the incapacitated as well as to places for the cure of the sick. Founded by Charles II, Chelsea Hospital for old soldiers opened in 1692; Greenwich Hospital, another of

---

[13] Thomas Guy, 1645?–1724, London bookseller, printer for Oxford University, MP, speculated successfully on the South Sea Bubble in 1720 and left his large fortune to a variety of good causes including a hospital.

Wren's masterpieces, was begun two years later to provide for sailors. At Newcastle Defoe described 'a large hospital built by contribution of the keel men, by way of friendly society, for the maintenance of the poor of their fraternity'.[14] When Thomas Wood, the Bishop of Coventry and Lichfield, died in 1692 he left £20,000 to build a hospital for old men that presumably provided retirement homes as well as geriatric care.

Given the state of contemporary pharmacology neither universities nor hospitals could promote significant medical advances. More characteristic of new approaches in this era was the abandonment of touching by the monarch for the cure of scrofula and the first attempts to inoculate against smallpox. Before the Glorious Revolution it was popularly held that sufferers of scrofula, a form of tuberculosis, could be cured by the royal touch. This power was ascribed both to religious authority, because the monarch was God's direct representative on earth, and to an innate mystical quality. It has been estimated that Charles II touched 90,000 sufferers in his reign (1660–85), but William and Mary pointedly discontinued the practice, so making a forceful statement about the limits to their power and removing a significant point of contact between the people and monarch. Anne revived it (even touching the young Samuel Johnson), but with her death the practice fell into complete abeyance. This casts light not only upon monarchy, but also upon perceptions of ill health and viable forms of cure, symbolizing a diminishing belief in the efficacy of what would now be characterized as superficial and external remedies.

Smallpox was, pre-eminently, a visual affliction, permanently disfiguring those who escaped its deathly embrace. In 1717 Lady Mary Wortley Montagu, writing from Turkey, noted that 'The Small Pox so fatal and so general amongst us is here entirely harmless by the invention of engrafting . . . There is a set of old Women who make it their business to perform the Operation . . . There is no example of any one that has dy'd in it . . . I am Patriot enough to take pains to bring this usefull invention into fashion in England'.[15] The following year she had her son successfully inoculated by the embassy's doctor—who later published a pamphlet on the treatment. More important, back in London she obtained the support of the Princess of Wales and in the summer of 1721 some criminals condemned to death were inoculated in a London prison. According to Voltaire, 'Once assured of the practical success of this test, the Princess had her own children inoculated: England followed

---

[14] Defoe, *Tour*, p. 535.

[15] *The Complete Letters of Lady Mary Wortley Montagu*, ed. R. Halsband, 3 vols. (Oxford, 1965), vol. 1, pp. 338–9. Lady Mary Wortley Montagu, 1689–1762, renowned for her intellect, free spirit, wit, and beauty; a productive but largely unpublished writer, now best known for her correspondence; she travelled with her husband when he was appointed ambassador to Constantinople in 1716.

her example'.[16] It was not, of course, quite so simple, but the lesson is instructive. A technique fashioned abroad was introduced by a layperson, worked on the anvil of maternal affection and the terror of the law, and championed by royalty. Doctors played their part, but it was a supporting rather than leading role.

BIRTHS, MARRIAGES, AND SEX

It has often been held that until the nineteenth century fertility was uncontrolled and 'naturally' high, thereby playing little part in changes of population size. Supposedly large families were the norm because of early marriage and ineffective contraception. This is now known to be somewhat mythical. For a variety of reasons family size was generally much smaller than we might imagine. Only a quarter of women both married before they were 20 and lived beyond the menopause, and even they bore an average of just seven children, not all of whom survived infancy. Most women married later and had fewer children because of sexual abstinence, *coitus interruptus*, the low chances of conception (especially as a consequence of breast feeding and poor nutritional status), incomplete pregnancies, and the death of husbands.

For women the average age at first marriage was about 26 in the final two decades of the seventeenth century, rose very slightly between 1700 and 1719 before declining significantly in the second half of the eighteenth century. This was well beyond sexual maturity, acting as a significant restraint upon population growth, helping to limit average family size to a little less than five. Men married on average a year later, at about 27 or 28, only about 15 per cent of men being married by their 21st birthday. Furthermore, people not only married late, a good many never married at all. This was especially so in the mid- to late seventeenth century when, by one speculation, for those born in 1641, over one in five were unmarried by the mid-1680s. This proportion fell thereafter, celibacy among 40 year-olds in the first decade of the eighteenth century being around one in ten. Yet late age at marriage and such high levels of marriage avoidance were not, as might be expected, associated with high levels of illegitimacy, for at the turn of the century only about 2 per cent of births took place out of wedlock. At that date marriage was late, often avoided, but still provided the social context for raising a family—the very purpose of marriage was to procreate, with emotional solace for partners often being viewed as a secondary consideration. Consequently, in spite of the Prayer Book's comprehensive justification for the institution of marriage, fertility rates were depressed and late seventeenth-century England was demographically a society of restraint, not of rampant procreation. Only slowly did this change. As

[16] Voltaire, *Letters on England*, trans. L. Tancock (Harmondsworth, 1980), p. 55.

age at marriage began to fall and celibacy retreated, fertility levels responded positively, helping to fuel England's modest population growth in these years.

Few in late seventeenth-century England married other than for affection or love. Only among the elite, concerned with the descent of their vast wealth, did this frequently give way openly and routinely to calculation—such arranged marriages were often referred to as making an 'alliance' or 'treaty'. Even so parents knew the limits to their authority. When contemplating marriage as a law student in 1716, Dudley Ryder, the future Solicitor-General, met stiff resistance from his father: 'But he said if I was so deeply engaged in love as to interrupt me in my study or that I could not be easy without her, he could freely consent to my marrying of her'.[17] Doubtless the reasoning was, as Lady Mary Wortley Montagu remarked, that 'tis better to be privately happy than Splendidly Miserable' and that 'man and woman must run a great hazard of living misserably all their lives, where there is not a mutual inclination beforehand.'[18]

Entering into sexual relations and marriage was not something taken lightly, though nor were they the product of mere calculus. That love and passion had their parts to play in marriage is also suggested by the high proportion of so-called clandestine marriages. These legal but irregular marriages, held outside churches, accounted for a significant minority of all marriages and were especially prevalent in London. In and around the Fleet prison poor clergymen were conducting 50 to 60 clandestine marriages a week in the first decade of the eighteenth century and perhaps 80 by the 1720s. Clandestine marriages had a number of advantages for couples. Requiring only the consent of the partners and a licence, they were readily available, quick, cheap, and private. Secrecy helped keep costs down, but also suggests that couples often married against the wishes of parents or employers. As ever, therefore, marriage was a common inter-generational battlefield. The threat clandestine marriages posed to the Church's authority, and the socially co-ordinated control of inheritance, worried polite society particularly, though despite many attempts in this period the law of marriage was not overhauled until 1753.

As a sacred union, marriage was much more easily entered into than quitted. Divorce was only possible through an Act of Parliament and so available only to the wealthy and educated. Barely a handful of divorces were granted each year, most usually on the grounds of adultery, but they provided the public

---

[17] *The Diary of Dudley Ryder, 1715–1716*, ed. W. Matthews (1939), p. 327. Dudley Ryder, 1691–1756, studied at Edinburgh, Leiden, and Middle Temple, briefly an MP, Solicitor General 1733, Attorney General 1737, knighted 1740, Lord Chief Justice King's Bench 1754, and Privy Councillor.

[18] *Letters of Lady Mary Wortley Montagu*, vol. 1, p. 178; *The Letters and Papers of the Banks Family of Revesby Abbey 1704–1760*, ed. J. W. F. Hill, Lincoln Record Society, 45 (1952), p. 15.

with voyeuristic entertainment of a high order—the 2nd Earl of Macclesfield divorced his wife in 1698 after she bore two children fathered by Earl Rivers. Cuckolded husbands sometimes sued their rival for damages, in 1689 a gentleman from Buckinghamshire was reportedly awarded £5,000 in this way and the 12th Duke of Norfolk obtained 100 marks from a Mr Jermain. But most marriages which disintegrated did so much more privately and modestly, with separation the best that could be hoped for—parish records often note husbands who had abandoned their family. In such circumstances legal remarriage was impossible until one of the partners died, but such religious and legal stringency was too much for many and bigamy was not uncommon.

Not only in England, but for most of Western Europe, the nuclear rather than the extended family was the norm. Families usually consisted of no more than two generations—of parents and children—with most people establishing their own home at marriage. Though this was a distinctive cultural phenomenon it also meant that marriage was intimately tied to the context not only of emotions and sexuality but also of economic opportunities. The ability to set up an independent household particularly depended upon the availability and cost of lodgings, the ability to make at least some modest savings with which to furnish the new home, and the real value of income opportunities (their availability, reliability, and rewards relative to prices). It is noticeable here that marriage was highly seasonal, peaking first in April and May and then in October and November. Partly this followed the remnants of a bygone religious calendar, especially the prohibition of marriage in Lent, but mainly it followed the rhythm of the agricultural year. The first peak followed the heavy demands of lambing and calving, the second the busy work of the harvest. Plentiful and relatively well-paid work was too valuable to miss for most betrothed couples, providing the final monies to float their union. Over the longer term, moreover, economic niches had been hard to come by in seventeenth-century England because of a lack of sustained economic growth. The doubling of population between 1540 and the start of the civil war had put enormous pressure upon resources. Work became scarce, prices rose, State instituted charity expanded, disaster threatened. Some parts of the country were worse hit than others, but in such an environment and within the constraints of prevailing value systems, marriage became less accessible for many —not to mention the resistance of some poor law administrators to 'pauper marriages'. Whatever the pull of emotions, for many couples economic uncertainty forced either an avoidance or postponement of marriage. To the poor agricultural labourer, faced with high rents and often only casual employment, marriage became a relatively expensive luxury. Only as economic fortunes slowly improved after the Restoration did this change, and then only gradually.

Relatively late age at marriage was culturally driven but economically influenced. It was also partly institutionalized. The apprenticeship of boys (and some girls) for seven years from about 14 provided valuable skills but required celibacy—the sexual antics of apprentices was something of an obsession of contemporary moralists. Similarly, in the countryside young people might be taken on as servants and labourers, living in the household of the farmer, so long as they remained single. The heyday of apprenticeship had passed by the 1690s, but in some towns and cities, such as Coventry, Norwich, Sheffield, and London, it was still important. Service in husbandry was if anything growing in significance in this period, both in terms of the number of jobs and the length of contract, as agricultural expansion encouraged farmers to secure labour supplies on a more predictable basis.

Late marriage was not inversely correlated to levels of sexual experience. The majority of young people fell outside the constraints of service and apprenticeship, and the requirement of celibacy was in any case unlikely to prevent sexual encounters. The low rate of illegitimacy in this period is in fact no evidence of sexual abstinence or of abortion, for being only a measure of those born out of wedlock it is just as much an indicator of mores regarding bastardy, particularly of the willingness of expectant unmarried parents to wed to preserve the reputation of themselves and their child. It is notable, therefore, that around 1700 between 15 and 20 per cent of first births were pre-nuptially conceived (three times the level of France at the same time) suggesting that a much higher portion of young people must have been sexually active before marriage. There was nothing new in that, though there is some evidence that an unusually large number of couples began full sexual relations after rather than before they had decided to marry. Demographically England may have been relatively restrained, but it was not in practice a bastion of Puritan morality. Unwanted pregnancies did occur and bastards were born, which with the prevailing double standard harmed the reputation of the mother more than the father. Few avenues for escape existed and desperate remedies were sometimes taken. Steele claimed that 'There is scarce an Assizes where some unhappy Wretch is not Executed for the Murder of a Child . . . Not to mention those, who by Unnatural Practices do in some Measure defeat the Intentions of Providence, and destroy their Conceptions even before they see the Light.'[19] This exaggerated the frequency of infanticide and of the number of women executed for killing their child (indeed there seems to have been an increasing reluctance to convict women for infanticide over the period), but it is likely that mortality rates were higher among illegitimate than legitimate children and that abortion may have been common, crude and secretive as it was.

[19] *The Guardian*, ed. J. C. Stephens (Lexington, Kentucky, 1982), p. 366.

Couples certainly sought to control their fertility, both to encourage and to avoid pregnancies. Though medical knowledge of reproductive processes was rudimentary, there was a common fund of opinion to be drawn upon. It was, for example, generally believed that a woman had to enjoy sex in order to conceive. Only later in the eighteenth century did developments in embryology cast doubt upon this. Reproduction was linked, therefore, to the wider wellbeing of the partners, to physical and psychological happiness. Charms and potions, as well as love and lust, had their part to play. Attempts to ward off pregnancies rested upon magic, herbalism, the withdrawal method, and sheaths. Sexual knowledge was, though, limited. In 1699 a soldier suffering from venereal disease 'seduced' two daughters aged 7 and 9 of an Uxbridge innkeeper because, 'according to the common Opinion in these cases', he believed sexual intercourse with a virgin would cure him.[20] No less striking, in the autumn of 1726 Mary Toft of Godalming in Surrey claimed to have given birth to seventeen rabbits. Her story fascinated many and was given some credit. She was soon brought to London where Lord Hervey reported that 'All the eminent physicians, Surgeons, and Men-midwifes in London are there Day & Night to watch her next production.'[21] Toft claimed that her monstrous births were caused by being frightened by rabbits when weeding in the fields while pregnant. To many onlookers the view that psychology might overpower physiology was entirely plausible, though the hoax was exposed by December. The battle of beliefs spread extensively, even leading to a report that 'Several Higglers from Cambridgeshire, Suffolk, and other Parts, affirm, they have lost above a hundred Pounds a Man by the detestable Rabbet-breeding Woman; they being under Contracts to take of the Warreners, weekly, a certain Number, which afterwards came to bad Markets, and they could not dispose of them'.[22]

After 1689 moralists frequently assaulted the sexual standards of the people. Lewdness was allegedly everywhere, the stench of the farmyard morals of the Restoration court having overpowered society as a whole. 'Vice' was indeed one of the age's watchwords. Perhaps there had been some small shift in attitudes. More probably, irregular behaviour was more noticeable and more noticed than ever. In particular, the great growth of London in the seventeenth century provided plentiful evidence of relationships only occasionally encountered in rural backwaters. So many people in so small a space provided sexual opportunities aplenty and the possibility of their generally anonymous enjoyment: 'now the most Scandalous, Inhuman, Unnatural, and Beastly Offences,

[20] The Post Boy, 31 October–2 November 1699, [p. 2].
[21] Quoted in D. Todd, Imagining Monsters: Miscreations of the Self in Eighteenth-Century England (Chicago, 1995), p. 1.
[22] Mist's Weekly Journal, 24 December 1726, [p. 3].

stalk abroad at Noon day'.[23] Prostitution and a nascent homosexual sub-culture flourished, soon attracting adverse comment. Yet what made post-Revolution London distinctive was the attempts to stem such developments. Notably, the Reformation of Manners societies, the first of which was founded in 1691, were at their zenith in the first quarter of the eighteenth century prosecuting an annual average of 1,300 prostitutes in London for 'lewd and disorderly' conduct.[24] Rather than their clients it was often poor young women with no other means of support than selling their bodies who were particularly targeted by the Society. Certainly there was a clash of values here, and not only between the women and their prosecutors. In York in 1725 'Three young Ladies of Pleasure were . . . ordered by the pious Magistrates to be whipp'd out of the different Gates of that City; but the Nature of the Crime was such, that they met with as many Friends as Spectators, so that the Executioner durst not perform his Duty.'[25] Such 'pious Magistrates' were of course uncovering an old not a new problem. They were far less successful in finding active homosexuals, though sodomy was as widely condemned as prostitution (lesbianism attracted little comment). There is no doubt that homosexuals in London were better organized and more visible than elsewhere. '*Sodomites* (who have been but rarely heard of in this Nation till the last Age) . . . have their appointed Places of Meeting for their acting their abominable Villanies, and to encrease their Numbers'.[26] There were well-known cruising grounds, such as the Royal Exchange and Lincoln's Inn Fields, and 'molly houses', taverns, and alehouses for homosexual rendezvous. Outside London, evidence of organized homosexuality is harder to find though institutionalized male society—the armed services, Church, universities, and Inns of Court—provided particular opportunities. At Oxford it was claimed that 'among the chief men in some of the colleges sodomy is very usual and the master of one college has ruined several young handsome men that way, that it is dangerous sending a young man that is beautiful to Oxford.'[27]

PEOPLE ON THE MOVE

England was a land of villages interspersed with the lures of urbanization and, increasingly, international opportunities. Consequently, if some people died in

[23] *The Tryal and Condemnation of Mervin, Lord Audley, Earl of Castle-Haven. At Westminster, April the 5th 1631* (1699), Preface.

[24] For a further discussion of these societies, see below, pp. 238–9.

[25] *Mist's Weekly Journal*, 8 May 1725, [p. 2].

[26] [J. Wedgwood], *An Account of the Progress of the Reformation of Manners, in England, Scotland, and Ireland, and Other Parts of Europe and America* (12th edn., 1704), p. 25.

[27] *Diary of Dudley Ryder*, p. 143.

the village of their birth many did not. Both internal and international migration had their impact upon England's population history. Moreover, contemporaries worried incessantly about people on the move. Parishes hated the idea of having to provide for the poor from elsewhere and vagrants were seen not as poor migrants in search of work but idle rogues wallowing in the luxury of social irresponsibility. Hawkers and peddlers roamed on the very margins of society, prompting legislators occasionally to attempt their extinction. Emigrants were a net loss to national prosperity, yet immigrants threatened Englishness, citizenship, and order. The social ideal was of a fixed, immobile, and ordered society, the reality was something else altogether.

The absolute level of migration within England in this period is impossible to establish accurately. Depositions at ecclesiastical courts, apprenticeship indentures, and poor law records, amongst other sources, allow a sketch of the types of mobility that existed to be attempted. What is clear is that this was a mobile society, with about two-thirds of people moving to live beyond the parish of their birth at least once in their life in the late seventeenth and early eighteenth centuries. Most people, however, moved fairly small distances, only one in ten migrants travelling more than 40 miles. Nearly three-quarters of apprentices at Sheffield in this period were born within 15 miles of the city. Only London was magnetic enough to attract migrants from across the British Isles.

There were, of course, a variety of motives behind geographical mobility. Some moved because of their jobs, but eventually returned home—such as chapmen, soldiers, and sailors, as well as seasonal workers harvesting fruit and hops. Others moved for career reasons, to undertake apprenticeship, attend university, or join the Inns of Court. In this period, with economic improvements tending to outstrip the growth of population, subsistence migration was becoming slightly less common. Even so, in 1700 a city like Norwich was attracting around 400 migrants per annum and London perhaps 8,000, many of them desperately poor. At this date between a half and two-thirds of all town dwellers in England were in fact migrants. High rates of urban mortality and perceptions of the opportunities for work and charity in towns were powerful stimuli here. It is notable that more women than men made the move from countryside to towns, mainly reflecting the gender imbalance in work opportunities. In agriculture, though both sexes were employed, more jobs were available for men than women, whereas in towns domestic service was frequently undertaken by women (usually young and unmarried). Larger towns were usually composed of significantly more women than men—at the start of the eighteenth century the ratio may have been 92 men per 100 women (at birth males slightly outnumber females). About two-thirds of migrants to town were aged less than 30, and they were often single.

Though neither emigration nor immigration were especially numerous in this period both exercised a powerful influence upon contemporary perceptions of national well-being. More emigrated than immigrated, the net outflow numbering perhaps 5,000 per annum. (This understates somewhat the outflow of the English, for it counts as immigrants those arriving from other parts of the British Isles.) Aside from the exodus of English Jacobites in 1688 and 1689 (many more Irish Jacobites fled to France in 1691) and the deaths of soldiers and sailors on service overseas, most left for a new life in North America. Many of these were men—records of emigrants from Liverpool in the eleven years after 1696 show 72 per cent were men and 28 per cent women. Similarly, records of baptisms for England in 1700 show nearly 105 males per 100 females, but because so many men died abroad the sex ratio at burial in England was 98 to 100. In the seventeenth century a typical form of emigration was indentured servitude, whereby a migrant contracted to work for a master for a given period, usually seven years, in return for the cost of passage and, usually, bed and board. But the outflow of emigrants by this route was badly disrupted by war between 1689 and 1697 and 1702 and 1713. In parts of the Caribbean and some of the Thirteen Colonies labour shortages became more acute and cheap labour hard to find. Planters saw imminent stagnation unless alternative sources could be tapped, looking to tropical west Africa for slaves.[28] The darkest days of the Atlantic slave trade were now dawning.

Few commentators applauded emigration, for the number of labourers was seen as central to economic well-being. Immigration was another matter and subjected to intense political debate. For the Whigs, 'Whereas the increase of people is a means of advancing the wealth and strength of a nation; and whereas many strangers [i.e. foreigners] of the Protestant or Reformed religion out of due consideration of the happy constitution of the government of this realm, would be induced to transport themselves and their estates into this kingdom, if they might be made partakers of the advantages and privileges which the natural-born subjects thereof do enjoy'.[29] Many questioned the social consequences of this and a strong strand of xenophobia often reared its ugly head. As one visitor noted 'the British people . . . look on foreigners in general with contempt'.[30] To many, Englishness was challenged by strange faces, languages, manners, and religions, with the nationality and religion of William III and the Hanoverians giving this a significant political dimension. Jacobites loved to depict England being picked bare by foreign parasites—'we saw old England, so famous for our good and excellent laws and happy constitution, swarming

---

[28] See below, pp. 266–8.   [29] 'An Act for Naturalizing Foreign Protestants', 7 Anne, c. 5.
[30] *A Foreign View of England in the Reigns of George I and George II. The Letters of Monsieur César de Saussure to his Family*, trans. and ed. Madame van Muyden (1902), p. 177.

with Dutch blood-suckers that thirsted after our estates'.[31] Yet attitudes were mixed. Defoe pointed out that over the centuries England had received wave after wave of immigrants to the extent that 'A true-born Englishman's a contradiction,/ In speech an irony, in fact a fiction.'[32] And the English could look upon foreign Protestants as brothers, supporting Crown-sponsored charity briefs for them to the tune of nearly £200,000 between 1686 and 1703.

Parts of English society in the early eighteenth century were unusually cosmopolitan. Some 50,000 French fled to England in the late seventeenth century as Louis XIV sought to Catholicize his country—mainly Huguenots, often highly skilled, they generally lived together in large cities. A good number of Dutch settled in London, brought by trade, finance, or William. A small Jewish community was developing, perhaps numbering 1,000 in London in 1695. A taste for 'exotic' servants led to the presence of perhaps as many as 10,000 non-Caucasians, often blacks and sometimes slaves. And in 1709 13,000 poor Palatines suddenly arrived in England, bringing attitudes towards foreigners to a head. Such large numbers could not be easily found homes or jobs—a newspaper report published in the midst of this influx thought only a quarter had a trade. A large camp on Blackheath became their temporary residence (presumably disrupting England's one and only golf club). Charitable collections were instituted, and £20,000 was raised in London alone, but attitudes soon soured. By July 1709 'People are generally very angry here at soe many Palitanes being brought over . . . And they begin to make reports as if they wou'd bring a Plague among us for they die in heaps at Black heath'.[33] Some of the Palatines were found places in England; some 3,000 were shipped off to Ireland; another 3,000 went to America and 1,000 to the West Indies, though many died en route; and many returned to Germany.

GREGORY KING'S ENGLAND

Towards the end of the seventeenth century 'political arithmetic', 'the art of reasoning by figures, upon things relating to government', enjoyed something of a vogue in England.[34] The foremost exponent of this art was the former herald Gregory King, who loved playing with numbers, true or not, drawn variously from personal observation, taxation records, and guesswork. Writing

---

[31] *Memoirs of Thomas, Earl of Ailesbury Written by Himself*, 2 vols. (1890), vol. 2, p. 441.

[32] D. Defoe, 'The True-Born Englishman', in G. de F. Lord (ed.), *Anthology of Poems on Affairs of State: Augustan Satirical Verse, 1660–1714* (New Haven, 1975), pp. 633–4.

[33] *The Wentworth Papers 1705–1739. Selected from the Private and Family Correspondence of Thomas Wentworth, Lord Raby, Created in 1711 Earl of Strafford*, ed. J. J. Cartwright (1883), p. 96.

[34] *D'Avenant Works*, vol. 1, p. 128.

TABLE 1. *Gregory King, 'A scheme of income and expence of the the several families of England calculated for the year 1688'*

Number of families	Ranks, degrees, titles, and qualifications	Heads per family	Number of persons	Family income p.a. £	Income per head p.a. £	Expence per head p.a. £	Increase per head £
160	Temporal lords	40	6,400	2,800	70	60	10
26	Spiritual lords	20	520	1,300	65	55	10
800	Baronets	16	12,800	880	55	51	4
600	Knights	13	7,800	650	50	46	4
3,000	Esquires	10	30,000	450	45	42	3
12,000	Gentlemen	8	96,000	280	35	32.5	2.5
5,000	Persons in offices	8	40,000	240	30	27	3
5,000	Persons in offices	6	30,000	120	20	18	2
2,000	Merchants and traders by sea	8	16,000	400	50	40	10
8,000	Merchants and traders by land	6	48,000	200	33	28	5
10,000	Persons in the law	7	70,000	140	20	17	3
2,000	Clergymen	6	12,000	60	10	9	1
8,000	Clergymen	5	40,000	45	9	8	1
40,000	Freeholders	7	280,000	84	12	11	1
140,000	Freeholders	5	700,000	50	10	9.5	0.5
150,000	Farmers	5	750,000	44	8.75	8.5	0.25
16,000	Persons in sciences and liberal arts	5	80,000	60	12	11.5	1.5
40,000	Shopkeepers and tradesmen	4.5	180,000	45	10	9.5	0.5
60,000	Artisans and handicrafts	4	240,000	40	10	9.5	0.5
5,000	Naval officers	4	20,000	80	20	18	2
4,000	Army officers	4	16,000	60	15	14	1
511,586		5.25	2,675,520	67	12.9	12	0.9

							Decrease
50,000	Common seamen	3	150,000	20	7	7.5	−0.5
364,000	Labouring people and out servants	3.5	1,275,000	15	4.5	4.6	−0.1
400,000	Cottagers and paupers	3.25	1,300,000	6.5	2	2.5	−0.25
35,000	Common soldiers	2	70,000	14	7	7.5	−0.5
849,000		3.25	2,795,000	10.5	3.25	3.45	−0.2
	Vagrants		30,000		2	3	−1
849,000		3.25	2,825,000	10.5	3.15	3.38	−0.23
	So the GENERAL ACCOUNT is:						
511,586	Increasing the wealth of the kingdom	5.25	2,675,520	67	12.9	12	0.9
849,000	Decreasing the wealth of the kingdom	3.25	2,825,000	10.5	3.15	3.38	−0.23
1,360,586	Nett totals	4.05	5,500,520	32	7.9	7.56	0.34

Source: Adapted from G. King, *Natural and Political Observations and Conclusions upon the State and Condition of England, 1696* (1804), pp. 48–9.

at a time when finding money to fund wars was a pressing concern, and inclined to see England slipping into the abyss of national bankruptcy, he was prone to pessimism. Yet if his findings are not robust they nevertheless provide an important introduction to English economy and society in 1700. His most significant contribution was his famous social table drawn up in the 1690s depicting England in 1688.

In its details King's table is often demonstrably inaccurate—he did what he could, but the roundness of many of the figures suggests he knew of the limitations involved. So, for example, the average family income of peers of the realm is likely to have been closer to £6,000 than the £2,800 King asserted and the numbers of freeholders and farmers appears to have been exaggerated. Such criticisms and adjustments are themselves highly speculative, but at the broadest level it is possible that national income was not the £43.5 million that King suggested but nearer £54.5 million. Informed guesswork by historians has concluded that agriculture accounted for 37 per cent of this, industry 20 per cent, commerce 16 per cent, rent and services 20 per cent, and government 7 per cent.[35] England in 1700 was, therefore, far from simply an agrarian society and was already a mixed economy with prominent industrial and commercial sectors. This indeed was a point much noted by contemporaries thinking about the peculiarity of England. Not only did some argue that 'Trade is fitted to the Nature of our Country' as an island nation, others also noted that 'an *Estate's a pond, but a Trade's a spring*'.[36] All European societies were agrarian, but only England, Holland, and Venice might also be labelled as commercial. Commonly England was described as a 'trading nation', a designation which drew its initial force from the high regard for overseas trade but which also, as Defoe noted, encompassed the inland trade, 'the foundation of all our wealth and greatness; it is the support of all our foreign trade, and of our manufacturing'.[37]

If the details of King's table are unreliable, its organization is rich in significance. Clearly King's scheme is hierarchical, but one ordered both by status and income. Thus because of differences of annual income he distinguished two levels of office holders, merchants, clergymen, and freeholders. To King, the organization of English society had a highly plutocratic element. No less significant, however, was his use of the family as the primary unit of social analysis, by which he meant the wider household of resident kin and

---

[35] N. F. R. Crafts, *British Economic Growth during the Industrial Revolution* (Oxford, 1985), p. 16. For a critique of such estimates, see J. Hoppit, 'Counting the Industrial Revolution', *Economic History Review*, 53 (1990), pp. 173–93.

[36] J. Addison, *The Freeholder*, ed. J. Leheny (Oxford, 1979), p. 224; D. Defoe, *The Complete English Tradesman* (Gloucester, 1987), p. 375.

[37] Defoe, *The Complete English Tradesman*, p. 222.

servants. Indeed, in King's scheme the plutocratic structure of society was linked to a hierarchy of family size, hence the large number of people in the families of temporal lords. A society viewed in familial terms was also, importantly, a patriarchal one, categorized on the basis of the occupation of the head of the household, most usually the man. Yet it is striking that King employed a much more finely graded view of society at the top than at the bottom. In the top half of society he identified twenty-one ranks, but in the bottom half only five. Betraying many of the assumptions of the elite, King's social categories were crude for the majority but much more subtle for the minority. Such prejudices are laid bare by his belief that just over a half of the population spent more than they earned and so 'decreased the wealth of the nation'. Inequality was marked and fundamental and, implicitly, only transfer payments from the rich to the poor kept famine and catastrophe at bay. Something like 42 per cent of national income was taken by the top 10 per cent of earners, the bottom 40 per cent of earners taking only 15 per cent. To King the fundamental social division was not between classes, but between those who reliably had access to the means of subsistence and those who did not. Yet if King's perception of proximity to poverty as a fundamental social fact cannot be questioned, his assumption that ultimately the poor were a drain on the nation can.

UNCERTAIN HIERARCHIES

English society in this period was fluid not fixed, dynamic not timeless. Certainly, social structure is not something that can be described easily or precisely, not least because many changes were slow and subtle. Three serious problems face the historian here. First, evidence of social structure was overwhelmingly generated by the elite, looking down from their mountains of wealth upon the majority working in the plains of hardship (King believed 70 per cent of people were manual workers). What ordinary English people thought of their society is much harder to uncover. Second, contemporaries provided not one way of seeing their society, but many. Such multiplicity is itself full of meaning, suggesting the different ways society could be conceptualized and the difficulties of abstracting out some 'national' general picture from the complexity of actual experience. Finally, depictions of social structure are liable to resemble a photograph rather than a moving image, thereby losing those movements that constituted the essential social experiences of people at the time.

All contemporaries had a clear sense that society was hierarchical. Most crudely this was based upon status. At the pinnacle stood the royal family, followed by the five degrees of nobility: dukes, marquesses, earls, viscounts, and barons. 'Next to the Nobility, let us take a View of the *English Gentry*, which keeps a middle Rank betwixt the Nobles and the Common People. Of which there are three Degrees; *viz. Knights, Esquire,* and *Gentlemen.*'[38] These last three degrees were supposed to be formally limited, but in practice the label of gentleman was in the midst of a prolonged process of recasting, subtly challenging many ideas of order. Miege noted that noblemen 'may be called a Gentleman' yet 'On the other side any one that . . . has either a liberal or genteel Education, that looks Gentleman-like (whether he be so or not) and has wherewithal to live freely and handsomely, is by the Courtesie of *England* usually called a Gentleman.'[39] In this view status was being eroded by evolving conventions. Beneath these 'middle Rank' was the 'Commonalty . . . Yeomen, Merchants, Artificers, Tradesmen, Mariners, and all others getting their Livelihood after a Mechanick Way.'[40] The crudity of this social category is impossible to ignore. The mass of society were simply lumped together in Miege's scheme of things, as in that of King and others. To Macky 'The Degrees of People in *England* are divided into five Classes. The Peers of the Realm. The Baronets and Knights Batchelors. The Esquires. The Gentlemen. The Commoners.'[41]

   The depictions of society by Miege and King fail to provide evidence of the ways society worked as a living organism, of those interests, duties, dependencies, changes, and interactions which structured day-to-day life. This is best considered in relation to the distribution of authority and power according to age, sex, and economic interest. In all three the prevailing, though far from universal view, was that there were natural or divinely ordained hierarchies at work. Few at the time were committed to the view that all people had equal rights and opportunities, though philosophers were already much concerned with explaining why civil society was so distinct from a state of nature. It was expected that most people were disabled in some way, the young should be subservient to the old, women to men, and the poor to the rich. Full citizenship was available to few. According to one cleric, 'every Family (the original indeed and model of Bodies Corporate, Cities, and Commonwealths) must have its proper Superiour, whom all the rest must needs obey.'[42]

   Compared with today, English society at the start of the eighteenth century had a relatively large proportion of young people. If it was true that 'They have

---

[38] G. Miege, *The New State of England under our Present Monarch K. William III* (4th edn., 1702), part 2, p. 152.

[39] Miege, *New State of England*, part 2, p. 154.

[40] Miege, *New State of England*, part 2, p. 154.

[41] [J. Macky], *A Journey Through England*, 2 vols. (2nd edn., 1722), vol. 2, pp. 236–7. John Macky, *d.*1726, writer and government spy, his *Memoirs of the Secret Services of John Macky, Esq* (1733) contains useful observations on leading politicians of the period 1689–1705.

[42] W. Fleetwood, *The Relative Duties of Parents and Children, Husbands and Wives, Masters and Servants* (1705), pp. 167–8.

an extraordinary Regard in *England* for young Children, always flattering, always caressing, always applauding what they do', the young were also seen as dependent and generally requiring discipline.[43] Supposedly, wisdom and authority were acquired with age. If economically valuable, the young were often viewed as headstrong and passionate, lacking the capacity for fully reasoned judgement. Moreover, 'youth' was not merely a question of age, but also of status. Most obviously, apprentices and servants in husbandry lay absolutely under their masters' control—'An Apprentice is a Sort of Slave'.[44] Marital status was a key issue here, with bachelors and maids viewed as 'youths' even into their twenties but husbands and wives as adults almost regardless of age. In a similar way much of the social ideology and many of the institutional arrangements of the period significantly favoured men over women. Many families, though by no means all, practised primogeniture, the inheritance of wealth by the eldest son. At marriage women became legally subject to their husbands, their property his: 'the Father is also superiour to the Mother, both in Natural Strength, in Wisdom, and by God's appointment'.[45] Women who murdered their husbands, as with servants who killed their masters, took not only a life, but challenged the social order and were charged with petty treason. A double standard of sexual morality for men and women was a commonplace, if one that was none the less contested. Women were routinely excluded from civil and military office, from apprenticeship to most trades, from the universities, the workings of the law, and the franchise. Finally, if to be young or a woman limited social function and authority so did poverty. Many contemporaries stressed that riches alone allowed the acquisition of education, the trappings of politeness, and the exercise of civility, supposedly the prerequisites of reasoned judgement and the powers of government. Thus to the Earl of Ailesbury 'The common sort' were 'a giddy and unthinking people'.[46] In the elite's view, full citizenship went with the ownership of property, most usually land. It was assumed that people without such resources were liable to influence from any quarter prepared to strike a bargain. So, for example, in the counties the exercise of the vote had long been limited to the forty shilling freeholders in an attempt to ensure that electors acted independently and judiciously. Inequalities in the distribution of power and authority was closely correlated to inequalities in the distribution of wealth and income.

Social ideals were largely expressed by those who were old, male, and rich. At bottom, their justification for the inequalities at the heart of English society

---

[43] H. Misson, *Memoirs and Observations in his Travels Over England* (1719), p. 33.

[44] Misson, *Memoirs and Observations*, p. 3.   [45] Fleetwood, *Relative Duties*, p. 59.

[46] *Memoirs of Ailesbury*, vol. 1, p. 242. Thomas Bruce, 1655?–1741, succeeded as 2nd Earl of Ailesbury 1685, a courtier of James II, imprisoned on suspicion of Jacobitism, and in exile 1696–1741.

rested upon paternalistic ideas of human frailty rooted deep within biblical tradition, arguments about the benefits of a social division of labour, and a stress upon the burden of duties allegedly felt by everybody. This last point was a critical part of the elaborate skein of self-justification spun by the elite. Wealth brought not only ease, but the obligation to govern. Patterns of subordination entailed not only obedience but also reciprocal duties and interdependencies: 'God's provident Care is very remarkable in making the Rich and Poor thus mutually needful and helpful to each other'.[47] In this way English society was viewed in practical terms as one organized on a local basis, with leading landowners playing vital economic, legal, religious, and political roles. Thus they could appear as active paternalists not indolent parasites, labouring as JPs, providing employment, supporting the church, and dispensing charity.

As ever, social ideals failed to mirror precisely social reality. In any case, social ideals were themselves mutable and debatable and some of the fundamental inequalities of the age were increasingly coming into question. The aged may have been revered, but they were also mocked. Old women still became liable to the charge of witchcraft, even though legally it was an offence now in its death throes. Those too old to work were a heavy burden upon charity and poor relief. And an increasingly literate culture gradually eroded the importance of old people as conduits of oral culture and received knowledge. Misogynistic expectations also failed to doom all women to a life of quiet subservience. Some women did quit unhappy marriages, travel in search of prospects, assert their independence, inherit and own property, learn and practise trades, and exert some political influence (be it at court, as in the case of Sarah Churchill's influence over Queen Anne, or at the head of a food riot). Even the double standard was coming to be condemned, notably by Steele in 1713: 'the Man of Gallantry cannot pursue his Pleasures without Treachery to some Man he ought to love, and making despicable the Woman he admires . . . When it is thoroughly considered, he gives up his very Being as a Man of Integrity, who commences Gallant.'[48]

Many among the elite were also concerned that the relationship between rich and poor was being subverted in practice. Some, like Defoe, saw the poor as a whole becoming increasingly and persistently disorderly. The 'miserable Circumstance of this Country is now such, that, in short, if it goes on, the Poor will be Rulers over the Rich, and the Servants be Governours of their Masters; the *Plebeii* have almost mobb'd the *Patricii* . . . Order is inverted, Subordination

---

[47] R. Moss, *The Providential Division of Men into Rich and Poor, and the Respective Duties thence Arising* (1708), p. 5.
[48] *The Guardian*, p. 90.

ceases, and the World seems to stand with the Bottom upward.'[49] He explained this by reference to the growing prosperity of the poor and to the evil influence of rising levels of alcohol consumption upon their behaviour and habits. Others noted how urbanization eroded old social ties and encouraged new and generally unwelcome habits.

IDENTITIES AND INTERESTS

To most English people in this period social structure was not conceptualized, it was experienced. Such experiences were richly varied and are best considered in relation to those different communities or interests people considered themselves belonging to. Such communities were both real and imagined, the latter, because of the impact they could have upon behaviour, being no less significant than the former. Feelings of belonging, and of exclusion, operated at a number of overlapping levels: geographical, political, religious, occupational, cultural, generational, and sexual.

Whatever the propensity of people to move in this period it is easy to sympathize with the contemporary view that 'a *Kingdom* is but a Collection of Families, and Parishes'.[50] Such a stress upon the particular and the local seems right, for people were attached to their neighbours and villages. It is telling, for example, that 'country' and 'county' were still virtually interchangeable at this date. Among the majority dialect and accent were significant identifiers. Local customs could powerfully bond communities together. This might literally define the boundaries of a social world: it 'is still observed in some *Country Parishes*, to go round the *Bounds* and *Limits* of the *Parish*, on one of the three Days before *Holy Thursday*, or the Feast of our Lord's Ascension'.[51] Celebration of local saints' days and annual parish feasts were common. Sport could cut across social boundaries, but keep within regional ones. County cricket matches were sometimes played; at Chipping Camden the annual multi-event 'Costwolds games', founded in 1604, were still going. Among the elite the shire was both an administrative unit and a broader social framework. For them, something approaching a county community still existed, where peers were 'like little kings, according to the good they do and the extent of their bounty'.[52] They might be greeted by massed ranks of the gentry on horse when returning after a long absence; their rites of passage (birth, coming of age, marriage,

[49] [D. Defoe], *The Great Law of Subordination Consider'd; or, the Insolence and Unsufferable Behaviour of Servants in England Duly Enquir'd into* (1724), p. 17.

[50] W. Kennett, *The Charity Schools for Poor Children Recommended in a Sermon* (1706), p. 22.

[51] H. Bourne, *Antiquitates Vulgares; or, the Antiquities of the Common People* (Newcastle, 1725), p. 203.

[52] Saussure, *A Foreign View of England*, p. 209.

and death) were often public and widely celebrated events; and their political influence was generally respected and sought after. Towns, with their assembly rooms and theatres, were increasingly becoming focal points of provincial polite society.

Localism was overlaid by national concerns. National history, especially that since the accession of Elizabeth, was a potent force and one widely remembered. Anniversaries of the execution of Charles I on 30 January, the Restoration of Charles II on 29 May, and William's landing and the Gunpowder plot on 5 November were generally celebrated, the last as an element of popular anti-Catholicism. Royal birthdays were similarly observed (William's was on 4 November). Two long periods of war, from 1689 to 1697 and 1702 to 1713, provided further opportunities for experiencing national events. The identification of France (and to a lesser extent of Catholic Ireland and Highland Scotland) as an enemy helped point up the peculiarities of the English; the burden of manning, funding, and supplying the war was felt everywhere; and splendid victories were a cause for national celebrations that were carefully orchestrated by the monarch, with proclamations instituting days of thanksgiving and fasting (the first were virtually public holidays) regularly issued by both William and Anne.

The largest community of interest was that provided by the Anglican church which had a massive presence in English life. If a parish frequently defined a local community of interest, the Church of England was equally a national and uniquely English establishment. Theologically distinctive (neither Lutheran nor Calvinist), many of its ideas and much its structure was fully integrated with English society. The monarch was its head; bishops sat in the House of Lords; and the cathedral close was at the very heart of many cities. Religious ceremonies and the religious calendar provided a framework for people's lives. Virtually everyone celebrated Christmas and Easter, just as 'no one can amuse himself here on Sundays, which are observed as strictly as in any place in the world'.[53] Baptisms, marriages, and burials were usually conducted at church. And the spiritual succour provided by the church was vital to many people, not least in helping them to come to terms with the great uncertainties of life. Yet not everyone was a part of this community, with Dissenters and Roman Catholics in particular standing apart. Excluded from civil society by the Test and Corporation Acts, their services and doctrines literally separated them from the rest of society, albeit incompletely, and helped forge an identity of interest among the majority.

---

[53] *London in 1710: From the Travels of Zacharias Conrad von Uffenbach*, trans. and ed. W. H. Quarrell and M. Mare (1934), p. 36. For a discussion of church observance, see below, pp. 208–10.

As has been seen, fundamental to the structure of English society in this period was the relationship between status and the extreme inequality in the distribution of income and wealth. Though such inequalities were rooted in economic facts of life, they were also highly visible. Patterns of consumption vividly identified people, making them members of certain communities and outsiders to others. If the rich drank wine, the poor resorted to small beer and cheap gin. If the rich shaved their heads, trading lice for elaborate wigs, the poor kept their own hair and its unwelcome visitors. Patterns of consumption were, in fact, as finely graded as the social hierarchy. Ordinary people, with little opportunity to consume much beyond day-to-day necessities, nevertheless were able to enjoy those customs, festivals, wakes, and sports which helped to realize a social community clearly distinguished from that of their more prosperous neighbours—who indeed frequently condemned such activities. For example, in some places at New Year there was 'mumming', the changing of clothes between men and women; at Valentine's day 'It is a *Ceremony*, never omitted among the Vulgar, to draw Lots, which they Term *Valentines*'; and on midsummer's eve people often gathered before large fires in the streets to celebrate.[54] This was far removed from the world of the coffee-house, the waters of Bath, the Inns of Court, and the assize ball.

In Bedfordshire, and we can reasonably suppose elsewhere, 'The Commonalty hate the yeomen, these care but little for their gentlemen, and these are envious towards the nobility'.[55] Such a view suggests the primacy of economic factors above others, of labour struggling for jobs and wages, farmers for output and prices, and landowners for fattened rent rolls. Yet for the poor labourer expressing an identity on the basis of such a common experience was difficult, though not impossible. In 1725, for example, farmers near Portsmouth put a stop to gleaning, the valuable customary right which allowed villagers to clear the fields of remaining corn and straw after the farmer had finished his harvest. The poor 'apply'd to the Mayor for Relief, thinking he could help them; but were answer'd, that it was not in his Power', which led to the farmers being stoned and terrorized.[56] Here ordinary people contested a change in traditional arrangements imposed from above, resorting first to legal redress from the authorities and to violence only as a last resort. There was respect for authority but it was limited. Law and violence, actual or threatened, were the main forces by which the politically impotent found a voice, expressed their experience, and limited the condescension of the elite. The propensity of the poor to transmute into a mob was widely commented upon, especially from above—and a mob (a contraction from '*mobile vulgum*') not only stood outside

---

[54] Bourne, *Antiquitates Vulgares*, p. 174.   [55] *Memoirs of Ailesbury*, vol. 2, p. 442.
[56] *Mist's Weekly Journal*, 14 August 1725, [p. 2].

hierarchy and order but challenged it. It was a fairly small step from the mischief of the mob to the terror of the riot. Yet such violence was not mindless, for 'even in tumultuous assemblies the mob ever reasons well, and seldom do they rise but when oppressed and weighed down.'[57]

Tensions between capital and labour were real enough, but divisions within such broad categories and bridges across them must not be ignored. For example, some amongst the elite came to decry the growing power of the 'monied interest', of bankers, insurance brokers, and stockjobbers, accusing them of leaching the life out of landlords and farmers as well as attacking the age-old political hegemony of the 'landed interest'. But some economic interconnections denied such distinctions. Most prominently the woollen interest provided a bond between landlords, farmers, merchant manufacturers, and those labourers who toiled away at spinning, weaving, dyeing, and carding. Similarly, the little Englandism of Spitalfields silk workers, aghast at the rising tide of cotton imports from India, may have challenged the mercantile capitalism of the East India Company but they also struck a cord with many Tories and landowners. Economic changes were, indeed, transforming the arrangement and alignment of interests. The close association of wealth and income with status meant that the socially ambitious among old and new wealth alike could not afford to ignore what new opportunities were available, be they in countryside, town, or colony. And economic interests might require a degree of formal expression if regulatory frameworks were to be adjusted to their benefit. The heightened role of Parliament after 1688 and the rising burden of taxes did, indeed, encourage interest-group politics to develop, heightening the distinctiveness of some economic identities, such as those lobbies associated with Irish commerce and West India plantations.

At heart, patterns of power and citizenship in early eighteenth-century England rested upon the distribution of property and religious persuasion. These factors overlay all other communities and interests. But no more than overlay. Powerful social identities occasionally revolved around local experiences, cutting across the boundaries of the ownership of or dependence upon property. National identity was sometimes a powerful experience that united rich and poor. People were, therefore, members not of one community but of many.

THE UNCERTAIN LIFE OF THE POOR

Gregory King believed that just over half of all people earned less than they spent. No less striking, to many contemporaries it was meaningful to categorize

---

[57] *Memoirs of Ailesbury*, vol. 2, p. 383.

the bulk of working people as 'the poor' or 'the labouring poor', labels demonstrating that even when in work many struggled to survive. For the poor, making ends meet was the enduring aspiration, not the pursuit of dramatic social advancement. Yet it is important to note that King's 'poor' did not all live in poverty but was rather that part of society that was *liable* to fall into poverty. So, at the very start of our period, about 30 per cent of the population was judged unable to pay the hearth tax and it has been estimated that each year around 15 per cent of the population was in receipt of some sort of charitable aid. Whether poverty became a more or less frequent experience in these years is impossible to determine with certainty though it appears to have become more pressing in towns. Many complained of an epidemic of begging in the capital in this period and in 1716 a report on London concluded that 'the Poor are rather increased in this great City of late than diminished'.[58] In Liverpool, the average annual levy for poor rates in the early 1690s was just over £60, but by the 1720s had risen to nearly £1,000, an increase far greater than that of the port's population or trade. Such evidence had an immediacy to contemporaries that vividly coloured their reactions to the causes of poverty and proposed solutions, making them see not only its symptoms but its causes as largely urban. In fact rising absolute numbers of poor in towns sometimes meant declining relative numbers because of population expansion, just as much rural poverty was expressed in terms of migration to towns.

Many years ago Phelps Brown and Hopkins concluded that for building craftsmen in southern England, wages may have risen by up to one-fifth from the 1680s to the late 1720s relative to prices. Such improvement may well have taken place, but the evidence is far from robust. First, it relates only to adult, male, skilled workers. Given the important economic role played by women and children, it is less an individual's than a family's standard of living that is significant. Second, it cannot safely be assumed that experiences across the skill spectrum were similar. In the more rapidly growing towns of the north of England the gap between the wages paid to craftsmen and their labourers widened over the late seventeenth centuries, mainly because of the rise in the former, though in London's high-wage economy the gap remained constant. Third, it rests upon unverifiable assumptions about underemployment and makes no allowance for unemployment. Much fragmentary material suggests that few enjoyed reasonably full employment. Fourth, it says nothing about the possibility of significant regional variations in wages and prices. Yet if the wage rates paid to labourers in London rose by 20 per cent between *c.*1685 and *c.*1725, at Carlisle, Beverley, Chester, Durham, Hull, Lincoln, Penrith, and York they were stagnant. Further, the rate at London was twice that at Hull

---

[58] *The Weekly Journal, or British Gazetteer*, 17 March 1716, p. 360.

which was in turn 20 per cent above that of Lincoln. Finally, the Phelps Brown
and Hopkins series ignores non-waged forms of income such as payment
in kind and perks. The fluidity of wages was indeed such as to undermine
attempts to enforce statutory wage regulation by JPs.

Modest population growth in this period, along with somewhat quicker
improvement in the agrarian, industrial, and commercial sectors of the economy, meant that, on balance, more resources were available to society. Prices
for some foodstuffs slowly fell, helping towards some small rise in standards of
living. Though this modest improvement was enjoyed by many it was not
enjoyed by all. Paradoxically, areas of economic vibrancy often suffered as too
many migrants competed for too few jobs. No less significant, England in this
period had a growing proportion of society who might be classed as dependants, those aged less than 15 and more than 59, who were usually unable to
maintain themselves and so relied in part upon the productive members of
society. In 1671 the ratio of dependants to adults of working age stood at 624
to 1,000 and in 1711 it was 730, a rise of nearly 17 per cent which suggests that
in life cycle terms there was an increasing reliance upon working adults.

Keynes famously remarked that '*In the long run* we are all dead'.[59] Indeed,
for most people in the pre-modern world short not long-term material considerations took priority. All economic life was much more vulnerable to
the weather than nowadays. Its fluctuations, together with the passage of the
seasons, significantly impacted upon the demand for labour and the supply of
goods. Income and, especially, prices were liable to dramatic swings, most
obviously with harvest fluctuations. Of the thirty-nine wheat harvests between
1689 and 1727 some nine were bad or worse (five in the 1690s), fourteen good
or abundant, with the remainder about average. Bad harvests influenced
employment in agriculture, food processing, and distribution, but the main
effect was to push up prices, dragging more and more people into poverty.
Good harvests had the opposite effect. Heavy frosts could bring the construction industry and water mills to a standstill. Floods could destroy livestock,
crops, and buildings. Warm spring rains might help germinate newly sown
crops yet make some roads impassable. Storms were an obvious threat to shipping and commerce, with 'The Greatest, the Longest in Duration, the widest
in Extent, of all the Tempests and Storms that History gives any Account'
occurring on 26 November 1703.[60] In the New Forest alone 4,000 trees were
uprooted; Bishop Kidder of Bath and Wells and his wife were killed in their
bed by falling masonry; houses were flattened everywhere; and the Royal Navy

---

[59] J. M. Keynes, *A Tract on Monetary Reform* (1923), p. 80.

[60] [D. Defoe], *The Storm: or, a Collection of the Most Remarkable Casualties and Disasters which
Happen'd in the Late Dreadful Tempest* (1704), p. 11.

lost 1,706 men drowned. Apocalyptically some thought the end of the world was nigh, and churches were full to overflowing at the commemorative public fast held two months later.

Other sources of instability in the economy were man-made. Fire, especially in towns, was a constant hazard. New Alresford in Hampshire in 1689, Warwick in 1694, Whitehall Palace in 1695, Bermondsey in Surrey in 1699, and Buckingham in 1725 were all badly damaged by fire—there were some 92 major fires in provincial towns in this period. This, though, was the last era of such great conflagrations. The increasing use of brick and tile in building, which was notably stimulated by the great fire of London in 1666 and by discriminatory fire insurance premiums 'charging "double for Timber"', was gradually to reduce such threats.[61] No less serious was the disruption caused by war. The burden of extra taxation, the mobilization of a family's principal earner, the dislocation of overseas trade through the closure of foreign markets and the predatory activities of privateers, the diversion of resources to supply combatants, and the swamping of labour markets at the onset of peace with discharged soldiers and sailors all served to dislocate (both positively and negatively) the peacetime economy. Financial dislocation was also marked on at least two occasions. First, in 1696 a general recoinage temporarily yet severely disrupted the exchange economy, producing real hardship. At Manchester, 'The cuntry is in so great distresse for want of current money, that without some speedy supply, all traffick will cease. Our markets cannot be continued. The poor have been, in severall markets, tumultuously mumuring; and we are, I think, in great danger of greater unquietnes.'[62] Then, in 1720 the most disastrous stock market collapse of the eighteenth century, centred upon the pricking of the South Sea Bubble, led to a credit squeeze which hit some hard: 'The ruin is general, and every man has the miserable consolation to see his neighbour undone.'[63]

Somewhat more than a half of English people in this period would experience poverty at some point of their lives. If relatively few suffered abject poverty for months on end, the real hardship many periodically endured and always feared can hardly be exaggerated. There was no one means of making ends meet, rather many small ones which together constituted what in another context has been called an 'economy of makeshifts'.[64]

[61] E. L. Jones, S. Porter, and M. Turner, *A Gazetteer of English Urban Fire Disasters, 1500–1900*, Historical Geography Research Series, no. 13 (1984), p. 61.

[62] H. M. C., *Kenyon*, p. 409.

[63] J. Trenchard and T. Gordon, *Cato's Letters: or Essays on Liberty, Civil and Religious, and Other Important Subjects*, ed. R. Hamowy, 2 vols. (Indianapolis, 1995), vol. 1, p. 44.

[64] O. H. Hufton, *The Poor of Eighteenth-Century France, 1750–1789* (Oxford, 1974), chs. 3 and 4.

In the first instance the poor tried to help themselves. Neighbourliness and a spirit of hospitality had a real meaning in many communities. Friends, relations, and fellow worshippers might all be able to help briefly. Short-term difficulties might be bridged by resort to credit, with shopkeepers and innkeepers well used to allowing customers time to pay. In fact contested debts drew people into the law in considerable numbers—over four years at the start of our period nearly 40 per cent of the population of King's Lynn, then a prominent port, were in court over debts and everywhere the gaols were full of debtors. To make ends meet the poor might also resort to the economic margins and powerful customary rights. 'Custome is a law or right, not written, which being established by long use and the consent of our ancestors, hath been and is dayly practised.'[65] Common land could be used to keep some livestock upon. Gleaning was valuable to many. Some workers received limited perks as a wage supplement. The taking of rabbits, hares, and waterfowl, in contravention of the class-based game laws, was widespread. Woods, forests, and wastes were liable to exploitation by villagers searching for food and fuel. One Lincolnshire landowner complained about having to 'continue to keep a more than ordinary strick eye over the woods whilst nutting time lasts'.[66] Ships cast ashore might be plundered by wreckers who viewed them as 'God's goods'; in north Norfolk, 'the farmers, and country people had scarce a barn, or a shed, or a stable; nay, not the pales of their yards, and gardens, not a hogsty, not a necessary-house, but what was built of old planks, beams, wales and timbers, &c. the wrecks of ships, and ruins of mariners' and merchants' fortunes.'[67] Food riots were a common reminder to the authorities of the plight of the poor, of the disruption caused by new lines of commerce, and of the obligation of paternalistic regulation of the market. In May 1693 'poore women in Oxon market [were] clamoring again at the price of corne; pelting millers, mealmen, bakers, etc., with stones' while at Shrewsbury 300 rioters 'made proclamation against carrying corn out of the nation, which might occasion a famine'.[68] Later that year rioters at Northampton seized corn and sold it at a price they held to be reasonable.

Time and again contemporaries emphasized the obligation of the rich to provide for the poor in their hour of need, perhaps because traditions of

---

[65] R. Gough, *The History of Myddle*, ed. D. Hey (Harmondsworth, 1981), p. 64. Or, 'Custom, that unwritten Law, By which the People, keep even Kings in awe'. C. D'Avenant, *Circe a Tragedy* (1677), p. 17.

[66] *The Letters and Papers of the Banks Family*, p. 18.

[67] *The Diary of Mr Justice Rokeby* (1888), p. 28; Defoe, *Tour*, p. 94.

[68] *The Life and Times of Anthony Wood, Antiquary, of Oxford, 1632–1695*, vol. 3, ed. A. Clark, Oxford Historical Society, 26 (Oxford, 1894), p. 422; Luttrell, *Brief Historical Relation*, vol. 3, p. 88.

hospitality were gradually being eroded. Charity, organized or not, was common, especially in the towns. If many were prepared to give a few pennies here and there, prominent examples of philanthropy can also be found: in February 1692 William III gave £1,000 to the poor of St Martins-in-the-Field in London; during his London shrivalty Charles Duncombe gave over £5,000 to imprisoned debtors; in 1709 the Duke of Newcastle bought corn to be distributed, along with bread, to the poor of Nottingham, Mansfield, and Newark; in 1716 it was reported that 'Mr. Feast a great Brewer in Whitecross-Street [London] has given 400 chaldrons of Coals to such poor People that he found were hinder'd from working in the hard Frost'; the devout high churchman, Edward Colston, a prominent Bristol merchant who accumulated a part of his fortune on the back of the invidious slave trade, gave away at least £70,000 (his monument lists gifts in excess of £120,000), much of it for almshouses, schools, and hospitals for the poor.[69] Such generosity bears witness to the hardship many faced, to the structured inequality at the heart of society, and to perceptions of the importance of good works by the well-to-do.

Though philanthropy was considerable, it was usually unpredictable and could not be assumed with any certainty by the poor. There were however thousands of small parochial charities, often organized through the vestry, that provided some support for the poor. Occasionally charities were more substantial, as with Thomas Guy's gift to build a hospital. On the national stage, charity briefs were issued by royal warrant to allow collections to be made, often at church, for a variety of good causes. Two-thirds of the 336 briefs issued in this period collected for victims of fire—that for Warwick raising £11,000—providing for many a form of cover in an era when fire insurance was still in its infancy. Other catastrophes also elicited considerable sums. In 1715 and 1716 over £24,000 was raised for farmers who had suffered through a cattle disease that ravaged south-east England and in 1723 some £10,000 was raised for the sufferers of coastal flooding in Lancashire. Yet, by itself, such *ex post facto* help often reached the poor too late and it is notable that financially the most successful briefs were specifically for distressed foreign Protestants.

In their hour of need, most poor people looked not to charity but to the poor law, a system of relief organized on a parochial basis whereby a rate was levied upon the more prosperous to be dispersed among the impoverished. The system had been framed in the last years of Elizabeth's reign and by 1689 was

---

[69] *The Weekly Journal*, 4 February 1716, p. 326. Charles Duncombe, d.1711, banker and politician who refused to aid James II before his flight in 1688, MP, knighted 1699, and Lord Mayor of London 1708. John Holles, 1662–1711, Gentleman of the Bedchamber to William III, married heiress to Newcastle dukedom 1690 and created Duke of Newcastle in 1694, Lord Privy Seal 1705–11. Colston, 1636–1721, educated Christ's hospital, London, and MP for Bristol 1710–13.

in operation across the nation, managing to provide a frayed safety blanket between the poor and utter destitution. Its greatest strength was its statutory basis, flexibility, and low overheads. Unpaid parish officials usually knew well enough who was needy and who was able, just as the poor seem to have had a good appreciation of their legal entitlements. Apprenticeships could be organized for the young, work found for the idle, and pensions provided for the aged or the infirm. Including dependants, by 1700 the system was able to relieve some 4–5 per cent of the population on a permanent basis, considerably more intermittently. About £400,000 was being raised per annum for relief, of which 10 per cent was in the capital. (This total was probably three times that of disbursements from charities, though still probably less than 1 per cent of national income, or only about half the annual peacetime expenditure on the Royal Navy.)

The sums raised by the poor rate constituted a remarkable achievement in welfare provision and speak volumes of contemporary social attitudes. Yet the poor law was also subjected to fierce criticism. One complaint was that the dependence upon parochial authority created an antipathy to outsiders who might fall into poverty, thereby eroding commonweal and neighbourly trad-itions. People on the move, 'vagrants', were frequently viewed with suspicion, and the ability to receive relief away from one's parish of 'settlement' was strictly circumscribed. Moreover, those in receipt of relief were to an extent stigmatized. The poor law thus had its role to play in defining the very limits of local society, of insiders and outsiders, of the wanted and the loathed. Moreover, there was growing concern, evidenced by the newly instituted Board of Trade's investigation into their operation in 1696, that the poor law was becoming increasingly burdensome yet no more successful. Already, a cen-tury before Malthus, there were those who saw the poor law not as a solution but as part of the problem of poverty. 'There is no Nation I ever read of who by a Compulsory Law, raiseth so much Money for the Poor as *England* doth . . . but our Charity is become a Nusance, and may be thought the greatest Mistake of that Blessed Reign in which that Law passed, which is the Idle and Improvident Mans Charter.'[70] Partly as a consequence of such attitudes, many attempts were made to overhaul the system of relief, attempts which ultimately rested upon the elite's tendency to view poverty in black and white terms. Defoe was typical. 'The Poverty and Exigence of the Poor in *England*, is plainly deriv'd from one of these two particular Causes, *Casualty* or *Crime*.

[70] Quoted in S. Macfarlane, 'Social Policy and the Poor in the Later Seventeenth Century', in A. L. Beier and R. Finlay (eds.), *London, 1500–1700: The Making of the Metropolis* (Harlow, 1986), p. 253.

By Casualty, I mean Sickness of Families, loss of Limbs or Sight, and any, either Natural or Accidental Impotence as to Labour . . . The Crimes . . . are, 1. Luxury. 2. Sloath. 3. Pride.'[71] In this view poverty had little or nothing to do with inflation or unemployment, interest rates or liquidity, for among the able poor like as not it was caused by a moral failing.

The 'criminal' or 'undeserving' poor have always taxed the imagination of policy makers. One response in this period was to stigmatize poverty, hoping to shame dole seekers into 'honesty'. An Act passed in 1697 required that those in receipt of relief wear a badge to advertise their status, though such branding met substantial passive disobedience and was generally ignored. A second attack on the undeserving poor, and one in use since the middle of the sixteenth century, was to discipline them in quasi-prisons known variously as 'houses of correction' or 'bridewells'. Here the habits of industry could be (it was supposed) thrashed into them and the vices of indolence exorcised. To many contemporaries in the 1690s such an approach looked very attractive, the calls for 'workhouses' or 'colleges of industry' often becoming very loud. The main obstacle was financial, for bricks, mortar, and staff, unlike unpaid overseers, did not come cheap. Individual parishes rarely had the resources to make such additional investments. Thus, beginning in Bristol in 1696, supra-parochial institutions, usually known as corporations of the poor, had to be formed if this solution was to be adopted. It was further hoped that in due course such institutions could become self-supporting through the sale of goods produced by those taking relief within. By 1711 fifteen cities had followed this path. Yet such indoor relief always proved to be an expensive and hotly debated remedy. The monies raised by the sale of produce always fell well short of the running costs of the institution. Further, Defoe for one pointed out the likely distortion to employment prospects elsewhere if such corporations became widespread. He argued that no new work would be created, rather it would simply be diverted from the private to the public economy. Consequently, by the death of Anne the original hopes for corporations had been replaced by one which stressed their disciplinary function alongside that of dissuading all but the truly necessitous from taking relief. From the 1710s these proliferated widely such that, aided by the Workhouse Test Act of 1723 (which allowed relief to be denied to those unwilling to enter the workhouse) and the significant backing of the Anglican Society for the Promotion of Christian Knowledge, there were nearly 2,000 workhouses in England by the 1770s.

[71] [D. Defoe], *Giving Alms no Charity, and Employing the Poor a Grievance to the Nation* (1704), p. 25.

CONCLUSION

In the century before 1660 England had struggled to cope with a doubling of its population, indeed the generation immediately preceding the Glorious Revolution had been one of demographic decline. But thereafter growth, slow at first but later much quicker, became the norm, transforming society in the process. Such increase was only possible because sustained economic growth was also established, not that anyone in the England of George I anticipated an 'industrial revolution'. Life was still dominated by natural resources and natural forces. If there was improvement it was painfully slow and interrupted by the disasters of foul weather, war, and disease. Yet there were too many signs of change for it to be useful to describe England as 'pre-industrial' or 'traditional'. Localism though still strong was being eroded. Hierarchy was only in part dependent upon ancient and codified notions of status. New sources of wealth were coming into being. Industry and trade were slowly growing and agriculture's relative importance gradually diminishing.

In 1700 England was neither simply an '*ancien régime*' nor a 'class society', though evidence of both can be found. Rather it was a society which was painfully aware that old conceptions of social structure fitted social reality increasingly poorly. Belief in hierarchy and order were as strong as ever, but society was too fluid to be contained within any neat categorization or series of expectations. Limited geographical and social mobility, caused by both economic problems and opportunities, undermined traditional ideas of order just as much as religious pluralism threw into doubt the notion of a unitary civil society. Novel developments had their friends and enemies, but crucially none could see where these developments would lead or where they might end. Rather, just as the political world was full of uncertainty in these years so was the very fabric of society. Hobbes's warning, therefore, had lost some but by no means all of its potency.

CHAPTER 4

A Bloody Progress

England, more accurately Britain, was involved in two major wars in this period, the Nine Years War and the War of the Spanish Succession. Waged on both sea and land, these were long and intense struggles, involving most West European powers. In both wars Britain and her numerous allies faced the might of France and, for the first time in centuries, year after year deployed large armies on the continent, eventually with conspicuous success. If militarily both wars were ultimately inconclusive, Britain entered the Nine Years War as a junior partner but left the War of the Spanish Succession as a great power. There was however nothing inevitable about this and such success was dearly bought and often reluctantly achieved, requiring new priorities to be established, precious resources to be diverted, strategic innovation of a high order, and much bloodshed. Only after the event did it come to look like a great achievement.

These wars were European—not British, still less English. This cannot be stressed too highly, for they took Britain into the heart of Europe in ways that had been unimaginable even in the glory days of the Hundred Years War. Of course England had her own reasons for fighting, but so did every power, such that she was only partly in control of her destiny. If her star was rising, the night sky of war was badly cluttered with competing ambitions, as a satirical doggerel from early in the War of the Spanish Succession well illustrates.

The Powers of Europe engaged All at All.
France aims at All.
Spain expects All.
Portugal helps All.
Italy suffers All.
The Emperor ventures All.
The Empire neglects All.
The Palatine sacrifices All.
Bavaria shams All.
The Pope winks at All.
Savoy stakes All.

England and Holland pays for All.
Denmark trades with All.
Sweden gets nothing at All.
Poland loses All.
Cologn has lost All.
Mantua hopes to redeem All—but
Tis believed will get nothing at All.
God overrules All,
Or else the Devil would overrun us All.[1]

War did not overrun England, though at times it nearly did so. Rather, it enabled her to confirm the Revolution settlement, further develop some of its consequences, enhance her international status, and underscore her colonial prospects and pretensions. Together the Glorious Revolution and the wars that followed in its wake took England out of a dark age of civil strife and, for better and for worse, set her on a course towards her imperial meridian.

THE CAUSES OF THE NINE YEARS WAR

Through the sixteenth and early seventeenth centuries Bourbon France and Habsburg Spain vied for supremacy in Europe. France's victory in that struggle was symbolized and extended by the accession to the French throne of the youthful Louis XIV in 1661. The Sun King, who reigned until 1715, was certain not only of France's greatness but also of her role as Catholic champion in the twilight years of the Counter Reformation. Thus he sought to strengthen France externally and internally. Expansion to the 'natural' frontiers of France was one ambition (the *Réunions* policy), as was the heightening of monarchical power within France by eradicating competing sources of authority, including religious pluralism. If the mountains of the Pyrenees and Alps and the waters of the Mediterranean, Atlantic, and Channel provided secure enough frontiers, France's eastern border was less certain, especially abutting the Rhineland and, most critically of all, Flanders. The integrity of the adjoining Spanish Netherlands had been eroded by the loss of the northern provinces with the establishment of the Calvinist Dutch Republic by the early seventeenth century and the continued weakening of Habsburg authority. In 1672 Louis launched a major offensive that almost overpowered the whole area. Only desperate Dutch resistance, led by William of Orange, averted annihilation. But if the Republic survived, French victory could not be avoided. By the 1678 Treaty of Nijmegen, France gained significant new territories along its north-eastern frontier to add to those granted in 1668 at the Treaty of Aix-la-Chapelle.

[1] *Verney Letters of the Eighteenth Century from the Mss. at Claydon House*, ed. M. M. Verney, 2 vols. (1930), vol. 1, p. 99.

William, Prince of Orange, was born in 1650, the year of his father's death. Though William's mother was a daughter of Charles I of England his father and grandfather had been Stadholders of the Dutch Republic and he forever saw himself as Dutch and Protestant. Much of his adult life was given over to limiting the power of France, particularly through establishing an effective barrier or buffer in Flanders. Indeed, though an unemotional man, his hatred of Louis and France was deeply heartfelt. In 1672 he had seen French pressure cause the Dutch Republic to peer into the chasm of civil war, he faced France in battle many times, and in 1682 he looked on helplessly as Louis ordered dragoons into Orange, his small principality on the east bank of the Rhône to the north of Avignon. The walls of the town were dismantled, homes ransacked, women raped, and William's right to call himself a sovereign Prince effectively eradicated. (Orange was to be formally ceded to France in 1713.) No Prince could forgive or forget such a barbarous humiliation.

Between the peace at Nijmegen in 1678 and William's invasion of England a decade later, European powers wove patterns of alliances in an attempt to establish international security. But the fabric they made was ripped apart by the unpredictability of France and England. From 1679 France moved into a number of areas on its eastern and north-eastern frontier, including Luxembourg, Lorraine, Orange, and the Spanish Netherlands, bringing to an end with the *truce* of Regensburg (Ratisbon) in 1683. Further, in 1685 Louis revoked the Edict of Nantes, prompting a mass exodus of Huguenot refugees to his Protestant neighbours. Not only the Dutch Republic but Spain and the German states wondered where the Sun King intended to draw the line. In July 1686 several German states, the Emperor, Spain, and Sweden united against France by establishing the League of Augsburg to defend treaties dating back to 1648. Undeterred, Louis pressed on, in August 1687 instituting aggressive anti-Dutch trade measures in contradiction of the Treaty of Nijmegen. He did not aim to provoke a Dutch reaction, indeed he believed that the provinces were so disunited that William would be unable to mobilize any effective opposition. It was a fatal miscalculation, for by striking at the heart of Dutch prosperity he questioned the Republic's very existence. Commercial war was to the Dutch a mere prelude to full war, a belief that hardened when on 24 September 1688 Louis, piqued at his failure to control the appointment of a new Elector of Cologne and Liège, sent a French army towards the Rhine, besieging Philippsburg. Over the following winter the French laid waste to the Palatinate.

In such an environment England's strategic significance was clear to all, but especially to the French and the Dutch. To the Republic, an Anglo-French alliance might easily create an impenetrable barrier to the west and the loss of many of her most prized markets. Louis would be able to concentrate all his efforts on an assault into the Spanish Netherlands and, perhaps, upon the Republic itself. But as an ally of the Republic England would provide a potent threat to France. Yet in the middle of 1688 it was not possible to predict English policy. If James had many sympathies for Louis the political nation had come to view France as a serious threat to European liberty and Protestantism. Thus William's aim in invading England, as stated in his Declaration, was to give English anti-French sentiment powerful expression in a 'free Parliament', thereby preventing an Anglo-French compact being forged at this critical juncture. That important but limited ambition was however transformed by James's flight, for England could now be drawn into active opposition to France. And if William were made King, then England had to be prepared to defend that grant—James had fled to France and it was to be expected that Louis would support his restoration, both for reasons of French strategic interest and those of kingly regard. Defence of the new monarchy could not passively await a French supported Jacobite invasion, it had to seek to prevent one ever setting sail by tying up French resources as completely as possible. This could best be done by actively waging war on France. Thus, with James's flight, Dutch and English interests became as one.

England declared war on France on 7 May 1689 and France soon faced formidable allied opposition. The Grand Alliance constructed in 1689 and 1690 first joined the Dutch Republic to the Empire of Leopold I (effectively Austria), then to England, Spain, Savoy, Brandenburg, Saxony, Hanover, and Bavaria. The expressed aim was that 'There shall by no means any peace be concluded before the peace of Westphalia, and those of Osnaburg, Munster, and the Pyreneans, have . . . been vindicated'.[2] This Western European war, begun with the French invasion of the Palatinate the previous September, lasted until the Treaty of Ryswick in 1697 and hence is accurately known as the Nine Years War—though it is also called the 'War of the Grand Alliance', 'War of the League of Augsburg', and 'King William's War'. French aggrandizement, as much perceived as real, was at its heart. This had territorial, commercial, and religious dimensions, though the importance of the latter can be easily exaggerated. Though some English propagandists claimed that it was a war of religion, Spain and the Empire, leading Catholic powers, allied with Protestant England and the Dutch Republic, indeed Leopold I was keen for William to ensure toleration for Catholics in England. Yet from an insular English perspective religion undoubtedly bulked large. James's assaults on the Protestant establishment in Church and State were the main reasons for the passive

[2] C. Jenkinson (ed.), *A Collection of all the Treaties of Peace, Alliance and Commerce between Great Britain and Other Powers*, 3 vols. (1785), vol. 1, p. 287. The treaties referred to had ended the Thirty Years War (1618–48) and attempted to establish a Western and Central European balance of power.

disobedience to his authority in late 1688, such that when Englishmen fought to prevent James's restoration they fought to defend liberties they held to be peculiarly Protestant. In 1689 James and Louis quickly melded as one in the consciousness of many Englishmen. Louis's Catholicism, absolutism, and quest for *gloire* were inseparable as causes of slavery and loss of liberty in France. His support for James might easily be seen, therefore, as an attempt to rob England of its freedom: 'France is in the Bottom of all Slavery, and that was to be brought upon us.'[3] Thus when James II landed at Kinsale in Ireland on 12 March 1689, beginning his most forceful attempt to reclaim his kingdoms, he came with the French ambassador, the Comte d'Avaux, and French officers. As Evelyn remarked a few weeks later 'tis apparent how this poore Prince is menag'd by the French'.[4] Almost as soon as the news of James's landing reached London, Parliament's reluctance to declare war on France evaporated.

WAR IN IRELAND, 1689–1691

If James still believed himself to be King after his flight in December 1688, then he had to depose William and Mary. Realistically this could only be done by a French sponsored military conquest, though in 1689 Louis could not spare the resources for a direct full-scale invasion of England. Yet it was important for James to move quickly. He had to act as if he were still King and so began his attempt to reclaim his throne in Ireland, preferring that battleground to Scotland because it was more distant from the new regime's forces and because, compared to Scottish Presbyterians, the Catholic majority there would warmly welcome him. Indeed, on his way to Dublin 'All along the road, the country came to meet his majesty with staunch loyalty, profound respect, and tender love'.[5] He planned to build a powerbase in Ireland, somewhat independent of France, by accumulating the men and materials for an attack on England, perhaps via Scotland. There were however three main weaknesses in such a plan: a powerful Protestant minority in Ireland would be likely to offer stiff resistance and provide a basis for an English counterattack; in England James would be further tainted by his use of Irish Catholics; and, as Ireland lacked the materials fully to supply a force to invade England, dependence upon France would still be considerable.

---

[3] A. Grey, *Debates of the House of Commons, from the Year 1667 to the Year 1694*, 10 vols. (1763), vol. 9, p. 391.

[4] *The Diary of John Evelyn*, ed. E. S. de Beer, 6 vols. (Oxford, 1955), vol. 4, p. 635.

[5] *A Jacobite Narrative of the War in Ireland, 1688–1691*, ed. J. T. Gilbert (Dublin, 1892), p. 46.

War in Ireland was decisive both to the course of the Glorious Revolution and to British and Irish history over the longer term—memories of the battles and sieges are central to the mythology of Ulster Protestantism to this day. Those memories are of a land campaign, for although James depended heavily upon French supplies only one of the eight major convoys met opposition from the Royal Navy. On 1 May 1689 the English and French navies met in Bantry Bay, County Cork, the English, having failed to prevent the French from unloading their supplies, unconvincingly claimed a victory. In the early stages of the land war it looked as if major confrontation might be avoided as the somewhat ragged Jacobite army of 40,000 men swept across the country. On 14 March 1689 Ulster Protestants were routed at the 'break of Dromore', County Down. By late April 'all people of the Protestant profession have lost the greatest part of their substance.'[6] Only Derry and Enniskillen stood out as major points of opposition to James. The former was soon ineffectually besieged, but more successfully blockaded. With large numbers of refugees in the city, food soon ran short and starvation was imminent when on 28 July William's ships broke through to relieve the city. At Enniskillen, by contrast, the Protestants were able to go on the offensive, especially under Thomas Lloyd, nicknamed 'Little Cromwell'. On 7 May they secured a minor victory over Jacobites at Belleek to be followed on 31 July, the day the siege of Derry was lifted, by a more considerable victory over 3,000 Jacobites at Newtownbutler in County Fermanagh. Such resistance at Derry and Enniskillen created huge problems for James, for the weaknesses of his army were painfully exposed and time was created for William to send the reinforcements which were eventually to provoke James to flee to France for the second and last time in his life.

On 13 August 1689 an English force landed in Bangor Bay, County Down, led by the elderly Duke of Schomberg, a half-German, half-English Protestant who had been a marshal in the French service until the revocation of the Edict of Nantes. Most of his troops were English, but the failure of the English army in late 1688 could hardly inspire much confidence. Raw and inexperienced as they were, he placed more faith in the two battalions of Dutch infantry and four regiments of French Huguenots he brought. The army rapidly seized Carrickfergus in County Antrim before turning south towards Dublin. Bad weather and lack of supplies halted the march at Dundalk in County Louth and inexperience soon took a heavy toll. By 25 September 'The weather has been extraordinarily bad and our camp being in a cold place, our men fall daily sick in great numbers.'[7] Large numbers 'died like rotten Sheep', 'especially of the

---

[6] H. M. C., *Report on the Manuscripts of the Earl of Egmont*, vol. 2 (Dublin, 1909), p. 190.
[7] *Calendar of State Papers Domestic, February 1689–April 1690*, ed. W. J. Hardy (1895), p. 272.

English . . . we computed we had lost more than three fourths of them.'[8] Little wonder then that Schomberg avoided battle with the approaching Jacobite forces—always an important skill for a commander uncertain of his army's ability to win a battle. James hesitated. With deteriorating weather both sides soon withdrew to winter quarters.

The failure of James to take control of the whole of Ireland in 1689 was, in retrospect, a great setback to him. Opposition had initially been relatively slight and determined, well planned action could have suppressed it. Lack of resolve by James was only partly responsible, the disorganization of his army being more significant. But as in November 1688 he showed poor powers of leadership. The Jacobite failure at Enniskillen and Derry enabled William's regime to set about retrieving the situation. Not that Schomberg or his troops covered themselves in glory in the remnant of the campaigning season available. However, their presence, rapidly diminishing though it was, did prevent new Jacobite assaults on the Protestant enclaves that remained. That enabled the winter to be spent putting William's army in good order. Reorganization took place alongside the addition of English, Huguenot, Dutch, and Danish manpower—the latter were mercenaries. By April this polyglot army comprised 37,000 troops. James, dependent upon France, was able to do rather less. In March a French convoy landed about 6,500 troops, about half of which were Germans and Walloons. But almost as many Irish troops left to serve Louis on the continent, giving James a force totalling about 25,000. Thus if by the start of the campaigning season both forces were prepared for conflict on a much larger scale than had taken place in the previous year, the numerical balance of military might now clearly favoured William.

Towards the end of 1689 William decided that he had to take personal command of the campaign in Ireland. He implicitly doubted Schomberg's capacities—the Duke was, after all, in his mid-seventies—and, not for the first or the last time, exaggerated his own military abilities, though not his strategic vision. Decisive action was needed to eradicate the Jacobite menace to allow him quickly to concentrate his attention, and the resources of his new kingdom, on the continental war. He prepared hard, hoping to leave for Ireland via Scotland in March. He was held back by difficulties in Parliament over funding and a Regency Bill to put the administration in Mary's hands in his absence. Not until the start of June could he leave London. He made his way with the Prince of Denmark to Chester, arriving at Carrickfergus on 14 June—he saw more of his kingdoms in this one campaign than over the whole of the rest of his reign.

[8] R. Kane, *Campaigns of King William and the Duke of Marlborough* (2nd edn., 1747), p. 2; R. Parker, *Memoirs of the Most Remarkable Military Transactions from the Year 1683, to 1718* (1747), p. 20.

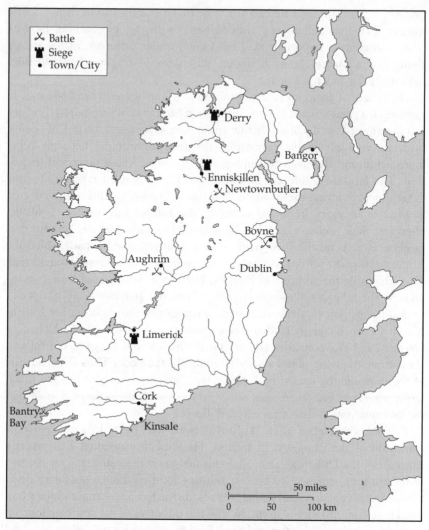

Map 1. The Irish war, 1689–1691

His position was now, on paper at least, superior to his rival. In the circumstances James should have played a long game, avoiding battle, holding what
he had until his position improved. He misjudged again. On 1 July the armies
met just to the west of Drogheda, on the banks of the river Boyne. William was
in the thick of things and though Schomberg was killed James' army was forced
from the field, retreating westwards. Despite fierce fighting, casualties at the

Boyne were not heavy compared with other battles of the era—perhaps 1,500 Jacobite troops were killed, wounded, or captured, their opponents losing about 500. If to English eyes the Boyne was 'a success next to a miracle' because the Jacobite troops had made a strong showing and retreated in reasonable order, what made the battle decisive was James's reaction to it.[9] He deserted his army, made rapidly for Dublin, and left for France from Kinsale on 4 July. Rarely had he moved so quickly and he was never to see his kingdoms again. Even a Jacobite concluded 'that the king had no solid reason to quit Ireland upon the loss he sustained at the Boyne in his troops.'[10] Whereas William committed himself totally and absolutely to his cause James did not.

James's departure marked the beginning of the end of the Irish war. The Jacobites were abandoned and they felt it. One of the Danes in William's army thought that 'The enemy are completely scattered and it appears that the war in Ireland will soon be over.'[11] He was wrong, for remarkably the Jacobites, inspired by Patrick Sarsfield, managed to hold off final defeat for more than a year, maintaining serious centres of resistance in the west. William's call for Jacobites to surrender unconditionally was ignored. A month after the Boyne, William failed to take Limerick, losing some 2,000 men in the process. He left Ireland early in September and its subjugation to others. On 23 September the Earl of Marlborough arrived with over 5,000 troops and soon took Cork and Kinsale, the main ports used by France to supply the Jacobites. Yet France continued to provide limited support, still seeing Ireland as a second front by which to attack the Anglo-Dutch alliance. Gradually the Jacobites were cornered and on 12 July 1691 were decisively defeated at the Battle of Aughrim. There William's forces, led by the Dutch general Baron von Ginkel, killed the French Jacobite commander, St Ruth, and up to 7,000 others at a cost of 2,000 killed and wounded. With the signing of the Treaty of Limerick on 3 October 1691 Jacobite resistance to the new regime ended and 'this great revolution of publicke affaires in these 3 kingdoms' was completed.[12] By its terms not only the French but some 12,000–15,000 Irish soldiers left for France, the 'Wild Geese' who with their descendants were to give distinguished service to the French army. That they had been unable to do the same for James was not for lack of zeal on their part. Neither James nor Louis gave them the support their bravery deserved.

[9] 'A Brief Memoir of Mr Justice Rokeby, Comprising his Religious Journal and Correspondence', *Publications of the Surtees Society*, 37 (1861), p. 46.

[10] *A Jacobite Narrative*, p. 104.

[11] *The Danish Force in Ireland, 1690–1691*, ed. K. Danaher and J. G. Simms (Dublin, 1962), p. 43.

[12] 'Rokeby Memoir', p. 48.

THE NINE YEARS WAR AT SEA

If only James had waited, for just two days before the Battle of the Boyne the French secured a victory over the Anglo-Dutch navy off Beachy Head, Sussex. If it was not as decisive an engagement as the Boyne, it was a bloodier one. The larger French fleet (75 ships of the line against the allies' 56) sank seven English and ten Dutch ships, many after Torrington gave up the fight and, in the words of the English Secretary of State, 'deserted the Dutch'.[13] Not only the Dutch were furious with Torrington: 'The best acct of it yt I cd learn is, that our fleet did not fight, while the Dutch were torn to peeces . . . Ld Torrington is most miserably reproached by ye mobile'.[14] In due course Queen Mary felt bound to write a humiliating letter to the Dutch States General apologizing. Torrington's aim, to preserve the English fleet and so prevent a French descent, was certainly justifiable, but his defeat, leaving the French in control of the Channel, merely fuelled invasion fears. A rumour quickly spread that the French had sacked Hastings in Sussex and just along the coast at Rye there was 'Nothing seen but fears & consternations; sending of goods out of Towne'.[15] In London Evelyn noted that 'The whole Nation now exceedingly alarm'd by the French fleete braving our Coast even to the very Thames mouth'.[16] Such was the anxiety that across the country prominent Catholics and Jacobites were arrested lest they should lead internal support to the French. The second Earl of Clarendon, a minister to both Charles II and James II, and Pepys, the elderly one-time diarist, were clapped up in the Tower.[17]

An invasion failed to materialize for three reasons. It had not been part of Louis's initial strategic plan. He had hoped that the war would very quickly secure France's eastern frontiers and restoring James was of only secondary concern to him. Consequently, not until later in the war did a Franco-Jacobite invasion of England attract him, and by then he had lost the naval supremacy won at Beachy Head and adopted a different maritime strategy. Second, the

[13] H. M. C., *Report on the Manuscripts of the Late Allan George Finch, Esq.*, vol. 2 (1922), p. 334. Arthur Herbert, 1647–1716, entered navy 1663, MP 1685, commanded William's invasion fleet 1688, First Lord of the Admiralty 1689, created Earl of Torrington 1689, acquitted at court martial 1690.

[14] *Correspondence of the Family of Hatton, being Chiefly Letters Addressed to Christopher First Viscount Hatton, A.D. 1601–1704*, vol. 2, ed. E. M. Thompson, Camden Society, New Series, 23 (1878), p. 156.

[15] *An Astrological Diary of the Seventeenth Century: Samuel Jeake of Rye, 1652–1699*, ed. M. Hunter and A. Gregory (Oxford, 1988), p. 204.

[16] *Evelyn Diary*, vol. 5, p. 27.

[17] Henry Hyde, 1638–1709, son of Charles II's leading minister, succeeded as 2nd Earl of Clarendon 1674, Privy Councillor 1680, Lord Privy Seal 1685, adhered to James II after 1688. Samuel Pepys, 1633–1703, diarist and reformer of Royal Navy.

French fleet was soon weakened by illness. Third, despite the losses at Beachy Head the combined naval resources of the Dutch and the English (the Maritime Powers) were still greater than those of France—the Republic put out three ships to every five from the Royal Navy. Looking only at battleships larger than 1,000 tons, in 1690 France had 68 with a total displacement of 104,000 tons, compared to 85 Anglo-Dutch ships displacing 129,000 tons. In the ensuing naval race France initially did well, for by 1695 she was almost on equal terms with the combined might of the Maritime Powers' larger ships. But by then French control of the Channel had gone and in the Mediterranean was being challenged.

The major turning-point was the Anglo-Dutch victory off Barfleur on the Cherbourg peninsula. Over the winter of 1691–2 plans were laid for a Franco-Jacobite landing on England's south coast. This could only be secured by reconfirming French authority in the Channel. Yet the Battle of La Hogue (or, strictly speaking, La Hougue) lasting six days from 19 May, was an unequal battle. Some 99 allied ships, with over 6,700 guns, defeated a French fleet of just half the size and firepower. By the end of the battle fifteen French ships had been sunk, including the Soleil Royal, the pride and joy of the whole navy. No English ships were sunk. Though the French fleet was far from being destroyed (over half of the fleet was not engaged in the battle), victory repaired English naval pride and established the Royal Navy as pre-eminent in Europe, a position usually maintained for the succeeding two centuries. Indeed, though the Dutch had made significant contributions to the battle, the English had taken the leading role and it remained the Royal Navy's greatest victory until 1759.

The reaction of the French navy to La Hogue was to withdraw and take stock, first to St Malo and then to Brest. Though it did subsequently sally forth, by the end of 1694 the fleet spent most of its time in its bases, avoiding battle. Bad harvests, economic dislocation, and the demands of the land war saw a cut of about 50 per cent in the programme for ship building. By the second half of the war England was building almost three times as many warships. Yet France was not abandoning naval warfare. Rather, partly prompted by the great military theorist Marshal Vauban, it dramatically and successfully changed its strategic direction to concentrate upon a privateering war, a *guerre de course*. By this means private enterprise was commissioned to attack Anglo-Dutch commerce, both by using their own ships and leasing some of the King's ships, aiming to undermine the commercial basis of the allied war effort. From ports large and small allied shipping was harried, seized, and ransomed, not only off the French coast but in the North, Irish, and Mediterranean seas. French privateers had in fact been out since the start of the war. For example, in 1689 one Lancaster merchant noted that 'the sea was overspread with the

French privateers and ships of warr, which quite put a stop to the commerce by sea betwixt London and this county'.[18] But after La Hogue there were many complaints that 'The French privateers are very numerous and bold' and certainly large numbers of ships were taken.[19] In 1693 it was claimed that 1,500 ships worth £3m had already been lost. From 1688 to 1697 ships from St Malo, a major privateering port, were responsible for 1,275 prizes and ransoms. All told perhaps 3,000–3,500 allied ships were taken in the course of the war, enabling captains such as Jean Bart to become French heroes.

Though the allies also resorted to privateering it was on a much lesser scale and there was, in any case, a tension between the Dutch, who wished to continue trading with France during the war, and Britain who did not. The main defence against privateering was an effective convoy system. But with the vagaries of the winds, the variable speeds of vessels, and the seasonality of some cargoes, this was difficult to organize, particularly far from home waters. Convoys, moreover, revived the predatory instincts of the French navy. In June 1693 the massive Smyrna convoy of 400 ships to Turkey, 'the finest fleet that had appeared on the *British* seas, in the memory of any man then living', was attacked off Lagos, on Portugal's southern coast, by vessels from the main French fleet out of Brest.[20] Some 92 merchants vessels, with cargoes said to be worth over £1m, were destroyed or captured, causing despair amongst London merchants to plumb new depths. So while the French lost at La Hogue, giving up naval supremacy to the allies, for them the *guerre de course* was undoubtedly a good war.

The failure of the Smyrna convoy encouraged a radical rethinking of British naval strategy. Two decisive moves were made. First, if the French fleet would not engage with the allies, then it had to be attacked in port, a line of reasoning which led to a dismally unsuccessful assault on the French naval base at Brest in June 1694—a failure aided by an apparently duplicitous Marlborough, who in May had effectively confirmed the plan to the French. Second, given the value of English and Dutch trade to southern Europe and Turkey, and the threat posed by the French navy out of its southern port of Toulon, a Royal Naval presence in the Mediterranean was highly desirable. By July 1694 an allied fleet of 41 English, 24 Dutch, and 10 Spanish ships had concentrated off Gibraltar, ready to make their way around Spain's southern and eastern coasts to help see off a French attack on Barcelona. Over the winter 1694–5 the Royal Navy's Mediterranean fleet refitted at Cadiz using English supplies, an

[18] *The Autobiography of William Stout of Lancaster, 1665–1752*, ed. J. D. Marshall (Manchester, 1967), p. 94.

[19] N. Luttrell, *A Brief Historical Relation of State Affairs from September 1678 to April 1714*, 6 vols. (Oxford, 1857), vol. 2, p. 556.

[20] Parker, *Memoirs*, p. 40.

operation that taxed to the full the State's administrative capacity. For the Maritime Powers opening a theatre of war in the Mediterranean was a dramatic extension of the geographical scope of the war, underlining the significance of economic factors to war and of the ability of the allies to stretch to the full the French war effort.

By March 1695 the French for reasons of 'frugality' decided 'to have no fleet at sea this year'.[21] Though the *guerre de course* continued the French fleet played very little part in the remainder of the war—though there were careful plans laid for a Jacobite invasion of England in 1696. With no enemy to fight, the fleets of the Maritime Powers resorted to the protection of trade and to the ineffectual bombarding of French coastal towns—when an attack was made on Dunkirk in August 1695 four English ships and one Dutch were lost against only slight damage to the port facilities and privateers. By 1696 the Royal Navy was at a loose end and suffering a shortage of manpower and provisions. In a failed attempt to find sailors a short-lived national register of seamen was instituted. This was symptomatic of the effective sterility of the battle fleet aspect of the Nine Years War. It was not a war of huge set-piece naval battles where fleets tore one another to pieces. War at sea was much more effectively undertaken by smaller ships preying upon enemy merchantmen. The Royal Navy had established a certain supremacy over the French navy and demonstrated the uses of operating in the Mediterranean, but with regard to the outcome of the war such achievements were secondary.

THE NINE YEARS WAR ON LAND

Britain invested heavily in the naval war and many people agreed with one MP's declaration after La Hogue that 'I am for . . . His Majesty to take care of the sea and let your confederates take care of the land'.[22] In terms of England's limited war aim of the securing of the new regime this was highly defensible, for it required only the prevention of a Franco-Jacobite invasion. Moreover, a 'blue-water strategy' was highly attractive to an island nation, heavily dependent upon overseas trade and with a large mercantile marine—unquestionably with the Republic England was best placed to operate at sea on the allies' behalf. The Navigation Acts, first instituted in the Interregnum and vigorously adhered to ever since, required that England's colonial trade was carried in English ships manned by Englishmen, assets to be called upon by the Royal

---

[21] H. M. C., *Calendar of the Stuart Papers Belonging to His Majesty the King*, vol. 1 (1902), p. 100.

[22] *The Parliamentary Diary of Narcissus Luttrell, 1691–1693*, ed. H. Horwitz (Oxford, 1972), p. 243.

Navy in war to provide the nation's 'wooden Walls'.[23] Moreover, very nearly 45 per cent of England's expenditure upon the war was on the Navy and the number of men it bore rose from over 22,000 in 1689 to a peak of over 48,500 in 1695. Yet if such a commitment prevented an invasion and offered some limited protection to English commerce in the end it could little influence the wider European causes of the war, the contested definition of France's eastern frontier. After failure in Ireland and at La Hogue France committed the bulk of its resources to the land war. This became the critical theatre and William was determined that England should play to the full its part there. Thus for the first time in centuries English troops spent campaign after campaign on the continent.

In November 1688 the royal army of 40,000 men had collapsed. Riven by internal divisions, some of its senior officers deserted James for William, and the army's retreat from Salisbury became a shambles. Putting the pieces back together again was no easy task and in any case few of the men had ever fired a musket in anger. In such circumstances the prospect of serving on the continent, or even in Ireland, was distinctly unappealing and early in 1689 'A general discontent, next to mutiny, began to spread it self through the whole English army.'[24] The officers, many of whom had served abroad (for France, Spain, the Republic, and the Empire), helped to avoid the total disintegration of the army. Only one regiment, the Royal Scots, actually mutinied and they were soon brought back into the fold. Purges of the Irish, the Catholics, and the disloyal, especially among the officer corps, helped to produce a more closely knit force. But there was little time to do more, for by May 1689 some 10,000 English troops had been sent to Flanders and in August Schomberg arrived in Ireland with his multinational force that included about 9,000 English troops. Thereafter the restoration of the English army took place gradually and uncertainly in the middle of campaigning. Even so, the army was never able to find enough men to fight the good fight and heavy recourse was made to the employment of foreign troops. Indeed, through most of the war about 25 per cent of those on the paper establishment of the 'English army' were in fact Dutch, German, Danish, and Huguenot troops.

On land the focal point of the Nine Years War was the Spanish Netherlands, with the Rhineland, Catalonia, and Ireland (until 1692) important supplementary regions of conflict. The dominant motif of the war was the size of the forces that were assembled. Armies of up to 100,000, far larger than anything Europe had ever seen before, faced one another, though they engaged only rarely. This inflation was caused by the capacity of the allies to draw troops

---

[23] [J. Macky], *A Journey Through England*, 2 vols. (2nd edn., 1722), vol. 2, p. 31.
[24] G. Burnet, *History of his Own Time*, 6 vols. (Oxford, 1823), vol. 3, p. 349.

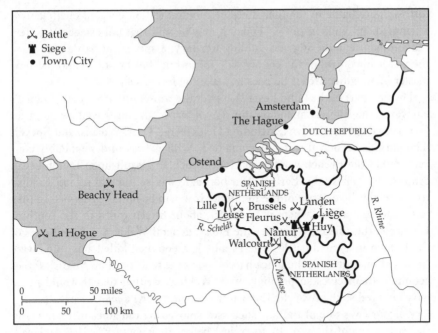

MAP 2. Main sieges and battles of the Nine Years War

from a number of sources, from the militarization of French society, and by a technological equality amongst combatants that placed a premium upon brute numbers. In fact, the very scale of the commitment precluded speedy and decisive action. Armies moved slowly and their direction was determined more by the need to find food for men and forage for horses than military advantage. Most campaigning took place between April and October because of the lack of fodder for cavalry horses and draught animals over the winter months and the deplorable state of roads when subjected to the weight of all those boots and hooves. Equally significant, because provisioning was much easier by water than land, the waterways of the Spanish Netherlands assumed such a critical importance that they were defended by formidable fortresses—for example, the Scheldt, which enters the sea at Antwerp, was commanded by Dendermonde, Ghent, Oudenarde, and Tournai. The Meuse, Senne, and Sambre were similarly fortressed. Moreover, the French had, under Vauban's command, fortified their frontier from Dunkirk through Ypres, Lille, Tournai, Le Quesnoy, Maubeuge, to Dinant, with a secondary line of fortress towns behind these. The Dutch too had their defensive lines, though these were less formidable. War in the Spanish Netherlands became, in effect, a war for command of such fortresses and defences, for armies which entered territory beyond an untaken fortress were liable to see their lines of communication cut and encirclement attempted. As Vauban put it 'Today it may be said that only siegecraft offers the means of conquering and holding territory; a successful battle may leave the victor in control of the countryside for awhile, but he still cannot become master of an entire area if he does not take the fortresses.'[25]

The first part of the Nine Years War over the winter of 1688–9 saw France's entry into the Rhineland and a campaign of terror that destroyed hundreds of German villages and towns, including Heidelberg, Trier, Worms, and Speyer. Though the French threat was contained, William was understandably concerned that the French would soon repeat such an assault upon Dutch urban centres. In March the Earl of Marlborough was sent with 10,000 English troops to aid the defence of the Republic. It was to be mid-August before they saw concerted action when at Walcourt, about fifteen miles to the south of Charleroi, the allied army under the Dutch general Waldeck got the better of the French in a small battle. The French lost 600 men killed and 1,400 were wounded or captured, the allies had 600 or so casualties. The English forces acquitted themselves surprisingly well, Waldeck writing that 'I would never have believed so many of the English would show such a *joie de combattre*.'[26]

Walcourt was one of the few successes enjoyed by the allies in Flanders in the early years of the war. In 1690, just before their victory at Beachy Head, the French vanquished Waldeck at Fleurus, just to the north-east of Charleroi. In August of the same year Duke Victor Amadeus II of Savoy was defeated by the French at Staffarda in Piedmont. Early in the following campaign the French took Mons and in September again defeated Waldeck, this time at Leuse. This turn for the worse was confirmed early in 1692 when Marlborough was dismissed as Commander-in-Chief of the English army, almost certainly for Jacobitical activities. Then the fortress at Namur, 'reckon'd the strongest place in the *Spanish Netherlands*, and a Man must say, the very Key of it', fell to the French in June 1692 and in August William barely managed to hold his own at the Battle of Steenkerk.[27] Little wonder that towards the end of May 1693 Evelyn worried that 'The French in Flanders [were] much superior to the Confederat forces', a superiority decisively demonstrated on 29 July 1693 n.s. with the heavy defeat of William at Landen (Neerwinden).[28] By the end of 1693 Charleroi and Huy had also fallen to the French. In Italy the French defeated

[25] S. Le Prestre de Vauban, *A Manual of Siegecraft and Fortification*, trans. G. A. Rothfrock (Ann Arbor, 1968), p. 21.

[26] Quoted in D. Chandler, *The Art of Warfare in the Age of Marlborough* (2nd edn., Tunbridge Wells, 1990), p. 113.

[27] E. D'Auvergne, *A Relation of the Most Remarkable Transactions of the Last Campaigne . . . 1692* (1693), p. 26.

[28] *Evelyn Diary*, vol. 5, p. 142.

Savoy at Marsaglia in October. The allies suffered combined casualties well in excess of 50,000 in these engagements. The French were inching eastwards in Piedmont and Flanders and they were also making some headway in Catalonia. The allies were close to defeat.

Success in Ireland and at La Hogue, combined with William's extraordinary commitment to the alliance, helped avert outright defeat. William's leadership, helping to keep the alliance together, was especially important, for unity was always likely to be tested by contradictions between collective aims and particular interests. As one chronicler noted 'Alliances are attended with great Inconveniences, and . . . the Operations of Allied Armies cannot be so Active and Brisk, as when they are the Results of one Single, Wise, and Absolute Head'.[29] Spain and the Empire were reluctant to contribute significantly to the military confrontation with France—the former because of ill government, the latter because of war with the Turks—and early on Savoy began to look seriously for a separate peace. William gritted his teeth, convening regular meetings of ministers of the alliance at The Hague to discuss joint objectives. He could point out that the longer the allies continued together the greater would be the erosion of French resources. Certainly the allies fielded impressively large armies that the French struggled to match. In 1691 the Empire, Spain, Brandenburg, and England each supplied 20,000 men, the Dutch Republic 35,000, Savoy and Bavaria 18,000 each, Saxony 12,000, the Palatinate 4,000, Hesse-Cassel 8,000, Swabia and Franconia 10,000 each, Liège and Württemberg 6,000 each, the Bishop of Münster 7,000, and the Hanoverians 16,000, a combined paper total of 210,000 of which the British share was less than 10 per cent. Such resources ensured that the French victories of 1690–3 were never followed up very far and were always liable to be reversed.

In truth after 1692 the Nine Years War was one of attrition. On the field the combatants were too equally matched to allow victories sufficiently decisive to end the war, and taking fortresses was a slow and painful process. The turning-point came in late 1693 with the failure of the harvest in parts of France. By the start of 1694 one French soldier claimed France was suffering from 'the severest famine known for many centuries' and an English diplomat noted that 'the French garrisons are destitute of bread and money'.[30] So significant was this that she was unable to mount offensive manoeuvres of any consequence in the 1694 campaign. Militarily it was a remarkably uneventful campaign, only the fall of Huy to the allies standing out. But it was clear that the initiative had passed to William, a shift confirmed in January 1695 by the death of aged but

[29] E. D'Auvergne, *The History of the Campaigne in the Spanish Netherlands, Anno Dom. 1694* (1694), p. 2.
[30] *The Chronicles of an Old Campaigner: M. de la Colonie, 1692–1717*, trans. W. C. Horsley (1904), p. 37; H. M. C., *Calendar of the Manuscripts of the Marquis of Bath*, vol. 3 (1908), p. 17.

able French commander the Duke of Luxembourg and by the decision of the French to invest in new defensive trench lines. From the French perspective if 1694 'was not as brilliant or as glorious as those preceding it' then 'The campaign of 1695 was not favourable to France', largely because of the success of the allies in taking Namur, strategically sited at the confluence of the Meuse and Sambre rivers.[31] Since it had been seized by the French in 1692 all of Vauban's skills had be turned to making Namur as impregnable as possible, raising its garrison to 16,000 men. Many foolishly reckoned it could not be taken. It was, though it took over two months, a massive allied force, and heavy losses to achieve it. It was claimed that 'it may justly be rank'd among the most Famous Sieges Register'd in History'.[32] William was in the very thick of the siege, rightly seeing victory at Namur as a vital blow to French prestige. If Namur was not safe, then none of Vauban's fortresses were.

The French spent the winter of 1695–6 further improving their defensive lines. They were not to be needed for England was finally buckling beneath the financial strain, a crisis encapsulated and escalated by the recoinage of 1696. Funds were short for the payment of troops and contractors alike. Moreover, troops were tied up in England by the threatened Franco-Jacobite invasion and the plot to assassinate William uncovered in February 1696. Then in June Savoy made a secret separate peace with France that became public at the Treaty of Turin in August, freeing some 30,000 French troops. War in Italy effectively ended, allowing France to concentrate upon the Spanish Netherlands, the Rhineland, and Spain. Military stalemate was the order of the day through most of the year. In the following year France made some inroads into the Spanish Netherlands, taking Ath and Alost, and in Spain where Barcelona fell in August. But through 1696 and 1697 both sides were waiting for peace. Namur in 1695 had been the last notable military confrontation of the war.

A FRAGILE PEACE

The Nine Years War was a European war with an English dynastic dimension and as a European war it decisively established that concerted allied power was able to contain France. Louis had made only limited gains and at very great cost. It was this failure rather than clear advances by the allies that was crucial. It was no part of their war aims to conquer France, rather simply to hold her

---

[31] *Chronicles of an Old Campaigner*, p. 39.
[32] E. D'Auvergne, *The History of the Campagne in Flanders, for the Year, 1695* (1696), p. 171.

to the borders as agreed at various treaties between 1648 and 1678. The English and British dimension went no less well for the allies. James spent the majority of the war a mere pensioner of France, consigned to inactivity and marginal relevance at St Germain. Thus the Treaty of Ryswick, signed on 10/20 September 1697, benefited William and the allies more than Louis. Most of the *réunions* were given up. France left the Rhineland and their forts there were to be razed. Only Strasbourg remained French. In the Spanish Netherlands France returned the fortresses of Luxembourg, Chimay, Mons, Courtrai, Charleroi, and Ath, and the Republic was allowed to control Namur and Ypres as part of a buffer. In Catalonia it gave up Barcelona. Dinant was returned to Liège. The Dutch gained a commercial Treaty. And Louis recognized William as King of Great Britain and Ireland, promising not to 'not give or afford any assistance, directly or indirectly, to any Enemy . . . of the said King of Great Britain'.[33] He thereby renounced James's claims, refused future support to the Jacobites, and acknowledged the success of the Anglo-Dutch alliance as a powerful force in the European balance of power.

For England, ill used to the heavy burdens of foreign war, peace was a great relief. 'The Bells rung all yesterday in most parts of this City, as well as the day before, upon the welcome News of Peace.'[34] When William returned to London in November he observed that 'It is impossible to conceive what joy the peace causes here.'[35] People looked forward to demobilization, lower taxes, new commercial opportunities, and political tranquility. Diplomats were far less sanguine. Portland reported that Ryswick 'will ease our affairs in England, provided we do not rely on, and trust to it too much, and we place ourselves in a condition to ensure and preserve it'.[36] The uncertainty was caused by worries over who might succeed the childless and ailing Charles II as King of Spain. This unhappy product of excessive Habsburg inbreeding had succeeded his father in 1665 when he was only 4. There had never been much hope that he would produce an heir and his crown would have to descend through a female line. Spain possessed a formidable empire and considerable resources, the distribution of which was bound to weigh heavily in the European balance of power. The situation was worsened by the fact that both France and the Empire had good claims to the Spanish Crown. Louis XIV had married Charles II's eldest sister, Maria Theresa and the Emperor, Leopold, had married Charles's youngest sister Margaret Theresa. Both sisters had renounced

---

[33] From the Treaty of Ryswick, reprinted in Jenkinson (ed.), *Collection of Treaties*, vol. 1, p. 300.

[34] *Post Boy*, 14–16 September 1697, [p. 2].

[35] *Letters of William III and Louis XIV, and of their Ministers*, ed. P. Grimblot, 2 vols. (1848), vol. 1, p. 137.

[36] *Letters of William III*, vol. 1, p. 125.

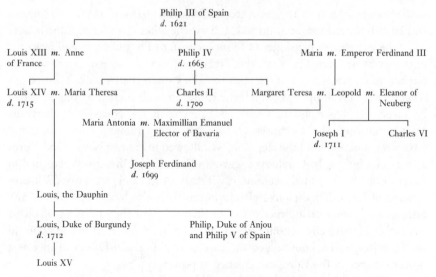

FIG. 2. The Spanish succession

claims to the Spanish Crown when they married, though Margaret's renunciation was somewhat more binding. Unlike Louis, Leopold's marriage to the infanta failed to produce a son, though he had a daughter, Maria Antonia, who married Max Emmanuel of Bavaria. She too was forced to give up any claim to Spain when she married.

The diplomats at Ryswick well knew that so much was at stake with the Spanish succession that it could easily lead to war. But at this juncture both William and Louis genuinely wanted peace and took an early lead in trying to find a compromise. That Louis looked to deal with William rather than Leopold evidenced the power of the Anglo-Dutch alliance in European and colonial affairs. With princely arrogance Louis and William set about cartographic surgery, cutting up the Spanish empire, giving pieces to interested parties in the hope of establishing powerblocks so finely balanced that war was unthinkable. By this Partition Treaty, signed on 11 October 1698 n.s., Spain, the Netherlands, Sardinia, and the Spanish empire in America were assigned to Joseph Ferdinand, the son of Max Emmanuel of Bavaria and Maria Antonia, the daughter of Leopold. The French Dauphin was given Naples, Sicily, part of the Basque country, and interests in Finale and Tuscany. Leopold's second son was given the duchy of Milan. In balance of powers terms such a settlement was remarkably even-handed, demonstrating on Louis's part a real desire for peace. But it was a Treaty of breathtaking over confidence, failing to involve not only Leopold but Charles II and the Spanish, who had no wish to see their empire dismembered. The Treaty was undermined in two major ways: on 14 November 1698 n.s. Charles made a will leaving the whole of his inheritance to Joseph Ferdinand and then this 'Bavarian baby' died on 6 February 1699 n.s.

Louis and William had to start all over again, but with Spain and the Empire now fully alerted and with no real prospect of the Spanish succession being equally divided between Habsburg and Bourbon. The second Partition Treaty, signed in March 1700, gave Spain, its American empire, and the Spanish Netherlands to Leopold's younger son, Archduke Charles and Spain's Italian lands to the Dauphin. As the Emperor's territorial ambitions were mostly in Italy this partition was unacceptable to him. And Charles II and his court again declared their own wishes (though the Pope had been consulted) in a new will which left the Crown intact to Philip of Anjou, the second son of the Dauphin. Shortly thereafter, on 1 November 1700 n.s., Charles, showing no respect for the calculations of foreign powers, died.

Implementing the second Partition Treaty, required the unthinkable, that William and Louis make war on the empire. After some deliberation Louis accepted Charles II's will and the inheritance of his grandson, so breaking the Treaty signed so recently with William. Though Leopold would never accept this, initially both England and the States General recognized Philip V as King of Spain. All depended upon whether Philip became his own man or a tool of Louis. The Spanish Regents did not help by initially giving Louis equal authority in Spanish matters to that of his grandson. Louis made matters worse by stating that Anjou still had a claim on the French throne, thereby threatening the formation of a Franco-Spanish behemoth. For the Anglo-Dutch alliance the dangers of Philip's accession lay in the fate of the Spanish Netherlands and Spain's commercial empire. Fatally, Louis managed fully to justify such fears, moving French troops into fortresses in the Spanish Netherlands in February 1701 and gaining from Spain concessions for French traders. Unquestionably the drift to war had begun. The Imperial army, led by Prince Eugene, moved successfully into Italy in the summer of 1701, forcing France to act and William to react. France mobilized and William, his own health failing, began to make full use of Marlborough in the delicate diplomatic negotiations required to construct an alliance powerful enough to resist France. Marlborough, who had returned to favour in 1698, was chosen not only for his ability but because his wife, Sarah, was Anne's close confidante. By employing him William was establishing the means to continue his policy of English involvement in an anti-French coalition beyond his death. If from an English perspective the Nine Years War belonged to William, the War of the Spanish Succession was to belong to Marlborough.

On 7 September 1701 n.s. a new alliance was signed between the Empire, Republic, and Britain. It claimed that Louis had 'usurped the possession of the entire inheritance' of Charles II, had 'invaded by his arms the provinces of the Spanish Low Countries and the duchy of Milan', was ready to move against Anglo-Dutch commerce in the Mediterranean and Caribbean, and that 'the kingdoms of France and Spain are so closely united and cemented, that they may seem . . . as one and the same kingdom'. The Treaty committed the Grand Alliance to obtaining the Spanish succession for the Emperor, 'a barrier, separating and distancing France from the United Provinces', and commercial advantages for the Maritime Powers in Spanish America.[37] Thus Europe was brought to the very edge of war. Yet at this stage England had little enthusiasm for renewed conflict. Insularity ensured that many were reluctant to give weight to balance of power considerations. But then, in an unexpected twist, Louis decided to raise the stakes, adding to the issue of the Spanish inheritance that of the British succession by recognizing James II's son as King of Great Britain and Ireland after his father died on 16 September 1701 n.s. This broke Ryswick, further provoked William, and from an English perspective returned religious and dynastic considerations to centre stage. In Louis's own words to the Pretender 'I will subordinate all material and political considerations for the sake of true religion. Remember then that it is your religion that makes you King'.[38] By recognizing the Pretender, Louis primed the weapon of Jacobitism for the coming war, but also strengthened the Anglo-Dutch alliance. In England therefore the causes of the War of the Spanish Succession were hardly different from those that had led to the Nine Years War, the preservation of the nation from 'Popery, Tyranny, Universal Monarchy'.[39]

It is striking that William's death on 8 March 1702 had no immediate effect on British foreign policy. Mobilization had already begun and two days later Marlborough was made Captain-General. On 4 May Great Britain, Austria, and the United Provinces declared war against France. Through the winter of 1701–2 the allies had been joined by some of the German states, notably Brandenburg-Prussia, Hanover, the Palatinate, Münster, Hesse-Cassel, and Baden. Only the first of these made an active contribution to the war effort, though the others were places in which troops might be raised. It was a strong coalition, but on paper not a dominant one. France was in any case far less isolated than at the outset of the Nine Years War. Not only Spain but also Savoy, Bavaria, and Cologne were her allies. France need not worry about her Pyrenees frontier, might reasonably hope to make the Mediterranean its own, was secure on its south-eastern border, and had allies well sited to attack

[37] *Collection of Treaties*, vol. 1, pp. 326–8.

[38] *The Jacobite Threat—England, Ireland, Scotland, France: A Source Book*, ed. B. P. Lenman and J. S. Gibson (Edinburgh, 1990), p. 79.

[39] *Defoe's Review*, facsimile edn., 22 vols. (New York, 1938), vol. 4, p. 235.

Austria and the Republic. With such well balanced sides, the War of the Spanish Succession was to be hard fought and long. But if in many respects it was indecisive it was, nevertheless, the war which clearly established Britain as a great power. Though Austria also did well, Britain was the one nation to emerge from over a decade of conflict with its reputation dramatically enhanced.

THE WAR OF THE SPANISH SUCCESSION AT SEA

As in the previous war, the allies' navy was dominated by ships of the Maritime Powers. Formally the Royal Navy was again to contribute five ships to every three from the Dutch fleet, though in practice the latter's contribution was somewhat less. Yet though 46 per cent of Britain's military expenditure in this war was upon the Royal Navy, there were even fewer major engagements than in the Nine Years War. The determining factor was not the ambition of the Admiralty, but, once again, the unwillingness of the French to seek dramatic naval confrontations. Such avoidance was undoubtedly prudent for, as Table 2 shows, the French navy started the war clearly smaller than the combined might of the allies and came to fall even further behind. From an initial position of inferiority French naval strategy sought not to build ships to match the allies but to be able to protect connections with the Franco-Spanish empires in the Americas and, once again, to attack Anglo-Dutch commerce. Little thought was given to a Franco-Jacobite invasion, though in 1708 a significant force did set sail only to be dispersed by a combination of the chasing English fleet, ill preparations, and the weather. From 1709 until the end of the war no new ships were added to the French navy. The cornerstone of French naval strategy through the war was to concentrate upon a privateering war, a war which, if anything, was even more concerted and successful than in the Nine Years War.

TABLE 2. *Size of main battlefleets of the War of the Spanish Succession* (000 tons displacement)

	Britain	Dutch Republic	France	Combined allied superiority in %
1695	152	84	190	24
1700	174	97	176	54
1705	170	94	167	58
1710	171	101	158	72
1715	168	84	102	147

Source: J. Glete, *Navies and Nations: Warships, Navies and State Building in Europe and America, 1500–1860*, 2 vols. (Stockholm, 1993), vol. 1, p. 226.

Less than a week after the declaration of war a London newspaper was reporting that 'The Sea already swarms with French privateers'.[40] They soon reaped a rich harvest. For the war as a whole the French Conseil des Prises considered over 2,000 ransoms and 4,500 prizes. Once the privateering war was fully under way over 500 allied ships were being seized annually and in 1707, 1709, and 1711 over 700. About three-quarters of these were taken in the Atlantic approaches or the Channel. Despite convoys and the theoretical naval superiority of the allies, sailors, merchants, and shipowners came to view losses and the escalating cost of marine insurance as inevitable: 'losses must be expected this war time, which if one should happen the profit of many years would be gone att once.'[41] Naturally English shipping interests complained long and hard, and following a parliamentary inquiry in 1707 three new counter measures were instituted: a home cruiser force of at least 43 ships was established; to encourage English privateers the Crown's ancient right to a share in prize proceeds was abolished; and a bounty was offered for the seizure of enemy men-of-war and corsairs. There was in fact a vigorous English privateering war, 232,000 tons being licensed, three times the level of the Nine Years War. But though they managed to take over 2,200 prizes this was only about a third the number taken by French privateers. Yet despite these disruptions a good deal of England's overseas trade continued to be possible, the average level during the war years being some 87 per cent of that for 1699–1701.

Though the privateering war was the most important aspect of the war at sea maritime concerns were powerfully influential in other ways. First, the Dutch were so dependent upon trade with France that in only one year, 1703–4, did they agree to British demands to suspend commercial contacts. This was a cause of much tension both between the Maritime Powers and within the Republic itself. Second, the value of colonial trade led warfare, albeit low scale and intermittent, to spill over into North America and the Caribbean. Finally, at the start of the war the Maritime Powers were concerned to emulate their policy of the previous war by establishing a strong presence in the western Mediterranean and a base on the Iberian peninsula. With Portugal notionally allied to France in 1702 and Spain effectively hostile this could only be done by force. In August and September 1702 an Anglo-Dutch fleet of 50 ships with nearly 14,000 infantry and marines attempted to take Cadiz. The strategic and logistical ambition of this descent was remarkable, but it failed dismally and the looting of the troops left a powerful impression upon the Spanish. However, on its return the fleet encountered the Spanish American fleet in Vigo bay on

[40] *Post Boy*, 7–9 May 1702, [p. 2].

[41] *Atlantic Merchant-Apothecary: Letters of Joseph Cruttenden, 1710–1717*, ed. I. K. Steele (Toronto, 1977), p. 12.

Spain's north-west coast. Some fifteen French and three Spanish men-of-war and seventeen galleons were taken or destroyed and 'treasure' amounting to £200,000 was seized (some of which was later ordered to be coined with 'Vigo' stamped beneath the Queen's head). This was a serious blow to Franco-Spanish naval pretensions and a cause of much celebration in London. No less significant was the impression it left upon Portugal, for it helped to persuade King Peter II to join the Grand Alliance in March 1703. John Methuen, the English ambassador in Lisbon, took a leading role in the negotiations, determined to find a base for the allied fleet, partly with the aim of promoting commercial interests, not only in the Mediterranean but in South America. But the amity was dearly bought. If it cost little to guarantee Portuguese independence, reluctantly recognized by Spain in 1668, it was more expensive to promise to transfer some Spanish territory to Portugal and to restore the Portuguese empire in South America. That, however, was cheap compared to agreeing to send the Emperor's second son, Archduke Charles, to Portugal and to help place him on the Spanish throne by force. An army of 12,000 men and subsidies to the Portuguese were to be provided. This dramatically expanded the objectives and commitments of the allies. Now a whole new theatre of war was to be opened and there was to be 'No peace without Spain'. If it was desirable for the allies to have one of their number as future King of Spain—the Spanish empire was always a honeypot to the Maritime Powers—it was to prove beyond the capacity of the allies to achieve these new objectives. As with the Partition treaties the Methuen treaties (three were signed in 1703) showed a complete disregard for the wishes of the Spanish, idle day-dreaming that led to much bloodshed.

In the short term the Portuguese alliance was highly beneficial. From Lisbon an allied fleet sailed into the Mediterranean in the summer of 1704 with no fixed plan but to harry and, if possible, engage the French Toulon fleet. On 3 August n.s. the fleet's 1,200 guns bombarded Gibraltar, firing off about 40,000 rounds—rather more Dutch than English. As the Spanish port was defended by only 50 guns and 430 men it was an unequal and, on the part of the allies, unheroic struggle. Gibraltar was taken and plundered, its inhabitants fleeing. Though it was a small port it offered oversight, though not quite command, of the Straits and thus of trade into and out of the Mediterranean. France soon attempted its recapture, leading to the only naval battle of any significance of the war. The Battle of Málaga, fought on 24 August n.s., was heated yet inconclusive: 'They both did fight, they both were beat, / They both did run away' ran one ditty.[42] But the withdrawal of the French fleet to Toulon, where it

<hr />

[42] 'On the Greatest Victory Perhaps that Ever Was or Ever Will Be by Sir George Rooke', in *Poems on Affairs of State: Augustan Satirical Verse 1660–1714*, vol. 7. *1704–1714*, ed. F. H. Ellis (New Haven, 1975), p. 18.

generally remained for the rest of the war, and the retention of Gibraltar allowed the allies to claim victory. But if the Rock was strategically significant it was in practice too small to allow the allied fleet to winter in the Mediterranean, thus in September 1708 Minorca was taken by a small force under the command of General James Stanhope to afford use of Port Mahon. If neither base could prevent French privateers taking nearly 700 vessels in the Mediterranean during the war, by becoming British possessions in 1713 they visibly symbolized her naval potency and imperial aspirations.

THE WAR OF THE SPANISH SUCCESSION ON LAND

The Spanish Netherlands, Germany, Italy, and Spain were all major areas of confrontation between the allies and France in the War of the Spanish Succession. Few comprehended the strategic interrelationships between these arenas. Louis, used to thinking big, undoubtedly did, to the extent that he was able to save France from outright defeat despite major setbacks. On the allied side only two men matched him for breadth of vision, Prince Eugene of Savoy, the French-born Austrian commander, and Marlborough. In so far as the war had a dominant figure it was John Churchill. With Eugene he fully understood the causes of the military stalemate in the Nine Years War as the obsession with defensive lines and fortresses. In reaction, mobility of arms and calculated risks were their hallmarks, allowing them to defeat the French on the battlefield time and again and push them from fortress after fortress. Marlborough's military record in the war was, indeed, almost unblemished: 'he never fought a Battle, which he did not gain, nor laid siege to a Town which he did not take.'[43] Strongly supported by Godolphin's financial prowess at the Treasury, the duumvirs (as they were known) attained for Britain real military might for the first time since the Hundred Years War.

Marlborough was, in many respects, a deeply unattractive character. His limitless ambition led him into disloyalty to both James II and, to a lesser degree, William III just as his beauty bred vanity and his success unbridled avidity. Early in his career he used his body to gain money and position, later he lusted impotently after a decisive campaign with which to end the war. Throughout his correspondence reeks of self-pity. Yet a man who began life amongst the provincial gentry of Civil War England and ended it as a duke of the realm, living in a magnificent palace given to him in thanks for his great victory at Blenheim, must have had numerous abilities and virtues. He was charming, thorough, determined, tireless, patient, brave, and, above all, imaginative. He was not content, as William ultimately had been, to contain France

[43] Parker, *Memoirs*, p. 214.

nor to follow in the ruts of earlier military practice. He wanted significantly to reduce French power and to do this he led from the front, politically, diplomatically, and militarily, both in Britain and abroad. No one matched his personal commitment to the allied cause. He inspired many and rightly was widely seen as one of the giants of the age—some 67,000 lines of panegyric verse were written celebrating his achievements.

In 1702 though Marlborough was militarily inexperienced he was William's chosen successor as the leading figure on the English side of the Anglo-Dutch alliance. That counted for much. The Republic, following William's lead, was prepared to give him overall command of allied forces in the Spanish Nether-lands, but required that strategic considerations be agreed with their field deputies, a limitation that frequently created tensions. Once again, indeed, though Marlborough was the leading military figure in the alliance, the war was very much a collective enterprise and one where Britain's direct military con-tribution was relatively small. In 1702 the Empire was meant to put 82,000 men into the field, the Dutch 100,000 and the British 40,000. However, Britain only sent just over 13,000 to the continent, buying in foreign troops to make up the deficit. Even at its peak, in 1709, only 28,000 Britons were serving under Marlborough. Subsidies—mainly to Savoy and Portugal—and the purchase of foreign troops accounted in fact for over a fifth of Britain's expenditure on the land war, reaching an absolute peak of £875,000 in 1710.

The level of Britain's commitment of forces to the land war and the prox-imity of conflict to the Dutch frontier undoubtedly weakened Marlborough's hand in his dealings with the Republic. In 1702 he quickly discovered how reluctant they were to follow his adventurous lead. The field deputies wished to utilize defensive lines, build secure fortresses, and edge forwards away from the Republic's borders. Marlborough on the other hand sought decisive en-gagements with the French, looking for success in battle to enable quick and deep penetration of the Spanish Netherlands and then France itself, believing that, when the moment was right, a victorious battle was 'of far greater con-sequence to the common cause than the taking of twenty towns'.[44] On four occasions in 1702 he manoeuvred the allied forces into a position for battle only for Dutch reluctance to hold him back. In 1703 he was also restrained from forcing the Lines of Brabant. Yet the field deputies were not wholly unrealistic in their assessment, for to them Marlborough looked more like a royal favourite than a great general. In 1702 and 1703 that was only slowly to change as Marlborough oversaw a series of successful sieges. In October 1702 Stevens-weert, Venlo, Roermond, and Liège were all taken. In May 1703 Bonn fell and in August Huy. These successes secured the Republic's eastern frontier and took

---

[44] W. C. Coxe, *Memoirs of John, Duke of Marlborough*, vol. 1 (2nd edn., 1820), p. 250.

the conflict onto the Rhine, but otherwise the campaigns in 1702 and 1703 were largely indecisive. As Marlborough noted in July 1703 'The French are very cautious, and the Dutch will venture nothing, soe that unless itt happens by accedent I think there will be noe battaile'.[45]

It was decisive action elsewhere that provided Marlborough with the opportunity for his first great victory. Italy had been in fact the first area to see armies on the march, Prince Eugene, a latter-day Hannibal, leading an Imperial army through the Alps to Vicenza in May 1701. On 1 September n.s. the Imperialists defeated a French army at Chiari and on 1 February 1702 n.s. at Cremona the French commander, Villeroy, was captured. In July a new theatre opened when an Imperial army under Prince Louis of Baden crossed the Rhine and took Landau and in September neighbouring Bavaria allied with France and seized Ulm. France now viewed war in southern Germany and northern Italy as of critical significance, hoping to defeat the Empire and so devote its attentions to the Maritime Powers. At the Battle of Höchstäd in September 1703 the Imperial army was decisively defeated by the French and Bavarians. The defection of the duchy of Savoy to the Grand Alliance in the following month merely confirmed the fluidity and importance of this theatre. To perpetuate the Grand Alliance the Maritime Powers would have to come to Leopold's aid in 1704. This might be done in many ways, by providing men and supplies, by launching a diversionary attack in, say, Lorraine or, audaciously, engaging with the French and Bavarians directly in southern Germany. Typically Marlborough chose the last option.

Early in the 1704 campaign Marlborough decided to take an army from the Dutch frontier, march south down the Rhine, cross east to the Danube, rendezvous with Eugene's Imperial army, and attempt a decisive encounter with the French and Bavarians. Remarkably he kept the Republic in the dark over his plans, setting out on 19 May n.s. for the 400-mile march with about 19,000 troops, about three-quarters of whom were British. By the time the army met the Imperialists, who had 30,000 men, Marlborough's army had grown to 40,000 strong, diluting the British presence to about a third. On 2 July n.s. the allies turned on the enemy's army at Schellenburg and in a bloody encounter gained control of Donauwörth. Moving into Bavaria the allied army then destroyed everything in its path in a vain attempt to force the Elector, Max Emmanuel, to change sides—Marlborough oversaw the futile and awful destruction of some 500 villages. And then on 13 August came the decisive encounter Marlborough had yearned for. At the village of Blenheim, a slightly smaller allied force crushed a Franco-Bavarian army of 56,000 men. Marlborough

---

[45] *The Marlborough–Godolphin Correspondence*, ed. H. L. Snyder, 3 vols. (Oxford, 1975), vol. 1, p. 210.

jubilantly reported to Godolphin that 'we doe flatter ourselves here, that the victory we obtained . . . is greater than has been known in the memory of man; for we have taken all their canon, their general, and taken about 1,500 officers, and above 8,000 soldiers, besides a very great sla[ugh]ter, soe that Tallard's army is ruined.'[46] Perhaps 20,000 French and Bavarians were killed and wounded, with 12,000 casualties on the allied side. Victory was followed up with the taking of Landau, Trier, and Trarbach, the latter two providing bases from which France might be invaded via Luxembourg or Lorraine.

Marlborough's march to the Danube was a breathtaking achievement and Blenheim was a major battle both for Europe and England. One of Marlborough's officers at Blenheim summed up the wider significance as having 'decided the Fate of the Empire, fixed the Imperial Crown in the House of Austria, and was the first fatal Blow that *Lewis* XIV had received during his whole Reign.'[47] This was soon appreciated in London, undermining those advocates of a largely blue-water strategy. And though only a quarter of the allied army and a fifth of its casualties at Blenheim were British, the battle was seen as much as an English or British triumph as a confederate one. Partly that was due to patriotic fervour, but it was also due to the accurate perception of Marlborough's decisive contribution. He had shown wonderful and inspiring military vision, demonstrating Louis's vulnerability to bold action.

The War of the Spanish Succession was, however, too large to be decided by a single battle or the genius of one man. In retrospect Blenheim was not as decisive as it initially appeared, not least because the war had expanded into the Iberian peninsula in 1704. In any case, the French army remained a formidable force and through 1705 was able to thwart most of Marlborough's hopes at an invasion of the Gallic heartland. Though there were engagements, stalemate resulted in the Netherlands, on the Rhine, and in Italy. Marlborough blamed the Dutch for lack of ambition, concluding by the end of the campaign that 'Europe must be saved by England'.[48] That was surely asking too much, as Marlborough must have known, but in 1706 he did his utmost to validate it. On 23 May n.s. Marlborough won his second great battle, at Ramillies, about fifteen miles north of Namur. The French army retreated in disorder to lick its wounds at Lille. Less bloody than Blenheim the victory came early enough in the year to promise other successes and allowed Brabant and Flanders to reject French rule. Louvain (Leuven), Brussels, Antwerp, and Ghent were all soon entered peacefully by the allies. Ostend, Menin ('one of *Vaubon's* master-pieces'), Dendermond, and Ath were all taken.[49] In Spain the allies, after successes in

---

[46] *The Marlborough–Godolphin Correspondence*, vol. 1, p. 350.
[47] Kane, *Campaigns*, p. 56.
[48] *The Marlborough–Godolphin Correspondence*, vol. 1, p. 507.
[49] Parker, *Memoirs*, p. 135.

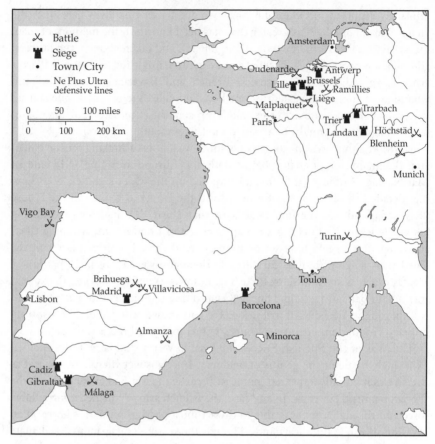

MAP 3. Main sieges and battles of the War of the Spanish Succession

1705 in Catalonia, including taking Barcelona, captured Madrid on 26 June n.s.
In Italy Eugene won a great victory at Turin on 7 September n.s., forcing the
French army to retreat across the Alps and effectively acknowledge defeat in
that theatre. For the allies this was to prove the high water mark of the war.
Their original war objectives had largely been attained.

   Louis made serious offers of peace in 1706. But Britain and the Empire mis-
takenly held out for more, exaggerating the allies' capacity for war. The soft
underbelly of the allied cause was Spain, the new ambition adopted in 1703, for
they could never commit sufficient resources to achieve their aim of putting
Charles on the throne. However, successes at Gibraltar, Málaga, Barcelona,
and Madrid obscured this vital point. Thus, once France and her Spanish ally
responded to the allied threat they were gradually able to win back most of

what had been lost. In October 1706 the Duke of Berwick, the bastard son of James II by Marlborough's sister, Arabella Churchill, recaptured Madrid for the French cause, leading the Lord Treasurer 'to lament the condition of our affairs in Spayn, which grow worse and worse every day'.[50] In the following April Berwick defeated the allies in a major battle at Almanza in south-east Spain. Now 'No peace without Spain' was virtually unattainable, becoming a great millstone around the necks of Marlborough and Godolphin. And though great efforts were made to remove it, including a failed diversionary descent on Toulon in 1707 and a fresh attempt on Madrid in 1710, in mid-December 1710 the allies were twice defeated, at Brihuega and Villaviciosa, finally ending their hopes of success in Iberia.

If failure in Spain was complete and ignominious, success in the Spanish Netherlands was less clear-cut. Though the campaign in 1707 was relatively uneventful, in 1708 Marlborough won a third major battle at Oudenarde. This was his least bloody victory—less than 10 per cent of the allies' 3,000 casualties were British. Yet though important, by 1708 war in the Spanish Netherlands was becoming increasingly like that of the Nine Years War, an attritional one centring upon the taking of key fortresses, sieges which involved heavy losses for the allies. For example, though victory at Oudenarde enabled the allies to besiege and take Lille and Ghent, the former cost them about 12,000 casualties (again the British share being less than 10 per cent). Moreover, the winter of 1708–9 was very hard in many parts of Europe, leading to famine. Not only France was close to breaking-point. Marlborough reported in late January 1709 that 'We have dayly complaints from the frontier, of numbers of poor country people on their side as well as ours which dye for want'.[51] Louis dispatched his foreign minister Torcy to The Hague to make peace. The allies pressed for everything and Louis agreed to most—to cede Newfoundland, dismantle Dunkirk's defences, withdraw troops from Spain, and give up most of his conquests on France's eastern frontier. But he was required to help the allies eject his grandson from Madrid or else face renewed war within two months. With Philip V widely accepted as King in Spain, Louis was being asked to wage a futile war against common sense and his own blood. He would not do it and the chance for peace was lost.

'No peace without Spain' helped the war to drag on for four more years. Neither side was able to overpower the other. The importance of fortresses and the continued ability of France to field massive armies precluded the possibility

---

[50] James Fitzjames, 1670–1734, born and educated in France, created Duke of Berwick 1687, served in the French army, rising to rank of Marshal of France, supported the Anglo-French alliance of 1716, killed besieging Philipsbourg. *The Marlborough–Godolphin Correspondence*, vol. 2, p. 721.

[51] *The Marlborough–Godolphin Correspondence*, vol. 3, p. 1210.

that Marlborough could deliver a knockout blow to end the war. New French defensive lines were constructed. Still, the allies did move forward to the very borders of France, taking Tournai and Mons in 1709, Douai, Béthune, St Venant, and Aire in 1710, and Bouchain in 1711. Like Lille, these were hard-won gains, entailing total allied casualties of about 30,000 to French losses of about 16,000. The conclusive demonstration of the military stalemate came with Marlborough's final, pyrrhic, victory in battle at Malplaquet on 11 September 1709 n.s., the very antithesis of Blenheim. If the allies notionally won 'It was as bloody a battle as has been fought, either this war or the last.'[52] Marlborough himself described it was 'a very murdring battel', noting that 'The French has never during this warr faught so well'.[53] Grim evidence of the skill of the French army is obtained from the casualty lists, the 20,000–24,000 allied killed and wounded being twice the level of French losses—about 10 per cent of allied losses were British. France may have lost the battle, but it won both the grudging admiration of her opponents and sufficient confidence to fight on.

Despite his great victories, Marlborough was never able to render the French army an irrelevance and found himself increasingly unable to avoid the deadly mire of siege warfare. If, even after Malplaquet, he was able to achieve notable successes, not least the remarkable manoeuvring of the allied army unopposed past the French *Ne Plus Ultras* defensive lines in August 1711, forcing a peace more beneficial than those offered in 1706 and 1709 was beyond him. Whatever his genius, his greatest failure was his inability or unwillingness to recognize such an unpalatable fact.

THE PEACE OF UTRECHT

The War of the Spanish succession was a 'great' war. Huge armies were raised, mighty battles fought, and formidable fortresses besieged. Such military effort made unprecedented demands upon the materials and men of the combatant nations and upon those areas unfortunate enough to have war waged on their doorstep. Not surprisingly, one by one the main powers became exhausted by the effort involved in going beyond limited war aims. After 1703 the Dutch Republic found its borders secure and concentrated upon obtaining a 'barrier' of defensive fortresses in the Spanish Netherlands with which to keep the French forever at bay. Such a barrier was negotiated with Britain in 1709 and was effectively in place by then. After 1706 the Empire had evicted France from Italy and expected to widen its authority on the peninsula. France had

---

[52] A. Crichton, *The Life and Diary of Lieut. Col. J. Blackader* (Edinburgh, 1824), p. 351.
[53] *The Marlborough–Godolphin Correspondence*, vol. 3, pp. 1360 and 1363.

already tried to make peace in 1706. And by 1708, after the disasters of
Almanza and Toulon, the limitations of British military prowess and the
unattainability of all of her ambitions encouraged anti-war opinion in London.
Much of that opinion was politically inspired, the Tories lashing out at
Marlborough and Godolphin's quest for glory. But it was also rooted in the
defensible belief that Britain could get little more out of the war and, indeed,
now had considerable gains to lose. By 1709 it was claimed with some reason
that 'the generality of the nation long for a peace'.[54] It says much about
Britain's heightened international significance that many of the stimuli to
ending the war emanated from a battle for power at the heart of English
political society.

In London Anne's opinion was crucial. So long as she retained faith in
the judgement of Marlborough and Godolphin then an alternative military
strategy was unthinkable. Slowly, however, that faith was lost. It was marked by
a growing gulf in 1708 between the Queen and her favourite Sarah Churchill,
the Duchess of Marlborough. Anne came increasingly under the sway of lowly-
born Abigail Masham who provided a conduit for the machinations and desires
for peace of Robert Harley. These bore fruit with Godolphin's dismissal on
8 August 1710. In the late summer of that year there was something close to a
revolution in the government as the Whig supporters of the duumvirs, including Marlborough's son-in-law Sunderland, were ousted to be replaced by
Harleyites and Tories, a revolution confirmed by a general election in October.
The battle for the will for war had been lost—and the new government pressed
for peace with unseemly haste.

The movement towards peace was intensified by the death on 17 April 1711
n.s. of Emperor Joseph, who had succeeded Leopold in 1705. Joseph died
childless, so the empire passed to his brother, Charles, the allies' pretender to
the Spanish Crown. If, however, Charles were to gain Spain, then Habsburg
power in Europe would be dangerously enhanced. Why, many wondered, was
a Habsburg leviathan preferable to a Bourbon behemoth? Now the Tories had
no scruples in seeking peace. Henry St John, one of the Secretaries of State,
opened secret negotiations with Torcy in the summer of 1711, with peace preliminaries signed on 27 September. By these Spain was given up, but Britain
gained Newfoundland, Nova Scotia, Gibraltar, Minorca, and the Asiento contract to supply Spanish America with slaves. However, the mighty figure of
Marlborough and a Whig majority in the House of Lords stood in the way of
peace itself. In a concerted propaganda campaign Marlborough was criticized
and ridiculed. In November, justifying the need for a speedy peace, Jonathan
Swift produced one of his most brilliant polemics, *The Conduct of the Allies*.

[54] H. M. C., *Calendar of the Manuscripts of the Marquis of Bath*, vol. 1 (1904), p. 197.

A central objective of Swift's attacks was to question the motivation of Marlborough: 'whether this War were prudently begun or not, it is plain, that the true Spring or Motive of it, was the aggrandizing of a particular Family [the Churchills], and in short, a War of the *General* [Marlborough] and the *Ministry* [the Whigs], and not of the *Prince* or *People*'.[55] On 31 December Marlborough was dismissed as Captain General, soon to be replaced by the Duke of Ormond, who was now a Tory and later a Jacobite. With little regard for constitutional propriety, in a few days in December 1711 and January 1712 Anne created twelve new peers to ensure the passage of the peace through the House of Lords. Soon after Marlborough went into voluntary exile, returning only after the Hanoverian accession in 1714. But after 1711 he never again commanded power as he had in his prime. Gradually his body and mind collapsed. It was a pitiful end to a remarkable career.

By reaching a separate agreement with France, Britain preferred self-interest to honouring the Grand Alliance—soon and for long after being remembered as 'Perfidious Albion'. She effectively abandoned her allies, leaving them with little option but to join her at the peace talks that began at Utrecht on 29 January 1712 n.s. The desertion was taken further still when in May Ormond received 'restraining orders' requiring him to avoid serious military engagements. Amazingly the orders were communicated to the French but not to Britain's allies. Thus Britain's war effort petered out in 'the last and most inglorious Campaign of this war, which is a blot and dishonour to the *British* Nation.'[56] In July France defeated the Dutch at Denain and went on to recover Le Quesnoy, Bouchain, and Douai, setbacks that had been unthinkable until Marlborough's dismissal. With further reverses possible the Dutch were forced to agree to peace. A new Barrier Treaty with Britain was signed in January 1713 leading the way to the conclusion of the peace of Utrecht in a series of treaties in the spring and summer. Only the Emperor held out, finally giving up the war the following March at the Peace of Rastatt.

The map of Europe after Utrecht and Rastatt was significantly different from that of 1702. The Spanish Netherlands had become the Austrian Netherlands and the Empire had made significant gains in Italy, especially Milan and Naples. The King of Spain, Philip V, was the grandson of the Sun King. The Dutch were given barrier fortresses in the Netherlands. Max Emmanuel of Bavaria was handed Sardinia and Victor Amadeus of Savoy obtained Sicily. France gave up some of its fortresses in Flanders, notably Ypres, Menin, and Tournai and had to dismantle Dunkirk's defences. Britain received Hudson Bay, Nova Scotia, and Newfoundland in Canada and St Kitts

[55] J. Swift, *Political Tracts, 1711–1713*, ed. H. Davis (Oxford, 1973), p. 41.
[56] Parker, *Memoirs*, p. 202.

in the West Indies. Louis returned to the Empire all lands on the east of the Rhine, but kept Alsace and Strasbourg to the west. Spain ceded Gibraltar, Minorca, and the Asiento to Britain. And France pledged itself to the Hanoverian succession to Anne—the Pretender was not to live in France, nor to receive French aid for any attempted restoration.

Britain ended up by making peace without Spain and to some it looked like failure.

> Why so many Battles did *Marlborough* win?
> So many strong Towns why did he take in?
> Why did he his Army to *Germany* lead,
> The Crown to preserve on the Emperor's Head?
> Why does he the Honour of *England* advance?
> And why has he humbled the Monarch of *France*
> By passing the Lines and taking *Bouchain*,
> If now at the last we must give up *Spain*,
> If now we must give up *Spain*.[57]

In truth, however, Britain had gained much. The succession was secured, the empire extended in North America and the Mediterranean, naval supremacy established, France contained and reduced, and a new European balance of power constructed. Britain had played a leading role in both war and peace and was now acknowledged as one of the leading European powers. How different this was from the reign of Charles II, when an enemy fleet had sailed up the Thames and the King had been a pensioner of France. Certainly Britain lost much pride in getting to the peace table, but the substantive losers at Utrecht were Spain and France. 'Spain was made to pay the bill for all the rest' and an era of French expansionism was closed.[58]

WAR, STATE, AND SOCIETY IN ENGLAND

For most of the reigns of William and Anne, England was deeply engaged in war. But significant though Marlborough's victories were the domestic contributions to and consequences of Britain's military achievements were no less dramatic or important. Taxes were levied, loans raised, supplies gathered, trade disrupted, and men mobilized, maimed, and killed. Britain was able, beyond all prior expectation, to wage war on a grand scale and, indeed, to wage it remarkably effectively. But in so doing, permanent changes were wrought at

---

[57] A. Mainwaring, 'An Excellent New Song, Called Mat's Peace, or the Downfall of Trade', in *Poems on Affairs of State*, ed. Ellis, pp. 508–9.
[58] *Chronicles of an Old Campaigner*, p. 377.

the heart of political society. Building on developments first set in train in the 1650s, the nature of the State, and of the relations between it and the populace, was significantly expanded and altered, assuming in most respects the form followed until Britain waged something akin to total war against France between 1793 and 1815.

In neither war did one side vanquish the other. Consequently, the material aspects of waging war were very prominent, a point widely appreciated. 'The mystery of war in having the last loaf, our ancestors understood.'[59] In both wars England did just that, in the process dramatically expanding the scale and scope of the domestic State. In the ten years before the Glorious Revolution total government expenditure was usually about £1.7m a year. During the Nine Years War this had risen to £4.9m per annum and in the War of the Spanish Succession to £7.8m, with about three-quarters of expenditure in war years devoted to the military. With so few State assets to sell, financing this huge expenditure could only be done through increasing revenue or by borrowing. In the Nine Years War loans provided 33.6 per cent of expenditure and in the War of the Spanish Succession 31.4 per cent. The new regime, having inherited no national debt, had not only introduced one but by 1698 had amassed one of £17.3m and which, by 1714, had reached £36.2m. Clearly the financial burden of both wars was huge, such that to provide the additional taxes and loans to fund them required what historians have, with reason, called a 'financial revolution', a revolution of both income and debt.

There was little chance of being able to raise sizeable loans in the years immediately after the Revolution. The Crown had for many years been a poor debtor and the possibility of the Jacobite restoration, which would have rendered debts to the Williamite regime worthless, made any loan far too risky. Until William and Mary were well established, loans were unlikely to provide significant sources of additional funds. Increased tax revenues provided the basis of the financial revolution, an increase that rested more on higher levels of contribution than growth in the economic base—in the 1680s 3–4 per cent of national income was levied as taxes, but by 1710 this had reached about 9 per cent. Such an increase was not achieved painlessly, but it was achieved without any serious threat of a tax revolt, partly because it had parliamentary legitimacy, partly because the burden was spread about. During the Nine Years War customs duties provided 22 per cent of current revenue, excises on commodities such as beer some 25 per cent, and taxes on land and other forms of wealth or indicators of status some 42 per cent. In the War of the Spanish Succession there was a slight shift away from the latter, the shares being customs 25 per cent, excise 32 per cent, and land and assessed taxes 38 per cent.

---

[59] H. M. C., *The Manuscripts of his Grace the Duke of Portland*, vol. 3 (1894), p. 535.

If customs and excise were 'regressive' taxes, tending to hit the poorer hardest, land and assessed taxes hit the rich harder and were 'progressive'. Thus to a considerable extent the wealthy apparently shouldered a significant share of the tax burden of these expensive wars.

Through both wars legislators were asked to consider a wide range of new demands upon the nation. Raising customs duties was a natural course to take. Less easy was the extension of the excise which the political nation disliked because it depended upon officials under the command of central government not local powerbrokers for its collection. Such suspicions were overcome because the alternatives were no better and because the excise, levied at point of production rather than point of sale, was a 'silent' and productive tax. Salt, malt, spirits, and hops were among the new commodities taxed. In the absence of an income tax, no less significant was the gradual transformation of the poll tax into the land tax by 1698, the administration of which rested with the landowners themselves. This linked centre and locality directly, involved local sources of authority in the needs of State, was cheap, and did away with heavy-handed State tax collectors. The level of the land tax was, indeed, to become the litmus test of a government's respect for the landed interest. Direct taxes were also levied upon hackney coaches in 1694, burials, bachelors, births, and marriages in 1695, houses in 1696, and hawkers in 1697.

Administering revenue gathering, raising loans, and waging war necessarily required a considerably enlarged State bureaucracy. In 1690 the customs service had 1,313 employees but by 1716 about 1,750, a rise of a third. For the excise service the increase was much greater, from 1,211 to 2,247. The paperwork of the Admiralty and Navy boards doubled during the Nine Years War and perhaps doubled again in the next war. Several new offices were established in 1696: the Board of Trade, the Inspector-General of Customs, and the Register of Shipping. Though by modern standards the State was still small in 1713, to contemporaries it was larger and more intrusive than it had ever been before and it did not shrink significantly with peace. Customs and excise officers were spread through the country, visible signals of a growing State apparatus. Yet the opposition this provoked, not least from smugglers, was limited both because of parliamentary endorsement and administrative efficiency. High standards of public service were the norm and the sins of corruption, peculation, pluralism, and venality were not widespread by the standards of other European powers. Between 1691 and 1697, 1702–4 and 1711–14 Commissions of Public Accounts scrutinized the State's budget in an attempt to ensure everything was in order.

The English State was remarkably fortunate in the calibre of the majority of its administrators. In key departments something close to permanent civil service was being forged. Men such as Lowndes, author of the maxim 'Take care of the pence, and the pounds will take care of themselves' and Secretary at the Treasury from 1695 to 1724, and Blathwayt, Secretary at War 1683–1704, served long and hard.[60] If there was a dominating administrative presence, however, it was Sidney Godolphin, at the head of the Treasury from 1690–6 and 1702–10. A Cornishman, born in 1645 of a royalist family, he served all monarchs from Charles II to Anne, though he gave up James reluctantly in 1689 and maintained some contact with him in the 1690s. Having lost his wife in 1678 he devoted himself to work, diverting himself only through an addiction to Newmarket races. By one character sketch he was 'a very cunning man, modest in his behaviour, speaks not much' and by another, more partisan, 'a man of few words, but of a remarkable thoughtfulness and sedateness of temper; of great application to business . . . He affected being useful without popularity'.[61] Indeed he tirelessly oversaw the dramatic expansion of key areas of the State, providing an element of integrity, continuity, and predictability in a very uncertain environment. He was in a very real sense Marlborough's partner and together the duumvirs oversaw the glory days of the War of the Spanish Succession. It is clear that Marlborough's dismissal and Godolphin's death the following year marked the end of an era.

Whether collected by local amateurs or officers of the State, all taxes were levied by vote of Parliament. However, the costs of the war outstripped the ability of Parliament to tax or the nation to pay. Yet parliamentary legitimacy was able to provide the pillars upon which the bridge between income and expenditure of the new national debt was built. The Crown had long been used to borrow to make ends meet. Such loans had, however, been as much personal as governmental and had been temporary rather than long-term commitments. There was no permanent national debt, secured by parliamentary taxation, drawing upon the reserves of public credit. In 1693 this changed when the treasury borrowed £1m by promising to repay lenders an annuity of 14 per cent (there was also a tontine element to this loan). In the following year a 'Million Lottery' was established, the prizes for which were to be paid for out of future duties on salt and liquor—hence this debt was 'funded'. The funded debt was soon to become common and effectively permanent. It took its best known institutional form in 1694 when the Bank of England was established to provide

---

[60] A. Partington (ed.), *The Oxford Dictionary of Quotations* (4th edn., 1992), p. 431. William Lowndes, 1652–1724, employed in the Treasury from 1679, as Secretary from 1695, MP for most of the period from 1695. William Blathwayt, 1649?–1717, diplomatic positions prior to 1683 when appointed Secretary at War, Clerk of Privy Council 1689, Secretary of State with William III in Flanders, MP 1685–8 and 1693–1710, built fine house, Dyrham Park, Gloucestershire.

[61] *The Wentworth Papers, 1705–1739: Selected from the Private and Family Correspondence of Thomas Wentworth, Lord Raby, Created in 1711 Earl of Strafford*, ed. J. J. Cartwright (1883), p. 131; *Memoirs of Sarah, Duchess of Marlborough Together with her 'Characters of her Contemporaries' and her 'Opinions'*, ed. W. King (1930), pp. 235–6.

a loan of £1.2m. In less than two weeks over 1,200 people, including William and Mary, invested in the new bank. At this stage the Bank of England was a private company conducting a limited range of financial services, not the least of which was the creation of paper credit for the government. It was, from its inception, closely allied to the government and to the needs of war—the deputy governor, Michael Godfrey, on a visit to discuss business with William, was killed in the trenches outside Namur in 1695. The national debt in general and the Bank of England in particular were soon seen as great buttresses to the Revolution settlement, as Addison depicted in a brilliant allegory.

I saw towards the Upper-end of the Hall, a beautiful Virgin, seated on a Throne of Gold. Her Name . . . was *Publick Credit*. The Walls, instead of being adorned with Pictures and Maps, were hung with many Acts of Parliament written in Golden Letters. At the Upper-end of the Hall was the *Magna Charta*, with the Act of Uniformity on the right Hand, and the Act of Toleration on the left. At the Lower-end of the Hall was the Act of Settlement, which was placed full in the Eye of the Virgin that sat upon the Throne. Both the Sides of the Hall were covered with such Acts of Parliament as had been made for the Establishment of publick Funds. The Lady seemed to set an unspeakable Value upon these several Pieces of Furniture, insomuch that she often refreshed her Eye with them, and often smiled with a Secret Pleasure, as she looked upon them; but, at the same time, showed a very particular Uneasiness, if she saw any thing approaching that might hurt them.[62]

The financial revolution, particularly the creation of the permanent national debt, was one of the age's most remarkable and enduring achievements. Yet it was not one without difficulties and, indeed, failure. In the early years, given the uncertain grip of William and Mary on the throne and the scale of the loans required, high rates of interest had to be offered to bait lenders. The loans of 1693 and 1694 were at 14 per cent, over double the statutory maximum for private debts and even in 1698, after Ryswick and French recognition of the new government, a loan of £2m had to offer interest rates of 8 per cent. Only during the War of the Spanish Succession was the government able to borrow at rates close to the general market rate. Even so, by that date much expensive debt had been contracted and Godolphin faced increasing difficulty in meeting existing commitments and raising new loans. Early in 1710 he had to offer 9 per cent interest rates and there had been a dangerous expansion of the unfunded debt since 1706. No less indicative of the experimental and fragile nature of the early stages of the financial revolution was the failure to establish a Land Bank in 1696 and the dislocation surrounding the recoinage in the same year. The former, a politically inspired anti-Bank of England initiative, attempted to tap the solidity of landed wealth to raise loans. Its flotation

<hr>

[62] *The Spectator*, ed. D. F. Bond, 5 vols. (Oxford, 1965), vol. 1, p. 15.

flopped as spectacularly as that of the Bank had soared. The recoinage was necessitated by heavy clipping of the old coins. Heavy remittances abroad to pay for the war effort—some £938,000 in bullion was sent to Europe 1689–95—provided a good deal of the pressure behind this. A lucrative trade was conducted, despite the execution of many clippers. Following the advice of John Locke, and against that of the Master of the Mint, Isaac Newton, a highly disruptive scheme was devised that provoked a crisis of commercial confidence, a dramatic decline in exchange transactions, and real want through the country.

The form of the financial revolution was decided at Westminster and there-fore hotly debated. Moreover, those who believed that Britain was unneces-sarily involving itself in overseas affairs were likely to condemn taxes and the national debt as anti-English. Higher taxes were disliked, but the national debt could be likened to planting usury at the heart of civil society, to line the pockets of a few financiers. It was complained by some, especially in the Nine Years War, that the national debt was more concerned to tie creditors to the regime than in finding money. Some questioned the justice of bequeathing heavy debts to future generations. Swift brilliantly summed up such views: 'Let any Man observe the Equipages in this Town; he shall find the greater Number of those who make a Figure, to be a Species of Men quite different from any that were ever known before the Revolution; consisting either of Generals and Colonels, or of such whose whole Fortunes lie in Funds and Stocks: So that *Power*, which . . . was used to follow *Land*, is now gone over to *Money*; and the Country Gentleman is in the Condition of a young Heir, out of whose Estate a Scrivener received half the Rents for Interest, and hath a Mortgage on the Whole'.[63] The City of London as a financial centre certainly benefited from helping to provide the means for waging war and many bankers, stockbrokers, and merchants were firm advocates of the Revolution settlement. This undoubtedly gave the City an enhanced authority, precisely indicated in June 1710 when 'some of the Dons of the City and the Bank' tried but failed to pre-vent Anne from abandoning Godolphin and the Whigs.[64] Harley, wearing the landowners' badge, was apoplectic: 'This is a matter of a very extraordinary nature, that private gentlemen . . . should have the presumption to take upon them to direct the sovereign.'[65] In fact City financiers now bestrode public and private finance and had to act in both.

Higher levels of taxation were the most obvious way in which the war was directly felt in England. Increased customs and excise duties hit everyone,

[63] J. Swift, *The Examiner*, ed. H. Davis (Oxford, 1966), p. 5.

[64] H. M. C., *The Manuscripts of the Marquess of Townshend* (1887), p. 67.

[65] H. M. C., *The Manuscripts of his Grace the Duke of Portland*, vol. 4 (1897), p. 545.

indeed England was more heavily taxed than France, but were stomached because they were hidden, levied away from point of sale, and parliamentary. The second impact was upon commodity markets, for to supply the military with transport, arms, clothing, food, and shelter required a huge diversion of resources. The third direct impact was upon labour markets. The State needed to find not only sailors and soldiers, but carriers, shipbuilders, blacksmiths, and the like. For example, numbers employed in the royal dockyards rose from 1,800 early in 1689 to a peak of 4,200 at the end of the war and to 5,800 by 1712. More dramatic was the need to find men for the armed forces. At average levels of mobilization the navy was voted 40,000–42,000 men in both wars, levels for the army being 76,000 in the Nine Years War and 92,000 in the following war. These were well above peacetime levels, in 1715 there were only 13,000 men in the navy and 19,000 in the army. Though some who served in the forces were foreigners, because of death, discharge, and desertion much larger numbers of Britons served in the armed forces than these totals suggest. Probably at least 15 per cent of men of serviceable age were in the armed forces in these wars, an unprecedented militarization of society, though still less than that of the Dutch Republic or France. Finding such a significant portion of the workforce was not easy. The navy faced a very competitive market for men, for in wartime wages in the merchant marine rose sharply and royal proclamations calling for seamen were frequently issued through both wars. Bounties were also offered but were often inadequate such that the press was often resorted to, though often with indifferent results—landmen notoriously took time to find their sea legs and the press was widely disliked and opposed. The army found it no easier to find men, though bad harvests and hard winters were a great help. Volunteers were assiduously sought out in the dead winter months by offering a bounty of £2 to every recruit, comically depicted in Farquhar's 1706 play *The Recruiting Officer*. Such methods were inadequate to the heavier demands of the War of the Spanish Succession. Impressment of the ablebodied unemployed was introduced in 1704 and continued for most of the remainder of the war. Though relatively small numbers were conscripted, in 1709, for example, the pressed outnumbered volunteers by nearly six to one among the new recruits. Such coercion, ripping young men away from their families and friends, naturally caused popular opposition and recruiting officers were always wary of possible mob resistance.

War had then a highly disruptive effect on English society. The State taxed heavily and took many men. Markets for many commodities were skewed by government contractors. French privateers badly disrupted overseas trade. Among the political nation this provoked heated debate and stylized outrage. Yet what is striking is how little evidence there is of popular opposition to the war in England, though petty outbursts, often Jacobitical, can be found. More commonplace were the celebrations of military successes and the demonstra-tions of hostility towards France which, if choreographed by the elite, were often genuinely popular. In the Nine Years War there were seven days for pub-lic thanksgiving and in the next war ten, all generally respected, helping to focus people on the national struggle being waged. For example, at Chester, celebrating Blenheim, 'The day of thanksgiving, calm and fair, the Bells and joy began early . . . The Dean preaches . . . before a vast number . . . universal joy and illuminations fill and beautify the town.'[66] Many people undoubtedly viewed these wars as just and necessary. France was a dangerous enemy, to be defeated at almost any cost. Moreover, by defending the providential deliver-ance of 1688–9, the achievements of Ryswick, Utrecht, and Marlborough's great victories could be seen as confirming England as the chosen nation, the modern Israel.

CONCLUSION

In the early sixteenth century Henry VIII had tried and failed to establish England as a European military power to be reckoned with. And, though in the seventeenth century the Royal Navy was widely respected, England was usu-ally seen as too weak and divided to weigh heavily in the complex calculations over the European balance of power. The Glorious Revolution changed that. William's invasion in 1688 forced England into Europe and an era of unpre-cedented warfare. For the best part of a quarter of a century the twin demands of securing the Protestant succession and limiting the power of France required England dramatically to develop her military capacity and act on a stage she had little experience of. This she did with remarkable success, not only by hugely expanding her own military capacity but also by paying large subsidies to allies. By the Treaty of Utrecht she was acknowledged as a leading European and colonial power, with a Mediterranean presence that continues to this day.

Though the reasons for England going to war in 1689 and 1702 were widely regarded as just, the conduct of the war and the nature of her achievements were viewed much less certainly. Many reminisced about England's previous isolationism and low taxes. Undoubtedly building up military might was costly. Two questions were constantly being asked: might the costs be reduced and would the benefits they brought place the nation in profit. From afar it might seem that such questions were simplistic and wrong headed, that war and the Protestant succession were inseparable and the achievements in battle

[66] *The Diary of Henry Prescott, LL. B, Deputy Registrar of Chester Diocese*, vol. 1, ed. J. Addy, Record Society of Lancashire and Cheshire, 127 (1987), p. 19.

marked the beginning of a period of 'greatness'. At the very least, however, that is to be somewhat wise after the event. Contemporaries had real choices before them in the conduct England's international affairs, choices that dominated the political worlds of both William and Anne. The intensity of political debate in those reigns drew much of its strength from the consideration of alternative strategies and aspirations. Certainly Britain's path to great power status was to be as uncertain politically as it was militarily.

CHAPTER 5

The Political World of William III

Like James II, William towered over the landscape of England's government, setting the political agenda to a degree unmatched by his next two successors. His intelligence and unwavering sense of purpose set him apart from kith and kin, as contemporaries well knew: 'King William thinks all, Queen Mary talks all, Prince George drinks all, And Princess Ann eats all.'[1] On the larger European canvas he was, alongside Louis XIV, the most remarkable monarch of his generation. Yet even William's considerable abilities could not ensure that royal policy was dominant in England. Indeed the unity shown in the crisis months of 1688–9 soon disappeared, to be followed by a prolonged battle between competing views of the national interest. Times without number King and Parliament were at loggerheads, to the extent that a whiff of anarchy occasionally drifted in the air. England's time of troubles was not ended by the Glorious Revolution, and though it did immediately ease some sources of friction it is only with hindsight that the changes in the conduct of politics in the 1690s can be seen to have led towards a dramatically more stable political system.

At heart the political instability of William's reign was due to the significance of the issues at stake. Establishing the Revolution settlement, conducting a major war, raising unprecedented levels of taxes, establishing the national debt, and securing the Protestant succession, among many other important matters, were always going to be hotly debated. But the political temperature was raised to such extreme levels because Parliament now had a huge presence in government, with long annual sessions providing plentiful opportunities not only to frame policy but also to reflect upon what had been done. Further, William generally worked through rather than around Parliament. Parliament may have driven him to distraction but he never, as Charles II and James II had, denied its significance or role. Yet its new found authority posed problems. Not least, a working relationship between executive

---

[1] 'The Diary of Abraham de la Pryme, the Yorkshire Antiquary', *Publications of the Surtees Society*, 54 (1870), p. 49. Prince George of Denmark was the husband of Princess Anne.

and legislature had to be established. But because there were markedly different views as to what constituted England's best interests, such a relationship
could not easily be built upon agreed policies. William, therefore, often altered
the composition of ministries in the hope of providing a measure of control
over Parliament and, when that failed, resorted to general elections to attempt
to find a more accommodating legislature. Yet it must also be remembered that
Parliament had to find its feet after twenty years of royal disfavour: Commons
and Lords had to learn to work together, just as within each House the wide
variety of opinions that existed precluded the establishment of a single legislative point of view. In such an environment, party politics became central,
though not all-important, for if Whig and Tory predominated there were those,
especially in the Commons, who might best be labelled 'independents' (called
by contemporaries the 'country party') who followed broad principles but no
clear programme. Such independence meant that all politicians—William, his
ministers, and Whig and Tory leaders—were attempting to traverse a political
world that was imperfectly mapped, though by 1702 the main features had all
been much more accurately identified.

DUTCH WILLIAM AND THE ENGLISH

The coronation of William and Mary took place on 8 April 1689 at
Westminster Abbey. Though the ceremony was 'performed with exceeding
great splendour, order & quietnesse' the majesty of the event was somewhat
illusory.[2] Compton, the Bishop of London, conducted the service because
Sancroft, the Archbishop of Canterbury, would not accept the Revolution.[3]
Other notable absentees further underlined the equivocal nature of the settlement and others attended only very reluctantly. Moreover many viewed, or
came to view, William with suspicion, though for various reasons—because of
their attachments to James, the unpalatable terms of the Revolution settlement,
William's policies, and because William endeared himself to few at the personal
level. Such suspicions were widely and deeply felt, to the extent that William
spent much of his reign struggling, not always successfully, to get his way. For
a time this struggle was partly masked by the fog of war, but with peace in 1697

  [2] R. T. Gunther (ed.), *The Life and Work of Robert Hooke*, Early Science in Oxford, 10
(Oxford, 1935), p. 113.
  [3] Henry Compton, 1632–1713, son of 2nd Earl of Northampton, gained some military experience, Bishop of Oxford 1674 and London 1675, Privy Councillor 1676 but dismissed 1685
through mutual hostility with James II, culminating in his active support for William's invasion
1688, his disappointment at not being promoted to Canterbury led to a distancing from William's
regime, active in support of foreign Protestants, collector of foreign plants. William Sancroft,
1617–1693, student, Tutor, Bursar, and Master Emmanuel College, Cambridge, Archbishop of
Canterbury 1678 who clashed with James II over religious policy but deprived by William 1690.

it was clear for all to see. In the last few years of his life he waged a near constant battle with the political nation, a battle that exhausted and exasperated England's last monarch to be blessed with keen intelligence.

Had William been gracious, amusing, entertaining, and accessible then some of the hostility he encountered might have been dissipated. But he was no such thing. Though his reputation for physical bravery preceded him, he gave a poor first impression of himself. His hook nose, sunken eyes, and foreign accent were joined to a constant asthmatic cough. Indeed, physical frailty prompted him effectively to abandon the old palace at Whitehall for the tranquillity and clean air of Hampton Court and Kensington. Necessarily this set him somewhat apart, though he was in any case temperamentally unsuited to lead and promote a court society that might have tied notables to his personage. He lacked the grace and patience to ingratiate himself socially with the elite and found polite conversation as dangerous as the battlefield and trench which he faced more readily. However, he well knew the value of rewarding his supporters with dignities, offices, and pensions—it says much that, for a King so distant from polite society, the annual cost of his court was nearly 40 per cent higher than James's and was not surpassed by either Anne or George I. In fact, William had a rather materialist and non-spiritual conception of kingship. His authority was based upon determination and constant endeavour rather than appeals to the word of God. He shouldered, in any case, a great burden of work, not only as King of England and military commander but also as Dutch Stadholder. Thus often 'he was shut up all the day long', cutting him off from the great and the good.[4] Moreover, as an outsider he had to learn to operate within a new political system and, like many good students, he studied so quietly as to appear indifferent of English affairs. This was not helped by the fact that he forever valued his Dutch confidants above those English he was obliged to depend upon. He characterized England's elite as factious, ingenuous, and selfish. As a man of destiny, certain of his role as Europe's saviour from French expansionism, he found the English insular and short-sighted. Yet these were the men he had to work with and his real feelings could not readily be shown. Thus from one perspective he displayed iron self-control – 'He is very stately, serious, & reserved'.[5] To his critics, however, 'He had a dry morose way with him, seldom having a merry countenance, and when he had it not becoming him' and was 'so ill-natured and so little polished by education, that neither in great things nor in small had he the manners of a gentleman.'[6]

[4] G. Burnet, *History of his Own Time*, 6 vols. (Oxford, 1823), vol. 4, p. 147.

[5] *The Diary of John Evelyn*, ed. E. S. de Beer, 6 vols. (Oxford, 1955), vol. 4, p. 612.

[6] *Memoirs of Thomas, Earl of Ailesbury, Written by Himself*, 2 vols. (1890), vol. 2, p. 502; *Memoirs of Sarah, Duchess of Marlborough Together with her 'Characters of her contemporaries' and her 'Opinions'*, ed. W. King (1930), p. 81.

Though the Glorious Revolution challenged the very heart of kingship—hereditary succession and passive obedience—William was in no doubt that he was the very mainspring of government and as much King as his predecessors. He believed that he should formulate and direct policy, especially regarding foreign affairs, such that ministers were his servants and Parliament mainly an instrument to bring his plans to fruition. He valued kingly prerogative highly, though he had little time for the theatre of royalty. This was at one with the difficulties he had in trusting other people. He was loath to allow his wife to exercise authority except in the area of ecclesiastical preferments, never appointed a Lord Treasurer, and treated his Secretaries of State as mere 'hired kind of clerks'.[7] Few English politicians did he rank as indispensable. Such distrust was central to his outlook, having been nurtured in the fractured world of Dutch politics and further developed in England by the Jacobite threat and the strength of partisanship and parochialism. By his standards the best politician was the able administrator and dispassionate analyst. His own abilities were, in any case, considerable. He spoke four languages, including English, understood three others, and 'had a memory that amazed all about him, for it never failed him: he was an exact observer of men and things'.[8]

Clearly William had little time for the petty prejudices of Westminster politics and at times his frustration came close to driving him back to the Republic. He was soothed by other considerations. Most important of all, England's resources were essential for him to pursue his European ambitions. At heart William was a realist with enough modesty to enable him, unlike James and however grudgingly, to recognize that his authority was limited. He knew that he had to work with the English and silently suffer some of Parliament's impertinences. Second, he knew that in the end most in England preferred him to James—he was Protestant and never abandoned Parliament or the law. It is notable that when the crunches came—not only in 1689, but also when his wife died in 1694, when a Jacobite plot to kill him was uncovered in 1696, and when the question of the succession and the European balance of power was reopened in 1700 and 1701—the overwhelming majority of the political nation fell in behind Dutch William. He was, so to speak, easier to love as an idea than as a man. He never ceased to believe that he held the high moral ground and, indeed, presented his regime as a crusading one. Third, he looked ever forwards, rarely backwards. Thus, in the right circumstances, he was willing to forget past indiscretions, using many of James's cronies in 1689 and 1690 and welcoming Marlborough back into the fold towards the end of his reign. Fourth, he spent a good part of his reign in the Republic, not only waging war,

[7] *Letters of William III and Louis XIV, and of their Ministers*, ed. P. Grimblot, 2 vols. (1848), vol. 1, p. 191.

[8] Burnet, *History*, vol. 4, p. 548.

but escaping from the trials and tribulations of Westminster. Though he was gradually somewhat Anglicized he was able to remain true to his origins— Hampton Court was remodelled to provide a little corner of Holland. Finally, though he was something of a loner, there were those to whom he could divulge his inner feelings. His emotional world was secular not spiritual, for in purely personal terms friendship and love meant more to him than heaven and hell. In England, two Dutch favourites, Bentinck, the Earl of Portland, and then Keppel, the Earl of Albemarle, both provided solace.[9] For a time he took Elizabeth Villiers as his mistress and the depression he experienced when his wife died in 1694 also suggests that there was more intimacy between them than some evidence suggests.

None the less, through his reign there was a tension, amounting almost to mutual distrust, between William and a goodly part of England's political nation. Exploring the changing nature of that tension is the central thread of the political history of this period. Yet such tensions did not preclude major developments. William clearly attained his fundamental objectives: establishing his regime and the Hanoverian succession while decisively allying England with Holland to check France. Parliament too achieved much. It became a permanent part of the governmental process, witnessed a remarkable growth in legislative activity, and introduced unprecedented levels of executive accountability. Though neither recognized it at the time, William and England's political nation slowly and painfully edged towards a *modus vivendi*.

THE HYDRA OF OPPOSITION

The political world of William III was undeniably disordered. If the intractability of the issues involved and the nature of William's kingship were two key factors at work a third was provided by the complex arrangement of opposition groupings. Such complexity was not immediately apparent. Superficially, at one end of the political spectrum were the Jacobites, longing to restore James in William's place, and at the other republicans who wished to abolish or significantly reform monarchical government. Most, however, occupied the middle ground. Nearest to the Jacobites were the Tories and indeed some, though by no means all, Tories were Jacobites. Nearest to the republicans were Whigs. Such a depiction, even allowing for its overgeneralization, is

---

[9] William Bentinck, 1649–1709, helped to negotiate marriage of William and Mary, was active in preparations for invasion in 1688, trusted by William for much other diplomatic work, resigned positions within royal household in pique at Albemarle's rising star, successively Lord Cirencester, Viscount Woodstock, and Earl of Portland. Arnold Joost van Keppel, 1669–1718, came to England with William 1688 and returned to Holland on his death, fighting in major battles in War of the Spanish Succession, created Earl of Albemarle 1697.

inadequate on two main counts. First, the nature of Whig and Tory changed in the 1690s, not least as the former, sucked into executive politics, had to rethink some of their political principles. Second, there were those politicians, the 'country', who saw themselves as standing above party, seeking not office but efficient and good government. They constituted not a party but a point of view, and one that might, as circumstances allowed, appeal to both Whig and Tory.

Jacobites were potentially William's most serious opponents, for by definition they denied his crown. Yet Jacobitism was never monolithic and, because of its need for secrecy, was by its very nature of uncertain size and significance. There were those Jacobites prepared to have James back unconditionally, the so-called 'Non-compounders'. Other Jacobites argued that James had to court popularity by offering concessions and guarantees, not least because he was never willing to consider renouncing his faith. Moreover, some Jacobites were deadly serious, others far less so. Few could doubt those who followed James into exile from England (probably numbering hundreds, possibly a few thousand), or actively plotted from England for his return. But there were also those who might take up the Jacobite banner for reasons other than to restore James. Politicians such as Shrewsbury, Godolphin, and Marlborough established links with the Jacobite court to guard their position in the event of James's return. Their Jacobitism was shallow and self-serving. Even so, the suspicion must be that committed Jacobitism was more common among the political elite than the nation at large. Among some a culture of Jacobitism flourished, partly sustained through celebrating the birthdays of James and his son, buying portraits, and reading the exiled King's latest 'Declaration'. And certainly popular Jacobitism existed, as, for example, the Yorkshire yeoman who proclaimed that 'There is no King but King James . . . I wish prosperity to King James and all his forces' or the Hertfordshire schoolmaster who was fined for declaring 'King James is my lawful king and I ought to respect him.'[10] But shouting up Jacobitism was also a convenient and potent anti-establishment rhetoric. For example, before six people were executed at Tyburn in London in September 1690 they made themselves merry with drink, calling on the crowd to 'send for king James back', thereby rejecting the authority that was about to place a rope around their necks.[11] There is in fact little evidence that Jacobitism was popular among ordinary folk in the 1690s. The Jacobite Earl of Ailesbury told James II to his face in exile that 'his

[10] *Quarter Sessions Records*, ed. J. C. Atkinson, North Riding Record Society, 7 (1889), p. 108; *Hertford County Records*, 1 and 2. *Notes and Extracts from the Session Rolls*, ed. W. J. Hardy, 2 vols. (Hertford, 1905), vol. 1, p. 408.

[11] N. Luttrell, *A Brief Historical Relation of State Affairs from September 1678 to April 1714*, 6 vols. (Oxford, 1857), vol. 2, p. 103.

Majesty was esteemed . . . by men of honour, but that amongst the generality in England his name was nowise in reputation.'[12]

Jacobites were divided in terms of their commitment to a restoration and in terms of the methods for attaining such a restoration, much turning upon the extent of dependence upon France. Some Jacobites argued that the throne could only be retaken by a massive, French sponsored, invasion. However, dependence upon France put the movement at Louis's whim and further exacerbated the problem of James's religion. Others planned for a palace coup or a popular uprising. Such a range of views might not have mattered had the Jacobite court at St Germain been able to provide a clear lead. However, James showed little relish for the task and channels of communication between him and his followers were inevitably fractured and unpredictable. Much Jacobitism in England took place independent of St Germain and was, therefore, so ill-co-ordinated that its left and right hands might not only be ignorant but at odds with each other.

In a sense it was the perceived and not the real scale of the Jacobite threat to William's regime that mattered and there is no question that William was forever worried by the possibility of plots, risings, and invasions. Serious threats were perceived in 1691–2, 1696 (twice), and 1697. Seizures of arms, horses, papers, and suspects were a commonplace, often under the watchful gaze of Dutch troops. Yet the fact is that there was no rising, invasion, or actual attempt on William's life. And though William was fully prepared to arrest malefactors, intercept the mails, employ spies, and buy support, it is remarkable how little Jacobite blood he shed in England. In the end this was because Jacobitism lacked sharp teeth. Its logistical problems were considerable, but, more important to most English people, nothing could mask or excuse James's religion or his dependence upon Louis. Furthermore, few in England savoured the prospect of another civil war. It is notable, therefore, that the Jacobite threat significantly diminished after 1696. So long as war continued Jacobites reasonably hoped either that William's regime would dig its own grave, through excessive taxation and conscription, or that James would lead an invasion of his motherland. With peace, and Louis's recognition of William, prospects for a restoration shrank dramatically. By 1699 it was unkindly (but accurately) observed that 'Ther is no good nues for poor Jacobites . . . their hops must be in the next world'.[13]

Even those who accepted William as King had many reasons to question his policies. Many Tories were uncomfortable with the Revolution because as a

---

[12] *Ailesbury Memoirs*, vol. 1, p. 335.

[13] *Verney Letters of the Eighteenth Century from the Mss. at Claydon House*, ed. M. M. Verney, 2 vols. (1930), vol. 1, p. 44.

party they had largely come into being in the late 1670s to defend the royal prerogative, hereditary succession, and ideas of passive obedience. In the main
they had turned their back on James only because he had turned his on the
Anglican hegemony. To Tories, William might only be recognized as a King
in fact rather than by right. Further, though they valued his Protestantism,
they were suspicious of his Calvinism and, though many endorsed the anti-
French alliance, of his committing English resources to a continental land war.
Profoundly compromised by their passivity in 1688 they now became suspicious of William's use of the royal prerogative to further his European objectives and were very worried about the erosion of the position of the Church of
England. The Whig party had cut its teeth between 1679 and 1681 in the failed
attempts to exclude James from the succession and they had suffered badly at
the hands of both Charles II and James II. Some of their leaders had been executed for plotting (real and imagined), many had been forced from local and
national office, and a good number had prudently gone into exile on the
Continent. Thus by 1689 the Whigs had an indelible distrust of the Stuarts, a
fact which in the end drew William towards them. Moreover, though they
were as profoundly anti-Catholic as the Tories, they were markedly more tolerant to Protestant Dissent and thus more sympathetic to William's religious
outlook. However, though they enthusiastically supported the offer of the
Crown to William it was less clear what form of kingship they envisaged. Many
were deeply suspicious of the royal prerogative and stressed the need for a shift
of authority from the executive to the legislature to produce a better balanced
political system. Indeed, at the extreme some Whigs had been so disillusioned
with Charles and James that they were republicans. Certainly William initially
viewed the Whigs as commonwealthmen and was loath to trust much to them.
Yet in time the proximity of his views to theirs on the succession, religion, and
the European war forced an accommodation. In the process many Whigs also
shifted their ground and became much more willing to embrace executive
government.

In 1689 political commentators usually viewed Tories as allies and Whigs as
enemies of the Crown. But through the 1690s the map of political ideology was
redrawn. Tories found more and more reasons to question the royal prerogative and to oppose the particular policies pursued by William. The Whigs, having more in common with the new King, found their radicalism compromised
by office and undermined by the growth of parliamentary government to the
extent that in the 1690s it is possible to identify a new generation of court
Whigs. But not all Whigs were prepared to abandon their roots, Robert Harley
being the most notable example. Reared in the tradition of Puritan radicalism,
he feared the Stuarts specifically and executive government more generally. To
him fully trusting monarchy was very difficult and good government had to

come from or be watched for by men who were truly independent, the country gentlemen. But as the Whigs were drawn into government in the 1690s Harley did not lose that belief. In his view political office often led to corruption and a loss of virtue. For a time he championed the country cause before, in due course, finding himself within the Tory party. Yet it was not Harley that had gone from one extreme to another, but the parties as they came to terms with the altered world of post-Revolution politics.[14]

Many contemporaries were uncertain about the legitimacy of party politics, for it conjured up painful memories of the factionalism of the Interregnum and the dark days of the 1680s. Moreover, given the shifts in ideology, party was liable to be viewed as a cover for the lust for office and private profit. With the expansion of the size and cost of government through the 1690s, it was to be expected that among the political elite some were suspicious and disenchanted with the political order. Wary of the expansion of the central State, they argued for relative local autonomy and the full accountability of the executive, a viewpoint presented especially forcefully after 1696. In 1700 one perceptive observer noted that 'Though the English are nearly all divided into Whigs and Tories, there are many country members in Parliament who have never joined with these parties to the extent of closely espousing either. These men speak and vote in the House according to their lights, which rarely reach beyond the shores of their own island.'[15]

Contemporaries only faintly perceived the shift in political alignments that took place in the 1690s. It was not anticipated, pre-determined, or desired. It was also obscured because it was overlaid by personal animus to William and leading politicians such as Carmarthen, Somers, and Portland. Parties were, in any case, somewhat indistinct entities. They lacked formal structures of authority and responsibility. Nor did they have central offices, think tanks, or conferences to thrash out policy (though Christ Church, Oxford, may have been a hothouse of Tory thinking). Indeed, counting the strength of parties in William's parliaments is very difficult—neither the Whigs nor the Tories had formal membership lists, records of debates are sparse, and only rarely do we know how MPs voted on particular issues. The best estimates available are shown in Table 3. The significance of such counts should not be exaggerated, for both MPs and peers retained a high degree of political independence, a point that was crucial in allowing the Tories to change direction. It is harder still to estimate the popularity of the parties amongst the electorate and wider public, not least because of the infrequency of contested elections. All in all,

[14] See Chapter 9.
[15] Quoted in G. S. Holmes and W. A. Speck (eds.), *The Divided Society: Parties and Politics in England, 1694–1716* (1967), p. 19.

TABLE 3. *Party strength in the House of Commons, 1690–1701*

	Tories	Whigs	Unclassified
1690	243	241	28
1695	203	257	53
1698	208	246	59
1701 (Jan./Feb.)	248	220	45
1701 (Nov./Dec.)	240	248	24

Note: Figures relate to the position immediately after each election, but exclude the outcome of disputed returns. These provisional estimates have been kindly made available by the 1690–1715 House of Commons section of the History of Parliament.

even with the benefit of hindsight, it is very difficult to describe accurately the complex political world of the 1690s. It was, and is likely to remain, one of the most confused periods of England's political history.

ESTABLISHING THE REGIME, 1689–1690

On 13 February 1689 William and Mary were offered the Crown by the Convention assembly that had been elected the previous month. Ten days later this was further legitimized when the assembly, passing its first Act, transformed itself into a Parliament. It was through the Convention, which was dissolved on 6 February 1690, that the first steps were taken towards finding a workable mode of government. It was not an easy body for William to deal with, for it contained many who were unhappy with the settlement which had been reached. His immediate objectives were easily stated: establish his authority across the British Isles and involve Britain in war with France. Howsoever determined and independent he was, he knew that to achieve this he had to work through the usual channels of political power. The first crucial decision to be made was who to employ in this task. This was a question not only of personnel but also of party and, thus, of the whole tenor of the government, both civil and religious. To favour the Whigs was to favour a party that was traditionally suspicious if not actually hostile towards the royal prerogative. To favour the Tories was, however, to favour many who had been tainted by James's policies and were profoundly uncertain of the legitimacy of the new regime. In fact he attempted to establish a government that was above party, hoping to build upon the unity that had deprived James of support at the end of 1688. He saw himself as a 'Trimmer', as one who moved between the parties and if the Whigs were in a majority in the Privy Council the Tories held a number of key posts: Danby, once Charles II's leading minister, was made Lord President (and became Earl, later Marquis, of Carmarthen); Godolphin was put into the Treasury Commission; and the Earl of Nottingham was the Secretary of State for the north.[16] In between, so to speak, was the Marquis of Halifax, also a self-proclaimed 'Trimmer', now made Lord Privy Seal. William took it for granted that this mixed ministry would be able to deliver votes in the Convention, where there was a majority for the Whigs but substantial numbers of Tories. But by employing some of James's servants William cast doubt upon the very Revolution which had brought him to power—though it is notable that those servants were exorcised from the lord lieutenancy and principal judicial offices. To Whigs and republicans they were 'Perfidious wretches who joyned in the attempt of enslaving and undoing the nation' lamenting that they 'are not called into question, and . . . are not only received into mercy, but into favour.'[17] It was, moreover, naive of William to expect Whig and Tory ministers to put their differences to one side and work single-mindedly to promote his policies.

After the offer of the Crown the immediate task facing the Convention was to neutralize perceived threats to the new government, both domestic and international. At home Jacobites and Roman Catholics were viewed as the main worries. By Act, habeas corpus was suspended, Catholics were banished from the capital and disarmed, and new oaths of allegiance replaced those to James. Only the last of these caused serious debate. What form of commitment to the new monarchs could reasonably be required? Both Houses produced proposals before deciding that William and Mary were due allegiance because they were monarchs in fact (*de facto*) rather than by right (*de jure*), an outcome suggesting that the Convention was far from Whig controlled and reasonably pragmatic in its wish to tie as many as people as possible to the new regime. Such an oath would expose and identify men of professed principle, both Jacobites and those who were more vaguely unenthusiastic towards William, but it was an oath a majority could take with a reasonably clear conscience. Secondary threats to the new regime were posed by renegade army units and Dissenters. The former were dealt with by the establishment of martial law in a Mutiny Act. Parliamentary suspicions that an army might become an instrument of independent royal authority were satisfied by placing martial law

---

[16] H. C. Foxcroft, *The Life and Letters of Sir George Savile, Bart. First Marquis of Halifax*, 2 vols. (1898), vol. 2, pp. 207, 252. Thomas Osborne, 1631–1712, successively baronet, Earl of Danby (by which title he is most commonly known), Marquis of Carmarthen, and Duke of Leeds, Privy Councillor 1673 and as Charles II's leading minister adopted anti-French and pro-Dutch foreign policy but signed invitation to William and central to the rising in the north, 1688, a major ministerial figure to 1695. George Savile, 1633–1695, Marquis of Halifax. Opposed Bill for exclusion of James from succession but in communication with William in 1680s, opposed repeal of Test Act, a central figure in resolution of political crisis of 1688–9.

[17] *The Life and Times of Anthony Wood, Antiquary, of Oxford, 1632–1695*, vol. 3, ed. A. Clark, Oxford Historical Society, 26 (Oxford, 1894), pp. 308–9.

beneath the civil courts and limiting the life of the Act to only six months. Despite their reputation for republicanism, the threat from Dissenters was a different sort for most of them were content with William as King—on 2 January some ninety Nonconformist ministers had pledged loyalty to him. The worry, rather, was the renewed threat they posed to the Anglican supremacy. Dissenters had long been seen as challenging the stability of political society, for as outsiders they questioned its established conventions and often advocated different structures of authority, most extremely republicanism. Such a challenge was imagined by Anglicans to be the more serious in the environment of constitutional uncertainty existing in England in the first half of 1689. Not least there was a concern not to allow moderate Dissenters into the Church at a time when the new oaths threatened to decimate the Anglican clergy. William undoubtedly wanted Dissenters to be accommodated or 'comprehended' within the established Church, but the Convention had enough Tories (or members of the 'Church party' as it was sometimes called) to see off the proposal. It was sent to Convocation where it was foredoomed to die. Its failure demonstrated the weakness of the royal will and the independence of Parliament, though the passage of the Toleration Act, which gained the royal assent on 24 May, was a blow to the Anglican supremacy.

The limitations of royal control over Parliament in 1689 were demonstrated in three other ways. First, when all is said and done the Bill of Rights was perceived to be a statutory limitation upon the Crown. Specifically, it ended the Crown's power to dispense with laws and to keep a standing army in peacetime (though it appears not to have been invoked when this issue came to the fore after 1697), while generally it clarified a number of constitutional conventions. Second, on 25 March 1689 William had urged Parliament to pass an Act pardoning all but a few of the worst malefactors from the previous two reigns. He preferred only to look forward, wanting old wounds to be healed quickly. Though the Commons did consider the issue there were too many Whigs with painful memories of persecution for headway to be made. To them, their very identity was bound up with the sufferings of their colleagues at the hands of Charles and James. To abandon those martyrs was to question one of the foundations of their political philosophy. It was, of course, also a matter of opportunism, for their sights were trained upon those Tory opponents who had done the dirty work of imposing royal authority from 1679 to 1688. But, finally, the most direct challenge to William was the manner in which supply was found for the nation's military commitments and the support of his government. Money was found, but only slowly and reluctantly. Few liked having to send £600,000 to the Dutch to pay for the invasion the previous November and suspicion that the money which had already been granted to the government was being ill used was stimulated by Jacobite success in Ireland

and evidence of corruption. The Commons demanded that Privy Council papers be made available to settle the matter, an extraordinary intrusion by the legislature into the executive though at one with long-standing hopes that a revived Privy Council would prevent the misuse of royal authority by ministers. It is a sign of William's weakness that in July he had to agree to this.

By the middle of 1689 William complained that 'the Commons used him like a dog' and that he was 'so weary' of Parliament that 'hee could not bear them'.[18] On 20 August he brought the parliamentary session to a close, soon confessing 'I see that I am not made for this people, nor they for me'.[19] The recess provided only a brief respite, for William needed too much money to survive without Parliament for long. On 19 October the second and final session of the Convention began. In legislative terms it conducted little business, passing just nine public and eight private Acts. Some progress was made—the Bill of Rights was passed without undue debate and William made available evidence of government finances in return for which Parliament provided supply. But William viewed the investigations of the Commons into the campaign in Ireland as an intrusion into his business and again the Commons failed to pass an Indemnity Bill. Moreover, Whig malice came to the fore when they attempted to attack Tories in local government through the so-called Sacheverell clause to a Bill (not ultimately enacted) regulating corporations. To him that signalled the bankruptcy of the present distribution of power and so on 27 January he prorogued Parliament, dissolving it on 6 February.

Though William never lamented its passing, the Convention had achieved much: the transfer of the Crown, a new oath, the Bill of Rights, the Toleration Act, a Militia Act and reasonably plentiful supply were, by any standards, major accomplishments. The era of legislative quiescence that had begun in the 1670s had been decisively concluded. The Jacobite advance in Ireland had been halted and English troops sent to the Dutch Republic's aid. Yet William was exasperated both by the effort involved in attaining these goals and in his failures both to preserve the royal prerogative untouched and pass an Act of Indemnity. Partly this was wishful thinking. It was to be expected that working out the consequences of the Glorious Revolution through Parliament would be disputatious and disordered, protracted and partial. The political system was, in effect, being recast. Even so, William's relations with the Convention were fractured because his chosen ministers were unable to control it, because of stresses between the two Houses, and, more significantly, because the Commons was deeply split. The unity of January and February 1689 had in fact been somewhat illusory, a temporary state brought about by

---

[18] Foxcroft, *Halifax*, vol. 2, pp. 207 and 224.
[19] Quoted in S. B. Baxter, *William III* (1966), p. 255.

revulsion towards James's government and force of circumstances rather than agreement as to the form and policies of future governments. Furthermore, because party organization and discipline was ill-developed grandees struggled to control the rank and file of Whig and Tory parties. It was, however, the Whig majority in the Convention that especially troubled William, for he found them obsessed with settling old scores and determined to encroach upon his authority. He believed they were quasi-republicans, a 'Commonwealth party . . . [and] that at the best, they would have a Duke of Venice'.[20] William's Tory ministers, especially Nottingham, urged that a general election would produce a Parliament more sympathetic to the royal will.[21] The Whigs, however, complained that his use of Tory ministers was ill-advised. Their attacks upon the executive were in part designed to force William to depend entirely upon them and their leaders. At heart Whigs damned Tories as Jacobites. Shrewsbury, the youthful Whig Secretary of State, told William bluntly that 'the tories, who many of them, questionless, would bring in king James, and the very best of them . . . have a regency still in their heads; for though I agree them to be the properest instruments to carry the prerogative high, yet I fear they have so unreasonable a veneration for monarchy, as not altogether to approve the foundation your's is built upon.'[22] Neither party could suit William perfectly, a point he came only gradually to recognize, but in the short term he looked more towards the Tories than to the Whigs.

THE FAILURE OF THE MIDDLE WAY

The general election for the new Parliament was held in February and March 1690. Some 40 per cent of constituencies actually experienced a poll, a high figure by contemporary standards. These were partisan struggles, notable for the involvement of churchmen on the Tory side. Certainly the Whigs lost ground, voters seeing them as a source of political instability, particularly by challenging the Anglican establishment. Remarkably, London returned four Tories in place of four Whigs, a clear sign of a split amongst the Whigs and in the Commons the Tory Sir John Trevor was made Speaker. William, however, was unwilling at this stage to abandon trimming for party government, though

[20] Foxcroft, *Halifax*, vol. 2, p. 203.

[21] Daniel Finch, 1647–1730, 2nd Earl of Nottingham, a leading figure in debates of 1688–9, Secretary of State 1689–93, 1702–4, leading High Church Tory under Queen Anne.

[22] *Private and Original Correspondence of Charles Talbot, Duke of Shrewsbury*, ed. W. Coxe (1821), p. 15. Charles Talbot, 1660–1718, 12th Earl and only Duke of Shrewsbury, converted to Protestantism 1679, landed with William 1688, Secretary of State 1689–90, exasperation at political intrigues kept him out of politics 1700–10 but played important role at death of Anne in securing Hanoverian succession.

he did shift towards the Tories.[23] Many Whigs kept their posts, though some were replaced by Tories and courtiers. Halifax and Godolphin had already resigned and Shrewsbury was soon to do so. The leading ministers were now certainly Carmarthen and Nottingham, the latter unequivocally Tory.

The new Parliament met on 20 March 1690 and William hoped that its business could be quickly conducted so that he could go to Ireland to repulse James. His determination is evidenced by his willingness to introduce an Act of Grace to obtain the indemnity he had repeatedly sought from the Convention. To go to Ireland he needed further money and to establish a form of government to operate in his absence. Surprisingly, the former was found more easily than the latter. Party manoeuvring slowed progress, as Whigs struggled to exercise some authority in what for them were reduced circumstances. In particular, they forwarded a highly controversial and abortive Bill that would have required the abjuration of James and debate also surrounded a measure to confirm the Convention's parliamentary status. Debate over the regency provided further opportunities of mischief to those who viewed William's kingship as limited and conditional. One Bill, 'framed in such a manner that the Prince of Orange would be no sooner out of the kingdom than he would cease to be King until his return, and would need a fresh Act of Parliament to re-establish him', appealed both to Jacobites and to radical Whigs.[24] Still, therefore, there were those on both sides who were uncertain that the settlement was settled. But Shrewsbury's resignation on 28 April signalled recognition by the Whigs of their diminished power in the new Parliament and ministry. In this climate the passage of a moderate Regency Act and the Act of Grace were readily accomplished and on 23 May William adjourned Parliament. Six weeks later he defeated James on the battlefield at the Boyne.

William's campaign somewhat revived his fortunes not least because he saw that he could leave the administration under the gaze of his wife. On his journey to Chester he was widely fêted and his victory at the Boyne was generally celebrated, though the gloss was taken off by news of the navy's defeat off Beachy Head. In domestic political terms his military defeat of James strengthened his hand against extremists on both flanks, for his regime could now be seen to work. To radical Whigs and republicans William had shown the value of committed kingship and a willingness to make minor concessions, such as the provision of financial records, to attain his main objectives. Moreover, as

---

[23] John Trevor, 1637–1717, barrister and knighted 1671, MP from 1673, Master of the Rolls and Speaker 1685, dismissed from judicial post 1688 but reinstated 1693.

[24] H. M. C., *Report on the Manuscripts of the Late Allan George Finch, Esq.*, vol. 2 (1922), p. 279.

prospects of James seizing back his throne dramatically receded, the hopes of his English supporters withered. Jacobitism now became a long game. However, if William had to a limited extent shifted the ground underneath Jacobites and radical Whigs he was not much closer to establishing productive relations with Parliament. His opponents had been wounded rather than disarmed and his policy of trimming meant that uncoordinated opposition from both wings remained a daily threat. No less significant, all politicians saw how unwilling the King was to devolve policy making upon them. From 1690 to 1694 the mixed ministry was only notionally headed by Carmarthen, for despite his experience and stature William was reluctant to trust him and continued to shoulder a huge burden of government himself. Carmarthen was also unable to establish an effective working relationship with some of the other leading Tories, notably Nottingham and Godolphin. Until 1693 the ministry was fractured and multi-faceted, following no clear line of policy than that of attempting to fall in behind William and his overriding desire to find money and men to wage war.

William returned to England at the start of September 1690, opened Parliament on 2 October and closed it on 5 January. It was not, in truth, a memorable session, for besides finding money for the war major legislation was limited. However, the creation of a Commission of Public Accounts was a pointer to the future preoccupation with making the executive financially accountable. The uncovering of a Jacobite conspiracy on 31 December that implicated even some Whigs also stands out as evidence of the heady cocktails of political principles that were then a commonplace. The session was, though, devoid of the intense partisanship which had marked earlier sessions. In this climate it was significant that William spent most of 1691 in the Republic, removing from the domestic political scene the focal point of opposition groupings. Thus, even his appointment in April of a new archbishop and several bishops to fill the places of the ejected non-jurors failed to whip up a really fierce storm.

William returned to England on 19 October 1691 and three days later a new parliamentary session was opened. Over the following four months it passed only fifteen public Acts. Curiously, the final failure of Jacobitism in Ireland with the signing of the Treaty of Limerick on 3 October, subtly changed the terms of debate at Westminster. Having extinguished immediate threats to the new regime, which had generally if reluctantly been accorded a high priority, debate could now shift to the significance and desirability of the continental war, an issue on which a range of opposition opinion could partially come together, especially when framed in terms of value for money and financial probity. Hence the role of the Commission of Public Accounts, and the united actions of Clarges and Musgrave (Churchmen) and Foley and Harley (Whigs), began to loom large.[25] Typical was a debate on 19 November when detailed consideration was given to William's request for 65,000 troops for the coming campaign. In the Commons Foley complained bluntly that 'I do not see any necessity for so many men' and Clarges worried that 'the naming a number of men to us is the same as naming the sum . . . This is only what the Parliament of Paris do . . . this sort of proceeding by naming a sum takes away our liberty.' In doing this they doubted William's military judgement and assessment of the national interest and raised the constitutional issue of Parliament's function. The successful retort was similarly framed: 'His Majesty is a great captain, and since he thinks 65,000 men necessary, I that am but a private man cannot but think there is weight in it . . . if the French should invade you I believe there is hardly any would think much of a great charge to oppose them.'[26]

The activities of Foley and his allies, both within and outside the Commission of Public Accounts, were seen by contemporaries as evidence of an emerging 'country party' critique of the court which drew support from many shades of opinion. In a sense this provided an additional political perspective to the Whig–Tory dichotomy. But if a court–country or executive–independent distinction became a central feature of the political world, it is harder to see these positions as constituting 'parties'. However, this was not the only cause of friction between William and Parliament in the 1691–2 session: William vetoed a Bill that would have removed his authority to dispense with judges at will; the Commission of Public Accounts was kept alive by attaching ('tacking') a clause to a money Bill, so preventing the Lords, which was more liable to follow the court's bidding, from rejecting the measure; and a Bill to regulate treason trials, which would have required of the government higher standards of evidence in such trials, was perceived as a weakening of the regime's security.

William's control of Parliament was very incomplete in the 1691–2 session. He was also struggling elsewhere, for on 21 January 1692 he stripped Marlborough of all his posts. Though the King gave no reasons for this, it appears to have been due to Marlborough's Jacobitical activities and to his attacks on the role of Dutch officers in the English army. However, so close was Marlborough and his wife to Princess Anne that the commander's dismissal finalized a rift which had gradually opened up between the King and his sister-in-law. Such a rift might have easily widened to pose a serious threat to William's crown. Though he believed he was due the same protection afforded his predecessors, he also knew that this would only come in time.

---

[25] Sir Thomas Clarges, c.1618–95. Sir Christopher Musgrave, c.1631–1704, 4th Baronet, MP 1661–1702. Paul Foley, c.1645–99, from a Nonconformist background, MP for Hereford, and Speaker 1695–8.

[26] *The Parliamentary Diary of Narcissus Luttrell, 1691–1693*, ed. H. Horwitz (Oxford, 1972), pp. 30–2.

Paradoxically, success in Ireland forced James and his supporters to focus their efforts upon a seizure of power in England, through an invasion, rising, or coup, or some combination of the three. In the short to medium term, Jacobitical activity in England might, if anything, have become more common in England after the Treaty of Limerick. In such an environment the King found it difficult to know whom he could depend upon and in the spring he brought some more Tories into office, hoping to commit them to his regime. It was to prove a forlorn experiment.

William was out of England on campaign from early March to mid-October 1692. On his return he 'was received with the greatest demonstrations of joy by Bonefires ringing of Bells discharge of Canon and universall Lumination'.[27] He may have been reasonably popular to Londoners, but politicians were much more jaundiced, not least because the war was going badly. Granted the Royal Navy now commanded the Channel, but merchant shipping was being incessantly harried and William had suffered setbacks at Namur and Steenkirk in the summer. The parliamentary session from 4 November 1692 to 14 March 1693 was fractious and finally convinced William to begin to abandon trimming. Ministers of all shades were subject to abuse and though reasonably generous funds were found, attempts were also made further to reduce royal authority. Notable contests included: another attempt to introduce an oath that William and Mary were rightful monarchs; a Bill to prevent MPs taking office once elected, which passed easily through the Commons and was only narrowly defeated in the Lords; a Bill to force the monarch to call parliamentary elections every three years, which William vetoed; and a clause supporting the right of Privy Councillors to order the arrest of suspected traitors was lost in the Commons. It was clear to William that his ministers had too little control over Parliament and, indeed, that the executive was prey to the unpredictable will of the legislature. For their part the parties were 'all weary of the king's way of balancing himself between them.'[28] A new course would have to be charted and it was at this time that he began to take advice from the Earl of Sunderland who pressed for the ministry to be handed over to the Whigs. He argued that too many Tories were Jacobites for William to depend upon that party and that 'Whenever the government has leaned to the Whigs it has been strong, whenever the other has prevailed it has been despised.'[29] Initially, the

[27] *The Portledge Papers Being Extracts from the Letters of Richard Lapthorne, Gent, of Hatton Garden London, to Richard Coffin Esq. of Portledge, Bideford, Devon, from December 10th 1687–August 7th 1697*, ed. R. J. Kerr and I. C. Duncan (1928), p. 150.

[28] *The Diary and Autobiography of Edmund Bohun Esq.*, ed. S. Wilton Rix (1853), p. 113.

[29] Quoted in Holmes and Speck (eds.), *The Divided Society*, p. 12. Robert Spencer, 1640–1702, 2nd Earl of Sunderland, educated Christ Church, Oxford, a minister under Charles II who converted to Roman Catholicism before returning to the Church of England, a noted schemer, Lord Chamberlain and Lord Justice 1697.

King was unwilling to follow this advice, though soon after the end of the session he did call on the great Whig lawyer Somers to be Lord Keeper and Sir John Trenchard to be one of the Secretaries of State.[30] During the summer, with William again away on campaign, Sunderland worked behind the scenes to formulate a scheme for managing Parliament, including the co-option of some key individuals.

The major breakthrough came soon after William's return at the end of October. With the war continuing indifferently—the notable setbacks were the destruction of the Smyrna convoy and the Battle of Landen—his Tory ministers were pessimistic about the prospects of obtaining the funds he desired. This forced his hand and on 6 November he decided to dismiss Nottingham, the Tory Secretary of State, one of the few ministers he had trusted. William's willingness to contemplate party government and to look to the Whigs was now clear and soon bore fruit, for by Christmas Mary noted how things had gone 'pretty well, far beyond what could be hoped'.[31] Plentiful funds were found for the war, including later the legislation creating the Bank of England. It was not all plain sailing however, for William decided again to veto a Place Bill, provoking a fierce parliamentary storm. The Commons resolved that whoever had advised William to veto the Bill was 'an enemy to their majesties and the kingdom' and lectured him on the use of that prerogative.[32] William needed no such lesson, his evasive reply provoking a remarkable outburst from Foley who complained, 'The king tells us, "He has a great regard to our constitution;" but it appears not that he understands our constitution.'[33] Clearly William's relations with Parliament had improved only to a limited degree and he began to court the Earl of Shrewsbury, a prominent Whig and former Secretary of State, further signalling his shift away from the Tories. On 2 March 1694 Shrewsbury was back in office, this time as Secretary of State for the northern department. More Whig appointments followed, notably Montagu as Chancellor of the Exchequer, in the admiralty board and in the higher ranks of the customs and excise services.[34] Something close to a Whig government was now in being, with Carmarthen and Godolphin the only notable Tories still employed. The question was whether Parliament could be better managed

[30] John Trenchard, 1640–95, MP from 1679, active in schemes to keep James from throne, fleeing to continent 1685, knighted 1689.

[31] *Memoirs of Mary, Queen of England (1689–1693)*, ed. R. Doebner (1886), p. 61.

[32] W. Cobbett (ed.), *The Parliamentary History of England*, 36 vols. (1806–20), vol. 5, p. 830.

[33] Cobbett (ed.), *Parliamentary History*, vol. 5, p. 835.

[34] Charles Montagu, 1661–1715, a student and Fellow Trinity College, Cambridge, MP, Lord of the Treasury 1692, introduced Bill founding the Bank of England 1694 and Chancellor of the Exchequer 1694–9, raised to peerage in 1700 and then in 1714 made Earl of Halifax, unsuccessfully impeached 1701 and out of office under Anne but first Lord of the Treasury on accession of George I.

by this route and what price the Whigs would charge William, especially over constitutional matters.

THE WHIG JUNTO

Militarily, politically, and personally 1694 was something of a turning-point in William's reign. On the battlefield French progress was halted and an allied fleet patrolled the Mediterranean. Thus when Parliament met on 12 November it proved reasonably amenable to the King's call for money. In part, the easing of relations between William and Parliament was due to his willingness to depend upon the Whigs. However, one cost of this was that on 22 December he finally gave his assent to a Triennial Bill, so limiting his powers of dissolving Parliament. Why William changed his mind is uncertain, but he may have struck a deal with Shrewsbury in March, reckoning that it was a relatively minor concession that would significantly improve his standing among MPs. Certainly the tempers of many Whigs, among them Foley and Harley, had cooled. In practice, however, it was a concession that ushered in an age of intense electoral politics, involving the wider nation in events at Westminster more frequently and in a rather unpredictable way. In the nineteen years between 1694 and 1716, when the Septennial Act was passed, there were ten general elections, six of them due to the limit set in the Triennial Act. William's second Parliament, from 1690 to 1695, lasted much longer than any other elected until 1715. Gradually but radically the parameters of political life, kingly, ministerial and parliamentary, were, therefore, changed after 1694.

The death from smallpox of Mary on 28 December, aged only 32, was a personal tragedy felt deeply by William. He was devastated and for awhile his own fragile health was feared for. Though their marriage lacked the cloying affection of Anne and George, Mary suited William admirably. He wanted sole authority and his wife happily complied, believing 'that women should not medle in government'.[35] While he was abroad she oversaw government in a firm but essentially passive manner. Only in religious matters was she really active, rightly seen as 'a Nursing Mother' to the Church of England.[36] She directed the important task of filling the many bishoprics vacated by the non-juring schism and death, and actively promoted a campaign to reform the nation's manners. Mary was, of course, William's most direct hereditary link to the throne and her unimpeachable English and Anglican credentials tempered his Dutch and Calvinist origins. Necessarily, therefore, her death also

[35] *Memoirs of Mary*, p. 23.
[36] *The Diary and Letter Book of the Rev. Thomas Brockbank 1671–1709*, ed. R. Trappes-Lomax, Chetham Society, New Series, 89 (1930), p. 76.

posed questions of his rule. Jacobites could proclaim that the demise of the joint monarchy established in 1689 allowed the nation to reconsider the whole question of the succession—in London the guards at Whitehall were doubled and in Bristol 'Jacobites . . . made publick rejoycings, by ringing of bells, &c.'[37] This was very much the minority response, for Mary's death and lavish public funeral on 5 March 1695 (Wren designed her mausoleum and Purcell composed some of the music) prompted a general and genuine outpouring of national grief. William also effected a reconciliation with Anne, so closing off a potentially serious opening for Jacobitical intrigue. Undeniably, however, William was faced with new problems, especially over the government of the country while he was on campaign and English sensibilities over his preference for all things Dutch. The sense that an era was drawing to a close was strengthened in early April by the death of the arch-trimmer, Halifax.

By the time of Mary's funeral William had put most of his faith in the Whigs. Yet this did not stop the Commons still being highly independent, particularly over questions of morality in public life. There were continued attempts to pass a Place Bill in the 1694–5 session and, more dramatically, there were a series of investigations into alleged corruption, further evidence of the significance of the country frame of mind in the House. The Speaker of the Commons, Sir John Trevor, was found to have received 1,000 guineas from the City of London to help smooth the passage of a Bill for the Relief of London Orphans. On 12 March he was stripped of his post and expelled from the House. It says much that Foley fought off the claims of the court's candidate to be the new Speaker. Another story of corruption was uncovered with regard to the East India Company's efforts to renew its charter. This time the Duke of Leeds (as Carmarthen had become in May 1694) was implicated and the Commons initiated his impeachment. Though for want of time and an absent witness this could not be prosecuted, it effectively marked the end of a remarkable political career. The scandals which had been uncovered also sounded the death knell of this long Parliament. William could not risk the questions being revived in the following session, thus before he left for the Republic he had already decided upon a dissolution and a general election.

William was on campaign from 12 May to 10 October 1695, the highlight of which was the recapture of Namur. In his absence he left the government in the hands of seven Lords Justices, mostly Whigs, though also including Godolphin. It was a system which worked well enough. It is notable that William refused to make any use of either Anne or her husband. Nor was Sunderland employed, preferring to play the part of the minister behind the curtain. The day after William returned he formally dissolved Parliament,

---

[37] Luttrell, *A Brief Historical Relation*, vol. 3, p. 423.

though many had already been forewarned. Then in a highly calculated move to enhance the standing of the ministry's supporters he went on a successful three-week progress through central England. In fact, the election was less contentious than that of 1690, only seventy-nine constituencies actually going to a poll. Nor was it one that was clearly fought along party lines, local issues often being more significant than national ones. On balance the Whigs did better than the Tories, but the independent minded Foley was once again chosen as Speaker in the Commons and it was clear that William's Whig ministry could not hope always to get its way. It was a difficult session, particularly on the financial front. Large funds were required, both for current expenditure and to make up the shortfall from previous years, and the coinage was now so rotten that a total recoining was planned. A country opposition to the ministry was also gaining ground, not least because of the skills of Robert Harley. The Whig leadership found on several occasions that it could not command a majority in the Commons and it looked as if Sunderland's plan was, after a promising start, coming to nought. And beyond Westminster lurked Jacobitism which might ignite the incendiary discontent which existed. Years of high taxes and the spiralling national debt had caused real hardship to many; English blood was being spilled in foreign fields; and now utter chaos surrounded the recoinage.

On 24 February 1696 Westminster was thrown upside down when William told Parliament that a plot had been uncovered to assassinate him and so leave the way open for a French invasion to put James back on the throne. Some 300 Jacobites were soon arrested. This was no sham plot, though it is not clear that its instigator, Sir John Fenwick, knew of the plan to assassinate William. It was though the first Jacobite plot to produce a countrywide reaction.[38] General revulsion was felt at the murderous intent and the willingness of Jacobites to use French arms. Moreover, the involvement of the Duke of Berwick, who had visited London, directly implicated James. This was a defining moment of William's kingship. Evelyn perceptively noted that 'tho many did formerly pitty K. James's Condition, this designe of Assasination, & bringing over a French Army, did much alienate many of his Friends, & was like to produce a more perfect establishment of K. William'.[39] Without kingly prompting, William's active supporters seized upon this opportunity further to cement his authority. In the Commons an 'association' declaring William 'as rightful and lawful king' and threatening action against his enemies was drawn up. This was not only a shift from *de facto* to *de jure* kingship, but effectively required the abjuration of James as well. Initially, signing it was supposedly voluntary but

---

[38] John Fenwick, c.1645–97, MP for Northumberland 1677, brigadier general 1686.
[39] *Evelyn Diary*, vol. 5, p. 233.

already on 25 February eighty-nine MPs who had refused had been flushed out into the open. By mid-March it was noted that 'People go on heartily with associating' and in April legislation made the oath mandatory for office holders.[40] It was claimed, perhaps with some exaggeration, that 'every one signs it with the greatest alacrity imaginable.'[41] In fact, the King dismissed three Privy Councillors for refusing—Nottingham, Normanby, and Seymour—and by the end of July one Lord Lieutenant, 86 JPs, and 104 Deputy-Lieutenants had also been dismissed.[42] This was the most thoroughgoing purge of the disaffected from local and central government in the whole reign. Yet it is testament to the authority of William's regime that so little Jacobite blood was spilled in retribution. Seven plotters were executed immediately; five more were sentenced by Act of Parliament to life imprisonment; and in January 1697, six months after his arrest, Fenwick was executed, a delay due to his attempt to implicate Marlborough, Godolphin, Shrewsbury, and admiral Russell in Jacobitical activity.[43]

The assassination plot undoubtedly boosted the position of William and the Whigs and was a step towards one-party rule. It is remarkable that William was confident enough of his position to leave England early in May 1696 to go on campaign. In October 1696 Godolphin resigned from government, further strengthening the Whig's position. In 1697 the advancement of Somers to Lord Chancellor, Montagu to first Lord of the Treasury, and at the end of year James Vernon, Shrewsbury's secretary, to be Secretary of State in place of the moderate Tory Trumbull, emphasized this shift. The so-called Junto lords—Somers, Russell (Earl of Orford), Wharton, Montagu (later Earl of Halifax) and, later, Sunderland—held regular meetings to agree policy and tightened relations with the wider Whig party which usually met at the Rose Tavern in Covent Garden. Something akin to party government now existed, though William's continued reliance upon Sunderland demonstrated his unwillingness fully to commit himself to the Whigs. It was then, perhaps, not surprising that Parliament continued to vote considerable supplies and, indeed, the control of

---

[40] *The Lexington Papers; or, some Account of the Courts of London and Vienna at the Conclusion of the Seventeenth Century*, ed. H. Manners Sutton (1851), p. 192.

[41] 'The Diary of Abraham de la Pryme', p. 92.

[42] John Sheffield, 1648–1721, 3rd Earl of Mulgrave, 1st Duke of Buckingham and Normanby. Served in army under Charles II, foolishly courted Princess Anne 1682, Privy Councillor 1685 and restored 1702, Lord Privy Seal 1702–5, Union Commissioner 1706, patron of poets, buried Westminster Abbey. Edward Seymour, 1633–1708, MP 1661, Speaker 1673, Privy Councillor 1673, succeeded to baronetcy 1685, Lord of Treasury 1692.

[43] Edward Russell, 1653–1727, Earl of Orford. Military career, joining William in 1680s, MP from 1689, First Lord of the Admiralty 1694–9, 1709–10, 1714–17, a Lords Justices 1697, 1698, 1714, Union Commissioner 1706, created Baron of Shingey, Viscount Barfleur, and Earl of Orford 1697.

the ministerial Whigs was now strong enough to bring about the demise of the Commission of Public Accounts in February 1697. Only Fenwick's attainder provided a clear focal point for the opposition. Indeed, arguably the 1696–7 session was the least contentious of William's reign. Yet William continued to face huge problems in attaining his principal objectives, the containment of France and forcing from Louis a recognition of his crown. The 1696 campaign had not been as successful as the previous year and the defection of Savoy in August enhanced French prospects for the future. William acknowledged that England could not support for much longer its war effort and at Ryswick in May 1697, a month after the end of the parliamentary session, efforts were begun to find an acceptable peace.

COURT AND COUNTRY

Peace came as a great relief to King and country. In celebration, early in December 1697 a great firework display was held in St James's Square in London where a triumphal arch, capped by the figures of peace, conduct, concord, and valour, was built. But several were killed by the brilliant pyrotechnics and 'all ended in smoake and stinke.'[44] Such an ambiguous celebration was entirely appropriate, for peace brought to government not accord but a renewed and more complicated factiousness.

The peace signed at Ryswick in September 1697 dramatically changed the context of English domestic politics. Most important, Jacobite prospects had been dashed when Louis recognized William as King. It was not to be expected that Jacobitism would simply disappear as a fact of political life, but its immediate task was largely one of keeping alive the flame while there was so little prospect of James's return. For a time Jacobitism became little more than a loose affiliation of the nostalgic, toasting an impotent King stuck over the water. Moreover, the success of William at Ryswick took the wind from the sails of those at both ends of the political spectrum. He had not only seen off the threat of the Jacobites (and therefore of 'high' Tories), but also of the fairly minor challenge of republicans. Further, his increasing use of Whigs had made many from that party come to value more highly the importance of a strong executive and so throw doubt upon some of the fundamental tenets of their earlier political world-view. In short, the meaning of Whig and Tory was, in a sense, uncertain and peace provided a breathing space for a more thorough rearrangement of alignments that had been underway since the early 1690s.

[44] *Correspondence of the Family of Hatton, being Chiefly Letters Addressed to Christopher First Viscount Hatton, A.D. 1601–1704*, vol. 2, ed. E. M. Thompson, Camden Society, New Series, 23 (1878), p. 230.

The most serious problem facing William's government was one of satisfying the unrealistically high expectations of a people who had longed for
peace—a problem no less serious than those also faced in 1713, 1815, 1918, and
1945. The country looked forward to lower taxes and demobilization, to the
rapid establishment of 'normality'. Central to this was the presumption that
there would be a withering away of the central State and a return to local independence. Such hopes were always likely to be frustrated. Indeed, the last five
years of William's reign saw relations between King, Parliament, and people
plumb new depths. Four factors were at work. First, not only did it take time
to return soldiers and sailors home, but William, ever distrustful of Louis,
believed a standing army was needed to assure the regime's security. Linked to
this, the uncertainty of the Spanish succession maintained a highly unstable
international situation and created parliamentary suspicions of the King's
handling of British interests. Second, significant tax revenues were needed to pay
for the funded national debt which had been established. Customs and excises
did not fade, they and their collectors were all too visible and keenly felt. This
had the effect of focusing attention upon the Crown's use of resources, especially William's generosity to his favourites. Third, with a twist of biological
fate and the death of the Duke of Gloucester, the succession question was
reopened. Finally, these three factors so dislocated the executive's attempts to
manage Parliament that three general elections were fought in William's final
years. New Parliaments undermined any hopes of creating a stable relationship
between executive and legislature. These four factors provided an ideal climate
for the coming together of different strands of anti-executive country opinion
that had caused such difficulties in 1692 and 1693. Thus the last five years of
William's reign were distinguished by Whig and Tory divisions being overlaid
by no less powerful court and country distinctions.

The first peacetime parliamentary session began on 2 December 1697 and
was to be long and contentious. The tone was set early on over the standing
army question. Instigated by Harley the Commons decided to reduce the army
to the level current in 1680, about 8,000 men. As William had specifically told
Parliament that it was his 'opinion, that, for the present, England cannot
be safe without a Land-force', by which he meant a substantial force, the
Commons was clearly contradicting the monarch.[45] This was the start of a
long-running battle of wits between the Crown and country opinion. On the
country side there were two main considerations, cost and the uses of military
authority. It was the latter which caused controversy, though the Bill of Rights
and the annual Mutiny Acts had all stressed Parliament's responsibility for
a peacetime standing army. In the country view a standing army under royal

[45] Cobbett (ed.), *Parliamentary History*, vol. 5, p. 1166.

authority was a potential tool of arbitrary authority: 'if we look through the World, we shall find in no Country, Liberty and an Army stand together'.[46] To the King this was patently unrealistic and 'fanciful', believing that the Franco-Jacobite threat remained of such menace that a large army was needed both to deter and to defend.[47] Court supporters rightly, if a little timidly, pointed out that the militia, under country control, was simply inadequate to the task of confronting insurrection or invasion, but the tide of opinion could not be turned. William was clearly defeated over the question of the standing army in 1697–8, as he was to be in future sessions. His only solace was that lack of funds prevented full disbanding and a force of 16,000 was maintained.

After the battle over the standing army many MPs turned on ministers. Sunderland's backroom manoeuvrings were widely commented upon and his impeachment was rumoured. The great survivor flinched at the prospect of fighting for his political life, resigning in late December, much against William's wishes, though still offering the King advice subsequently. Opposition sights then trained upon Montagu, though less effectively. And with Shrewsbury incapacitated through ill health, the Junto was now some-what rudderless, a position worsened by William's all-too-evident refusal to confide in them in fully. With such a long leash the Commons began to run about wildly. On 22 February 1698 William complained to Heinsius in Holland that 'Parliament is now engaged in private animosities and party quarrels, and thinks very little of public affairs. God knows when this session will terminate.'[48] That was a little unfair, not least because William at last received a grant of £700,000 per annum for the civil list for life, but certainly it was aston-ishing how quickly the control exerted over parliamentary business in the previous session had been lost. When the session ended on 7 July William soon left for the Republic, an act which in peacetime was hardly calculated to endear him to English opinion. 'His countenance was expressive of the joy which he felt at going to Holland: he took no pains whatever to conceal it from the English, and, to say the truth, they speak openly about it.'[49] He did not return until five months later in early December. No less striking, in his absence a contentious general election was held in which he showed remarkably little interest. The King gave every sign of being disillusioned with the world of English domestic politics.

---

[46] 'An Argument Shewing, that a Standing Army is Inconsistent with a Free Government, and Absolutely Destructive to the Constitution of the English Monarchy', in *A Collection of State Tracts, Publish'd on Occasion of the Late Revolution in 1688 and During the Reign of King William III*, 3 vols. (1705–7), vol. 1, p. 569.

[47] *Letters of William III*, vol. 1, p. 148.   [48] *Letters of William III*, vol. 1, p. 197.

[49] *Letters of William III*, vol. 2, p. 91.

In the elections divisions between Whig and Tory were now joined by 'a strange spirit of distinguishing between the court and country party'.[50] It is, however, not at all clear that there was a country party in existence. Rather, there was what has been called a country 'persuasion' or frame of mind—which included the belief that government should be frugal and efficient, a dislike of high taxation (especially the prospect of a general excise), a concern for the liberties of the subject (as in treason trials and habeas corpus), a wish for frequent parliaments to ensure independence and accountability, a preference for the militia over the army, and a desire for moral reform (such as clamping down on vice and Sabbath breaking). Generally there was a clear concern to make government fully accountable, a concern which might initially appear profoundly anti-ministerial and essentially negative and defensive. However, the leading advocates of the country platform, such as Harley, Foley, and Clarges, appreciated the need not only to oppose but also to engage in government. They were convinced of the need for a high level of public service, which enjoined upon backwoods MPs the obligation to participate fully in the legislature's activities. Moreover, the country view never really doubted that the executive constructed policy. There is no question that the country view could cut across Whig and Tory divisions, drawing support from both. But as an oppositionist stance, by the end of the 1690s, with many Whigs having entered the political mainstream, those adopting country positions, both in the Commons and in the wider political nation, were more usually Tories.

Somers was correct to note the significance of the country view in the 1698 general election. However, it is also clear that voters, showing a strong preference for the Revolution settlement, tended to turn their back upon those who had not signed the 1696 association. This point should not be lost sight of. In his last years William faced much vocal opposition, but little of this was Jacobitical in any meaningful sense, a point the King failed fully to appreciate. Still, when the new Parliament met in early December 1698 opposition soon became very aggressive. Though the court managed to get its candidate, Sir Thomas Littleton, elected as Speaker in the Commons, MPs soon turned to the task of further reducing the size of the standing army. William hoped to keep 10,000 on foot, including his Dutch guards, but the Commons voted for 7,000 none of which could be foreigners. There were high feelings on both sides and in Parliament there were 'six set battles' between the two.[51] John Trenchard's *A Short History of Standing Armies in England*, published in

[50] *Letters Illustrative of the Reign of William III. From 1696 to 1708. Addressed to the Duke of Shrewsbury by James Vernon, Esq. Secretary of State*, ed. G. P. R. James, 3 vols. (1841), vol. 2, p. 143.
[51] H. M. C., *The Manuscripts of S. H. Le Fleming, Esq.* (1890), p. 354.

November, had in exaggerated form set out the opposition case.[52] Indeed it was claimed that 'This is not an affair conducted merely by those who are opposed to the Court: the whole nation concurs in it.'[53] Thus the Commons voted against the King, who in turn reacted very extremely, drafting an abdication speech that he never delivered. There is no doubt that he gave serious thought to returning permanently to the Republic and giving up Britain, but equally there was still no question that uncertainties surrounding the Spanish succession and continued anxieties about French expansionism required William to preserve the Anglo-Dutch alliance. William also chided his ministers for failing him (which, given his unwillingness to take them fully into his confidence, was somewhat unfair). Indeed, in the absence of a firm lead from the King or the ties of close party affiliation William's ministers could not be expected to establish a clear working relationship between executive and legislature. The government was now something of a ragbag, the days of the Junto's supremacy having clearly passed.

On 1 February 1699 William gave his assent to the Disbanding Bill. As he did so he flatly told parliamentarians that 'the nation is left too much exposed'.[54] His kingly authority had been successfully challenged, providing a signal for such a heterodox opposition to besiege other parts of the fortress of government: the Admiralty Commission was censured; a Place Bill was framed and several office holders expelled from the Commons; and, not for the first time, consideration was given to those Irish estates forfeited by rebels which William had disposed of. All this helped to distract the attention from finding adequate supplies, not least to pay the government's creditors. To the King such behaviour was an abdication of public responsibility and he looked forward to the end of 'this misserable session'.[55] William felt keenly the loss of his Dutch guards, just as the retirement of his old friend Portland, piqued at the influence of Albemarle, only increased the King's sense of isolation. Weary of England he again spent four months in Holland though, given the difficulties he had faced, it is little wonder that before he left he sought to introduce some fresh blood into the ministry in the hope of governing more successfully through Parliament in the next session. He looked to return to the middle way that had been unsuccessfully attempted in the first four years of the reign. In particular, three Tories were conscripted: the Earl of Jersey succeeded Shrewsbury as Secretary of State; the Duke of Leeds, for long inactive, was

---

[52] John Trenchard, 1662–1723, son of Somerset landowner, educated Trinity College, Dublin, called to bar; became independently wealthy in 1690s, allowing time for writing on politics, wrote with Thomas Gordon *Cato's letters* 1720–3, MP in 1722.

[53] *Letters of William III*, vol. 2, p. 224.

[54] Cobbett (ed.), *Parliamentary History*, vol. 5, p. 1193.

[55] *Letters of William III*, vol. 2, p. 324.

replaced as Lord President by the Earl of Pembroke; and Viscount Lonsdale became the new Lord Privy Seal.[56] Also Russell, the Earl of Orford, had resigned so that of the original Junto only Somers and Montagu remained in government.

Parliament might only be managed by a minister fully supported by the King and who was following an agreed policy agenda. However, William felt unable to trust fully those in his government and by the start of the new session on 16 November 1699 he wanted nothing from Parliament other than supply and silence. Yet this allowed the Commons to decide upon the issues and terms for debate. Most remarkable was the major role played by Harley in ordering financial matters from beyond the ministry. Yet the opposition was not always able to get its way. For example, Burnet's role as Preceptor to the Duke of Gloucester was unsuccessfully attacked, though more significant were early attacks on Somers, accusing him of promoting piracy, unsuccessful though they were. With Orford and Shrewsbury, Somers had, early in 1697, used a royal grant and his own money to commission Captain Kidd to protect East India Company ships from predators in the Indian Ocean. But Kidd had himself turned pirate, only to be caught in America and returned to London for questioning and trial. After nine hours of debate it was decided not to endorse the view that the patent was 'dishonourable to the k[in]g against the laws and statutes of the realm against the law of nations destructive to trade and commerce and invasive of property'.[57]

Attacks on the King were more successful and focused upon the issue of the Irish forfeited estates, a target that had already been attacked through a Commission of inquiry. The Commons sought to restore to the public those Irish lands which William (personally or in his name) had granted to his generals, mistress, Dutch favourites, and friends since the Treaty of Limerick. The Commons decried the enrichment of private individuals when the public purse was not only empty but deeply indebted—some exaggeratedly valued the estates at about £1.5m. William for his part insisted that at the very least he was by custom due one-third of the lands forfeited, a point the Commons was unwilling to concede. By March 1700 it was noted that 'How the King & Parliament will A gree A bought the forfeited lands in Iorland no man can tell, ther is such great contest & fircness on both sides'.[58] The question was

[56] Thomas Herbert, 1656–1733, 8th Earl of Pembroke, dismissed as Lord Lieutenant of Wiltshire 1687, held a number of high offices in the Admiralty, helped negotiate the Treaty of Ryswick, a Union Commissioner 1706, Lord Lieutenant of Ireland 1707–8. John Lowther, 1655–1700, succeeded to baronetcy 1675, MP from 1676, barrister 1677, created Baron Lowther and Viscount Lonsdale 1696.
[57] *The Parliamentary Diary of Sir Richard Cocks, 1698–1702*, ed. D. W. Hayton (Oxford, 1996), p. 40. William Kidd, d. 1701, Scottish, lived at Boston, Massachusetts.
[58] *Verney Letters*, vol. 1, p. 73.

complicated because the ideological purity of the original Bill had been compromised: it had been attached to a financial measure to prevent the Lords amending it; on an unprincipled basis some grantees or purchasers were exempted; and an unconnected place clause had also been attached. In the Lords, where William's word still retained some force, amendments were made, thereby bringing on a major confrontation between the two houses. One aspect of this was that the Commons turned upon the role of William's Dutch favourites, Portland and Albemarle, resolving on 10 April that no foreigners should serve in the King's councils. Only after much heated debate was the Bill passed.

William immediately ended the session, refusing to make the normal closing speech thanking Parliament for its efforts, reckoning it 'the most dismal session I have ever had'.[59] Perhaps irritated by Somers's unwillingness to support the royal cause he forced the Lord Chancellor's resignation soon after, so breaking the final tie to his days of dependence upon the Junto. By June Harley complained that 'It was now a general complaint we had no ministry, no right management of public affairs'.[60] The collapse of the limited measure of parliamentary control that the Junto had been able to enjoy was due to many factors, among them the accidents of illness and the personal preferences of many leading politicians. But the most significant were William's unwillingness really to marry himself to his ministers and the changing nature of opposition in the Commons. Peace and the absence of a meaningful Jacobite threat allowed the executive to be attacked from all angles, including the middle ground. Indeed, for about three years William lost control of that middle ground to the country view. He only managed to regain some command over it once the central issues of 1688 and 1689, the Protestant succession and European liberty, had again come to the fore.

THE PROTESTANT SUCCESSION AND EUROPEAN LIBERTY

William was in the Republic from early July to mid-October 1700. Soon after he arrived there the Duke of Gloucester, Anne's only heir, died, immediately reviving the succession question. Soon after he returned Charles II of Spain died and Louis ignored the second Partition Treaty that had been secretly negotiated with William. Europe teetered on the brink of war. Together these whims of fate set the seal on William's last years. The King himself was certain that Britain should add Sophia of Hanover and her heirs to the line of succession and continue to play a central role in an anti-French alliance. It speaks volumes of contemporary political priorities that there was relatively slight

[59] *Letters of William III*, vol. 2, p. 398.
[60] *Letters Illustrative of the Reign of William III*, vol. 3, p. 90.

opposition to William's broad objectives but that Parliament seized to the full the chance to cut the King and his ministers down to size.

The difficulties of the 1699–1700 parliamentary session along with Sunderland's behind-the-scenes advice convinced William that he needed to reinvigorate his ministry and attempt tighter control over Parliament. He began by shifting towards the Tories, appointing both Godolphin and Rochester in December 1700.[61] On the face of it this was unlikely to succeed, for the King could not have expected the Tories to embrace enthusiastically the prospect of a new war. However, William also sought to strengthen his position in Parliament more directly by calling a general election which was held in January and February 1701. If only eighty-six constituencies went to the polls the party dimension was clearer than it had been two years earlier, especially over foreign policy, where the Whigs were more prepared to support an aggressive foreign policy than the Tories. Evelyn noted that 'There was extraordinary strivings among the Candidats'.[62] But there was no clear swing towards either, creating the possibility of a factious session. Still, the court managed to get Harley, now a central figure on the political scene, elected as Speaker of the Commons and both Houses, replying to the speech from the throne, urged William to establish the alliances necessary to maintain the European balance of power. They went on to vote the government higher peacetime revenues than ever before. And the Act of Settlement, establishing the succession to the Crown in the House of Hanover, passed through Parliament without a division, despite the efforts of Jacobites and republicans who 'joyn in every thing . . . to oppose the settlement of the crown'.[63]

It was not all plain sailing. A raft of restrictions on future Hanoverian monarchs were included in the Act of Settlement, prompted by perceptions of William's inadequacies as King, especially his absences abroad, Calvinism, dependence upon Dutch advisers, and ability personally to engage the nation in war to defend other powers. Thus the Act of Settlement committed the nation to a significantly more limited form of monarchy. A further strand of this criticism of William was expressed by hostility towards the two Partition treaties he had negotiated with Louis. The second Treaty had been made public in July 1700 and had been loudly condemned even before Charles II died. William's dominating role could not be directly assailed because of the fig leaf convention that 'the King can do no wrong', but those ministers who had signed the treaties might be.[64] On 28 March Portland was impeached, to be followed on 14 April by Somers, Orford, and Halifax. Though only Somers and

---

[61] Laurence Hyde, 1641–1711, 1st Earl of Rochester, second son of 1st Earl of Clarendon, held many offices under Charles II and James II, supported a regency in 1689, readmitted to Privy Council 1692, Lord Lieutenant of Ireland 1700–2.

[62] *Evelyn Diary*, vol. 5, p. 441.   [63] *Cocks Diary*, p. 69.   [64] *Cocks Diary*, p. 91.

Orford were tried, and though both were easily acquitted, there is no doubt that all these impeachments were thinly veiled attacks on William and his policies. But there was also a clear party political dimension, with the Tories exploiting their strength and the dilemma of the Whigs over whether to support William's foreign policy or their traditional distrust of kingly prerogative. It is notable, therefore, that the Kentish petitioners, who on 8 May had called for the King's foreign policy to be supported, were clapped into custody by an officious Commons. Across the nation many sympathized with the gentlemen of Kent and the discord soon became general. As one York cleric observed, with war imminent 'we had dreadful apprehensions of being devoured by the French and by one another at home'.[65]

The parliamentary session ended on 24 June and again William spent the summer and early autumn in the United Provinces. He had made three significant changes to his ministry before he departed. If the new faces were not Tory, neither were they Whig, demonstrating once again the King's preference for the middle way. Marlborough was restored to his command of the army and given responsibility for negotiations with the Republic; Sir Edward Northey became Attorney General; and the Duke of Somerset was made one of the Lords Justices.[66] In William's absence there were three significant developments: there was 'a furious Civil *Paper*-War, between the respective Sticklers for the old and new Ministers'; the Grand Alliance between Britain, Holland, and Austria was signed; and on 6 September James II died and his son was recognized by Louis XIV.[67] War now looked inevitable and Sunderland, working behind the scenes and from outside the ministry, told William, as he had in 1693 and 1694, to throw in his lot with the pro-war Whigs. He pressed the King to negotiate with Somers, 'the life, the soul, and the spirit of his party, and can answer for it'. This the King did, though in turn the former Lord Chancellor argued that it was necessary 'to begin a war with a new Parliament' and pressed for a dissolution.[68] That this was pure party politics is clear for, as Godolphin pointed out to Marlborough, William had received from the existing Parliament (elected less than a year previously) generous supplies and an invitation to enter into alliances. To the Tory Godolphin the Whigs were 'an angry party, who breath nothing but violence

[65] *The Rev. Oliver Heywood, B.A., 1630–1702; his Autobiography, Diaries, Anecdote and Event Books*, ed. J. H. Turner, 4 vols. (Bingley, 1885), vol. 4, p. 168.

[66] Edward Northey, 1652–1723, barrister 1674, Attorney General 1701–7 and 1710–18, knighted 1702, MP 1710. Charles Seymour, 1662–1748, succeeded as 6th Duke of Somerset 1678, sided with William 1688, Speaker of House of Lords 1690, Union Commissioner 1706.

[67] A. Boyer, *The History of William III*, 3 vols. (2nd edn., 1703), vol. 3, p. 498.

[68] P. Yorke (ed.), *Miscellaneous State papers from 1501 to 1726*, 2 vols. (1778), vol. 2, pp. 446, 453.

and confusion when the whole power of the government is not entirely in the hands of their own creatures.'[69] Such arguments failed, for a week after William returned he called a general election, provoking Godolphin to resign.

The election did not result in a crushing victory for the Whigs, though some Tories were ousted. One foreign envoy noted that 'It seemed astonishing that in the midst of the popular ferment against the Tories, whom many look on as the secret enemies of the state, so many of them should have been returned to Parliament' and credited their success to greater unity.[70] William for his part was now clearly siding with the Whigs, with the Earl of Carlisle put into the treasury and the Earl of Manchester replacing Hedges as Secretary of State.[71] Rochester was to be removed as Lord Lieutenant of Ireland, though William's death reprieved him. But the balance of forces in the new Commons was such that the court failed to get its candidate elected Speaker and Harley once again took the chair. Given Harley's public spiritedness this was not a disaster for William and it is notable how rapidly the Commons voted through new taxes. William had implored them that 'the eyes of all Europe are upon this Parliament; all matters are at a stand, till your resolutions are known' and the legislature did not fail him.[72] Having only convened on 30 December 1701 by the middle of February 1702 it had already agreed to find £3,600,000, to raise the land tax to four shillings, and levy a malt tax. It is also notable that a Bill requiring the abjuration of the Pretender was also passed. This was less significant than requiring the abjuration of his father, but, unless the warming-pan myth was embraced, it required a categorical rejection of the hereditary succession and, in practical terms, Hanover to be embraced. James II, by his death, had once again managed to unite his opponents. As is so often the case, the threat of war dissolved many political divisions.

On 23 February, William was thrown from his horse when it stumbled on a molehill in Richmond park. Though he broke his collarbone, it was a minor accident, almost commonplace. However, he caught a fever and by 6 March his life was feared for and only two days later, early in the morning, he died, aged just 51. England had lost a remarkable King, the Dutch Republic its unifying Stadholder, and Orange its last Prince. Briefly the nation was shocked and the presses ran off a good number of elegies. But deep mourning was rare. At Worcester there were 'few mourners', at Bath 'so short a sorrow', and in

---

[69] *The Marlborough–Godolphin Correspondence*, ed. H. L. Snyder, 3 vols. (Oxford, 1975), vol. 1, p. 32.

[70] Quoted in Holmes and Speck (ed.), *The Divided Society*, p. 20.

[71] Charles Montagu, *c.*1660–1722, 1st Duke of Manchester, son of 3rd earl, fought in Ireland 1690. Charles Hedges, d. 1714, knighted 1689, Judge of Admiralty Court 1689–1714, first entered House of Commons 1698.

[72] Cobbett (ed.), *Parliamentary History*, vol. 5, p. 1330.

Buckinghamshire 'severall expressions of Joy publickley spock'.[73] Despite his considerable virtues Dutch William had never endeared himself to many of his subjects. Yet both friends and enemies readily acknowledged his greatness. According to the Jacobite Duke of Berwick, 'I cannot deny him the character of a great man, and even of a great King . . . He had a very extensive understanding, was an able politician, and was never discouraged in his pursuits, whatever obstacles he might meet with. He was very rigid, but not naturally cruel: very enterprizing, but no general.'[74] On the other side William was viewed as 'A Prince whom Providence had raised up, not only to restore and support our Religion and Liberties in particular; but also to check the pride and ambition of *Lewis* the Fourteenth, who had combined with King *James* to enslave *all Europe*.'[75] He had 'reviv'd the martial Spirits of our English Nation, and restor'd us to our ancient Reputation abroad.'[76]

CONCLUSION

Despite the considerable opposition he faced, William achieved much as King. He retained his crown; guided the nation through a protracted war; established Britain as central to the anti-French alliance; committed the nation to the Hanoverian succession; oversaw the transformation of public finances; altered the relationship between Church and State; and worked with Parliament. This last point distinguished him from Charles II and James II. They preferred to use the legislature only occasionally, managing to reign without it for long periods. William had no such choice. And though he was not always able to get his way—witness his failures over triennial parliaments and Irish estates—he was able to avoid a fundamental breakdown in relations between Crown and Parliament. That was not easy, for he was a foreign invader who spent vast amounts of English tax revenues abroad. Fundamental to his success was his Protestantism and his appreciation of the need to rule through Parliament via English ministers. These were no small matters, for James had failed on both counts. Moreover, as time passed, William was able to tie more and more of the political nation to his regime. By his death over a fifth of the peers in the Lords owed their titles to him; over two-thirds of bishops were his appointees; the number of placemen in the Commons was about 130; the Commission of Peace in the counties had grown by about one-third; and as the national debt

---

[73] H. M. C., *The Manuscripts of his Grace the Duke of Portland*, vol. 4 (1897), p. 35; *Verney Letters*, vol. 1, p. 107.

[74] *Memoirs of the Duke of Berwick. Written by Himself*, 2 vols. (1779), vol. 1, pp. 156–7.

[75] R. Parker, *Memoirs of the Most Remarkable Military Transactions from the Year 1683, to 1718* (1747), p. 68.

[76] *Post Boy*, 7–10 March 1702, [p. 1].

grew so more and more wealthy people committed themselves to William's regime.

Only a quarter of the MPs returned after the election of late 1701 had sat in the Convention Parliament in 1689. This was more than a mere change of personnel. At the start of his reign William had dealt with politicians whose outlook was dominated by memories of the 1670s and 1680s, especially by fears of royal intentions over religion, Parliament, the courts, and the independence of local government. By 1701 he was dealing with politicians who knew him and his intentions well. None seriously worried that Parliament could now be dispensed with, the Church of England disestablished, or local government reconstructed. Indeed, changes in the nature of Whig and Tory and of the rise to prominence of the country persuasion bear witness to the remoulding of political conventions undertaken in the heat of the 1690s. By the time of William's death there was no possibility that politics might now be conducted as it had under James.

CHAPTER 6

Wars of Words and the Battle of the Books

Few contemporaries considered the importance of ideas as deeply as John Locke.[1] In 1690 he observed that 'EVERY Man being conscious to himself, That he thinks, and that which his Mind is employ'd about whilst thinking, being the *Ideas*, that are there, 'tis past doubt, that Men have in their Minds several *Ideas*'. He believed that ideas came 'in one word, From *Experience*: In that, all our Knowledge is founded; and from that it ultimately derives it self.' Such experiences might be of '*external, sensible Objects; or about the internal Operations of our Minds, perceived and reflected upon by our selves* . . . These two are the Fountains of Knowledge, from whence all the Ideas we have, or can naturally have, do spring.'[2] For two generations before 1700 that first fountain was fed from a deep reservoir. Most obviously these were the political crises which peppered the period, requiring hard thinking about the distribution of power, the role and form of the established Church, and the nature of civil society. Few could ignore such questions, just as few could ignore the impact of trade and travel which brought England increasingly into contact with new customs, ideas, products, animals, and plants. Less generally: scientists were delving deep into the complexities of the solar system and the natural world; textual critics were looking afresh at the writings of ancients and moderns; antiquaries and historians were digging deeper and deeper into England's past; and economists were developing a range of ways of thinking about the bases of prosperity. A prolific press after the Glorious Revolution only served to underscore the significance of this ferment of ideas.

In the study of ideas it is usual to concentrate upon the written word, an understandable approach given the stature and significance of works such as

---

[1] John Locke, 1632–1704, philosopher. Educated Christ Church, Oxford, member of first Earl of Shaftesbury's household, in exile 1683–9, on his return publishing a series of key texts: *Letter Concerning Toleration* (1689); *Two Treatises of Government* (1689, dated 1690); *An Essay Concerning Human Understanding* (1690). Contributed to the debate over the recoinage in 1695–6 and was a member of the new Board of Trade in 1696. Many of his ideas were the subject of intense controversy.

[2] *An Essay Concerning Human Understanding*, ed. P. H. Nidditch (Oxford, 1979), p. 104.

those of Locke and Newton.[3] However, the particularities of such a view must be appreciated. Most obviously, in this period only a minority could read and many ideas were communicated orally or visually. Clearly there were significant differences between scientific discussions at the Royal Society, storytelling among alehouse habitués, and rioters exclaiming their *raison d'être* against the agents of authority. All worlds of ideas are worthy of the historian's attention, but for reasons of evidence those expressed in print are the most easily recovered. However, the history of ideas also concentrates upon books and pamphlets because of a desire to trace with some precision certain intellectual traditions or dynamics—such as providentialism, republicanism, or astronomy. Such approaches provide pathways through the mass of printed materials to have survived but, because of the lure of teleology and anachronism, at the danger of imposing an agenda that contemporary writers themselves might only faintly recognize. They, it should never be forgotten, were more usually moulded by what had gone before than what they hoped might come after.

EDUCATION

Contemporaries well knew the significance of learning, few doubting Bacon's opinion that 'Knowledge and human power are synonymous'.[4] Yet if many longed for education, there were those who thought that access to ideas ought to be socially restricted. Most obviously, the provision of education was seen as part and parcel of the social hierarchy. To many among the elite, people warranted an education commensurate with their status, such that both the poor and women were to kept in a state of relative ignorance. In this view only gentlemen needed a full education though, as might be imagined, there were plenty who rebelled against such presumptions. Many gentlemen took it for granted that "'Tis of dangerous ill Consequence for People to *judge* of those Things, that are above their *Capacity*, and beyond their *Reason*.'[5]

---

[3] Isaac Newton, 1642–1727, scientist, educated King's school, Grantham, and Trinity College, Cambridge, Fellow of Trinity and Lucasian Professor of Mathematics from 1668, published his greatest work *Philosophae Naturalis Principia Mathematica* in 1687 and another great work, *Opticks*, in 1704, President of the Royal Society from 1703 to 1727, spent much of the period after 1689 as a public servant, notably as Master of the Mint from 1699, resigning his professorship in 1701.

[4] *Novum Organum. Aphorisms Concerning the Interpretation of Nature and the Kingdom of Man* (Chicago, 1990), p. 107. Bacon, 1561–1626, polymath, successively MP, Solicitor and Attorney General, Lord Keeper and, in 1618, Lord Chancellor, he fell from grace in 1621. He wrote many works of a philosophical nature.

[5] O. Dykes, *English Proverbs, with Moral Reflexions* (3rd edn., 1713), p. 155.

In the middle ages the written word was largely the preserve of clerics. Though the intellectual significance of the Church and its representatives remained enormous in the early eighteenth century, the literate world was being dramatically reconstituted with the spread of printing. Especially from the late sixteenth century a symbiotic relationship developed between increases in the output from the presses and the numbers able to read. By 1714 perhaps 45 per cent of men and 25 per cent of women could read—though writing was more restricted. Such figures mask both geographical and social variations. Literacy was higher in towns than the countryside and there was a close correlation between income and the ability to read and write. Of course, relatively few among the poor could read, but there is plenty of evidence of a genuinely popular market for literature. One rector thought it quite reasonable 'to buy some small Books (as ye Xtian Monitor . . .) to be given to Poor Families' and a French visitor noted how in London 'Workmen habitually begin the day by going to coffee-rooms in order to read the latest news.'[6] Indeed, there existed an extensive trade in chapbooks, cheap works aimed at a mass readership, that were peddled high and low by thousands of chapmen (2,500 were licensed in 1697–8). Consequently, even the poorest households might own printed works. Almanacs were especially popular, providing astrological inspired predictions of events, including the weather, and information about the likes of fairs, saints days, regnal years, and the farming calendar. Ballads and historical legends also sold well, but religious works—especially the Bible, *Pilgrim's Progress* (1678–84), and *The Whole Duty of Man* (1658)—were probably those most often bought by ordinary people. Even those who could not read, moreover, might have access to the written word by listening to readings, often at inns and coffee-houses.

If most towns had a school in this period, few villages did. Local authorities were under no obligation to provide schools and were as likely to put the poor to apprenticeship as set them before a teacher. Traditionally grammar schools, of which there were some 500 in 1700, had aimed to educate all comers, more especially the poor, but gradually they had become socially more exclusive. A more significant source of education was provided by the numerous charity schools which existed. These had come into being through the seventeenth century, but were encouraged with especial enthusiasm from the 1690s. Many in the Church believed that literacy might strengthen people's faith by making accessible the joys of the Bible. Such schools might be funded by local benefactors or even by collections at church. They were frequently small and

---

[6] *The Rector's Book, Clayworth Notts.*, ed. H. Gill and E. L. Guilford (Nottingham, 1910), p. 129; *A Foreign View of England in the Reigns of George I and George II. The Letters of Monsieur César de Saussure to his Family*, trans. and ed. Madame van Muyden (1902), p. 162.

ephemeral, depending upon the enthusiasm of teachers—men and women—
for their success. In the 1690s the recently founded Society for the Promotion
of Christian Knowledge (the SPCK) sought to coordinate and further stimulate this effort as a buttress to the Anglican establishment. In Bishop Kennett's
words such schools might be 'little garrisons against Popery', catechizing the
young and providing a rudimentary education.[7] In 1704 there were 54 such
schools in London, but by 1734 there were 132, educating over 3,000 boys and
nearly 2,000 girls. One newspaper reported that there were 1,221 such schools
across the British Isles in 1716, educating 30,000 children.[8] Even if such figures
are correct, clearly charity schools educated only a small proportion of children. Certainly many people acquired the skills of reading, writing, and arithmetic outside of school and often over a period extending well into adulthood,
not least because many children worked from the age of 7. Their education
remained unstructured and informal, depending heavily upon self-help—
exploiting the enthusiasm and experience of parents, listening to sermons, and
watching nature at work. Probably many villages were like Chipstead in Surrey
where there 'is no school of any account, nor endowment for one. John Ship
and Mark Provost, two poor men, teach a few children to read English, and one
of them teacheth to write.'[9] Such an education might have been rough and
ready, but it was no less important for that.

An altogether different educational world was available to those with time
and money to spare. This was a free market. The State had no educational policy in the modern sense, just as there were no national exams and few formal
qualifications to be achieved. Tradesmen and merchants needed to acquire a
facility with languages and arithmetic, usually resorting to academies, cram-
mers, and teach-yourself guides. In and around London a vibrant market in
educational provision flourished in this period, led by academies such as those
at Soho (founded c.1690) and Hackney (founded 1685). Dissenters were in the
vanguard of the educated middling sort, the Quaker William Stout noting that
'when out of busnes, [I] passed my time in reading religious books, or history,
geography, surveying or other mathamatical sciences.'[10] Gentleman were part
of a somewhat different educational culture. The education of the elite took
place at home, under the gaze of parents and tutors and, for boys, also at grammar and public schools, university, the Inns of Court, and on the grand tour.

[7] Quoted in M. G. Jones, *The Charity School Movement: A Study of Eighteenth Century
Puritanism in Action* (Cambridge, 1938), p. 14.

[8] *The Weekly Journal, or British Gazetter*, 2 June 1716, p. 427.

[9] *Parson and Parish in Eighteenth-Century Surrey: Replies to Bishops' Visitations*, ed.
W. R. Ward, Surrey Record Society, 34 (Guilford, 1994), p. 16.

[10] *The Autobiography of William Stout of Lancaster, 1665–1752*, ed. J. D. Marshall (Manchester,
1967), p. 96.

Not qualifications but manners, acquaintances, and experience were sought—the cultivation of judgement and right reason, what contemporaries often called 'virtue', rather than the accumulation of particular bodies of learning. Concern for the education of boys set the terms of reference here. The 'Gentleman, whose proper calling is the service of His Country . . . is most properly concerned in Moral, and Political Knowledge; and thus the studies which more immediately belong to His calling, are those which treat of virtues and vices, or Civil Society, and the Arts of Government, and so wil take in also Law and History.'[11]

If schools often provided a reasonably structured environment for learning, the function of universities was then in some doubt. Not only did very few attend Oxford and Cambridge, England's only universities, but numbers were also falling through the period, reaching a nadir in the middle of the eighteenth century—in the 1720s Oxford was admitting about 300 freshmen per annum, compared to over 500 in the 1630s. Those who did attend usually arrived aged about 17 and remained only for a year or two. It is important, however, not to see the function of England's universities in this period in modern terms. Usually only those intent upon a career in the Church stayed the course, and most college fellows had also been ordained. In this sense universities in part served as Anglican theological colleges. The gentry, on the other hand, often viewed them as finishing schools: at Oxford 'the young men go there rather for the sake of its having been said they have been at the University than for any advantages to improve them in knowledge.'[12] In this role the universities competed with the Inns of Court, the grand tour, and the developing London season. It is notable, therefore, that a Bill to establish a college for gentlemen in Westminster in 1700 was in part killed off by stiff opposition from Oxford's establishment, worried that it would lose prospective students and shrivel into nothing more than a seminary. Whether that was likely might be doubted, for a similar threat was posed by the Inns of Court. On the face of it the Inns offered the elite a structured environment for making valuable connections and friendships, allied to the powerful lures, both good and bad, of the capital. Yet they too had fallen upon hard times as membership roles, income, and the quality of legal training were all in decline.

As the student body at the universities became socially more exclusive through the late seventeenth and early eighteenth century it is possible that there was a commensurate reduction in the proportion seriously attending to their studies. At Oxford 'plebeians' accounted for 52 per cent of matriculants in

[11] J. Locke, *Some Thoughts Concerning Education*, ed. J. W. and J. S. Yolton (Oxford, 1989), p. 319.
[12] *The Diary of Dudley Ryder, 1715–1716*, ed. W. Matthews (1939), p. 133.

the late 1620s, but only 27 per cent by 1711, and whereas about three-quarters of poorer students took a degree, among nobles and gentlemen commoners only 3 per cent did so, the latter figure perhaps accounting for Burnet's view that at university many 'lost the learning they brought with them from schools'.[13] Another common complaint was of drunkenness, though it might be doubted if students are more restrained today. And, as today, those students who sought a challenging education could easily find one in the quads. William Stukeley, a student at Corpus Christi, Cambridge, in the first decade of the eighteenth century, had his tutor 'read to us in Classics, Ethics, Logic, Metaphysics, Divinity, & . . . in Arithmetic, Algebra, Geometry, Philosophy, Astronomy, Trigonometry.'[14] Amongst others he read Grotius, Pufendorf, and Locke, then all at the cutting edge of philosophical enquiry. His college provided him with a laboratory and he pillaged the surrounding countryside for specimens for his exercises in botany and biology. He was in some respects an exceptional student, but it shows what was possible at England's junior university.

Stukeley's diverse studies were characteristic of the education of gentlemen from an early age. There was only a loosely formulated core curricula. Languages provided not only a social and intellectual sign of distinction but also a necessary tool. Latin, needed for a career in the Church, courts, or medicine, was a prerequisite for scholarship, providing with French the international language of discourse. In Locke's library, for example, 39 per cent of books were in English, 37 per cent in Latin, and 18 per cent in French. Early in the period, major works of scholarship, including Newton's great work on gravity *Philosophiae Naturalis Principia Mathematica* (1687), continued to be published in Latin, though by 1727 this was much less true. Though fewer were competent in Greek than Latin there were those, like Shaftesbury, who viewed it as 'the fountain of all; not only of polite learning and philosophy, but of divinity also, as being the language of our *sacred oracles*.'[15] It was also expected that the well educated were widely educated, with a competency in both the arts and the sciences. One father wished his son to study 'Logick, Ethicks, Physicks, Metaphysicks, & Divinity'.[16] Rigid distinctions between disciplines were unheard of and if the classics loomed large a place was often found for modern studies.

---

[13] H. C. Foxcroft (ed.), *A Supplement to Burnet's History of My Own Time* (Oxford, 1902), p. 500.

[14] 'The Family Memoirs of the Rev. William Stukeley, M. D.', *Publications of the Surtees Society*, 73 (1880), p. 21.

[15] *Letters of the Earl of Shaftesbury, Author of the Characteristicks, Collected into one Volume* (1746), p. 35.

[16] *The Flemings in Oxford being Documents Selected from the Rydal Papers in Illustration of the Lives and Ways of Oxford Men*, vol. 2., ed. J. R. Magrath, Oxford Historical Society, 62 (Oxford, 1913), p. 262.

THE WORLD OF LEARNING

It was one thing to acquire learning, another to produce it. Here too the universities were hardly glorious role models. It was frequently complained that the universities had slipped into a dark age by 1700, providing a lead in debauchery and dissipation rather than erudition and education. Certainly there were problems and some made calls for 'a speedy reformation'.[17] Politically they were hard hit by the Revolution, some 62 fellows being ejected for failing to take the various oaths to the new regimes. Oxford in particular became heavily politicized in favour of the High Church and was tainted by Jacobitism. Less extremely, the universities remained integral to the Anglican establishment. They set themselves against opening up fellowships to the unordained and looked unappealing to those of more heterodox views. The established Church also had a strong arm: Edmond Halley, the astronomer, was for a time denied a professorship at Oxford because of worries about his faith; in 1710 William Whiston was deprived of his professorship in mathematics for his views on primitive Christianity; and, refusing to take the oaths to the Hanoverians, the antiquary Thomas Hearne was turned out of his fellowship and denied access to the Bodleian Library in Oxford.[18] Nor did the universities always keep up with, let alone stimulate, the most recent developments. In medicine, for example, Oxford had been notably dynamic in the seventeenth century, but stagnated from about 1690 so that an decreasing proportion of an expanding profession received their training in the ancient universities. Moreover, much of the best academic work took place away from the universities and which could not, consequently, easily claim to provide the nation's intellectual lead. This must not be exaggerated, for it reflected as much the strength of the wider gentlemanly spirit of enquiry as a hardening of the arteries of research at Oxford and Cambridge. Though we may chuckle at the opinion that 'we have had *history* professors who never read any thing to qualify them for it, but *Tom Thumb*, *Jack* the *gyant-killer* . . . and such-like valuable records' we must not forget the stature of such academics as Isaac Newton or Richard Bentley the eminent philologist.[19] A new professorship in

[17] *The Life of the Reverend Humphrey Prideaux, D. D. Dean of Norwich, with Several Tracts and Letters of his* (1748), p. 199. He went on to propose 58 articles for such a reformation.

[18] Edmond Halley, 1656–1742, scientist, especially astronomer. Educated St Paul's school, London, and Queen's College, Oxford, Savilian Professor of Geometry at Oxford 1703, Astronomer Royal 1721–42, predicted the return in 1758 of the comet that bears his name. William Whiston, 1667–1752, Lucasian Professor of Mathematics in Cambridge 1703–10. Thomas Hearne, 1678–1735, undergraduate and Fellow of Edmund Hall, Oxford, antiquary, 1712–16 second Keeper of Bodleian Library.

[19] [N. Amhurst], *Terræ-Filius: or, the Secret History of the University of Oxford*, 2 vols. (1726), vol. 1, p. 48; similarly one man was supposedly denied a Fellowship at Merton College, Oxford,

Arabic at Oxford in 1717 and the establishment by George I in 1724 of the regius professorships of History at Oxford and Cambridge are visible signs of change. Another signal that the universities were far from moribund is provided by the notable architectural commissions of the period, such as the Peckwater quad at Christ Church, Oxford, Hawksmoor's work at All Souls College, Oxford, and Gibbs's Senate House at Cambridge.

Research was far from confined to Oxford and Cambridge. At home, much depended upon the initiative of 'amateur' individuals. A culture of gentlemanly enquiry, which had been established earlier in the seventeenth century, flourished in this period. Clergymen, doctors, lawyers, and landowners often actively involved themselves in a world of ideas that centred on their small libraries, cabinets of curiosities, gardens, and inns. Many went on tours to gather data and establish contacts. In 1708 Stukeley set out from his home in Holbeach in Lincolnshire 'to converse with the Physicians of any Note & eminence' in King's Lynn, Stamford, Lincoln, Newark upon Trent, Northampton, and Peterborough.[20] Coffee-houses and taverns provided convenient places for gentlemen to meet and discuss, with newspapers and periodicals read aloud and debated. Almost literally, a 'republic of letters', the international and national correspondence of interested gentlemen, provided an intellectual lifeline that was probably the main means by which new ideas were initially circulated and explored. England's pre-eminent natural historian, John Ray, though rarely straying far from his house in Black Notley in Essex, nevertheless managed to keep in contact with other intellectual leaders such as Hans Sloane.[21] From Oxford the Welshman Edward Lhwyd, an antiquary, circulated 4,000 printed 'Queries' to elicit information.

At first blush, there was a burgeoning of clubs and societies to promote science and the arts in this period. The Oxford Philosophical Society had been founded in 1682 and in 1717 the Society of Antiquaries was re-established further to promote the study of the nation's rich past. In London there were 'an Infinity of CLUBS, or SOCIETIES, for the Improvement of Learning', such as the Spitalfields Mathematical Society and the informal botanic club based at

'because he was too precise and religious and therefore not fit to make a societic man. This is the custom of most elections in the Universitie.' *The Life and Times of Anthony Wood, Antiquary, of Oxford, 1632–1695*, vol. 3, ed. A. Clark, Oxford Historical Society, 26 (Oxford, 1894), p. 424. Richard Bentley, 1662–1742, educated St John's College, Cambridge, chaplain to Bishop of Worcester 1690, Keeper of royal libraries 1694, Master of Trinity College, Cambridge, 1700–42 where he came into bitter conflict with the fellows.

[20] *Family Memoirs of Stukeley*, p. 42.

[21] John Ray, 1627–1705, educated Braintree Grammar School, and Catherine Hall and Trinity College, Cambridge, held various academic appointments at Trinity, which he resigned in 1662, unable, despite his Anglican orthodoxy, to break his prior oath to the Interregnum regime; spent the rest of his life collecting, cataloguing, and classifying specimens, mainly of plants and insects.

the Temple coffee-house.[22] Certainly local gentlemen were beginning to club together to graze on ideas that interested them. In Lincolnshire, which seems to have part of a regional 'hot spot' for such things, the Spalding Gentlemen's Society, established in 1710, was meeting weekly by the end of our period and, only twenty miles away, there was a Stamford Society by 1721. But such societies were not to be common until the middle of the eighteenth century and the history of the Royal Society demonstrates the limitations of such associational endeavours. Founded in 1662 and Europe's first learned society, it quickly established a reputation as a centre of learning. Newton, Halley, Wren, Evelyn, and Sloane were just some of the famous men of ideas among its fellowship after the Revolution. Its *Philosophical Transactions* was the pre-eminent journal for new work, both in the sciences and much of the humanities. Yet all was not well. In the 1690s and 1700s it fell into cliquishness and became for a time as much a social club as a learned society (Gresham's College, established in 1579, had also lost its way by this time). In 1710 a foreign visitor complained that 'Now scarcely anything is done by them', putting it down to a decline in the quality of the fellowship who were now composed of 'apothecaries and other such people as know scarce a word of Latin'.[23] Voltaire, in many respects an Anglophile, agreed with such a prognosis, ascribing it to the Society casting its net too widely, mingling 'literature and science indiscriminately. It seems to me better to have a specialized academy for literature, so that there is no confusion'.[24]

The relative weakness of the institutional framework of the world of learning is further evidenced when attention is shifted to consider the state of libraries and museums. Public libraries were conspicuous by their absence from all but a score of towns in 1700, though efforts were then made (again under the aegis of the SPCK) to establish parochial libraries for the clergy. By this means 64 libraries were established between 1705 and 1729, though they were modest affairs, usually with only 80 or so volumes. There was no national reference library and the university libraries at Oxford and Cambridge were not yet major institutions (at both many books were still chained), with the latter described in 1701 as 'full indeed of Books, but that is owning to the Smallness of it'.[25] Most major libraries were privately owned, though often they were available to the dedicated scholar. At the Revolution probably the leading library was that formed by Sir Robert Cotton early in the seventeenth

---

[22] [J. Macky], *A Journey Through England*, 2 vols. (2nd edn., 1722), vol. 1, p. 287.
[23] *London in 1710: From the Travels of Zacharias Conrad von Uffenbach*, trans. and ed. W. H. Quarrell and M. Mare (1934), p. 99.
[24] *Letters on England*, trans. L. Tancock (Harmondsworth, 1980), p. 115.
[25] *The English Travels of Sir John Percival and William Byrd II: The Percival Diary of 1701*, ed. M. R. Wenger (Columbia, Missouri, 1989), p. 69.

century and maintained by his heirs. A major collection of around 30,000 volumes was created by John Moore, the Bishop of Ely. When Moore died George I bought the collection and donated it to Cambridge's University Library, more than doubling its holdings overnight. Robert Harley, the politician, began collecting voraciously in 1705 and soon amassed 6,000 manuscripts and 40,000 books. Thomas Rawlinson, the son of a Lord Mayor of London, had reputedly collected 200,000 volumes by his death in 1725.[26] Around the turn of the century a number of peers, including Lord Somers, the Duke of Devonshire, and the Earl of Sunderland, began to form major libraries as a signal of their intellectual and financial virility. A similar picture emerges with regard to the collection of artefacts and scientific specimens. Aside from a menagerie at the Tower of some lions and other big cats, the hard work was again done by private individuals. Elias Ashmole had given his collection to Oxford in 1677 leading after a few years to the establishment of a museum which still thrives. Thoresby, the Yorkshire antiquary, waxed lyrical on Charleton's museum in London that had cost perhaps £8,000 to form. It was 'perhaps the most noble collection of natural and artificial curiosities, of ancient and modern coins and medals, that any private person in the world enjoys.'[27] Hans Sloane had by the start of the eighteenth century begun to collect what was, in 1753, to become the heart of the British Museum (he acquired much of Charleton's collection). Prompted by Lords Halifax and Somers and Bishop Nicolson of Carlisle, attention was also directed in the first two decades of the century towards better preserving and ordering the public records.

Undeniably, the world of learning afforded few visible openings for women. Excluded from many schools, both universities, and almost all learned societies—they became full members of the Royal Society only in 1945—it is easy to imagine them wallowing in relative ignorance. Certainly, powerful sexual stereotypes existed, with women often characterized as lacking the same capacity as men for reason and being less able to acquire learning. No less certainly, less attention was paid to the education of girls than boys, as the sexual composition of literacy attests. As one man observed, 'Women are thought generally by nature to be much inferior to man in Understanding; but I believe the difference lies chiefly in education, by which they give us very great odds.'[28] It was, however, one thing to be formally excluded from seats of learning, another to be denied access to the world of ideas. If few women became notable scholars in this period—Elizabeth Elstob the Anglo-Saxonist and Mary Astell the political philosopher are notable exceptions—there is good evidence that many

[26] Born 1681, educated Cheam, Eton, St John's College, Oxford, and the Middle Temple.
[27] *The Diary of Ralph Thoresby*, ed. J. Hunter, 2 vols. (1830), vol. 1, p. 299.
[28] *The Works of John Sheffield, Earl of Mulgrave, Marquis of Normanby, and Duke of Buckingham*, 2 vols. (1723), vol. 2, p. 270.

read and debated vigorously. How could they be prevented from reading or listening? It is also interesting to note that publications began to appear aimed either in whole or in part at women. John Dunton's *Athenian Mercury* (1690–7) expressly welcomed questions to be answered in future editions from women, Addison and Steele's periodical the *Spectator* (1711–12, 1714) clearly envisioned women readers, and John Tipper's *Ladies' Diary* (1704–1840) and Ambrose Philip's *Free Thinker* (1718–21) were specifically written with women readers in mind. These were all works of some intellectual pretension and demonstrate the ways some women, largely those among the more prosperous classes, could become involved in new trends. Even making allowance for journalistic licence, Steele's observation that 'the great Improvements Women have made of Education, there being hardly any Science in which they have not excell'd' carries some weight.[29]

PRINTING AND PUBLISHING

Until 1695 England had a highly regulated press, with both the quantity and nature of what was printed subject to control. The Licensing Act which expired in that year required all works to gain government approval before publication and limited printing within England to no more than twenty master printers of the Stationers Company of London and the university printers. Further, the number of apprentices, journeymen, and presses per printer was regulated and only four type founders were permitted. It says much about the relationship between the Church and the world of ideas that vacancies among the ranks of the master printers and the type founders were filled on the recommendation of the Archbishop of Canterbury and the Bishop of London. Furthermore, what might be printed had to obtain a licence. Despite such restrictions it is important to stress that few of the revolutionaries of 1688–9 believed in free speech, categorizing ideas as highly combustible matter whose dissemination had to be carefully controlled. They need only look back to the 1640s and 1650s and to events such as the Putney debates to be assured of that. Yet in 1695 the Licensing Act lapsed, not because of forceful arguments for a free press such as those Milton had made earlier in *Areopagitica* (1644), but because censorship was seen to be impracticable. In 1692 the Whig licenser had been expelled for licensing Anthony Walker's *A True Account of a Book Entituled Eikon Basilike* and in 1693 his successor, Bohun, was dismissed for licensing the pamphlet *King William and Queen Mary Conquerors*. The

---

[29] Quoted in G. D. Meyer, *The Scientific Lady in England 1650–1760: An Account of her Rise, with Emphasis on the Major Roles of the Telescope and Microscope* (Berkeley and Los Angeles, 1955), p. 72.

problem was that in the highly charged atmosphere of parliamentary politics after 1688 deciding what should and should not be published depended to a considerable extent upon relatively random fluctuations in party influence over the executive. In such an environment somewhat arbitrary censorship came to be viewed as worse than allowing uncontrolled publishing.

The lapse of the Licensing Act was followed by an explosion of printed matter issuing from the presses, be it books, pamphlets, sermons, journals, or newspapers. It is difficult to put accurate numbers to this explosion, but if library holdings are an indication between 1660 and 1688 about 1,100 titles were published per annum, between 1689 and 1727 about 2,000, and between 1728 and 1760 some 2,300—that is to say increases between the succeeding periods were 82 and 15 per cent, suggesting a particularly dramatic surge in publishing in the generation after the Glorious Revolution.[30] Little wonder then that one foreigner noted how '*England* is a Country abounding in printed Papers'.[31] The proliferation of newspapers vividly illustrates the dynamism of this print culture. Before 1695 there existed only the government's newspaper of record, the dry as dust *London Gazette*. In 1695 it was soon faced in London by three tri-weekly newspapers (the *Post Boy*, *Post Man*, and *Flying Post*). These were modest affairs, printed in double columns on both sides of a single sheet of paper. But they were soon taken out into the nation with the mails, channelling not only national but much international news into the far corners of the realm. And by providing a new and powerful link between the metropolis and provinces they helped to reconstitute the domain of the printed word. In 1702 the first daily paper, the *Daily Courant*, was founded. These London papers provided the material for a growing provincial press. Outside London there had been no newspapers before 1695, but at least 51 were established between 1700 and 1727. Admittedly many of these were short-lived ventures, but some, such as the *Worcester Post Man*, *Newcastle Courant*, and Norwich's *Transactions of the Universe*, survived for many years. Perhaps 70,000 copies of newspapers a week were being sold on the eve of the introduction in 1712 of a Stamp Act that sought, with limited success, to control their incidence.

London remained the centre of the print industry through the period. Though provincial presses were established, their most significant productions

[30] Figures derived from the online *English Short Title Catalogue*, searched in May 1999. This is a union catalogue of works published before 1800 in England or in the English language outside of England now held in all major and many other libraries in Britain, Ireland, and North America. Despite the scope of the database these figures must be used with caution. For example, though the catalogue is well-established it continues to grow as new libraries are searched; a one-page broadsheet has the same status as a multi-volume book; older books are less likely to have survived; series have largely not been included; and new editions are counted separately, even if changes from the original were very slight.

[31] H. Misson, *Memoirs and Observations in his Travels over England* (1719), p. 203.

MAP 4. Provincial towns and cities with newspapers before 1728

were newspapers. The university presses were not yet the powerhouses that they were eventually to become. Oxford University Press may have moved into the splendour of its Clarendon building in 1713, but it was a decision that rested upon a commercial miscalculation about the profitability of Clarendon's *History of the Great Rebellion* (1702–4). Cambridge University Press was effectively controlled by the Stationers' Company until 1698 when it was re-established under the guidance of university curators. Most scholars, including Newton, a Fellow of Trinity College, Cambridge, published in London—in his library, as in Locke's, over 85 per cent of the books published in Britain issued from London. After 1695 the vibrancy of London's commercial world allowed the opportunities of the new order to be seized quickly and, for the most part, successfully. Profit and loss was, therefore, the dominant determinant of patterns of publishing. Almanacs, bibles, chapbooks, newspapers, and the like always outnumbered works with serious intellectual pretensions. This was the era which gave rise to the idea of Grub Street, the publication of salacious, sensationalist, and often low-brow works. More esoteric or scholarly works struggled to be viable given their smaller markets, short print runs, and high unit cost. Little use was made of serial publication, though periodicals did flourish, but subscription publishing, whereby purchasers bought in advance of publication and had their names listed inside, became an ever-increasing means of breaking this constraint, especially in the early eighteenth century. Subscribers not only supported a needy author and printer but also publicized their patronage and worth. In the 1720s well over a hundred works were published by this route and in the 1730s over 300.

The warmth of political passions that had undermined the credibility of the Licensing Act also provided a reading (and listening) public eager for news and opinion. Many of the influences at work are nicely illustrated by a report on the uses to which Swift's *Examiner*, a sophisticated apology for Harley's Tory government of Anne's last years, was put. A letter to Harley from Scarborough in Yorkshire in December 1710 reported that the *Examiner*

has done excellent service in these . . . parts, and proves . . . a weekly antidote to that weekly poison so industriously scattered through the nation by those two public libellers and incendiaries 'The Observator,' 'The Review,' and others. The honest parson [here] . . . takes abundance of pains to apply the remedy where it is wanted. Mr. Hungerford sends him the 'Examiner' down every Thursday: its comes hither on Sunday and after evening service the parson usually invites a good number of his friends to his house, where he first reads over the paper, and then comments upon the text; and all the week after carries it about with him to read to such of his parishioners as are weak in the faith, and have not yet the eyes of their understanding opened; so that it is not doubted but he will in time make as many converts to the true interest of the State, as ever he did to the Church.[32]

Quite apart from the partisan nature of the print culture of this period, this letter vividly demonstrates the ways 'readership' might be much larger than circulation figures. Both coffee-houses and taverns might effectively serve as libraries where public readings and debate took place. And though politically charged works were probably those which were most in demand, we can assume that history, literature, and religion were also wanted. There is little question that the nature of England's reading public was dramatically transformed after

[32] H. M. C., *The Manuscripts of his Grace the Duke of Portland*, vol. 4 (1897), p. 641.

1695. Among journals perhaps 2,000 copies of each of Addison and Steele's *Spectator* (1711–12 and 1714), 1,600 of Swift's *Examiner* (1710–11), and 425 of Defoe's *Review* (1704–13) were sold. Polemical works were best-sellers: Sacheverell's *Perils of False Brethren* (1709) sold *c*.100,000, Molesworth's *Letter to Sir Jacob Banks* (1711) *c*.60,000, Defoe's *True Born Englishman* (1701) *c*.80,000, and Steele's *The Crisis* (1714) *c*.40,000.

One French visitor in the early eighteenth century believed that because England was 'a Country of Liberty' 'Freedom of Thoughts and Sentiments' was general.[33] Unquestionably many came to see the freedom of the press as an 'indisputable Birthright of every free Briton'.[34] Yet the efflorescence of the press after 1695 did not please all. An unregulated press was seen by many as socially destabilizing, as new and perhaps radical ideas corroded the ideological framework of the status quo. Bolingbroke complained in 1712 of the 'melancholy consideration that the laws of our country are too weak to punish effectually . . . factious scribblers', stressing the need to differentiate between 'licentiousness' and 'liberty'.[35] In fact, between 1695 and 1714 there were fifteen Bills brought into Parliament aimed at establishing some control over what was printed. However, all but one failed because censorship was seen to be impracticable and because there were those (such as Locke had done) who strongly argued the case for a free press. The one successful Bill, the Copyright Act of 1710, simply clarified issues of intellectual property and required the deposition of works at nine libraries (including all the British university libraries). Nevertheless, if the press was not directly controlled, it worked within limits. As with Swift's *Examiner*, governments soon appreciated the need to have their own voice. Harley was in the vanguard here, employing Defoe and Swift, and it was a lesson Walpole soon learnt, buying out the oppositionist *London Journal* in 1722 to turn it into a government rag. In 1712 and 1725 the government used taxes to raise the prices of newspapers in a partly successful attempt to drive some out of business and others into political respectability. And through the period authors, publishers, and printers might be prosecuted for seditious libel. Defoe, for example, was pilloried in 1703 when his satiric *The Shortest-Way with the Dissenters* was judged a seditious libel. Many books and pamphlets were ordered to be burned by the common hangman, dramatically (if unpersuasively) pointing up their supposed heretical content. Parliament alone prosecuted forty-five works between 1695 and

[33] B.-L. de Muralt, *Letters Describing the Character and Customs of the English and French Nations* (2nd edn., 1726), p. 2.

[34] V. Snell, *Loyalty the Duty and Interest of Every Private Subject. A Sermon Preach'd at the Assizes in Wisbech . . . May 18 1725* (1727), preface (no pagination).

[35] *Letters and Correspondence, Public and Private, of the Right Honourable Henry St. John, Lord Viscount Bolingbroke*, ed. G. Parke, 2 vols. (1798), vol. 1, p. 600.

1714 and the university authorities were also keen book burners and censors. In 1715 Cambridge's vice-chancellor designated only four publications which might be taken by the town's coffee-houses, proscribing works such as the *Examiner* and *Spectator* so that students should supposedly 'have news without politics'.[36] Claiming authorship of a work remained a somewhat risky business—in 1715 a reward of £1,000 was offered for the capture of the unknown author of the *English Advice to the Freeholders of England* (1715)—such that many authors continued to prefer anonymity or pseudonymity.[37] The press was undoubtedly more free after 1695, but it was far from being unconstrained.

A growing press and widening access to literature were related to each other and had profound effects upon the intellectual environment of post-Revolution England. At the broadest level the strength of oral traditions existed alongside an ever-growing culture of the text. Necessarily, given the distribution of literacy and the ownership of printed works, this had profound social connotations. The well-to-do often frowned upon the superstitions of the poor, seeing orality as ignorance. The role of 'Legendary Stories', 'lucky Omens', or unwritten customary rights was contrasted with the reasoned literary culture of the more prosperous.[38] In fact, however, given ever-widening access to the printed word the relationship between oral and literary cultures evolved at every social level. For many this was most keenly worked through over religion. More and more households came to own copies of the Bible, tracts, sermons, and catechisms. But this was not merely a private matter of faith for it also bore upon a reader's view of priests, sermons, and services. Moreover, newspapers and pamphlets became important ways in which new ideas were spread about a wide range of activities, from farming to politics, from sex to war. Such new ideas were often unsuccessful, but their very existence could require a rethinking or justification of assumptions and commonplaces. The act of writing for the printed page in itself required the ordering of observations and ideas (and some regularization of spelling and grammar) that might previously have been held as a more casual assemblage, such that the growth of published works in this period was part and parcel of a wider concern better to understand the world in which people lived and died. By no means was this always in the direction of 'reason' and 'enlightenment' for the publication of ballads and chapbooks could give more shape and significance to the worlds of magic, alchemy, ghosts, and fairies.

---

[36] *The Private Journal and Literary Remains of John Byrom*, ed. R. Parkinson, Chetham Society, 32 and 34, 2 vols. (1854–5), vol. 1, p. 31.

[37] The author was Francis Atterbury, the High Tory/Jacobite Bishop of Rochester.

[38] H. Bourne, *Antiquitates Vulgares; or, the Antiquities of the Common People* (Newcastle, 1725), pp. xii and 41.

EXPANDING EXPERIENCES

Both at home and abroad there was a significant growth of Englishmen and women on the move in this period. An increasing number of such journeys were driven by a quest for the new. If and when they returned travellers brought back experiences, impressions, images, and specimens which, no matter how slightly, changed the world they had originally travelled from. This was not intellectually neutral in its consequences. Gradually, as increasing knowledge was acquired of England and many other countries, ideas about the natural and the man-made world had to be rethought, perhaps rephrased, or even recast. Such a challenge was not new in this period, but the widespread availability in print of travel journals, geographies, and natural histories was— a quantitative change which had important qualitative consequences.

Topographical descriptions of England proliferated in this period, often showing much concern for antiquities and sometimes based upon distinguished earlier authors. In 1695 a new edition of Camden's *Britannia* was published under the guiding hand of Edmund Gibson, later Bishop of London; and between 1710 and 1712 the Oxford antiquary and sourpuss Thomas Hearne brought out Leland's *Itinerary*. Naturalists and antiquaries such as Ray and Aubrey went on tours to gather information for their work. And travelogues began to appear in increasing numbers—such as King's *A Journey to London* (1698) or Macky's *A Journey Through England*, which first began to appear in 1714. Among the best known was Daniel Defoe's *A Tour Through the Whole Island of Great Britain*, published in three volumes between 1724 and 1726. On the title-page Defoe wrote that he aimed to provide 'A Particular and Diverting Account of Whatever is Curious and worth Observation', particularly urban centres, 'Customs, Manners, Speech', economic activity, and 'Publick Edifices'. This was to be no mere catalogue for he also included 'Useful Observations upon the Whole'. Such works allowed a better appreciation of the distinctive nature of England and of the significance of its varied parts to the national whole. The stress upon variety was one contemporaries made much play upon, producing and devouring numerous county natural histories such as Charles Leigh's *The Natural History of Lancashire, Cheshire and the Peak* (1700) and John Norden's *Speculi Britanniae Pars Altera; or a Delineation of Northamptonshire* (1720).

In truth, such depictions of the domestic scene were comfortable and unthreatening. Celia Fiennes thought such travels raised the 'Glory and Esteem' of England, curing 'the evil itch of over-valueing foreign parts'.[39]

---

[39] *The Journeys of Celia Fiennes*, ed. J. Hillaby (1983), p. 19.

Certainly increasing numbers of gentlemen were traipsing around the Netherlands, France, Italy, Switzerland, and the German-speaking states, dreaming
amongst the ruins of the classical world, marvelling at the glories of the Renaissance, socializing with local worthies, and signing up painters, sculptors, and
musicians. Such continental sojourns helped to tie England into the wider
European context of ideas, habits, and fashions, but in truth involved relatively
few (albeit often highly influential) and a good many who were dilettante rather
than virtuosi. In fact, the grand tour largely aimed to reconfirm ties to what was
already known, 'to fit the Past with the Present' in Congreve's telling phrase,
be they the glories of Rome or the marvels of Titian.[40] And though much
reportage of European countries was informative, that of superstitions among
Catholic peoples was often used to underscore England's supposed superiority
as a Protestant nation. It was reports of distant climes, Africa, Asia, and the
Americas, which provided the real challenge. Considerable ignorance and
prejudice existed at the start of our period. With regard to Asia, for example,
the Bible and ancient authorities such as Herodotus and Ptolemy still held sway.
The Travels of Sir John Mandeville, put together in the fourteenth century, was
reprinted ten times in England in the late seventeenth and early eighteenth
centuries. The limitations of such sources, however, were becoming ever clearer
as more and more ships plied the oceans and more and more travellers wrote
up what they had seen and thought. Something approaching an explosion of
works began to issue from the press, among them *A Collection of Curious Travels
and Voyages* published by John Ray for the Royal Society in 1693, Patrick
Gordon's popular and wide-ranging *Geography Anatomiz'd or the Geographical
Grammar* (1693), John Churchill's four-volume *A Collection of Voyages and
Travels* (1704–5), John Harris's two-volume *Navigantium Atque Itinerantium
Bibliotheca* (1705), and the *Atlas geographus* issued in parts from May 1708. If
many of the travel books lacked scholarly pretension many were substantial
enough and attained some stature.

Accurately assessing the significance of this wave of experiences and impressions is impossible, not least because there was no coordination in the studies
of distant lands. Neither the Crown nor the Royal Society provided much of a
lead and there was no Kew Gardens or British Museum to collect and catalogue what had been found. What mattered was the initiative of the individual
scholar, such as Sir Hans Sloane, or what the market for literature would bear.
And if that market occasionally sunk under the weight of bulky geographies
or travelogues it was often buoyed up by works such as *The Arabian Nights
Entertainments: Consisting of One Thousand and One Stories* (1704) and Defoe's
Robinson Crusoe (1719). Shaftesbury complained in 1710 that 'Histories of

---

[40] W. Congreve, *Letters and Documents*, ed. J. C. Hodges (1964), p. 62.

Incas or Iroquois, written by friars and missionaries, pirates and renegades, sea-captains and trusty travellers, pass for authentic records and are canonical with the virtuosi of this sort'.[41] Moreover, travel, or knowledge of a wider world, did not necessarily broaden the mind. Lady Mary Wortley Montagu, perhaps tongue in cheek, thought that

after having seen part of Asia and Africa and allmost made the tour of Europe, I think the honest English Squire more happy who verily beleives the Greek wines less delicious than March beer, that the African fruits have not so fine a flavour as golden Pipins, and the Becáfiguas of Italy are not so well tasted as a rump of Beef, and that, in short, there is no perfect Enjoyment of this life out of Old England. I pray God I may think so for the rest of my Life . . .[42]

Still, serious scholars did raise questions about the ever-widening natural and man-made worlds. Botanists had to come to grips with new plants just as theologians struggled with the proliferation of religions. North America set perhaps the greatest challenge. From one perspective it provided some material with which to think through ideas of a state of nature and the noble savage ('in the beginning all the World was *America*'), from another the chaos that attended the absence of civilization and Christianity.[43] The visit in 1710 of four leaders of the Iroquois tribe (as with the negro slaves that had begun to appear in England) brought the point vividly home. Some found their racial stereotypes confirmed by such encounters, others found them confronted. Such a range of reactions was characteristic of responses to travelling and wider knowledge. Images of and ideas about the world were becoming more detailed and varied, producing both more and less certainty.

THE TWILIGHT OF THE SCIENTIFIC REVOLUTION

On 19 March 1727 Sir Isaac Newton died aged 84 and, consonant with Voltaire's view that such a man was born but once a millennium, was given a State funeral and buried in Westminster Abbey. Lucasian professor of Mathematics at Cambridge when only 26, author of two great scientific treatises, for many years President of the Royal Society, he was also briefly an MP and, for much longer, Master of the Mint. In England his career and achievements mark the culmination of the remarkable efflorescence of intellectual endeavour that had taken place through the seventeenth century and which is

[41] Quoted in P. J. Marshall and G. Williams, *The Great Map of Mankind: British Perceptions of the World in the Age of Enlightenment* (1982), p. 61.

[42] *The Complete Letters of Lady Mary Wortley Montagu*, ed. R. Halsband, 3 vols. (Oxford, 1965), vol. 1, p. 444.

[43] J. Locke, *The Two Treatises of Government*, ed. P. Laslett (Cambridge, 1991), p. 301.

conveniently, if a little inaccurately, called the Scientific Revolution. Though that Revolution was demonstrably a European one, England played a very full part. Alongside Newton stood the astronomers Flamsteed[44] and Halley, the naturalists Ray and Grew, the chemists and physicists Hooke[45] and Boyle,[46] and many others. With some justification the English prided themselves in the belief that they led the scientific world by the end of the seventeenth century, needing to defer to none: 'great Brittain deserves to be the Academy of the Universe.'[47]

In the first instance the Scientific Revolution was driven by a desire for knowledge of man and his world, what was called 'natural philosophy', and to root that knowledge firmly in observation rather than speculation. In the English context the most forceful (though far from the only or the original) advocate of the empirical approach had been the polymath and one-time Lord Chancellor Francis Bacon. Further, he, like most contemporaries, took science to be wholly catholic in its subject matter. The foundation of the Royal Society at the Restoration gave considerable institutional substance to a methodology that put more weight upon induction than deduction, what was sometimes called an 'experimental philosophy'. The power of observation had in a very real sense been transformed by Hooke's development of the microscope by 1665 and improvements in the quality of telescopes that was symbolized in 1675 by the appointment of Flamsteed as Astronomer Royal and the building of Greenwich Observatory. Yet, in practical terms, a purely inductive method was impossible. Pathways for research could only be established speculatively, not the least of which at the time were the mechanical theories deriving from René Descartes.[48] Nevertheless, many would have agreed with the view put forward in 1722 that 'a right Method of Reasoning, are become the happy Characters of this Age'.[49]

[44] John Flamsteed, 1646–1719, educated Derby Free School and Jesus College, Cambridge, ordained 1671, first Astronomer Royal 1675, meticulous cataloguer of 3,000 stars, argued with Halley and Newton about publishing his findings.

[45] Robert Hooke, 1635–1703, educated Westminster School and Christ Church, Oxford, active in the Royal Society, Professor of Geometry at Gresham College 1665, eclectic interests, coined the term 'cell'.

[46] Robert Boyle, 1627–91, son of the Earl of Cork, educated at Eton College, active in Oxford in the 1650s and 1660s (but holding no academic post), instrumental in establishing the Royal Society in 1660 (declining its Presidency in 1680), established 'Boyle's law' relating the volume of gas to pressure and heat, much concerned with theological matters.

[47] The Letters and Papers of the Banks Family of Revesby Abbey 1704–1760, ed. J. W. F. Hill, Lincoln Record Society, 45 (1952), p. 12.

[48] French philosopher cum mathematician, 1596–1650. His ideas became very influential and on the Continent remained in vogue well into the eighteenth century.

[49] W. Beckett, A Free and Impartial Enquiry into the Antiquity and Efficacy of Touching for the Cure of the King's Evil (1722), p. 62.

Another potent contributor to scientific enquiry in the seventeenth century was an increasing interest in exploring the mathematical bases of human understanding. The work of Newton on calculus and gravity, the efforts of the Political Arithmeticians, the actuarial studies of Halley and de Moivre, even Wren's architecture, all bear witness to the new power of numerical thinking. As John Arbuthnot put it in 1700, 'The advantages which accrue to the mind by mathematical studies consist chiefly . . . first, in accustoming it to attention; secondly, in giving it a habit of close and demonstrative reasoning; thirdly, in freeing it from prejudice, credulity, and superstition.' Following Bacon, he believed that 'All the visible works of God Almighty are made in number, weight, and measure; therefore to consider them we ought to understand arithmetic, geometry, and statics'.[50] More widely, not only literacy but numeracy had been increasing through the early modern period. Symbolically, a Royal Mathematical School (concerned to train up good navigators) had, through a grant of £7,000 from Charles II, been attached to Christ's Hospital in 1673 and by Ryder's time mathematics was 'a study in vogue among the great men'.[51]

In terms of intellectual achievement, Newton's *Principia* was the most significant contribution to the scientific world in the late seventeenth and early eighteenth centuries. Building upon the work of others, and aided into print by Halley, he geometrically demonstrated how the laws of motion and gravity ordered the planetary system. Though improved telescopes were showing increasing detail in the night sky (such as Saturn's rings) Newton's work allowed the unity of that complexity to be comprehended, though he admitted that 'the cause of gravity is what I do not pretend to know'.[52] Newton's findings concluded a line of enquiry that can be traced directly back to Copernicus in the sixteenth century, making him in Voltaire's words the 'destroyer of the Cartesian system'.[53] In truth, few could follow the *Principia* (Cambridge students joked that neither could Newton) and it was left to his followers to popularize its key findings and confirm his reputation as 'the Miracle of the present Age, [who] can look through a whole Planetary System; consider it in its Weight, Number and Measure'.[54] Such achievements were vividly brought home when in 1715 and 1724 Halley predicted a lunar eclipse of the sun and published *in advance* maps of England describing the area from which it could be viewed. At the time this made a more popular impression than his accurate

---

[50] 'An Essay on the Usefulness of Mathematical Learning', in G. A. Aitken (ed.), *The Life and Works of John Arbuthnot* (Oxford, 1892), pp. 410 and 413.

[51] *Ryder's Diary*, p. 150.

[52] *The Correspondence of Richard Bentley*, ed. J. Wordsworth, 2 vols. (1842), vol. 1, p. 61.

[53] *Letters on England*, p. 68.

[54] *The Spectator*, ed. D. F. Bond, 5 vols. (Oxford, 1965), vol. 4, p. 442.

prediction that the comet which had last appeared in 1682 (and which is also depicted in the Bayeux tapestry) would return in 1758.

Newton's *Opticks*, where he discussed the nature of light, was somewhat more accessible than his *Principia*. It was simple to copy his experiment and use one prism to split white light into the seven colours of the spectrum and to use another prism either to combine them into white light again or to show that the seven colours could not be further divided. Though Newton misunderstood the causes of this, plumping for the role of corpuscles rather than waves, he had shown another way in which the natural world could be disassembled to aid comprehension. This was vividly illustrated through the work of John Ray in cataloguing plants, animals, and insects. Arguably his greatest achievement was the three-volumed *Historia Generalis Plantarum* he produced between 1686 and 1704 and which attempted to classify nearly 19,000 species of plants. In a similar vein Flamsteed meticulously charted the heavens, his magnum opus, *Historia Coelestis Britannica* being published posthumously in 1725. Constructing a taxonomy that could be applied to whole aspects of the natural world shows an intellectual ambition to understand and order that was entirely characteristic of the period.

John Ray waxed eloquent upon the scientific advances of the seventeenth century. In 1690 he declared that he was

full of gratitude to God that it was His will for me to be born in this last age when the empty sophistry that usurped the title of philosophy and within my memory dominated the schools has fallen into contempt, and in its place has arisen a philosophy solidly built upon a foundation of experiment . . . It is an age of noble discovery, the weight and elasticity of air, the telescope and microscope, the ceaseless circulation of the blood through veins and arteries, the lacteal glands and the bile duct, the structure of the organs of generation, and of many others—too many to mention: the secrets of Nature have been unsealed and explored: a new Physiology has been introduced. It is an age of daily progress in all the sciences . . .[55]

Yet it might be doubted whether the scientific endeavours, not only of this period but of the Scientific Revolution more generally, affected more than a tiny intellectual elite. If Newton and his contemporaries only sought intellectual advances, then the question is ill-posed. Yet the issue of the wider utility of science did concern contemporaries. Some headway was made at the border of science and instrument makers, and propagandists such as John Houghton attempted to disseminate new ideas of a practical nature, as in his *A Collection for the Improvement of Husbandry and Trade* (1692–1703). The high priority given to England's shipping also produced developments. In 1688 Halley

[55] Quoted in C. E. Raven, *John Ray, Naturalist: His Life and Works* (2nd edn., Cambridge, 1950), p. 251.

produced a map of ocean trade winds and in 1698, sponsored by the Crown, set sail to investigate magnetic variation in the Atlantic, producing in 1701 a map of the results for navigators. In 1714 Parliament passed an Act establishing a reward of £20,000 for discovering a reliable way of measuring longitude, though it was not to be claimed for many years. Yet in an area such as medicine few advances were achieved, despite all the bodies that were dissected. The uses of science in this (as in any) period are, not however, fully tested by attempting to set a commercial value on investigative or experimental work. Rather, given the absence of any meaningful distinction between pure and applied science, the growth of scientific enquiry in the seventeenth century had a wider cultural influence which encouraged people to look for new ways of tackling old problems and of utilizing the new found resources of the Americas and Asia. So, the development by Thomas Savery of a crude steam engine water pump to drain mines in 1699, or Darby's discovery ten years later of a means of smelting iron with coke rather than charcoal, were symptomatic of an intellectual environment rather than particular bodies of ideas. By 1727 that environment was markedly different from that of a century earlier. It was more curious, more ambitious, and more at odds with the traditional explanatory structures of the Graeco-Roman and Christian traditions. Even since 1689 there had been developments, what has been called 'The rise of public science', where science became an important part of gentlemanly society at large and a basis for many speculative projects (from supplying London with water to raising shipwrecks).[56]

It is often assumed that the Scientific Revolution ended either in giving birth to or by mutating into the 'Age of Reason'. There are many problems with such an assumption, not least that the 'Age of Reason' cannot easily be defined or identified and, as we shall see, many of the central players of the Scientific Revolution assaulted secularization. What is less disputable is that the heyday of scientific endeavour appears to have passed by the early eighteenth century. The decline of the Royal Society was demonstrative of such a change, as was Newton's career subsequent to publication of the *Principia*. He left Cambridge, eventually resigning his chair, was heavily involved in the recoinage of 1696 (Halley was also active at the Chester mint), was Master of the Mint from 1699, and set himself to defending his intellectual reputation. In this last role he was little short of a vainglorious bully: as President, he exploited the Royal Society to rubbish Leibniz's reasonable claims to have developed calculus contemporaneously with himself; he gave short shrift to Hooke's important work on optics (which ascribed correctly to the idea of light waves); and later became

[56] L. Stewart, *The Rise of Public Science: Rhetoric, Technology, and Natural Philosophy in Newtonian Britain, 1660–1750* (Cambridge, 1992).

embroiled in a bitter clash with the astronomer Flamsteed. Yet Newton's personal failings cannot provide a sufficient explanation for a change in intellectual climate. Two factors were perhaps crucial to the course of scientific endeavour. First, the ever-increasing body of knowledge of the natural world, with reports of and specimens from all corners of the globe constantly arriving, kept many intellectual frontiers in a constant state of flux. Not least, huge problems of taxonomy were set by the discovery of yet more species of flora and fauna. Second, to comprehend this ever-growing world, the detail of which was also becoming ever greater, required increasing specialization by scientists if projects were to remain realizable and creditable. In that sense the Scientific Revolution could not be constantly sustained upon the terms forged in its seventeenth-century heyday. Its methodological imperatives required it to evolve and in the process to *appear* to diminish.

ECONOMICALLY SPEAKING

The methodological imperatives of the Scientific Revolution had no limit with regard to subject matter and exerted an influence well beyond 'natural philosophy', particularly in what contemporaries called 'Political arithmetic'. The term had been coined around 1671–2 by Sir William Petty and he meant it to be interpreted literally. The two great political arithmeticians at work after 1688, Gregory King and Charles Davenant, were both concerned to explore matters of relevance to governments—tax revenues, national income, population, and the like—by employing Petty's quantitative methods. Petty was a great evangelist on this point, believing that 'The Method I take to do this, is not very usual; for instead of using only comparative and superlative Words, and intellectual Arguments, I have taken the course . . . to express my self in Terms of *Number*, *Weight*, or *Measure*'.[57] In an era without a census or a Central Statistical Office, such an approach was limited by available evidence, but political arithmeticians made highly imaginative use of what little they had. The London bills of mortality or tax records might be used to make demographic calculations. Studies of religious practice, such as Sir Peter Pett's *The Happy Future State of England* (1688), could call on Compton's ecclesiastical census gathered in 1676. Some sources of information had also been developed. Commercial data had been significantly regularized through the establishment in 1696 of the Inspector Generalship of Customs, and improvements in the efficiency of the excise service had also made available more data relating to industrial output. Less routinely, the government was beginning to survey its

---

[57] *The Economic Writings of Sir William Petty*, ed. C. H. Hull, 2 vols. (Cambridge, 1899), vol. 1, p. 244.

colonial resources to plan for their defence and in 1721 the Board of Trade surveyed the population and trade of all of the nation's overseas possessions.

Political arithmetic was pursued both purposefully and incidentally. In the
first category none rivalled King and Davenant. Both sought to specify the
scale and distribution of the nation's resources so that public finances could be
put on a more secure footing in the exceptionally demanding times of war in
which they worked. Indeed, much of their best work was done while they were
public servants—an interesting document has King justifying his calculations
in response to Harley's sceptical comments. King's work was especially imaginative, providing not only his social table but also estimates of amounts of different types of land, the distribution between urban and rural populations, and
breakdowns of agriculture's arable and pastoral output. King and Davenant
were such prominent figures that it is easy to forget that there were others who
also occasionally turned their mind to number crunching, such as Houghton's
paper on the relationship between county acreages, tax levels, and housing
submitted to Parliament in 1693. Perhaps most important, the House of
Commons came, as a matter of course, to call upon the customs and excise services to provide it with data, often highly specific, to aid in its deliberations
over duties, taxes, and regulations. Hardly less significantly, the Board of
Trade, established in 1696, routinely sought to collect and order data. Though
it mainly concerned itself with overseas trade and the utilization of colonial
resources, in its early years it also surveyed the numbers of people obtaining
poor relief.

Political arithmetic did not attempt a comprehensive assessment of the
whole of the economy. King and Davenant were not econometricians, indeed
political arithmetic did not really see itself as being a branch of what we call
'economics'. Rather they were men who liked to play with numbers in the hope
of finding the best ways of funding the great wars of the period. However, it
was one thing to use statistics, quite another to establish their primacy. The
quality of the underlying data was often suspect, allowing many opportunities
for pricking the bubbles of calculation. It is telling, for example, that in the
debate over the Anglo-French Commercial Treaty drawn up in 1713 the estimate of the balance of trade employed was one that had been produced forty
years earlier. Probably the most accurate work was undertaken by demo-
graphers. The pioneer here had been John Graunt who with great skill statistically analysed London's bills of mortality in 1662 and in 1693 Halley undertook
a comparable exercise on data relating to Breslau provided for him by Leibniz.
Consideration of issues such as life expectancy gained added urgency in the
1690s by the use of annuities and tontines as part of the burgeoning national
debt because information about survival rates at different ages was vital in
putting such loans upon a reasonably secure footing. Later work by de Moivre

on questions of risk and chance in the 1710s and 1720s laid a number of the actuarial bases upon which insurance companies were soon to depend.

Though political arithmetic was profoundly limited evidentially and thematically, it did create some new ways of looking at human problems. The concept of national income which Petty and King developed, crude though it was, attempted a comprehensive valuation of the national economy and of its components that was more precise than the vague assertions which had hitherto held sway. No less significantly, work on life expectancy began to show that though to an individual mortality appeared random, among large communities there were clear patterns to be discerned. It was a big step to move from a world where death might occur tomorrow to establishing the statistical probabilities of lifespans. Of course there were those who remained profoundly suspicious of the quantitative approach to social and political issues, decrying its crude materialism and limited agenda. Such a reaction was voiced most potently by Swift in 1729 in his short work 'A modest proposal for preventing the children of poor people in Ireland, from being a burden to their parents or country'—employing the cold language of the social scientist he satirized political arithmetic by calculating the benefits to Ireland of killing and eating young children. But though the golden age of political arithmetic passed with the death of King in 1712 and Davenant in 1714, it continued to play a significant role in many spheres through the eighteenth century.[58]

There were, of course, many other ways contemporaries addressed questions of the organization of society. Closest to political arithmetic was a flourishing literature dealing with economic issues. Often that literature has been viewed as 'mercantilist', supposedly an influential, intellectually conservative, and highly unrealistic body of thought. Though such a view has proved long lived it is inaccurate. Its strength can be traced back to its originator, Adam Smith, who invented it in 1776 to provide a straw man to be cut down by the knight of free trade. To Smith the mercantile system was predicated on the belief that, in a commercial economy without gold or silver mines (such as England), economic well-being could be measured by its bullion stocks. In turn, increasing those stocks could only be achieved by ensuring exports outvalued imports, and systems of duties, regulations, and monopolies were erected to produce such an end. According to Smith the prime movers in this system were merchants and their cronies who brought undue pressure to bear upon governments to introduce policies that were often detrimental to the interests of consumers.

[58] Some have argued a different case. The view adopted here is based upon J. Hoppit, 'Political Arithmetic in Eighteenth-Century England', *Economic History Review*, 49 (1996), pp. 516–40.

'Mercantilism' was not a concept employed in England around 1700, it was invented retrospectively to give order to a confused situation. As such it does usefully point up some of the assumptions upon which economic thought was based around the start of the eighteenth century. England was frequently characterized as a commercial nation, peculiarly blessed to exploit international opportunities. 'Trade is the *Life Blood* that runs through the Veins of the Nation, that moves, maintains, and enlivens the whole Body of the People from the meanest Cottage, to the *Royal Throne*.'[59] Equally, there was much worry about the balance of trade. And nobody thought that sustained economic growth could be based upon continuous improvements in productivity. Though much effort was put into 'projects', technological change was invariably seen as providing limited and short-term benefits. Fundamentally, the world economy was often seen as a fixed cake, where one nation could only increase its share at the expense of another.

'Mercantilism', however, is a term with many weaknesses. It ascribes a coherence and sense of identity to ideas that were actually produced in a wide range of non-programmatic ways. Second, in framing what we would call economic policy, governments naturally attended to external trade, but they were also heavily influenced by the need to fill their own coffers, maintain domestic social stability (including the promotion of agriculture), and ensure the nation was adequately protected against external threats. Much economic thought and economic policy was given over to issues such as emigration and immigration, public and private finance, weights and measures, roads and rivers, patents and projects. It is interesting to note how little use was made in this period of data on bullion flows, a situation at odds with a dominant mercantilist ideology. Third, there was a very confused relationship between economic ideas and policy-makers. Merchants and chartered companies vied for the ear of government with landowners, industrialists, guilds, corporations, and other vested interests. Further, it is notable that merchants and monopolies were increasingly coming into conflict in this period, a conflict which saw many advocate free trade in what were effectively Smithian terms. Ideas of the exploitation of international comparative advantage and the benefits of extensions of the division of labour began to be aired, most powerfully in Dudley North's *Discourses upon Trade* (1691) and Henry Martyn's *Considerations on the East India Trade* (1701). Both the Royal Africa Company and the East India Company came in for sustained criticism in this period, admittedly sometimes for political reasons. One line of reasoning was simply economic, that 'The success and improvements of trade depend wholly upon supplying the commodities cheap

[59] J. Whiston, *The Causes of our Present Calamities in Reference to the Trade of the Nation Fully Discovered* (1696), p. 3.

at market . . . Now it is impossible that any company can do this upon equal terms with a private merchant'.[60] Another, more missionary view, reading more like 1846 than 1696, was that 'All monopolies, restraints of trade to companies exclusive of all others, are narrow thoughts that spring up in narrow souls, and contradict the great designe of God almighty, which is to civilize the whole race of mankind, to spread trade, commerce, arts, manufactures, and by them christianity from pole to pole'.[61]

PHILOSOPHICAL POLITICS

Central to the political turmoil of the seventeenth century were different ideas about the nature of and relationship between civil and ecclesiastical authority. It was, indeed, a century of remarkable intellectual fertility and ferocity over such issues. Not only was blood shed over ideas but the whirlwind of debate, literary and oral, drew in all sections of society. The presses churned out volume after volume of political argument and it has been estimated that some 5,000–6,000 polemical pieces were published between 1689 and 1714. By Anne's reign a range of periodicals from across the political spectrum provided a constant stream of commentary. As might be expected, in the first place attention was directed towards comprehending the Revolution and its aftermath and only once it was implicitly accepted that the new regime was likely to remain intact did consideration shift to the nature of the new leviathan of the fiscal-military and, after 1707, British State.

Many reacted to the chaos that had run through the reigns of Charles I and his two sons by stressing that man was and had to be a sociable animal. Hobbes, with the significance he attached to materialism and self-interest, was something of a bogeyman by the late seventeenth century. He was further seen as having originated freethinking, the dangerous creed of subjecting all aspects of civil society to the glare of scepticism and reason. In 1666 Parliament blamed him both for the fire of London and the plague, and in 1683 his *Leviathan* (1651) was burned by Oxford University. Other freethinkers, such as Spinoza in the first rank and John Toland in the second, were also widely condemned. Yet though such thinkers might be deplored, they could not be ignored, not least because their ideas had to be countered with at least some semblance of rational argument. The key questions raised were, what were the ties that bound politico-religious society together and where did sovereign power reside?

---

[60] J. Trenchard and T. Gordon, *Cato's Letters: or, Essays on Liberty, Civil and Religious, and Other Important Subjects*, ed. R. Hamowy, 2 vols. (Indianapolis, 1995), vol. 2, p. 645. The title of this edition was 'Monopolies and Exclusive Companies, how Pernicious to Trade'.

[61] *The Diary and Autobiography of Edmund Bohun Esq.*, ed. S. Wilton Rix (1853), p. 134.

Several answers were provided. The majority of political thought in the 1690s was founded upon assumptions derived from scriptural and historical authority. However, a minority, generally republicans, put those authorities effectively at nought and looked to first principles. At this extreme some believed that originally God had established all men equal in a state of nature. Only through the rise of private property and exchange did hierarchy emerge. In this view, political systems were man-made, effectively based upon a contract of rights and responsibilities for both rulers and ruled. Reason not faith should be the guiding light. The foremost exponent of such an approach was John Locke whose *Two Treatises of Government* (1689, though dated 1690) sought to demolish patriarchal theories and to establish the 'Original, Extent, and End of Civil-Government'. In his view 'Reason, which God hath given to be the Rule betwixt Man and Man' provided 'the common bond whereby humane kind is united into one fellowship and societie'. His emphasis upon reason meant that '*Voluntary Agreement gives . . . Political Power to Governours* for the Benefit of their Subjects, to secure them in the Possession and Use of their Properties' and that there was a right of resistance against a tyrannical ruler.[62]

The *Two Treatises* is a remarkable book, unquestionably the greatest work of political thought published in this period. Shaftesbury admired Locke because 'No one has done more towards the recalling of philosophy from barbarity, into use and practice of the world, and into the company of the better and politer sort'.[63] And because the *Two Treatises* attached so much significance to ascertaining universal principles rather than depending upon historical precedence it has remained a potent text. Yet it is easy to misunderstand its significance in the England of William III and Anne. In the first place it was mainly written before 1683 and passed comment upon the Glorious Revolution rather indirectly. Moreover, except among some Whigs, even as a contribution to the intense debate of the 1690s it made little impression and was generally ignored until 1703 (though in Oxford in 1695 it was reported to have made 'a great noise').[64] Partly this was because Locke sometimes followed other authors, among them Tyrrell and Pufendorf; partly it was because other authors, such as Sidney, gained a wider currency; more important, the very radicalism of the ideas was unpalatable to many. Locke was himself well aware of how dangerous his thinking might appear and was under no illusions about the risks that he ran—from exile in 1683 he had watched helplessly as Algernon Sidney, another great theorist, was executed partly because he had dared to challenge Filmer's *Patriarcha*. The *Two Treatises* was published anonymously

---

[62] Locke, *Two Treatises*, p. 383.   [63] *Letters of Shaftesbury*, p. 2.
[64] H. M. C., *The Manuscripts of S. H. Le Fleming, Esq.* (1890), p. 335.

and Locke resolutely refused to acknowledge them as his (though many confidently ascribed them to him).

At the other extreme to Locke were those who believed that God had made society rigidly hierarchical, with a hereditary monarch at its head, holding sovereign power. As God's earthly representative the monarch was due complete obedience; active resistance was an anathema, though obedience might be passive rather than energetic. This had been a commonplace among supporters of Charles II and James II, not least among the Anglican clergy before the crisis of 1688. It was forcefully articulated in Filmer's *Patriarcha*, written before the first civil war though only published in 1680. After the Revolution such a position was more difficult to maintain (and it is notable that Filmer was largely ignored), but the High Church did not abandon it, for obedience was seen as a precondition for maintaining an orderly society. Tory, or what would now be called 'conservative', political thought remained alive and well in the 1690s and 1700s. As Thomas Sherlock put it in 1704, 'To maintain the Establish'd Form of Government, is the First and Highest Duty of Men Acting in Society.'[65] No one theorist of the Tory/High Church view stands out in intellectual terms, but there is no doubt that it was widely and effectively espoused, not least because it was seen as the best means of maintaining the supremacy of the Church of England—though Filmer's ideas were on the wane. Potent examples include the substantial support shown for Sacheverell when he was prosecuted in 1710 for his famous sermon against 'false brethren', and the fact that between 1689 and 1700 six of the nine sermons to the House of Commons commemorating the execution of Charles I spoke out against the deposition of kings.

Tory or High Church ideology was authoritarian, occasionally dictatorial. It was an ideology of certainty and of a particular truth. Others wavered, believing that political society should accommodate as wide a range of opinion as possible. In essence this vacillation derived from the belief that if there was no question about the legitimacy of Protestantism, the scriptures were at particular points too debatable to afford the Anglican Church, or the monarch at its head, the right of unquestioning devotion. Indeed, to Gilbert Burnet, the leading exponent of such views, 'The *Supream Authority* must . . . be . . . with those who have the *Legislative Power* . . . but not with those who have only the *Executive*; which is plainly a *Trust*, when it is separated from the *Legislative Power*; and all *Trusts*, by their nature import, that those to whom they are given, are accountable.'[66] A less prescriptive and exclusive political society was

<hr>

[65] Quoted in M. A. Goldie, 'Tory Political Thought 1689–1714', Ph.D. thesis (University of Cambridge, 1978), p. 20.

[66] G. Burnet, *A Second Collection of Several Tracts and Discourses, Written in the Years 1686, 1687, 1688, 1689* (1689), p. 120.

envisaged. In this latitudinarian or 'Low Church' view Dissent was legitimate and limited religious toleration was necessary to involve everyone in the commonwealth. Citizenship in this scheme was earned by true piety. This had a historical dimension, the reign of Charles II being seen as so vicious and debauched that it was the duty of the godly to clean the Augean stables.

A more latitudinarian view of civil society was not far removed from one that gave great weight to historical example and legal precedence. One form of such an approach was to attempt the revival of the purity of the ancient constitution, a position that had been used to oppose all the Stuart monarchs. In such thinking, if only those political relationships which had existed at the dawn of Parliament were restored, then civil society might again take a settled form. This gave great authority to the common law and increasingly such an emphasis often went hand in hand with a belief in legislative sovereignty. One important difficulty contemporaries faced when looking to the past as a guide to the present was that determining just what happened in the mists of time was often unclear and hotly debated. Among many uncertainties were questions over the original nature of the common law and Parliament, and of how and why statute law and judicial precedence had over time acted upon the authority of common law. Because such questions could not be conclusively answered, despite the best efforts of historians and archive grubbers, it was possible for ancient constitutionalism to be used to support both a conservative and a radical vision of civil society.

Historically inspired thinking about political society looked at a wide range of examples. One rich mine was the ancient world, with Rome providing particularly impressive examples of both effective and ineffective authorities. Many, looking to this classical past, came to emphasize the importance of ensuring that those holding political power acted virtuously as much as advocating particular political structures. Central to this interpretation was the belief that only those who knew their society intimately and were intellectually and economically independent could avoid the lure of executive corruption and frame policies that were unambiguously for the national good. Such ideas might be traced back directly to classical authorities such as Aristotle but more often they were also placed in the context of Machiavelli and James Harrington. In *The Commonwealth of Oceana* (1656) Harrington had provided a sociological analysis of political action that inspired much thinking in the late seventeenth century. Extensions of the state apparatus in the 1690s and the creation of a new form of wealth holding with the development of private ownership of shares in the national debt were seen as highly disruptive and dangerous, threatening to overturn the natural order. It is not surprising that as the changes in the 1690s were extended rather than reversed such ideas came to have a long-term significance, ranging from such works as Andrew

Fletcher's study of the relative merits of standing armies and militias in 1698 to the publication of Harrington's collected works in 1700, the *Examiner*, Trenchard and Gordon's *Cato's Letters* (1720–3), and, finally, Bolingbroke's assault upon Walpole in the *Craftsman* from 1726. Typical was the view that 'It is melancholy to consider that Power follows Property, when we consider at the same Time into what vile Hands that Property is fallen, and by what vile means'.[67] Such 'civic humanist' discourse, as it has been called, generally decried the corrosive effects of luxury and corruption upon the body politic and placed faith in gentlemen landowners.

In many respects neo-Harringtonian and civic humanist ideas returned to the issue of self-interest versus public spiritedness that had so concerned Hobbes. Such issues were, of course, not only discussed within the framework of political ideas. They also involved perceptions of economic activity and the nature of reason and personal morality which were to a considerable extent wider philosophical matters. Major developments in these areas came from the pens of Locke, the third Earl of Shaftesbury, and Mandeville. Here Locke's seminal work was the *Essay Concerning Human Understanding* (1690). As in the *Two Treatises* he laid great stress upon the role of reason, particularly exploring the importance of acquired knowledge rather than innate ideas. Yet though Voltaire declared that 'Never, perhaps, has a wiser, more methodical mind, a more precise logician existed than Mr Locke' to some Englishmen Locke appeared to challenge the importance of revealed religion.[68] A similar difficulty was encountered by Shaftesbury. His *Characteristicks of Men, Manners, Opinions, Times*, 3 vols. (1711) sought, amongst other things, to present philosophy as an alternative to the Church as the main way in which morality was established and regulated. He hoped that a culture of politeness that was reasoned and scholarly would take root among gentlemen, directing them in their role in society. It was a vision far removed from the iconoclastic Bernard Mandeville whose satire and apparent amorality resonated powerfully through succeeding decades. The sting in Mandeville's argument is neatly summed up in the full title to his most famous work, *The Fable of the Bees: or, Private Benefits, Public Vices*, which was first published in 1714, but controversial only when he appended to it an attack upon charity schools a decade later. He aimed to 'shew the Impossibility of enjoying all the most elegant Comforts of Life that are to be met with in an industrious, wealthy and powerful Nation, and at the same time be bless'd with all the Virtue and Innocence that can be wish'd for in a Golden Age'.[69] As he argued in the fable 'whilst Luxury Employ'd a

---

[67] *A Collection of all the Political Letters in the London Journal, to December 17, Inclusive, 1720* (1721), p. 4.

[68] *Letters on England*, p. 62.

[69] *The Fable of the Bees*, ed. P. Hart (Harmondsworth, 1970), pp. 54–5.

Million of the Poor, And odious Pride a Million more. Envy it self, and Vanity Were Ministers of Industry'.[70] Such ideas assaulted both the secular and spiritual conceptions of virtue widely employed at the time. That alone would have been enough to ensure that he was heaped with scorn. The reaction was the more severe because Mandeville wrote with great immediacy and imagination. Like Hobbes, some of whose ideas he shared, he simply could not be ignored.

ANCIENT AND MODERN

A deep reverence for the past existed in England in this period, especially for the ancient world and the national history. Awareness of the classical legacy, be it aesthetic, political, or ideological, retained a strong grip on polite society. Much of that grip was textual. Latin and Greek were not yet dead languages and the education of gentlemen (and some gentlewomen) continued to place considerable emphasis upon reading masterpieces in the original by the likes of Aristotle, Homer, Livy, Sophocles, and Virgil. Translations of the classics began to appear, such as Dryden (1700) and Pope's (1715–20) different versions of Homer's *Iliad*. The grand tour was in part designed to bring gentlemen face to face with some of the greatest physical remnants of Greek and Roman civilization. But the ancient world was not merely a preoccupation of the elite. The intersection of the Roman world with the rise of Christianity concerned everyone and was brought home especially vividly at Easter. And Roman Britain had left a rich legacy. The antiquity of many prominent towns was traced back to the Roman occupation, Hadrian's wall loomed large (it was then known as the Picts's wall), and occasionally other physical remnants reared their head: Defoe was shown 'some old Roman coins' near Tadcaster and on the road to York 'saw plainly the Roman highway'; and in January 1712 a Roman mosaic pavement was discovered at Stunsfield near Woodstock in Oxfordshire which quickly became a popular tourist sight.[71] Such findings prompted some members of the Society of Antiquaries to form a Society of Roman Knights in 1722 to study Roman Britain—remarkably two women became members. But the Society was short-lived and it was left to individual scholars to press on, notably Alexander Gordon whose *Itinerarium Septentrionale* (1726) surveyed Scotland and northern England and John Horsley who worked through the 1720s to produce a detailed appreciation of Roman Britain that was finally published in 1732.

To the elite the ancient world was studied not only because of its contribution to the origins of the contemporary world but because it provided eternal

[70] *The Fable of the Bees*, p. 68.
[71] D. Defoe, *A Tour Through the Whole Island of Great Britain*, ed. P. Rogers (Harmondsworth, 1978), p. 518.

truths which no one aspiring to gentility could do without. Such truths might be specific bodies of knowledge (such as the classical orders of architecture, Pythagorean mathematics, or Aristotelian logic), the dramatic fables of mythology, or the lessons of history. Not the least of those lessons was understanding how and why empires and civilizations rose and fell. A cyclical rather than linear (still less progressive) interpretation of history was common. In this the rise of ancient civilizations was due to social discipline, military might, and conquest, and the fall to the collapse of Spartan values under the weight of luxury, corruption, and effeminacy. Employing the ideas of the Roman historian Sallust, Addison presented the case with typical elegance: 'When a Government flourishes in Conquests, and is secure from foreign Attacks, it naturally falls into all the Pleasures of Luxury; and as these Pleasures are very expensive, they put those who are addicted to them upon raising fresh supplies of Mony, by all the Methods of Rapaciousness and Corruption'.[72] Some believed that such an explanation provided a clear template for England's empire, others that it provided a more general warning for civil society.

Not everyone was convinced of the importance of the classical world, indeed doubts had long been expressed. Its paganism was one obstacle but another was the willingness of some to see the modern world's achievements as often superior to those of Greece and Rome, if only by reference to the analogy of dwarfs standing on the shoulders of giants. There was, indeed, an intense intellectual debate—not only in England but also in France—between the 'Ancients' and the 'Moderns' in this period. It began with Sir William Temple's 'An essay upon the ancient and modern learning' (1690) and involved, on the side of the moderns, such intellectual heavyweights as William Wotton, Richard Bentley (a distinguished classical scholar), and Humphrey Wanley. That this was no mere academic exercise but a debate that touched many is evidenced by Swift's pro-ancient *A Tale of a Tub* (1704), one of his earliest and most brilliant satires—according to Atterbury, another ancient, 'The town is wonderfully pleased with it.'[73] Characteristic of Temple's position was that he knew 'of no new philosophers that have made entries upon that noble stage for fifteen hundred years', classifying Descartes and Hobbes as decidedly second-rate. It says much about the vulnerability of such view that, only three years after publication of Newton's *Principia*, Temple concluded that 'There is nothing new in astronomy to vie with the ancients, unless it be the Copernican system'.[74] John Ray privately summarized the contrary case.

---

[72] *The Spectator*, vol. 1, p. 234.

[73] *The Miscellaneous Works of Bishop Atterbury*, ed. J. Nichols, 4 vols. (1789–90), vol. 1, p. 318. Swift had been secretary to Temple for a time and was his literary executor.

[74] J. Swift, *A Tale of a Tub and Other Works*, ed. A. Ross and D. Woolley (Oxford, 1991), p. 157.

In summe the ancients excel the moderns in nothing but acuteness of wit and elegancy of language in all their writings, in their poetry and oratory. As for painting and sculpture, and music and architecture, some of the moderns I think do equal, if not excel, the best of them, not in the theory only, but also in the practice of those arts; neither do we give place to them in politics or morality; but in natural history and experimental philosophy we far transcend them. In the purely mathematical sciences abstracted from matter, as geometry and arithmetic, we may vie with them; as also in history; but in astronomy, geography, and chronology, we excel them much.[75]

The moderns produced detailed critiques of ancient knowledge, often finding plentiful evidence of ignorance and misunderstanding. In the face of this onslaught the ancients had to shift their ground somewhat, stressing the uncertainties of much knowledge, new and old, and the timeless moral significance of the best ancient learning. It was not, of course, a debate that could be positively resolved one way or another, not least because the two sides employed different criteria. But that it took place at all and that the moderns scored so many points is rich in significance. It marked, in truth, a significant step on the road to the idea of progress which was to become such a central part of many people's intellectual baggage in the nineteenth and twentieth centuries.

Not only the ancient world but England's history were subject to intense scrutiny in this period. As we have seen, this was partly politically inspired as the past was ransacked for precedents to apply to current crises. In particular, this might lead deep into the study of the Anglo-Saxon Church and law, feudal relations after the Norman conquest, the medieval origins of Parliament, and the development of Anglicanism in the sixteenth and seventeenth centuries. It is noteworthy that an important contribution to historical scholarship in this period was made by the non-jurors and that there was no fixed border between the study of history, philology, politics, or theology. Probably the best work of historical scholarship to appear in the period, though written earlier, was Clarendon's *The History of the Rebellion and Civil Wars in England begun in the year 1641*, 3 vols. (Oxford, 1702–4) which provided a Tory view of recent history. Still, not all history was so obviously politically inspired. Much effort was spent upon producing editions of original documents, including Thomas Rymer's *Foedera*, 15 vols. (1702–11), which reprinted alliances and papers relating to foreign policy, John Smith's edition of Bede's *Ecclesiastical History* (1722), and Edmund Gibson's work on the Anglo-Saxon Chronicle. Equally, it says much that the position of the Historiographer Royal passed from men of literature such as Thomas Shadwell and John Dryden in the 1670s and 1680s to serious historical scholars such as Rymer and Thomas Madox in the

---

[75] *The Correspondence of John Ray*, ed. E. Lankester (1848), p. 229.

early eighteenth century. A number of general histories began to appear such as *A Complete History of England* (1706), in three tedious volumes and with 780 subscribers.[76] More notable was James Tyrrell's *The General History of England, as well Ecclesiastical as Civil*, 3 vols. (1696–1704).

A concern for England's past also involved much archaeological and anti-quarian endeavour, often by major scholars. William Nicolson and Edmund Gibson made notable contributions, not least by revising Camden's *Britannia*; John Evelyn produced a major work of numismatics; John Aubrey dabbled in almost anything he could lay his hands on; and William Stukeley developed an interest in druids, spending months spread over many years at Stonehenge and Avebury making 'innumerable drawings & measurements'.[77] Much of the best work in these fields was done on a county or local basis, by men committed to setting relics in their specific geographical and historical context such as Thoresby in Yorkshire, Gough in Shropshire, and Aubrey in Wiltshire. Sub-stantially overlapping with natural history, much of this work never reached the printed page, but was passed from gentleman to gentleman in the post or over beer. Such antiquarianism is often paid little credit today, but then it provided an accessible, frequently immediate, and appealing way into Eng-land's past.

NEW LEARNING, PROVIDENCE, AND PROPHECY

In the twentieth century it has become usual to see science as fundamentally atheistical, the very bedrock of a non-spiritual world-view. From that per-ception it is a small step towards interpreting new learning in the seventeenth and early eighteenth centuries as a major contributor to secularization. Some contemporaries certainly thought so. Locke, for example, was often accused of being an atheist, whose ideas were 'a snare of the devil, thrown among sharp wits and ingenious youths to oppose their reason to revelation, and because they cannot apprehend reason, to make them sceptics, and so to entice them to read other books than the Bible'.[78] Yet many scientists—Ray and Flamsteed for example—had been ordained, and the majority of scholars were educated deep within the Anglican establishment, not least through a university education where clerics dominated the fellowship and life centred as much upon the chapel as the library or common room. Yet the worry that the new learning in general, and science more particularly, encouraged dangerous heterodoxy

---

[76] This is usually ascribed to White Kennett, but he admitted only to the last volume being his. See J. Levine, *The Battle of the Books: History and Literature in the Augustan Age* (Ithaca, 1991), p. 310.

[77] *The Family Memoirs of Stukeley*, p. 52.

[78] *Literary Remains of John Byrom*, vol. 1, p. 7.

never went away, despite the best efforts of the Church's supporters, not least because in the end science did pose awkward questions of Christianity.

Many in the period attempted to wed science to religion. Most commonly they were made compatible by asserting that only God could have created the enormous riches of the earth and the extraordinary complexities of the wider universe: 'the *Laws of Nature are the Laws of God*.'[79] In this view even if man lived in a clockwork universe God was its mechanic—Newton himself believed that the solar system must have had an 'Author'.[80] For many, every discovery of a new part of the machine or of how it operated merely served to heighten the glory of God. As Ray put it, 'If the number of Creatures be so exceeding great, how great nay immense must needs be the Power and Wisdom of him who form'd them all!'[81] Indeed, in this light scientific enquiry became a duty of the good Christian. Man was 'made as 'twere on purpose to observe, and survey, and set forth the Glory of the infinite *Creator*, manifested in his Works!'[82] Not to search after the truths of the physical world was to abandon the quest for spiritual fulfilment. At heart such an unsceptical position was providentialist, a common basis of many people's outlook.

Such views were often loudly proclaimed in the annual lecturers endowed by Boyle which began in 1692. Robert Boyle, who died in 1691, had been at the forefront of attempts to ensure that science embraced Christian orthodoxy. Evelyn thought that 'religion . . . runs through all [Boyle's] writings . . . and show how unjustly that aspersion has been cast on philosophy, that it disposes men to atheism.'[83] Under the terms of the endowment the Boyle lecturers were to argue for the Christian faith against infidels of all shades, such as atheists, pagans, Jews, and Muslims. Not all the lecturers engaged with the significance of the new science, but a number did, especially Richard Bentley and Samuel Clarke. And the high quality of the men chosen meant that when printed the lectures usually reached a wide audience. Reading them became a common part of gentlemanly education by the second decade of the eighteenth century. Indeed, it can reasonably be claimed that the utilization of Newtonian thinking by some of the lecturers had a much greater impact than the *Principia* itself —it is especially noteworthy that Bentley's lectures were translated into Latin, German, French, and Dutch and Derham's into Dutch, Swedish, and German.

[79] *The Athenian Oracle: being an Entire Collection of all the Valuable Questions and Answers in the Old Athenian Mercuries* (1703), p. 199.

[80] *Bentley Correspondence*, vol. 1, p. 49.

[81] J. Ray, *The Wisdom of God Manifested in the Works of the Creation* (1691), p. 8.

[82] W. Derham, *Physico-Theology: or, a Demonstration of the Being and Attributes of God, from his Works of Creation* (2nd edn., 1714), p. 259.

[83] *Diary and Correspondence of John Evelyn*, ed. W. Bray, 4 vols. (1850–2), vol. 3, p. 349.

Undoubtedly the relationship between science, religion, and society was in a considerable state of flux in this era. Again, Newton nicely illustrates the point. In the late eighteenth century the visionary poet and painter William Blake depicted Newton as a god-like geometer astride the earth. Such an image of Newton as the arch rationalist, the destroyer of divination, has been long-lived, but it is very largely wrong. Neither his writing nor reading bear it out. Looking at his working library, the largest category of holdings, over a quarter, were theological. The next largest category, about one-tenth, was what we would call 'chemistry' but which was dominated by works relating to alchemy—as one contemporary noted 'alchemy . . . lures on most lovers of chemistry.'[84] Just as the great man spent many years working on scriptural matters, theological and chronological, so he had long been fascinated by what we know to be forlorn attempts to turn base metals into gold. He saw no incongruity or incompatibility between those interests and his work on gravity or optics. He believed that mathematical explanations were applicable only to limited fields of enquiry and was certain of the need for speculative enquiry elsewhere, hence the alchemy. Indeed, he went further, believing, as many did, that prophecies could reasonably be attempted, offering many himself. It may appear odd, but Newton's interest in alchemy, theology, ancient chronology, and prophecy simply cannot be divorced from his authorship of the *Principia* and *Opticks*. More widely, in this period reason and unreason, fact and faith, cannot easily be separated.

The Scientific Revolution, far from simply overturning old ideas and beliefs often placed new ideas alongside them. Examples include the responses of astrology and prophecy to intellectual developments in the period. Clearly discoveries in astronomy in the seventeenth and early eighteenth centuries cut the ground from beneath astrology as an explanatory and predictive system. With the motion of planets and stars now reasonably understood in terms of gravitational pull, it became difficult to sustain the belief that changes in the night sky had any other significance or irregular import. Yet astrology did not disappear, especially among the labouring poor, and a significant (if decreasing) number remained attached to the view that, rightly interpreted, particular types of evidence allowed prophecies to be made of the future. One form of evidence was providential. God provided signs, both in the Bible and, hardly less significantly, in natural phenomena, such as the minor earthquake that hit southern England in 1692 or the dramatic appearance of the aurora borealis in 1716. Even the landing of a 'vast great' salmon from the Thames near Whitehall 'some People judge to be Ominous'.[85] Other sources of prophecies

---

[84] *London in 1710: From the Travels of von Uffenbach*, p. 29.
[85] *The Weekly Journal, or British Gazetteer*, 27 July 1717, p. 793.

were often magical or mystical, found in ancient documents or perhaps dreams. Bishop Lloyd of Worcester and St Asaph gained 'the name of the Old Prophet', for example predicting in 1711 a 'war of religion which will last till the final destruction of Pope and Popery' and almanacs continued to offer numerous predictions.[86] Few abandoned their Christian faith and for them there was still some room for miracles and prophecies whatever proponents of the clockwork universe might say.

CONCLUSION

A revolution in ideas took place in England between the deaths of Francis Bacon in 1626 and Isaac Newton in 1727. This culminated not only in particular intellectual discoveries such as the role of gravity but also in the dramatic growth of debate and discourse, especially after 1695. Contemporaries were amazed but such fertility, and no matter how much they worried about it there could be no turning back of the clock. As more and more works sprang from the press, they often made their way deeper and deeper into society. This cannot be thought of simply in terms of the ploughman with his chapbook, the landowner his newspaper, and the scholar his turgid tome. Ideas knew no boundaries and floated on the thermals: in church, court, and inn. Moreover, if they acquired a certain permanence on the printed page, they became malleable around the kitchen table or in the coffee house. If the literary world was ever expanding, the spoken intellectual world of early Georgian England remained vital and alert.

The breadth of intellectual enquiry in the period cannot be overstressed. The established order was reconsidered not only in politico-religious terms, but also with regard to material, scientific, and historical issues. The scope of this endeavour has often been lost sight of. It was an endeavour with a wide appeal, not least because disciplinary boundaries were still highly permeable. Even among serious scholars, contemporaries did not yet worship at the altar of specialized knowledge. Moreover, ideas and learning did not take place in an unworldly vacuum, shut off from the Glorious Revolution, the battle over the nature of the established Church, the contest for the Protestant succession, or the waging of war. The flourishing periodical press provided a particularly potent means by which new ideas were popularized and disseminated. Addison, after all, was 'ambitious to have it said of me, that I have brought Philosophy out of Closets and Libraries, Schools and Colleges, to dwell in Clubs and Assemblies, at Tea-Tables, and in Coffee-Houses.'[87]

---

[86] *Memoirs of Thomas, Earl of Ailesbury, Written by Himself*, 2 vols. (1890), vol. 1, p. 254; H. M. C., *The Manuscripts of his Grace the Duke of Portland*, vol. 5 (1899), p. 128.

[87] *The Spectator*, vol. 1, p. 44.

Undeniably publications of the quality of the *Opticks*, *An Essay on Human Understanding*, and the *Spectator* had profound implications, forcing a re-thinking of many beliefs. But new ideas did not always sweep all before them. They wrestled, often unsuccessfully, with the old. As one Danish onlooker put it, 'the English proceed slowly . . . but investigate thoroughly'.[88] Moreover, we should be wary of believing that the change in intellectual climate was permanently progressive in character, leading inexorably to the glories of the Enlightenment. Astrology and prophecy had been diminished but not extinguished. We have seen how the Scientific Revolution took a somewhat different course in the early eighteenth century and similar changes also took place with regard to political arithmetic, economics, and historical research. Such changes were often integral to the nature of intellectual endeavour, but they also reflect the fact that the uncertainties of seventeenth-century England had provided a peculiarly fertile ground for new thinking. The ferment of ideas in Newton's England was partly generational. As that generation passed, so the stimuli to intellectual endeavour became increasingly commercial. The age of patronage, of Hobbes and Locke, overlapped with, but was quite different from, that of the *Spectator* or Dr Johnson's *Dictionary* (1755).

---

[88] *Ludvig Holberg's Memoirs: An Eighteenth Century Danish Contribution to International Understanding*, ed. S. E. Fraser (Leiden, 1970), p. 42.

CHAPTER 7

Faith and Fervour

Few contemporaries could imagine a life without Christianity. It gave them hope and understanding, experience and identity. Very few denied that 'God is spirit, light, and life, infinitely wise, good, just, strong, all-knowing, all-present, all-powerful, the creator and maker of all things visible and invisible.'[1] But because man was flawed, 'apt to run into corruption and misery', belief in Jesus and his resurrection provided the means of salvation.[2] Surrounded on all sides by uncertainties—of the afterlife, weather, economy, social order, and health—God provided a massive rock of wisdom and dependability. As one pious dame put it, 'I adore the Patience, Wisdom, Power, and Goodness of GOD, that protects my sinful and unprofitable Life so long.'[3] Such sentiments were commonplace at the time, providing a reference point for virtually all Christians. Yet, though foreigners often remarked that England was highly tolerant of religious opinion, those reference points were also keenly debated in the context of the nature and role of organized religion. Though often the eye is more seared by the heat than blinded by the light of those debates, it must not be forgotten that those struggles were so significant precisely because of the supreme importance of religion to people personally.

Christianity was not, of course, merely a matter of individual salvation. It had a prominent role in defining public morality and in providing ways of conceptualizing wealth creation and political authority. More dramatically, questions about the true nature of the reformed Church that had raged since the break with Rome under Henry VIII were given fresh impetus by the religious causes of the Glorious Revolution. James II's promotion of Roman Catholicism and his politic indulgence towards Protestant Dissent had terrified the Church of England and its supporters. The accession of William III could not completely calm the situation. The Church's abandonment of James II in 1688

---

[1] A. Conway, *The Principles of the Most Ancient and Modern Philosophy*, ed. A. P. Coudert and T. Corse (Cambridge, 1996), p. 9.

[2] J. Locke, *The Reasonableness of Christianity*, ed. I. T. Ramsey (1958), p. 75.

[3] *An Account of the Life and Death of Mrs. Elizabeth Bury, who Died, May the 11th 1720. Aged 76*, ed. S. Bury (3rd edn., 1721), p. 145.

compromised central tenets of its political philosophy that cast grave doubt upon its self-identity and confidence. Moreover, William did not wish merely to restore the religious *status quo* of the 1670s. Like James, though for different reasons, he saw the social and political value of religious toleration and of a less dictatorial State Church. Many in the Church willingly fantasized about the potentially damaging consequences of his Calvinist upbringing and, after 1701, worried that the Hanoverian succession would permanently reduce their Church's significance. This anxiety was further exacerbated by worries over popular religious behaviour following the Toleration Act of 1689 and over the intellectual challenges to orthodoxy presented with particular force in this era. The generation after 1689 experienced, therefore, debates over religion hardly less intense than those which had raged so fiercely in the middle of the sixteenth century and during the Interregnum. Yet by the early 1720s religious debate had markedly subsided and, despite continuing concern with relief for Dissenters, the Methodist revival of the mid-century, and momentary outbursts such as that surrounding the 'Jew Bill' in 1753, it was not until the eras of the American and French Revolutions that religious questions once again formed a significant active element in social and political controversies.

CHURCH AND SOCIETY

The Church of England was legally established as the national Church and given huge privileges commensurate with that elevated status. At its head stood the monarch; bishops sat in the House of Lords; and, under the terms of the Test and Corporation Acts (1661 and 1673), all holders of civil and military offices, as well as students and tutors at Oxford and Cambridge, were required to be communing members such that even some Dissenters wanting to hold office felt bound to conform occasionally. Its hierarchy of dioceses, archdeaconries, and parishes covered the whole country and its clergy were central figures in the community. Parish clergy were looked to as spiritual and community leaders and much local administration, including the repair of roads and the operation of the poor laws, took place through the vestry. People supported the Church through the payment of tithes and were subject to its disciplinary strictures and structures, not least through the Church courts. For most villages the church provided an architectural centrepiece to the community. Like it or not, no one could ignore the Church of England.

As an institution the Church of England had a massive social presence in this period and over 90 per cent of the population might formally be counted as its members. Fundamentally this rested upon its spiritual function, providing the wherewithal for people's salvation. Though some looked to other religions for this they were but a small minority. Most people were baptized at their parish church and in adolescence might confirm their membership. By attending church services people sought spiritual succour but also publicly demonstrated their faith and underwrote a powerful and socially diverse community. It was entirely natural to them to structure important parts of their lives around the Church of England. This took place most obviously through the rites of passage—baptism, confirmation, marriage, and burial. But the Church's calendar, Lent, Easter, the harvest festival, and Christmas, all bulked large. In certain respects indeed the Church most people experienced had hardly changed over the centuries. Much still centred upon services in the parish church and the ministrations of the priest. Legally all were meant to attend some form of religious service on Sundays and to observe it as a day of rest. In most villages two services were held on Sundays and perhaps one or two in the week, though in towns they were somewhat more frequent. The centrepiece of these services was provided by the sermon, simple psalm singing (hymns were more popular among Dissenters), and the lessons. Communion was rarely offered more than monthly, and more usually only three or four times a year.

Just how edifying and popular church services were is hard to determine. Evidence of disrespect can be found—one man was charged with 'defiling the house of God in pissing in the parish Church'—but it is unlikely to be typical.[4] Only tidbits of information provide an insight into popular religious observance. It is clear that few resorted to churches on holy days, seeing Sunday services as the mainstay, one commentator ascribing the decline in holy day observance 'to the backwardness of the People, who either thro' false and superstitious Notions, or an immoderate pursuit of Worldly Profit and Pleasure, are not easily drawn together to Worship God on these days.'[5] Further, if most were baptized, married, and buried in church and attended services with some regularity a good number avoided catechism, confirmation, and communion. In Pewsey, Wiltshire, only about 20 per cent of adults took communion in 1709–10; Bishop Green of Ely estimated for his diocese that at Easter 1728 the figure was not quite 12 per cent; and numerous clergymen would have agreed that 'Many of age seldome or never communicate at all.'[6] Such low figures ran directly counter to the strictures of divines who implored the need for frequent communion. Most who took communion, moreover, did so only once or twice a year, not the minimum of three times required by the canon of 1604. Explaining this is difficult, but may be due to a popular

[4] Quoted in C. E. Davies, 'The Enforcement of Religious Uniformity in England, 1668–1700, with Special Reference to the Dioceses of Chichester and Worcester', D.Phil. thesis (University of Oxford, 1983), p. 318.

[5] [J. Johnson], *The Clergy-Man's Vade Mecum: or, an Account of the Ancient and Present Church of England; the Duties and Rights of the Clergy; and of their Privileges and Hardships* (1706), p. 152.

[6] *Buckinghamshire Dissent and Parish Life 1669–1712*, ed. J. Broad, Buckinghamshire Record Society, 28 (1993), p. 149. Thomas Green, 1658–1738, Fellow of Corpus Christi College, Cambridge, 1680 and Master 1699–1713, Bishop of Norwich 1721–3 and of Ely 1723–38.

perception that the sacrament of communion was reserved for the respectable, entailing as it did a repentance for past sins and a sacred obligation to future good conduct upon pain of eternal damnation, undertakings many felt unable to make. Frequently communing members of the Church tended to be from the more prosperous sections of the community.

Religious practice depended heavily upon the abilities and enthusiasm of the exclusively male priesthood, of whom there were about 12,000 serving some 9,500 parishes. Though priests came from a wide variety of backgrounds, often from the ranks of craftsmen and tradesmen, in contrast to a century before an overwhelming majority were now graduates of Oxford or Cambridge—in Leicestershire in 1714 only 3 per cent of incumbents had no degree. Most were ordained in their mid-twenties, found a parish after a few years, and served it until death. They saw themselves as the agents of a vital organism and were dedicated to its prosperity. Few, however, could hope for advancement or promotion. For most it was a life of toil, with only modest material rewards, undertaken for the very best of reasons. Their function was truly pastoral, involving the care not only of souls but often the education of the young, the maintenance of the poor (often as trustees of small local charities), and the health of the infirm. They were real pillars of the community. Quite rightly the quality of the priesthood was widely seen as a critical factor in the Church of England's mission and many of England's 22 bishops strove to ensure that only those with adequate testimonials and requisite abilities were ordained.[7] Certainly far from all who presented themselves for the priesthood were admitted. Bishops also sought to keep a close eye upon what the clergy did. Most undertook periodic visitations of their diocese. In 1690 Simon Patrick, newly consecrated as Bishop of Chichester, thought little of touring his diocese in the midst of the serious invasion threat.[8] In 1700 William Lloyd, recently arrived as Bishop of Worcester, travelled through much of his diocese, meeting with his clergy and confirming as many as 10,000 young people, and was soon heavily involved in local electoral politics.[9] Wake, Bishop of Lincoln, also confirmed large numbers and pioneered printed questionnaires to be circulated and completed by his clergy in advance of his visitations, providing an important source of reference, an innovation subsequently copied by many eminent divines.[10]

[7] Wales had four dioceses (Bangor, Llandaff, St Asaph's, and St David's); there was also the see of Sodor and Man.

[8] Simon Patrick, 1626–1707, educated Queens' College, Cambridge, Bishop of Chichester 1689 translated to Ely 1691, early member of SPCK.

[9] William Lloyd, 1627–1717, educated Oriel and Jesus College, Oxford, Bishop of St Asaph 1680, Lichfield and Coventry 1692, and Worcester 1700, renowned for his prophesying.

[10] William Wake, 1657–1737, educated Christ Church, Oxford, Canon of Christ Church 1689–1702, Bishop of Lincoln 1705, Archbishop of Canterbury 1716, left his library to Christ Church.

Despite political divisions, the spiritual, administrative, and personal abilities of those on the episcopal bench in this period were often considerable.
Including the sees in Wales and Sodor and Man a total of 85 men held office
for at least a part of this period. Like the clergy as a whole, they came from a
range of backgrounds; roughly two-thirds had been educated at Oxford, the
remainder at Cambridge;[11] and most obtained their sees in ripe middle age (and
so over 40 per cent had been born before the Civil Wars). Bishops did not
retire, they died in office, though with almost a third transferred from one see
to another only a half served a see for more than ten years. Their work was
extensive, requiring care of the diocese and parliamentary politics. Few could
hole up in their palaces, they had to be peripatetic, not least in spending several months each year in London. Not all, however, were as industrious or
committed as Burnet, Gibson, or Sharp.[12] The Calvinistic Thomas Barlow,
Bishop of Lincoln from 1675 to 1691 may have visited his cathedral just once
during his tenure and the controversial Benjamin Hoadly, Bishop of Bangor
from 1716 to 1721, never visited his diocese.[13] And ten bishops were deprived
of their sees: eight as non-jurors in 1689–90; Watson of St David's in 1699 for
'Simony, Exaction and False Certifying'; and Atterbury of Rochester in 1723
for Jacobitical activities.[14]

Whatever efforts bishops might take, most clergymen ministered in relative
isolation, allowing in some cases serious problems to arise and to flourish
unchecked—few dioceses had a system of rural deans in operation and a plan
to revive them in 1711 did not reach fruition. Lloyd urged one vicar to 'be
more diligent in the Dutys of his place by Catechising ye youth and administering ye Sacrt, &c., and not to tipple and frequent Alehouses.'[15] Sharp,
Archbishop of York, chided another in fulsome terms:

[11] The exceptions were Burnet of Salisbury, who did not attend university, though he became
a professor at Glasgow, and Wilson of Sodor and Man who attended Trinity College, Dublin.

[12] Gilbert Burnet, 1643–1715, leading supporter of William III, born Aberdeenshire, educated
Marischal College, Aberdeen, Fellow of the Royal Society 1664, published *History of the Reformation in England*, 3 vols. (1679–1714), ministered to Lord Russell at his execution in 1683, spent much
of next five years on Continent, outlawed by James II 1687, accompanied William 1688, Bishop
of Salisbury 1689, attended William on his deathbed, his *History of his Own Time* (1723–34) is
a valuable Whig interpretation. Edmund Gibson, 1669–1748, Fellow Queen's College, Oxford,
1694, noted scholar and active when Librarian at Lambeth Palace, Bishop of Lincoln 1716–23
and of London 1723–48, worked closely with Walpole until they split in 1736 over the Quaker's
Tithe Bill. John Sharp, 1645–1714, educated Christ's College, Cambridge, refused to read
Declaration of Indulgence 1688, Archbishop of York 1702, Union Commissioner 1706.

[13] Thomas Barlow, 1607–1691, educated Queen's College, Oxford, Librarian of the Bodleian
in Oxford 1642–60, accepted William III in 1689. For Hoadly, see below, note 71.

[14] *The Post Boy*, 3–5 August 1699, [p. 2]. Thomas Watson, 1637–1717, Fellow St John's
College, Cambridge, opposed William's government.

[15] *Diary of Francis Evans, Secretary to Bishop Lloyd, 1699–1706*, ed. D. Robertson, Worcester
Historical Society (Worcester, 1903), p. 32.

It is complained to me, that you have for some considerable time used your parishioners very ill in your performance of divine offices among them. As for sermons, you rarely give them any; and as for the divine service of the Church, you begin it so uncertainly as to the hour, and you perform it so indecently as to the manner, as if you really had a mind to shew your hearers that you are so far out of charity with them, that you do not desire that they should receive any benefit, even by their saying of their prayers.[16]

Yet such shortcomings suggest personal rather than structural failings. Just as every sermon could not be a finely honed masterpiece, so not every incumbent could be above reproach. More significant was the problem of clerical poverty, for many livings provided very little income, not least because some had surrendered tithe income. If there were rich livings, many were decidedly poor. In 1704 out of 9,180 livings paying the Crown 'first fruits and tenths' some 3,826 (42 per cent) were worth less than £50 per annum, and 1,216 (13 per cent) less than £20 per annum.[17] In consequence, some, so to speak, turned to work at the plough or the forge to make ends meet. To some this degraded the ministry (though it might also be said to have narrowed the gap between a cleric and his flock): 'There are a vast many poor Wretches, whose Benefices do not bring them in enough to buy them Cloaths. This obliges 'em to look out for other Ways, and those often sordid ones, to get their Bread; and thus the Ministry grows scandalous.'[18] A more serious consequence of clerical poverty was the encouragement it gave to ministers to hold more than one living, inevitably giving rise to non-residence. In Ely diocese only four in ten parishes had a resident minister in 1728; in Leicestershire in 1714 a similar proportion of livings were held in plurality. In this it is important to note that the Church imperfectly directed its own destiny, for it controlled only about a quarter of appointments to livings. Over half were held by private individuals, about a tenth in the hands of the Crown, with the remainder controlled by bodies such as Oxford and Cambridge colleges. Advowsons had long since become a piece of property to be bought and sold, liable to all the benefit and mischief that the free market could muster.

Pluralism and non-residence necessarily diminished the opportunity for a cleric to play a full part in the life of the community. He might ride into a parish to conduct services and then ride out again. To some parishioners, not always the poorest, the Church was indeed somewhat remote and forbidding, less an agent of salvation than an arm of authority. On the one hand the Church

---

[16] T. Sharp (ed.), *The Life of John Sharp*, 2 vols. (1825), vol. 1, p. 156.

[17] First fruits and tenths had become by this date the payment by the incumbent of his initial year's income to the Crown. In 1704 there were an additional 1,975 (usually poor) livings which were not so charged and so excluded from these figures.

[18] H. Misson, *Memoirs and Observations in his Travels Over England* (1719), p. 36.

was politically potent, not least because 'The religion by law established is such a vital part of the government, so constantly woven and mixed into every branch of it, that generally men look upon it as a good part of their property too'.[19] This meant that to most people bishops, clergy, and church courts were integral to the political authority and hierarchy which governed and sometimes dictated their lives. If that provided a sense of order it might also raise the hackles. Clerical views on personal morality—from sexual activity to Sunday trading, swearing to drinking—sometimes ran counter to those of parishioners, and prosecutions at church courts for immoralities of one sort or another continued to run at significant levels and necessarily antagonized some. Burnet was clear that the clergy had 'to watch over Souls, to keep them from error, and to alarm them out of their sins, by giving them *warning* of the Judgments of God', an obligation a small but increasing number further fulfilled by sitting on the judicial bench.[20] Intellectually the Church still exerted considerable influence through its dominance of the universities and, as has been seen, attempted to police the wider world of ideas. The Church was, of course, also a substantial landowner, liable to be bracketed in the eyes of poor labourers with the Crown and peerage. Further, the payment of tithes to the clergy might be viewed as a form of taxation and which, judging from the flow of litigation and legislation engendered, was widely unpopular.[21] It was rightly noted that 'The church of England . . . is a political society . . . united in the king as head, and organized by the bishops, for the executing those laws or government which he chuses' and the authority of the Church was most vividly demonstrated through the episcopal bench.[22] Sitting in Parliament, prelates made laws that affected all; the cathedral close dominated many cities; and splendid episcopal palaces provided vivid reminders of dramatic social inequalities and to some raised doubts about the spirituality at the heart of the Church's hierarchy—if most sees had an income of under £1,000 per annum Canterbury was worth some £5,000, Winchester over £3,500, York about £2,500, and London perhaps £2,300. Defoe noted 'that the Bishop of Durham is a temporal prince, that he keeps a court of equity, and also courts of justice in ordinary causes within himself. The church of Durham is eminent for its wealth; the bishopric is esteemed the

[19] Edward Hyde, Earl of Clarendon, *The History of the Rebellion and Civil Wars in England Begun in the year 1641*, ed. W. D. Macray, 6 vols. (Oxford, 1888), vol. 1, p. xlii. This volume was first published in 1703.

[20] G. Burnet, *A Discourse of the Pastoral Care* (1692), p. 4.

[21] Excluding proposals concerned with particular parishes, in this period Parliament passed five Acts dealing with tithes and considered sixteen others.

[22] 'The Amicable Reconciliation of the Dissenters to the Church of England . . .', in *A Collection of Scarce and Valuable Tracts, on the Most Interesting and Entertaining Subjects*, ed. W. Scott, 13 vols. (2nd edn., 1809–15), vol. 9, p. 408.

best in England; and the prebends and other church livings, in the gift of the bishop, are the richest in England.'[23]

THE CHURCH OF ENGLAND AND NATIONAL IDENTITY

Though 'Anglican' and 'Anglicanism' only entered common usage in the nineteenth century, the Church of England was the national Church and intimately tied up with national identity. However, that relationship was complicated and somewhat uncertain. The connection between religion and national identity was transformed by the Reformation, particularly the negative dimension whereby national enemies were identified. In general terms this took the form of anti-Catholicism—in particular that England was quite different from, say, Spain, France, and Ireland—though it was often personalized through hostility to the Pope and, by 1689, Louis XIV. In English eyes, Catholicism was intimately bound up with absolute and arbitrary government (hence suspicion of James II) and English liberty was frequently contrasted to French slavery. But the connection between Anglicanism and Englishness was confused by concern over the Sun King's ardent advocacy of an aggressive Counter Reformation. Most notable here was his revocation of the Edict of Nantes in 1685 which led to the arrival of 50,000 Huguenots in England. Moreover, Louis was seen to encourage other Catholic powers to persecute their Protestant subjects. In 1686 the Duke of Savoy attacked 15,000 Protestant Vaudois (Waldenses), leading to the deaths of many, the conversion of some, and the migration of the rump into Switzerland. To many such assaults were part and parcel of a general threat to European Protestantism.

In the beginning of the last age, the protestant interest in Europe was more than a match for the Roman Catholick . . . But now, instead of this, is not the protestant power destroyed almost over Europe? The whole kingdom of Bohemia entirely popish? Are not the protestants of Poland, Austria, Moravia, utterly destroyed? Is not their destruction now carrying on, and almost finished in Hungary? . . . The protestants of Bavaria, Hamburgh, Cologn, Wurtzburgh, and Worms, are all destroyed. In France, the Spanish Low-Countries, Savoy, and Vaudois, after long and mighty struggles, the religion is utterly extinguished. Against the poor Palatinates the persecution is now carrying on with its usual barbarity . . .[24]

Even allowing for the polemical flourishes this is characteristic of the siege mentality common to many Protestant powers until Louis's death in 1715.

---

[23] D. Defoe, *A Tour Through the Whole Island of Great Britain*, ed. P. Rogers (Harmondsworth, 1978), p. 533.

[24] 'The Case of England, and the Protestant Interest', in *A Collection of Scarce and Valuable Tracts*, vol. 9, pp. 593–4.

That English anti-Catholicism and anti-Gallicanism were highly personalized in terms of Louis is hinted at by the proposal, unsuccessfully advanced by some French clergy just two years after he had died, that the French and English Churches unite.

If Anglicanism was peculiarly English, then the Church of England could also be viewed an integral part of a wider Protestant community. It is notable that many willingly subscribed to Crown sponsored charity briefs in aid of their persecuted Protestant brethren. At the end of the seventeenth and start of the eighteenth centuries such briefs raised £64,713 for Huguenots, £59,146 for Irish Protestants, £27,606 for the Vaudois, £22,038 for the Palatines, and £19,548 for Orange Protestants. William and Mary did much to encourage this, giving the Huguenots £39,000 between 1689 and 1693 and prompting a Royal Bounty of £15,000 per annum, supplied by Parliament from 1696. This Bounty helped thousands of Huguenots and survived into the nineteenth century, though George I reduced support to a little over £8,500 per annum. Generous though such donations were, they do not simply evidence the existence of a supra-national unity between English and European Protestantism, for such financial help also expressed many people's view that England was a uniquely favoured Protestant nation. Relatively safe in its island position and having seen off the Catholic challenge of James II, its military successes after 1689 only served to underscore such feelings of superiority. From this perspective England was a chosen nation, a modern Israel, and the Church of England God's chosen repository for the true religion. To many of its adherents, Anglicanism was a part of European Protestantism, but ultimately superior to kindred churches.

The varieties of European Protestantism helped to accentuate the distinctive role of the Church of England as the national Church. This was felt particularly strongly with regard to Scotland, where the Glorious Revolution led to the establishment of Presbyterianism as the national Church, with episcopalians pushed to the margins. The Union of 1707 pointed up, and to some also challenged, the distinctiveness of the Church of England's national status. To many, non-Anglican varieties of Protestantism were seriously flawed theologically, politically, and socially. To High Anglicans and Tories only the Church of England accurately interpreted the scriptures and the patristic writings, adopted the correct means of fulfilling the Church's mission, and secured the social hierarchy. Indeed, some antagonism was shown towards foreign Protestants, especially to the religious zealots of New England and the poor Palatines who flooded into England in 1709—after all, William III and George I, as Calvinist and Lutheran respectively, could be charged with failing to understand the real national interest. Proposals for the naturalization of foreign Protestants brought such sentiments vividly to the fore and were bitterly contested. If foreign Protestants might be judged beleaguered brethren, they might also be styled the bastard offspring of the true Reformation. No less of a problem was posed by those English who stood outside Anglicanism.

DISSENSION, DISSENT, AND RECUSANCY

Within England the supremacy of the Church of England was widely though far from universally endorsed. Many believed that its membership ought to encompass the whole population and full citizenship be refused to those who chose to deny its supremacy. Yet largely for reasons of principle three substantial groups fell outside its orbit: the non-jurors, Protestant Dissenters, and Roman Catholics. Though together these accounted for only about 8 per cent of the population their significance was disproportionately large, for they denied the hope of religious homogeneity and were believed to represent schism and faction, seriously weakening a political and social fabric already somewhat threadbare after many decades of wear and tear.

The non-juring schism largely occurred in 1689 and 1690 when the new oath of allegiance to William and Mary was introduced.[25] On point of principle about 400 clergymen held that their oaths to James II were still in force despite his flight, such that to take the new oath would be to break a sacred undertaking. At their head was the Archbishop of Canterbury, William Sancroft, and seven other bishops—Robert Frampton of Gloucester, Thomas Ken of Bath and Wells, John Lake of Chichester, William Lloyd of Norwich, William Thomas of Worcester, Francis Turner of Ely, and Thomas White of Peterborough.[26] It says much about the depth of these men's principles that five of them (Sancroft, Ken, Lake, Turner, and White) had been among the Seven bishops unsuccessfully prosecuted by James II in the summer of 1688 for challenging his Declaration of Indulgence to Dissenters and Roman Catholics. Most non-jurors were suspended in August 1689 and deprived on

---

[25] See above, pp. 34–6.

[26] Robert Frampton, 1622–1708, educated Corpus Christi College, Cambridge, Bishop of Gloucester 1680, offered see of Hereford near the end of his life. Thomas Ken, 1637–1711, Fellow of New College, Oxford, Bishop of Bath and Wells 1684, Queen Anne offered to restore him and gave him a pension. John Lake, 1624–1689, educated St John's College, Cambridge, Bishop of Sodor and Man 1683, Bristol 1684, and Chichester 1685. William Lloyd, 1637–1710, educated St John's College, Cambridge, Bishop of Llandaff 1675, Peterborough 1679, and Norwich 1685. William Thomas, 1613–89, educated Carmarthen Grammar School and St John's College, Oxford, Fellow Jesus College, Oxford, Bishop of St David's 1677 and Worcester 1683. Francis Turner, 1637–1700, Fellow of New College, Oxford, Master of St John's College, Cambridge, 1670–9, Bishop of Rochester 1683, Ely 1684, after 1689 often arrested for Jacobite activity. Thomas White, 1628–98, educated St Johns College, Cambridge, Bishop of Peterborough 1685.

1 February 1690.[27] Undeniably they remained members of the Church of England and held the high moral ground even though there were jurors, notably Sherlock, who devised elaborate justifications for taking the new oaths. For the survivors, refusing the new oaths in 1696, 1702, and 1714 provided opportunities to perpetuate the memory of their integrity, though James II's death prompted some to take the oaths to William.

In a sense, the non-jurors constituted a small church within a church, though one with plenty of allies among the jurors. Theologically they were distinguished by their absolute commitment to the Thirty-nine Articles and a belief in the divine right of kings. On this basis, some illegally established and served their own congregations. Few were prosecuted, not least because many were content to act quietly in the background. Ken's replacement at Bath and Wells reported the case of one non-juring vicar who remained in his parish and 'continued to supply the place, and prayed for the King and Queen, and behaved himself very well.'[28] Some, however, were less discreet and remained active Jacobites, notably Turner. Indeed, in 1694 James II approved two non-jurors to be consecrated as 'bishops' of Thetford and Ipswich. Consequently, the non-jurors retained a separate identity which allowed them, despite deaths and desertions (especially following the death of James II in 1701), to remain a small force to be reckoned with well into the eighteenth century. As such they were a potent reminder to the Church of England of how severely tested its principles had been in the crisis of 1688–9 and of how many had, ultimately, sacrificed those principles at the altar of pragmatism.

If the non-juring schism was a product of the Glorious Revolution another arose from long-established Protestant nonconformity. Impassioned debates over the nature of the reformed church dated from the mid-sixteenth century. Those debates reached fever pitch in the Interregnum, but at the Restoration the strength of the desire for episcopacy and the isolation of faction led to a religious settlement that deprived nearly 1,000 clerics of their livings and introduced various legal requirements binding full citizenship to religious conformity. William III, Burnet, and others hoped in 1689 to reduce nonconformity to a tiny rump by 'comprehending' moderates within the established Church and allowing those outside a measure of toleration to practise their faith relatively unhindered.[29] Though toleration was enacted, the project of comprehension failed because of considerable opposition within the Church. Many conformists, mindful of the weakening effect of the non-juring schism and the

---

[27] Lake and Thomas died before they were deprived.

[28] *The Life of Richard Kidder, D. D., Bishop of Bath and Wells Written by Himself*, ed. A. E. Robinson, Somerset Record Society, 37 (1924), p. 86.

[29] See above, pp. 31–2.

generally unsettled nature of the nation, were hostile to any dilution of the principles of the Church necessary to accommodate Dissenters. 'The Kingdom is yet in such a ferment, and many things so unsetled, that to change now in the Church, is like altering Military Exercise in the midst of a Battle.'[30] Many indeed were determined not to compromise the theological integrity of the Church of England in the ways necessary to incorporate moderate Dissenters, though in doing so such Churchmen effectively perpetuated heterodoxy and disunion.

Many in the Church feared Dissenters, not least because vivid memories of the giddy days of the 1640s and 1650s allowed the religiously unorthodox to be stigmatized as progenitors of faction and disorder. And just enough visionaries proclaimed their insights through the period to keep such concerns alive. If 'Quakers now are nothing like what they were formerly . . . They do not quake, and howl, and foam with their mouths . . . but modestly and devoutly behave themselves', small bands of Sabbatarians (who believed Saturday was the day of rest), radical millenarians, and Philadelphians all stood decisively outside the religious mainstream.[31] In 1694, for example, there was 'A greate Rising of People in Buckinghamshire, upon the declaration of a famous Preacher . . . that our Lord Christ appearing to him . . . told him he was now come downe, & would appeare publicly at Pentecost & gather all the Saints Jew & Gentile, & leade them to Jerusalem, & begin the *Millenium*'.[32] Lodowick Muggleton, the leader of the radical Muggletonian sect of the Interregnum, died as late as 1698. The Philadelphians, a religious sect who held various mystical beliefs, flourished briefly in the closing decades of the seventeenth century. For a few years after 1705 the so-called French Prophets, refugees from the Cévennes, attracted small but vocal support in a number of towns. More generally, the rejection of episcopacy by Dissent maintained the connection in the popular imagination between nonconformity and political radicalism, to the extent that Nonconformists were frequently attacked by mobs at moments of high political tension. Such moments might also reflect upon the religion of William III and George I, and it is notable that at the coronation of the latter many meeting houses were attacked and destroyed, stimulating the passage of the Riot Act in 1715. It was, moreover, feared that nonconformity was proliferating in this period, not least because under the terms of the Toleration Act some 2,500 meeting houses were registered with the episcopal authorities and Justices of the Peace between 1691 and 1710.

[30] T. J. Fawcett, *The Liturgy of Comprehension 1689: An Abortive Attempt to Revise the Book of Common Prayer*, Alcuin Club Collection, 54 (Southend-on-Sea, 1973), p. 45.

[31] 'The Diary of Abraham de la Pryme, the Yorkshire Antiquary', *Publications of the Surtees Society*, 54 (1870), p. 53.

[32] *The Diary of John Evelyn*, ed. E. S. de Beer, 6 vols. (Oxford, 1955), vol. 5, pp. 177–8.

Nonconformity posed no real social threat for three reasons. First, it was heterogeneous, united only by its Protestantism and its anti-episcopalianism. All sects established a separate identity and presence and only occasionally were they able to present a united front. In 1695 'the heats among the Dissenters grew perfectly scandalous' and in 1719 they were unable to agree to a joint subscription to Trinitarian doctrine as Presbyterians and General Baptists began to drift towards Unitarianism.[33] Second, after the Restoration Dissent had gradually become more organized, regulated, and, to an extent, respectable. If there had been no weakening of their faith, there had been of their proselytizing. Congregations became more inward looking, concerned for self-discipline and self-fulfillment. The deaths of John Bunyan, a great evangelist for Independents, in 1688 and of the Puritan Richard Baxter in 1691 marked the end of an era.[34] Further, Dissenting leaders went out of their way to demonstrate their loyalty to all of the monarchs in this period. Finally, Dissent was in certain fundamentals weak. Most obviously, the Test and Corporation Acts, requiring conformity for office holding, formally placed them outside political society, even if in practice they often circumvented such restrictions by occasional conformity. Though many hoped that these laws would be repealed, the only attempt seriously considered in Parliament in this period was the failed measure of comprehension in 1689. Politically, Dissent remained on the defensive for most of the time, though Quakers did succeed in getting the recognition of their refusal to swear oaths. Not the least of the weakness of Dissent was its general lack of popularity, accounting in total for only one in sixteen people (rather more women than men). A snapshot of the scale of Dissent is provided in Table 4. Such figures are somewhat misleading because of the uneven regional distribution of Dissent. Some counties had almost no chapels or meeting houses, others many. Crudely speaking, Presbyterians were more numerous in the west than the east, Independents and Particular Baptists in the south than the north, and General Baptists in the south and east. Congregations were more frequently urban than rural. However, in some counties Dissent drew significant numbers of members from among poor agricultural labourers and nonconformity cannot accurately be depicted as being solely confined to the commercial classes (both the contemporary

[33] E. Calamy, *An Historical Account of my Own Life, with Some Reflections on the Times I have Lived in (1671–1731)*, 2 vols. (1829), vol. 1, p. 356.

[34] John Bunyan, 1628–88, born Bedfordshire of poor parents, on parliamentary side in Civil War, preaching at Bedford Independent congregation from 1657, spent much of 1660–72 in Bedford prison because of his faith, his most famous work *The Pilgrim's Progress* (1678 and 1684). Richard Baxter, 1615–91, born Shropshire, ordained 1638, on parliamentary side in Civil War, discontented with episcopacy in England, active in negotiations over the Church 1660–2, declined Bishopric of Hereford after the Restoration.

TABLE 4. *Numbers of Dissenters in England, c.1715*

	Number	Percentage of total population
Presbyterians	179,350	3.4
Independents	59,940	1.1
Particular Baptists	40,520	0.8
General Baptists	18,800	0.4
Quakers	39,510	0.8
ALL DISSENTERS	338,120	6.4
TOTAL POPULATION (1715)	5,246,260	

Source: M. Watts, *The Dissenters: From the Reformation to the French Revolution* (Oxford, 1978), p. 270; E. A. Wrigley and R. S. Schofield, *The Population History of England 1541–1871: A Reconstruction* (1981), p. 533.

Anglican establishment and some historians have sometimes been over influenced by the prominence of large Dissenting congregations in and around London).

If anything, the popularity of Dissent was stagnant in this period. In 1689 a circular letter sent to many Baptist congregations bewailed 'the present condition our churches seem to be in, fearing that much of the former strength, life and vigour, which attended us is much gone'.[35] In Essex the number of Quakers fell from around 2,400 in *c.*1680 to 1,650 in *c.*1720, a decline of 30 per cent. The number of MPs who were Dissenters fell from 93 in the Restoration period to only 42 in the slightly shorter period 1705–27. And in London some 50 Dissenting ministers conformed between 1714 and 1731. Dissent's weakness was partly political, partly theological. Doctrinal divisions and developments, particularly over Trinitarian questions, kept sect from sect and overwhelmed the enthusiasm and vitality that had been so important in their earlier expansion. There was also a decline in the importance of those Dissenters, the 'middle way men', who hoped to be accommodated within the established Church, such that as a whole Dissent became less mainstream. Some, however, managed to keep the flame alive. Pre-eminently, Isaac Watts inspired many by his learning, devotion, and hymn-writing. His *Hymns and Spiritual Songs* (1707) and *The Psalms of David* (1719) helped further to develop a strand of nonconformity which rejected asperity and ceremonial austerity—hymn-singing was rare in parish churches.[36] Note might also be made of Edmund Calamy (1671–1732), an effective historian for nonconformity,

---

[35] Quoted in M. D. MacDonald, 'London Calvinistic Baptists 1689–1727: Tensions Within a Dissenting Community under Toleration', D. Phil. thesis (University of Oxford, 1983), p. 33.

[36] Isaac Watts, 1674–1748, educated Dissenting Academy at Stoke Newington, Pastor of Independent congregation in London 1702–12, opposed imposition of Trinitarian doctrines on Dissenting minister in 1719.

and Philip Doddridge (1702–51) who wrote many hymns and, especially in his last twenty years, laboured to unite the sects.

The third major challenge to the established Church was provided by Roman Catholicism. There were in fact relatively few English Catholics, perhaps 60,000 or around 1 per cent of the total population (served by c.650 clergy), though significant numbers were to be found in Lancashire. Consequently, the challenge supposedly posed was based upon bitter memories and vivid imaginings. Naturally this took its origins from the Reformation, when the Church of England had broken with Rome. The theological dimension to this, that the Roman church was based upon invention and superstition, materialism and deception, should not be undervalued. Enthusiasts for the Church of England depicted it as securely based upon scripture, authoritative patristic writing, and piety. It was a true Church and the Pope was often labelled as the anti-Christ. From another, nationalistic angle, the allegiance Roman Catholics owed to the Pope might be construed as disloyalty, an accusation that was also levelled at many Irish. The policies of James II brought such thinking into the very heart of English society. The domestic causes of the Glorious Revolution were pre-eminently religious, albeit frequently expressed politically through James's assaults on the Church's monopoly in civil and military affairs. His flight and the attempts by him, his successor, and supporters to reclaim his crown doomed Catholicism to be tarred with the Jacobite brush.

Anti-Catholicism was one of the most potent ideologies in post-Revolution England, manifesting itself at all levels of society and sometimes in extreme forms. The title of a pamphlet from 1700 tells its own tale: *Reasons Humbly Offer'd for a Law to Enact the Castration of Popish Ecclesiastics, as the Best Way to Prevent the Growth of Popery in England.* More moderately if Catholics, like Dissenters, were subject to the Test and Corporation Acts, as in Ireland a raft of legislation specifically sought to isolate and punish them, encouraging conversion. In 1689 they were banished 10 miles from London (an order repeated in 1692 and 1696), disarmed, and any benefices they held vested in the universities; in 1692 they were subjected to a double tax; in 1695 they were excluded from large parts of the legal profession; in 1700 a wide-ranging 'Act for the Further Preventing the Growth of Popery' was introduced to be underscored in 1714 by another general anti-Catholic measure; in 1715 Catholics were required to register their names and estates; and after the failure of the Atterbury plot in 1722 a new levy was imposed. Such penal laws usually emanated from the Church and its warmest supporters—in 1699 Dryden, a Catholic, noted that William III 'is very Unwilling to persecute us . . . But the Archbishop of Canterbury is our heavy Enemy'.[37] Such splits were significant, for if the intent behind anti-Catholic measures was clear and heartfelt,

[37] *The Letters of John Dryden*, ed. C. E. Ward (Duke, 1942), p. 112.

prosecuting Catholics depended upon the enthusiasm of Justices who often found it hard to act against honest neighbours. As one French visitor observed, 'There are a great many Acts of Parliament . . . against Popery and Papists; but those Laws are not strictly executed.'[38] To a considerable extent those Catholics prepared to worship quietly and to show what allegiance they could to the new regime were usually left in peace. One Berkshire Catholic neatly summarized his potential loyalty: 'I am, by the grace of God, an English Catholic, and as such believe that it is my duty to be actively obedient where I can, without offence to God, and passively where I cannot, to whatever government God permits to come over me, and that non-resistance in all cases is one of the characteristic marks of a Christian; and that therefore I would willingly take an oath of fidelity to King George.'[39]

Not all Catholics were as submissive. Quite apart from their religious ties to James II, many followed the non-jurors and refused to swear allegiance to the new regime. In this view the Glorious Revolution was sinful: 'God damn the Protestants for Heathens, they cut off the King's Head, and now they have turned the Father out'.[40] Some Catholics engaged in Jacobite plots and actively supported the '15. Indeed, Catholicism and Jacobitism together offered the means of expressing hostility to the established authorities that were sometimes demonstrated by crowd activity. In 1716 'Papist and Jacobite Mobs' challenged the Thanksgiving day for the suppression of the '15, wearing 'rue and Thyme in their Hats as a Badge of Rebellion'.[41] Such cocking a snook at the established order took courage, but braved loyal mobs rather than the rule of law. Popular anti-Catholicism was considerable, especially in the towns, and had developed in a highly stylized way. Revolving around an extensive calendar of Protestant deliverance were ritual processions and the burning in effigy of noted Catholics—usually James II, his son, Louis XIV, and the Pope. In November 1696, for example, with searches underway in the capital for Jacobites and their arms, the anniversary of the birthday of Elizabeth I was celebrated 'with great Solemnity, viz. Ringing of Bells, firing of Guns, Bonefires, Fire-works, &c. And the Pope, according to Custom, was burnt by the Mob.'[42] The 5th of November, the anniversary of the failed Gunpowder plot and William III's landing, had already assumed considerable magnitude.

[38] Misson, *Memoirs and Observations*, p. 204.

[39] E. E. Estcourt and J. O. Payne (eds.), *The English Catholic Nonjurors of 1715: Being a Summary of the Register of their Estates* ([1882]), p. 8.

[40] *The Post Boy*, 20–22 August, 1696, [p. 2].

[41] *The Weekly Journal, or British Gazeteer*, 9 June 1716, p. 435. The herbs 'signifying that the King should rue the time that he ever beat the rebels'. *The Diary of Dudley Ryder, 1715–1716*, ed. W. Matthews (1939), p. 253.

[42] *The Post Boy*, 17–19 November 1696, [p. 2].

About 7 a-Clock on the 5th of November last, a Detachment was sent from the Roebuck to . . . where the Images lay; as soon as every Man had his proper Charge given him, and Links lighted, Old Infallibility [the Pope] was brought out. Next came his unfortunate Son, Perkin [the Pretender], drest in a black Coat, Scarlet Stockings, and a pair of Wooden Shoes on his left Shoulder: their Old Friend the Devil serv'd for their Life Guard, and brought up the Rear. In this manner we march'd along . . . our Company increas'd to some Thousands; we continu'd . . . back to our Bonfire, which we went round, and then committed [the effigies] to a Fiery Tryal, amidst the Acclamations of a vast Concourse of People, crying No Popery, No Pretender; King GEORGE and the Royal Family for Ever.[43]

As this suggests, most in England were proud of the national Church; it was part of their birthright, identity, and means of salvation. It was to be protected, celebrated, and enjoyed.

A WEAKENING FAITH?

Christians have always held to the view that mankind is weak, prey to any temptations the devil might conjure up. Such concerns were, however, cried out with particular vigour and frequency after 1689. Irreligion was seen to be on the rise, and faith increasingly the preserve of a devoted minority. In 1699 Evelyn complained of 'Atheism, Dissensions, prophenesse, Blasphemy among all sorts' and in 1711 Convocation, the Church's governing body, published *A Representation of the Present State of Religion, with Regard to the Late Excessive Growth of Infidelity, Heresy, and Profaneness*.[44] This complained of 'that Deluge of Impiety and Licentiousness, which hath broke in upon us, and overspread the Face of this Church and Kingdom' (p. 3). Contemporaries advanced three main explanations for this supposed spiritual decay: that more and more were worshipping Mammon rather than God; that the Toleration Act had undermined the foundations of religious observance; and, finally, that scepticism and freethinking encouraged some to deny doctrines fundamental not only to the Church of England but even to Christianity.

It was a common complaint that England was increasingly being submerged beneath a torrent of luxury and vice. Many believed that 'In Proportion as our Zeal for Religion decayed, Our Corruptions and Vices increased'.[45] Most usually the origins of this were traced back to the Restoration court of

---

[43] *The Weekly Journal, or British Gazeteer*, 10 November 1716, p. 570. The Roebuck Inn was the meeting place for the 'Loyal Society'; Perkin Warbeck had claimed the throne in 1491 by pretending to be one of the murdered Princes in the Tower; wooden shoes were the common symbol of French poverty and slavery.

[44] *Evelyn Diary*, vol. 5, p. 366.

[45] F. Atterbury, *Sermons and Discourses on Several Subjects and Occasions*, 4 vols. (7th edn., 1761), vol. 2, pp. 129–30. This comes from a sermon preached in 1707.

Charles II whose loose living was legendary and whose bastard offspring unintentionally perpetuated the memory. His sexual antics, extravagance, and crypto-
Catholicism were supposed to have encouraged corruption and vice. In this
view, James II's Catholicism could not but perpetuate these failings. Nor,
it was often argued, did the Glorious Revolution bring any respite, a vicious
spiral of luxury being particularly encouraged by Toleration and the national
debt. After the collapse of the South Sea Bubble, Berkeley lamented that 'it
is very remarkable that luxury was never at so great a height, nor spread so
generally through the nation, as during the expense of the late wars'.[46]

Luxury was evidenced less by conspicuous consumption than behaviour
falling outside the usual moral norms—it is interesting how little concern there
was to institute sumptuary legislation. Thus it was less luxury than vice which
raised concerns: gambling, drunkenness, sexual immorality (extra-marital
liaisons, prostitution, and homosexuality), Sabbath breaking, and swearing.
Whether such 'vices' were actually increasing is impossible to know. One visitor certainly believed that 'the people of this country are very fond of liquors'
and that 'Englishmen are mighty swearers'.[47] There is some evidence of
increasing alcohol consumption in this period, and in the 1720s concern was
already being expressed at the growing amount of gin being consumed in
London which was counted 'destructive to the Lives, Families, Trades and
Business of such Multitudes, *especially to the lower poorer Sort of People*'.[48]
More important, especially in large towns 'vices' became more visible. Not
only the riotous antics at taverns, gaming houses, and brothels, but the frivolity
of the stage and masquerades were often condemned. It is certainly clear that
the pious elite were prone tautologically to view vice as a sign of irreligion and
irreligion as a cause of vice.

There may have been a decline in active religious participation in this
period. Many at the time quickly blamed the Toleration Act, for though it still
required that all attend a place of worship on Sundays this was normally
impossible to enforce. Whereas previously absences from the parish church
could easily be checked up on, now licensed meeting-houses provided a cover
to escape the clutches of all organized religion. For good measure, it was often
complained that when people ignored church or chapel they whiled away the

---

[46] G. Berkeley, 'An Essay Towards Preventing the Ruin of Great Britain', in *The Works
of George Berkeley Bishop of Cloyne*, ed. T. E. Jessop, vol. 6 (1953), p. 76. George Berkeley,
1685–1753, educated Kilkenny and Trinity College, Dublin, philosopher, held various posts at
Trinity College, Dublin, Bishop of Cloyne 1734.

[47] *A Foreign View of England in the Reigns of George I and George II. The Letters of Monsieur
César de Saussure to his Family*, trans. and ed. Madame van Muyden (1902), pp. 165 and 193.

[48] 'The Charge of Sr. *Daniel Dolins*, Kt. to the Grand-Jury, and Other Juries of the County of
Middlesex . . . the Seventh Day of October 1725', in *Charges to the Grand Jury 1689–1803*, ed.
G. Lamoine, Camden Society, 4th series, 43 (1992), p. 208.

time in the alehouse. As early as 1692 one cleric was certain that the Toleration Act would 'in a short time . . . turn halfe the nation into downe right athiesme.'[49] Six years later the Archbishop of York complained to a clergyman of the negligence of some of his parishioners, 'neither attending prayers nor sermon, nor any other ordinances of religion . . . they *do not serve God at all.*'[50] Just how common such rejections were is difficult to pin down. No doubt many clergymen preached to large congregations, but in some places there is evidence of a real decline. At Bucknell in Oxfordshire the number of communicants declined by over 40 per cent between 1699 and 1709. At Clayworth in Nottinghamshire perhaps 85–90 per cent of parishioners of an age to communicate did so before the Glorious Revolution, but by 1701 the proportion had fallen to perhaps only 55 per cent.[51] Whether or not such figures were general cannot be said, but certainly the Church was nervous about the spiritual and disciplinary consequences of Toleration. Whereas previously non-attendance had frequently been prosecuted in the ecclesiastical courts now such business dropped away markedly. In some of those courts the total volume of business was unaffected by Toleration, though usually an increasing proportion was given over to matters of personal behaviour and parochial administration. At others, however, there was a significant falling off of total business. At Chester consistory court the annual level of cases fell by a half between the 1680s and 1730; at Worcester there was an equally marked decline either side of 1689; and at Carlisle the number of presentments fell by nearly 40 per cent between 1704–8 and 1724–6.

It is clear from the complaints over the spread of vice and non-attendance that the elite was frequently dissatisfied with popular religious activity and the nature of England as a Christian society. In some measure that dissatisfaction was rooted in presumptions about the tendency of the 'vulgar' towards viciousness or the consumption of a heady cocktail of pagan, mystical, and Christian beliefs. In this view popular religion was inclined to ignorance, making them 'the Slaves of Superstition and Sin, and have all the While no true Dependance upon God'.[52] Such a view was marked by a social arrogance that was common

[49] *Letters of Humphrey Prideaux Sometime Dean of Norwich to John Ellis Sometime Under-Secretary of State 1674–1722*, ed. E. M. Thompson, Camden Society, New Series, 15 (1875), p. 154.

[50] Sharp (ed.), *The Life of John Sharp*, vol. 1, p. 207. See also *Calendar to the Session Books, Session Minute Books and other Sessions Records 1658–1700*, ed. W. Le Hardy, Hertfordshire County Records, 6 (Hertford, 1930), p. 426.

[51] These figures are tentative, resting as they do on assumptions about the village's total population, its age distribution, and the pattern of communicating at Easter time. The data is derived from *The Rector's Book, Clayworth Notts.*, ed. H. Gill and E. L. Guilford (Nottingham, 1910).

[52] H. Bourne, *Antiquitates Vulgares; or, the Antiquities of the Common People* (Newcastle, 1725), p. 75.

but not ubiquitous among the elite. In truth, however, there was no hard and fast divide between an elite and a popular religion in this period.[53] Some indeed noted that the rich were prone to particular failings—luxury, gambling, duels, and the avoidance of the Christian duties of charity and hospitality. Moreover, enthusiasm for providentialism, proverbialism, and millennialism crossed all social boundaries. Some light is shed on the social morphology of religiosity by exploring attitudes towards witchcraft and suicide.

For many centuries witchcraft had been viewed as an integral part of the devil's work which Christianity had constantly to struggle against. In the sixteenth and early seventeenth centuries Parliament had legislated against witchcraft and significant numbers of women (and a few men) had been prosecuted and executed. Gradually, however, there was some weakening of the idea of eternal damnation and a rethinking of the nature of witchcraft. In this view, witches took on a quite different appearance. Addison answered his rhetorical question 'Whether there are such Persons in the World as those we call Witches?' decisively in the negative. His reasoning was entirely material: 'When an old Woman begins to doat, and grow chargeable to a Parish, she is generally turned into a Witch, and fills the whole Country with extravagant Fancies, imaginary Distempers, and terrifying Dreams. In the mean time, the poor Wretch that is the innocent Occasion of so many Evils begins to be frighted at her self, and sometimes confesses secret Commerces and Familiarities that her Imagination forms in a delirious old Age.'[54] Such thinking was not new, but to find it in a major publication such as the *Spectator* is symptomatic that it had now become fairly common or at least acceptable. Prosecutions for witchcraft in England tailed off in the second half of the seventeenth century, with grand juries being told that 'their being no such Practice now' as 'Witchcraft, Sorcery or Inchantments', with the legislation concerning witchcraft finally repealed in 1736.[55] This was somewhat different from Scotland where prosecutions remained at significant levels into the early eighteenth century while reports from New England of the trials at Salem in 1692 were published in the London press. Yet if among the elite scepticism became the usual reaction to witchcraft, some villagers continued to accuse old women in time-honoured ways. How frequently this occurred is unclear, but the element of terror that continued to be involved should not be underestimated. Early in 1700, at St Albans in Hertfordshire, 'The Mob learnedly debating' a confrontation between an old woman and an apprentice 'conclude

[53] See E. Duffy, 'The Godly and the Multitude in Stuart England', *The Seventeenth Century*, 1 (1986), pp. 31–55.

[54] *The Spectator*, ed. D. F. Bond, 5 vols. (Oxford, 1965), vol. 1, pp. 480 and 482.

[55] 'The Charge of Whitlocke Bulstrode, Esq; to the *Grand-Jury*, and Other Juries, of the County of *Middlesex* . . . Held, April 21st, 1718 . . .', in *Charges to the Grand Jury*, p. 98.

that the Boy was bewitch'd' and proceeded to drag her through a river before taking her, nearly dead, before a Justice of the Peace who was forced 'to appease them' and place her in custody where she soon expired.[56] Few accusations took such a violent form, but clearly the reasonings of the judiciary and legislators sometimes ran counter to popular opinion.

Changing ideas about witchcraft can usefully be set alongside attitudes towards suicide. Until the Restoration suicide was commonly seen as self-murder and, in breaking the commandment not to kill, a crime against God. Harsh punishments were meted out. The suicide's goods were liable to be seized and the body denied a Christian burial, to be put instead in an unmarked grave at a cross-roads with a stake driven through it. Gradually, however, more and more suicides were judged by coroner's juries to be insane rather than wicked. In 1700 it was said that 'There is a General Supposition that *every one* who kills himself is *non Compos*, and that nobody wou'd do such an Action unless he were Distracted.'[57] At the King's Bench the proportion of suicides declared *non compos mentis* rose from just 7 per cent in 1660–4 to 40 per cent by 1714, and at Norwich from 29 per cent between 1670 and 1699 to 91 per cent in the 1720s. Such a shift, which was certainly not complete by 1727, had much to do with medical and philosophical ideas, though it also throws light upon a gradual reinterpretation of the role of the devil. A willingness to rationalize suicide in terms of a person's mental state rather than as a demonstration of the black arts was not a small shift.

Rethinking witchcraft and suicide is symptomatic of an increased readiness during this period to question the traditional bases of not only Anglican but, indeed, of Christian belief. If few religions go long without some challenge to their creeds and doctrines, the Church of England found itself especially subject to frequent and potent intellectual threats after the Glorious Revolution. For the most part those threats were based upon the application of reason and close textual criticism to scriptural and patristic authority leading, in the Church's eyes, to the growth of a variety of faiths that were often, inaccurately, denoted as atheistical. Very few, in fact, can be counted as true atheists, for the complete rejection of God was almost universally seen as 'one of the most Irrational Principles in the World'.[58] Rather this period saw the growth of Arianism, Socinianism, and, particularly, Deism. Central to Arianism was its denial of the divinity of Christ; Socinianism rejected Trinitarian doctrines, and thus also the divinity of Christ, providing a central pillar to Unitarian

---

[56] *The Post Boy*, 16–18 January 1700, [p. 2].

[57] Quoted in M. MacDonald and T. R. Murphy, *Sleepless Souls: Suicide in Early Modern England* (Oxford, 1990), p. 133.

[58] [D. Defoe], *The Storm: or, a Collection of the Most Remarkable Casualties and Disasters which Happen'd in the Late Dreadful Tempest* (1704), preface (no pagination).

thinking; and Deism stressed the existence of one Supreme Being and that true religion was natural religion.[59] Though all three had distinct theological identities, the labels were often used loosely and indiscriminately against anyone who employed scepticism and reason to question the fundamental tenets of the Established Church.

John Locke was at the forefront of attempts to place Christianity on a rational basis, the very title of his pamphlet *The Reasonableness of Christianity* (1695) proclaiming his thinking. God, Christianity (more especially Protestantism), and man were all fundamentally rooted in reason. He was certain that the essence of Protestantism was simple and readily accessible to all. In his own eyes this did not lead him into nonconformity and he readily took the sacrament in order to hold office, though he enthusiastically endorsed religious toleration, which he thought 'to be the chief characteristical mark of the true Church' and a means by which 'all may be brought together into one body.'[60] This and the emphasis Locke placed upon reason rather than revelation encouraged his critics inaccurately to label him 'a Socinian or an atheist'.[61] In some measure this was because of his close association with John Toland, 'eminent for railing in coffee houses against all communities in religion, and monarchy', whose *Christianity Not Mysterious*, published in 1696, was a central work of Deism.[62] Toland proudly proclaimed that 'I acknowledge no ORTHODOXY but the TRUTH' and denied that this was to be found in the 'wonderfully corrupted and adulterated' patristic writings. To him, only by applying reason to the scriptures could truth be found: *'there is nothing in the Gospel contrary to Reason, nor above it; and that no Christian Doctrine can be properly be call'd a Mystery.'*[63]

Scepticism was also manifested in concern about the accuracy and authenticity of the scriptures and patristic writings. Through the seventeenth century

---

[59] 'Arianism' originated with the ideas of Arius (c.250–c.336). 'Socinian' derives from the Latinized surname of Lelio Sozini (1525–62) and his nephew Fausto Sozzini (1539–1604); Unitarian tracts were published in England by John Biddle (1615–62). Deism in England gained great impetus from Lord Herbert of Cherbury's *De Veritate* (1624).

[60] J. Locke, 'A Letter Concerning Toleration', in *Political Writings*, ed. D. Wootton (Harmondsworth, 1993), p. 390; *The Correspondence of John Locke*, ed. E. S. de Beer, 8 vols. (Oxford, 1976–89), vol. 3, p. 689.

[61] *The Private and Literary Remains of John Byrom*, ed. R. Parkinson, Chetham Society, 32 and 34, 2 vols. (1854–5), vol. 1, p. 7.

[62] R. T. Gunther (ed.), *Life and Letters of Edward Lhwyd*, Early Science in Oxford, 14 (Oxford, 1945), p. 278. John Toland, 1670–1722, Irish, converted from Roman Catholicism to Protestantism when aged 16, educated at Glasgow, Leiden, and Oxford, forged a number of links on the continent, partly as a keen supporter of the Hanoverian succession.

[63] J. Toland, *Christianity Not Mysterious: or, a Treatise Shewing, that there is Nothing in the Gospel Contrary to Reason, Nor Above it: and that no Christian Doctrine can be Properly Call'd a Mystery* (1696), pp. 175, 2–3, and 6.

many had struggled to attach a chronology to a close reading of the Old Testament and other ancient texts. Though this was often undertaken by men of undoubted orthodoxy, such as Mills and Bentley, their work exposed tensions, contradictions, and gaps in the fundamental sources upon which the Church of England rested.[64] The supremacy of the biblical text, which was so central to the Protestant identity, could only be maintained by an act of faith or by ignoring the problems which had been uncovered. Newton spent many of his last years upon just such a struggle in the 'labyrinth and abyss of infinity', neutering his work on chronology having apparently realized that his findings might be interpreted as supporting Deism.[65] Others were prepared to speak out, most notably William Whiston (1667–1752) who was, by turns, a millenarian, a Newtonian, and an Arian. Educated at Cambridge, ordained into the Church, and chaplain to the Bishop of Norwich in 1696, he published in that year the highly popular *New Theory of the Earth*, employing Newtonian ideas to explain the origins of the earth and the deluge, as well as to predict the end of the world. In 1703 he was appointed Newton's successor as Lucasian Professor at Cambridge. However, his research into the early church led him to deny that the Church of England was coterminous with Primitive Christianity, provoking his eviction from Cambridge in 1710. Soon after he published *Primitive Christianity Revived*, 4 vols. (1711) and between 1715 and 1717 he organized a small Society for Promoting Primitive Christianity which met weekly in London. Some sense of the importance attached to the nature of primitive Christianity and whether the Church of England was therefore the true Church is evidenced by the fact that among those who attended Whiston's Society were Benjamin Hoadly (in turn Bishop of Bangor, Hereford, Salisbury, and Winchester) and Arthur Onslow, the future Speaker of the House of Commons. Whiston also met regularly with Queen Caroline and at her behest received a stipend of £40 per annum.

Toland and Whiston were far from lonely voices. Samuel Clarke (1675–1729), Matthew Tindal (1655–1733), Charles Blount (1654–93), and Anthony Collins (1676–1729), to name only the most prominent, also produced notable works that questioned some of the Thirty-nine Articles and many of the fundamental bases of the Church's authority—its services, clerical (especially episcopal) structure, and political role. In these far from unified attacks the Church was seen as a human invention designed not to aid salvation but to give priests power over the general population: 'that the name *Church* signifieth only a Self-interested Party, and that the Clergy have no Godliness but

---

[64] John Mills (often Mill), 1645–1707, Fellow of Queen's College, Oxford, 1670–82, Principal of St Edmund Hall, 1685–1707, New Testament textual critic.

[65] Voltaire, *Letters on England*, trans. L. Tancock (Harmondsworth, 1980), p. 86.

Gain.'[66] Many Churchmen were concerned that such ideas were becoming widely held. In 1692 Bentley worried that 'Atheism is so much the worse that it is not buried in books; but is gotten . . . that taverns and coffee-houses, nay Westminster-hall and the very churches, are full of it' and Burnet complained of the 'growing *Atheism* and *Impiety*, that is daily gaining ground'.[67] Locke, however, observed that 'The greatest part of mankind have not leisure for learning and logic, and superfine distinctions of the schools. Where the hand is used to the plough and the spade, the head is seldom elevated to sublime notions, or exercised in mysterious reasonings', though perhaps he might better have considered how widely disseminated freethinking works were.[68]

If the heavy tomes of the freethinker lacked much of a readership at the base of society, there was a significant impact among the elite, as Whiston's little Society demonstrates. Though the authorities burned some radical works, it is interesting to note how little legal action was taken against freethinking. For example, the Blasphemy Act of 1698 (which is still in force) criminalized unitarian ideas, but implicitly allowed many other strands of unorthodoxy. Moreover, some believed that latitudinarians within the Church were themselves fomenting radical religious thinking. Tillotson, Archbishop of Canterbury between 1691 and 1694, was accused of contributing 'more to the spreading and rooting of atheism than fifty Spinosa's, [or] Hobbs's'.[69] In 1701 Harley anonymously chided Tenison, Tillotson's successor, for being 'entirely under the influence of those who have . . . for many years been promoting, first Socinianism then Arianism and now Deism in the state, they have propagated notions which destroy all government'.[70] Most famously, in March 1717 Benjamin Hoadly, Bishop of Bangor, preached a sermon before the King that sought to prove that the gospels offered little or no evidence for any visible Church authority. To many, for a bishop to deny scriptural authority for his own office was hypocritical and outrageous, 'For no Heresy can ever be held so fatal, as that which denys the Power of the Clergy', provoking a heated debate known as the Bangorian controversy, where Hoadly's dissimulation only further blackened his reputation.[71] It says much, however, that Hoadly was

---

[66] [W. Stephens], *An Account of the Growth of Deism in England, with Other Tracts of the Same Author* (1709), p. 8.

[67] *The Correspondence of Richard Bentley*, ed. J. Wordsworth, 2 vols. (1842), vol. 1, p. 39; Burnet, *Discourse of Pastoral Care*, p. xxii.

[68] Locke, *Reasonableness of Christianity*, p. 76.

[69] 'Remarks Upon the Present Confederacy, and Late Revolution in England', in *A Collection of Scarce and Valuable Tracts*, vol. 10, p. 519. John Tillotson, 1630–1694, educated Clare Hall, Cambridge, Fellow 1651 but deprived 1661, favoured comprehension.

[70] H. M. C., *Calendar of the Manuscripts of the Marquis of Bath*, vol. 1 (1904), p. 53.

[71] *The Letters of Thomas Burnet to George Duckett 1712–1722*, ed. D. N. Smith (Oxford, 1914), p. 132. Benjamin Hoadly, 1676–1761, fellow Catharine Hall, Cambridge 1697–1701.

translated to Hereford in 1721, Salisbury in 1723, and to Winchester in 1734. Anglican heterodoxy had entered the mainstream.

THE HIGH CHURCH REACTION

Between 1690 and the latter stages of the Bangorian controversy many Anglicans believed that their Church was in crisis. Fraught by internal divisions and weakened by the religion of two foreign monarchs, the perceived fertility of Dissent, vice, non-attendance, and scepticism all felt like massive blows. Yet the Church was too considerable merely to take these on the chin, too rooted to move out of their range, and too sure of its own rightness to turn the other cheek. Rather, its supporters felt obligated by God to protect and nurture what they were sure was the true Church. To them it was not a responsibility which could be abrogated. They enthusiastically challenged criticism, and sought to reinvigorate and reform the Church in a variety of imaginative ways.

Following the precept that the best form of defence is attack many Anglicans confronted opponents by force of argument and political power. Such assaults were usually made by those then called the 'High Church', which gives an accurate impression of its self-assured superiority but which should not mask the contemporary meaning of 'high' as 'strong'. The intellectual defences the High Church mounted were much more substantial than has usually been recognized, though they struggled 'to reconcile the *Revolution*' to 'Notions of *Passive-Obedience*, *Non-Resistance*, and the *Divine-Right of an Hereditary-Monarchy*'.[72] They stressed three features. First, that human reason was too imperfect fully to comprehend God's work. Thus true religion had to rest in part upon revelation, 'not in contradiction to Reason, but by way of difference and distinction.'[73] Daniel Waterland (1683–1740), Master of Magdalene College, Cambridge, from 1714 and John Sharp, Archbishop of York from 1691 to 1714, were prominent proponents of this line of thinking. Second, emphasis was placed upon the wisdom of tradition and of the importance of fixed points of reference for religious practice. Finally, though the supremacy of the scriptures was unchallenged, the patristic authorities, rightly interpreted, provided a clear legitimation for the Church's authority. Centrally, bishops, priests, and deacons were God's agents through the apostolic succession; the Church not only provided the worldly means for salvation, but had a missionary duty which required it to be powerful. Forceful advocates of some

---

[72] W. Kennett and others, *A Complete History of England*, 3 vols. (1706), vol. 3, p. 518.
[73] [M. Astell], *The Christian Religion, as Profess'd by a Daughter of the Church of England* (1717), p. 91.

or all of these ideas included Francis Atterbury (1662–1723), Bishop of Rochester from 1716–23, William Beveridge (1637–1708), Bishop of St Asaph from 1704, and, most famously, Henry Sacheverell (c.1674–1724), one-time Fellow of Magdalen College, Oxford.

The High Church reaction was purposeful, loud, and, occasionally, shrill. One of its most important outlets was in the Canterbury Convocation, a body comprised of 22 bishops in the upper house, and 145 clergy in the lower.[74] Significant tensions between the two houses existed, with the upper house often coming under attack from the High Church lower house. Certainly many in the lower house had non-juring and non-comprehending sympathies and viewed numerous prelates as weak latitudinarians—little wonder that Burnet, Bishop of Salisbury, complained that 'litle good is to be expected from the Sinodicall meetings of the Clergy'.[75] Much blame was heaped upon William III for this, despite the fact that, having left ecclesiastical appointments in the hands of his wife and a Commission, in his reign the episcopal bench comprised all shades of establishment opinion. Undoubtedly, however, his two appointments as Archbishop of Canterbury, Tillotson and Tenison, were in many respects low church. William, in fact, managed largely to avoid disputes with and within Convocation, for during his reign it only met in 1689 and 1701. Convocation's weakness was that, having surrendered the power to tax the clergy in 1664, it had no leverage with which to pressure the monarch to summon it into existence. Indeed, dispute raged over Convocation's precise constitutional standing. In 1697 Atterbury asserted that 'It is plain, that convocations ought to be held as often as parliaments' and, though his scholarly frailties were fully exposed by Gibson and Wake, the accession of Anne in 1702 and her High Church leanings did indeed institute a period of near-annual sittings.[76] As a consequence, until the accession of George I the lower house of Convocation became an important forum for High Church activity, giving vent to opinion that had previously often been expressed in a somewhat disjointed way. That it was a loose cannon only served to underscore the intense feelings of many among the clergy. As Godolphin observed in 1704, 'a discreet clergyman is almost as rare as a black swan.'[77]

Under Anne the High Church reaction soon advanced in Parliament, though it met stiff opposition until the Tories came to power in 1710. A key

[74] The Convocation of York was less significant, and comprised a single chamber of 55 members.
[75] A Supplement to Burnet's History of My Own Time, ed. H. C. Foxcroft (Oxford, 1902), p. 498.
[76] 'A Letter to a Convocation-Man, Concerning the Rights, Powers, and Privileges of that Body', in A Collection of Scarce and Valuable Tracts, vol. 9, p. 425.
[77] H. M. C., Bath, vol. 1, p. 63.

battle ground was over the practice of occasional conformity, whereby Dissenters took communion once a year to qualify themselves for office holding. To Churchmen and their supporters such behaviour was hypocritical, dishonest, and sinful and, if allowed, further weakened the Anglican supremacy. Concerted attempts were made in 1702, 1703, and 1704 to legislate against the practice and failed only narrowly—some Whigs and latitudinarians saw occasional conformity as a means of unifying the Protestant interest in 'peace, quiet, and love', almost as a means of bringing in comprehension by the back door.[78] In December 1705 the House of Lords rejected by 61 votes to 30 a High Church motion that the Church was in danger. So long as the latitudinarian or whiggish bishops held the balance of power in the upper house of Convocation and in both houses of Parliament, the High Church reaction could make little practical headway. In 1709 and 1710, however, the parliamentary context began to change as war-weariness mounted. That change reached its crescendo in the notorious Sacheverell affair, which Burnet rightly described as 'one of the most extraordinary transactions in my time'.[79]

The Sacheverell affair began in earnest on 5 November 1709 when the High Churchman preached before the Corporation of London in St Paul's cathedral, offering his audience less a sermon than a ninety-minute tirade.[80] In frequently vulgar terms he lambasted Whigs and Dissenters for what he saw as the deplorable state of the nation and the Church. He attacked the Whig view of 1688–9 and believed that Toleration had led to the growth of 'Heresy and Schism', and occasional conformity to the abandonment of principle, effects which together threatened to overturn Church and State. 'False Brethren' had entered the mainstream, such that 'Atheism, Deism, Tritheism, Socinianism, with all the hellish principles of Fanaticism, Regicide, and Anarchy, are openly professed and taught'.[81] There was little new in Sacheverell's intemperance— he had given a similar sermon four years earlier—and had the sermon been left only to ring in the ear of his audience then little might have come of it. But it was published on 25 November and, in the climate of late 1709, made a dramatic impact, quickly going through 11 editions, selling perhaps 100,000 copies, and reaching a much wider audience still. Sales were helped by the decision of the Whig government to impeach Sacheverell for high crimes and misdemeanours. In this the government badly miscalculated, for it raised the stakes dramatically. However, even the normally unflappable Godolphin, who can hardly be described as a Whig, was personally stung by the sermon and was determined to exact revenge. But Sacheverell's trial soon exploded out of

[78] S. Patrick, *The Auto-Biography* (Oxford, 1839), p. 185.
[79] G. Burnet, *History of his Own Time*, 6 vols. (Oxford, 1823), vol. 5, p. 420.
[80] Henry Sacheverell, 1674–1724, student, Fellow, and Bursar, Magdalen College, Oxford.
[81] T. B. Howell (ed.), *A Complete Collection of State Trials*, vol. 15 (1812), cols. 89 and 83.

control, with Godolphin wishing 'it never had begun'.[82] Wren oversaw the conversion of Westminster Hall to accommodate the huge crowds; tickets were
in such short supply that they were soon traded on an active black market;
the Queen attended incognito; Sacheverell was escorted to the trial each day
by aides and supporters; and the mob began physically to attack the 'false
brethren' such as Dissenters that Sacheverell had chided. For the period it was
a lengthy trial (27 February to 20 March 1710), providing a great show-
piece debate over the nature and consequences of the Glorious Revolution.
Sacheverell was supported by Atterbury and the former Solicitor General Sir
Simon Harcourt, and among the prosecution's big guns was the young Robert
Walpole.

Sacheverell was found guilty by a majority of just seventeen Lords (69 to
52). The Queen's opinion, 'that there ought to be a punishment but a mild
one', was shared by the judges.[83] Sacheverell was suspended from preaching
for three years and his sermons were to be burned. Though he had been found
guilty such an outcome was widely interpreted as a Pyrrhic victory for the
Whigs, an endorsement of the doctor, and a great fillip to the High Church
cause. Toasts, bonfires, and dozens of loyal addresses to the Queen celebrated
his principles—one gentleman distributed 1,710 loaves of bread to the poor,
each inscribed on the side '*Sacheverell 1710*'.[84] Sacheverell's popularity was
huge, and his legal costs of £800 fell nearly £1,600 short of the donations he
had received. He was given a lucrative rectory in Shropshire and his journey
there was little short of a victory progress, involving ten civic receptions. While
at Oxford he rode round the surrounding districts, 'stirring up the people who
hold him in such honour that they flock to him in hundreds, especially the
women'.[85] At the same time Anne began to abandon the Whigs and the October
general election produced a crushing victory for the Tories. The High Church
moment had arrived.

The zenith of the High Church reaction was reached in the last four years
of Anne's reign. In 1711 Parliament at last legislated against occasional conformity, requiring conformists to take communion at least three times a year; in
1712 the General Naturalization Act of 1709 was repealed, closing England as
safe haven for foreign Protestants; and in 1714 the Schism Act was passed in
an attempt to stamp out the Dissenters's schools. In this environment Jonathan
Swift was in his element and did much to champion the cause. Yet the overlap

[82] *The Marlborough–Godolphin Correspondence*, ed. H. L. Snyder, 3 vols. (Oxford, 1975),
vol. 3, p. 1428.
[83] *The Diary of Sir David Hamilton, 1709–1714*, ed. P. Roberts (Oxford, 1975), p. 6.
[84] Quoted in G. Holmes, *The Trial of Dr Sacheverell* (1973), p. 240.
[85] *Oxford in 1710, from the Travels of Zacharias Conrad von Uffenbach*, ed. W. H. and
W. J. C. Quarrell (Oxford, 1928), p. 41.

which existed between extreme Toryism, the High Church, and Jacobitism meant that everything depended upon the health of the Queen. When George I succeeded in 1714 the days of an effective High Church reaction were numbered. By December the King issued a warning against 'public opposition between preachers' and 'That none of the clergy in their sermons or lectures presume to intermeddle in any affairs of state or government'.[86] Within two years he had overseen the appointment of seven bishops, most prominently the translation of Wake from Lincoln to Canterbury (which he held until 1737), with Gibson taking his place at Lincoln, and the appointment of Hoadly to Bangor. All three were exponents of limited toleration, though only Hoadly can be categorized as unorthodox. Against the background of the Jacobite rebellion of 1715–16 and the political isolation of the Tories, this recasting of the episcopal bench decisively reduced the significance of the High Church. After its inconclusive meeting in 1717 Convocation was dissolved, not meeting in earnest again until 1852, and in 1719 both the Schism and Occasional Conformity Acts were repealed. After 1722 the Treasury even paid a semi-secret subsidy to Dissenting churches. The twists and turns provoked plenty of mocking, from the ballad 'The Vicar of Bray' (1720), which told the tale of a cleric who changed his colours continuously in order to retain his Berkshire benefice, to Matthew Prior's poetic prediction from 1709.[87]

> Among the *High Church Men*, I find there are several
> That stick to the *Doctrine* of *Henry Sacheverell*;
> Among the *Low Church* too, I find that as Odly,
> *Some pin all their* Faith *on one* Benjamin Hoadly.
> But we *Moderate Men* do our *Judgment Suspend*,
> For God only knows where *these Matters* will End;
> And *Salisbury Burnett* and *White Kennet* show,
> That as the Times vary, so *Principles* go.
> And Twenty Years hence, for ought you or I know,
> 'Twill be *Hoadly* the high, and *Sacheverel* the low.[88]

---

[86] 'Directions to Our Archbishop and Bishops for the Preserving of Unity in the Church, the Purity of the Christian Faith Concerning the Holy Trinity; and also for Preserving the Peace and Quiet of the State', E. Cardwell (ed.), *Documentary Annals of the Reformed Church of England*, 2 vols. (Oxford, 1839), vol. 2, p. 366.

[87] Matthew Prior, 1664–1721, educated Westminster school and St John's College, Cambridge, where he became a Fellow 1688, entered House of Commons 1701 and held fast to the Tories, many diplomatic posts, especially in negotiating the Treaty of Utrecht, active poet, imprisoned 1715–17.

[88] 'Dr Sacheverell and Benjamin Hoadly', in *Poems on Affairs of State: Augustan Satirical Verse 1660–1714*, vol. 7. *1704–1714*, ed. F. H. Ellis (New Haven, 1975), pp. 359–60. White Kennett, 1660–1728, was a leading Low Churchman and Bishop of Peterborough 1718–28.

Unable effectively to channel its passions through Parliament or Convocation, after 1714 the High Church entered a prolonged period of limited influence. It was nicely marked by the decline in observance of the statutory anniversaries for the martyrdom of Charles I and the Restoration (on 30 January and 29 May respectively). Yet neither did latitudinarians sweep all before them. Attempts to repeal the Test and Corporation Acts failed, there was no serious push for comprehension, clerical dominance of the universities was unchallenged, and the attempt to secularize parochial local government through the Select Vestries Bill of 1716 was defeated. Nor did the ideology which informed the High Church outlook quickly wither on the vine. It remained an important element among the range of opinions which characterized the eighteenth-century Church.

RENEWAL, REPRESSION, AND REFORM

The limited achievements of the High Church reaction should not detract from the fact that in many other ways the challenge of irreligion was purposefully tackled in this period. Fearful of divine retribution, much effort was put into reinvigorating true religion within English society. Attention was directed towards improving the spiritual education of the young, increasing the availability of pious literature to all, rescuing poor clergymen from want, improving the quality of the ministry, providing more places of worship, and stamping out vice. Such was the combined scale of these efforts that they constitute vivid evidence of the centrality and vitality of Protestantism generally and Anglicanism more particularly within English society.

A significant new feature of the religious landscape of late seventeenth-century England was provided by voluntary religious societies. Initially these sprang up from within the Church of England—especially in London where they had first appeared in 1678 and by 1714 somewhat more than a quarter of the capital's Anglican churches were involved with them. The societies aimed to aid the spiritual quest of members (usually middling sort) through mutual self-help. Though somewhat tangential to the formal structures of the Church, they in no direct sense challenged it, indeed the societies demonstrate the religious enthusiasm which existed within the mainstream. It was an enthusiasm embraced by the post-Revolution order, certain that 'a general reformation of the lives and manners of all our subjects' was necessary for complete political security and religious fulfilment.[89] In this environment three major

[89] 'His Majesty's Letter to the Right Reverend Father in God Henry Lord Bishop of London, to be Communicated to the Two Provinces of Canterbury and York', in *A Collection of Scarce and Valuable Tracts*, vol. 9, p. 589.

voluntary initiatives were launched: the Society for Promoting Christian Knowledge (SPCK), the Society for the Propagation of the Gospel (SPG), and the societies for the Reformation of Manners.

The SPCK was founded in early 1698, largely through the efforts of Thomas Bray.[90] In November 1699 the Society's first circular letter to provincial clergy complained of the 'visible decay of Religion' and the 'monstrous increase of Deism, Prophaneness, and Vice', ascribing this to 'the barbarous ignorance observable among the common people, especially those of the poorer sort, and this to proceed from want of due care in the education of the Youth'.[91] Thus it set about encouraging catechizing, promoting charity schools, and distributing uplifting literature, all to be directed by local societies and correspondents. Catechizing and primary education became particularly closely associated in the charity schools the Society encouraged. The growth of such schools has already been discussed, but it is also notable that between 1690 and 1710 there was a surge in the publication of new catechisms or catechetical works.[92] The SPCK targeted not only the young but also those it judged to be vulnerable to sin and vice. In March 1701 it was 'Ordered that 800 of the King Cautions against Swearing . . . be distributed amongst the Hackney Coachmen'; later that year 1,000 copies of a paper against drunkenness and 1,000 against 'Uncleanness' were sent to naval admirals to be given to seamen; and soon after 5,000 copies of Woodward's *The Soldier's Monitor* were printed.[93] To assist in just such endeavours Bray also sponsored the foundation of the SPG in 1701 which, in contrast to the domestic focus of the SPCK, particularly concerned itself with looking to provide for colonial Anglicans and to undertake some missionary work. As with the SPCK this was very much an Anglican body, enjoying the enthusiastic support of the likes of Tenison, Compton, and Sharp.[94] Though neither society was very large—in 1710 the SPCK had about 159 members and the SPG about 226, with significant overlap between the two—the generous financial support they enjoyed and the intensity of their proselytizing made them highly visible. A huge amount of effort was channelled through both societies and by 1705 Burnet was, perhaps wishfully, already celebrating 'More constant Prayers, more frequent Communions, more diligent Catechising. Visiting the Sick. Schools of Charity.'[95]

---

[90] Thomas Bray, 1656–1730, educated All Souls College, Oxford, travelled to Maryland to help organize the clergy 1699, never held high office in the Church.

[91] *A Chapter in English Church History: Being the Minutes of the Society for the Promotion of Christian Knowledge for the Years 1698–1704*, ed. E. McClure (1888), p. 36, note.

[92] See above, pp. 169–70.   [93] *Minutes of the S. P. C. K.*, pp. 122, 138, and 148.

[94] Thomas Tenison, 1636–1715, student and Fellow Corpus Christi College, Cambridge, Bishop of Lincoln 1691–4, Archbishop of Canterbury 1694, active supporter of Hanoverian succession.

[95] Quoted in C. Jones, 'Debates in the House of Lords on "The Church in Danger", 1705, and on Dr Sacheverell's Impeachment, 1710', *Historical Journal*, 19 (1976), p. 766.

Although taking root in the same soil of spiritual renewal and quest for primitive Christianity that had supported the SPCK and the SPG, the Reformation of Manners societies were in many important respects distinct, though there was some common membership between the three. First, though arising from within Anglicanism—the first Reformation of Manners society was established in Tower Hamlets in London in 1691—by 1694 they had admitted Dissenters as members. Consequently, whereas few Churchmen failed to embrace the SPCK and the SPG on grounds of principle, many refused to have anything to do with the reformation societies and those who did often had a Dissenting background. Second, the *modus vivendi* of the Reformation of Manners societies was primarily disciplinary, seeking to enforce the numerous laws which already existed against all forms of vice. Members searched the streets with blank warrants and employed (occasionally unreliable) informers in order to prosecute thousands of men and women before the civil authorities. Pressure was also brought to bear on local government to obliterate dens of iniquity, which to such kill joys might include, as at Bristol, 'Stage playes, Musick houses, Lotteryes, [and] Gameing houses'.[96] The Reformation of Manners societies were distinguished, therefore, by their resort to secular authority to enforce a rigid moral code. Coercion not persuasion was their watchword and received some encouragement through royal proclamations issued in 1692, 1698, 1699, 1702, and 1703. The main thinking behind the reformation societies was that unless vice was checked 'they may bring down the heaviest judgments of God upon us' and, secondly, 'Where Men are no more restrained by the Principles of Religion . . . Nature must break out, and undisciplined Appetites and Passions must work the Dissolution of Society and Government'.[97]

Though Reformation societies were founded in a number of towns they were absent from many others and made their most dramatic impact in London where, for a time, ill-doers had to keep ever alert for these private enforcers of legal morality. Prostitutes, charged with lewd and disorderly behaviour, were a favoured target, as Table 5 shows. The impressive scale of this wave of prosecutions bears ample witness to the fervour and fury at the heart of the Reformation of Manners societies. However, it also meant that there were sometimes bitter battles with ordinary people—in London two members of

---

[96] *Reformation and Revivial in Eighteenth-Century Bristol*, ed. J. Barry and K. Morgan, Bristol Record Society, 45 (1994), p. 22.

[97] 'His Grace the Lord Archbishop of Canterbury's Letter to the Right Reverend the Lords Bishops of his Province', in Cardwell (ed.), *Documentary Annals*, vol. 2, p. 347; G. Burnet, 'A Sermon Preached at Whitehall, Before the King and Queen, on the 29th of April, 1691, Being the Fast Day', in Burnet, *A Third Collection of Several Tracts and Discourses Written in the Years 1690, to 1703* (1703), p. 20.

TABLE 5. *Prosecutions initiated by London Societies for the Reformation of Manners, 1708–1724*

	Swearing and cursing	Sabbath breaking	Drunkenness	Lewd and disorderly	Keep bawdy house	Gaming	Total
1708	626	1,187	150	1,255	51	30	3,299
1709	575	1,523	42	794	32	10	2,976
1715	263	1,066	46	1,152	36	8	2,571
1716	102	621	14	1,066	9	8	1,820
1717	400	524	25	1,927	33		2,909
1718	205	492	17	1,253	31	8	2,006
1720	114	615	11	1,189	14	16	1,959
1721	161	709	13	1,197	15	4	2,099
1722	201	653	8	1,223	35	104	2,224
1723	96	648	5	1,622	36	42	2,449
1724	108	600	12	1,951	29	23	2,723

Source: R. B. Shoemaker, 'Reforming the City: The Reformation of Manners Campaign in London, 1690–1738', in L. Davison, T. Hitchcock, T. Keirn, and R. B. Shoemaker (eds.), *Stilling the Grumbling Hive: The Response to Social and Economic Problems in England, 1689–1750* (Stroud, 1992), p. 105.

the reformation societies were killed while attempting to make arrests. To people on the street, moreover, prosecutors targeted the poor and ignored the immorality of the rich, prompting the view that the reformation societies were merely part of the hypocrisy and authority of majesty rather than an attempt at religious revival. To that extent their tactics were inevitably counter-productive and alienated some from both church and meeting-house. Though some, not least William and Mary, also advocated the strategy of the elite reforming itself to provide a salutary example to the rest, this was largely invisible to those who lived in fear of the constables and informers employed by the Reformation of Manners societies.

Though it is uncertain that the religious societies made a significant difference to popular religious practice, they provide considerable evidence of the vitality of Anglicanism in this period. Great imagination and industry was displayed. Moreover, the societies were not the only signs of vitality. As has been seen many bishops carefully oversaw the work of their clergy through visitations. The output of printed sermons, which rose from about 1,000 per decade before the Revolution to nearly 2,500 by the end of Anne's reign before slowly declining thereafter, shows how readily the Church embraced the vibrant print culture world. Significant effort was also put into the physical fabric of the Church. St Paul's cathedral was finished and over the period 1689–1727 some 126 charity briefs were issued (all but 8 after Anne's accession) to raise money to build, extend, or repair churches—about 31 per cent of all charity briefs. Concern about the inadequacy of church provision was greatest in London. In 1711 the lower house of Convocation told the Commons that in the capital there were but 46 churches or chapels (compared to 75 Dissenting meeting-houses and 13 French congregations) which could accommodate only about half of the Anglican population. As a result, it was enacted that, 'computing 4,750 Souls to each Church', the capital be supplied with 50 new churches to be paid for out of a duty on coal shipments.[98] That only 12 were eventually built is evidence of extraordinary architectural ambition rather than a lack of commitment. Churches as remarkable as Nicholas Hawksmoor's St Anne, Limehouse, St Alfege, Greenwich, and Christ Church, Spitalfields or James Gibbs's (a Catholic!) St Mary-le-Strand were no mean achievements. Attempts were also made to improve the worldly circumstances of the Anglican clergy. As has been seen, relative poverty afflicted many at the start of the period. One modest response saw the expansion of the charitable Sons of the Clergy, providing aid to the widows and children of clergymen. Founded in 1655, granted a royal charter in 1678, in 1688 it was helping 209 widows and by 1721 621, a threefold rise made possible by generous bene-factions, especially £18,000 from Dr Turner, President of Corpus Christi, Oxford, in 1714. Such clerical self-help was an important part of the Church's identity, underscored by the annual festival in support of the charity through the period—held from 1697 in the splendour of the new St Paul's cathedral. More significant, however, was the institution of Queen Anne's Bounty in 1704.[99] Under this scheme the Queen gave up the revenues of first fruits (fur-ther endearing herself to the High Church) by putting them into a fund to be distributed among the poorer clergy. Administratively this was a consider-able undertaking, requiring the evaluation of 9,180 clerical livings (to which Gregory King contributed) and the accumulation of considerable sums. Between 1705 and 1736 some £580,926 was raised, though the first augmenta-tion of a poor living was not made until 1714 (some 6,400 grants were made over the next century).

CONCLUSION

In the 1720s relative calm and moderation surrounded religion. The threat of Roman Catholicism had been contained at home and abroad; Dissent was able to do little more than mark time; and the shock of Deism and unorthodoxy, having failed to penetrate deep into society, had gradually weakened. The Church of England had not collapsed because of James II's assaults, the non-juring schism, the Toleration Act, or occasional conformity. It remained a cen-tral part of political and civil society with the bulk of the population continuing

---

[98] *Journals of the House of Commons*, 16 (1708–11), p. 583.
[99] Such a scheme had been suggested to William and Mary by Gilbert Burnet.

to enter it at baptism. Yet the quiescence of the 1720s also reflected a mood of conservatism born of bitter experience. Attempts by the State to promote religious homogeneity and orthodox spiritual intensity that had begun at the Reformation had now reached their limit and, to an extent, were tacitly acknowledged to have failed. If political, economic, and social authority were all still closely tied to Anglicanism—the Test and Corporation Acts remained on the statute book until the early nineteenth century and Dissenters generally made headway only in local government and society—religious pluralism was reluctantly acknowledged even within the heart of the Church.

Whether secularization aided the cooling of religious passions by 1727 is difficult to assess on two main counts. First, whether in this period society became less spiritual, either personally or institutionally, is a moot point. Certainly priestcraft was attacked, Newtonianism offered the possibility of a non-spiritual world-view, and attendance at church may well have waned. But the siren cries against irreligion that can be found in abundance in the period often sound remarkably similar to those also to be found in, say, the 1590s, the 1650s, the 1790s, and the 1840s. Such 'moral panics' often had much more to do with political and social questions than purely religious ones. Second, the contemporary debate over religious unorthodoxy was, as has been seen, hot and fiery, not dispassionate and civil. Consequently, it was not so much that God, Christ, or the Church were less significant by 1727, rather that there was more uncertainty as to just what their significance was. In time that may have contributed to a markedly more secular outlook but few at the time anticipated, still less relished, such an outcome.

CHAPTER 8

England, Britain, Empire

Over the centuries England's relationship with Scotland and Wales has gone through many twists and turns. Nor has Britain's island situation ensured splendid isolation, for the surrounding seas have all been bridges as well as barriers. These geographical peculiarities of English history were strikingly analysed in 1701 by Defoe in his poem 'The True-Born Englishman', reminding that though some of the lineal ancestors of the English were ancient Britons, due account had to be paid to the impact of successive waves of invaders —Roman, Saxon, Danish, Scots, Picts, Irish, and Norman. 'From this amphibious ill-born mob began/ That vain ill-natured thing, an Englishman.'[1] Language and law, customs and surnames, had been blended over many centuries, a process that was still continuing as the interests of Huguenot refugees and Dutch invaders were thrown into the pot. By the early seventeenth century, however, England had already turned the tables on the rest of the British Isles and was also beginning to export her interests overseas, especially across the Atlantic. Thus to some, even to the Irishman John Toland, 'Tho I commonly use the word *England* in its proper sense, yet I sometimes understand by it all the *British* Dominions'.[2]

England was the most powerful polity within the British Isles in this period, a position never doubted by governors and opinion makers in London. Yet if that led to various constraints being laid or imposed upon other countries, there was little consistency either in their form or success. The nature of political attachments varied; English military might was utilized only occasionally; and the Anglicization of Ireland, Scotland, and Wales was distinctly limited. The British Isles was not in practical terms a unified and coherent English empire. Indeed, the relationship was never unidirectional, for English interests were liable to be influenced by those of her neighbours. Wider afield, England was unusual in the extent to which she attempted to establish 'plantations'

[1] D. Defoe, 'The True-Born Englishman', in G. de F. Lord (ed.), *Anthology of Poems on Affairs of State: Augustan Satirical Verse, 1660–1714* (New Haven, 1975), p. 628.
[2] *The State Anatomy of Great Britain* (9th edn., 1717), p. 46.

in America (meaning both the West Indies and North America) in the seventeenth and eighteenth centuries. Yet contemporaries were struck by the equivocal nature of that empire to England—that her colonies often voiced ambitions for greater independence, that many inhabitants were not English by origin, and that they were prey to attack from European competitors, indigenous people, and the natural environment. Though by 1700 England's empire was clearly larger than it had been a century earlier, contemporaries were as much impressed by its problems as by its potential. Closely managing and maintaining England's imperial jurisdiction while attempting to wage two great wars in Europe was simply impossible.

AN IMPERIAL DOMAIN

With the death of the childless Elizabeth in 1603 the Crowns of England and Scotland were united in the person of James VI and I. His English inheritance brought with it the kingdom of Ireland, the principality of Wales, and a fanciful claim to France. This monarchical empire was extended over the course of the seventeenth century with the development of colonies in the West Indies and North America. By 1689 England was part of a complex and uncertain concoction of kingdoms and domains, a compound made only more volatile by the Glorious Revolution. Though James II had pursued his unpopular policies across his imperial jurisdiction, provoking widespread hostility, it was not a foregone conclusion that all parts would emulate England and acknowledge the joint monarchy of William and Mary. If the course of the Revolution was dominated by events in England, those in Ireland, Scotland, and North America also had a wide significance. The Glorious Revolution was never merely English; it was also British, European, and imperial.

This monarchical empire was united under one Crown, but not by one rule, religion, economy, social structure, or national identity. Wales, the nation most closely integrated with England, nicely illustrates some of the points of unity and division. One symbolic connection was that the eldest son of the monarch was titled the Prince of Wales—in this period the future George II was the first to hold the title (though it was also claimed for the Pretender between 1688 and 1701). More importantly, Wales sent MPs to Parliament, was part of the legal system whose final court of appeal was the House of Lords, was substantially Anglican, sent its favoured sons to Oxford, and paid customs and taxes to London. The abolition of the Council of Wales in 1689 signified this institutional harmony. Economically the links were evidenced by the 'great herds of black cattle . . . [that] fill our fairs and markets, even that of Smithfield', and the involvement of English commerce in the considerable trade issuing out of the Severn estuary and Pembroke.[3] Nor was Wales the site of very significant Jacobite activity. One Welshman was even prepared to claim that 'we are Englishmen, and must, like good patriots, stand by our country'.[4] Yet outside the gentry class most Welsh experienced a distinctive cultural milieu of history, music, ballads, and literature and were, to a considerable extent, untouched by life on the other side of Offa's Dyke. Welsh was the strongest of all the Celtic languages in the British Isles, used by perhaps 90 per cent of the population. Indeed, Wales's Celtic heritage was put on a secure scholarly footing through the efforts of Edward Lhwyd whose *Archæologia Britannica* (1707) showed the common Celtic ancestry of Breton, Irish, Cornish, and Welsh languages.[5] In practice the English were relatively powerless in Wales, typified by the failure of the SPCK to make headway with its charity schools by the late 1720s. Welsh independence kept alive a tradition among some English to belittle their neighbours, portraying them as rustic and uncivilized. An extreme view characterized its mountains as 'the fag end of the Creation; the very Rubbish of *Noah's Flood*' and the Welsh language as 'inarticulate and guttural . . . more like the Gobling of Geese, or Turkeys, than the Speech of Rational Creatures.'[6]

Wales managed to strike a successful balance between integration and independence, yet it was never held up as an ideal to be emulated by the other parts of the Crown's imperial domain. In 1689 Scotland, Ireland, and the colonies were distinguished from Wales by having their own legislatures and by the minority status of Anglicanism. Consequently, each had their own view of the Glorious Revolution and of the nature of their relationship with England. In Scotland James's numerous supporters fought for him with their lives in 1689–90 and 1715–16. As we have seen, James sought to reclaim his throne by force of arms through Ireland in 1689.[7] And in some colonies James's flight in 1688 led to armed rebellion. Many in Ireland, Scotland, and the colonies viewed England as a predatory power, largely self-interested in its dealings with them, yet also affording military aid, a language of liberty, and commercial opportunity. In turn, England looked upon each as a political problem to be solved and an economic resource to be exploited. Yet if security and prosperity were the twin motives at the heart of English perceptions of the benefits

---

[3] D. Defoe, *A Tour Through the Whole Island of Great Britain*, ed. P. Rogers (Harmondsworth, 1978), p. 377.

[4] W. Cobbett (ed.), *The Parliamentary History of England*, 36 vols. (1806–20), vol. 5, p. 985.

[5] Edward Lhwyd (sometimes Lhuyd), 1660–1709, educated Jesus College, Oxford, Keeper of the Ashmolean Museum 1690–1709, Fellow of the Royal Society 1708.

[6] 'A Trip to North-Wales', pp. 2–3, in E. Ward, *Five Travel Scripts Commonly Attributed to Edward Ward*, ed. H. W. Troyer (New York, 1933).

[7] See above, pp. 93–7.

of close and controlled ties with Scotland, Ireland, and the colonies, there was never a coherent imperial mission and English political responsibility for relations with these areas was highly fragmented.

For centuries London had worried that foreign invaders would use Scotland and Ireland as a gateway to England. That worry only increased after 1689, with the scale of the Jacobite threat ensuring that considerable resources were needed to pacify the British Isles as a whole. In part that was achieved by force of arms and physical intimidation. Yet military might was employed only occasionally. England did not for long station large armies and expend huge sums of money in ensuring Scottish and Irish obedience, not least because of the competing demands for money and men made by war against France. If it was occasionally possible to contain Scottish and Irish challenges militarily, such a solution could not be sustained over the long term. It was too expensive and uncertain. Rather England sought to govern the British Isles by use of allies who were happy to tie their future to London. Lowland Scots and Protestant Irish provided significant means of control. Yet that control was always more limited than might at first appear. Both countries retained a high degree of independence, even though Scotland lost its Parliament in 1707. English political ambitions were concentrated upon neutralizing the Jacobite threat, not upon governing, say, the everyday lives of Highland clansmen.

It is, indeed, remarkable how infrequently English politicians considered what might now be called imperial questions and of how responsibility was split between various officers. Dependence upon the Crown as a pivotal figure and office was necessarily rendered less certain by changes in the nature of monarchical authority after 1689. Further, monarchs undoubtedly saw England as the lifeblood of their dominion, William's single campaign in Ireland in 1690 being the only visit by a monarch in this period to another part of the British Isles (Anne had briefly visited Scotland in 1681). Moreover, the few royal officials in Ireland, Scotland, and the colonies often lacked authority, being highly dependent upon local political authorities. Operating at a distance of hundreds or thousands of miles and many weeks from their masters they could not be asked to follow a tightly prescribed line of policy. Matters were also confused by the situation in London. Before the Union in 1707 no minister in London had overriding responsibility for relations with Scottish, and, over the whole period, Ireland came under the jurisdiction of Lord Lieutenants who usually spent little time in the kingdom. Multiple responsibilities were most marked in colonial affairs, a situation encouraged by the variegated origins of different colonies. Policy making was divided in no very clearly defined way among the Crown in Privy Council, Parliament, and the Secretaries of State. If administratively after its foundation in 1696 the Board of Trade provided a central forum, it lacked executive authority and officers in the

Customs, Admiralty, War Office, and Treasury departments might all act in their own areas, while in ecclesiastical matters the Bishop of London was responsible for the new world.

Many in England looked longingly upon overseas empire as a means of national salvation. Spanish America and Dutch commerce were the great exemplars here. Yet in so far as England had an imperial plan it was largely economic in conception, though with important subsidiary strategic dimensions. That plan, first formulated in the middle of the seventeenth century, is remembered as the 'navigation system' and by it England tried to tie colonial consumption, production, and trade securely to its own interest—Ireland and, until 1707, Scotland were kept firmly outside. Through the Navigation Acts passed in 1651, 1660, and 1696 colonies were rarely allowed to trade except with England and that trade had to be conducted in English ships with English seamen (for which purpose the colonies were defined as English). It was hoped that colonies would reduce English dependency upon imports from European competitors such as tobacco from Spain and naval stores from the Baltic—in 1705 the Naval Stores Act sought through bounties to encourage the production of masts, pitch, and tar in North America. Moreover, if these goods were sent in an unprocessed form they would generate employment opportunities in England. Further, colonial imports surplus to English demand might then be re-exported to Europe, helping trading balances and promoting the shipping industry against Dutch dominance of the carrying trade. A powerful mercantile marine was, in any case, seen as a prerequisite for a powerful navy, '*Shipping* being our Security'.[8] It was also hoped that the colonies would provide significant markets for English goods and become complimentary to the English economy. One feature of this was to protect key parts of the domestic economy, especially agriculture and the woollen industry which was well represented in Parliament. This might mean preventing imports of certain commodities even if they could be produced more cheaply abroad. On the English side the presumption behind the navigation system was of colonial dependence upon and subordination to the needs of the mother country. In this view as England had prepared and seeded the plantations only she might reap the harvest.

England lacked the wherewithal to commit substantial resources to cajole and coerce its empire. Thus it is instructive that in this period it took the greatest legislative pains over commercial matters, passing numerous laws to perfect the navigation system. In 1696 William, defeating an attempt by Parliament to wrest control from him, appointed the Board of Trade to oversee commercial, especially colonial, issues. The Navigation Act of the same year, 'for the better

---

[8] W. Wood, *A Survey of Trade* (1718), p. 152.

securing and regulating of the plantation trade', was a further attempt at a degree of centralization of colonial policy.[9] To check smuggling and illicit trade it strengthened the customs service and prepared the ground for the establishment in the following year of eleven Vice-Admiralty courts on the western seaboard of America and in the West Indies. By the death of George I a further twenty-seven Acts were passed at Westminster dealing with different aspects of the commercial relationship between England and her empire (the period 1660–88 had seen only five such Acts).

The empire of which England was a part may have been forged on the fire of security and plenty but it was also tempered by the connections of people and ideas. People moved in every direction, both within the British Isles and between those islands, Africa, the West Indies, and North America. This was the flesh and blood of empire, be they free migrants, indentured servants, transported convicts, or slaves. Yet coming from so many different backgrounds, moving for very different reasons, and experiencing such different new lives, created a more not less heterogeneous identity in which 'British' had no very clear or deep meaning. England might have believed itself to be the linchpin of these societies, yet not only in Wales, Ireland, and Scotland but also across the Atlantic many were deeply ambivalent about their feelings towards England. Did, for example, New England Puritans relish and respect the High Church credentials of Anne, or Indians and slaves their subjection to George I? Once planted in foreign soil English institutions, customs, laws, and cultures started to develop a life of their own. England may have been at the heart of the British empire, and believed that empire was ruled over by its monarch, Parliament, and laws, but political and military dominance did not bring absolute control, even in the sphere of overseas trade where its grip was strongest. It was an empire of many separate interests, many identities, all loosely collected together under one monarch, but often pulling in several directions at once.

THE SCOTTISH CHALLENGE, 1689–1705

The Stewart family had provided Scottish monarchs since the fourteenth century and Scotland was proud of this unbroken line of descent. Yet ironically it had been the fertility of James and the birth of the Prince of Wales in the summer of 1688 which set in train the events leading to William's invasion and James's flight. From France James continued to lay claim to all his realms. In Scotland that claim was given weight not only by his Stewart ancestry but also by his familiarity with Scottish life, acquired during his residency there from 1679 during the Exclusion crisis in England. The Scots knew James and James

---

[9] 7 and 8 William and Mary, c. 22.

knew the Scots to a degree unmatched by any subsequent monarch until at least Victoria. Yet that knowledge produced just as passionate a mix of loyalty and hatred as was to be found south of the border. That cauldron of opinion was further spiced by the strength of Scottish Presbyterianism and the significance of the Highland–Lowland divide. As a result eighteenth-century Scotland remained the most important centre of Jacobitism within the British Isles.

Scotland, delighted to have resisted English expansionism over the centuries, had retained a high degree of independence after the union of the Crowns in 1603. Thus Edinburgh no less than London experienced a lively debate in the early months of 1689 over the nature of the desired political and religious settlement. It says much that though Scottish politicians also offered the throne to William and Mary their experience of the Glorious Revolution was altogether distinctive. For example, it was explicitly claimed that Scottish monarchical government was restricted and that James far from having 'abdicated', as the English fictionalized, was being cast off by his people. The Claim of Right, the Scottish equivalent to England's Bill of Rights, complained that James had altered the kingdom 'from a legal limited Monarchy, to an arbitrary despotick Power . . . whereby he hath forefaulted the right to the Crown, and the Throne is become vacant.'[10] More significant, however, was the assertion of religious and legislative independence.

Because of the significance of Calvinism, the Reformation in Scotland had taken a different course from that in England and Presbyterianism had come to enjoy such widespread support through all social groups that it was, indeed, an integral element of Scotland's national identity. Thus to many in 1689 the aim was not only to reverse James's policies in favour of Roman Catholics but also to prevent the supremacy of English-style episcopalianism. In July 1689 the Scottish Convention Parliament passed an Act abolishing prelacy and in 1690 those ministers ejected in 1662 who were still alive were restored to their parishes and Presbyterian church government was established, purging many episcopalians in the process. Because of his own religious background and his desire to turn his attention as quickly as possible to war with France such a settlement suited William more than the English political and religious establishment and underscored national distinctions. However, at the same time the Scottish Parliament was able to increase its independence by abolishing the Lords of the Articles who had hitherto controlled much of its business. Consequently through the 1690s, faced by republicans, Jacobites, radical Presbyterians, and powerful magnates, William found it next to impossible to manage Scotland. For the first time since the Civil Wars England was faced by

[10] W. C. Dickinson and G. Donaldson (eds.), *A Source Book of Scottish History*, vol. 3 (2nd edn., Edinburgh, 1961), p. 203.

a neighbour able to give voice to its own political will, though only rarely was that voice heard and respected.

Westminster was particularly worried that Scottish political independence would provide the ideal climate to ripen Scottish Jacobitism. The fear was well founded. In 1689 a Jacobite army under Viscount Dundee had attempted to reverse the Revolution.[11] He raised his standard in April but, able to gather a force of only a little over 2,000 men, mostly Highlanders, he was limited to guerilla warfare before a final fling of the dice. On 27 July he defeated the new regime's army at Killiecrankie in the southern Grampians near Pitlochry. However, Dundee was himself killed in the battle and within a month his small force had been defeated at Dunkeld. Though another small encounter took place at Cromdale in Strathspey on May Day 1690 and many clans remained in a state of military preparedness until 1691 the conflicts that constituted this so-called 'Highland War' had effectively lasted but five months. None, however, believed that Scottish Jacobitism had been eradicated. It was particularly strong in the Highlands, where out of 50 clans some 28 were Jacobite. Of those 28, it is worth noting, none were predominantly Presbyterian, only 6 were Roman Catholic and 14 were episcopalian (the remainder being of mixed denomination). Scottish Jacobitism, partly rooted in the Scottish credentials of the Stuarts, also gained strength from the distinctive nature of Highland society and the reaction of that society to the particularly radical nature of the Revolution settlement reached in Edinburgh. In fact in some respects the divide between Highland and Lowland was as significant as that between Scotland and England—in the 1720s it was claimed, with only slight exaggeration, that 'The Highlands are but little known even to the Inhabitants of the low Country of Scotland'.[12] The relative social and economic autonomy of the clans and their use of Gaelic set Highlanders apart from the more Anglicized lowlanders.

Divisions within Scottish society were displayed most awfully on 13 February 1692 when thirty-six members of the MacDonald clan were massacred by Scottish government troops at Glencoe, on the pretext of having failed to meet the new year deadline for the clans to swear allegiance to William and Mary. In the massacre Scot killed Scot, effectively on the orders of a Scotsman, John Dalrymple, Master of Stair and Secretary for Scotland.[13] The Glencoe massacre was not part of an English plan to exterminate the clans, not least

---

[11] John Graham of Claverhouse, c.1649–89, student at St Andrews, served with William in the 1670s, Scottish Privy Councillor 1684, created Viscount Dundee 1688.

[12] [E. Burt], *Letters from a Gentleman in the North of Scotland to his Friend in London*, 2 vols. (Edinburgh, 1974), vol. 1, p. 4.

[13] John Dalrymple, 1648–1707, committed to the new regime following the flight of James II in 1688, succeeded as Viscount Stair in 1695, Privy Councillor 1702, created Earl of Stair 1703.

because such an ambition was well beyond her limited means at the time. Rather, it reflected the poor control exercised by William and English ministers over Scottish affairs in the 1690s. Where William was culpable was in obstructing calls for an inquiry until 1695 and, when Dalrymple was exposed by that inquiry, in indemnifying and rewarding him. Nothing could more clearly have demonstrated the poverty of the King's knowledge of Scottish affairs or his contempt for Scottish opinion. In this, as ever, he was his own man, giving primacy to European balance of power considerations, but was probably encouraged by English anti-Scottish feeling. That sentiment, with deep historic roots, was only encouraged by the progress of the Glorious Revolution north of the border. It was a commonplace that 'Never two Nations that had so much Affinity in Circumstances, have had such Inveteracy and Aversion to one another in their Blood.'[14]

In the years following the Glorious Revolution Scotland was only partly and reluctantly part of Britain. The freeing of her Parliament from the control of the Lords of the Articles in 1689 wrecked any prospect William might have had of exerting his royal will through Edinburgh. Instead legislators frequently flexed their muscles, challenging William's prerogatives and calling his ministers to account. More widely, though many Scots served in William's armies on the continent that was due both to a sense of duty and economic necessity. Lacking a developed industrial base or a significant overseas commerce, the Scottish economy was particularly prey to the vicissitudes of the weather upon agricultural output. In 1695 the harvest failed in what was to be the first of seven so-called 'ill years' of dearth and want (not all years were bad in fact). In 1698 it was claimed that 'many thousands of our people who are at this day dying for want of bread' and tens of thousands fled abroad, mostly from the south and west and mainly to Ulster.[15] Those who saw these disasters readily ascribed some responsibility to the English policy of protecting and nurturing its own economy. In this view England had hindered economic development in Scotland by excluding it from the growing colonial trade and by imposing duties in the early 1660s upon the import into England of Scottish coal, beef, linen, hides, yarn, salt, and cattle. Given that England was Scotland's most important trading partner (the reverse was not the case), this closed off a potential channel of economic advancement. Not surprisingly Scottish opinion reacted strongly to such exclusion (though Scotland also excluded or limited the import of certain English commodities) and sought ways out. Attempts at establishing Scottish colonies in New Jersey and South Carolina had already

---

[14] [D. Defoe], *The History of the Union of Great Britain* (Edinburgh, 1709), p. 1. Pagination to this volume is confusing and this is from the first section.

[15] A. Fletcher, *Political Writings*, ed. J. Robertson (Cambridge, 1997), p. 56.

been attempted when in 1695 the Company of Scotland trading to Africa and the Indies, the so-called 'Darien Company', was incorporated by Scottish Act of Parliament. Initially this was an Anglo-Scottish enterprise, aimed at allowing merchants from both countries to cut into the monopolies of the English East India and Royal Africa Companies. However, reaction to this threat was so strong in London—William believed his interests had been ignored and Parliament presented him with a strong address against the new Company —that English cooperation was closed off, thus leaving Scottish capital as the sole support of the fledgling enterprise. Moreover, when in 1698 the Company attempted to establish a colony at Darien in Spanish territory at the southern end of the isthmus of Panama London ordered its Caribbean colonies not to provide aid and assistance. Prey to mosquitoes and Spanish forces, by 1700 all three expeditions to Darien had failed to gain a foothold at enormous cost of life and capital.

SCOTLAND, UNION, AND REBELLION

The failure of the Darien scheme cruelly exposed the limited benefits to Scotland of a considerable but still incomplete degree of political independence. In the union of the Crowns Scotland's voice counted for relatively little, allowing English interests to predominate. Painfully aware of such impotence, the death of Anne's son, the Duke of Gloucester, in July 1700 presented Scotland with the important choice of whether the line of succession should be the same as England's. Feelings in favour of independent action were intensified when, with complete lack of sensitivity and political judgement, Westminster passed its Act of Settlement in June 1701 without consulting Scotland. Led by the brilliance of Andrew Fletcher of Saltoun and a 'Country party' coalition in Parliament, anti-English opinion entered a golden age. 'All our affairs since the union of the crowns have been managed by the advice of English ministers . . . we have from that time appeared . . . more like a conquered province, than a free independent people.'[16] By this view the time was now ripe to reclaim true Scottish independence by breaking the union of the Crowns: 'though we suffer under many grievances, yet our dependence upon the court of England is the cause of all, comprehends them all, and is the band that ties up the bundle.'[17] Others, not always as principled, soon joined the bandwagon. Anglo-Scottish relations had reached a crossroads.

[16] Fletcher, *Political Writings*, p. 132. Andrew Fletcher, 1653–1716, succeeded as Laird of Saltoun 1665, travelled in the Dutch Republic and France, participated in Monmouth's rebellion at accession of James II, fled abroad, returned to Scotland 1688, Member for Haddingtonshire in Scottish Parliament 1703, published a number of works on Scottish politics.

[17] Fletcher, *Political Writings*, p. 145.

English political opinion never wavered in its view that for security reasons a degree of union with Scotland was necessary. William, conscious of the weakness of ties based only upon a union of the Crowns, and therefore upon the health and fertility of a few individuals, had long harboured hopes of closer links. He recommended union in 1689 and 1690, and in 1700 recommended 'some happy Expedient for making [England and Scotland] One people.'[18] He repeated the call only days before he died and it was soon taken up by Anne. In 1702–3 Commissioners from both countries met in London to try to find the basis for a fuller union. Though to the Earl of Mar the discussions succeeded 'pritty well' and 'the English are fair enoch hitherto' mounting opposition in Scotland put a stop to progress.[19] Indeed, calls for Scottish independence were reaching new heights. In 1703 the Edinburgh Parliament passed three measures asserting national independence: the Act Anent Peace and War established the need after Anne's death for Scottish parliamentary consent for waging war and making treaties and alliances; the Wine Act challenged the English ban on the import into Britain of French wines; and the Act of Security threatened a non-Hanoverian succession unless Scottish parliamentary, religious, and commercial freedoms were guaranteed. Though initially royal assent was withheld from the Act of Security it was passed in 1704 because the English treasury was desperate to secure Scottish taxes. The prospect that at Anne's death Scotland might reject the Hanoverians rapidly concentrated English minds, as did the realization of the depth of Scottish anti-English sentiment demonstrated by the execution on trumped-up charges of piracy of the captain and two officers of a ship, the *Worcester*, which had innocently sought shelter in the Forth. At this juncture English paranoia only added to the sense of purpose, Lord Haversham warning in December 1704 that the Scottish 'common people . . . are very numerous and very stout, but very poor. And who is the man that can answer what such a multitude, so armed, so disciplined, with such leaders, may do . . . And there will never be wanting all the promises and all the assistance France can give.'[20] England's response was to flex its muscles. Pressure was exerted on the Scots in March 1705 by the Alien Act which appointed Union Commissioners and threatened

---

[18] *Journals of the House of Lords*, 16 (1696–1701), p. 514. John Erskine, 1675–1732, 6th/11th Earl of Mar, Scottish Privy Councillor 1696, Union Commissioner 1705, Secretary of State for Scotland 1713–14, Scottish representative peer 1707, 1708, 1710, 1713, advocated repeal of the Union 1713, instigated the Jacobite rising of 1715–16, joined the Jacobite court after the rising failed.

[19] H. M. C., *Report on the Manuscripts of the Earl of Mar and Kellie* (1904), p. 227.

[20] Cobbett (ed.), *Parliamentary History*, vol. 6, p. 370. John Thompson, 1647–1710, Baronet 1673, initially supported William III, created Baron Haversham 1696, Lord of the Admiralty 1699–1701, joined Tories.

that unless Scotland adopted the Hanoverian succession by December then any Scot in England would be treated as an alien and the Scottish trade in livestock, coal, and linen to England would be stopped (at the same time Westminster was seeking to encourage the Irish linen industry). In the event, in this earnest trial of strength, Scotland only agreed to appoint its Commissioners on condition that the Alien Act was repealed (which Westminster agreed to on 27 November).

The Union Commissioners convened in London between April and July 1706, the two sides conducting almost all their negotiations by paper rather than face to face. In all 25 articles of Union were drawn up, which were ratified by the Scottish Parliament in January 1707 and then by Westminster on 6 March. As if to mark a great victory the guns of the Tower of London were fired to celebrate the achievement. The key features of the Union included establishing: a single kingdom of 'Great Britain' with the succession vested in the Hanoverians; a single Parliament at Westminster by expanding the Commons and Lords to include 45 MPs from Scottish constituencies and 16 elected Scottish peers; a British free trade area and the use of English standards of coins, weights, and measures within it; an equality of status of Scots and English in colonial trade; and a unified fiscal system based upon that already in place in England. Also of note, no change was made to Scotland's legal system, Presbyterian settlement, universities, burghs (towns with charters), or heritable jurisdictions (hereditary criminal jurisdictions). Scotland's last Parliament was dissolved in April and the Union came into effect on 1 May 1707. With the merging of the flags of St George and St Andrew the united kingdom of 'Great Britain' was born.

In England the Union was subject to remarkably little discussion. The House of Commons ratified the articles almost without debate and in the Lords opposition was decisively in the minority, though figures such as the Bishop of Bath and Wells issued dire warnings: he 'was altogether against the Union . . . he could no better compare it, than to the mixing of strong liquors, of a contrary nature, in one and the same vessel, which would go nigh to be burst asunder by their furious fermentation'.[21] Yet Scottish opinion was so bitterly divided that union was never a foregone conclusion. A lively debate was conducted with over 530 pamphlets, sermons, poems, and treatises on the question put into print. The view from Alloa was that 'generally there appears ane aversione at ane incorporatione with England be the conditions thereof never so favourable or plausible'.[22] Nationalist sentiment rang strongly and many, like Lord Belhaven, shuddered at the prospect of the death of '*our Ancient*

---

[21] Cobbett (ed.), *Parliamentary History*, vol. 6, p. 568.   [22] H. M. C., *Mar*, p. 274.

Mother CALEDONIA'.[23] Scotland would lose its Crown and Parliament; the number of its constituencies was to be reduced from 157 to 45; and its peerage was denied parity of status with their English counterparts. That the Scottish Parliament ultimately voted for its own abolition and the Union was partly due to bribery and corruption. A British and a Scottish dukedom to Queensberry and Roxburghe respectively helped ensure powerful support and Scotland was given a generous financial settlement: nearly £400,000, the 'equivalent', was granted to the Scottish revenue to cover the share of the English national debt it acquired with the Union, to compensate the creditors of the Darien scheme, and to reimburse those Scots who lost out from the adoption of the English coinage; and £20,000 cash was given to cover the expenses and arrears of office holders.[24] But many voted for the Union because they believed that without it Scotland would remain stuck in what they saw as the mire of an outmoded society and a stagnant economy. And though the Union was clearly not a federal one, nor was Scotland totally subsumed within England. Scottish exceptionalism was protected to a degree. Moreover, there were those, like Defoe, Harley's agent in Scotland from October 1706 to December 1707, and the Earl of Cromartie who passionately argued for the new State. 'May wee be Brittains, and down goe the old ignominious names of Scotland, of England.'[25]

Opinion in London was generally content with the Union for it settled the succession question, eradicated the problems posed by a Scottish Parliament, and ensured that the new arrangements would be dominated by English interests. Most in England probably looked down upon their northern neighbours and the Union had, if anything, made Westminster even less interested in Scotland. But if, from this perspective, Scotland 'was a beggar, and whoever married a beggar could only expect a louse for a portion' then, with Jacobitism, that louse was to prove very irritating.[26] Indeed, the Union gradually fomented Scottish Jacobitism. In March 1708 Louis XIV, anxious to distract allied attentions in Flanders, made available over 30 ships and 6,000 men to sail to Scotland with the Pretender in a concerted attempt to utilize Jacobite sentiment there. That the fleet was commanded by a man who never believed it

---

[23] Defoe, *History of the Union*, section 4, p. 34. John Hamilton, 1656–1708, 2nd Baron Belhaven, imprisoned 1681 for comments on the Duke of York, supported Darien scheme, advocate of Act of Security 1703, imprisoned 1708 on suspicion of Jacobitism.

[24] James Douglas, 1662–1711, succeeded as 2nd Duke of Queensberry 1695, educated at Glasgow University, joined William III 1688, created Duke of Dover, Marquis of Beverley, and Baron Ripon 1708, third Secretary of State 1709. John Ker, d. 1741, succeeded brother as 5th Earl of Roxburghe 1696, created Duke of Roxburghe 1707, Scots representative peer 1707, 1708, 1715, 1722, a Lords Justice when George I was abroad.

[25] H. M. C., *Mar*, p. 242.

[26] Quoted in W. Ferguson, *Scotland's Relations with England: A Survey to 1707* (Edinburgh, 1977), p. 201.

could succeed, overshot the entrance to the Forth by many miles, sailed home without landing any troops, and failed to prompt significant risings of support in Scotland, should not detract from the fact that even after the Union England's backdoor was still wide open. As Vanbrugh remarked, in 1708 Scotland was 'quite at Liberty to chuse wch Side they think best'.[27]

Neither Anne nor her ministers had a clear view as to how to manage Scotland after the Union. In 1708 the Scottish Privy Council was abolished in a somewhat cavalier fashion, in the hope of operating through leading Scottish magnates. In 1709 the Scottish Secretary was replaced by a third principal Secretary of State with specific responsibility for Scotland (though the post was abolished in 1725). Yet governing Scotland from London could only be done in the most general way, and because Edinburgh no longer functioned as a significant centre of government decision-making Scottish political society was badly fragmented and disordered, providing a seedbed of dissent. That soil was fertilized by imposing on Scotland the English treason law in 1709 and three years later, in the midst of the English High Church reaction, legislation introducing toleration for episcopacy, effectively breaking guarantees made to the Kirk in the Union. This also had the effect of demonstrating the minority status of the Scottish MPs and peers at Westminster—the Duke of Hamilton was also personally slighted by Parliament.[28] Thus in 1713 when proposals were put forward to extend the English malt tax throughout Britain voices were raised about reversing the Union. Scotland was learning what England had long known, that the decisions of one Parliament were not binding upon its successors.

Anne's death provided its greatest test. Scottish patriotism was rooted in a reverence for its ancient monarchy and now the country was to be governed by a German Prince of England's choosing. Many turned to Jacobitism as a means of reversing the Union. However, though they must have anticipated Anne's death when it happened it was reported from Edinburgh that 'the chiefs of the Jacobite party here . . . have been strangley surprised and taken unawares at the Queen's death'.[29] The delay of thirteen months between that surprise and the raising of the Jacobite standard by the embittered and self-seeking Mar at Braemar speaks volumes about the nature of Scottish discontent. It may have been heartfelt and full of potential, but it lacked strong leadership, adequate coordination and, vitally, significant foreign support. Though Edinburgh castle was attacked and a Jacobite army reached Preston, the rising fizzled out after

[27] *The Complete Works of Sir John Vanbrugh*, ed. B. Dobreé and G. Webb, 4 vols. (1928), vol. 4, p. 18.
[28] James Douglas Hamilton, 1658–1712, Scottish representative peer 1708–12, Privy Councillor 1710, created Duke of Brandon 1711, killed in duel by Lord Mohun.
[29] H. M. C., *The Manuscripts of his Grace the Duke of Portland*, vol. 5 (1899), p. 498.

the inconclusive encounter at Sheriffmuir on 13 November 1715, where Mar's 4,000 Jacobites failed to overrun 1,000 troops loyal to the Hanoverians under the Duke of Argyll.[30] Stuart ill-planning brought the Pretender to Scotland a month later and for six weeks he did little before turning round and sailing out of Montrose. He would never again set foot in the British Isles.

A fuller account of the English dimensions of and reactions to the '15 will be provided below.[31] Here, however, it must be noted that opinion in London took the rising very seriously. For example, under the terms of the Barrier Treaty 8,000 Dutch troops were sent to England and Scotland and Swiss mercenaries were also employed. Yet though the '15 fully exposed the continuing weakness of English policy over Scotland, it did not lead to a significant strengthening of that grip. There was too little patronage available to the government in Scotland to tie people into the future of the Union; the Commission of police established in 1714 to keep an eye on the Highlands, Roman Catholics, and the poor was never very effective; and most Scottish Jacobites returned home unpunished after the '15—though a good number were transported to America and two peers, Kenmure and Derwentwater, were executed in London.[32] Moreover, an attempt to seize the estates of rebels soon ran into the sands of deception and dissimulation. Some effort was made to ensure Hanoverian military dominance, especially in the Highlands. Lieutenancies and Highland companies were established and a Disarming Act passed in 1716. However, it is illustrative of the difficulties the government faced that the attempted disarming failed completely and, indeed, was used as a money-making venture by some malcontents.

After the '15 policy-makers in England viewed Scotland primarily as a Highland 'problem', the essence of which was the 'uncivilized' nature of the people and the scale of political dissent. In 1724 Wade, the new military commander in Scotland, reckoned that 12,000 of the 22,000 men in arms in the Highlands were 'ready, whenever encouraged by their Superiors or Chiefs of Clans, to creat new Troubles and rise in Arms in favour of the Pretender.'[33] One initiative already in train was to attempt to calm the situation

[30] John Campbell, 1678–1743, military career, succeeded as 2nd Duke of Argyll 1703, advocate of the Union, created Duke of Greenwich 1719, Field Marshal 1736.

[31] See pp. 392–7.

[32] William Gordon, d. 1716, 6th Viscount Kenmure, induced to join Jacobite rising by wife, pleaded guilty to charge. James Radcliffe, 1689–1716, 3rd Earl of Derwentwater, raised at St Germain as companion to the Old Pretender, returned to England 1710, his youth and character made his execution unpopular.

[33] J. Allardyce (ed.), *Historical Papers Relating to the Jacobite Period, 1699–1750*, 2 vols. (Aberdeen, 1895), vol. 1, p. 132. George Wade, 1673–1748, long military career, MP for Bath 1722–48, made Lieutenant General 1727 and Field Marshal 1743.

by strengthening religious instruction. However, though the Scottish Society for the Promotion of Christian Knowledge, founded in 1709, was operating 78 schools by 1727 and had in 1725 begun to receive £1,000 per annum from George I's royal bounty committee to fund itinerant preachers, it resolutely resisted the use of Gaelic which still had general currency in the Highlands, thus significantly restricting its impact. Attempts were also made to stimulate the Scottish economy. By 1727 £30,000 had been accumulated from a variety of sources and placed under a board of trustees for manufactures who dispersed grants to the fishing, linen, and woollen industries. Further efforts were also made under Wade's direction to subdue the Highlands by again attempting the disarming of the clans and by establishing an effective chain of barracks linked by new roads. Wade was sure that such roads 'Contribute to civilize the Highlanders' and by 1727 that between Inverness and Fort William was already complete.[34] Such policies achieved some success, but were probably subsidiary to the influence of increasing commercial pressures upon traditional ways of life. Thus when the Highlands erupted again in 1745–6 only 18 clans joined the Jacobite side compared to 26 in 1715–16.

Defoe, one of the more knowledgeable English observers of Scottish affairs and strongly pro-Union, concluded at the end of our period that the Union

has seemed to secure [Scotland] peace, and to increase her commerce. But I cannot say she has raised her figure in the world at all since that time, I mean as a body. She was before considered as a nation, now she appears no more but as a province, or at best a dominion; she has not lost her name as a place; but as a state, she may be said to have lost it . . . I might enlarge here upon the honour it is to Scotland to be a part of the British Empire, and to be incorporated with so powerful a people under the crown of so great a monarch; their being united in name as one, Britain . . . But I should be told, and perhaps justly too, that this was talking like an Englishman, rather than like a Briton . . .[35]

Defoe, of course, was hardly alone in failing to make the adjustment. The Scottish economy remained relatively unimportant to England and Scottish political problems generally uninteresting to those in Whitehall and Westminster. In fact the limited positive effects often ran in the opposite direction. Scots were joining the army and diplomatic service in great numbers and Scottish MPs and peers enriched London life, to the chagrin of some English: 'They seem to be men very fit for business, intriguing, cunning, tricking sort of men.'[36] It was of course one thing to forge a political union, quite another to change attitudes and eradicate prejudices.

---

[34] Allardyce (ed.), *Historical Papers*, vol. 1, p. 162.   [35] Defoe, *Tour*, p. 446.
[36] *The Diary of Dudley Ryder, 1715–1716*, ed. W. Matthews (1939), p. 88.

IRELAND—INDEPENDENCE AND DEPENDENCE

Ireland alone among James II's dominions responded positively to his policies after 1685, especially among those Catholic landowners, professionals, and business interests who had avoided Protestant depredations. And though James fled England, he soon turned to Ireland as the best hope of reclaiming his realms, arriving in March 1689. Prospects of Irish independence from England briefly beckoned to the Catholic majority. From 7 May to 18 July the Jacobite 'Patriot Parliament' assembled in Dublin and set about reversing some of the plunder undertaken by English and Scottish Protestants since the Civil Wars, particularly the land seizures. But on the very first day it met, Jacobite forces were checked at Belleek by Enniskillen Protestants. Until the conclusion of the Treaty of Limerick, signed on 3 October 1691, war dominated life in Ireland.[37] Though defeated, Irish Catholics came out of the conflict with much greater credit than James. That relative achievement and a frequently exaggerated awareness of the threat they posed coloured their treatment both at Limerick and subsequently. Under the military articles of the Treaty the Irish army and their dependants were allowed to go into exile in France to continue to fight in James's service, with perhaps 12,000–15,000 taking up this option. Under the civil articles Catholics were to enjoy the religious liberties experienced in Charles II's reign and guarantees were given to the property and professional rights of the vanquished. That these clauses were seen as too generous by some, and too harsh by others, indicates the breadth and depth of opinion which existed. It is also suggestive that, determined to exercise its authority to the full and unconcerned with Catholic opinion, the wholly Protestant Irish Parliament never fully ratified the Treaty.

At first glance there appears to have been considerable similarity in the nature of Anglo-Irish and Anglo-Scottish relations in the 1690s. Dublin and Edinburgh had their own parliaments which both enjoyed some real independence. Both were separate kingdoms ruled over by a monarch who enjoyed jurisdiction across the British Isles. Both were excluded from England's burgeoning empire. And both suffered because of English prejudices. On this last point, Ireland, like Scotland, was regarded with considerable indifference, that 'It has been usual with the gentlemen of England hitherto to think that the state of Ireland did not concern them, and that it was policy to keep this country low.'[38] More usually, as with the Scots and the Welsh, it also entailed cruel ethnic caricatures. By this the Irish were uncultured, stupid, irrational, lazy, fanatically devoted to Catholic superstitions, 'notorious *Thieves*', and

---

[37] For a brief account of the conflict, see above, pp. 93–7.
[38] H. M. C., *The Manuscripts of his Grace the Duke of Portland*, vol. 3 (1894), p. 479.

unnaturally fecund, 'they ingender as thick as *Fly-blows*'.[39] Even Swift, an Irishman by birth, bemoaned in 1713 that he was 'condemned to live again in Ireland . . . I am banished'.[40]

As with Scotland, many in England looked to ensure that Ireland failed to challenge domestic prosperity or provide a haven for international Jacobitism. To protect English agriculture, the import of Irish cattle had been stemmed in the Restoration period. Many Irish responded by turning over their pastures to sheep, but then found that in 1699, at the behest of England's west country woollen interests, Westminster put a stop to Irish and American woollen imports. English opinion so valued the domestic woollen industry that it was not prepared to risk any threat to it. From London there was little doubt that the needs of the Irish economy were subordinate to those of England. To Defoe, 'No Nation in the World has those Opportunities to Injure our Trade as they; the Goodness and Quantity of their Wooll . . . the Cheapness of Land, and consequently the Plenty of Provisions, are things that might easily have drawn all our Trade for Woollen Goods in time to that Nation.'[41] Political security was sought by attempting to control the independence of the Irish Parliament and ensuring the continued ascendancy of the Protestants in Dublin. These twin objectives were to prove somewhat incompatible with the consequence that, like Scotland, Ireland enjoyed a good deal of independence during this period.

Most of England's problems in Ireland arose not in its dealings with the Catholic majority, who were largely ignored, but with the Protestant minority, the so-called ascendancy. Perhaps one-quarter of Ireland's population of about 2m in 1700 were Protestant, but in Ulster many of these were Presbyterians of Scottish descent—some 50,000 arrived between 1689 and 1715. The Church of Ireland had only 600 priests (about a third of the number of Roman Catholic priests), was poorly endowed, and made only feeble efforts to convert Catholics. The power of the Protestant ascendancy was rooted, therefore, in Anglican control of the political processes and landownership. Though Catholics could vote until 1728 none sat in any Dublin Parliament in this period and Presbyterians were subject in 1704 to a sacramental test which pushed them to the political margins until relief measures began to be passed for them from 1719. Catholics had owned 59 per cent of land in 1640 but this

[39] 'A Trip to Ireland', pp. 5–6 in Ward, *Five Travel Scripts.*

[40] *The Correspondence of Jonathan Swift*, ed. H. Williams, 5 vols. (Oxford, 1963–5), vol. 1, p. 346. Jonathan Swift, 1667–1745, born Dublin, educated at Kilkenny School and Trinity College, Dublin, secretary to Sir William Temple 1692, moved between London and Ireland until he became Dean of St Patrick's Dublin 1713 after which he visited England only briefly; a poet, journalist, essayist, and brilliant satirist.

[41] *Defoe's Review*, facsimile edn., 22 vols. (New York, 1938), vol. 4, p. 85.

had been reduced to only 22 per cent by 1688 and was further reduced to 14 per cent in 1703. In a somewhat disjointed way, the Protestant ascendancy passed a series of 'penal laws' attempting to ensure that Catholics posed no threat to them. Amongst others, in 1695 Catholics were denied the right to hold arms or to own a horse above the value of £5; in 1697 Roman Catholic bishops and regular clergy were banished; in the same year obstacles were put in the path of Catholics inheriting the estates of Protestants; in 1703 Catholics were disabled from purchasing land or taking out long leases and were required to indulge in partible inheritance; and in 1709 a Protestant informing on a Catholic landowner who was avoiding penal legislation would be rewarded with a grant of the estate involved. Such legislation emanated from Dublin but was agreed to in London and was largely consistent with English anti-Catholic measures.[42] However, if the intent of the penal laws was clear, their implementation was more uncertain. So long as Catholics were denuded of political and economic power only occasional efforts were made to force them from their faith or convert them into English speakers.

If the Protestant ascendancy routinely saw itself as thoroughly English and their Roman Catholic countrymen as Irish, few in England employed that distinction without hesitation. Swift, for example, was confident that the members of the ascendancy had an equality of status with those across the Irish Sea and 'ought to be on as good a foot as any subjects of *Britain*, according to the practice of all other nations, and particularly of the *Greeks* and *Romans*.'[43] There was, indeed, a fierce battle of political will on this point through much of the period. Much of the confusion arose because of the means that had been found to circumvent Poynings's law (1494), which attempted to restrict the independence of the Dublin Parliament. This was exacerbated in the 1690s because for the first time in over a generation the Irish Parliament was meeting on a regular biennial basis and undertaking a good deal of business. Consequently, the elite in Ireland viewed its Parliament, in both its legislative and judicial capacities, as co-existing with but not subordinate to Westminster. Only gradually did English ministers devise the means for managing the Dublin Parliament, by utilizing local 'undertakers' to direct affairs as best they could. Even so, tensions remained. Matters were brought to a head in a series of cases over legal appeals on Irish questions where the Lords in both Dublin and London claimed ultimate jurisdiction. Famously, Molyneux, even flying the kite of no taxation without representation, articulated the case for Irish independent action in 1698: '*Ireland*, tho' Annex'd to the Crown of *England*, has always been look'd upon to be *a Kingdom Compleat within it self*, and to have all Jurisdiction to an *Absolute* Kingdom belonging, and Subordinate to no

---

[42] See above, p. 221.   [43] *Swift Correspondence*, vol. 3, p. 132.

Legislative Authority on Earth.'[44] At Westminster the House of Commons condemned Molyneux's book and officiously asked William to make it clear to Ireland that it was dependent upon England.

The self-government of the Protestant ascendancy was cried up long and loud in this period, reaching a crescendo in the 1720s under the inspiring leadership of Swift who, once he had become resigned to his banishment, began to develop and champion a powerful vision of Irish nationalism. In 1720, noting that 'Oppression makes a wise man mad', he proposed an Irish boycott of English manufactured goods.[45] However, his greatest triumph came in 1723 and 1724 when he wrote a series of stinging attacks, his *Drapier's Letters*, on the patent to supply Ireland with small coins, 'Wood's halfpenny'. He complained that Ireland had not been consulted in this, that no new coins were needed, and that the patentee, Wood, had obtained the grant by bribing the King's mistress with £10,000. To many in Ireland national interests were being sacrificed on the altar of English jobbery. Swift described the coins as '*Filthy Trash*' and '*Dross*', urged people to refuse to pass them, and articulated a vigorous case that Ireland was not 'in some State of Slavery or Dependence'.[46] Various groups of tradesmen agreed and publicized their defiance. In the face of widespread civil disobedience and parliamentary difficulties Wood's patent was cancelled in August 1725.

The débâcle over Wood's halfpence clearly demonstrated the limits of English authority in early eighteenth-century Ireland. Despite the passage of the Declaratory Act in 1720, which asserted the superiority of Westminster over the Dublin Parliament, England had to operate through and with the Protestant ascendancy to obtain its objectives. However, it is also worth noting the limits of the ascendancy's voice on events in London. In the first place, the death of the Duke of Gloucester in 1700 provoked no succession crisis in Ireland, despite the emphasis put upon her status as a kingdom by Protestant opinion there. The ascendancy silently followed the course determined in London. Partly that was due to a lack of leadership, such as Fletcher provided in Scotland at the critical moment—Molyneux had died in 1698 and the Irish Parliament did not meet between 1699 and 1703. Partly, however, it was due to the lack of bargaining power on the ascendancy's side. Jacobitism,

---

[44] W. Molyneux, *The Case of Ireland's being Bound by Acts of Parliament in England Stated* (1977), p. 103. William Molyneux, 1656–98, educated Trinity College, Dublin, entered Middle Temple 1675, Fellow of the Royal Society 1685.

[45] 'A Proposal for the Universal Use of Irish Manufacture, in Cloaths and Furniture of Houses, &c.: Utterly Rejecting and Renouncing Every Thing Wearable that Comes from England', in J. Swift, *Irish Tracts, 1720–1723*, ed. H. Davis (Oxford, 1968), p. 18.

[46] *The Drapier's Letters to the People of Ireland Against Receiving Wood's Halfpence*, ed. H. Davis (Oxford, 1935), pp. 14, 68, and 78.

emasculated by the flight of the Wild Geese after Limerick, and by continued French recruitment of young men after 1691, posed too distant a threat to concern London and require them to cultivate the Protestant minority. It is also notable, therefore, that in 1703 calls from the Irish Parliament for a union with England were completely ignored. Similarly, in 1709 nothing came of the 'great Talk of an Union, between Great-Britain and Ireland, as a necessary Consequence of that with Scotland'.[47]

Though it could do so only to a limited degree, England preferred to ignore Ireland. It treated it less as a colony than as a dependency or province. It is notable that little conscious effort was made to construct a supra-national identity. With some truth the Earl of Ailesbury suggested that 'It is wonderful, but true, that the English hate the Irish, and they are quits with them; and 'tis the same between the English and the Scotch, as also between the Scotch and Irish . . . we English love no nation but our own'.[48] Yet when all was said and done England and Ireland lacked that residue of mutual respect which tied England and Scotland. On both sides of the Irish Sea, for example, the expectation was that Irish talent would come to England to find fulfilment, not vice versa. And many did, among them Jonathan Swift, John Toland, Richard Steele, and George Farquhar. Those English who made the reverse journey usually did so to take up civil or religious positions, expecting their stay to be temporary but lucrative.

AN EMPIRE OF TRADE

England's overseas empire was formally constituted by its colonial possessions in America—both in the Caribbean and on the North American mainland— and informally by its trade in goods, ideas, and peoples, not only across the Atlantic but also round the Cape, into the Indian Ocean, and beyond. If France aimed at 'Universal monarchy', England aimed at 'Universal Trade', to 'Convince the Doubtful World that the *English Lyon* is awake'.[49] The commerce in commodities, perceptions, and people impacted with ever-increasing significance upon England through this period and left a deep imprint not only in colonies but in tropical West Africa. Though at the time opinion in England viewed this empire of trade as wholly beneficial domestically, it had a huge cost in terms of European imperial rivalry that fed wars through much of the eighteenth century, not to mention the assaults on the people's health by the influx of tobacco and sugar.

---

[47] *Post Boy*, 8–10 December 1709, [p. 1].

[48] *Memoirs of Thomas, Earl of Ailesbury, Written by Himself*, 2 vols. (1890), vol. 1, p. 268.

[49] D. Thomas, *An Historical Account of the Rise and Growth of the West-Indies Colonies, and of the Great Advantages they are to England, in Respect to Trade* (1690), p. 8; J. Whiston, *The Causes of our Present Calamities in Reference to the Trade of the Nation Fully Discovered* (1696), p. 10.

TABLE 6. *Empire and English foreign trade, 1700–1731* (£000 per annum)

Imports from	1700–1	1730–1	Per cent increase
British Islands	285	325	14
North America	372	655	76
West Indies	785	1,586	102
Asia	775	943	22
Africa	24	43	79
All overseas trade	5,819	7,386	27

Exports to	1700–1	1730–1	Per cent increase
British Islands	144	275	91
North America	256	351	37
West Indies	205	374	82
Asia	114	116	2
Africa	81	105	30
All overseas trade	4,461	5,203	17

Source: P. Deane and W. A. Cole, *British Economic Growth, 1688–1959* (2nd edn. Cambridge, 1969), p. 87.

Note: 'British Islands' comprises Ireland, Isle of Man, and Channel Islands.

It is indicative of the importance attached to overseas trade and commercial duties that in 1696 the administration of the English customs service was improved sufficiently to provide for the first time reasonable evidence of the volume of the nation's overseas trade on an annual basis. The contribution to England of its overseas trade in general, and of its connections with the constituent parts of the British empire, is outlined in Table 6. Such figures are not, of course, definitive—smuggling and administrative incompetence provide one source of errors, the valuations put upon commodities another, while no account is taken of trade between England and Wales and Scotland. Nevertheless, the table provides a guide to broad orders of magnitude. At the beginning of the eighteenth century the British empire provided about 39 per cent of England's imports and markets for 18 per cent of her exports. By the middle years of Walpole's premiership those proportions had risen to 48 and 24 per cent respectively. Moreover, these were rising shares of an ever-larger cake, total English imports rising by 27 per cent between 1700 and 1731 and exports by 17 per cent. England's economy was being stimulated to a high degree by this imperial trade, and to contemporaries looked much more significant than domestic sources of expansion, thereby apparently vindicating the benefits of the navigation system. By one contemporary estimate that trade furnished 'a full third part of the Whole Trade and Navigation of England. Here is a great Nursery of Our Sea Men, and the Kings Customs depend mightily thereon.'[50] So highly prized was that trade that it only heightened England's determination to keep French, Spanish, and Dutch competitors at bay.

The immediate economic effects of this imperial trade were felt through the employment of dockers, processing facilities, seamen, ships, and financial services. Labour and capital were exploited to the full. That was felt principally in London, the port of entry and exit for nearly two-thirds of shipping to and from the New World in the 1720s, but also had an increasing impact in Bristol, Liverpool, Whitehaven, and Glasgow. One consequence, therefore, was to create developing centres of economic gravity on England's western seaboard and an alternative trans-Atlantic perspective to the traditional one across the Channel and North Sea. Economic effects, however, were felt well beyond the ports. The infrastructure of internal commerce—warehousemen, carriers, boat and bargemen, innkeepers, shopkeepers, and hawkers—was deeply involved, as were producers of exported goods. Birmingham, for example, 'so famous for all manner of Iron-Work', was beginning to send its products down the Severn in search of distant markets.[51] As might be expected, however, most people experienced the dynamic effects of the empire of trade through the consumption of goods and the changes they brought in hearth and home—especially sugar from the West Indies and tobacco from Virginia and Maryland, but also including dyestuffs, rice, furs, fish, spices, tea, and textiles. As one analyst put it in 1715 'it appears that our Sugar and Tobacco Collonys are of greatest advantage, and deserve most regard.'[52] Slowly what had once been luxury goods were becoming decencies to be enjoyed across a wider spectrum of society. Some turned from small beer to coffee, others from honey to sugar, or woollens to richly coloured silks.

Trade with America and Asia was peculiar not only because of the commodities involved but also because it took place over such long distances, posing particular problems that fundamentally determined the nature of the interplay between England and the wider world. Those who plied the oceans were away for months on end and many never returned home. Merchants similarly waited anxiously for returns on their huge outlays of capital and credit. Storms, whales, pirates, disease, and uncharted shallows threatened labour and capital alike. Consequently, the ambitions of decision-makers in England sometimes went unfulfilled. Moreover, it also meant that ship captains, plantation agents, colonial merchants, and royal officials operated with a high

---

[50] M. G. Hall, L. H. Leder, and M. G. Kammen (eds.), *The Glorious Revolution in America: Documents on the Colonial Crisis of 1689* (New York, 1972), p. 67.

[51] [J. Macky], *A Journey Through England*, 2 vols. (2nd edn., 1722), vol. 2, p. 169.

[52] *Colonial Records of North Carolina, 2, 1713 to 1728*, ed. W. L. Saunders (Raleigh, North Carolina, 1886), p. 156.

degree of discretion and independence, ensuring the mutual dependence of 'core' and 'periphery'. Nevertheless, the oceans were not barriers, they were links and means of communicating—her safe havens tellingly known as 'roads'. Each year hundreds of ships successfully crossed the oceans, often sailing from distant port to distant port. If a sixty-day voyage from Plymouth to Barbados seems agonizingly slow today, it must be put into the contemporary perspective of overland travel often averaging just twenty miles a day. Moreover, improvements were being made to the quality of connections between England and her trading world. Developments in marine insurance, centring on Lloyd's coffee-house, ship design and construction, and navigational aids all helped. Journey times were also tending to decrease and a greater volume of traffic meant news could be communicated more immediately, though the Post Office Act of 1711 did raise costs. Transatlantic packet boat services were established for military reasons in 1702 and 1710 and by 1730 it took London news ninety days to appear in the *Boston News-Letter*, compared to over 160 at the start of the century. The Atlantic was huge and forbidding, but to contemporaries it was also comprehensible, increasingly accessible, and alive.

SLAVES AND SUGAR

In 1721 George I received a major summary from the Board of Trade on the state of Britain's colonies and plantations. Drawn from reports by officials in the colonies, including estimates of population, trade, and resources, they provide a good example of eighteenth-century political arithmetic in action. One conclusion came out particularly clearly, that the Caribbean islands not continental America was of greater commercial value to Britain. Using this report it is possible to calculate that in the trans-Atlantic trade, North America provided just 26 per cent of Britain's imports and took 49 per cent of her exports, but the Caribbean 74 and 51 per cent respectively. On the population side, however, rather the reverse was true. In 1700 the white population of England's colonies in North American was about 234,000 but in the West Indies only about 32,000. These findings were far from new and only served to confirm the well-established perception that in financial terms it was the small islands of the West Indies that ought particularly to concern policy-makers in London, but that the social and, hence, political ties between North America and Britain were the more considerable.

England had moved into the Caribbean in 1624 when it laid claim to part of St Christopher (St Kitts). Over the next decade or so it acquired a number of other Leeward Islands, including Barbados in 1627, and seized Jamaica in 1655. Though only the last of these was of any great size, there was to be no further territorial expansion in the region until the middle of the eighteenth century. It says much that though the white population of these islands was very modest in 1700 some 222,000 emigrants had arrived from the British Isles over the previous seventy years, compared to 145,000 in North America. Partly this was because of the depredations of the natural environment, Jamaica, for example, being characterized 'As Sickly as an Hospital, as Dangerous as the Plague, as Hot as Hell, and as Wicked as the Devil. Subject to Turnadoes, Hurricanes and Earthquakes'.[53] Indeed, many settlers viewed the islands as temporary not permanent homes, looking either to move on to the mainland colonies or to return home. 'Our Planters—those especially of the warmer Climate consider England their Native Country, to which they are at last to return.'[54] This fundamentally influenced the character of England's Caribbean experience. For many the West Indies were resources to be exploited rather than societies to be nurtured and enjoyed. Christopher Codrington (1668–1710) was one of the few to leave a large impact both in the Caribbean and England. Governor of the Leeward Islands in succession to his father, at his death he left £10,000 pounds to All Souls College, Oxford (to build a library to house his book collection which he also donated) and funds for the SPG to establish a college at Barbados (still in existence).

In the middle of the seventeenth century it became clear to English colonists that sugar was commercially the greatest asset to be drawn out of the West Indies and soon the islands were given over to monoculture. By the end of the 1660s England and Wales were importing about 26.2 million lbs per annum of sugar, mostly from the Caribbean; by the early 1700s this had risen to 42.5 million lbs; and by the second half of the 1720s was perhaps 92.6 million lbs. Some of these imports were re-exported, thus domestic per capita consumption rose from about 2 lbs per annum in the 1660s to 13 lbs per annum by the end of our period (today's figure is about 50 lbs). This growth was not matched, however, by a comparable growth in English exports to the West Indies—which obtained much of what was needed from the mainland colonies. However, English commerce was integral to the growth of the West Indian sugar economy by shipping slaves from West Africa to meet the huge demands for labour on the plantations. Accurate figures of the scale of that deadly trade are unavailable, but the best guesses suggest that the trade grew markedly in the late seventeenth century and that between 1720 and 1729 British vessels took on board some 243,000 slaves in Africa and delivered about 211,000 to America (only 15 per cent going to the mainland colonies), the difference (13 per cent) being accounted for by death in the 'middle passage'. No other country was as

---

[53] 'A Trip to Jamaica', p. 13, in Ward, *Five Travel Scripts.*
[54] H. Martin, 'Observations Upon the Acct of Exports and Imports for 17 years Ending Christmas 1714 Delivered to the Board of Trade 1717/8', Public Record Office, CO 390/12/11.

1. View of William, Prince of Orange, entering London, 18 December 1688

This Dutch print shows William, standing in the middle ground, left of centre.

Englands Happiness Reviv'd;

OR,

A Farwell to Popery,

To the Tune of, *Souldiers Departure.*

NOw he in the West is Landed,
whom we have expected long,
Tracing Famous Alexander,
with an Army stout and strong:
Trumpets sounding, and Drums beating
And the Romans still repeating
when to have their Overthrow.

Now they must to Purgatory,
to be Purged of their Sins,
Father Petres shall go before them,
to make room to let them in:

Lord Jeffrys shall to their Chancellor,
to decide their woful Cause,
And the Pope must grant them Pardon,
for Transgressing 'gainst our Laws.

No Whitsen ever penned
such stranger Wonders done before,
Within two Months the Nations Conquer'd
all that Fools did dote about.
Now the Triple Crown is Totter'd,
and is shaking too and fro,
And a Peace falls without fighting,
like the Walls of Jerico.

Where's our Heads and Trustees?
where's our holy Martyrs now?
Will they ne're rise up from Destruction,
to whom so often we did bow?
Where's our Plots and Counter-ploting
to destroy the Herrick Sheep,
Where's our Jesuits running trotting,
wondering how to escape the Deep.

Orange is bitter in the tasting,
but for Health is very good,
There has some thousands lain a Wasting,
on the White have understood.
Had not the Nobles of our Nation,
on this Curst cast a Snuff,
And brought Orange o're this Ocean,
to be planted in our Isle.

And when Orange Prince was landed,
with several Lords of high degree,
Then the Nation stood amazed,
wondering what the Event would be.

Then soon their Plot it was discover'd,
when the Same did once begin,
And the Snare for us prepared,
they themselves did fall therein.

Romish Groups in our Nation,
now of late crept in amain,
And a dark Cloud lays like to cover
our true light that still remaining.
But on the fourteenth of October,
the bright Sun did bow its Head,
Which I saw was a fore-runner
of some great ones banished.

In the Western Equinoctial,
two Religions stood on strife,
But the Gallants gave dissatisfaction,
lest one the other should beguile.
But the one on false foundation,
brought dishonour and disgrace,
And Babylons abomination,
must no longer here take place.

Printed in the Year 1689.

933

2. *England's happiness reviv'd; or, a farwell to Popery, 1689*

A cheap wood-cut ballad. These images were reproduced in many ballads of the period, that on the right shows William and Mary by an orange tree.

3. *England's-memorial. Of its wounderfull deliverance from French tirany and Popish oppression, 1688*

A strong and upright orange tree (whose branches support the coats of arms of other Protestant powers) and the sinking Church of England are overseen by God's providential eye. James II's crown (I) and Lord Chancellor Jeffrey (K) are hit by falling oranges. On the edges are Louis XIV (G) and Roman Catholic schemers (H and N).

4. *Ready mony the prevailing candidate, or the humours of an election, 1727*

A satire on bribery and corruption in parliamentary elections.

5. Skimmington-triumph, or the humours of horn-fair, c.1720

A scold and her husband are mocked by the 'rough music' of their neighbours.

6. *Francis de Wit, View of London from Southwark,* c.1710

A Dutch depiction of the capital. Most of London is shown here, from Whitehall on the left to the Tower on the right.

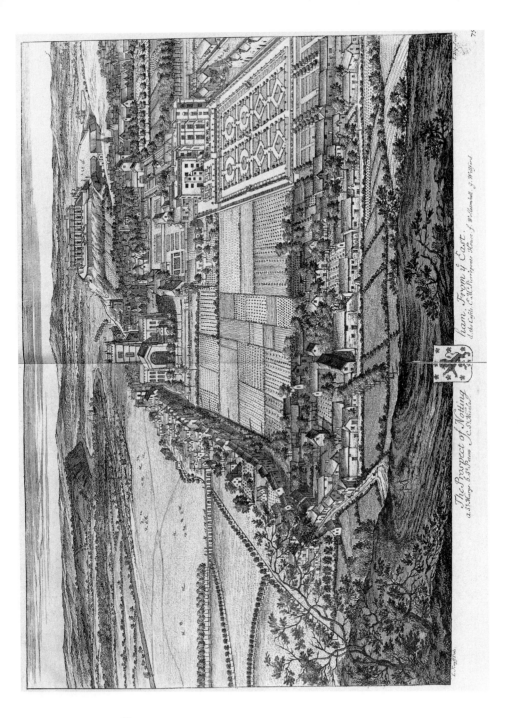

The Prospect of Notting[ham], From ye East.
a. S.t Marys. b. S.t Peters. c. M.r Pierreponts House. f. W.dumhall. g. Wilford.
d. the Castle. e. M.r Pierreponts House. f. W.dumhall. g. Wilford.

7. *Johannes Kip and Leonard Knyff, The prospect of Nottingham from ye east, 1707*

A plate from *Britannia Illustrata* (1707). In the centre of the city is 'Mr Pierreponts House' and in the background is the castle.

8. The usurper's habit, 1691

This shows Louis XIV wearing a coat made up of various towns and territories he has attempted to seize.

9. The execution of conspirators at Tyburn, 1696

This German print places Tyburn on the wrong side of the Thames and appears to depict old St Paul's which was destroyed in the fire of 1666.

10. *The compleat auctioner*, c.1700

The titles of some of the books on sale can be made out and include 'Poems by the Earl of Rochester', 'Ogilby's Asia', 'Culpeper's Dispensatory', and 'Aristotle's Masterpiece' (a sex manual).

11. *Edmond Halley, A description of the passage of the shadow of the moon over Europe, as it may be expected May 11th 1724*

Halley produced a map of the eclipse in 1715 for England alone. This geographically more expansive prediction asks for observations to be sent to him and closes with the sentence 'We wish our Astronomical Friends a Clear Sky.'

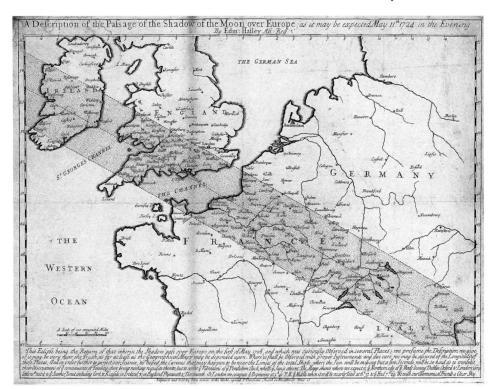

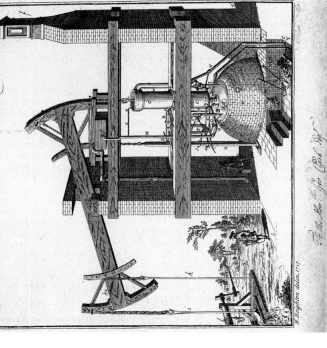

12 (left). William Emmett, The front or west end of the cathedral church of St Pauls London, 1702

Sir Christopher Wren's baroque masterpiece.

13 (above). Henry Beighton, The engine for raising water (with a power made) by fire, 1717

A primitive steam engine, most often used for draining mines.

14. *The Jacobites hopes, or Perkin rideing in triumph, 1709*

The Old Pretender is drawn by the asses of non-resistance and passive obedience, tigers of tyranny and arbitrary power, and dragons of slavery and popery, accompanied by figures and symbols of Roman Catholicism, superstition, and oppression. They are crushing property, moderation, toleration, and liberty.

15. *William Hogarth,*
The South Sea Bubble,
1721

A satire on the great
stockmarket folly. Honour
(D) is being broken on the
wheel and honesty (E) is
being whipped. Even
clerics (C) join the mania.
The dwarf-like figure in
the middle foreground is
probably the poet
Alexander Pope.

16. Colen Campbell and H. Hulberg, Castle Howard, Yorkshire, 1725

This illustration from *Vitruvius Britannicus* shows a very elaborate design which if never fully built nicely illustrates the ostentation of the Earl of Carlisle and the vision of his architect, John Vanbrugh.

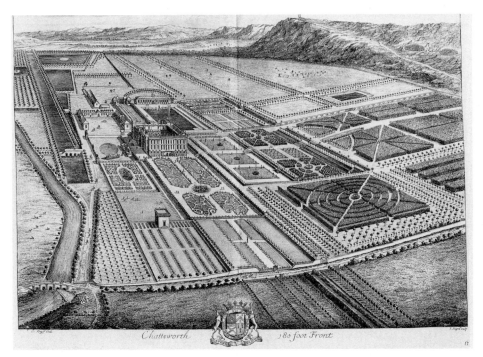

17. Johannes Kip and Leonard Knyff, Chatsworth House, Derbyshire, 1707

This plate from *Britannia Illustrata* (1707) shows a good example of formal gardening.

18. *The coffehous mob, 1710*

The civility and fractiousness of the masculine coffee house culture is here well caught.

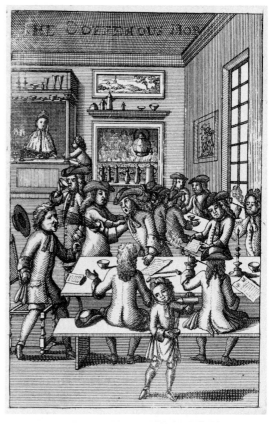

19. *William Hogarth, Masquerades and operas* or *Bad taste of the town, 1724*

Hogarth mocks the rage for opera and masquerades and, in the background, the architectural purity and exclusivity of the Earl of Burlington. In the foreground the works of Congreve, Dryden, Jonson, Otway, and Shakespeare are being carted away and sold as waste paper.

Masquerades and Operas. Burlington-gate.

The Diabolical Maskquerade, 1725.
Or the Dragons-Feast as Acted by the HELL-FIRE-CLUB, at Somerset-House in the Strand.

Thus impious Wretches, without fear or shame,
Feast & sing Praises in the Devil's Name;
Deride those sacred Powers they ought to dread,
And live, as if in Hell, before they're dead.

Defy Eternal Vengeance, as they sit,
And, deal about vile Blasphemies for Wit;
High Altars raise to LUCIFER the proud,
And, Indian like, adore him as their God.

Well may a Kingdom suffer that can see
Such Evils practis'd with impunity;
Nor can we hope to prosper, till we mend,
Do Justice first and Heav'n will prove our
Friend.

Sold by B. Cole, at the Lock of Hair next Furnivals Inn, in Holborn London & Y Printsellers.

20. *The diabolical maskquerade, c.1725*

An attack on the Hell Fire clubs that emerged in about 1720.

21. *The funeral procession of the celebrated Mr Jonathan Wild thieftaker-general of Great Britain and Ireland; together with a list of ye principal Priggs hanging in effigie who were taken by him, and convicted and executed upon his information. To which is annex'd his lamentation in Newgate, 1725*

heavily involved in the slave trade, Britain taking about a half of all slaves shipped from West Africa in this period. Before 1698 the Royal Africa Company had a monopoly on this trade, but in that year it was thrown open and the Company soon drifted towards bankruptcy. Until the 1730s most slave traders were London-based, but already by the 1720s Bristol and Liverpool merchants were of rapidly growing significance. Thus was forged the so-called 'triangular trade', whereby English manufactured goods were shipped to Africa, slaves from thence to the Caribbean, and plantation sugar to North America and Britain. Little wonder that it was noted that the *'Labour of Negroes* is the principal Foundation of our *Riches* from the *Plantations'*.[55]

Economic factors drove the slave trade. In the West Indies the shortage and high cost of white labour created the demand; in West Africa local authorities made available a plentiful supply at an attractive price. Increasingly, therefore, on the sugar islands the numerical balance between free white and black slave shifted in favour of the latter, moving most dramatically on Jamaica from about 1:1 in 1675 to about 1:11 in 1722. Once in the West Indies the slaves found themselves part of a plantation system which, with sugar prices on a downward trend except during wartime, was highly competitive. Consequently slaves were pushed hard, frequently beyond the limit, in a regime notable for its severity. A majority of slaves worked on large plantations, often owned by absentees and run by managers who were largely assessed by the standard of slave productivity not human longevity. There is no question that white looked down on black. By the Barbados slave code blacks were 'an heathenish, brutish and an uncertaine, dangerous kinde of people'.[56] Even as educated a man as Hans Sloane, who had made a scientific expedition to the West Indies, after describing various punishments meted out to slaves, including 'Gelding, or chopping off half of the Foot with an Ax', believed 'These Punishments are sometimes merited by the Blacks, who are a very perverse Generation of People, and though they appear harsh, yet are scarce equal to some of their crimes'.[57] He noted that some slaves committed suicide in the belief that they returned home when they died, something that singularly failed to touch his conscience.[58]

[55] Wood, *Survey of Trade*, p. 179.

[56] Quoted in R. S. Dunn, *Sugar and Slaves: The Rise of the Planter Class in the English West Indies, 1624–1713* (1973), p. 239.

[57] H. Sloane, *A Voyage to the Islands of Madera, Barbados, Nieves, S. Christophers and Jamaica, with the Natural History . . . of the Last of those Islands*, 2 vols. (1707 and 1725), vol. 1, p. lvii. Sloane, 1660–1753, studied at Paris and Montpellier, Fellow of the Royal Society 1685 and its Secretary 1693–1712, President of Royal College of Physicians 1719–35, Baronet 1716, purchased manor of Chelsea 1712 (hence street names in London SW1), created large collection of specimens that was a basis for the British Museum.

[58] Similarly, in 1698 one periodical reported that some slaves 'will hang themselves, no creature knows why. I have been told they will sometimes starve themselves out of revenge to their

Slavery occurred in many parts of the early eighteenth-century world, often among non-Europeans. Western Europe, however, was unusual in the extent of its involvement in slavery and its use on colonial plantations. England, largely emulating Spanish and Portuguese examples, adopted tried and tested methods in the West Indies. Moreover, it should be remembered that slave owners had an interest of sorts in the well-being of their slaves and that the trans-Atlantic world was a harsh one on all sides and among all peoples. For example, demographically neither blacks nor whites reproduced themselves in the West Indies, and if 13–20 per cent of slaves died in the middle passage the rate for transported convicts from England was between 10 and 15 per cent and among ordinary passengers was perhaps 6 per cent. Such points provide a necessary context but in no way justify the slave trade. Moreover, given so many contemporaries, including foreigners, cried up England as a land of liberty her involvement in the slave trade cannot but give rise to charges of hypocrisy. Contemporaries who were prepared to scream out against Louis XIV's use of Protestant galley slaves were mute on the lot of ever-increasing numbers of plantation slaves. Few in London contemplated the Christianizaton of slaves, fewer still their liberation—Thomas Bray, the founder of the SPG, accepted slavery as an institution. Ignorance about the scale and nature of the trade fails adequately to explain this, for some slaves were brought into England as servants and exotic appendages. Many continued to lack freedom and were treated as chattels. One advertisement (many might be cited) described a runaway as dressed in 'grey livery lined with yellow, about . . . eighteen years of age, with a silver collar about his neck, with these directions: "Captain George Hasting's boy, Brigadier in the King's Horse Guards." '[59] By 1727 there was no excuse for ignorance of the slave trade: it was knowingly sustained by economic opportunism and racial stereotypes.

Because the slaves and the sugar they produced were highly prized, the West Indian colonies, so distant from England, were prey to attack from foreign powers and pirates. France posed an increasing menace, with war in Europe between 1689 and 1713 making England's colonies fair game. In 1689, for example, 130 Irish on St Christopher rebelled in support of James II, allowing France to seize the whole of the island. In 1706 the French plundered St Christopher and Nevis, laying waste to many plantations, giving rise to parliamentary compensation in 1711 totalling £103,000. Yet if such conflicts tied up precious resources they did not lead to a significant redrawing of the imperial map in either 1697 or 1713. It says much that the greatest change was at

masters.' J. Houghton, *A Collection for the Improvement of Husbandry and Trade*, 4 vols. (1727–8), vol. 2, p. 328.

[59] Quoted in F. Shyllon, *Black People in Britain, 1555–1833* (1977), p. 11.

Utrecht when France gave up its half of the small island of St Christopher. In contrast to English anti-French policy in Canada, no policy of expansion in the Caribbean was formulated in London. Nor did London have to worry about strong separatist tendencies in the West Indies given the vulnerability of their small and dispersed white populations to attack from France and Spain. Sir Dalby Thomas was proud to proclaim that West Indians of English origin or descent 'are and ever must be English-Men'.[60] Moreover, the West Indian colonies were vulnerable to the depredations of pirates. While war was waged most pirates sheltered behind the legitimacy afforded by privateering. But with peace in 1713 piracy flourished in the Caribbean as never before. Assessing the scale of this 'golden age' is difficult, but one infamous pirate, Batholomew Roberts, seized about 400 vessels between 1719 and 1722. This was the age of the notorious pirates Edward Teach, better known as 'Blackbeard', and Mary Read.[61] But the success of the pirates in the 1710s prompted London to attempt their extirpation from 1718. By the mid-1720s the ships of the Royal Navy and the justice of the Vice-Admiralty courts had done their job and the hey-day of piracy had passed.

NORTH AMERICA

English expansion into North America began a little before and carried on well after it gained its Caribbean possessions. For example, the colonies of Virginia and Carolina had been named in celebration of Elizabeth I and Charles II respectively; New Amsterdam had been seized from the Dutch in 1664; the Hudson Bay Company established in 1670; and Pennsylvania and Georgia founded in 1681 in 1733 respectively. In comparison with the West Indian colonies, parts of North America offered settlers the possibility of large amounts of land, a more temperate if continental climate, and a less stressful disease environment (though 'seasoning' still took its toll). Thus the white population rose from perhaps 55,000 in 1650 to 223,000 in 1700, reaching 538,000 by 1730. Some of this was based on migration from the British Isles, but some was also due to natural growth. The first great wave of migration had been between 1630 and 1660, but except in wartime there were few periods without some significant movement. People moved for a variety of reasons, to escape religious and political persecution or high prices and a lack of economic opportunities—'Bishops, Bailiffs, and Bastards, were the three Terrible

---

[60] *An Historical Account*, Dedication, [p. iii].

[61] Teach's long black beard, interwoven with coloured ribbons, was as famous as his butchery. He died resisting arrest in 1718. Mary Read passed herself off as a man for a time, enabling her to serve in the army in the War of the Spanish Succession; after arrest she claimed to be pregnant, dying in prison in 1720.

Persecutions which chiefly drove our unhappy Brethren to seek their Fortunes in our Forreign Collonies.'[62] Puritans had moved into New England in the 1630s; royalists and indentured servants into Virginia from the 1640s to the 1670s; Quakers into Pennsylvania after 1681; people from the north Midlands and Wales into the Delaware Valley from c.1675 to 1725; and Scots and Ulstermen into the Appalachian backcountry after c.1718.

The demographic diversity of the North American colonies was matched in the political, economic, social, religious, and cultural spheres. Some, such as Carolina, were founded as royal endeavours; others, such as Maryland, were proprietory colonies, in this case the property of Lord Baltimore; and others, such as Virginia, had been initiated by chartered companies. If some, therefore, readily acknowledged the Crown's fiat, others stressed a high degree of political independence. Matters were complicated by the weakness and minority status of Anglicanism in the colonies. Indeed, many had fled to the colonies to escape from religious proscription in England. Finally, there were dramatic economic contrasts based on different economic resources, climate, and degrees of involvement in England's navigation system.

In this period few English-speaking people lived in what is now Canada. In 1720 there were perhaps 10,000 in total, manning the trading posts around the Hudson Bay and the coastal villages of Newfoundland and Nova Scotia. But they drove a valuable trade in furs and fish—London received about 150,000 beaver skins from North America in 1693–4, and much of the fish was sent direct to valuable markets in southern Europe. To the south the New England region had a population of about 170,000 in 1720 (few of whom were slaves) and with an economy dominated by farming and fishing drove significant trades, especially in the export of food, whale products, and wood, with England, southern Europe, and other New World colonies. It provided something of a hub for commerce in the western North Atlantic. A similar situation existed in the middle colonies (Delaware, New Jersey, New York, and Pennsylvania) whose population was about 103,000, about a tenth of which were slaves. The combined population of Virginia and Maryland in 1720 was 158,000, nearly a fifth of whom were slaves, working on tobacco plantations which sent much of their output to England. Finally, Carolina had a population of some 39,000 in 1720, over a third of whom were slaves, but was not heavily involved in Atlantic commerce, though rice and indigo exports were beginning to assume some significance by the end of the period.

With characteristic lack of judgement James II looked scornfully upon the heterogeneity of England's American colonies. He feared the weakness of royal will there, and also longed for greater religious toleration to provide a seedbed

---

[62] 'A Trip to New-England', p. 3, in Ward, *Five Travel Scripts.*

for the germination of Roman Catholicism. Determined to introduce order and authority under centralized control he instituted the Dominion of New England in 1686, abolishing local representative assemblies and employing governors sure to do his bidding. Such policies and personnel were bitterly resented by independent-minded colonists, especially in Massachusetts. Thus when news of the Glorious Revolution gradually made its way across the Atlantic some seized the opportunity to throw off the newly-forged shackles. Three armed risings took place in 1689, first in Massachusetts, then in New York, and finally in Maryland, and in all much resort was made to the language of liberty. In this many colonists proclaimed their English credentials, of liberty as a birthright and of a hatred of slavery, sentiments which were to be repeated many times in succeeding decades. And in practical terms the colonies did enjoy a high degree of autonomy. All had legislative assemblies, making most of the law required by local circumstances, and which, because of their control of tax gathering, were generally able to limit the authority of the royal governors. To the English such colonies could be represented as 'little commonwealths', liable 'to make laws without having any regard as to their being repugnant to the laws of England.'[63]

London continued to harbour hopes through the 1690s and 1700s of regularizing its relations with the American colonies. In 1697 Penn submitted a plan of union to the Board of Trade which was taken up in the following year by Charles Davenant.[64] Whitehall was especially concerned with the independence of proprietory and chartered colonies and Bills aiming to resume their titles by the Crown were introduced into Parliament in 1701, 1702, and 1706. All failed, in part because of powerful colonial lobbying at Westminster. The most articulate defence of their rights was put forward in a pamphlet in 1701. Though acknowledging England as 'their lawful Mother', and in no way calling for full independence, the author criticized the credentials of colonial governors and the Board of Trade, and queried whether Acts passed at Westminster always ran in the colonies, or only those 'wherein the Plantations are particularly named.'[65] The solution posited, but itself unrealized, was to constitute a general assembly of the mainland colonies (a form of congress), the residence in England of an agent from each colony to represent their interests, and the appointment of a Commissioner to collect information about America

[63] H. M. C., *Portland*, vol. 5, p. 199.

[64] William Penn, 1644–1718, educated Christ Church, Oxford, but sent down for nonconformity becoming a Quaker 1667; persecuted for his faith he established Pennsylvania 1682 as a refuge for Quakers, but lived there only briefly, worked with James II over toleration making reasonable relations with the new regime difficult to establish.

[65] Anon., *An Essay upon the Government of the English Plantations on the Continent of America*, ed. L. B. Wright (San Marino, California, 1945), pp. 16, 23.

and to send it back to London. The failure of the Bills for the resumption of titles was also due to the unwillingness of parliamentarians to challenge property rights and to the tacit acceptance of ministers that the Crown's grip on the American colonies was weak. As with Scotland, London had little patronage available and could not afford to keep large numbers of men in arms to badger and oppress. Ultimately obedience to English commands could only be based upon an identity of interest. So if the navigation system sought to establish an economic interdependence, the political sphere was characterized by *laissez faire*. In religion too metropolitan Anglicanism exerted little sway in the colonies. Efforts were made to send more ministers, especially because of Bray's work. Yet of the seventy-seven ministers sent to Maryland between 1690 and 1729 only a little over a half were English or Welsh and a fifth soon deserted the challenge, turning to other occupations or returning home.

If a sense of a common English identity bound many in the colonies to acknowledge London's residual authority, many were also grateful for the military aid that England could provide in time of need. Threats were felt from the French, especially in the area from the St Lawrence valley to the Atlantic seaboard, and from some native peoples along the shifting boundary of white settlement. The French population in North America was comparatively small, perhaps 70,000, but as in the West Indies European conflict spilled over onto mainland America, with both sides utilizing Indian allies. In 1690 Anglo-American forces were defeated at Quebec; France established its colony in Louisiana in 1699; and in May 1711 some sixty-nine ships, manned by 6,000 seamen and carrying 5,000 troops, sailed from England to help in a disastrous attempt to conquer Canada. In both wars there was considerable loss of life in the colonies—often at the hands of Indian allies of the European powers—especially in Maine, New Hampshire, and Connecticut. The ceding to Britain of Nova Scotia and Newfoundland at Utrecht meant relatively little to those further south. Their vulnerability, arising largely from the population being thinly scattered over a thousand or so miles of territory, made them fully aware of the benefits of being part of the British empire.

If France posed a near constant threat to colonists, relations with the Indian nations were much more varied and changeable. Many were loyal allies and provided valuable trading contacts. Others were hostile, because of the invasion of their lands or because of treaties they had made with the French. Consequently, Indians might be described as 'inhumane savages', unbounded 'by any laws of reason or religion', and were liable to have their lands seized, their persons enslaved, or bounties put upon their heads.[66] Others, however,

---

[66] *Calendar of State Papers Colonial Series, America and West Indies, June 1708–1709*, ed. C. Headlam (1922), pp. 42 and 49.

showed them deep respect. Often admired physically, the simplicity of their life and its peculiar freedom was sometimes looked upon longingly. If some believed they were the descendants of the ten lost tribes of Israel, others were happy to describe their societies as 'Nations' or 'Cantons', albeit inclined to violence.[67] With justice one traveller believed that 'They are really better to us, than we are to them', another that 'they are . . . very kind and obliging to the Christians'.[68] England had little missionary zeal here, and few were converted either by the considered efforts of the New England Company (founded 1649) or the SPG. In contrast to Spanish America too few missionaries went to the New World to have a significant impact. Rather Indians were seen as people to be used in whatever way best served the interests of people on the spot, be they national and military or personal and commercial. Not only profitable political and economic alliances were instigated, for in Nova Scotia the vulnerability of British settlers led to a policy of encouraging intermarriage by land grants.

EASTERN PROMISE

In this period, as England's colonies were all in the New World, it could not yet be said that the sun never set on her empire. But the tentacles of trade were already fast involving English commercial interests in Asia, almost exclusively under the umbrella of the East India Company. And if in political terms English interests were but a midge troubling the powerful Moghul and Chinese empires, the East India Company's trade, which grew significantly over the seventeenth century, had some considerable domestic importance. Much debate was given over to the costs and benefits of imported Oriental products and the power of the East India Company.

The East India Company had been established in 1600 to trade between England and the Indian and Pacific oceans. So considerable were the perceived risks of this trade that the Company was founded as a joint-stock enterprise and given a monopoly to exclude domestic competition, though Dutch, Portuguese, and French traders remained a serious threat. The Company was lured on by the prospect of selling Eastern goods in domestic and European markets rather than the hope of selling English exports. There was nothing inevitable

---

[67] *Royal Instructions to British Colonial Governors, 1670–1776*, ed. L. W. Labaree, 2 vols. (New York, 1935), vol. 2, p. 463.

[68] J. Lawson, *A New Voyage to Carolina*, ed. H. T. Lefler (Chapel Hill, 1967), p. 243; G. Thomas, 'An Historical and Geographical Account of Pensilvania and of West New Jersey', in *Narratives of Early Pennsylvania, West New Jersey and Delaware, 1630–1707*, ed. A. C. Myers (New York, 1912), p. 316.

about the success of this trade, but by the 1690s about 13 per cent of England's imports came from Asia, a level sustained through the period. Mostly these were from India, initially from Bombay and Madras in particular, but by the 1720s nearly one-half of the Company's imports came from Bengal, about a fifth from Madras, and a tenth from Bombay. Imports from India largely comprised cottons, silks, spices, and indigo, all of which found a ready market. Gradually they were joined by tea and porcelain from China which by the 1720s provided a tenth of the Company's imports. If goods from the East found a ready market in England the Company struggled to find outlets for English manufactured commodities in the East, leading to the shipment of huge amounts of treasure (often picked up at Cadiz) to balance the trade— in the 1720s this amounted to an average of £537,000 per annum.

The East India Company had a relatively small physical presence in Asia. In 1713 it had ten sizeable bases, 'factories', but that at Calcutta, the gateway to Bengal, had an English population of only a few hundred. Like all European traders, the Company operated largely because of the tolerance of and the benefit provided to local powers. The use of naval power might be threatened, but this was risky, as the Company discovered when it adopted a more aggress-ive stance in Bengal in 1688–91 and met with stiff opposition. That some of the Company's servants in the East already saw themselves as representatives of England's government only heightened the risks. Moreover if in the East the Company was fairly small, in England it was very considerable and the East India Company was the largest business enterprise operating in this period. Though it did not build or operate its own ships, it was a substantial employer of dockers, porters, warehousemen, salesmen, clerks, and the like, especially in London; it drew upon large amounts of capital; and it became an integral part in the management of the national debt in the 1690s, such that to be a director of the Company was to be a member of England's commercial and political elite. Such prominence, however, attracted the envy and suspicion of those excluded from the charmed circle or threatened by the Company's commercial success.

By 1689 the East India Company was vulnerable to attack at home, both because of its trading success and because of the close links that its governor, Sir Josiah Child, had established with James II.[69] Frequent expression was also given to concerns over the heavy export of bullion and of the limitations of monopoly trading rights. Both were said to detract from England's best inter-ests: 'that we should send out Bullion to any place to buy Goods to be spent in Luxury . . . cannot well be for the Interest of the Nation, nor the best way to

---

[69] Josiah Child, 1631–99, son of a London weaver, created baronet 1678, at the East India Company he was famed for his bullying and bribery, published *A New Discourse of Trade* (1668).

gain or retain Riches'.[70] Merchants and their allies pressed hard to be let into the trade to ensure exports and imports of manufactured goods moved closer to parity, so ending or reducing bullion exports. On the political front, the Company, by looking to buy political support, opened itself up to charges of corruption which became the more intense when, with its charter due for renewal, it came under close parliamentary scrutiny in the early 1690s. Despite vigorous lobbying and bribing the original Company could not prevent the formation of a New East India Company in 1698 that had offered a financially desperate government a loan of £2 million at 8 per cent. In theory the old Company was to be wound down, but it very quickly seized an unbreakable lifeline by investing £315,000 in the new Company, easily making it the largest shareholder. In 1702 the two Companies agreed to merge, though this union was not completed until 1709. Consequently, the trade remained a monopoly and interlopers continued to be dealt with severely, one, for example, being fined £3,900 in 1723.

A further source of controversy over trade with Asia concerned the volume of cheap silk, cotton, and calico imports which it was alleged threatened the market for domestically produced woollen and silk goods. From the middle of the 1690s a medley of English interests, including popular concern over wages and employment, pressed for restrictions to be put upon the imported textiles. In early 1697 'the Weavers, who live about *Spittle-fields*, came to the Parliament-House with their Wives and Children, praying (though in a rude manner) to have the Bill pass for the prohibiting the Importation of Wrought silks, & c, from *India* and *Persia* . . . in their return they abused several Shopkeepers, that hung out any *Persian* or *Indian* wrought Commodities, and at last they endeavoured forcibly to enter the *East-India* House in *Leaden-hall street*'.[71] With the battle being waged between the Old and New Companies legislation came into force in 1701 restricting the import of a wide range of silk and cotton goods. Customs duties were raised on imported plain calicoes in 1701, 1704, and 1708 to be followed in 1712 with an excise on domestically printed calicoes. Such measures signify both the strength of demand for the new fabrics and the powerful opposition of vested interests. Even so the situation remained unsettled. In 1719 famous riots occurred where it was reported that women wearing foreign silks and calicoes had their clothing ripped from their backs or doused with acid. Consequently, in 1721 legislation put a total ban upon the wearing of calico goods. Once again, therefore, England's overseas interests were held to be decisively subordinate to her domestic prosperity.

[70] [J. Pollexfen], *England and East-India Inconsistent in their Manufactures. Being an Answer to a Treatise, Intituled, An Essay on the East-India trade* (1697), p. 57.

[71] *Post Boy*, 21–3 January 1697, [p. 2].

In this case, curiously, the restrictions served to stimulate the English cotton industry which was to grow so spectacularly in the second half of the eighteenth century and, with bitter irony, to flood the Indian market in the nineteenth century.

CONCLUSION

In order to secure a new regime faced by resurgent representative institutions England tightened its grip on the other parts of the British Isles in this period, mostly markedly with Union in 1707 and by supporting the Protestant ascendancy in Ireland. Such a hold was primarily political and military. In many fundamental respects, however, the British Isles was a disunited kingdom. Most people employed local, national, and religious identities—they were, for example, Cameronians and Scotsmen not Britons. Their language, culture, history, religion, law, and economy were their own. Some attempts were made to construct a new 'British' persona, the figure of John Bull was first drawn in 1712, but these had made little headway by 1727. 'Rule Britannia' and 'God save the King' had still not been written and many Tories remained firmly attached to the idea of 'old England'. Overseas much the same was true. England often faced flourishing local representative institutions, and peoples who proclaimed their Englishness to underpin their claims to independence and freedom of action. London's attempts to control such behaviour were never more than partially successful.

Despite divisions within the British Isles and the British empire, three points of contact tied parts of them together. Protestantism provided one, though it was often also a point of contention and served to isolate Irish Roman Catholics and some Highland Scots. Parliament was another, pragmatic connection. The Irish, Scots, and Welsh, as well as colonial agents from America, developed the arts of lobbying at Westminster and Whitehall, both to obtain and obstruct legislation. A third point of contact was provided by the peoples of England's overseas empire. The Scots were particularly assiduous in contributing to the army and later to the diplomatic and civil services. What had begun as English plantations in the early seventeenth century had by the early eighteenth century become what was generally known as the British empire. Union in 1707 contributed to the development of that nomenclature, but it also arose from the gestation of expansionist ambitions which if hard to tie down either in time or place certainly involved Glasgow as well as London, Ulster as well as Bristol. By 1720 many parts of Britain, engaged in a single endeavour, looked longingly overseas for tranquillity, opportunity, and salvation. Domestically, however, the ideology of imperialism was largely expressed with reference to considerations of overseas trade. London did not yet have notable

'imperial' architecture; missionary activity was still slight; scientific expeditions were few and ad hoc; and there was relatively little consideration given to
the export of British institutions. This was decidedly not imperialism according to the nineteenth-century model: evangelicalism did not restrain the slave
trade; capital exports were inconsiderable; and gunboat diplomacy had not
been established. The early British empire was as weak as it was strong, as prey
to be influenced as to influence. And in 1727 there was little prospect that this
was ever to change.

CHAPTER 9

The Political World of Queen Anne

Anne's brief reign was full of achievements. Huge resources of money and men were mobilized to wage a war that successfully defended the Revolution settlement and an effective European balance of power. Marlborough's great victories at Blenheim, Ramillies, and Oudenarde established Britain's army as second to none in Europe and cemented the nation's pre-eminent role in the Grand Alliance. Britain's enhanced authority was acknowledged at Utrecht by the banishment of the Pretender from France, the recognition of the Hanoverian succession, and the acquisition of Gibraltar, Minorca, and Nova Scotia. Indeed, not least among the achievements of Anne's reign was that when she died George I came to the throne unchallenged. She left a State significantly larger and more powerful than that she had inherited. If the national debt had grown, so had the revenues to support it. Through her reign Parliament was an increasingly imposing legislative factory—notably the Union between England and Scotland was forged without provoking serious civil discord.

Yet Anne's was also a reign full of bitterness and failure. The Queen had no heir of her body and felt deeply the poignancy of being the last Stuart to be crowned. Moreover, because of the depth of political and religious divisions she was unable to unify her people in a common cause. Fundamental differences in definitions of the national interest were championed regarding war and peace, the role of the Church of England, and the importance of the Hanoverian succession. Signalling such divisions, major legislation dealing with occasional conformity, general naturalization, and placemen, was attempted time and again, in spite of the zealous opposition encountered. In this environment it is not surprising that elections were often fought with considerable ferocity. Local government was also occasionally purged by the centre, though in return the localities poured addresses and petitions into the centre in attempts to force issues. A prolific press, communicating events to society at large, helped to keep the political temperature very high. Nor did the newspapers want for stories. Looking at only Anne's last four years, for example, Sacheverell was impeached, Walpole, pre-eminent among a new generation of Whigs, thrown in the Tower, Harley stabbed, and Marlborough entered voluntary exile.

QUEEN ANNE

On St George's Day 1702 Anne was crowned at Westminster Abbey by the Archbishop of Canterbury. Anne relished to the full this conjunction: the saint's day emphasized the undiluted nature of her English blood, the presence of the archbishop her Anglican orthodoxy. Moreover, to set the intended tone of her reign she had the Archbishop of York preach to the text 'And kings shall be thy nursing fathers, and their queens thy nursing mothers' (Isaiah 49: 23) and later adopted Elizabeth I's motto (*Semper Eadem*). Such careful positioning decisively highlighted her virtues in comparison to her predecessor, designated successor, and the Pretender. None doubted that she was a legitimate heir to the throne and her accession was widely celebrated as heralding an age of restored unity within the realm. When she was proclaimed at Linton, to the south of Cambridge, 'her Majesty's Health was publickly drank . . . with Huzza's, Guns firing, Trumpets sounding Drums beating, Bells ringing, and the Country Musick playing, which continued all the day . . . such an unanimous Appearance was never seen in this County before.'[1] At Honiton in Devon on coronation day there was a

very pretty procession of three hundred women and girls in good order two and two, march with three women drummers beating, and a guard of 25 young men on horseback. Each of the females had a long white rod in her hand on top of which was a tassel made of white and blue ribbon (which they said was the Queen's colours) and bone lace, the great manufacture of the town. Thus they had marched in and about the town from ten in the morning, hurraing every now and then, and then weaving their rods. Thus they returned at 9, and then broke up very weary and hungry.[2]

Born on 6 February 1665 Anne was 37 when she was crowned, though for many of those years her accession had appeared unlikely or remote. She was after all only James II's second daughter. Moreover though her mother died when she was just 6, her father remarried in 1673 to Mary of Modena so that any male heir from this new union would head the line of succession. On several occasions her stepmother became pregnant, though not until June 1688 was a healthy heir born, the future Old Pretender. Moreover, her sister's marriage to William had threatened to produce heirs that would have taken the line of succession effectively out of Anne's way. Thus Anne was bred as a Princess, but not raised to be Queen—her education was decidedly limited. Furthermore, she keenly felt the isolation caused by the loss of her mother and the marriage of her sister, an isolation intensified by an insoluble conflict between

---

[1] *Post Boy*, 4–7 April 1702, [p. 2].
[2] *The Journal of James Yonge [1647–1721]*, ed. F. N. L. Poynter (1963), p. 210.

her Protestantism and her father's Catholicism. Throughout their lives neither father nor daughter ever compromised on matters of faith. Such family tensions over issues of inheritance and religion were, of course, public matters, being first shouted in her ears as a teenager when Parliament attempted to exclude James from the succession.

An element of stability was brought into Anne's life by marriage in 1683 to Prince George of Denmark.[3] Remarkably, in an age when such arranged marriages were more often honoured in the breach than in the observance, the couple soon became happy, loving, and intimate. George was, indeed, to provide Anne with an emotional rock she clung to until he died in 1708. There was a real meeting of minds here, though George was no Hamlet. 'I have tried him drunk and I have tried him sober and there is nothing in him' was Charles II's devastating evaluation of the Prince. By another characterization George was 'very fat, loves News, his Bottle, and the Queen'.[4] Yet if his intellectual limitations suited Anne perfectly marriage soon brought her new emotional turmoil. From late 1683 until her last miscarriage in 1700 the trials of maternity battered body and mind almost without respite, as seventeen pregnancies produced only one child who lived into infancy. And then in 1700 her last surviving child, the Duke of Gloucester, died. Her health, which had rarely been good, now became wretched as she found solace by gorging. Obesity, gout, and lameness set in, and she spent much of her reign unable to walk any distance. Physical incapacity and intimations of the peculiar significance of her own mortality enveloped the life of this last Stuart monarch.

Despite the trials and tribulations of Anne's life, like all the Stuarts she lacked neither opinions nor resolve. Raised under the watchful gaze of Bishop Compton, one of the seven who invited William to England in 1688, she never wavered in her belief of the essential rightness and superiority of Protestantism and of the very real threat posed by Catholicism. Her father's policies and the prospect that they might be continued by a son dismayed her deeply, leading her to play a significant role in the Glorious Revolution: she absented herself from the birth of her half-brother on 10 June 1688, effectively encouraging the warming pan myth to take a powerful hold; and soon after the Dutch invasion she abandoned her father, sided with the Anglican establishment, and joined the rising in the north in November, being 'fully perswaded that the Prince of Orange designs the King's safety and preservation'.[5] Doubtless like many she

---

[3] George, Prince of Denmark, 1653–1708, deserted James II's army 1688, created Duke of Cumberland 1689, notional head of army and navy 1702–8.

[4] Quoted in E. Gregg, *Queen Anne* (1984), p. 35; J. Macky, *Memoirs of the Secret Services of John Macky, Esq; During the Reigns of King William, Queen Anne, and King George I* (2nd edn., 1733), p. 3.

[5] *The Princess Anne of Demark's Letter to the Queen* (1688).

was surprised by the new scene introduced by her father's flight, but early in 1689 she quickly fell in behind the proposal for the joint monarchy of William and Mary. This was partly self-interested, a feature of Anne's personality easily ignored. Through the 1690s, despite a split with William and Mary from 1692–4, Anne never lost sight of the goal of her own accession. On her sister's death she and William became reconciled, though she never warmed to the King, and contacts she appears to have made with her father's court in France in the 1690s were probably designed to confuse her half-brother's prospects and ensure her own peaceful accession. She was, however, far from being a radical enthusiast for the Glorious Revolution. Like William she was hostile to any idea that the Crown's powers had been significantly changed by the settlement reached in 1689, arguing (correctly) that the Revolution had been brought about by Tories as well as by Whigs. Nevertheless, she eschewed notions of divine right and if a keen supporter of the Church of England made it clear that she would 'inviolably maintain the Toleration.'[6]

Formally Anne's authority was the same as William's. Indeed, at first blush she had many advantages over him as a ruling monarch: she was English, Anglican, resident, thrifty, and able to trust loyal advisers. But if much government revolved around her, little of it took its lead from her. She lacked William's intellectual, emotional, and physical independence. Sarah Churchill, the Duchess of Marlborough, a personally embittered observer to be sure, marvelled at the Queen's prodigious memory, but thought 'she chose to retain in it very little besides ceremonies and customs of courts and suchlike insignificant trifles'. Moreover, she 'has no Original Thoughts on any Subject; is neither good nor bad, but as put into: that she has much Love & Passion, while pleas'd, for those who please'.[7] The ladies of the bedchamber, especially Sarah Churchill and later Abigail Masham, played an important role in this— to circumvent some of the formality of royalty the Queen styled herself 'Mrs Morley' to Sarah, who responded as 'Mrs Freeman'.[8] Such dependency may have been exaggerated by contemporaries, but it significantly coloured their view of her capacities and responsibilities. Though she frequently attended cabinet meetings and often observed the deliberations of the House of Lords she was widely believed largely to follow the lead provided by her ministers. As one overseas visitor noted, 'foreigners have a much higher opinion of her

---

[6] W. Cobbett (ed.), *A Parliamentary History of England*, 36 vols. (1806–20), vol. 6, p. 452.

[7] *Memoirs of Sarah, Duchess of Marlborough Together with her 'Characters of her Contemporaries' and her 'Opinions'*, ed. W. King (1930), p. 230; *The Private Diary of William, First Earl of Cowper, Lord Chancellor of England* (Eton, 1833), p. 49. Sarah Churchill, 1660–1744, Maid of Honour to Anne 1672, married John Churchill 1678, with Anne in the crisis of 1688–9, Mistress of the Robes and Keeper of the Privy Purse 1702, was famously quarrelsome.

[8] Abigail Masham, née Hill, d. 1734. First cousin of Sarah Churchill; given control of Privy Purse after Duchess of Marlborough's dismissal.

parts than her own subjects'.[9] Consequently, whereas William was frequently subjected to bitter attacks in Parliament and the press Anne was earnestly fêted, gently mocked, or, more frequently, silently ignored.

Certainly Anne had no big idea which she relentlessly pursued through her reign. War with France, Union with Scotland, and the Hanoverian succession were already in place as central objectives when William died. This was the framework within which Anne worked and which she was unwilling and unable to alter. Her ambition was to maintain the figure of the monarch which she had seen diminished by William's actions and domestic political attacks upon him. Even here she struggled. If her speeches to Parliament were noted for the clarity of their delivery she lacked the charisma, wit, intelligence, or good health to energize her court. Nor did she have the common touch to enthuse her subjects. She put more effort into taking the waters at Bath and attending Newmarket races than in rousing the nation to arms. In fact her greatest source of power was over the appointment and dismissal of ministers in which, like William, she hoped to be able to stand above party.

All I desire is my liberty in encouraging and employing all those that concur faithfully in my service, whether they are Whigs or Tories, not to be tied to one or the other; for if I should be so unfortunate as to fall into the hands of either, I shall look upon myself, though I have the name of Queen, to be in reality but their slave; which as it will be my personal ruin, so it will be the destroying of all Government, for of putting an end to faction, it will lay a lasting foundation for it.[10]

In this, as in so much else, she was ultimately and sadly to be disappointed.

THE RAGE OF PARTY

The immediate political prelude to Anne's reign was provided by four deaths: of her son on 30 July 1700; of Charles II of Spain on 21 October 1700; of her father on 6 September 1701; and of William on 8 March 1702. The first raised the question of the Protestant succession, which was resolved to the satisfaction of England and the dissatisfaction of Scotland by the Act of Settlement, so initiating the Union controversy. The second, through Louis XIV's consequential recognition of the Pretender as James III, effectively joined together in English eyes the issues of the Protestant and Spanish succession, thereby ensuring her full commitment to the Grand Alliance. The third, followed by France ignoring the second Partition Treaty, meant that the Spanish empire was again up for grabs, bringing Europe to the edge of war. And, finally,

[9] *London in 1710: From the Travels of Zacharias Conrad von Uffenbach*, trans. and ed. W. H. Quarrell and M. Mare (1934), p. 116.

[10] *The Letters and Diplomatic Instructions of Queen Anne*, ed. B. C. Brown (1968), p. 196.

despite her limitations, the accession of Anne changed the domestic scene in ways that sharply focused attention upon the party basis of political life.

Those domestic changes were several. First, Anne's instinctive Toryism and deep commitment to the Church of England prompted others to seek to strengthen the Anglican establishment in Church and State, her religious traditionalism encouraging bitter assaults upon heterodoxy. Most significantly, whereas William had few dealings with the Canterbury Convocation, under Anne it operated alongside Parliament, helping to keep religious issues centre-stage. Second, her dynastic legitimacy initially took much of the wind out of the sails of English Jacobitism. Whereas Jacobites had attacked William in an unrestrained fashion, Anne provided a much more difficult target, for 'even the more moderate Jacobites were pleased to see at least a daughter of that good but unfortunate king [James II] on the throne.'[11] The death of James II in 1701 meant that his adherents had now to press less for a restoration than the estab-lishment of a young Prince raised in the bosom of Catholicism who had no direct experience of England. Consequently, English Jacobites most usually marked time, waiting for Anne's last illness. Thus it was not until after 1710, when her health became more precarious, that Jacobitical intrigue once again entered the political mainstream—though fears of plots remained strong through the reign. A final consequence of Anne's accession was that the removal of William as a source of dispute, and the relatively uncontroversial nature of Anne's authority and predilections, significantly de-personalized some political questions. An important element of this was that party politics in William's reign had been confused by the importance of court–country div-isions. But under Anne the country programme only occasionally came into the limelight, allowing the Whig–Tory dichotomy to appear more distinctly and forcefully. One explanation rises from the fact that the Queen's financial dis-cretion, insistence upon courtly propriety, and complete Englishness made charges of court corruption harder to credit. Another can be traced to the suc-cession of military victories attained under Marlborough's lead, which until c.1709 made criticism of the objectives and cost of the war difficult to sustain—though failure in Spain began to offer opportunities from 1707. Finally, given the close association established in the 1690s between the Tories and country programme, the relative strength of the Tory party after 1702 provided a clear outlet for criticism of the executive. Attention could now focus much more clearly upon issues and their party-political basis, though such a process had in fact been underway before her accession. Indeed Anne's reign saw party politics conducted with an intensity and clarity that is difficult to find in William's reign.

---

[11] *Memoirs of Thomas, Earl of Ailesbury, Written by Himself*, 2 vols. (1890), vol. 2, p. 525.

The four principal political problems of Anne's reign—war and peace, religion, the succession, and the Union—might all have been solved by a number of routes. Articulating those options and attempting to choose the most suitable produced intense debate, lending a distinctive voice to the period. The proliferation of political clubs (such as the Whig Kit Cat), newspapers, periodicals, books, and pamphlets developed and carried much of this debate, but the pulpit, judicial bench, and stage were also significant. It was periodicals which particularly stood out as new and powerful vehicles of political ideology in Anne's reign: Defoe's *Review*, the *Examiner* (especially when Swift was at its helm), Mainwaring's *Medley*, Tutchin's *Observator*, and Leslie's *Rehearsal* are only the most famous. Enabled by the lapsing of the Licensing Act in 1695, this efflorescence largely arose because new markets were perceived by both political and commercial interests. In particular Robert Harley, initially taking his lead from John Somers, looked to produce a range of propaganda to support his political objectives. Yet if often highly partisan, periodicals were far from being mere political rags. The writing was usually of a very high order and that political issues jostled alongside discussions of philosophy, economics, manners, aesthetics, and the like only serves to demonstrate the centrality of political discourse within polite society.

That discourse enveloped a spectrum of opinion but largely took place between the orange of the Whigs and the blue of the Tories. An introduction to the ideological polarity of Whigs and Tories in Anne's reign is provided by comparing two summaries of party positions on key issues produced in 1714, just after she died. At one extreme was the view of the arch-Tory and Jacobite Francis Atterbury.[12]

The Merits of the Church Party [i.e. Tories]	The merits of the Whigs
1 No new war, no new taxes.	1 A new war, six shillings in the pound, a general excise, and a poll-tax
2 No attempt against the church	2 A general and unlimited comprehension, without common-prayer book or bishops
3 No repeal of the conditions upon which the crown was settled upon the king	3 The repeal of the act of limitation of the crown
4 No foreigners in employment	4 An equal distribution of places between Turks, Germans, and infidels

[12] 'English Advice to the Freeholders of England', in *A Collection of Scarce and Valuable Tracts, on the Most Interesting and Entertaining Subjects*, ed. W. Scott, 13 vols. (2nd edn., 1809–15), vol. 13, p. 541. Francis Atterbury, 1662–1732, educated Westminster School and Christ Church, Oxford, Dean of Christ Church 1712, Bishop of Rochester 1713, deprived of offices and exiled for Jacobitism 1723.

5 No standing army	5 An augmentation of troops for the better suppressing of mobs and riots
6 No long parliament	6 The repeal of the Triennial Act
7 No restraint of the liberty of the press	7 An act to prohibit all libels in favour of the church or churchmen, and to enable free-thinkers to write against God and the Christian religion
8 No insulting the memory of the queen	8 An encouragement to all men to speak ill of the queen and her friends

Against this may be contrasted a Whig view. Amongst other things the Tories were charged with: aiding 'The persecution in King Charles and King James's reign; The blood of my Lord Russel, Colonel Sydney, Mr Cornish, & c.'; supporting 'King James, and his attendants popery and slavery'; protecting 'The dispensing power to set up will and pleasure, instead of law and justice'; forcing through a dishonourable peace in 1713; attacking the religious settlement of 1689; and, finally, supporting 'The Pretender, mass, and wooden shoes'. In sum, by this view the Whigs were for 'security of religion, liberty and property', the Tories sought 'No Church, no trade, no liberty, no property, no kingdom.'[13] As such points demonstrate, at the extremes the ideological basis of party politics under Anne had little to distinguish it from that under William. Positions upon the Exclusion crisis, the Revolution settlement, European war and its finance, the 1696 association, and the Act of Settlement provided the key historic reference points. Thus it was less the content than the form debate took and the context within which it raged that distinguished party politics before and after Anne's accession.

If political parties continued, as in the 1690s, to lack a formal basis, nevertheless they operated at all levels of English society in Anne's reign. At Westminster a high proportion of MPs and peers (perhaps eight out of ten) followed a consistent party line on controversial questions. Before the start of a session party leaders and managers met to work out strategy—the Whigs liked to mix this business with the pleasure of Newmarket races—and during sessions London taverns often hosted meetings to thrash out tactics. The terms of the Triennial Act also ensured that the electorate were frequently asked to judge such manoeuvres, with circular letters and regional whips attempting to hold the line. Five general elections were held in Anne's reign, generally producing Tory majorities (see Table 7).

[13] 'English Advice to the Freeholders of England [alternative version]', in *A Collection of Scarce and Valuable Tracts*, vol. 13, p. 558.

TABLE 7. *Party strength in the House of Commons, 1701–1713*

	Tories	Whigs	Unclassified
1701 (Nov./Dec.)	240	248	25
1702	298	184	31
1705	260	233	20
1708	225	268	20
1710	329	168	16
1713	354	148	11

Note: Figures relate to MPs for constituencies in England and Wales only, the position immediately after each election, and exclude the outcome of disputed returns. These provisional estimates have been kindly made available by the 1690–1715 House of Commons section of the History of Parliament.

Even if these elections produced polls only in a minority of constituencies the intensity of electoral politics should not be underestimated. English society was riven by party disputes, even at the level of local politics or outside the electorate. Burnet noted in the summer of 1708 that 'The parties are now so stated and kept up, not only by the elections of parliament-men, that return every third year, but even by the yearly elections of mayors and corporation-men, that they know their strength; and in every corner of the nation the two parties stand, as it were, listed against one another'.[14] Indeed, far more than in the 1690s the Commission of the Peace was redrawn along political lines. Between 1702 and 1704 significant numbers of Whigs were dismissed and replaced by Tories, though when the Whigs held the whip-hand between 1705 and 1710 the remodelling was less severe. With the Tory star ascendant again in 1710 a new wave of evictions and appointments followed, often in their favour.

Yet the political world of Queen Anne was not simply a question of Whig versus Tory. In first place the composition of ministries only occasionally reflected the balance of opinion in the country and Parliament. Marlborough, Godolphin, and Harley, the three leading ministers of Anne's reign, all stood to some extent above party and were prepared to use allies wherever they might be found. This was a position the Queen sympathized with, and which partially accounts for her enthusiasm for all three. If she was 'very certain there are good and ill people of both sorts' she also dreaded 'falling into the hands of either party'.[15] Moreover, there were still parliamentarians who were tied to the Queen and her ministers by blood, favour, or office. Finally, contemporaries also occasionally employed non-partisan ways of conceptualizing political activity. Most usually this was done by reference to the operation of 'interests',

[14] Quoted in G. Holmes, *British Politics in the Age of Anne* (revised edn., 1987), pp. 312–13.
[15] *Letters of Queen Anne*, pp. 153 and 172.

generally of individuals or families, and when particular pieces of legislation were under consideration of economic groups such as shipowners, landowners, or workers in the woollen industry. That politics was about personalities as well as policies, materialism as well as idealism, is undeniable. However, such interests were clearly subsidiary to the controlling influence of party politics. They lacked either the critical mass, temporal continuity, or breadth of vision to make a general impact on a nation faced by intense war and an uncertain Hanoverian succession.

THE NEW MINISTRY

Anne inherited a largely Whig ministry and a newly-elected Parliament with a small Tory majority that had been sitting for over two months. Though William preferred to employ ministers from both parties he had come to appreciate the value of weighting his administration in favour of the Whigs and had last done this in the winter of 1701–2, driving Godolphin to resign.[16] Though Anne also espoused the virtues of mixed ministries she clearly favoured the Tories, who seized the moment and put her under considerable pressure to purge Whigs from all levels of government. Certainly in the months after her accession many Tories were appointed to key posts, but they were more often of a moderate than extreme disposition, both because of her own independence and because of the views of her closest advisers—not least the harangues of her favourite, the arch-Whig Sarah Churchill, Lady Marlborough. The two critical appointments came early. Almost immediately Marlborough was made captain general and given the Garter, the Crown's highest honour, and was soon on his way to the States General to maintain the foreign policy objectives established by William. Unlike his wife Marlborough inclined towards Toryism, though it was often diluted by a sizeable measure of self-interest. Second, Anne decisively turned her back on her predecessor by appointing Godolphin as Lord Treasurer in early May, a post William had never filled. Godolphin, a moderate Tory by temperament, was also committed to the coming war with France. Other Tories were also brought into the ministry, such as the Earl of Nottingham and Sir Charles Hedges as Secretaries of State. The leaders of the Whig Junto—Somers, Halifax, Wharton, and Orford—were all removed from the Privy Council.

The new ministry suffered from one particularly serious weakness. Most of the principal members were peers, posing the tricky problem of managing the Commons. This was settled by the willingness of Harley, Speaker in

[16] See above, p. 163–4.

the Commons, to act in concert with Godolphin and Marlborough. Indeed, the three had met just before William's death to agree the means by which to smooth Anne's accession. Though Harley was not formally a member of the ministry his role was highly significant, providing its eyes and ears in the Commons. Widely respected for his knowledge of parliamentary ways and able to exert some measure of control over the operation of the Commons from the chair, he was also acutely sensitive to comings and goings at Westminster. Moreover, his background allowed him legitimately to appeal to moderates among both Whigs and Tories. A further role he played, however, was as confidant to Godolphin. With Marlborough usually away on campaign for over six months each year, and given the slowness and uncertainty of the mails, the Lord Treasurer often turned to Harley to work out ideas and to provide advice. If to the public the early government of Anne was in the hands of the duumvirs, Godolphin and Marlborough, in practice it was held by the triumvirs from the outset. In 1704 Harley was told that 'The Duke, the Treasurer and yourself are called the Triumvirate, and reckoned the spring of all public affairs; and that your interests and counsels are so united and linked together that they cannot be broken, nor in any danger of it during this reign.'[17]

Less than a month after William was buried, war was declared against France and before the end of May Parliament had been dissolved. With the new appointments in place, and Anne's explicit desire to favour strong supporters of the Church, the general election (brought on by her accession) in June and July was a triumph for the Tories—in the new Commons their majority exceeded one hundred. Yet the apparent unity of electorate and ministry was somewhat illusory. First, the moderate Toryism of Marlborough and Godolphin was at odds with the table thumping of many High Church Tories in both the Commons and Convocation. Leading High Church Tories, such as the Earl of Rochester, coveted the office and influence of the duumvirs and were determined to hold Anne to a strong anti-Whig line. Second, if the Tories dominated the Commons, in the Lords the Whigs were usually able to hold their own, so ensuring frequent and intense struggles between the two Houses. Third, though the Whigs had been routed in the polls the strength of the leadership provided by the Junto allowed them greater influence than mere numbers alone might suggest. Fourth, in Parliament Marlborough's policy of a continental land war found its natural allies among the Whigs rather than the Tories. All told, therefore, government was possible in the opening session of Anne's first Parliament only by the ministry calling upon support from all sides according to circumstances rather than hitching itself consistently to one or other party.

<hr />

[17] H. M. C., *The Manuscripts of his Grace the Duke of Portland*, vol. 4 (1897), p. 119.

Thus the session which began on 20 October 1702 and ended on 27 February 1703 had a good measure of trouble and strife. Such tension can be glimpsed in the refusal of the Commons to agree to Anne's request for a grant of £5,000 per annum to Marlborough when he was raised to a dukedom in December or in the attack by the Commons on Lord Halifax, once William's Whig Chancellor of the Exchequer, which was repelled in the Lords. But it came out especially strongly in the battle over the first Occasional Conformity Bill, aimed at excluding Dissenters from civil offices and purifying the communing membership of the Church. This had been introduced into the Commons by William Bromley, one of the members for the Anglican fortress of Oxford University, and with a clear Tory majority in the House was sent up to the Lords at the start of December.[18] There it faced stiff opposition from Whig leaders such as Wharton and Somers, who, concerned that such a measure might be 'tacked' to a money Bill—and therefore only able to be accepted or rejected by the Lords (not amended)—managed to get passed a motion on 9 December that tacking was unconstitutional. In fact, the Bill was amended in the Lords, with Godolphin and Marlborough voting for it only with great reluctance, leading to considerable 'clashing between the two Houses' and a failure to pass the Bill.[19] Hardly less significant was the debate over the relative merits of a land war versus a blue water strategy, with Marlborough's modest achievements in 1702 being set against the failure of the Cadiz expedition. By the spring of 1703, therefore, Anne's accession was acknowledged to have been something of a false dawn. Far from political divisions having been eradicated or weakened they were as strong as ever. Still, there had been progress: substantial supplies had been voted; the army and navy mobilized; and the duumvirs had established a working relationship with the Queen that was to remain operative for eight years.

Parliament had been prorogued in late February 1703 and was not to meet again until 9 November. Internationally, the Methuen Treaty and the commitment to 'no peace without Spain' transformed the scope of the war, though militarily the campaign was not very noteworthy. Closer to home Anne had refused her assent to the Scottish Act of Security, signalling the crisis that was to eventuate in the Union of 1707. Subtle developments were also taking place in the background of domestic political affairs, aimed at creating a climate of political moderation. As Marlborough later explained, 'There is nothing more certaine then . . . that either of the partys would bee tyrants if thay were lett alone; and I am afraid it is as true, that it will be very heard for the Queen to

---

[18] William Bromley, 1664–1732, educated Christ Church, Oxford, MP, Speaker of the House of Commons 1710, and Secretary of State 1713–14.

[19] *The Norris Papers*, ed. T. Heywood, Chetham Society, 9 (1846), p. 122.

prevent itt.'[20] One step was the enforced resignation from the ministry in February of the Tory hothead the Earl of Rochester, Lord Lieutenant of Ireland. Rochester had been a thorn in the side of the duumvirs since Anne's first days and Marlborough was easily able to persuade the Queen, who knew what the Whigs were capable of and personally disliked Rochester, that extremists of any colour were damaging to the national interest. Another step taken was to counterbalance Whig strength in the Lords by appointing four new Tory peers (Granville, Finch, Seymour-Conway, and Leveson-Gower). Whether this was enough to smooth troubled waters was uncertain. Through the summer of 1703 there was a significant correspondence carried out between Anne, Godolphin, and the Marlboroughs about the nature of the political parties and the way ahead for the ministry. The Duchess pressed the merits of the Whigs upon both her husband and the Queen, attempting to damn the Tories as a Jacobite party. Neither was convinced, marking a significant weakening of the duchess's influence upon the Queen. Marlborough declared to his wife that 'I hope I shall always continue in the houmor I am now in, which is to be governed by neither party, but to doe what I think is best for England, by which I know I shall disoblige both partys.'[21] For her part, Anne defended the Tories: 'I do not deny but there are some for the Prince of Wales, but that number I believe is very small, and I dare say there are millions that are called Jacobites that abhor their principles as much as you do.'[22]

The new session proved no less fractious than the last. A second Occasional Conformity Bill was introduced into the Commons on 25 November, only to be scuppered outright by the Whigs in the Lords. Though the duumvirs voted for it, behind the scenes they spoke against it. No less significantly, the Prince of Denmark, who held a seat in the Lords as Duke of Cumberland, having supported the first Bill, absented himself from the crucial vote, a clear indication of Anne's displeasure with the measure, encouraging other moderate Tories to stay away. Relations between the Queen and the Tories were undoubtedly damaged by this, though they were at least partially repaired by the announcement of Queen Anne's Bounty to support poor livings on 7 February. But the controversy over occasional conformity was symptomatic of the bad relations between the parties, expressed through disagreements between the two Houses that existed for the rest of the long session (it did not end until 3 April 1704). One major controversy surrounded investigation in February and March of the 'Scotch plot' of 1703 when Franco-Jacobites had attempted to foment the

[20] *The Marlborough–Godolphin Correspondence*, ed. H. L. Snyder, 3 vols. (Oxford, 1975), vol. 1, p. 197.

[21] *Marlborough–Godolphin Correspondence*, vol. 1, p. 240.

[22] *Letters of Queen Anne*, p. 228. This letter dates from June 1703, not 1707 as Brown suggests. See Gregg, *Queen Anne*, p. 432, n. 136.

Highlands. In the Lords Whigs hoped to expose failings in the handling of the affair by the Tory Earl of Nottingham, prompting the Commons to leap to his defence. Another heated exchange came in the case of *Ashby* v. *White*, an appeal heard in the Lords in January over voting at general elections at Aylesbury.[23] This was a dispute which operated at two particularly important levels. First, it was a contest for electoral control of Aylesbury between Sir John Pakington and Lord Wharton, respectively ardent advocate and critic of the Occasional Conformity Bills, and thus a trial of party strength.[24] Second, it set the judicial authority of the Lords against the Commons's exclamation of their right to determine the nature of the franchise.

The party disputes of the early years of Anne's reign must not be exaggerated. Between them the triumvirs were able to obtain the legislation necessary to wage war on an unprecedented scale. What infuriated them, Godolphin and Marlborough in particular, was the time and energy that had to be given over to this when they viewed such measures as absolutely essential and uncontroversial. Moreover, they both appreciated that domestic controversy weakened the enthusiasm of England's allies, especially Holland. As the duumvirs's exasperation mounted so privately thoughts of retirement began wishfully to be aired, though at the same time there continued the process of rethinking the nature of the ministry's support begun in earnest a year earlier. If that support could not be easily achieved by shouting up the national interest, then it would have to be bought by further ministerial changes.

HALCYON DAYS, 1704–1708

In April 1704 several leading Tories were eased out of the ministry, to be replaced by moderates who might best be called 'Harleyites'. It began on 4 April when Henry St John, the 25-year-old supporter of Harley and a favourite of Marlborough, was appointed Secretary of War.[25] Alarmed at the strengthening of the duumvirs's position Nottingham had earlier pressed the Queen to throw in her lot with the Tories: 'He was very positive that the Queen could not govern but by one party or the other' and that some Whigs were 'contemptible'.[26] It is testament to Anne's strength of character, the value she

---

[23] See above, pp. 46–7.

[24] John Pakington, 1671–1727, succeeded as 4th Baronet 1688, MP for Worcestershire 1690–5, 1698–1727, he opposed Anglo-Scottish Union.

[25] Henry St John, 1678–1751, educated Eton College and possibly Christ Church, Oxford, MP first in 1701, created Viscount Bolingbroke and Baron St John of Lydiard Tregoze 1712, attainted, lost titles, and fled to France and service of the Pretender 1714, broke with the Pretender 1716, pardoned 1723, but debarred from House of Lords, leading opponent of Walpole, wrote many important political works.

[26] *Marlborough–Godolphin Correspondence*, vol. 1, pp. 280–1.

placed in the services of the duumvirs, and her quest for moderation, that she rejected Nottingham's threats and took a different tack. She dismissed two prominent Tories, Sir Edward Seymour, comptroller of the household, and the Earl of Jersey, the Lord Chamberlain, leading Nottingham to resign.[27] Seymour was replaced by an ally of Harley, Sir Thomas Mansel, Jersey by the insignificant Earl of Kent, and Nottingham by Speaker Harley. This redrawing of the ministry was not so much a switch from the Tories to the Whigs as a move towards the middle ground that fully embraced the war. Harley valued his independence from party, but it was reasonably claimed that 'most people in the Protestant interest are pleased with his preferment.'[28] The Queen also came to place great store in his advice, so that as Sarah Churchill's star waned, Harley's waxed.

The new ministry soon had a strong following wind with the seizure of Gibraltar, the neutralization of the French fleet following the Battle of Málaga, and the successful march of the allied army to the Danube capped with the decisive victory at Blenheim. Optimistically the Earl of Peterborough hoped that 'Every body will now own the effects of the happy influence of those [the Queen] confides in. Malice and all cabals are defeated'.[29] It was not to be. First, Anglo-Scottish relations reached crisis point with Anne's agreement in July to the Edinburgh Parliament's Act of Security.[30] Second, it became clear soon after the new session opened on 24 October 1704 that both parties were intent on demonstrating their strength and value to the ministry by criticizing government policy, driving the Queen to resort to attending debates in the Lords in the hope that her presence would calm debates and offer the Lord Treasurer some protection. For a third time occasional conformity became the site of intense battles, though on this occasion the Tories misjudged their strength in the Commons, for an attempt to tack the Bill to the land tax failed by 251 votes to 134—for long after a Tacker was often taken to be 'a Man of Passion, a Man of Heat, a Man that is for Running the Nation upon any Hazards, to obtain his Ends'.[31] In the Lords the Bill met the same fate as its predecessor, but on this

---

[27] Edward Seymour, 1633–1708, succeeded as 4th Baronet 1685, active in the Commons from 1661, joined William III at Exeter 1688 but opposed offer of the Crown to him. Edward Villiers, 1656–1711, educated St John's College, Cambridge, created Viscount Villiers of Dartford 1691, diplomatic posts in 1690s, a Lord Justice of Ireland 1697–9, created Earl of Jersey 1697, Lord Chamberlain 1700–4.

[28] H. M. C., *Portland*, vol. 4, p. 86.

[29] *Private Correspondence of Sarah, Duchess of Marlborough*, 2 vols. (1838), vol. 1, p. 5. Charles Mordaunt, 1658–1735, leading soldier, sailor, and diplomat, Privy Councillor 1689, created Earl of Monmouth 1689, succeeded as Earl of Peterborough 1697, took a leading role in the war in Spain 1703–8, literary patron.

[30] For the progress of this crisis, see above, p. 252.

[31] *Defoe's Review*, facsimile edn., 22 vols. (New York, 1938), vol. 4, p. 99.

occasion Godolphin and Marlborough voted against it. The sense that the parties were stalemated between 1702 and 1705, both unable to gain the upper hand, was strengthened by the continued and ultimately indecisive deliberations between the Houses over *Ashby* v. *White* early in 1705. Only new issues or a general election might provide the means of breaking the deadlock.

Parliament was prorogued on 14 March and, under the terms of the Triennial Act, dissolved on 5 April. Anne and the triumvirs as ever wanted a moderate House to be elected, signalling this by their disapproval of tackers. Certainly in the general election, fought with considerable ferocity in May and June, the Whigs made some advances at the expense of the Tories, with the two parties close to parity in the new House of Commons. Alongside this were two significant changes in the ministry. The Tory Duke of Buckingham was replaced by the Whig Duke of Newcastle as Lord Privy Seal in March and two weeks before the new Parliament met on 25 October the Lord Keeper, Wright, responsible for the purge of so many Whigs from the Commissions of the Peace, was replaced by the renowned barrister Sir William Cowper, the Junto's favoured choice.[32] Together the election and these appointments marked a change in direction at the centre towards the Whigs, with Tory suspicions of the Queen's 'erroneous' political opinions now seemingly confirmed. Harley too was concerned about this shift to the Whigs, signalling a developing tension among the triumvirs. In September 1705 he warned Godolphin that 'If the gentlemen of England are made sensible that the Queen is the Head, and not a Party, everything will be easy, and the Queen will be courted and not a Party; but if otherwise—', effectively rebuking the Lord Treasurer for the path he now looked to be taking.[33] For their part the duumvirs appeared to calculate that experience since 1689 had demonstrated the bankruptcy of ministries wedded to trimming and moderation.

When Parliament met on 25 October the first clear indication of the balance of opinion in the new Commons came with the election of the Speaker. Godolphin's candidate, the moderate Whig John Smith, was elected, but Bromley, the High Church Tory who had formally instigated all three Occasional Conformity Bills, managed to obtain over 200 votes, dashing any hope the duumvirs might have had to utilize cross-party support.[34] As

[32] Nathan Wright, 1654–1721, educated Emmanuel College, Cambridge, and Inner Temple, Serjeant-at-Law 1692, knighted and made King's Serjeant 1697, Lord Keeper of Great Seal and Privy Councillor 1700. William Cowper, *c.*1665–1723, leading legal figure, becoming Lord Chancellor 1707–10, 1714–18; MP 1695–1700 and 1701–5; created Baron Cowper 1706 and Earl Cowper 1718.

[33] H. M. C., *Calendar of the Manuscripts of the Marquis of Bath*, vol. 1 (1904), p. 75.

[34] John Smith, 1655–1723, educated St John's College, Oxford, and Middle Temple, MP from 1678, Chancellor of the Exchequer 1708–10.

Godolphin later reflected, 'the Tories are more numerous in this Parliament than the Whigs, and the Queen's servants much the least part of the three.'[35] Soon the Tories sought to embarrass the ministry and the Queen by proposing that Sophia dowager Electress of Hanover be invited to England (to Anne it was a 'disagreeable proposal').[36] Though the motion was easily defeated in the Lords it had the effect of finalizing the process by which Anne turned her back on the Tories. It had taken but three and a half years. Further, she and her minister supported the Whig Regency Bill that aimed to put in place the machinery of government to operate between her death and the arrival in England of her successor (in April, as a further mark of her commitment to the Hanoverian succession, Anne gave the garter to the Electoral Prince). The limitations of Tory power were again demonstrated by the failure on 6 December of Rochester's motion in the Lords that the 'Church was in danger'. A further sense of development rather than stalemate was given with the repeal of the Alien Act in December, bringing the prospect of an Anglo-Scottish union markedly nearer.

If the 1705–6 session was not especially bloody, the supply Bills were passed easily for example, the 1706 campaign was. But Marlborough's victory at Ramillies and the capture of a number of key fortresses seemed once again to justify the strategy of the duumvirs. The conclusion of the Union Treaty in July, along with Prince Eugene's victory at Turin in late August, marked the summer as the zenith of Godolphin and Marlborough's ministry. But the summer also saw the rejection of French peace overtures because of Anne and Marlborough's desire to keep the Spanish monarchy intact, a decision that was to haunt much of the rest of the Queen's reign. Moreover, Marlborough's second great victory did nothing to calm domestic political tempers. In particular, the Whig Junto, having had a successful 1705–6 session, now pushed hard for office, threatening opposition should they be denied. They hoped to force the Queen to appoint the Earl of Sunderland, Marlborough's son-in-law, as Secretary of State in place of the Tory Sir Charles Hedges.[37] Anne was reluctant to favour one party and objected to Sunderland's extremism, 'I am afraid that he and I would not agree long together', and was strengthened in both objections by Harley.[38] But eventually she buckled beneath the reasons and threats (including resignation) brandished by Godolphin and the

---

[35] H. M. C., *Portland*, vol. 4, p. 291.   [36] *Letters of Queen Anne*, p. 176.

[37] Charles Spencer, 1674–1722, Whig MP 1695, married Anne Churchill 1700, succeeded as 3rd Earl of Sunderland 1702, active for the Hanoverian succession, Lord Privy Seal 1715, opponent of Robert Walpole, First Lord of the Treasury 1718, resigned in wake of South Sea Bubble. Charles Hedges, c.1650–1714, educated Magdalen Hall, Oxford, knighted 1689, MP from 1698, Judge of the Admiralty Court 1689–1701, Secretary of State 1700–6, Privy Councillor 1700.

[38] *Letters of Queen Anne*, p. 197.

Marlboroughs and appointed Sunderland on the 3 December, the opening day of the new parliamentary session. It was a pivotal moment in her reign. Serious splits had been evidenced between Harley and the duumvirs, the duumvirs and the Queen, and Sarah and the Queen, all at a time when the Whigs were pressing strongly for office and power.

The 1706–7 session once again saw the ministry depend heavily upon Whig support for the success of its measures. Tory opposition was almost always unsuccessful and considerable supplies were voted for the prosecution of the war, leading Godolphin to remark in April on 'The close of the best sessions of Parliament that England ever saw'.[39] It was remarkable, moreover, how little controversy the Union caused, in part because the Whigs outmanoeuvred their opponents by promoting a Bill to secure the Church of England after the Union. The Queen's presence at some of the Union debates in the Lords helped, once again, to keep discussion within touch of reason. Whig influence, however, was felt not in forming but in supporting or opposing policy. This second-hand role came out clearly when in the early months of 1707 their chosen candidates for the vacant bishoprics of Winchester and Chester and the regius professor of divinity at Oxford were overlooked by Anne who, asserting her independence, favoured three Tories, declaiming that 'Whoever of the Whigs thinks I am to be hectored or frighted into a compliance, though I am a woman, is mightily mistaken in me.'[40] The seriousness of the tensions involved, but also of the lack of decisive authority on Anne's part, is witnessed by the fact that the 'bishoprics crisis' rumbled on through most of 1707. In the process Anne snubbed not only the Whigs but also Godolphin and Marlborough. Her sense that the duumvirs were gradually turning their back on what in 1702 had been a common article of faith was, over the next twelve months, to be fully justified.

Serious divisions at the heart of government were exacerbated in 1707 by major allied defeats, first at Almanza in Spain in April and then in the summer with the disastrous attempt to take Toulon on France's southern coast. Even in Flanders Marlborough had made precious little headway. Such setbacks brought the conduct of the war into the heart of political debate where it was to remain for much of the rest of Anne's reign. The government found itself under attack from both flanks. Soon after the new session opened on 23 October an investigation was launched into the management of an Admiralty formally headed by Prince George of Denmark but in practice governed by Marlborough's Tory brother, Admiral George Churchill.[41] In December attention turned to consider the war in Spain, with the Lords adopting Somers's millstone motion

---

[39] *Marlborough–Godolphin Correspondence*, vol. 2, p. 754.

[40] *Letters of Queen Anne*, p. 231.

[41] George Churchill, 1654–1710, naval career began 1666, avaricious, MP from 1700–8.

of 'No peace without Spain' on 19 December. On 29 January 1708 the Tories and the independent or 'Country' Whigs in the Commons exposed serious discrepancies between the forces voted for the Spanish theatre by Parliament and the number of troops who had fought at Almanza. With further debates in store it was clear that to survive the ministry had to gain support from one of the parties, a weakness which was to be exploited to the full by the Whigs.

Harley rather than the Queen provided the major obstruction to the duumvirs' wish for the ministry to move closer to the Whigs, though his sentiments, moderate Toryism tempered by a desire for a high degree of independence, were very close to Anne's, and by the autumn of 1707 she had come to value highly his advice and friendship. In the dark days of December and January the ministry might only survive, therefore, by either Harley or the duumvirs gaining the upper hand. The triumph of Godolphin and Marlborough began when in January it was discovered that one of Harley's clerks, William Greg, had been engaged in treasonous activities, allowing the Secretary's reputation unreasonably to be blackened. Harley, sensing his isolation and the need to strengthen his position, counter-attacked. Addison neatly summarized the machinations and dramatic confrontations which led to the resignation of Harley on 10 February 1708, followed soon after by his friend the Comptroller Sir Thomas Mansel, Henry St John, Secretary at War, and Attorney General Harcourt.[42]

It is said Mr Harley and his friends had laid schemes to undermine most of our Great officers of State and plant their own party in the room of 'em. If we may believe common fame he himself was to have bin a Peer and Ld Treasurer . . . It is I believe very certain that the Duke of Marlborough and Lord Treasurer refused to sit any longer in Council with so wily a secretary and woud have laid down themselves if he had not been removed. It is said he had hopes of working his Ends by the Assistance of a Bed-chamber woman, whom it seems he had found out to be his Cousin [Abigail Masham].[43]

Central to Harley's fall was the ability of the duumvirs, spurred on by Sarah Churchill, to ride roughshod over the personal wishes of the Queen. It was a devastating experience for all. Harley and his allies were to spend two years in the political wilderness and the relationship between Anne and her two leading ministers was now firmly based upon necessity rather than trust or a sense of shared objectives. And Godolphin and Marlborough now depended upon the Whigs, though by appointing Boyle and Walpole as Secretary of State and

[42] Simon Harcourt, c.1661–1727, educated Pembroke College, Oxford, barrister Inner Temple, entered Commons 1690, Solicitor General 1702–7, Attorney General 1707–8, counsel for Sacheverell at his impeachment 1710, Privy Councillor 1710, created Baron Harcourt 1711 and Viscount 1721, Lord Chancellor 1713–14.

[43] The Letters of Joseph Addison, ed. W. Graham (Oxford, 1941), p. 91.

Secretary of War respectively they studiously avoided the claims of the Junto.[44] Symbolic of the new configuration, on 24 February the ministry was able to survive a third debate on Almanza only with Whig support.

WHIGS ASCENDANT, WHIGS DESCENDANT

The new domestic political scene depended heavily for its stability upon further military successes. In the short term the failure of the Franco-Jacobite invasion fleet in March 1708 had the salutary effect of concentrating minds before the conclusion of the session on 1 April and, under the terms of the Triennial Act, the dissolution of Parliament soon after. The general election held in May produced a clear majority for the Whigs for the first and only time in Anne's reign (with even the leading Tory St John losing his seat). Such a result only further encouraged the Junto to press for more ministerial changes in their direction and again Godolphin and Marlborough were much more willing to countenance this than the Queen. Such disagreements continued through the summer, even as Marlborough secured another notable victory at Oudenarde on 30 June. They were intensified by the belief of Godolphin and the Marlboroughs that Anne was continuing to make use of Harley's advice —the Queen flatly, but unconvincingly, denied it. Once again the duumvirs threatened to resign, perhaps partly in earnest but also partly because they felt that only such extremism could make the Queen accept the limited opportunities available to her ministers to secure a working majority in Parliament.

Anne showed remarkable resolve through the summer of 1708. But there is no question that all of the disagreements, not least those with Sarah which had ended in tears, had taken their toll. Matters, however, were soon to get much worse. In October the Prince of Denmark fell seriously ill and for five days and nights the Queen nursed and comforted him as he died. When the end came, on 28 October, she was distraught and inconsolable, for her marriage had been the one source of happiness and dependability in a life beset by trials. 'This prince was silent and quiet, and never appeared vigorous or active; but was singularly useful in keeping the Queen steady.'[45] With him gone she buckled to the Whig demands: Sir James Montagu, Halifax's brother, was appointed

[44] Henry Boyle, d. 1725, educated Trinity College, Cambridge, entered Commons 1689, Chancellor of the Exchequer 1701, Secretary of State 1708–10, created Baron Carleton 1714. Robert Walpole, 1676–1745, educated at Eton college and King's College Cambridge, succeeded to estate 1700, first in House of Commons 1701 and almost continuously MP for King's Lynn 1702–42, leading Whig politician holding many important posts, built grand house, Houghton in Norfolk.

[45] E. Calamy, *An Historical Account of my Own Life, with some Reflections on the Times I have Lived in (1671–1731)*, 2 vols. (1829), vol. 2, p. 115.

Attorney General, Somers Lord President of the Council, and Wharton Lord Lieutenant of Ireland.[46] Thus when the new session began on 16 November Junto peers were in the ministry for the first time since William's reign and able to command a majority in the Commons.

The parliamentary session which lasted until 21 April saw the climax of the Whig party's fortunes under Anne. Not only were Tories in a minority, but the policy of moderation espoused by the Queen and Harley had been dramatically overturned. Not surprisingly the Whigs seized the moment, passing in the new year their long sought after Act for Naturalizing Foreign Protestants, allowing persecuted foreign Protestants to find a ready home in Britain. Whig muscles were also flexed by passing an Act which introduced the English treason law into Scotland, a measure deemed necessary because of the failure to convict many Scots concerned in the abortive invasion of 1708. And in March Parliament drew up an address setting the conditions for a satisfactory peace: recognition of Anne's title and the Hanoverian succession by Louis XIV, the removal of the Pretender from French territory, the demolition of Dunkirk's defences, and the recall of Philip V from Spain. Such terms were to play a central part in the political struggle of the next four years. Indeed, soon after the end of the parliamentary session on 21 April 1709 Louis, despite his desperate situation, rejected allied peace terms, especially those concerning Spain. Godolphin reported to Marlborough that 'Though there did not want a great many people here to find fault with the peace while it was thought sure, yett upon yesterdays news of its [being] broken off, to show the generall opinion which the publick had of it, the stocks fell 14 per cent in one day. 'Tis true they had risen 20 per cent upon the news of the peace.'[47] The duumvirs had been outmanoeuvred by Louis and, with a very poor harvest being gathered in, public opinion was beginning to move decisively in favour of peace. Satirists bitterly reflected upon the state of the nation:

> In Sounds of Joy your tuneful Voices raise,
> And teach the People whom to thank and praise.
> Thank prudent Anna's providential Reign
> For Peace and Plenty, both of Corn and Grain:
> Thank the Scotch Peers for their firm, unbought Union;
> Thank Bishops for Occasional Communion:
> Thank the Stock-Jobbers for your thriving Trade;
> Thank just *Godolphin* that your Debts are paid:
> Thank *Marlborough's* Zeal that scorn'd the proffer'd Treaty;

---

[46] James Montagu, 1666–1723, educated Trinity College, Cambridge, barrister Middle Temple, entered Commons 1695, knighted 1705, Solicitor General 1707, Attorney General 1708–10.
[47] *Marlborough–Godolphin Correspondence*, vol. 3, p. 1271.

But thank *Eugene* that *Frenchmen* did not beat ye:
Thank your own selves, that you are tax'd and shamm'd;
But thank th' Almighty, if you are not damn'd.[48]

Unbeknown to the ministry and the Whigs their attachment to unrealistic peace terms was within a year to prove their undoing. Marlborough's costly victory at Malplaquet on 31 August led to the voicing of significant domestic opposition to the continental war and, contrary to the duumvirs's perception, strengthened French resolve with regard to the peace they sought. As a background to this, the influx of some 13,000 poor Palatines through the summer revived Tory fears of the subjugation by the Whigs of English interests to unnecessary continental objectives, in this case Protestant internationalism. Anne too appears to have had enough of the Whigs and the war. Badgered incessantly by the Duchess of Marlborough, forced by the Whigs to appoint Orford of the Junto as First Lord of the Admiralty, and, prompted by advice from Harley, she dreamed of freedom from her bondage.

Anne's room for manoeuvre was limited but real. It evidenced itself first because of her role as ultimate head of the military. In the summer of 1709 she demonstrated some measure of independence by refusing Marlborough's request that he be granted the captain-generalcy for his life, which to a man as vain and ambitious as the Duke was a grievous blow. Further, she stripped one of Marlborough's closest generals, George Maccartney, of some of his positions following a prosecution for rape and refused all blandishments to reverse her decision. Serious as these flurries were they were as nothing to the storm which broke out in early 1710. On 10 January the Earl of Essex died, leaving vacant two military posts which would normally have been filled by Marlborough's recommendation but which on this occasion Anne insisted on filling so as to demonstrate her authority. Marlborough was bound to feel the slight deeply, but one of Anne's choices, Jack Hill, was Abigail Masham's brother, further confirming to the paranoid Marlboroughs Anne's dependence upon this bedchamber woman. In high dudgeon Marlborough withdrew to Windsor Lodge, refusing for a time to attend cabinet meetings. He relented after ten days, and the Queen gave Hill a pension of £1,000 for life instead of the regiment. For both Anne and Marlborough it was a bargain dearly bought.

What neither the Duke nor the Duchess were capable of seeing was that the Queen's increasing hostility towards them was based upon a heartfelt sense of the national interest, particularly that peace not war should now be the immediate ambition. To them, more especially to Sarah, evil counsellors in the guise of Harley and his cousin Masham (Sarah and Masham were themselves

[48] Anon., 'The Thanksgiving', in *Poems on Affairs of State: Augustan Satirical Verse 1660–1714*, vol. 7. *1704–1714*, ed. F. H. Ellis (New Haven, 1975), pp. 374–5.

cousins) were corrupting Anne's judgement. As one of Sarah's kindred spirits wrote of Masham, 'She'as neither Beauty, Birth nor Sense,/ Yet does controul the Nation,/ A matchless Stock of Impudence,/ And blasted Reputation.'[49] Masham's role, however, was much exaggerated by the Duchess. The Queen valued her plain speaking, but was never under her control. However, Anne's continued reliance upon Harley's advice could only be interpreted by observers as a sign of lack of faith in the duumvirs. At some point in late 1709 it would appear that she had indeed decided upon a change in the ministry and that Harley was to be the agent to bring this about. They awaited an opening.

When the new parliamentary session opened on 15 November the Whigs appeared to be secure as ever following the exit of the last of the Tories, Pembroke from the cabinet. What they could not have foreseen was that they would soon be swamped by a tidal wave of public opinion provoked by the Sacheverell affair.[50] The rancid doctor's sermon had been preached on 5 November 1709 and the vote for his impeachment was taken on 13 December. Violent hostility to the Whigs and the ministry was, however, not apparent until his trial began on 27 February when rioting broke out in London. Significantly Marlborough was now out of the way in The Hague and Godolphin was overwhelmed, complaining that 'this uneasy tryall of Sacheverell does not only take up all my time, but very much impairs my health, and how it will yett end I am not at all certain.'[51] The last admission was crucial, for the Whigs, having aimed at conducting a show trial, found that moderate opinion in the Lords was unwilling to follow the Junto's lead. Sacheverell's light punishment was rightly taken to criticize the current distribution of political power. Crucially, this was not merely a metropolitan phenomenon, for at least 141 of the loyal addresses to the Queen from provincial clergy, gentry, and borough corporations cried out their attachment to her and what they viewed as moderation, sometimes calling for an election to allow the voice of the nation to be heard above the din of faction. (About 120 might be characterized as Tory, 21 as Whig.)[52] A clear disjunction had emerged between the ministry and Parliament on the one hand and the Queen and the political nation on the other. The days of the Whigs were numbered.

HARLEY, THE TORIES, AND THE PEACE

On 6 April 1710, the day after the end of the parliamentary session, Sarah Churchill had her last interview with the Queen. It marked the end of a remarkable personal and political relationship stretching back to the 1680s.

[49] A. Mainwaring?, 'Masham Display'd' (1708), in *Poems on Affairs of State*, ed. Ellis, p. 319.
[50] See above, pp. 233–4.   [51] *Marlborough–Godolphin Correspondence*, vol. 3, p. 1428.
[52] I am grateful to Colin Smith for this information.

None of Anne's subjects had been so honoured and rewarded as the Marl-boroughs, though the Duchess had always overstated her value to the Queen. Though Anne still fully appreciated the Duke's military and diplomatic significance she doubted whether he was capable of finding the peace the nation desired. In concert with Harley she decided to reconstitute her ministry, though not necessarily by replacing the duumvirs, and later to call a general election to secure a Tory and pro-peace majority in the Commons, even though the Parliament did not have to be dissolved until 1711. On 14 April she took her first hesitant step by, without consulting the duumvirs, dismissing the Earl of Kent as Lord Chamberlain and appointing the Duke of Shrewsbury in his place. Shrewsbury was a Whig by inclination and had served in the Junto administration in the 1690s, but 'King William was used to say, That the Duke of *Shrewsbury* was the only Man the *Whigs* and *Tories* both spoke well of.'[53] Furthermore, he soon attached himself to the Queen, leading Godolphin anxiously to complain that 'he may soon come to have as much influence with [the Queen] as [Godolphin] used to have'.[54]

Shrewsbury's appointment demonstrated Anne's independence, resolve, and desire to avoid moving from one extreme to another. Her next step was taken in mid-June, dismissing Sunderland, Marlborough's son-in-law, in favour of the moderate Tory, Lord Dartmouth, 'which was a surprise upon every body' though Godolphin had pleaded against it.[55] Naturally Marlborough took this personally, but he did not resign and it is not clear whether the Queen had further changes in mind beyond a general election to reduce the power of the Whigs. However, Sunderland's dismissal alarmed friend and foe alike. Immediately 'the fear of the City, was the loss of my Lord Godolphin, because he had been a great support to the Bank' and their representatives begged her not to 'change the Ministry, nor call a new Parliament'.[56] No less serious was the international consequence, for it brought to a stand the peace negotia-tions which had been on foot since February by encouraging French hopes for further ministerial changes and, thereby, better terms. The first effect likely strengthened Anne's natural hostility to all things Whig, and the second further reduced the chances of the duumvirs achieving the peace she desired. Ironically, it was calls from the allies to Anne not to undertake further minis-terial changes, calls prompted by the Whigs, that convinced the Queen that to protect English interests Godolphin would have to go, though she could not

---

[53] Macky, *Memoirs of the Secret Services*, p. 13.

[54] *Marlborough–Godolphin Correspondence*, vol. 3, p. 1478.

[55] H. M. C., *The Manuscripts of the Marquess of Townshend* (1887), p. 67. William Legge, 1672–1750, educated Winchester College and King's College, Cambridge, succeeded to Barony of Dartmouth 1691, Commissioner of Board of Trade 1702, Secretary of State 1710–13, created Earl of Dartmouth 1711.

[56] *The Diary of Sir David Hamilton 1709–1714*, ed. P. Roberts (Oxford, 1975), p. 11.

face dismissing him in person, granted him a lavish annual pension of £4,000 (never paid), and occasionally sought his advice subsequently. Deep in her heart Anne knew that, despite their disagreements, she was parting with a loyal and able servant and it says much of Godolphin's standing that his political enemies were unable to hound him far in retirement.

Godolphin was replaced by a Treasury board under the effective leadership of Harley as Chancellor of the Exchequer. Harley now pressed the Queen for a thorough reworking of the ministry in favour of moderate Tories or his personal allies, though Marlborough's military and diplomatic services were to be retained. In something akin to a ministerial revolution most Whig ministers resigned when on 21 September Anne declared that Parliament was to be dissolved without consulting them. If the new ministry was 'Harleyite' in complexion, the new House of Commons was strongly Tory, achieving a majority of about 150. Indeed, the 1710 general election set the tone of politics for the rest of Anne's reign. Campaigning was hard and furious, with over half of all constituencies going to a poll, and from the Whig perspective 'Great violence and sad disorders accompanied the elections in many places . . . news Papers were writ and scatterd to perplex the conciences of the people about the succession to the Crown, the state ministers Blackened, our successes abroad lessened and misrepresented, our losses aggravated, Passive obedience and Hereditary right and the crown preached upon.'[57]

Calling an early general election had been designed to negate the Whig majority in the Commons. But such was the scale of the Tory landslide that soon after the new Parliament met on 25 November Harley found himself faced by supporters baying for blood. To many Tories his ministry looked soft, prone to unnecessary and disadvantageous moderation. Crucially, the hybrid nature of Toryism in Anne's reign had become more not less marked since 1708, particularly as reactions to the war were complicated by the onset of military failure and increasing numbers became nervous about the Hanoverian succession and turned towards Jacobitism. Notable among Harley's Tory opponents was the so-called 'October club'. By February 1711 it was reported that

This loyal country club is a great disturbance to Mr. Harley, who finds they are past his governing; their Number is increased to a 150. They are most of them young gentlemen of estates that has never been in Parliament before, and are not very close, but declare to every body what they designe, to have every Whig turn'd out, and not to suffer that the new Ministry shou'd shake hands as they do with old.[58]

[57] *The Diary of James Clegg of Chapel en le Frith*, part 1, ed. V. S. Doe, Derbyshire Record Society, 2 (Matlock, 1978), p. 3.
[58] *The Wentworth Papers, 1705–1739. Selected from the Private and Family Correspondence of Thomas Wentworth, Lord Raby, Created in 1711 Earl of Strafford*, ed. J. J. Cartwright (1883), p. 180.

The new ministry's principal objectives were to secure a reasonable peace, put public finances upon a more secure footing, and to avoid Tory extremism. With regard to the peace they were prepared to ditch their allies and secure a separate agreement with France, abandon the condition of 'No peace without Spain' in return for commercial concessions in the Spanish empire, renounce the Anglo-Dutch Barrier Treaty of 1709, and, to keep on board Tory Jacobites, covertly to offer limited support to the Pretender's claims. Secret negotiations with France were opened in the summer of 1710 and had made reasonable headway by early 1711 before they were communicated to the Dutch in April. On the financial front, however, Harley was running into the sands of October club and Whig opposition in the Commons. Then, with a *cul-de-sac* approaching, on 8 March Guiscard, a French spy being interrogated in Council, attempted to assassinate Harley and seriously wounded him with a penknife. (Guiscard soon died of wounds inflicted by St John and the Duke of Ormond, and his pickled body was put on show for twopence a view.) The attack had the effect of stimulating a surge of loyalty towards Harley, providing the ministry with a breathing space, with much politics coming to a standstill. More than two weeks after the attack Swift noted how 'All things are at a stop in Parliament for want of Mr Harley'.[59] In this climate the October club failed in its politically highly charged attempts to legislate for a resumption of the land grants of William III and a grateful Queen celebrated Harley's return to full health by promoting him to the earldom of Oxford in May. At much the same time his Bill establishing the South Sea Company as a means of liquidating some £9 million of unfunded debt passed through Parliament, providing a Tory counterweight to the Whig dominated Bank of England and East India Company.

There is no question that by the summer of 1711 the administration centred upon the newly ennobled Robert Harley: 'he is the only true channel through which the Queen's pleasure is conveyed' complained St John.[60] Though he had been a key political figure since the mid-1690s, the period between 1710 and Anne's death marked his political apogee. As has been seen, he came from a Presbyterian and Whiggish background, but in the 1690s adopted the middle ground, tending if anything towards Toryism. Fleet of thought, an avid bibliophile, a politician to his very marrow, by Swift's friendly assessment 'Fear, avarice, cruelty and pride are wholly strangers to his nature, but he is not without ambition.'[61] In 1712 Prince Eugene, reporting to the court at Vienna, described him as 'an indefatigable man of business, of a lively and aspiring

[59] J. Swift, *Journal to Stella* (Gloucester, 1984), p. 144.
[60] *Letters and Correspondence, Public and Private, of the Right Honourable Henry St. John, Lord Viscount Bolingbroke*, ed. G. Parke, 2 vols. (1798), vol. i, p. 132.
[61] H. M. C., *Bath*, vol. i, p. 227.

spirit, and manages the caballing parties with that dexterity that he keeps in with both'.[62] Certainly he was 'generally allowed as cunning a man as any in England', such that his scheming and the growing hopes of Jacobites in Anne's last years lent the period a distinctive political complexion and earned him the nickname of 'Robin the trickster'.[63] His main political rival in these years was his younger colleague Henry St John, Secretary of State. Born in 1678, like Robert Walpole he was among the first generation to reach political maturity after 1688. Markedly more Tory in outlook than Harley, he was inclined to rush to judge and act. To Prince Eugene he was 'the bull-dog of the party . . . a bold and daring spirit, of an aspiring temper, of good parts enough'.[64] Keenly ambitious, St John nevertheless readily endeared himself to people of a similar point of view, inspiring them with his considerable wit, charm, and literary abilities.

In May 1711 Lord Rochester, Lord President, unexpectedly died, as did the Lord Privy Seal, the Duke of Newcastle, at the end of August. Their replacements, the Duke of Buckingham and Bishop Robinson of Bristol respectively, did not dramatically change the complexion of the ministry.[65] Though some October men were given junior offices Harley continued to attempt to chart a middle course. The other major development of the summer was Marlborough's brilliant circumvention of the French Ne Plus Ultra defensive lines at the end of July. By opening the real prospect of striking towards Paris it stimulated France to look more urgently for peace and secret peace preliminaries were signed between the two countries on 27 September, with St John having come to play a leading role on the British side. If the preliminaries delighted the Tories and dismayed the Whigs they also had the effect of energizing and giving a new sense of purpose to the Whigs after the shocks suffered since Sacheverell's trial. Indeed, Whig minority status in the Commons did not prevent Wharton and others from maintaining a vigorous party in opposition, not least through calls via the press to extra-parliamentary opinion. In a clear signal of the considerable importance attached to opinion 'out of doors' battle was once again joined in the presses over the peace.

The ministry's position was very strong. In the press it was championed by the pen of Swift, the most brilliant hack of his generation, in the *Examiner* and his *Conduct of the Allies* (November 1711). Moreover the ministry had a mighty majority to depend upon in the Commons. But the Lords was still, as it had been since the start of Anne's reign, something of a Whig stronghold

[62] H. M. C., *The Manuscripts of his Grace the Duke of Portland*, vol. 5 (1899), p. 156.

[63] *Wentworth Papers*, p. 132.   [64] H. M. C., *Portland*, vol. 5, p. 157.

[65] John Robinson, 1650–1723, educated Brasenose College, Oxford, Fellow of Oriel College, Oxford, Chaplain to Swedish embassy for twenty-five years, Bishop of Bristol 1710, plenipotentiary at Utrecht peace conference, Bishop of London 1714–23, Privy Councillor 1714.

where public opinion might be ignored. On 7 December, the opening day of the new session, the ministry's policy of 'peace without Spain' was defeated in the Lords by the Whigs and rebel Tories such as the disillusioned Nottingham (who in return demanded that the Whigs swallow their principles and pride and support the passage of the Occasional Conformity Bill soon after). This defeat immediately threw into confusion a major plank of the government's programme, threatening a very real impasse to which the ministry's response, with Oxford in the van, was that an extreme situation—the passionate need for peace, the passionate intransigence of the Whigs—called for extreme measures. On 31 December Marlborough was dismissed as Captain General and between 28 December and 1 January Anne created twelve new peers, including Samuel Masham (husband of Anne's confidante, Abigail), to ensure the success of the Tory peace in the upper house (there would have been thirteen, but Sir Michael Warton declined a peerage). There is no question that the Queen had the right to make such appointments *en bloc*, but it was certainly constitutionally extraordinary. When asked, Anne's doctor told her 'that I heard it openly said, that it was done to turn out dutyfull Servants, and that my Lord Oxford pack'd Jurys to carry Causes. That my Lord Hervey said it was unpresidented, that neither Edward the 2nd. nor Henry the 8th., That no Arbitrary or ruin'd Government ever did it'.[66]

Not the least of the divisions exposed by the peace preliminaries in late 1711 was that between Britain and her allies. In particular, Hanover sided with the Whig opposition and in January Prince Eugene visited London in a vain attempt to press the allies's claims. Matters became more complicated still when, following the death of Louis's son and heir in April 1711 his eldest grandson died on 7 February 1712. This left him with two grandsons, Philip V, whom Britain was now prepared to see crowned King of Spain, and the Duc de Berri, a young man in poor health. The prospect loomed that Philip might inherit both France and Spain. Yet the possibility of such a superpower did not deflect many Tories from their quest for peace (and in the event Philip renounced his claim to the French throne). In the first place, using somewhat flimsy evidence of peculation, in January attacks were launched against Marlborough and Walpole as advocates of continued military action—the latter being expelled from the Commons and briefly consigned to the Tower. Second, the army was put in the safe hands of the Duke of Ormond on 26 February and in May he received the 'restraining orders' requiring him to avoid battle or siege. This had been initiated by Oxford and St John, who had gained the Queen's consent, and effectively meant deserting the allies in the field. As a further signal of Oxford's desperation, to avoid censure in

---

[66] *Hamilton Diary*, pp. 35–6.

Parliament and to bring about the peace he had to resort to lying at critical points. Together with Philip's renunciation of the French throne and the lure of the commercial clauses in the proposed peace, that was enough to bring Parliament and a good deal of public opinion round in early June.

The 1710–11 and 1711–12 sessions had been unusually long and bitter as the structures put in place by the duumvirs since 1702 and the Whigs since 1708 were demolished and foundations dug for peace and a reinvigorated Church. Working from the basis of a substantial majority in the Commons, the Tories were gradually able to exert a strong grip over the political processes. But this could only be done by double dealing and abandoning their allies diplomatically and militarily, while deceiving many at home. Anne and, more especially, Oxford was at the heart of this, with both losing sight of their high standards of probity and attachment to moderation because they believed that the alternative to peace was national ruin. Both at home and abroad the stench of desperation and duplicity was to linger long in the air.

ANNE'S LAST YEARS

In the summer of 1712 Anne was only 47 and by her own poor standards her health was good. Yet, the peace negotiations had, once again, focused attention upon the fact that most but not all intended her to be the last Stuart monarch. Though the Treaty confirmed her title and the Hanoverian succession, and required the Pretender to leave France, Jacobites had little to hope for but the Queen's death, however distant it might be. Conscious that the very moment of her death would provide them with the best chance ever of attaining their objectives, Anne's last years were filled with intrigue and dissimulation. For their part, pro-Hanoverians and non-Jacobites were worried that all the future held was strife, chaos, and the real possibility of bloody civil war.

The history of Jacobitism between 1712 and 1714 must be a history particularly based upon fears as well as realities, fictions as well as facts. It suited both Whigs and Jacobites to play up the Pretender's prospects—to the former as a stick with which to beat the Tories, to the latter as a means of encouraging support from among the waiverers. Doubtless there were many who counted themselves as Jacobites in England, most usually from among the Tories. Some political leaders, such as Ormond and Bolingbroke, clearly leant towards Jacobitism.[67]

---

[67] James Butler, 1665–1745, educated in France, active against Monmouth's Rebellion in 1685, succeeded as Duke of Ormond 1688, Chancellor of Oxford University 1688, Lord High Constable at coronation of William and Mary, fought in Ireland, the Nine Years War, and the War of the Spanish Succession, Lord Lieutenant of Ireland 1703–5, 1710–11, and 1713, Commander in Chief of army 1712, leading Jacobite by 1714, impeached 1715, fled to France, involved in the '15 and the Spanish expedition of 1719, mainly lived at Avignon, buried in Westminster Abbey.

Many certainly believed by 1713 that detailed plans had been made for a Jacobite coup on Anne's death, underwritten by guarantees of support from significant numbers of the political elite. Yet when all is said and done the head of government remained, despite its misgivings, in favour of the Hanoverian succession. The evidence that Anne was in favour of her half-brother succeeding her is based only upon hearsay and is controverted by her own statements. In October 1712, for example, her doctor reported 'that I had seen my Lord Cowper, who was concern'd to hear that she had been ill and told me that Things look'd as tho' the Pretender was design'd, and all in Places, who are for him. Oh fye says she, there is no such thing.'[68] Equally, though Oxford certainly maintained contacts with the Jacobite court, his communications give every impression of being carefully designed both to string along the Pretender to prevent active preparations being made for his succession and also to buy support in the Commons from Tory Jacobites. Oxford's own behaviour seemed designed to ensure that none knew where his true loyalties lay. Cowper, a Whig and a shrewd judge, recorded a meeting where Oxford 'had written down Heads [of discussion] on a Paper, yet spake, as always, very dark & confusedly, interlaceing all he said with broken hints of Discoveries he had made'.[69]

A number of the domestic tensions of Anne's last years were played out by or through Oxford and St John. They had been unable fully to trust one another since coming back to power in 1710 and each sought to act behind the back of the other, though relations did not become seriously strained until June 1712 when St John was made Viscount Bolingbroke. St John had expected to be raised, like Oxford, to an earldom, but Anne was easily persuaded that his loose living ought to count against him. In September Oxford sought unsuccessfully to by-pass Bolingbroke by placing the remnants of the peace negotiations in Dartmouth's hands, producing major rows in the cabinet. However, these tensions were kept in the background, not least because the formal peace negotiations at Utrecht continued longer than had been expected and were not concluded until 31 March, so preventing Parliament from meeting until 9 April 1713 (the winter 1712–13 was the first since the revolution that Parliament had not sat). The death of Godolphin in September 1712 and the self-imposed continental exile of Marlborough in November also helped to calm the scene—it is notable that the end of Sacheverell's ban from preaching in March 1713 caused only a brief ripple of excitement.

Parliament sat from early April until 16 July 1713. With peace now achieved the political landscape was beginning to be redrawn in such a manner that Oxford found himself unable control the process. A Bill to extend the malt tax to Scotland, breaching the spirit of the Act of Union, led to fierce Scottish

---

[68] *Hamilton Diary*, p. 44.   [69] *Cowper Private Diary*, p. 54.

opposition nearly bringing about a defeat of the ministry. On 18 June the ministry was defeated in the Commons on its Anglo-French Commercial Treaty by 194 to 185 votes—a contest notable for the volume of pamphleteering involved. In this vote Whigs had successfully appealed to nearly eighty moderate, 'whimsical' (i.e. Hanoverian) Tories who were set against improving relations with France. Emboldened, the Whigs then managed to carry a motion in the Lords on 29 June calling for the Pretender to be removed from Lorraine, where he had sought sanctuary as a consequence of the Treaty of Utrecht. Though Anne did indeed issue letters calling for this, behind the scenes Oxford and Bolingbroke encouraged France and Lorraine to ignore the call.

Parliament was dissolved on 8 August, having run its three-year course. In the general election in September the Tories managed to increase their already substantial majority to over 150, many electors evidently being well pleased with the peace. That said, the election also served to expose some of the deep divisions which existed within the Tory party. One observer reflected that 'they give up the distinction of Whig and Tory, and bend all their thoughts to make new distinction between the Tories themselves, as Hanover Tory and Pretender's Tory, English Tory and French Tory, for trade or against it'.[70] In the new Commons perhaps 80 Tories were convinced Jacobites, slightly fewer were died-in-the-wool Hanoverians. Such divisions sat alongside a deepening chasm between Oxford and Bolingbroke. In July Bolingbroke had proposed that the ministry be reconstituted along strict Tory-party lines, challenging Oxford's preference for moderation. Though Oxford won this struggle— Bolingbroke was moved sideways to Secretary of State for the southern department—it left a strong residue of bad feeling. Moreover, Anne significantly heightened the explosive potential of this split. For some time she had become increasingly exasperated by Oxford's scheming, his failure to find adequate funds for her household, and his refusal to talk directly to any matter. Matters were brought to a head in September 1713 when the Queen refused his request for the revival of the Dukedom of Newcastle in his son's name after the latter's marriage to the Newcastle heiress, Lady Henrietta Holles.

By late autumn, a split ministry and a split party awaited the start of the new session on 16 February 1714. These worries were intensified when the Queen became seriously ill on 24 December and continued unwell through January. Though she recovered many believed her days were numbered, forcing her publicly to scotch rumours that she would be unable to open Parliament. Oxford and Bolingbroke now brought their separate negotiations with the Pretender to a climax by calling for his conversion to the Church of England. The powerlessness of the Jacobite court, shorn as it was of foreign aid, and

[70] H. M. C., *The Manuscripts of the Earl of Dartmouth* (1887), p. 319.

absolutely dependent upon allies in Britain, was now brutally exposed. James refused to convert and by the end of March the Duke of Berwick complained that Oxford and Bolingbroke 'runn on still on the same style about the relligion, but that confirmes me in the opinion, that no answer is ever to be made on that subject. Truly all this looks ill, for, after two or three years negociation, to propose at last an impossible thing, is what we call *une querelle d'Allemand*'.[71] The Pretender's Catholicism had long been sufficient to damn him in the eyes of many English and his refusal to convert, private though it may have been, did nothing to change that view.

When the new Parliament met, the Commons chose as their Speaker the Hanoverian Tory Sir Thomas Hanmer. A few days later Anne appointed the similarly disposed Sir William Dawes as Archbishop of York in place of Sharp who had just died. Both appointments were full of significance, one showing the temper of the legislature, the other of the monarch. Through the session strenuous efforts were made by the ministry to deny that it had any desire to abandon the Act of Settlement in favour of the Pretender. On 14 March, despite being ably defended by Robert Walpole, Richard Steele was expelled from the Commons for accusing the ministry of Jacobite sympathies in his highly popular *The Crisis*. In April both Houses narrowly declared that the Protestant succession was not in danger. And in the same month the Lords called for a proclamation offering a reward for the capture of the Pretender should he set foot in the kingdoms—though Anne prevaricated she complied on 21 June by offering £5,000. Such decisions, however, could not mask the depth of divisions which existed within political society, with one foreign observer even suggesting that 'Affairs are moving in such a manner that civil war is becoming inevitable in England.'[72] Matters were further intensified by the Hanoverian court. Concerned that the designated successor still had no support from the civil list and wishing, given the scale of Jacobite support in Parliament, to establish a physical presence in England a request was made for Prince George to be called to Parliament under his title as Duke of Cambridge, and at the end of April Hanover formally issued a request for a member of their electoral family to be invited to England. Both requests were denied and on 23 May Electress Sophia died, aged 84.

Extraordinary pressure was heaped upon Anne, Oxford, and Bolingbroke in April and May 1714, bringing what had long been a strained relationship to breaking point. Assaulted from all sides they could no longer fully trust one another. The final break in Anne's dependence upon Oxford came soon after Sophia's death, a break caused by his inability to curb the requests from

---

[71] H. M. C., *Calendar of the Stuart Papers Belonging to His Majesty the King*, vol. 1 (1902), p. 310.
[72] Quoted in Gregg, *Queen Anne*, p. 380.

Hanover for the residence of a member of the electoral family in England—
Anne reasonably interpreted such applications as proof that her own death was
seen as imminent. Her shift in sympathies was marked on 26 May when she
appointed the Earl of Clarendon, Bolingbroke's choice, as envoy to Hanover.[73]
With this backing Bolingbroke moved to unite the Tories behind the Schism
Bill which he personally introduced in the Lords, an extreme measure aimed
at stamping out Dissenters's educational facilities, calculating that if Oxford
supported it he would lose his moderate supporters and if he attacked it
he would lose his Tory supporters.[74] The Bill was passed in early July, with
Oxford's reluctant support, and was to be the last major piece of legislation of
Anne's reign. On 9 July, to protect Bolingbroke from Whig attacks over a commercial Treaty with Spain and corruption, the session came to a close. Little
wonder that he complained that 'These four or five months last past have
afforded such a scene as I hope never again to be an actor in. All the confusion
which could be created by the disunion of friends, and the malice of enemies,
has subsisted at Court and in Parliament.'[75] The confusion, however, was to
continue until the temporary calm brought about by Anne's imminent death.

   The close of the parliamentary session could not resolve the battle between
Oxford and Bolingbroke. Both exerted pressure on the Queen to dismiss
the other, leading her to complain that most of her ministers 'sought themselves, they had neither regarded her Health, Her Life, nor Her peace'.[76] That
it was Oxford who was sent packing (on 27 July) was in some measure due
to Bolingbroke successfully re-establishing good relations with the exiled
Marlborough. Anne's residual affection for the Duke, and the prospect that he
would be able to smooth relations with Hanover and the succession, decided
her to side with Bolingbroke. Oxford was never to hold office again and a year
later he was to be the victim of a vindictive impeachment. His had been a
remarkable political career, attempting in an age of intense ideological divisions
mainly to steer a middle course by reacting to circumstances as they occurred.
Anticipating Bismarck he believed that 'Wisdom in publick Affairs, was not
what is commonly believed, the forming of Schemes with remote Views; but
the making Use of such Incidents as happen.'[77] But in the cauldron of 1712–14
this required him to hide his true feelings so completely that he was increasingly
seen to be altogether unprincipled and untrustworthy. Few mourned his fall.

   Briefly it was expected that 'Lord Bolingbroke, and the Chancellor [Lord
Harcourt], are to rule the world, and it is said they will be swingeing Torys,

[73] Edward Hyde, 1661–1723, succeeded as 3rd Earl of Clarendon 1709.
[74] See above, p. 234.   [75] Bolingbroke Letters, vol. 2, p. 667.
[76] Hamilton Diary, p. 66.
[77] The Correspondence of Jonathan Swift, ed. H. Williams, 5 vols. (Oxford, 1963–5), vol. 1,
p. 238.

and not a Whig left in place a month hence'.[78] But Anne's concern for her own health under these political strains was soon proved to have been fully justified when she fell seriously ill in the early hours of 30 July. So unwell was she that almost immediately many recognized that this would be her last illness. On her deathbed she agreed to the proposal that Shrewsbury be the new Lord Treasurer. The Privy Council, aware that she was ailing fast, sought to secure the realm: ports were closed; the arms and horses of Catholics were ordered to be seized; troops moved towards London; Hanover's representatives brought into the Council's deliberations; messages sent to Hanover warning of the Queen's approaching death and requesting the Elector to come quickly; and a naval escort dispatched for his safe conduct. On the morning of 1 August the last Stuart monarch died aged only 49. The Council soon met and issued a proclamation of George's accession. 'All the nobility attended the proclamation, and there was not the least disturbance. The Parliament met, and the Lords and Commons took the oaths. Thank God everything is quiet'.[79] When the moment came few among the political nation refused to embrace the immediate implementation of the Act of Settlement and Regency Act. Despite all the plots and scheming to prevent it the Hanoverian age had begun.

CONCLUSION

When Anne died, over a quarter of a century had passed since the Glorious Revolution. They had been years so packed with incident and strife that superficially the nation was as divided as it had been in the winter of William's invasion, James's flight, and the establishment of the joint monarchy. Steele's expulsion from the Commons early in 1714 appeared to confirm that the political temperature was, after all these years, still at boiling point. But the political processes were now much stronger than they had been in 1688, much better able to bear such heats. What is remarkable about Anne's reign is that discord and controversy were normalized, not only within central and local government but also within the cultural milieu of political society. Though many longed for peace and quiet, debate was for the most part channelled into courses that did not erode the stability of the political system as a whole. In particular, the centrality of Parliament, re-established so decisively in 1689, went altogether unchallenged. It did act as a vast clearing house for ideas and interests, the place where competing ideals struggled for authority. Neither Anne nor her ministers could circumvent it (she employed her veto but once), while triennial elections kept it closely in touch with the electorate.

[78] H. M. C., *The Manuscripts of Lord Kenyon* (1894), p. 456.
[79] H. M. C., *Portland*, vol. 5, p. 482.

As the years passed so the old hands died away: Richard Cromwell (Lord Protector from 1658–9), Godolphin, Rochester, and Danby in 1712, Compton in 1713, Anne and Sharp in 1714, Burnet, Halifax, Wharton, and Tenison, in 1715, and Somers in 1716. Those who had served their political apprenticeships in the Restoration era were now slipping into a minority, to be replaced by those who knew James II and arbitrary authority only by repute and who had come to the fore in an age of toleration towards Dissenters, frequent elections, annual parliaments, terrible wars, heavy taxation, enormous national debts, and a burgeoning press. It was problems associated with these features of the political world which were so influential to their outlook. Of course worries over 'Popery and slavery' and the threat of a Jacobite inspired rebellion or civil war still chilled them to the marrow. But more usually they were concerned with perfecting the system of limited participatory politics which though it had evolved through the second half of the seventeenth century had only found a permanent place since the Glorious Revolution. War and questions over the Hanoverian succession had allowed only a few of the problems to be solved under Anne. With peace and single-party rule, most had been by 1727.

CHAPTER 10

Profits, Progress, and Projects

One of the defining characteristics of modern economies is their experience of self-sustained long-term per capita growth. Such an experience is rooted in the ability and willingness to forgo current consumption in order to invest in more productive processes. In that sense England's economy at the end of the seventeenth century was largely pre-modern. It was highly vulnerable to exogenous shocks (such as wars and bad weather); investment levels were low; growth rarely lasted for long; increasing output was much easier than increasing productivity; and material standards of living were still very low by modern standards. However, the economy was very far from being simply 'agrarian', 'traditional', or 'pre-industrial'. Not least if there was subsistence production consumers often bought what they needed—with specialized market-orientated manufacturing industry a commonplace; the service sector was of considerable size; and overseas trade, providing distant markets for home-produced goods and new consumer goods, such as tobacco, sugar, and tea, opened the domestic economy to the influence of international trading conditions.

In many respects England's economy in 1689 was surprisingly modern in form. But if industry, services, and trade also grew, such growth was undeniably slow, erratic, and unstable. One factor was the limited disposable income available to most people. Moreover, raising productivity by significant extensions of the division of labour or the utilization of labour-saving technology were far less important than increasing output by simply multiplying units of production. Furthermore, what growth there was often involved the regional relocation of economic activity, such that some places prospered while others decayed. Attempts at more rapid progress were often highly speculative and risky, prone to dramatic failures as well as real achievements. And as significant as any factor was the prevalence of a mental world which assumed stagnation and fluctuations rather than growth and certainty, which looked not to take risks but to achieve stability, and which worried incessantly about developments. Such worrying invoked criteria that were rarely only economic, frequently also social, moral, and religious. Consequently, though the State lacked the means successfully to enforce its vision of economic order and prosperity it frequently attempted to intervene in the market mechanism in pursuit of stability and justice.

CONSUMING NEEDS, CONSUMING PASSIONS

To establish his claim that 'The first and best Market of *England* are the Natives and Inhabitants of *England*' the pamphleteer Charles King conducted a simple exercise in political arithmetic. Taking Petty's estimate of national income as about £50m per annum he suggested that expenditure on retained imports was £4m per annum and on lodging about £3.5m per annum. Consequently, some £42m was annually spent upon 'the Product and Manufacture of our Native Country. Our own People are a constant Market for our own Product and Manufacture of so great a value.'[1] Though these figures are imprecise the rough orders of magnitude are plausible and suggest an important corrective. Valuable and relatively flexible as export markets undoubtedly were, on the demand side it was home consumption which buttressed England's economy. If the lure of running a vast trade to Latin America or China encouraged wild hopes of a dramatic increase in markets for manufactured goods, the relative dependability of the home market was, in practice, much more important. Little wonder that King gave consumers pride of place in his perception of the determinants of economic well-being.

Little information about household budgets is available to determine what people bought in this period. For many, of course, low incomes limited consumption mainly to necessities: food, shelter, clothing, and heat. However, foreigners frequently remarked on the relatively high standard of living enjoyed by England's poor, particularly noting the universal wearing of shoes and the absence of extreme malnourishment. 'The People in general are well cloathed, which is certain Proof of their living at Ease'.[2] If some complained that this encouraged idleness, others saw it as a vital component of the demand economy, stimulating exchange. Defoe was sure both that 'The Price of Labour in *England*, is allow'd to Exceed all the Nations in the World' and that this was 'the vast Hinge on which the Wealth of the Nation turns'.[3] Despite such observations the labouring poor lacked financial security and their ability to consume was especially vulnerable to the vicissitudes of price fluctuations. With expenditure on food accounting for a little over half the wages of labourers the cost of food was a fundamental determinant of their standard of living. Food prices

---

[1] C. King, *The British Merchant; or, Commerce Preserv'd*, 3 vols. (1721), vol. 1, pp. 165–6. He estimated the value of exports at £7m per annum. Little is known of King's life.

[2] B.-L. de Muralt, *Letters Describing the Character and Customs of the English and French Nations* (2nd edn., 1726), p. 10.

[3] *Defoe's Review*, facsimile edn., 22 vols. (New York, 1938), vol. 4, pp. 49 and 69.

TABLE 8. *Price index of agricultural and industrial products* (1640–1749 = 100)

	Grains	Livestock	Agriculture as a whole	Industrial
1680–9	92	98	97	98
1690–9	110	109	108	105
1700–9	91	108	99	103
1710–9	99	107	104	97
1720–9	101	105	101	93
1730–9	89	107	98	89

Source: 'Statistical appendix', in J. Thirsk (ed.), *The Agrarian History of England and Wales: vol. 5, pt. 2, 1640–1750* (Cambridge, 1985) p. 856.

rose sharply in the difficult conditions of the 1690s—war, the recoinage, and bad weather all took their toll—but fell in the following decade before another modest rise and fall. Table 8 provides an indication of changes, though such evidence is far from exact.

If prices fundamentally determined the living standards of many, their income might also fluctuate. Over our period wage *rates* of most labour barely changed on trend, such that changes in income were largely influenced by the availability of employment. The influence of short-term factors here, such as the weather, probably evened out over time, but there is evidence that more work was becoming available by the end of the period. It is possible that the industrial economy expanded by about 15 per cent between 1700 and 1725, agriculture by perhaps the same amount, and overseas trade by about 30 per cent. As population increased by only about 9 per cent at the time it is likely that economic expansion resulted from rises in average labour productivity and employment per person, giving greater income per worker (the supply and demand sides cannot be neatly separated).[4] A little more disposable income was finding its way into the pockets of many people, aided by the falls in the price of industrial goods indicated in Table 8. Of course some did rather better than this, some rather worse. And many continued to have non-wage sources of income such as payment in kind or access to common land on which to keep some animals.

Most people spent increased income on necessities or a few decencies: a little more food, beer, clothing, and household goods (sometimes second hand), perhaps some tobacco or sugar. If to the individual or family such increases were slight and uncertain, at the cumulative macro-economic level the consequences were far greater, providing an important stimulus to both the industrial and service sectors. At the individual level clearer changes were experienced by those with more disposable income, who were starting to

[4] For a discussion of the range of wage experiences, see above, pp. 81–2.

acquire durable and semi-durable goods in reasonable quantities. Inventory evidence, records of property at death (and thus concerning only those who had property to be disposed), helps chart such consumption patterns. In 1675 earthenware was mentioned in 27 per cent of inventories, but by 1725 57 per cent did so. For clocks the rise was from 9 to 34 per cent, for knives and forks from 1 to 10 per cent, and for looking glasses from 22 to 40 per cent. Such changes were both geographically and socially specific. London was at the vanguard of new patterns of consumption. For example, in 1725 62 per cent of London inventories record window curtains, but in rural areas the figure was only 10 per cent and for clocks the figures were 51 and 29 per cent respectively. Not surprisingly, patterns of consumption also reflected social inequalities in the distribution of income. So, for example, if across the period 1675 to 1725 51 per cent of inventories of members of the gentry record clocks, among small farmers and husbandmen only 4 per cent did so. Consumer goods were slowly filling the domestic environment of the middling sort, even if to the modern eye homes were often relatively bare, as some paintings of interiors clearly illustrate.

Contemporaries noticed such changes in patterns of consumption but were often anxious about their causes and consequences. Much comment was passed on the pursuit of luxury, the force of socially emulative consumption, and 'how wonderfully Fashions prevail on this Nation'.[5] Frequently, the long-term causes of these developments were ascribed to England's increasing involvement with the riches of Asia and the Americas, the medium-term causes to the example set by the debauched court of Charles II, and the short-term causes to the wars against France and the rise of national debt. Some panicked when considering this. Luxury had become a 'Plague', and 'Wisdom and Virtue' had been overtaken by 'insatiable Avarice'.[6] This was seen as socially pernicious: 'Among the *Benefits* we owe to *Trade*, there is One *Disadvantage*, unavoidably annexed to *It*—It *weakens* our *Humanity*, and *eradicates* an *open Confidence*, which most men are born with'.[7] Such criticisms did not go unanswered and a heated debate raged. Some celebrated the acquisitive spirit. 'It is not Necessity ... but ... the wants of the Mind, Fashion, and desire of Novelties, and Things scarce, that causeth *Trade*.'[8] Sir Dudley North thought that 'The main spur to ... Industry and Ingenuity, is the exorbitant Appetites of Men, which they will take pains to gratifie, and so be disposed to work, when nothing else

[5] J. Cary, *An Essay on the State of England, in Relation to its Trade, its Poor, and its Taxes, for Carrying on the Present War against France* (Bristol, 1695), p. 53.

[6] J. Dennis, *Vice and Luxury Publick Mischiefs: or, Remarks on a Book Intituled the Fable of the Bees; or, Private Vices Publick Benefits* (1724), pp. 26–7.

[7] W. Bond and A. Hill, *The Plain Dealer: being Select Essays on Several Curious Subjects ... Publish'd Originally in the Year 1724*, 2 vols. (2nd edn., 1734), vol. 1, p. 68.

[8] N. Barbon, *A Discourse of Trade* (1690), p. 72.

will incline them to it'.[9] This line was pushed to and beyond the limit by Bernard Mandeville in his famous piece of doggerel, 'The grumbling hive'.[10] He argued that the desire to consume stimulated economic activity which in turn heightened social interdependence because people had to buy from and sell to one another. Far from luxury undermining the civic order it strengthened it. Self-interest and sociability might both advance together.

One concern of moralists was that new patterns of consumption eroded vital visual markers of social hierarchy. Some worried (implausibly) that it was often impossible to distinguish a mistress from her maid because their clothing was so alike. Further, such emulative consumption could be seen as wasteful and unnecessary, a wholly inappropriate use of scarce resources. Such concerns had a long heritage, and in the sixteenth century there had been significant attempts to control consumption. Some now called for a renewed campaign, Swift urging Parliament 'To enact and enforce Sumptuary Laws against Luxury, and all Excesses in Cloathing, Furniture, and the like'.[11] But such calls met stiff opposition, others proclaiming the virtues of relative *laissez faire*. 'Countries which have sumptuary Laws, are generally poor'.[12] Restrictions on consumption were, in fact, few and far between. It speaks volumes that perhaps the most important limitation was the requirement, introduced in 1666 and not formally lifted until 1814, that people be buried clothed or wrapped in wool, in an attempt to stimulate the nation's staple industry. As has been seen the import of Asian textiles was undermined by legislation in 1700 and 1721. In 1698, 1709, 1717, and 1720 statutes attempted to control the consumption and hence the production of cloth buttons. Otherwise it was the failure to enact sumptuary legislation which is striking—including failed measures in the 1690s against selling cane chairs, building dovecotes, or wearing gold and silver in wartime. Except in highly specific instances it was no longer thought reasonable to attempt to control the consumers's needs and wants, a climate which encouraged among importers and manufacturers an increasing awareness of commercial opportunities, giving plentiful opportunities for product innovations and the sway of fashion and design. Many goods were increasingly being made as much to impress as to last.

[9] D. North, *Discourses upon Trade* (1691), reprinted in J. R. McCulloch (ed.), *Early English Tracts on Commerce* (Cambridge, 1970), p. 528. Dudley North, 1641–91, son of 4th Baron North, apprenticed to a merchant, worked in Smyrna and Constantinople, Sheriff of London and knighted 1682, worked in both the Customs and Treasury departments, wrote on economic matters.

[10] Bernard Mandeville, 1670–1733, born in Holland and educated in medicine and philosophy at Leiden, moved to London in the early 1690s; little known of his life in London except for his published writings.

[11] J. Swift, *The History of the Last Four Years of the Queen*, ed. H. Williams (Oxford, 1951), p. 95.

[12] North, *Discourses*, p. 529.

OVERSEAS TRADE

If powerful to the modern eye, King's view of the primacy of domestic demand convinced few contemporaries. In seventeenth-century England many agreed that 'Commerce is the Fountain of Wealth, the true Foundation of all real Greatness.'[13] By that standard England had advanced significantly over the course of the century. Indeed, in 1697 the newly established Board of Trade reported that 'We have made enquiries into the state of trade in general from the year 1670 to the present time, and upon the best calculations we can make by the duties paid at the Custom House, we are of opinion that trade in general did considerably increase from the end of the Dutch war in 1673 to *anno* 1688'.[14] If historians have been inclined to view that increase as part of a 'Commercial revolution', of a dramatic growth in the absolute and relative importance of overseas trade to England's economy, the report's authors did not feel that the available evidence allowed them to express that growth with any quantitative precision. Fortunately, the establishment of the Inspector General-ship of Customs in 1696 led to the collection of much more reliable trade data —if still far from completely accurate. Figure 3 presents that data visually.

Imports between 1699 and 1701 averaged £5.75m per annum and between 1726 and 1728 £7.02m, a rise of 22 per cent; for exports the figures were respectively £3.81m and £4.84m, a rise of 27 per cent; and for re-exports, that is for goods mainly imported from the colonies and Asia before being shipped on to Europe, £1.95m and £3.05m, an increase of nearly 57 per cent. Probably these increases were less than those experienced in the Restoration era, but it says much that, despite the disruption of two great wars, all three components of England's overseas trade maintained the momentum established after 1660, attaining greater size and significance than ever before. English industry was able to produce more and more goods at prices that found a ready market over-seas; at home people had more purchasing power to spend upon foreign goods; and the fruits of England's empire of trade were channelled by her merchants with increasing success into third markets. Of course, such dynamism was not merely due to developments in England's economy, but sometimes also to those among her trading partners. But it says much that sterling was either stable or strong against other currencies. Compared to the average for 1686–8 by the end of our period sterling bought 60 per cent more French livres, 15 per cent more Portuguese milréis, and 14 per cent more Spanish pesos.

---

[13] *Angliae Tutamen: or, the Safety of England* (1695), p. 3.

[14] J. Thirsk and J. P. Cooper (eds.), *Seventeenth Century Economic Documents* (Oxford, 1972), p. 568.

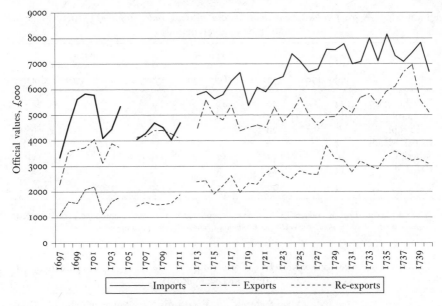

FIG. 3. English overseas trade, 1697–1740

Source: B. R. Mitchell, *British Historical Statistics* (Cambridge, 1988), p. 448

Internationally England's economy was becoming increasingly competitive and concerns of Dutch control of Europe's trade were gradually weakening.

The geographical nature of English overseas trade is outlined in Table 9. In Chapter 8 the importance of imperial connections to English trade was established, but Table 9 also demonstrates the continuing importance of European business.[15] Towards the end of our period continental Europe provided 55.2 per cent of imports and was a market for 77.2 per cent of exports and 72.6 per cent of re-exports. Trade through the Baltic, across the North Sea, and through the Straits of Gibraltar was fundamental to England's commercial prosperity.

The geographical patterns of English trade rested upon its commodity basis (see Table 10). The most important imports of manufactures were linens, calicoes, and silks, that is to say the products of industries that were as yet poorly developed in England. Similarly, imports of foodstuffs were largely of those that could not be produced at home. Sugar and wine were especially substantial, though tobacco, fruit, spices, tea, and coffee were also significant. Among raw material imports inputs for the domestic textile industries were especially important, notably silk, flax, hemp, wool, textile yarns, and dyes.

---

[15] See above, p. 263.

TABLE 9. *Geographical distribution of English overseas trade, 1699–1724* (percentage of all trade in given period)

	Imports		Exports		Re-exports	
	1699–1701	1722–4	1699–1701	1722–4	1699–1701	1722–4
NW Europe	24	20	42	30	58	64
N. Europe	10	9	6	4	4	2
S. Europe	27	26	33	43	11	6
British islands	7	6	4	6	10	9
America	19	25	12	15	16	18
East India	13	14	3	2	1	1
TOTAL	100	100	100	100	100	100

Source: R. Davis, 'English Foreign Trade, 1700–74', reprinted in W. E. Minchinton (ed.), *The Growth of English Overseas Trade in the Seventeenth and Eighteenth Centuries* (1969), pp. 119–20.

TABLE 10. *Commodity composition of English overseas trade, 1699–1724* (percentage of all trade in given period)

	Manufactures	Foodstuffs	Raw materials	Total
Imports 1699–1701	31	34	35	100
Imports 1722–4	28	36	36	100
Exports 1699–1701	81	11	8	100
Exports 1722–4	75	18	7	100
Re-exports 1699–1701	38	47	15	100
Re-exports 1722–4	41	46	13	100

Source: R. Davis, 'English Foreign Trade, 1700–74', reprinted in W. E. Minchinton (ed.), *The Growth of English Overseas Trade in the Seventeenth and Eighteenth Centuries* (1969), pp. 119–20.

Iron, steel, timber, and oil imports were also considerable. Through the period England's exports were mainly of manufactured goods which, in turn, were dominated by woollens—in 1699–1701 they accounted for nearly 69 per cent of all exports—with the so-called 'new draperies', lighter cloths aimed at the warmer southern European market, being the most dynamic element here. Re-exports of manufactured goods comprised overwhelmingly textiles, especially calicoes, silks, and linens, and foodstuffs, mainly tobacco, sugar, tea, and coffee.

Most of England's overseas trade was carried in English ships. The mercantile marine had grown significantly in the seventeenth century, from some 115,000 tons in 1629 to 323,000 tons in 1702, and the shipbuilding industry was prominent in many ports. Moreover, few foreign ships were involved in England's commerce and the Dutch could no longer count themselves as unchallenged in Europe's carrying trade. In 1718 foreign ships accounted for a mere 4 per cent by tonnage of entries into and clearances from English ports. Though over half of all English ships were owned in outports, London was the main conduit for overseas trade, in 1722–4 handling over 80 per cent of imports, 67 per cent of exports, and 87 per cent of re-exports. London was port to the nation's largest ships, and provided the best markets for insurance, labour, finance, business information, and imported commodities. There were, of course, other prominent ports—notably Bristol, Liverpool, Whitehaven, Newcastle, Whitby, Hull, Great Yarmouth, Ipswich, and Exeter—but they were very small in comparison to the capital. In 1702 some 140,000 tons of shipping was owned in London, with no other port owning more than 20,000 tons.

The majority of English overseas trade was conducted by private merchants, of whom there were 10,000 by King's reckoning. There is some evidence that such firms were increasing in size in our period, at least in London. For example, in 1676 the import of over 11,000 lbs of tobacco into London was handled by 573 firms but by 1719 twice the amount of tobacco was handled by just 117 firms (so the average amount handled by each firm rose tenfold). Prominent firms were coming into existence elsewhere, such as Twinings in the tea trade which was founded in 1706 and is still in business today. The biggest merchant firms were indeed the princes of the business world, prominent for the fortunes amassed, credit dispensed, risks taken, and power wielded. Such men were frequently celebrated for their accomplishments, 'a compleat *Trader* . . . should be . . . Proficient in *Languages, History, Geography*, and *Mathematicks*'.[16] Their prosperity sometimes attained near legendary status, 'for rich Furniture, plentiful Tables, Honourable living, for great Estates in Money and Land, [they] excel some Princes in some of our Neighbour Nations.'[17] There were just enough prominent examples of such successes to sustain this view and some fabulous fortunes were amassed. In point of fact, however, most mercantile businesses were small, limited by the resources (financial and physical) of an individual or two-man partnership. The largest concerns in overseas trade were those remaining regulated or joint-stock companies, mainly founded in the sixteenth and seventeenth century on the basis of having a monopoly of or control over trade to a given part of the globe. An undertaking such as the East India Company was a leviathan in an economy dominated by small-scale enterprises, a truly multi-national concern. Other prominent companies included the Royal Africa Company and the Levant Company. Increasingly, however, such businesses were chided for inefficiency and conservatism. 'Companies, generally speaking, can be of no advantage to the State, excepting only when private People are not able to attain the

---

[16] Bond and Hill, *The Plain Dealer*, vol. 2, p. 232.
[17] T. de Laune, *Angliæ Metropolis: or, the Present State of London* (1690), p. 301.

intended Ends'.[18] Many companies had, indeed, decayed or died by the start of the eighteenth century. For example, the Hudson Bay Company, Royal Africa Company, and Russia Company had lost many of their privileges in 1697, 1698, and 1699 respectively.

Clearly England's burgeoning overseas trade was an important stimulant to her domestic economy, encouraging export industries, including shipbuilding, processing industries, such as sugar refineries, infrastructural developments, such as carriers, and financial services, such as marine insurance. Much employment was created as a consequence. But overseas trade also created experiences. Most obviously, sailors were true citizens of the world. Their home ports and families felt their absences (though they probably accounted for only 5–10 per cent of the population in major ports), mourned those many who never returned, but enjoyed the income, tales, and goods brought back by those who did. Trade and cosmopolitanism went hand in hand, especially in the capital, London being 'so to speak, the market-fair of the human race' and its meeting point for traders and merchants, the Royal Exchange, 'the World in Epitome'.[19] But the social impact of overseas trade was felt far and wide. Sugar, tea, coffee, tobacco, silk, wine, and spices made their way into homes, inns, and coffee-houses across the nation. News of the arrival of ships was given a prominent place in many papers, sustaining England's self-perception as an island nation. Overseas trade was accorded considerable political importance. Merchants and shipowners were often prominent in local politics, over 100 parliamentary boroughs were ports or fishing villages, and sections of the trading community were already highly skilled in the arts of lobbying. In London, admittedly the largest port and the most powerful site of local government, of 62 aldermen elected between 1694 and 1714 some 36 had been overseas traders and 17 also served for a time as MPs.

Of course, the impact of overseas trade was not always positive. International trade was inherently risky. The two main wars of the period were initially highly disruptive and the Great Northern War (1700–21) often threatened to close access to the Baltic even though England was not a combatant; pirates menaced the Caribbean, Mediterranean, and Indian ocean; navigation was often inexact, not least because longitude could not be accurately measured; ill-packed cargoes might fester or become prey to rats; storms always threatened; foreign correspondents could not be closely controlled or their judgements easily assessed; and capital was tied up for many months before returns were made. Such factors influenced all involved in overseas trade, from sailors to

[18] I. Gervaise, *The System or Theory of the Trade of the World*, ed. G. H. Evans (Baltimore, 1954), p. 20.

[19] J. Beeverell, *The Pleasures of London*, trans. W. H. Quarrell (1940), p. 12; Muralt, *Letters Describing the English and French*, p. 80.

shipowners, merchants to warehousekeepers, carriers to consumers. It says much that merchants constituted the largest occupational group among bankrupts through our period, accounting for over 13 per cent of the nearly 6,600 businessmen legally declared bankrupt between 1701 and 1730.[20] Further, the expansion of overseas trade sometimes fell far short of domestic expectations—witness the insignificance of the South Sea Company's trade after its foundation in 1711 and the failure to export significant quantities of manufactured goods to Asia. Finally, some parts of overseas trade introduced an element of seasonality that led to dramatic swings in employment opportunities in the ports, be it because of the timing of the sugar harvest in the West Indies, the monsoon in India, or Atlantic trade winds.

THE INDUSTRIAL ECONOMY

Developments in overseas trade captured the imagination of contemporaries. But promoting colonies and importing commodities was only possible because England had goods and services to trade in return. In fact, England had a well-developed industrial base by 1700, accounting for perhaps one-fifth of national income. We have, however, no means of detailing with any precision the relative sizes of particular industries at a given point or the growth and decay of most industries over time. Rather, a picture has to be pieced together from contemporary qualitative descriptions and excise records which exist for a few industries. Despite such uncertainties, most contemporaries would have agreed that in industrial terms '*England* is founded upon Wooll-packs', that is to say the manufacture of a wide range of textiles made wholly or in part of wool.[21] Supposedly the woollen trades 'are brought by us to the utmost Perfection, none of our Neighbours pretend to equal us therein'.[22] Gregory King guessed that there were 11m sheep in England in the late seventeenth century, but even they were unable to meet the demands of domestic manufacturers and significant quantities of wool from Spain and Ireland were imported in most years. As a whole the woollen textile industries were probably growing slowly, but much of that growth was concentrated in the West Riding of Yorkshire, with other areas, notably in and around Exeter and Norwich, struggling to maintain their competitiveness. Other textile industries, such as linen, silk, and lace, while much smaller than most woollen textile

[20] The legal definition was a restricted one, and many more businesses than this will have become insolvent.

[21] J. Haynes, *Great Britain's Glory: or, an Account of the Great Numbers of Poor Employ'd in the Woollen and Silk Manufactures* (1715), p. 2.

[22] King, *British Merchant*, vol. 1, p. xxxiv.

industries, also appear to have grown slowly. For example, the silk industry, which depended completely upon imported raw materials, increased output by about a quarter between 1700 and the end of our period.

Though contemporaries stressed that the woollen industry was peculiarly suited to English circumstances historians have also noted the unusual significance of the coal industry. English coal production was around 177,000 tons per annum in the 1560s but by 1700 was 2.20m tons, a twelvefold rise.[23] That growth was sustained in the eighteenth century and by 1750 the figure had reached 4.30m tons. Both absolutely and relative to other countries this was an extraordinary performance, liberating England to a unique degree from reliance upon wind, water, and wood for energy. Indeed, England's coal output through our period may well have been greater than the combined total for the rest of the world. In 1700 four English coalfields produced over 100,000 tons per annum—Staffordshire, Yorkshire, Shropshire, and the North-east in ascending order. The last of these provided nearly half of national output, the majority of which was shipped down the east coast to the capital, requiring annually some 3,000 voyages from fleets of colliers. So valuable were these shipments that the London coal trade was heavily taxed, helping to fund the building of St Paul's cathedral, the 'fifty' new churches, Greenwich hospital, and the support of London orphans. Little wonder that seamen at Wapping described Newcastle as the '*Black-Indies*'.[24]

It has already been shown that about a third of England's imports were of manufactured goods and that these were mainly of textiles. Consequently, most other industrial goods were manufactured domestically—beer, starch, soap, salt, paper, candles, leather, iron, tin, glass, furniture, and pottery for example. England had both a developed and a diversified industrial base. Just how well these industries did is difficult to tell, but the signs are of modest advances in most but not all. Using excise data, and therefore ignoring domestic and illicit production, candle output rose by 15 per cent between 1711 and 1727, that of strong beer by 5 per cent between 1700 and 1727, and of soap by 10 per cent between 1713 and 1727. However, output of starch fell by 19 per cent between 1713 and 1727, probably because some raw materials were diverted into gin distilling (which rose by 118 per cent between those dates).

On balance English industrial output may have grown by about 15 per cent in the first quarter of the eighteenth century, that is to say at an annual

---

[23] Figures taken from J. Hatcher, *The History of the British Coal Industry*, vol. 1. *Before 1700, Towards the Age of Coal* (Oxford, 1993), p. 68. His figure for 1700 compares to 2.43m tons from the companion work of M. W. Flinn, *The History of the British Coal Industry*, vol. 2. *1700–1830, The Industrial Revolution* (Oxford, 1984), p. 26.

[24] J. Houghton, *A Collection for the Improvement of Husbandry and Trade*, 4 vols. (1727–8), vol. 2, p. 155.

compound rate of only 0.56 per cent, or rather less than a quarter of the average rate of growth experienced since 1945. Such a figure rests heavily upon guesswork and supposition, but it is broadly compatible with contemporary opinion. It is, of course, significant that there was growth rather than stagnation or decay and that a century before the climax of the industrial revolution there was already some modest expansion. Indeed, that revolution rested upon a variety of foundations that had gradually been laid since at least the early seventeenth century. But the slow rate of growth also points to the difficulties faced by early eighteenth-century industry in trying to improve output and productivity. In the first place those limits were due to the fact that much production took place via the rural domestic system of manufacture, where labourers took raw or semi-processed materials into their home to work upon when they could not find employment in agriculture. This helped to spread labour costs between industry and agriculture, so raising output per worker (over the long term this was so significant that it has been called an 'industrious revolution'), and allowed families to work together as a team, but it also meant that the techniques and technologies employed had to be cheap and easily acquired.[25] Workers had few skills and often only basic tools, while the unit of production was too small to allow the extensive division of labour. Moreover, though usually merchant manufacturers supplied materials and took back the finished goods they were unable to keep a close eye upon what was produced or when. This was the more serious in rural manufactures, as in most branches of the woollen industry, where workers might live some distance from their merchant manufacturer. Consequently, if it was relatively easy to expand total output through the domestic system of manufacture it was difficult to raise productivity per worker or to improve the quality of output. But even centralized production sometimes struggled to overcome such limitations. In the iron industry, for example, there were about 70 or 80 furnaces annually producing 29,000 tons of pig iron by 1727, which served at least 150 forges. However, this was too little to meet demand and iron imports totalling about 21,000 tons were needed to make up the shortfall. Partly this was due to the high quality of imported iron, partly to the technical difficulties of smelting iron ore by coke rather than the traditional fuel, charcoal. Though Abraham Darby had first used coke to smelt in 1709 it was not widely adopted until mid-century. If it is easy to exaggerate the problems of finding adequate sources of charcoal in early eighteenth-century England, the real lesson of this technical breakthrough is how few ironmasters appeared to have searched for technical improvements

[25] J. de Vries, 'Between Purchasing Power and the World of Goods: Understanding the Household Economy in Early Modern Europe', in J. Brewer and R. Porter (eds.), *Consumption and the World of Goods* (1993), p. 107.

as a matter of course. Whereas modern economies invest heavily and nearly continuously in technological developments, such a mentality was alien to the majority in our period.

Most industries depended upon rudimentary skills, muscle power, hand tools, and little fixed capital. Moreover, businesses were usually small, with limited funds and technical expertise, and faced an environment which looked uncertain and threatening rather than expansive and encouraging. Wars, bad harvests, storms, social strife, political disorder, and financial crises all occasionally loomed large, though the business cycle had not yet been born. Such problems were exacerbated because so much business was conducted by use of credit mechanisms based upon assessments of character as much as financial reserves and commercial acumen. 'True credit I call that which is founded on a right Principle, the knowing and considering whom is trusted by his Character and Abilities.'[26] Chains of credit were ubiquitous, linking producers, distributors, and consumers, such that one failure to repay could lead to serious problems elsewhere, trapping many in indebtedness and bankruptcy. As Defoe, himself a bankrupt, remarked, 'The best and most flourishing Tradesmen fall into Disasters . . . and such Men are standing Instances of the little Guard great Estates are to the surprises of Trade'.[27] Consequently, risk avoidance by emulating tried and tested techniques was a common approach, not experiment and innovation. Not that businessmen were adept at keeping track of their affairs, standards of accounting being notoriously poor.

Such a depiction of inflexibility and weakness must not be overdrawn. Industry was not stuck in the mire of traditionalism. There was some innovation, change, and growth. Cary was struck by 'the Ingenuity of the Manufacturer, and the Improvements he makes in his ways of working . . . there is a Cunning crept into Trades.'[28] One social dynamic was provided by the importance of non-conformists to the business community. What Voltaire noted of Quakers was generally true of Dissenters, they could not 'be members of Parliament nor hold any office . . . They are reduced to the necessity of earning money through commerce'.[29] Their non-classical education, social and religious mores, and networks well suited them to a business life. More generally, economic optimism did exist, as evidenced by publications such as John Houghton's *Collection for the Improvement of Husbandry and Trade*, published weekly between 1692 and 1703, which advocated and publicized the benefits of the new.[30] As we will see there was wave of patents taken out in the 1690s and

---

[26] *A Dissertation upon Credit* (n.d.), p. 1.   [27] *Defoe's Review*, vol. 6, p. 25.

[28] Cary, *Essay on Trade*, pp. 145–6. John Cary, d. 1720, a Bristolian, West Indian merchant, published a number of pamphlets on economic topics.

[29] *Letters on England*, trans. L. Tancock (Harmondsworth, 1980), p. 35.

[30] John Houghton, d. 1705, Fellow of the Royal Society 1680.

a good deal of entrepreneurialism through the period. And some important developments in business organization and new technology certainly occurred. Among the former, note should be made of Sir Ambrose Crowley's great iron-works near Newcastle, run from a London head office in part by a carefully compiled 'law book' of 94 management regulations.[31] Crowley's works were probably the largest in Europe at the time, with disputes settled by a court of arbitration, and workers protected by a social insurance scheme. In about 1718 Thomas Lombe built a silk-throwing mill, utilizing technology smuggled out of Italy.[32] Some five stories high and five hundred feet long, contemporaries marvelled at this prototype factory. Perhaps the most significant technical development was made in 1698 by Thomas Savery, who constructed a steam engine to drain mines, a development improved by Thomas Newcomen in 1712.[33] Thermodynamically inefficient though these were by 1733 there were about 100 Newcomen engines in operation. The steam age had been conceived, though it was take more than a century to come of age.

Most industrial developments, because so slow, were little reflected upon by contemporaries and what did catch their eye was often of secondary significance. Perhaps the most important was changes in the regional basis of industrial activity, what many historians now call proto-industrialization, and which contemporaries only faintly perceived. Industry had long been based upon regional specialization, especially for textiles, and thus dependent upon interregional trade. In England this had become especially marked since the sixteenth century, Defoe noting how 'manufactures . . . are made and wrought in their several distinct and respective countries in Britain, and some of them at the remotest distance from one another, hardly any two manufactures being made in one place.'[34] Continuing earlier trends, after 1689 the industries of some regions prospered, some declined, and others marked time. In broad terms there was already a shift of industrial dynamism towards the Midlands and north in this period, though London remained an important and innovative manufacturing centre. The iron industry of the Weald, once a major centre of ordnance production, was fast declining as areas such as Shropshire, the West Midlands, and South Yorkshire prospered; in textile production framework knitting was beginning to migrate from London to the East Midlands, and the energy of the West Riding sucked some of the vitality from the woollen

[31] Ambrose Crowley, 1658–1713, leading London business figure, serving as Sheriff and Alderman, knighted 1707, MP 1713.

[32] Thomas Lombe, 1685–1739, patented silk-throwing machine 1718, Sheriff of London and knighted 1727.

[33] Thomas Savery, c.1650–1715, engineer, especially hydraulics, Surveyor of Waterworks at Hampton Court 1714. Thomas Newcomen, 1663–1729.

[34] D. Defoe, The Complete English Tradesman (Gloucester, 1987), p. 226.

industries of East Anglia and southern England. The reasons for such changes are complex, but, aside from questions of demand and distribution, centred upon the availability and cost of labour which, with so much dual employment, was influenced both by agriculture and industry. Since the Restoration important agricultural developments (discussed in the next chapter) had their greatest impact upon southern and eastern England, leading to a relative labour shortage for expanding industries. Moreover, agriculture made somewhat less demand for labour in the more pastorally-orientated economies of the Midlands and north. Institutional and entrepreneurial factors were also important. Birmingham was proud of its lack of guild or corporate control, its tradition of religious toleration, and a flourishing artisanal culture. And the distant control exercised by London's Blackwell Hall factors over parts of the East Anglian and West Country textile industries probably meant that many commercial opportunities went unseen and undeveloped.

THE SERVICE ECONOMY

England's involvement in international trade and the regional nature of her agriculture and manufacturing required a well-developed means for the internal distribution and exchange of goods. The efficiency of this service economy was a crucial determinant of national prosperity and of the extent to which people were implicated in England's increasingly expansive commercial and industrial sectors. In fact, even in this age, before a developed system of turnpike roads, canals, and railways, most people had access to the products of interregional and international trade. Indeed, improvements in the economy's infrastructure made such access increasingly easy and secure. Thus when in 1731 Pope reflected on the quest to 'Bid Harbors open, public Ways extend . . . And roll obedient Rivers thro' the Land' he was inspired by developments that had for the most part taken place in the preceding four decades, one notable consequence of which was the erosion of significant regional price variations, strengthening the national basis of economic activity.[35]

Defoe observed that there were 'multitudes of people employed, cattle maintaine'd, with wagons and carts for the service on shore, barges and boats for carriage in the rivers, and ships and barks for carrying by sea, and all for the circulating these manufactures from one place to another, for the consumption of them among the people.'[36] Most movement by road was carried, but some walked 'on the hoof'. In the 1690s the roads to London suffered each

---

[35] A. Pope, 'Epistle to Richard Boyle, Earl of Burlington', ll. 197 and 202, in *The Poems of Alexander Pope*, ed. J. Butt (1996), p. 595.
[36] Defoe, *Complete English Tradesman*, p. 225.

year under the weight of about 87,500 beeves, 600,000 sheep, 150,000 hogs, and many thousands of turkeys. Inanimate goods were carried by packhorse or wagons, much of it locally orientated, some interregional. Naturally, county towns and provincial centres were the focal and staging points for this largely uncoordinated but extensive network. Even so much internal distribution was channelled through London, even for distant centres of manufacturing such as Birmingham, Sheffield, and Colchester. Routes began and ended at inns, with timetables already being printed. In 1690 there were about 350 weekly services leaving the capital for destinations at least twenty miles away, about half by packhorse, half by wagon. Such methods were not, of course, fast. In 1722 packhorses usually took five or six days to travel between London and Exeter, wagons six or seven days. There was little change in the efficiency of road transport in this period, though the number of services grew somewhat. Much depended upon the state of the roads which were of erratic quality because of variable maintenance by parochial authorities, the influence of soil, relief, and climate, and, particularly, different levels of usage. Some roads were certainly bad—Defoe singled out those in the Midlands—and stories can easily be found of unfortunate travellers wallowing in mud. But the main problems were caused by increasing traffic overwhelming the limited resources available to parishes to repair the roads. The answer just starting to be adopted was to turnpike roads, utilizing specific Acts of Parliament to allow a toll to be levied to fund the improvement and maintenance of heavily used roads. Though the main era of turnpikes was between 1750 and 1770 important developments took place earlier. The first new turnpike Act was in 1663, the second in 1695, and 81 were passed between that date and 1729 (there were also 38 failed attempts to obtain road Acts between 1689 and 1727). Thus by 1730 some 57 per cent of the mileage of the 13 major roads out of London had been turnpiked.

Road transport was relatively expensive, with coastal trade and inland navigation able to carry bulky goods more easily and cheaply. A pack-horse might carry 2 or 3 cwt and a wagon drawn by a team of horses about 30 cwt, but a single horse could haul a river barge of 600 cwt (30 tons). Such advantages, along with the growth of trade, stimulated considerable river improvement. In 1660 England had about 685 miles of navigable rivers, but by 1725 this had risen to 1,160 miles, much of which was added after 1689. As with turnpikes mostly this was brought about via an Act of Parliament, 34 such Acts being passed between 1689 and 1727. Among those improved were the Aire and Calder, the Trent, the Bristol Avon, the Great Ouse, and the Mersey, that is to say rivers serving some of England's most important non-metropolitan sources of industrial, commercial, and agricultural growth. It is worth stressing that these river improvements owed nothing to technical change, everything to perceptions of demand for traffic, especially of coal and corn.

However, that there were not as yet canals being built (that began in earnest in the 1760s) suggests that such demand could, as with road transport, still be satisfied within an essentially traditional structure of inland navigation. Much the same was true of coastal trade. England had a large fleet skirting its shores. The total tonnage of coasting ships belonging to outports rose from nearly 97,000 tons in 1709 to nearly 110,000 tons in 1730, a rise of just over 13 per cent, probably due as much to the growth in the size of the ships involved as their total number. These were widely scattered. Ignoring London, in 1723 there were nine ports with between 1,000 and 2,000 tons of coastal shipping, twelve with over 2,000 tons. The largest port was Scarborough, followed by Sunderland, Newcastle, King's Lynn, Great Yarmouth, and Whitby (all on the east coast and all involved in the coal trade). As with road and river improvements the period after the Revolution saw considerable efforts to enhance ports. And again this was often done by utilizing legislative authority, 37 Acts for new port facilities being passed in this period, often involving considerable capital outlay. England's first wet dock, Howland Great Dock at Rotherhithe, was opened in 1700 at a cost of £12,000; a new wet dock at Liverpool in 1715 cost £15,000; and near Bristol the docks at Sea Mills, begun in 1712, cost nearly £10,000.

If communications provided part of the link between producers and consumers another part was provided by the wholesale and retail outlets which covered the country. The number of those outlets is difficult to estimate, but Gregory King thought there were only 2,000 families who were 'merchants and traders by sea', compared to 8,000 who were 'merchants and traders by land', and 40,000 who were 'shopkeepers and tradesmen', though Defoe argued that 'the number is in a manner infinite'.[37] This wholesale and retail web contained much that was old and much that was new. Among the old were itinerant peddlers, hawkers, markets, and fairs, none faring particularly well in this period. There was much hostility to itinerant salesmen, either because they were argued to be vagrants or Jacobite agents—Scotch peddlers were especially distrusted. Between 1691 and 1695 the Commons considered at least five measures aimed at suppressing hawkers and peddlers (there had also been a number of attempts in the Restoration era). But these salesmen had their defenders. As Sir Christopher Musgrave told fellow MPs, to suppress them 'will hinder the consumption of your commodities, ruin many families, and deprive yourselves of many conveniences. Your wares and goods are now brought home to your doors.'[38] Such arguments held sway, for no anti-hawking legislation was enacted in this period. Markets and fairs, which England had 'in abundance', were also coming under pressure, though largely for

[37] See above, p. 70; *Complete English Tradesman*, p. 229.
[38] *The Parliamentary Diary of Narcissus Luttrell, 1691–1693*, ed. H. Horwitz (Oxford, 1972), p. 132.

commercial reasons.[39] In 1690 there had been perhaps 801 active market towns in England, with markets held on various days of the week. But these were gradually dying out as trade passed into the hands of shopkeepers and others. By 1720 numbers had fallen to 574, a reduction of 28 per cent. On the face of it fairs, which were usually annual events concentrating on agricultural produce, were more buoyant, reaching over 3,200 for England and Wales by the middle of the eighteenth century. Stourbridge fair, near Cambridge, was claimed to be 'not only the greatest in the whole nation, but in the world'. It had shops 'placed in rows like streets . . . Scarce any trades are omitted' and whole-sale booths selling 'vast quantities of Yorkshire cloths . . . with all sorts of Manchester ware, fustians, and things made of cotton wool', along with hops from Herefordshire, Lincolnshire wool, and 'all sorts of wrought iron, and brass ware from Birmingham; edged tools, knives, &c. from Sheffield; glass ware, and stockings, from Nottingham, and Leicester'.[40] But Stourbridge was unusual both for its scale and its vibrancy, for trade at many fairs was declining and others were mutating into sites of leisure rather than business.

One problem faced by both markets and fairs was the increasing tendency for wholesale trade to take place not publicly but privately by sample at inns, partly because of increasing specialization among middlemen, partly because of attempts to reduce transactions costs. Improved communications also enabled more trade to be handled in fewer markets and fairs. But markets and fairs were also losing retail trade to shops which, though they had long been a common-place in towns and cities (foreign visitors frequently commented on the splend-our of some of those in London), were gradually spreading into the villages of rural England. The advantages enjoyed by shops, whether a village general store or a specialist shop in the capital, were relative availability by being open six days a week, indoor comfort, and display. Moreover, the growth of shops encouraged, in turn, a heightened culture of consumption, especially the forces of acquisitiveness, fashion, and emulation.

Transport and distribution may have provided the mechanisms of internal trade, but they were lubricated by the oil of finance and information. Yet no formal or clearly organized capital market existed in this period. Very few businesses were founded on publicly traded share capital and there were far too few banks to service the needs of either business or personal users—London had only twenty-three in 1725. The Bank of England, founded in 1694, had an influence in and near London, but little elsewhere and moves to create alternative joint-stock banks were closed off by the Bank Act of 1708. However, in

[39] H. Misson, *Memoirs and Observations in his Travels over England* (1719), p. 77.
[40] D. Defoe, *A Tour Through the Whole Island of Great Britain*, ed. P. Rogers (Harmondsworth, 1978), pp. 102–5.

London goldsmiths and scriveners had long provided many financial services and some of these were now mutating into banks, with country gentlemen beginning to make some use of the deposit facilities offered by London's West End banks. Coutts bank, for example, dates from 1692, and was descended from the goldsmith's shop of George Middleton, just as the banks of Hoare and Martin emerged from similar sources in this period.[41] Nevertheless, such specialist intermediaries handled only a very small fraction of financial settlements and loans. Producers, distributors, and consumers usually had to fend for themselves. This was made the more necessary by the relative paucity of ready money, even after the great recoinage of 1696, the inevitable delays between production and consumption, and the perils of transporting cash along roads periodically infested with highwaymen.

The credit and debt necessary to lubricate the market economy was ad hoc, unplanned, and came from no single source. Producers and distributors expected both to give and receive credit, but loans were also made available by any with access to surplus funds. Widows and clergy were prominent lenders, and attorneys, with their inside knowledge of families's circumstances, often organized mortgages and other loans. However, the props used in the credit economy—such as bills of exchange, promissory notes, shop credit, and pawning—were not always strong enough to support the enormous weight of expectation put upon them. In large measure this was because so many loans were effectively unsecured, made simply on the expectation that they would be repaid. Such personal security was enormously flexible, usually enabling prospects to be seized readily, but prone to exaggerate perceptions of trading conditions. Once confidence began to disappear, perhaps because of the outbreak of war or a new Jacobite threat, then creditors might panic and turn on debtors *en masse*. In such circumstances liquidity disappeared and debtors often found that they could not pay. Such financial crises happened on at least six occasions in this period, in 1696, 1701, 1710, 1715, 1720, and 1726, each involving serious dislocation of the market economy. Little wonder that contemporaries characterized credit as fickle and a very mixed blessing. Neither the numerous attempts made in this period to overhaul the legal relationship between creditors and debtors, nor the establishment in 1699 of a joint-stock pawnbroker, the Charitable Corporation, stabilized the situation. Symbolically, the latter, with a notional capital base of £600,000 by 1730, collapsed in the following year as a result of reckless and corrupt undertakings.

One significant area of development in financial services was in the provision of insurance, marking not only a business opportunity but an important wider change in attitudes towards risks—that they could be calculated and hedged

---

[41] Richard Hoare, 1648–1718, knighted 1702, Sheriff of London 1709 and Lord Mayor 1712, MP for City of London 1710–15.

rather than left merely to chance or Providence. Much of this development was in fire insurance, some in marine insurance, relatively little in life insurance (though about sixty life insurance societies were founded 1696–1720). The first fire insurance office in England had been established in 1680 though developments were more rapid after 1689. In 1696 a company soon to be known as the Hand-in-Hand was founded and in 1708 Charles Povey set up the Exchange House Fire Office which by 1710 had mutated into the Sun Fire Office. These were soon to be followed by a number of other companies, often short-lived, until in 1720 the Royal Exchange Assurance and London Assurance were founded. Though some of these businesses prospered and survived the scale of fire insurance provision in the 1720s was still limited. Most coverage was in London where the majority of properties were still unprotected—a large company such as the Hand-in-Hand was issuing only 7,300 policies in 1704. Marine insurance had existed through the seventeenth century and was a more established business, mostly in the hands of some 200 specialist underwriters. They were given an identity of sorts by Edward Lloyd, after whose name the modern insurance market takes its name, when he founded a coffee-house in the 1680s where many of them met with shipowners, captains, and merchants. The institutional challenge to this market was provided by the joint-stock monopoly in marine assurance awarded to the London Assurance and Royal Exchange Assurance. In its first year the second of these companies underwrote £1.3m of marine risk and did business with almost 500 merchants. Even so much shipping was still unprotected by 1727 and as with fire insurance chance was still a vital part of the business world.

Information flows were another vital lubricant to the wheels of exchange, for transactions exclusively based on face to face encounters denote an economy unable to take advantage of distant opportunities. England's interregional and international trade already depended heavily upon an extensive postal system. As with other aspects of the service economy this system grew significantly after the Revolution, though of course the postal system was used by all, not just the business world. In 1688 postal receipts were about £90,000 and by 1724 £178,071. The London penny post, founded in 1680, was 'a mighty Encouragement to Trade and Commerce' in and around London, delivering over a million letters and parcels annually by 1702 via 600 'little offices', though the attempt by Charles Povey in 1709 to challenge the Post Office monopoly and introduce a half-penny service in the capital was suppressed.[42] From 1720 Ralph Allen, formerly postmaster at Bath, took over and developed the byeway and cross road posts, significantly enhancing the system and gaining a fortune in the process.[43] Letters kept buyer in touch with seller on an individual

[42] de Laune, *Angliæ Metropolis*, p. 345; Beeverell, *The Pleasures of London*, p. 50.

[43] 1694–1764. A local worthy and benefactor in Bath, friend of Alexander Pope, he was drawn upon by Henry Fielding for the character of Squire Allworthy in *Tom Jones*.

basis, but increasingly business news was also being carried by broadsheets and papers. The first stock price list, *The Merchant's Remembrancer*, had been published in 1681, but it was the arrival of John Castaing's *Course of the Exchange* in March 1697 which had a lasting impact. The 1690s saw a significant expansion of the business press, including, for example, Edward Lloyd's *Ships Arrived at, and Departed from Several Ports of England* begun in 1692 and which by 1726 had become *Lloyd's List*. By 1716 the London merchant could choose from seven weekly or twice-weekly business newspapers providing information about prices, ships, cargoes, and exchange rates. Some weeding out subsequently took place, but the business press was here to stay. Moreover, other newspapers, aimed at a more general reader, frequently carried business news, from the prices of certain goods to the arrival of the East India fleet.

Many developments in the areas of overseas trade, internal trade, financial services, and the business press centred upon London. Such developments had important international dimensions, involving both the capital and the nation in distant events and peoples. Foreign merchants and financiers lived and worked in London and capital flows from abroad, especially from the Dutch Republic, were an important feature of the post-Revolution era. Equally, London insurers, shipowners, and merchants were deeply involved in the trade of other nations, helping to bridge the deficit on the current account balance of payments. It says much about the strength of England's service economy that by 1727 the capital was vying with Amsterdam as the premier financial centre of northern and north-western Europe. That such a prospect had been unimaginable only sixty years earlier serves to show how significant developments had been since 1689.

BUBBLE ECONOMICS

In so far as the non-agrarian economy developed in this period it did so quietly, slowly, and hesitantly. But one aspect of change took on much more spectacular form, climaxing with the South Sea Bubble in 1720. The South Sea Company, founded in 1711, was initially championed by Harley and the Tories as an antidote to the Whig-dominated Bank of England and East India Company. The hope was that Tory financial probity would slay the dragon of Whig extravagance. With a capital base of £9.2m and the prospect of a lucrative trade to Spanish America it immediately became one of the leading commercial enterprises of the age. But an extensive trade never materialized (Britain had, after all, backed the losing side in Spain in the War of the Spanish Succession) and was effectively halted in 1718 by conflict between Britain and Spain. To survive the Company needed to exploit new opportunities and it went for broke. Prompted by John Law's Mississippi scheme in France, a highly ambitious plan was soon hatched to take over the whole of the national debt, though in the event the proposal which materialized was less comprehensive. The Bank was stung into retaliatory bidding with the government but the South Sea Company won out, offering the Treasury £7.5m. By Act of Parliament national debts to the value of £31m were effectively 'privatized'. The State continued to have to pay interest on this debt, but because this was at reduced rates the deal made much sense. But the Company could only meet its obligations by raising further share capital which would be much easier with a rising share price. Given that the underlying profitability of the Company's trade was perilous this could only be done by bluff, hyperbole, lies, and bribes. For a time it worked. At the start of 1720 the Company's stock was trading at around 130. In March, even before the passage of the South Sea Act, it was reported that 'The town is quite mad about the South Sea . . . one can hear nothing else talked of'.[44] By April the price had risen to over 300 and the speculative frenzy, encouraged by much dishonest activity on the part of the Company, was becoming ever more intense. On 2 June note was made of 'Surprizing scene in Change Alley. S. Sea in the morning above 900 . . . Professions & shops are forgot, all goe thither as to the mines of Potosi. Nobility, Ladys, Brokers, & footmen all upon a level. Great equipages set up, the prizes of things rose exorbitantly. Such a renversement of the order of Nature as succeeding ages can have no Idea of.'[45] By the end of June the share price reached its peak of over 1,000, but wise words of caution were being expressed. 'The demon of stock jobbing is the genius of this place . . . No one is satisfied with even exorbitant gains, but every one thirsts for more, and all this founded upon the machine of paper credit supported only by the imagination.'[46] Such high stock prices could not be sustained, however, once those imaginings were pricked by the sharp end of reality. At first the bubble lost air slowly, but by September the price was sinking fast, 'all is floating, all falling, the directors are curst, the top adventurers broke, four goldsmiths walked off'.[47] Others too lost heavily. Despair was general, suicides common. Defoe soon lamented those 'families . . . whose fine parks and new-built palaces are fallen under forfeitures and alienations by the misfortunes of the times'.[48] As an example of human failings run riot—credulity, avarice, dishonesty, vanity—the South Sea Bubble provided plenty of material for Hogarth to exploit in one of his early, masterly, satirical prints.

[44] H. M. C., *The Manuscripts of his Grace the Duke of Portland*, vol. 5 (1899), p. 593.
[45] 'The Family Memoirs of the Rev. William Stukeley, M. D.', *Publications of the Surtees Society*, 73 (1880), pp. 59–60.
[46] H. M. C., *Portland*, vol. 5, p. 599.
[47] H. M. C., *Calendar of the Manuscripts of the Marquis of Bath*, vol. 3 (1908), p. 489.
[48] Defoe, *Tour*, p. 111.

The South Sea Bubble was not an isolated puff but the extreme example of a generic type. In 1720 'the Inhabitants of *England*, and the Dominions thereunto belonging, ran Mad, and Transfer'd all their Wealth and Substance to Foreigners and Strangers—In that Year was . . . *England* Infested with numerous and monstrous Beasts of uncommon Nature . . . *Men call'd them BUBBLES.*'[49] The rise and fall in the price of South Sea stock was in fact followed in less extreme form by Bank and East India stock prices. Moreover, about 190 projects were floated in the twelve months to August 1720, concerned with a wide range of activities, from insurance to fisheries to water supply. Most of these were joint-stock enterprises, attracting investors by means of wild claims of future profits. This proliferation of company formation was in fact merely the latest stage of periodic bouts of 'projecting' which had first occurred on a significant scale in the early 1690s when the closing off of trading opportunities at the start of war created idle funds that could not yet look to the national debt for a home. Some of those funds found a refuge or a grave in Exchange Alley—there was as yet no formal stock exchange, trades being made in coffee-houses, especially Jonathan's and Garraways. Between 1689 and 1695 the number of joint-stock companies rose from 11 to 93 and Houghton's weekly *Collection for the improvement of husbandry and trade* was soon recording the share price of some 64 companies. This growth of enterprise was associated with a proliferation of inventive speculations. Patents, which provided publicity for new undertakings as much as protection for (often spurious) technical developments, increased in number sharply. Indeed, the total of 61 granted in 1691–3 was not surpassed in any other three-year period until the 1760s. Between this efflorescence and the bursting of the South Sea Bubble was indeed '*The Projecting Age.*'[50]

Though much projecting was highly speculative, real lessons can be drawn from the efforts made. In the first place the wide range of enterprises—among them 'Companies for Mines . . . Diving of many sorts . . . Glass-Bottles . . . Salt-Petre, Sword-Blades; Waters . . . Wrecks . . . Lifting-Engines, Drawing-Engines . . . Lotteries . . . New Settlements . . . Convex-Lights . . . Fisheries Royal and Private'—reflects on the breadth of economic activity in England.[51] Such speculation also bears witness to the strength of a certain type of entrepreneurialism, of a willingness to step outside the ruts of accepted practice, and the existence of a nascent investing public, even if the skills of projectors were more akin to those of the showman than the hard-headed businessman and many investors were naive and poor risk assessors. Most,

[49] Anon., *The Battle of the Bubbles: Shewing their Several Constitutions, Alliances, Policies, and Wars; from their First Sudden Rise, to their Late Speedy Decay* (1720), pp. 3–4.
[50] [D. Defoe], *An Essay upon Projects* (1697), p. 1.   [51] *Angliae Tutamen*, pp. 4–5.

however, failed, and the economic benefits were few and far between. Of the 93 joint-stock companies in 1695, for example, only 21 were left by 1717. Most enterprise did not need that form or scale of capitalization—though the capital valuation of English joint-stock companies rose from £4m in 1695 to £8m in 1703, and to over £20m in 1717.

If projects attracted the unwary their failure also led to widespread criticism and considerable efforts at regulation. Bubbles might be seen as 'down-right Cheats in their first Projection, as well as in their Execution'.[52] The market in shares was often depicted as unnatural, fragile, and founded upon dishonesty. Stockjobbers might be described as 'ravens', 'monsters', or 'pick-pockets', and the Royal Exchange as a '*Den of Thieves*'.[53] Earning money through investments was still liable to censure: it was mere gambling; the redistribution of wealth away from old landed families was decried; and share prices were characterized as transitory and fictitious, suffering unfavourable comparisons with the 'real' or 'intrinsic' worth of land. At moments of crisis social conservatism and economic traditionalism was voiced loud and clear. One preacher, surveying the causes of bankruptcies, took as his text 1 Timothy 6:9: 'But they that will be Rich, fall into Temptation, and a Snare, and into many foolish and hurtful Lusts, which drown Men in Destruction and Perdition.'[54] Another thought people should aspire only to 'so much as is necessary to supply all his real, not imaginary wants, in the station in which Providence hath placed him'.[55] Moreover, when bubbles burst they were depicted as having a debilitating effect, supposedly bringing ordinary life to a standstill, though in practice much economic activity went on as before. For example, if the South Sea Bubble involved some redistribution of property (from inexperienced or ill-informed investors, including Alexander Pope, to those with more inside knowledge and skill, among them Walpole and the Princess of Wales) numbers of bankrupts did not increase dramatically in 1720 and 1721 nor were patterns of trade or industry markedly disrupted.

These hostile reactions were sufficiently potent to aid the development of a legislative framework which sought to control the excesses of the enterprise culture—and it is interesting to note that many of the MPs involved in constructing this framework were also concerned with questions of moral reform. Private lotteries, which had proliferated in the 1690s, were the subject of six

[52] A. Hammond, *A Modest Apology, Occasion'd by the Late Unhappy Turn of Affairs, with Relation to Publick Credit* (1721), p. 15.

[53] J. Trenchard and T. Gordon, *Cato's Letters: or, Essays on Liberty, Civil and Religious, and Other Important Subjects*, ed. R. Hamowy, 2 vols. (Indianapolis, 1995), vol. 1, pp. 44–5; [T. Baston], *Thoughts on Trade, and a Publick Spirit* (1716), p. 5.

[54] E. Calamy, *A Sermon at the Merchants Lecture in Salters Hall on Decemb. the 7th. 1708. Upon Occasion of the Many Late Bankrupts* (1709), p. 3.

[55] S. Bradford, *The Honest and the Dishonest Ways of Getting Wealth* (1720), pp. 6–7.

Acts passed by 1727. Much attention was also given to stockjobbers. An Act passed in 1697 (but later amended in 1708), complaining that 'the Number of . . . Stock-Jobbers are very much encreased', restricted their number to 100 under the authority of the City of London, with 12 places reserved for aliens and a further 12 for Jews.[56] But the most famous restriction was the Bubble Act, passed in 1720. Under its terms joint-stock companies could only be established by obtaining an Act of Parliament or Crown charter. Though the Act was itself part of the jobbery at the heart of the South Sea Bubble—it was passed on 11 June 1720, well before the Bubble burst, being an attempt to stop capital being attracted away from the South Sea Company—it had the effect of contributing to the end of the age of projects. The law remained in place until 1825, helping to ensure that speculative mania regarding business formation was reined in. In fact, public opinion was so coloured by the scale of the fraud and incredulity of the South Sea Bubble that the summer of 1720 was a defining moment of early financial capitalism. Not until the railway age in the 1840s and 1850s were bubbles to be blown which bear comparison with those of 1691–5 and 1719–20.

POLITICAL ECONOMIES

As the episode over the South Sea Bubble demonstrates, contemporaries had good reason to believe that the economy needed guarding and nurturing if it was to survive the assaults of nature and of man. Fires and storms, disease and drought, war and pirates forever threatened. Moreover, the century of population growth that had ended in the middle of the seventeenth century had put such pressure on resources as to produce periods of intense crisis and social dislocation, breeding an outlook of caution and concern not ease and optimism. But that outlook, which had led to many attempts to regulate the economy in search of order, regularity, predictability, and justice was slowly changing. There were still those who held fast to the spirit of interventionism, but they were increasingly faced by vociferous opponents and silent disobedience. In an environment of slow economic expansion, ready access to legislative authority, and the demands of war, England's political economy was significantly reconfigured.

In theory major areas of economic activity were regulated. Local authorities were able to set wage levels for a wide range of manual workers, establish the rates for the carriage of goods, order public markets, control the mobility of poor labourers from parish to parish under the terms of the poor laws, and determine the prices of bread and beer. The acquisition of skills was notionally

[56] 8 and 9 William III, c. 32.

strictly limited by the terms of the 1563 Statute of Artificers and the power of guilds. And trade was bound by customs duties, protective barriers, and the Navigation Acts. Moreover, a disorganized pile of legislation confined particular trades or activities and subjected some to the burden of the excise. In practice, however, such controls were often faltering or failing. Presentments for market offences at Manchester, for example, declined by over three-quarters between the 1680s and 1730s despite the fact that the town was rapidly growing. Likewise, in 1689 Hertfordshire renewed wage regulation for eighty-three jobs of 'servants' and continued to do so annually until 1708 when the practice ceased, probably because the complexities of the labour market and the problems of enforcement made such attempts a thankless and near impossible task. Similarly, an Act passed in 1692, complaining that wagoners and carriers had 'raised the prices of carriage of Goods in many places to excessive rates to the great injury of Trade', allowed JPs to set the prices for the land carriage of goods.[57] However, if some counties quickly did this others, such as Middlesex and Staffordshire, did not and others complied only with the letter and not the spirit of the law. Use of the settlement regulations to control the movement of the poor was also difficult when so many on the move were honest folk in genuine search of work and whose cheap labour might be eagerly bought by employers. And if in many places guild and apprentice regulation remained strong in others they had already lost or were in the process of losing the battle for control of the 'mystery' of the trade. In London guilds found it hard to police an ever-expanding labour force as it sprawled beyond the City, and some growing industrial cities, such as Birmingham, had never had guilds. Economic changes often encouraged those outside guilds, 'foreigners' and 'strangers', to undercut those within. In particular, guilds concerned with wholesale trades— merchants, drapers, and mercers for example—suffered marked decline in this period, paradoxically indicating strength rather than weakness in these areas of activity, with manufacturing trades such as tailoring and shoemaking going the same way after c.1720.

The failure of such attempts at control bear witness to the slow expansion of the economy beyond the bounds of customary expectations, the relative infrequency of the problems which had brought such measures into existence in the first place, and to the difficulties of checking the actions of millions of buyers and sellers by the efforts of a small number of volunteer good citizens. Despite these shortcomings, political intervention in the economy far from dying away after the Revolution was stimulated by the dramatically increased potential for legislative action, the need to fund the wars, and by a continuing concern to encourage and stabilize a 'just' economy. The availability of Parliament after

---

[57] 3 William and Mary, c. 12.

TABLE 11. *Number of statutes concerning communications, the economy, and finance, 1660–1727*

	Communications	Economy	Finance
1660–88	23	67	70
1689–1714	90	135	244
1714–27	114	161	100

Source: O. Ruffhead (ed.), *The Statutes at Large*, 18 vols. (1769–1800), vols. 3–5.

1688 was, as has been seen, enthusiastically exploited by promoters of infrastructural changes. Such an expansion was part of a wider process, as is made very clear by Table 11 which provides evidence of Acts passed regarding communications, the economy, and finance. Taking these three categories of legislation together, in the Restoration era there were on average not quite six Acts per year; during the reign of George I this had increased to nearly twenty-seven, prompting some to complain about the 'vast Number of Acts of Parliament'.[58] This was not simply because more Acts were being sought but also because a higher proportion of attempts were being successful due to the greater availability of and predictability in the legislative process. It is possible, moreover, that there was a shift in the locale of some activity within the political economy from the executive, notably the Privy Council, to the legislature. Nevertheless, Parliament's role in economic activity was significantly expanded following the Glorious Revolution.

Much legislative action was limited in scope, often concerning local schemes. It was, therefore, largely ad hoc and disconnected, the product of particular groups or interests attempting to deal with specific opportunities or problems that had only a narrow impact. In fact it proved remarkably difficult to frame a more general political economy, mercantilist or otherwise. Economic ideas were heterogeneous and there was no single dominant view of the nation's economic interest. Debate was often heated, agreement rare. Moreover, Parliament was available to a wide range of interests, its development after 1689 encouraging the formation of lobbies that often contested initiatives with such skill as to defeat general measures and which also constituted a powerful anti-monopolistic force. Such groups or interests were never settled, frequently transitory, but often powerful. Nor were such groups limited to the politically enfranchised. Villagers and labourers might oppose 'improvements' with such force that they could not be ignored. They might attempt to enforce customary rights, traditional levels of pay and prices, or attack developments

---

[58] Baston, *Thoughts on Trade*, p. 79.

TABLE 12. *Economy legislation, 1689–1727* (percentages)

	Acts	Fails
Agriculture and land	20	20
Manufacturing	16	14
Internal trade	19	30
External trade	42	30
Food processing, mining and quarrying	3	6
	100	100

Source: O. Ruffhead (ed.), *The Statutes at Large*, 18 vols. (1769–1800), vols. 3–5; J. Hoppit (ed.), *Failed Legislation, 1660–1800: Extracted from the Commons and Lords Journals* (1997), pp. 160–306.

such as turnpikes. Even when measures were enacted the means of enforcement might be inadequate, such that 'Customs in Trade, frequently make Jests of Acts of Parliament, and will go on their own way'.[59] Consequently, the foundation of the Board of Trade in 1696 did not aid economic regulation as significantly as might have been expected. Though largely concerned with colonial affairs it also cast its gaze on the domestic economy and for much of our period was active and industrious in an attempt to define a public policy for the national good. Its relative failure, however, was due to the power of lobbies and political jobbery. It helped provide information but framed relatively few measures which were put into practice.

Some patterns in the political economy can, none the less, be discerned. One indication is provided by the subject composition of legislation dealing with the economy (see Table 12), including not only Acts but failed attempts considered in Parliament. Contemporary preoccupation with overseas trade is clearly indicated by this table, which partly explains the willingness of some to characterize the economic policy of this era as 'mercantilist'. The development of overseas trade was certainly often seen by contemporaries as the best hope for economic growth and was always accorded a high priority, not least because 'There are no doubt new Countries and Lands yet to be discover'd, new Colonies to be planted'.[60] Yet the development of foreign trade was usually also linked to the opportunities it would afford the domestic economy—such as building new ships, exporting more textiles, and processing sugar—and policy here followed no single clear path.[61] Equally, it is clear that much economic legislation did not concern overseas trade and that contemporaries took a broad

[59] *Defoe's Review*, vol. 6, p. 23.

[60] [D. Defoe], *The History of the Principal Discoveries and Improvements, in the Several Arts and Sciences: Particularly the Great Branches of Commerce, Navigation, and Plantation* (1727), p. 306.

[61] See above, pp. 192–4; also D. C. Coleman (ed.), *Revisions in Mercantilism* (1969).

view of where improvements might be attempted. Particularly noteworthy is the concern with internal trade, that is to say questions of wholesale and retail distribution, prices, consumption, and weights and measures.

The definition and regularization of 'markets' was indeed subject to considerable debate in this period. Most importantly, the Union of 1707 brought Scotland within the navigation system and created a large free-trade area. This was no small change for, as Adam Smith later noted, 'the Division of Labour is limited by the Extent of the Market.'[62] Furthermore, the economies north and south of the border were now to use the same units of currency, weight, and measure. Legislators had for some time been concerned with the existence of regional variations in weights and measures (a bushel was 9 gallons at Abingdon, 16 at Stamford, and 32 at Carlisle for example), seeing them as a hindrance to trade and a means by which consumers were exploited, and continued through our period to attempt to establish uniformity. It says much, however, that a proposed general reform in 1697–8, when leave was given for a Bill 'for the better preventing Abuses in Weights and Measures', failed, whereas a number of reforms of the standards used for particular commodities were passed.[63] Both governors and governed were also frequently concerned that the transparency of the market mechanism was being clouded by the tricks of 'that vile and pernicious Set of Men, who are called in the Language of our Laws, *Forestallers*, *Regrators* and *Ingrossers*'.[64] In times of high prices the poor frequently implored the authorities to stop the export of grain or the alleged price manipulations of farmers and middlemen. Notions of economic justice and the need for morality in the marketplace were common. The land market also came under the gaze of legislators, concerned that legality of title was often uncertain. Again it is worth noting that attempts to establish nationwide land or deed registries met stiff opposition, five such Bills failing in the 1690s. Attention then turned to local measures, registries being established in Middlesex in 1709 and in the West and East Riding of Yorkshire in 1704 and 1708 respectively (though Bills for Berkshire, Wiltshire, Surrey, and Huntingdonshire were all defeated in this period).

One further major area of economic policy making concerned finance—accounting for some 344 Acts. Needs of war meant that measures relating to customs and excise, public credit and the national debt accounted for 86 per

---

[62] *An Inquiry into the Nature and Causes of the Wealth of Nations*, ed. R. H. Campbell and A. S. Skinner, 2 vols. (Oxford, 1979), vol. 1, p. 31.

[63] *Journal of the House of Commons*, 12 (1697–9), p. 5.

[64] *An Essay to Prove, that Regrators, Engrossers, Forestallers, Hawkers and Jobbers of Corn, Cattle, and other Marketable Goods, Provisions and Merchanidizes, are Destructive of Trade, Oppressive to the Poor, and a Common Nuisance to the Kingdom in General* (1718), p. 10. Forestalling was undertaken by middlemen, buying goods before they had reached the market; regrating was buying goods in a market and then selling them there at a higher price almost immediately; engrossing was monopoly wholesale purchasing to enable higher prices to be charged.

cent of these. Though their economic effect was indirect it was nevertheless considerable, and in the realm of private finance significant improvements were also attempted with regard to the money supply and relations between debtors and creditors. The massive recoinage of 1696 provided, for a time at least, badly needed reliable tokens of exchange. Usury laws continued to set maximum interest rates that could legally be charged in the private economy, 6 per cent per annum to 1714, 5 per cent thereafter, demonstrating the continued strength of the moral dimension to economic questions, though the laws were frequently evaded. In 1704 legal security was given to promissory notes, easily created credit instruments that were increasingly important to the business world. But most important of all relations between debtor and creditor were subject to close attention. Until 1706 the law assumed that bankrupts were criminals rather than victims, to be punished rather than understood. Contrary views had been developing for some time, with one author distinguishing 'the Honest, the hardly Honest, and the Down-right Knave'.[65] Some observed that debtors in general and bankrupts in particular were so legally emasculated that the spirit of enterprise was strangled. As Cary noted 'Misfortunes may and often do befal industrious Men, whose *Trades* have been very beneficial to the Nation, and to such a due Regard ought to be had'.[66] In 1706 the law was changed such that the politic, fraudulent, and dishonest bankrupt was threatened by the prospect of the hangman's noose, but honest, decent, and god-fearing bankrupts received protection from imprisonment, freedom from any obligation for the debts contracted before they failed, and a proportion of their estate as a reward for good faith and to help them start afresh. Lesser debtors, however, continued to face the very real prospect of imprisonment. Indeed, the spirit of legal certainty was further extended by the statutory abolition of debtors's sanctuaries in 1697—areas of popular customary authority to which debtors fled to escape imprisonment and the rule of law.[67] Though this law was only partially successful it demonstrated the unwillingness of Parliament to countenance uncertainty in the realm of debtor–creditor relations. On the other hand efforts to establish small-debt courts were usually dismissed in this period, legislators being unwilling to challenge the authority and interests of those local courts that already existed.

CONCLUSION

In the 1590s England's economy barely survived a series of crises born of harvest failure and long-term population growth. If a Malthusian catastrophe

---

[65] *Observations on the Bankrupts Bill: Occasion'd by the Many Misrepresentations, and Unjust Reflections, of Mr Daniel De Foe, in his Several Discourses on that Head* (1706), p. 11.
[66] Cary, *Essay on the State of England*, p. 37.   [67] See below p. 489–90.

failed fully to materialize fears were renewed afresh with the dislocation of the Civil Wars and Interregnum. Such dark days led to the exodus of hundreds of thousands to the New World. But that exodus, quite apart from providing a safety valve of sorts, gave some hint of the economy's inherent flexibility and potential—that labour was mobile, capital available, horizons broadening. The century after the Restoration was to see that potential gradually realized. It first became apparent in the area of overseas trade, with England managing to find a place alongside the Dutch in the European carrying trade and the French and Spanish in the transatlantic trades. Yet that success rested upon the productivity of the domestic economy which was inching its way towards higher levels of output and productivity. By 1727 England was one of the foremost economies in Europe. With jingoistic pride and some justice Defoe exclaimed that England was the most '*Diligent* Nation in the World, vast Trade, Rich Manufactures, mighty Wealth, universal Correspondence and happy Success has been constant Companions of *England*, and given us the Title of an Industrious People, and so in general we are.'[68]

Such economic progress was never felt to be secure, nor was it always welcomed. Advance was often painfully slow, sometimes reversed, and when attempts were made to provoke more rapid change the results, as in the South Sea Bubble, could be disastrous. It is significant that the period saw the first concerted debates over the ethical basis of the exchange economy in general and economic growth more particularly. Those debates still resonate. The complaint that 'The *Power of Money*, is grown *absolute, arbitrary,* and *irresistable*', was hardly peculiar to this period, for it may be found frequently through the eighteenth, nineteenth, and twentieth centuries.[69] If the benefits of economic growth were widely recognized, the perceived dangers of unbridled capitalism were also a commonplace. Attitudes to consumption, self-interest, investment, and risk taking were still, for the most part, commensurate with an economy limited largely to evolutionary change. None looked forward to or anticipated an industrial revolution. Yet with hindsight some sense can be gained here that England was indeed at a crossroads, between the early modern economy of limited opportunity and the modern economy of reasonably rapid and long-term growth. Over the next century the economy was to be transformed and those changes came not as a bolt from the blue but from clouds that had long been gathering.

[68] [D. Defoe], *Giving Alms no Charity, and Employing the Poor a Grievance to the Nation* (1704), p. 26.
[69] O. Dykes, *English Proverbs, with Moral Reflexions* (3rd edn., 1713), p. 62.

CHAPTER 11

The Wealth of the Country

Impressive though England's commercial and industrial prowess was, in good measure it rested upon the solid foundation of agricultural well-being. In a pre-modern economy, with land such a central resource, agriculture was bound to play a vital part in the economy as a whole, not only in supplying food but also in providing industry with a wide range of raw materials (such as wool, leather, tallow, and hops), the economy as a whole with capital and credit, and industrial workers with occasional employment in the fields. Many of the uncertainties of life were caused by the rhythm of the seasons and the impact of good and bad harvest on prices, employment, and wages. Yet considerable as these influences were contemporaries were more impressed by the ways in which patterns of landownership played upon social and political structures. Famously in his *Two Treatises* John Locke explored the relationship between the distribution of property and the development of political authority, concluding that 'The great and *chief end* thereof, of Mens uniting into Commonwealths, and putting themselves under Government, *is the Preservation of their Property*.'[1]

Without doubt, by the early eighteenth century English landowners were highly adept not only at preserving but in extending their control over property. Yet in the heady and confused days of the 1650s such an achievement had looked very remote, so frayed had the relationship between property and power become during the Republican experiment. Though the Restoration managed to turn the clock back, both returning land to many who had been dispossessed and re-establishing most of the traditional links between landownership and political authority, from the 1670s renewed concern over the constitutional balance between the monarch and Parliament cast fresh doubts upon the security of that feat. In large measure those doubts stimulated the conservative elements of the Glorious Revolution. In 1688 and 1689 great care was taken to ensure that property was not questioned let alone threatened, and one important consequence of the rise of parliamentary government after that date was

[1] J. Locke, *Two Treatises of Government*, ed. P. Laslett (Cambridge, 1991), pp. 350–1.

to give property owners predictable, privileged, and potent access to political authority. Not only could they now keep a watching brief on the executive, but they were able to utilize the legislative process in pursuit of often highly personal ends, be it improving a river or reordering their estates.

Today the era from the Glorious Revolution to American independence in 1776 can appear to mark the apogee of landed power, a period of calm authority between the political disturbances that bedevilled the Stuarts and the new political and social challenges associated with the industrial revolution. Nothing seems to encapsulate that supremacy so much as grand classical country houses surrounded by 'natural' but deliberately evocative landscape gardens, creations which were both domestic settings and imposing pieces of social theatre. Yet the achievements of landed society were more muddled and contingent than might at first appear. The gentry, great and small, may have often paid homage at the shrine of tradition and revelled in inequality and conservatism, but they also worshipped at the altar of wealth accumulation. England had a commercial not a feudal elite, who viewed land both as an economic resource to be vigorously exploited and as a status indicator. Consequently it did not turn its back on opportunities and changes, but frequently embraced them. Wealth by itself was not enough, income had also to be generated.

THE LIE OF THE LAND

In 1700 the population of England was a little over 5 million, over 80 per cent of whom lived in the countryside. Though perhaps as many as a third of rural inhabitants were not directly employed in the fields, agriculture was never the less the mainstay of England's economy. The rhythms of the farming calendar and the well-being of crop and stock were felt far and wide. The fortunes of agriculture affected the employment prospects of many and the standard of living of all. Most contemporaries saw this as only right and proper. Land was permanent, natural, and god-given, 'the Earth being the very Womb that bears all, and the Mother that must nourish and maintain all.'[2] By contrast other forms of wealth were man-made, transient, and whimsical. Moreover, despite the basic uncertainties surrounding an agricultural economy that was fundamentally subservient to natural forces it was also claimed that 'The Soil here is so very fruitful' and 'The Air of this Island is so temperate'.[3] Indeed, England's agriculture, just like her trade and industry, was believed to be peculiarly

[2] L. Meager, *The Mystery of Husbandry* (1697), p. 3.
[3] [T. Cox], *Magna Britannia et Hibernia, Antiqua & Nova. Or, a New Survey of Great Britain*, 6 vols. (1720–31), vol. 1, p. 3.

favoured, able even in bad years to produce enough food to avoid serious short-ages, plentiful raw materials for many industries, and impressive amounts of wealth accumulation.

The benefits of benign conditions of soil, relief, and climate were, of course, not enjoyed everywhere. Gregory King guessed that the acreage of England and Wales was 39 millions, with 11 millions given over to arable, 10 millions to pasture and meadow, 3 millions to woods and coppices, 3 millions to forests, parks, and commons, and 2 millions for housing, gardens, rivers, lakes, roads, and ways, leaving 10 millions as barren heaths, moors, and mountains. Though these figures provide only rough orders of magnitude they suggest that only about two-thirds of land was given over to productive cultivation. Much land was too rough, too infertile, too wet, or too dry to be profitably farmed within the limits of available technology. Equally, regional variations in the natural environment directly influenced farming patterns. In particular, pastoral farm-ing predominated in the wetter west and cooler north, where ploughing was more taxing, crops less likely to ripen, and harvesting more at threat from rain. However, such a depiction is an over-simplification. Soil and relief might change from one side of a parish to another, from hill to vale. Nor could pas-toral and arable be rigidly separated. Everywhere, growing crops and raising livestock went hand in hand. Indeed, the use of animal manure was ubiquitous given the absence of artificial fertilizers and the considerable difficulties of improving soil by spreading marl, seaweed, ashes, or industrial by-products. Moreover, so great was the pull of the London market that providing it with fresh meat, milk, fruit, and vegetables impacted upon significant parts of the rural economy, even beyond the south-east. Together these factors produced a map of agricultural regions of bewildering complexity, of roughly thirty-one combinations of eighteen basic farming types. It is little wonder that contem-porary travellers were impressed by the variety of England's landscapes and of the extent of regional specialization in agriculture that they encountered. For example, Cambridgeshire was 'almost wholly a corn county', the heathlands of Surrey 'a sandy desert', Wiltshire and Gloucestershire were 'full of large feeding farms, which we call dairies', and in Leicestershire were 'the largest sheep and horses in England . . . most of the gentlemen are graziers'.[4] Kent was fast becoming the garden of England, Cheddar and Cheshire were famous for their cheeses, the best wool came from Lincolnshire and the Downs, and Herefordshire was a land of hop bines.

Such variety makes generalizations about the nature and fortunes of the agrarian economy hard to sustain. However, it is clear that most of English

[4] D. Defoe, *A Tour Through the Whole Island of Great Britain*, ed. P. Rogers (Harmondsworth, 1978), pp. 100, 156, 264, and 408.

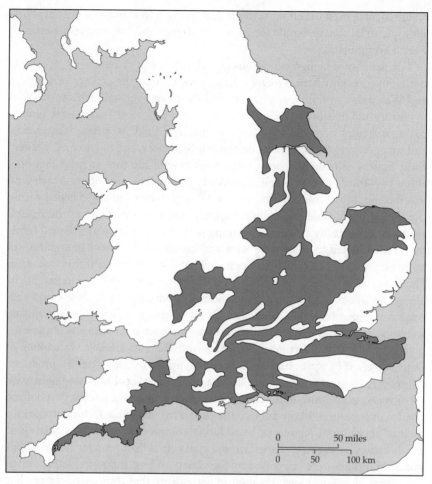

MAP 5. England's arable farming regions
After J. Thirsk (ed.), *The Agrarian History of England and Wales: vol. 5,*
1640–1750, pt. 1, Regional Farming Systems (Cambridge, 1984), p. xx.

Note: This simplified map shows areas where arable farming predominated, the remaining
areas being either largely pastoral or mixed.

agriculture produced for the market, even though some subsistence farming
survived—from villagers grazing a few animals on common land to the home
farm supplying a great house with herbs, fruit, vegetables, eggs, and meat.
Similarly, cultivated land was mainly privately owned, though its social distribution is uncertain. Perhaps 15–20 per cent of that land was held by the great
landowners, some 45–50 per cent by the middling and lesser gentry, 25–33 per

TABLE 13. *Indices of agricultural prices* (1640–1749 = 100)

	Grains	Other field crops	Livestock	All agricultural products
1640–79	107	96	91	99
1680–1709	98	101	105	101
1710–49	94	104	107	101
% change 1640–79 to 1710–49	−12.1	+8.3	+17.6	+2.0

Source: P. J. Bowden, 'Agricultural Prices, Wages, Farm Profits, and Rents', in J. Thirsk (ed.), *Agrarian History of England and Wales: vol. 5, pt. 2, 1640–1750, Agrarian Change* (Cambridge, 1985), p. 1.

cent by yeomen, family farmers, and other small owners, and 5–10 per cent by the Church and Crown. These shares were, however, slowly changing. Over the previous two centuries there had been a significant decline in the share of land held by the Church and Crown because of the Reformation and royal indebtedness. Though purchasers of these lands might be small or large landowners it was the strengthening of the position of substantial estates that was particularly marked. Great estates had existed since time out of mind, but they and the social inequalities they represented gained a heightened prominence in this period. Indeed, between the beginning and the end of the eighteenth century the great landowners and gentry probably accumulated a further 10 per cent of the nation's land. The existence of an active land market provided the opportunities for the purchase or expansion of estates and, given the high price land commanded, that meant those with significant cash reserves—be they the middling and upper gentry or those who had succeeded in the world of business. Land prices, which had reached a low point in the 1680s rose markedly in the 1720s, not least because the great demand for estates in 1720 provoked by the wealth transfers of the South Sea Bubble shattered notions of customary and near stable land prices. Whereas previously prices had usually been around twenty years purchase (that is twenty times the annual rental value) by 1730 estates were typically being sold for twenty-five years purchase.

Land prices reflected both its expected income and the balance between the amount coming up for sale and the extent of demand for it. The first factor mainly depended upon the prices of agricultural goods and associated rent levels. Table 13 provides an indication of price trends across the century from the middle of the seventeenth to the middle of the eighteenth century. Though agricultural prices as a whole were stable from 1650 to 1750 there were significant falls in the prices of grains and rises in the price of livestock. If the latter took place when the livestock population was rising, which was almost certainly the case, then this provided one stimulus for increasing land prices. However, there is also evidence that in the early eighteenth century demand for land was increasing, especially after 1713 with reductions in the burden of the land tax and of alternative investment opportunities in the national debt. More generally, purchasing power was enhanced by developments in the mortgage market through the late seventeenth and early eighteenth centuries and by the accumulation of investible funds in society as a whole, especially those outside the ranks of the landed gentry.

Land purchase was not the only reason for the relative strength of great estates by the early eighteenth century. Another was provided by landowners' use of legal devices to hinder heirs from selling all or parts of the inheritance. Most usually this took the form of 'strict settlements', by which heirs were made little more than life tenants, bound to hand on their estate intact to their own heir. Such settlements were relatively novel, only becoming common after the Restoration—in Kent and Northamptonshire, where they were especially common, the proportion of estates so settled rose from 63 per cent between 1660 and 1680 to 80 per cent between 1701 and 1720. Elsewhere proportions were somewhat less than this, and strict settlements were more common among the greater than the lesser landowners. Such settlements were, in fact, produced by the same attitudes which put such store in male primogeniture, of the inheritance of most or all of the estate by the oldest surviving son. Indeed, at times this concern with preserving a family's estate and name was little short of obsessional. Of course, patriarchs could not see into the future and heirs might fall so seriously into debt that an estate could be saved only by amputating an outlying limb. Nor did families always produce the heirs they wanted. In fact, for reasons which are very unclear, England's landed elite suffered something of a demographic crisis in the first half of the eighteenth century. At heart this crisis arose because so many avoided marriage. For example, among the children of peers born in the last quarter of the seventeenth century 22 per cent of men and 24 per cent of women never married. Moreover, as some marriages failed to produce children direct heirs were often lacking. So, for example, of the ninety-three Yorkshire baronetages created between 1611 and 1800 only forty-two survived into the nineteenth century. Similarly, for those owners of large estates in Hertfordshire, Northamptonshire, and Northumberland born in the second half of the seventeenth century some 41 per cent had no male heir. So serious was this lack of heirs that nationally the number of peers, baronets, and knights sank by 30 per cent in the first six decades of the eighteenth century, a pattern that appears to have been repeated among the gentry class as a whole. In such circumstances estates might be broken up or passed on to a daughter or distant heir. The frequency of the latter courses is evidenced by the growth in double or even triple-barrelled names, where heirs were obliged to perpetuate a family name that was in danger of dying out. Indeed, surname substitution, which was always rare on the Continent, became common in England only after 1688. The difficult struggle to maintain estates intact is also evidenced in dramatic fashion by the proliferation of Acts to allow the sale or reorganization of estates. There had been exactly 200 such Acts between 1660 and 1688, accounting for 36 per cent of all legislation. But between 1689 and 1714 there were 728, or 42 per cent of the total. It was little wonder that one MP 'inveighed much against private bills and the many mischiefs arising therefrom . . . and this House was taken up with private bills to destroy the settlement of estates in England' or that the House of Lords, worried about the amount of time being taken up, introduced standing orders in 1706 to stem the tide.[5]

Large estates were usually split into a number of farms and worked by tenant farmers employing wage labourers. Indeed, the relationship between landlord and tenant was central to the fortunes of English agriculture. Short-term leasehold arrangements had been gaining in popularity through the sixteenth and seventeenth centuries as landlords sought greater flexibility to set rents than was possible under copyhold (where land might be held for three lives). Fewer and fewer farming decisions were being made in manorial courts or collectively, more and more individually. Not least, open fields, where a strong spirit of co-operative endeavour survived, were gradually being enclosed long before the advent of large-scale parliamentary enclosure in the 1760s. Slowly market forces were intruding more directly into the agricultural sphere, an intrusion evidenced and in some measure brought about by the ever-growing significance of the estate steward. Such men were central pivots of agrarian society, the arbiter between landlord and tenant but holding a position which ultimately rested upon their ability to maximize an estate's potential. Stewards sought out good tenants and good practice, perhaps using tenancy agreements to prompt farmers to adopt something new and hopefully more profitable. Consequently they brought a degree of professional expertise to the countryside: 'It is not only necessary that a Steward should be a good Accomptant, but also that he should have a tolerable degree of Skill in *Mathematicks*, Surveying, Mechanicks, and Architecture'.[6] Rental incomes might be increased both by the stick and the carrot. Thus if the steward to the Duke of Norfolk was 'very remarkable for having raised the estate, to the great oppression and discontent of the tenants', others were gentler, allowing rent arrears to mount,

[5] *The Parliamentary Diary of Narcissus Luttrell, 1691–1693*, ed. H. Horwitz (Oxford, 1972), p. 323. The flow of such Acts may also have been reduced by the passage of 7 Anne, *c*.19, 'An Act to Enable Infants who are Seised or Possessed of Estates in Fee, in Trust, or by Way of Mortgage, to Make Conveyances of such Estates.'

[6] E. Laurence, *The Duty of a Steward to his Lord* (1727), p. 50.

recommending landlords undertake capital investment, or living among the farmers.[7] Either way, what evidence there is, and it is very limited, suggests that rents were rising on trend through the period, though there were years when farms were hard to let.

Far from all agriculture took place on great estates. The minor gentry owned much land and many landlords among them undertook day-to-day management of their estates, negotiated directly with their tenants, and rode with them to hounds. There was also a class of owner-occupiers, yeomen farmers or husbandmen, with enough land to support themselves and produce only a small surplus for sale. Then there were the villagers whose labour supported the whole edifice of landed society. Many of these were literally landless, unable to maintain themselves except by finding work. But many had some access to commons or wastes, often poor land subject to customary rather than profit-orientated practices. They enjoyed a degree of independence from the tyranny of the market. Such a life, often hard and insecure, frequently alarmed those of polite sentiments, challenging their faith in private property and order. From that perspective commoners lived 'in a very mean, low condition; at hunger and ease, for the most part; and for the best of them, they live an uncomfortable, moiling, and drudging kind of Life; what they get they spend . . . and this kind of miserable living they seem to be contented with, because they cannot better themselves.'[8] Another asserted that 'Commoners or Cottagers are generally Savage and Paganish'.[9] Faced by such hostility and by the rising tide of commercialization many commoners had to work hard to protect their way of life. If the odds were stacked against them they were, none the less, often able to struggle long and hard for their independence.[10]

THE FORTUNES OF AGRICULTURE

Soon after the Restoration contemporary descriptions of agricultural improvement began to proliferate and by the early eighteenth century had reached significant proportions. If many stressed the scope that remained for the spread of best practice many noted considerable advances already achieved. A typical eulogy claimed that 'The Improvement of Land, and the Study of Agriculture, have greatly contributed to render our Nation famous above all other Countries'; and another that 'experience has made the present age wiser, and

[7] 'The Journal of Mr. John Hobson, Late of Dodworth Green', *Publications of the Surtees Society*, 65 (1875), pp. 261–2.

[8] Meager, *Mystery of Husbandry*, p. 138.

[9] T. Nourse, *Campania Foelix: or, a Discourse of the Benefits and Improvements of Husbandry* (1700), p. 102.

[10] See below, pp. 359 and 486–90.

more skilful in husbandry'.[11] Such views were, of course, touched by a spirit of patriotism and separating fact from fiction is not always easy. It is particularly difficult to gain a quantitative sense of the scale of changes in output and productivity, for, apart from some runs of data of prices and the grain trade, only fragments of statistical evidence, whose representativeness is not always certain, have survived. All estimates are necessarily rough and tentative therefore.

Crop yields provide one of the best ways of estimating agricultural growth, and they suggest that land productivity had been rising slowly since the sixteenth century and continued to do so until the onset of somewhat more rapid growth in the nineteenth century. In Lincolnshire average yields of wheat in 1650 were 15.8 bushels per acre and a century later 20.0, while in Norfolk and Suffolk the figures were 14.5 and 20.0, giving rates of growth of 0.24 and 0.32 per cent per annum. Because those counties were far from backward, with many farmers following the most productive methods available, national rates of growth were probably somewhat lower. However, there is good evidence that not only productivity but also output was growing. Food shortages were very occasional, the product of individual bad harvests rather than structural inadequacies in the agrarian sector. Moreover, the evidence from the grain trade is that cereal crop output was growing more quickly than domestic demand. Indeed, at the time there was much more concern with low corn prices than with food shortages, a concern that, as Table 13 showed, was fully justified. Landowners and legislators looked about for means of soaking up rising corn production. One response, adopted in 1690, was to encourage the use of malted corn in making spirits by means of preferential duties. Though this helped to spark the gin age of the 1720s and 1730s, probably of greater significance were attempts to stimulate the export of corn. In 1672 the government introduced a system of bounties to encourage the export of wheat, rye, barley, and malt when their domestic price fell beneath certain specified levels. In 1689 the 'corn laws' were re-established, 'Forasmuch as it hath been found by experience, that the exportation of corn and grain into foreign parts, when the price thereof is at a low rate in this kingdom, hath been a great advantage not only to the owners of land, but to the trade of this kingdom in general.'[12] Good statistics survive of the scale of England's export of corn after 1700.

After 1760, with a rising population demanding more and more food, the export of grain dwindled and imports mounted. Indeed, the increasing plenty of the first six decades of the eighteenth century stand out as a highly unusual period in England's pre-modern agrarian history. Such was the extent of this

---

[11] R. Bradley, *A General Treatise of Husbandry and Gardening*, 3 vols. (1724), vol. 1, p. iv; Defoe, *Tour*, p. 193.

[12] 1 William and Mary, c. 12, 'An Act for Encouraging the Export of Corn'.

TABLE 14. *Decennial exports of English corn, 1700–1764* (in million quarters)

	Wheat and flour	Barley and malt	Rye	Total
1700–9	1.05	1.29	0.49	2.83
1710–19	1.05	2.32	0.32	3.69
1720–29	1.15	2.86	0.25	4.26
1730–39	2.94	2.21	0.16	5.31
1740–49	2.89	3.05	0.67	6.61

Source: A. H. John, 'English Agricultural Improvement and Grain Exports, 1660–1765', in D. C. Coleman and A. H. John (eds.), *Trade, Government and Economy in Pre-Industrial England: Essays Presented to F. J. Fisher* (1976), p. 49.

relative abundance that in most years in the 1720s grain exports accounted for over 10 per cent of the value of all other domestic exports. Much of this trade went via ports such as King's Lynn and Great Yarmouth, a good deal of it towards Holland, France, and the Iberian peninsula. At times so great was flow that there were worries about the supply of the domestic market. For example, at Colchester in 1696 'the Dutch factors coming to buy up great quantities of corn, the people began to mutiny'; and in 1725 it was reported from Romsey in Hampshire that 'The Mob has lately committed some Outrages here, and at several other Places . . . as at Winchester, Sarum, Southampton, and in the Isle of Wight, on Account of Corn being bought up for Exportation.'[13]

Estimating the output and productivity of other areas of agriculture is very difficult. Little can be done with regard to crops such as fruit, vegetables, and hops, and it is only possible to speculate about the course of animal husbandry. There is no doubt that animals were a commonplace, as Gregory King's wild speculations in Table 15 suggest. It is possible that the value of the output of meat and dairy farming in 1700 was about £19m, or just under a half the total value of agricultural output. For 1750 it has been estimated that this figure had risen by 40 per cent to £26.7m, or by 0.8 per cent per annum.[14] Given the relative buoyancy of livestock prices across the period 1660 to 1760 this rate of growth, which appears to have been higher than that achieved in arable production, reflects well on the flexibility and market orientation of contemporary farmers, though it is very unlikely that changes in the trend of output, productivity, and prices were immediately apparent to them.

[13] N. Luttrell, *A Brief Historical Relation of State Affairs from September 1678 to April 1714*, 6 vols. (Oxford, 1857), vol. 2, p. 629; *Mist's Weekly Journal*, 14 August 1725.

[14] These figures are only suggestions and depend upon many assumptions. They are taken from M. Overton, *Agricultural Revolution in England: The Transformation of the Agrarian Economy, 1500–1850* (Cambridge, 1996), p. 75.

TABLE 15. *Gregory King's estimate of English livestock, 1695*

	Annual increase	Total stock
Beeves and calves	800,000	4,500,000
Sheep and lambs	3,200,000	11,000,000
Pigs	1,300,000	2,000,000
Deer and fawns	20,000	100,000
Goats and kids	10,000	50,000
Hares and leverets	12,000	50,000
Rabbits and conies	2,000,000	1,000,000
Horses, foals, and asses	100,000	1,200,000

Note: These figures are no more than one person's guesses and might be badly in error. King failed to provide totals for geese, chickens, turkeys, and ducks. He valued their annual increase and total stock at £600,000 and £460,000 respectively, and thought 'tame fowl' was worth 6d. per pound.

Source: J. Thirsk and J. P. Cooper (eds.), *Seventeenth Century Economic Documents* (Oxford, 1972), p. 783.

What evidence there is suggests that both arable and pastoral farming were slowly growing in terms both of output and productivity in this period. Certainly it would seem that English agricultural workers were becoming increasingly efficient. Though total population doubled between 1600 and 1800, the number who could be classed as 'rural agricultural' rose by only 9 per cent despite the fact that food imports were still negligible. Thus output per worker in agriculture rose by perhaps 75 per cent across the two centuries, or annually by 0.3 per cent. Within Europe only Holland was able to match this. Almost everywhere else rising population growth was only possible by putting more and more workers into the fields and increasing the amount of land under cultivation. But in England growth involved rising output per worker and per acre. Consequently, the so-called 'agricultural revolution' of late eighteenth- and early nineteenth-century England evolved out of an agrarian structure that was already highly distinctive and had made significant strides forward. Moreover, agricultural rates of growth in the early eighteenth century are comparable to those in the industrial and service sectors explored in the previous chapter. In total England's whole economy continued to inch forward after 1689, though given agriculture's relative significance its rates of growth were especially influential.

English agricultural progress if marked was far from steady or universal. Variations in the weather played a particularly significant role, the 1690s particularly standing out as a decade of relative cold in a wider period that has been labelled the 'Little Ice Age'.[15] One powerful way of demonstrating such

[15] See M. Overton, 'Weather and Agricultural Change in England, 1660–1739', *Agricultural History*, 63 (1989), pp. 77–88.

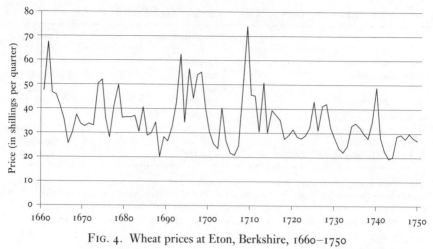

FIG. 4. Wheat prices at Eton, Berkshire, 1660–1750

Source: B. R. Mitchell, *British Historical Statistics* (Cambridge, 1988), pp. 754–5

variations is to look at fluctuations in the prices of agricultural goods, for ex-ample the course of wheat prices at Eton in Berkshire shown in Figure 4. Though prices in other parts of the country did not necessarily follow the same path as those at Eton, and prices of other agricultural products would have had their own history, Figure 4 usefully shows the high degree of fluctuations experienced between 1690 and 1715 and, by implication, the irresistible power of natural forces and the inelasticity of demand for basic foodstuff. Prices in over half of the years in that quarter century were either unusually high or unusually low, with prices appearing to have been more erratic than in the surrounding decades. Such swings provided a very unsettling environment, not only for farmers but also for labourers and landowners. As those years coincided with two great wars, when so much labour was mobilized and the land tax was invariably high, the agricultural sector felt not the warmth of steady if slow expansion but the chill of uncertainty. Nor were the only threats those posed by the weather, for farmers always feared being overrun by diseases and vermin that they were virtually powerless to prevent. In the spring of 1699 'a Coughing Disease gott among ye Horses (Universally thro'out ye Nation), of wch divers dyed'; nine years later there was 'a great distemper, almost universall among the horses'; and in 1714 cattle distemper reached England from the continent and was contained only by close control over markets and the destruction of infected herds—in Middlesex, Essex, and Surrey, where the disease was most common, 5,418 cattle and 439 calves were destroyed, for which farmers were compensated by the authorities.[16] The list of animals threatening crops, livestock, and stores was very long, with manuals urging farmers to wage war and extirpate the enemy: foxes were 'very prejudicial', badgers 'almost as pernicious', and moles 'noxious'; '*Crows, Ravens, Rooks* and *Magpies* are great annoyances to Corn'; and January was the time to 'Set Traps to destroy Vermin . . . Take Fowls, destroy Sparrows in Barns, and . . . kill Bullfinches'.[17]

Farmers looked out on fields and markets, therefore, which if wholly familiar were far from being predictable. Little wonder that 'The farmers in the country seem to be generally mighty sort of grumbling people that are never contented but always complaining.'[18] Moreover, because they could never be sure of their income flow they were as likely to be risk avoiders or risk sharers as risk takers. Hence in many places open field farming, where farmers might have several strips of land in different parts of a parish, retained a degree of popularity because it offered some equalization both of opportunity and risk. A spirit of communality and shared endeavour remained in places. Near Ashridge in Hertfordshire, for example, it was customary that 'when a stranger comes into a farm for the neighbours to come and assist him with their ploughs to plough his ground for the first time.'[19] Nor was the relationship between landlord and tenant farmer one solely resting upon an inflexible monetary calculus. When prices were low farmers might struggle to pay their rent through no fault of their own. Evelyn noted how in 1703 'Corne & Provisions on the sudaine so cheap that farmers are unable to pay their rents' and in 1724 one landowner reported that amongst farmers 'The cry of want of money is grievous'.[20] In such circumstances landlords who pressed too hard might find farms impossible to let, such that stewards and landlords often allowed arrears to mount or even to abate. Labourer, farmer, and landlord, whose interests were so often different, were therefore also tied together, their fortunes often rising and falling as one.

HUSBANDING RESOURCES

Despite the ups and downs that were such an inescapable feature of the agrarian economy the fact remains that gradually the sector slowly expanded

[16] *The Rector's Book, Clayworth Notts.*, ed. H. Gill and E. L. Guilford (Nottingham, 1910), p. 127; *The Marlborough–Godolphin Correspondence*, ed. H. L. Snyder, 3 vols. (Oxford, 1975), vol. 2, p. 966.

[17] J. Mortimer, *The Whole Art of Husbandry, or, the Way of Managing and Improving of Land* (1707), pp. 241, 242, 247, and [611]; Laurence, *Duty of a Steward*, p. 32.

[18] *The Diary of Dudley Ryder, 1715–1716*, ed. W. Matthews (1939), p. 112.

[19] *Ryder Diary*, p. 99.

[20] *The Diary of John Evelyn*, ed. E. S. de Beer, 6 vols. (Oxford, 1955), vol. 5, p. 528; *The Letters and Papers of the Banks Family of Revesby Abbey, 1704–1760*, ed. J. W. F. Hill, Lincoln Record Society, 45 (1952), p. 82.

and that such growth was partly the result of productivity gains consequent upon changes in the distribution of land and in what the land was used for. Responsibility for those changes was divided between farmers and landlords, with the latter taking a leading role. Indeed, it became common to celebrate and encourage the spirit of innovation among gentlemen. If it was widely agreed 'That Lands may be Improved, no Body can contradict' it was also claimed, with some snobbery and some truth, that 'From Farmers we may collect the common Practice in Husbandry . . . but it is from Gentlemen, who have given their Time and Thoughts to Improvements, that we can hope for the most useful Advices, founded upon Experiments they have made, from their Reason and Knowledge of natural Philosophy.'[21] As this hints, a gentlemanly interest in husbandry was rooted in the same intellectual and cultural soil that had produced the 'Scientific Revolution', and is indicated by a concern with agricultural issues in the Royal Society's *Philosophical Transactions*, Houghton's part-work publications, a slew of books and pamphlets on improvement, as well as the existence of 'several curious Societies of ingenious Men'.[22] Of course, in practice only some landowners and farmers strode boldly ahead. William Watkins of Myddle embodied the ideal, who though 'a person well educated, and fitt for greater employment' found 'his chief delight . . . in good husbandry, which is indeed, a delightfull calling', and set about transforming his farm, clearing it of weeds, marling the land, constructing new farm buildings, and employing 'many day labourers'.[23]

Perhaps the area of greatest concern to landowners was to enlarge their domain. Landowners expended much effort upon consolidating and extending their estates, introducing leasehold at the expense of copyhold, and enclosing open field and common land. These efforts were not new in this period, but the last of them in particular was championed more powerfully than ever before. Enclosure, the fencing or ditching of land while also bringing it more completely under individual proprietorship, had been generally condemned in the sixteenth century, both by the landed and the landless, not least because it was associated with the spread of sheep farming, which required less labour than arable farming—in More's famous depiction 'Your sheep . . . have become so greedy and fierce that they devour men themselves'.[24] But by 1700 there had been a marked change in opinion among the propertied, with enclosure often seen as a central means by which agriculture might be improved. It was asserted that 'common or open Fields . . . are great Hindrances to a

[21] G. Jacob, *The Country Gentleman's Vade Mecum* (1717), p. 1; Bradley, *General Treatise*, vol. 3, part 3, p. 48.
[22] Bradley, *General Treatise*, vol. 3, preface (no pagination).
[23] R. Gough, *The History of Myddle*, ed. D. Hey (Harmondsworth, 1981), p. 111.
[24] T. More, *Utopia*, ed. G. M. Logan and R. M. Adams (Cambridge, 1989), p. 18.

publick Good', for allegedly the system of manorial control and strip farming was resistant to change as well as wasteful of time and effort. Enclosure, by contrast, was said to stimulate growth and prosperity because private owner-ship supposedly encouraged responsibility, industry, and innovation, to the extent that one champion exaggeratedly claimed that '*Inclosure* encreases the Rent of Land sometimes Tenfold'.[25] Yet even advocates of enclosure recognized that it could not be done 'without prejudice to the Poor'.[26] Not least, worries about de-population remained. Nourse calculated that 600 acres of common land might support 120 people, 'which if inclos'd would not amount to above Eight Farms, each Farm containing about Seven Persons'. Further he and others supported the legal rights of commoners against 'private advantage', and argued the need for full compensation when such rights were altered.[27]

Though many gentlemen extolled the benefits of enclosure, it is striking that the period saw very little use of parliamentary statute to bring it about, despite, as has been seen, their extensive use of that route to reorder their estates and promote infrastructural developments. The first parliamentary act for enclos-ure had, in fact, been passed in 1604, but between 1660 and 1727 fewer than fifty more had been passed whereas between 1760 and 1800 there were over 1,800. It is possible that the propagandists for enclosure were in a minority and that the points Nourse made found wide support. If so, then some sense is gained of the limited authority of the landed elite. It was also the case that enclosure could encounter considerable popular opposition, perhaps with fences being destroyed or a landlord's ricks set ablaze. Defoe reported

an eminent contest here [Tring] between Mr Guy, and the poor of the parish . . . Mr Guy presuming upon his power, set up his pales, and took in a large parcel of open land . . . the cottagers and farmers opposed it, by their complaints . . . but finding he went on with his work . . . they rose upon him, pulled down his banks, and forced up his pales, and carried away the wood, or set it on a heap and burnt it; and this they did several times, till he was obliged to desist. After some time he began again, offering to treat with the people, and to give them any equivalent for it. But that not being satis-factory, they mobbed him again.[28]

With so little enclosure taking place by act of Parliament, that which did take place did so by private agreement, leaving a clear enough imprint upon the countryside but only a faint impression upon the sources. It is reasonably

[25] J. Laurence, *A New System of Agriculture: being a Complete Body of Husbandry and Gardening* (1726), p. 45.

[26] Meager, *Mystery of Husbandry*, p. 139.

[27] Nourse, *Campania Foelix*, p. 100; *Luttrell Parliamentary Diary*, pp. 409–10, which reports the debate over and defeat of a Bill to enclose a part of the New Forest.

[28] Defoe, *Tour*, p. 349. The encloser was Henry Guy, 1631–1710, Secretary to the Treasury 1679–88 and 1691–5. Following a charge of bribery, he later enjoyed a spell in the Tower.

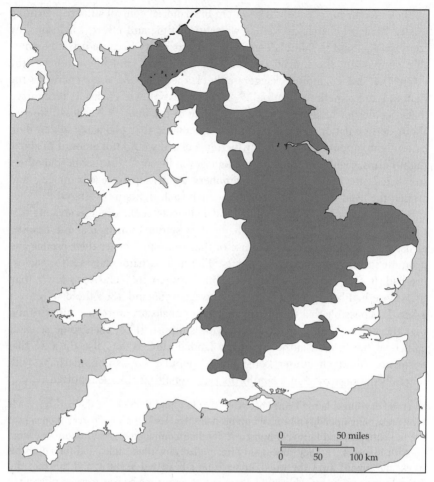

MAP 6. The main areas of open-field farming, *c*.1700
After E. C. K. Gonner, *Common Land and Inclosure* (1912).

Note: This simplified map shows areas where common or open field predominated.

certain that a little over a quarter of England's surface area was enclosed by Act
after 1740. Quite when the remaining three-quarters was enclosed by agreement is, however, far less clear, the process being spread out over many centuries and being heavily influenced by local circumstances. In particular, those
counties where open fields were common saw the least enclosure. Some counties, such as Lancashire, Cheshire, Cornwall, Devon, Kent, and Essex, were
already extensively enclosed by the end of the seventeenth century. Elsewhere
the pattern is uncertain. Despite the claim made in 1726 that 'great Quantities
of Ground . . . have been of late inclosed and are daily inclosing', in the south

Midlands, for example, it has been estimated that only 5 per cent of land was enclosed between 1675 and 1749, though in County Durham some 21 per cent of land was enclosed in the century 1650–1750.[29] Much depended upon the initiatives of individual landowners, and their ability to negotiate with other landowners and commoners. So, when the task looked daunting enthusiasm often quickly disappeared. After all, enclosure by agreement was, by definition, the product of negotiation in which legal rights had to be surrendered willingly and threats and bluster counted for relatively little.

Many landowners believed that enclosure provided the best environment in which to adopt new practices which might enable some of the constraints on levels of output and productivity to be broken. The most important constraint was one of maintaining soil fertility. In particular, continuous cropping of grains would gradually parch the soil of life, requiring land to be left fallow from time to time and animal manure applied (most easily by getting the animals onto the land). This last point meant that 'the arable Land must be proportioned to the quantity of Dung that is raised from the Pasture'.[30] But keeping large numbers of cattle and sheep from October to March, when grass was scarce, was so difficult that each autumn many were slaughtered, thereby limiting manure supplies and preventing continuous enhancements of soil fertility. At the time there were principally two related ways to break through these limitations: to grow different crops which complemented rather than exacerbated the effects upon soil fertility of growing wheat, barley, and other grains; and to find 'new' crops to feed to animals outside the growing season. It was beginning to be seen that 'a Crop of Beans and Pease do not (as most other grain) take *from*, but give Riches *to* the Land' and might be used in combination with grain crops to maintain soil fertility.[31] Certainly through the seventeenth century the range of crops available to farmers was expanding. Particularly significant were new fodder crops, be they 'artificial grasses', such as clover or sainfoin, or root crops such as turnips. Sheep might, for example, feed on a field of turnips by day and be 'folded' onto fallow land to manure it by night. It was, indeed, the spread of fodder crops which had the greatest impact, for '*an Encrease of the Stock is always a double Encrease of the Profit*; return'd to the Farmer these two ways, both in the Profit of fat Cattle, and in the *Improvement* of his Land for another Year.'[32] Yet given this and the fact that new fodder crops were often available from the early seventeenth century it is important to understand why they had only a limited impact before the middle of the eighteenth century.

[29] Laurence, *New System of Agriculture*, p. 46.   [30] Mortimer, *Whole Art of Husbandry*, p. 11.
[31] Laurence, *Duty of a Steward*, pp. 180–1.   [32] Laurence, *Duty of a Steward*, pp. 184–5.

One factor was simply that the benefits of the new fodder crops were not felt everywhere. In particular, root crops were ill-suited to heavier soils because they were so difficult to lift or dig up. Lighter and sandier soils made fewer demands upon labour and beast alike. This had important consequences for the regional geography of England's agriculture, tending to underline the pastoralism of large parts of the Midlands and the west. By contrast eastern and southern England, especially East Anglia, Kent, Sussex, and Hampshire, developed a mixed husbandry with a productive interplay between sheep and corn. Once arid tracts of Norfolk heath and Downland could now become significantly more productive. Indeed, it is possible that the most important development in English agriculture in the second half of the seventeenth century was in its regional realignment. However, it is important to stress that such changes were not simply consequent upon the adoption of new fodder crops. Earlier agricultural developments had played their part, as in the adoption by farms of 'up and down husbandry', that is breaking the rigid distinction between permanent pasture and tillage. Regional change also depended upon developments in non-agricultural employment discussed in the previous chapter, not least in changes in the availability of by-employment in rural domestic industries. Further, the dramatic absolute and relative growth of London in the seventeenth century had a profound impact upon the market orientation of farmers across many parts of England, for increasingly they knew that their surpluses would find a ready market in the capital. And, as with industry, agricultural regions could only specialize if there was a reasonable degree of market integration and an efficient distribution network, the development of which was certainly well underway by the second quarter of the eighteenth century.

Though the growth of such crops and the adoption of new rotations were applauded by many, farmers showed some resistance to their charms. In 1724 it was noted, for example, that 'The Husbandry of Clover has proved of great Advantage to several Parts of *England*, but is not yet so generally known as to be cultivated every where', and Defoe recognized that the cultivation of turnips was mainly limited to 'the east and south parts of England'.[33] Even in Norfolk and Suffolk, where rates of adoption were probably at their highest, diffusion was still limited in this period (see Table 16).

Though many farms made use of turnips and clover by the end of our period, they strictly limited the amount that they grew—accounting respectively for only about 7 and 2 per cent of the sown area. Yet by the 1830s these proportions had risen to a quarter. Not the least of the difficulties was that if new rotations were developed, most famously with the Norfolk four-course

---

[33] Bradley, *General Treatise*, vol. 2, p. 36; Defoe, *Tour*, p. 83.

TABLE 16. *Fodder crops in Norfolk and Suffolk farm inventories, 1660–1729*

	% noting turnips	Mean acreage of turnips on farms	% noting clover	Mean acreage of clover on farms
1660–69	1.6	—	0.7	—
1680–89	19.1	0.7	4.3	—
1700–9	40.2	1.3	11.7	0.1
1720–29	52.7	2.2	23.6	1.5

Source: M. Overton, 'Weather and Agricultural Change in England, 1660–1739', *Agricultural History*, 63 (1989), p. 83.

rotation (wheat, turnips, barley, and clover), it proved difficult to wean farmers away from belief in the efficacy of fallow, such that a significant proportion of land remained outside of intensive cultivation. We get some sense here of the limits to agricultural growth before the middle of the eighteenth century.

If the spread of new crops and rotations was limited it is also notable that the period saw relatively little development with regard to drainage, irrigation, selective breeding, or the application of new technology. Certainly the great age of fen drainage had passed by the late seventeenth century, indeed complaints were starting to be voiced that not all the drains were being adequately maintained. Farmers were also making limited use of irrigation by briefly flooding fields to enrich them with silt deposits (so-called 'water meadows'). Though the benefits of this process were generally acknowledged it could be expensive and was in any case only possible on fields close to rivers and streams. Nor did selective breeding make much headway—Robert Bakewell (1725–95) did not begin his work on sheep breeding until the 1740s, and the breeding of thoroughbred horses was also common only from that date, though Defoe believed that the army's need for chargers in the long period of war did lead breeders into new lines. Around 1700 many agriculturalists continued to believe that environment rather than heredity was the crucial factor in variations between animals, and indeed the increases in the sizes of animals which took place in the sixteenth and seventeenth centuries were probably the result of better nutrition. Similarly, few attempts were being made to use new machines or tools on farms. If different sorts of ploughs had been developed for different soil types, most work was still labour-intensive and back-breaking, from sowing to harvesting and hay making to milking. Developments in hand tools, as in the use of scythes rather than sickles, took precedence over attempts to mechanize farm processes. The demand simply was not there while labour remained relatively abundant—it is instructive that the seed drill, first promoted in 1731 by Jethro Tull (1674–1741), failed to become a commonplace until the mid-nineteenth century.

Four crucial factors restricted significant innovations in the agrarian sector: the ad hoc, amateur, and sometimes contradictory nature of new ideas; the high cost of certain developments relative to alternatives; variations in the natural environment; and farmers' attitudes. Some seized upon the last of these as the key, of 'the difficult Reception that these Improvements meet with, because of the Ignorance of some, and the wedded Opinions of the Generality to the Custom and Practice of their Neighbours'.[34] Certainly the spread of new ideas was as likely to take place in the bluster of conversation at the inn and market place as through the quiet contemplation of the words of an agricultural propagandist in the sanctuary of the farmhouse. But for a farmer to give weight to the opinions of a neighbour and to what he had actually seen was, arguably, more rational than following the urgings of an author of uncertain pedigree and authority. To ask farmers to break the habits not of a lifetime but of generations was to ask a lot. Moreover, propagandists were not always as innovative as might be supposed, one author being absolutely clear that 'Good husbandry requires every Farmer to keep his *Fallows* regular'.[35] Even if a farmer was willing to change he was often faced with a bewildering range of options. For example, the number of crops available to any farmer was so large there were many *possible* new rotations for any area, such that deciding on the best mainly depended upon trial and error over many years which few could undertake systematically.

Despite these limitations, despite the fact that change and growth was patchy and hesitant, this was an era when in many places agriculture moved forward. More food was being produced, to the benefit of domestic consumers—be it expressed through the preference for white over brown bread, porter over small beer, or the beef of old England ('We are the greatest *Flesh-pots* that ever liv'd' exclaimed one author).[36] There were no longer subsistence crises in England, as there had been in the sixteenth century and as there still were occasionally in Scotland and Ireland or on the Continent. Something like a national market for wheat and other grains had come into existence, such that shortfalls in one area might be made up by surpluses elsewhere, with prices following very similar paths between regions. Not until the darks days of the 1790s, when rapid population growth coincided with bloody war, would English agriculture struggle once again to supply the domestic market. For the time being a fruitful balance had been struck between man and land.

---

[34] Mortimer, *Whole Art of Husbandry*, introduction (no pagination).
[35] Laurence, *Duty of a Steward*, p. 189.
[36] O. Dykes, *English Proverbs, with Moral Reflexions* (3rd edn., 1713), p. 13.

THE LANDED INTEREST

One of the most important consequences of the Glorious Revolution was the involvement of Britain in an era of expensive Continental warfare, which could only be paid for by, for the first time, exploiting public credit through the establishment of a permanent national debt. Because that 'Financial revolution' centred upon the City, more particularly upon its bankers, great merchants, lawyers, and politicians, those groups came to have a new and greater political influence. No less significantly, the creation of a market for government debt secured upon parliamentary authority established a form of wealth that had hitherto been of negligible significance—now one might inherit stock just as one might inherit land or jewellery. One consequence was to provoke an intense debate about the very meaning of 'property', to the extent that the old adage that 'Power follows Property' was equally uncertain.[37] Indeed, the generation after 1688 saw the intimate relationship between landownership, social status, and political authority questioned for the first time, to the extent that some believed that the 'landed interest' itself was under threat.

In 1724 it was lamented that 'It is not many Years ago, since an unhappy Distinction was set on Foot, between the Landed and the Money'd Interest'.[38] Those who made that distinction most often did so to mourn the decline in the fortunes of the former, most prominently the advocates of the Tory and Country views, pre-eminently Swift.[39] Yet in at least three regards such a depiction of the decline of the landed interest was misleading. First the very distinction between the two interests was far from clear-cut, indeed it was rightly observed their 'Welfare *mutually* depend on each other'.[40] For example, the sheep from the fields of landowners provided the fleeces for woollen manufacturers (representing both capital and labour) who, in turn, supplied textiles to merchants to export. Equally, increasing numbers of landowners were spending large parts of their time in London, Bath, and other towns, often making full use of the developing financial and legal services of the 'monied interest' and enjoying the commodities of manufacturing industry and overseas commerce. And of course both the landed and the monied interests were heterogeneous and heterodox, not unitary and undivided. Landowner battled with landowner and merchant with merchant in attempting to define the public good and to implement the measures best suited to achieve that chimerical goal. In so doing merchant might ally with peer, banker with

[37] *A Collection of all the Political Letters in the London Journal to December 17, Inclusive* (2nd edn., 1720), p. 4.
[38] *Considerations on Publick Credit* (1724), p. 6.   [39] See above, p. 128.
[40] W. Wood, *A Survey of Trade* (1718), pp. 8–9.

bishop. Moreover, the landed interest was often deeply divided. If many were Tories or of a country disposition there were certainly Whig grandees. And if some were enthusiasts for developments such as enclosure others stood firmly against them. Second, the social values of polite society remained predominantly those of the landed elite, of, for example, education at Oxford, Cambridge, the Inns of Court, and the grand tour, of Anglican orthodoxy, and of the relationship between landownership and social status. Finally, it could reasonably be claimed that the landed interest remained 'the political blood of the nation'.[41] The ownership of certain amounts of property was effectively (and sometimes legally) a prerequisite for many positions of power and responsibility, and landowners continued to enjoy control over many of the most important offices of civil and military society.

Neither ministries nor Parliament ever ceased to be dominated by the upper echelons of the landed elite. Naturally members of the House of Lords always held large amounts of land, even if '*ex officio*' as in the case of bishops. Nor when creations were made were the Lords inundated by new blood: of the 72 new creations made between 1700 and 1739 only 10, or nearly 14 per cent, were not already directly connected to the peerage. Moreover, the patronage commanded by the landed elite was also substantial. The peerage effectively controlled 12 per cent of clerical appointments, the landed elite as a whole rather more. In 1702 perhaps 10 per cent of MPs owed their seats to direct peerage nomination, and the Property Qualifications Act of 1711 required MPs to hold substantial estates (though the effectiveness of the Act is questionable). Similarly, members of both the judiciary and the military were often headed by men from substantial landed families.

To say that landowners retained control of many positions of authority should not, however, be taken to mean that their authority was unquestioned or their will the law. Though advantageous policies were constructed for them, such as the corn laws, and the deference they commanded real enough, their power remained limited, conditional, and negotiable. One problem was set by the elite's perilous demographic fortunes, for the lack of heirs meant power did not always pass from father to son but was, so to speak, dropped by one family to be picked up by another. Moreover, in crude quantitative terms, for example, though the number of peers rose from 173 to 189 between 1700 and 1730, numbers of both baronets and knights fell, from 860 to 735 and from 290 to 150 respectively. That is to say the titled elite shrank in numbers by nearly 20 per cent in the first three decades of the eighteenth century, subtly changing patterns of social hierarchy in the process. It might also be claimed that the rise

---

[41] F. Atterbury, 'English Advice to the Freeholders of England' in *A Collection of Scarce and Valuable Tracts, on the Most Interesting and Entertaining Subjects*, ed. W. Scott, 13 vols. (2nd edn., 1809–15), vol. 13, p. 523.

of Parliament after 1688 was largely a rise in the Commons and that there was a real drift of political power away from the great estates. Certainly it is important not to exaggerate the extent to which the landed interest dominated or dictated the parliamentary process. The relatively open nature of parliamentary government, the dependence upon display and the rule of law rather than might to maintain order, and reliance upon local amateur JPs to govern and direct placed limits upon what the landed elite could and could not do. So, for example, much of the heavy burden of the cost of the Nine Years War and the War of the Spanish Succession was borne by the land tax. Determined to avoid the prying eyes of central government officials, the *quid pro quo* reached meant that landowners administered a burdensome tax upon themselves.

The development of the London season and leisure towns in the seventeenth century also began to change the nature of the authority of substantial landowners. If they wanted to spend a good deal of time in the capital, Bath, and the like, as they increasingly did, then they had to expect that this meant some loss of direct control in the localities. Similarly, the growth of parliamentary government after the Glorious Revolution, along with a quarter century of war, forced many landowners to absent themselves from their local power bases for considerable periods. Many were unable or unwilling to take the time or spend the effort and money needed to maintain a figure in their 'country' and to play an integral role in leading it, thereby devolving some responsibilities upon an emerging 'squirearchy' of lesser gentry. Indeed, the urban way of life was for some a conscious renunciation of the burdens of the countryside, be they financial or social. Many 'noblemen live in town to economise, and though they are surrounded with great luxury, they declare that in their country seats they are forced to spend far more, having to keep open house and table, packs of hounds, stables full of horses, and to entertain followers of every description.'[42] There is some evidence that at least since the Restoration, perhaps even from before, the reciprocity of paternalism and deference had more and more theatre about it and less and less substance. Traditions of hospitality were slowly changing as perceptions of social obligation mutated, not least as landowners' increasing 'sensibility' and 'politeness' jarred with old notions of paternalism and patriarchy. One noblemen, for example, complained 'I am very glad Christmas is Ended . . . Every day with the noise of Either Drums, Trumpetts, Hautboys, Pipes or Fiddles, some days 400 Guests, very few under 100, that besides the vast expense it has been very tiresome.'[43] Such a distancing can only have encouraged the people—the 'vulgar' in the elite's terms—to show increasing disrespect and indeed foreigners

[42] *A Foreign View of England in the Reigns of George I and George II. The Letters of Monsieur César de Saussure to his Family*, trans. Madame van Muyden (1902), pp. 208–9.

[43] *Verney Letters of the Eighteenth Century from the Mss. at Claydon House*, ed. M. M. Verney, 2 vols. (1930), vol. 1, p. 291.

were inclined to remark on the lack of social deference of the labouring poor, of the 'Pride' and 'Insolence' of people and of 'Their little Regard for the Grandees'.[44]

Despite their absences landowners remained, of course, at the pinnacle of local society. When they returned home they might be met by a guard of honour made up of gentlemen and citizens. A peer's rites of passage, from baptism, to coming of age, marriage, and burial, often assumed considerable local significance. And a certain rhetoric of paternalism remained in place. The rich were meant to respect the needs of the poor and could indeed be fulsome in their charitable efforts.[45] If the effort was made then it might pay dividends. In 1708 it was said of Lord Townshend that he 'florisheth much among us, for ye whole countey [Norfolk] is absolutely at his beck, an he hathe got such an ascendant here over everybody by his courteous carriage that he may doe anything among us what he will'.[46] That is to say, if the landed always had some authority, their power was also personal, liable to come and go according to their beneficence, consideration, devotion, and morality.

HOMES AND GARDENS

If landowners struggled to dominate society at large, they had less difficulty closer to home. The projection of personal authority in the local context preoccupied many and took its most striking form in building great houses and sculpting majestic gardens. From the landowner's point of view many would have agreed that 'of all injoyments, in the way of magnificence, building, with its appendage furniture, gardens, &c. are the most great and usefull; for the owner is honestly exhalted, and injoys plenty with vertue, and the exercise of business and arts'.[47] And publications such as *Britannia Illustrata*, by Johannes

[44] B.-L. de Muralt, *Letters Describing the Character and Customs of the English and French Nations* (2nd edn., 1726), p. 2.

[45] See above, pp. 84–5.

[46] *Letters of Humphrey Prideaux Sometime Dean of Norwich to John Ellis Sometime Under-Secretary of State, 1674–1722*, ed. E. M. Thompson, Camden Society, New Series, 15 (1875), p. 200. For a very similar sentiment, see *A Supplement to Burnet's History of My Own Time*, ed. H. C. Foxcroft (Oxford, 1902), p. 422. Charles Townshend, 2nd Viscount Townshend, 1674–1738, educated at Eton and King's College, Cambridge. A Whig, he married Robert Walpole's sister, was active in foreign affairs and agricultural improvement, hence the nickname 'Turnip Townshend'.

[47] *Of Building: Roger North's Writings on Architecture*, ed. H. Colvin and J. Newman (Oxford, 1981), p. 5. There was, of course, a contrary view: according to the Earl of Strafford 'a good seat is where there is great parks, fine woods, and plantations, and an extensive command for all kinds of country sports . . . I think any house good enough to sleep in, and the only magnificence the country neighbours have a notion off is your strong beer and beef.' *The Wentworth Papers, 1705–1739. Selected from the Private and Family Correspondence of Thomas Wentworth, Lord Raby, Created in 1711 Earl of Strafford*, ed. J. J. Cartwright (1883), p. 444.

Kip and Leonard Knyff, with its impressive 80 copperplates illustrating great houses and their gardens, emphasized the social as well as personal and aesthetic significance of such opulence. From another perspective, of course, the resources consumed by the building of homes and gardens, and the naked social ambition involved, speaks volumes of the yawning chasm between rich and poor, even if many jobs were created in the process. Not all landowners were like the Earl of Carlisle, demolishing a village to erect his pile (Castle Howard), but many placed formidable barriers between themselves and villagers, building walls, planting thickets, and guarding woods with guns, traps, and dogs. In this at least landowners often behaved not so much like quasi-princes as demi-gods.

The building of grand country houses mainly dates from the sixteenth century with the end of the elite's need for fortified residences consequent upon the relative security afforded by the Tudor regime. But it was particularly after the accession of James I in 1603 that country house building became fashionable and proliferated. Naturally the troubled years of the 1640s and 1650s put paid to many schemes, but the years after the Restoration in 1660 were full of activity. One survey of dated buildings concluded that activity rapidly increased to a decennial peak in the 1690s, before falling off somewhat thereafter and stabilizing through the second half of the eighteenth century. Looking at all houses built before 1739 which can be dated, some three-quarters were built in the century 1640–1739, mostly in the period 1670–1730.[48] This was apparent to contemporaries for, as the great architect Vanbrugh put it in 1708, 'All the World are running Mad after Building, as far as they can reach.'[49] The £50,000 the Earl of Devonshire spent on house and gardens at Chatsworth in the twenty years after 1686 was simply an extreme example of a relative common exuberance.[50] Country house building was one of this period's distinctive features.

Such trends are not in fact precise nor their significance clear, for it is difficult to date many buildings accurately, while to concentrate only upon new building ignores often very substantial renovations, and the quantitative approach ignores questions of style, function, and reception. There was, for example, considerable difference between building a suburban villa for a

[48] See R. Machin, 'The Great Rebuilding: A Reassessment', *Past and Present*, 77 (1977), pp. 33–56; C. Saumarez Smith, 'Supply and Demand in English Country House Building 1660–1740', *Oxford Art Journal*, 11 (1988), pp. 3–9 identifies a rise in country house building in his period, peaking in the 1720s.

[49] *The Complete Works of Sir John Vanbrugh*, ed. B. Dobrée and G. Webb, 4 vols. (1928), vol. 4, p. 25.

[50] William Cavendish, 1640–1707, succeeded as 4th Earl 1684, active for William in 1688, created Duke of Devonshire 1694.

London merchant and Blenheim Palace for the Duke of Marlborough, and if the cost of the latter was put at £287,000 by its architect, at times employed over a thousand in its construction, and took two decades of intermittent activity to complete, then the collective significance of villas was probably no less impressive. Macky, for example, counted 200 'little Country Houses' in the 'large Village' of Stratford, some five miles from London.[51] Yet it was because a villa was only 'a quasy lodge . . . to retire to injoy and sleep, without pretence of entertainement of many persons' and lacked the grandeur and ostentation of great houses that for the most part they failed to excite either contemporaries or the modern heritage industry.[52] It is the likes of Blenheim, Castle Howard, Chatsworth, Dyrham, Houghton, Petworth, and Uppark which are best remembered. Only one villa, the Earl of Burlington's Chiswick House, is usually talked of in the same breath, emphasizing the significance of architectural criteria in which the vernacular is a lesser form of life.

In terms of architectural excellence this was the age of Wren, Talman, Archer, Vanbrugh, Hawksmoor, Campbell, Burlington, Gibbs, and Kent. Born in 1632, Sir Christopher Wren was by 1689 the elder statesmen of English 'architects'—the term was rarely used at the time and did not acquire professional connotations until much later. Designer of St. Paul's Cathedral, many of London's churches after the great fire, notable buildings at both Oxford and Cambridge, and many royal works, among them the Royal Hospital at Chelsea, and parts of Greenwich hospital, Hampton Court, and Kensington, his standards and styles provided reference points for all architects in this period. Most usually Wren's architecture has been categorized as a move away from the classicism of Inigo Jones towards the 'baroque' style perfected by his independent spirited disciples, Vanbrugh and Hawksmoor. Certainly Wren was influenced by the French architecture of the court of Louis XIV, but his tastes were eclectic, mainly deriving from the interplay of the technical—of the mathematical relationships between dimensions, spaces, and effect—and the classical. (Echoing Petty, his motto was *'Pondere Numero et Mensurâ'*, by weight, number, and measure.) He was well versed in the 'rules' governing classical architecture where, for example, particular orders —Doric, Ionic, Corinthian, and Composite—provided a limited palate of supposedly unquestionable taste from which to design. His work at Hampton Court and Kensington was, perhaps, especially influential at the time, Defoe claiming that 'With the particular judgment of the king [William], all the gentlemen in England began to fall in; and in a few years fine gardens, and fine houses began to grow up in every corner'.[53]

[51] [J. Macky], *A Journey Through England*, 2 vols. (2nd edn., 1722), vol. i, p. 24.
[52] *Of Building: North's Writings*, p. 62.   [53] Defoe, *Tour*, p. 175.

Vanbrugh's Castle Howard and Blenheim Palace, and Hawksmoor's Easton Neston (Northamptonshire) are much more distinctive voices than Wren's, and certainly can usefully be categorized as 'English baroque'—so long as this is taken to be a particular expression of classicism and it is remembered that the term is a latter-day invention. 'A concise definition of the Baroque is almost impossible . . . Put most simply, it is the reverse of Classical harmony found in Palladianism; an essential element is a sense of drama . . . Often it is expressed in a sense of movement in a façade as opposed to harmony, of contrasting planes, insistent skyline and varied sense of scale.'[54] Certainly the theatrical effect of Vanbrugh's great buildings must be stressed, as it certainly struck contemporaries who well knew of his skills as a playwright.[55] He designed Blenheim as both 'a private Habitation' and 'a Royall and a National Monument' with 'ye Qualitys proper to such a Monument, Vizt. Beauty Magnificence, and Duration', and to see the palace for the first time via Hawksmoor's Triumphal Arch on the edge of Woodstock village is awe-inspiring.[56] But the majesty did not impress all. Famously the quarrelsome and selfish first Duchess of Marlborough came to hate Vanbrugh with such a passion as to ban him from viewing his creation. More importantly there were those who were hostile to it aesthetically. The Earl of Ailesbury complained that 'the house is like one mass of stone, without taste or relish', and Blenheim contradicted a growing preference for architectural restraint and obedience to classical ideals.[57] That preference had existed for some time, North privately noting in 1698 how 'in all country seats of late built, the same method is practis't, to the abolishing grandure and statlyness of that sort the former ages affected', but early in the eighteenth century it came to be championed in such a way as to be subsequently characterized as the 'Palladian revival'.[58]

Few architects have been as influential as Andrea Palladio (1508–80). Most famous for his villas in the Veneto, his study of classical architecture published in his *Four Books of Architecture* (1570) remained for over two centuries an essential work of reference for those with grand designs. In England both Inigo

---

[54] G. Worsley, *Classical Architecture in Britain: The Heroic Age* (New Haven, 1995), p. 71.

[55] John Vanbrugh, 1664–1726, son of a London tradesman of Flemish descent. Studied in France, served in the army, prisoner in the Bastille, author of *The Relapse* (1697), *The Provok'd Wife* (1697), *The Country House* (1705), and other plays, manager of the Haymarket theatre for two years, knighted in 1714. Nicholas Hawksmoor, *c*.1661–1736, from a family of farmers in Nottinghamshire. When 18 began to work for Wren, held a number of public offices, such as Clerk of Works at Greenwich. Best known for his six London churches, including Christ Church, Spitalfields. He provided much technical and imaginative support for Vanbrugh at both Castle Howard and Blenheim.

[56] *Vanbrugh Works*, vol. 4, p. 45.

[57] *Memoirs of Thomas, Earl of Ailesbury, Written by Himself*, 2 vols. (1890), vol. 2, p. 587.

[58] *Of Building: North's Writings*, p. 63.

Jones (1573–1652) and Wren drank from this well of ideas, but it was particularly in the early eighteenth century that Palladianism became the touchstone of architectural taste. Such standards were vigorously but certainly not solely championed by Colen Campbell (d. 1729), a Scot, and Richard Boyle, the 3rd Earl of Burlington (1695–1753). Creatively this took notable form at Wanstead House, Essex, Stourhead House, Wiltshire (both by Campbell), and Chiswick House, Middlesex, modelled on Palladio's Villa Rotunda outside Vicenza. But for their reference points they looked back not only to Palladio, but more immediately to Jones. What gave the movement greater momentum and influence was the fact that in part Palladian ideals were transmitted by the printed page. Leoni's edition of an English translation the *Four Books* was published between 1715 and 1719; between 1715 and 1725 Campbell published *Vitruvius Britannicus* in three volumes, surveying British architecture and championing the new standards; in 1727 William Kent edited the *Designs of Inigo Jones* (many taken from Burlington's collection); and in the following year classical references were rounded off by Castell's *The Villas of the Ancients Illustrated* (dedicated to Burlington).[59] From the 1720s neo-Palladianism was in the ascendant, with both the baroque and the gothic pushed to the margins, though not completely suppressed. Indeed so powerful and prescriptive did this movement become that it has been labelled 'the Palladian dictatorship'.[60]

The Palladian revival was about more than an architectural style, it was also about the image the landed elite projected, as much to itself as to society at large, and of a deliberate distancing from the grandeur, theatre, one might say craftsmanship of the baroque. This was not merely a question of façades, but also of interiors and gardens. Thus the elaborate carvings of Grinling Gibbons and the decorative paintings of Verrio, Laguerre, and Thornhill were, by 1727, inclined to be viewed as belonging to a bygone age.[61] But it is in the realm of gardening that changes in the nature and form of ostentation and luxury were most obvious. At the start of the period the gardens of country houses were often formal, regimented, and angular—with Dutch now joining earlier French influences. Much play was made of symmetry and geometry, of the

[59] William Kent, 1684–1748, began as a coach painter, went to Rome, returning under the patronage of Burlington to work as an architect, painter, and landscape gardener.

[60] H. M. Colvin, *A Biographical Dictionary of British Architects, 1600–1840* (3rd edn., New Haven, 1995), p. 27.

[61] Gibbons, 1648–1721, notable work at St Paul's Cathedral, Windsor castle, Kensington Palace, and Trinity College, Cambridge. Antonio Verrio, 1639–1707, born Italy, did much work at Hampton Court, where he died. Louis Laguerre, 1663–1721, born Versailles, godson of Louis XIV, originally assisted Verrio, also worked at Chatsworth and Blenheim. James Thornhill, 1675–1734, painter, worked on dome of St Paul's, and at Greenwich, Sergeant Painter to George I, knighted 1720, MP from 1722.

subjugation of mother nature by force of human will. Beds of orderly flowers, rows of clipped yew, straight gravel paths, and neat lawns were the stock-in-trade. Water did not flow freely, but was forced through fountains and cascades into dug canals. Beyond the gardens of the great houses led long dead-straight avenues of trees, either free standing or cut out from heavily wooded areas, giving the eye no choice of view, no horizon to survey. Many of the parks depicted in *Britannia Illustrata* give the impression of the landowner imposing himself violently upon the landscape, and making his house the focal point of all. London and Wise, and their nursery of 40,000 plants at Brompton Park near London, were the leaders of this form of gardening, helping to professionalize landscape gardening.[62] Such regularity could produce marvellous and inspiring effects, notably at Hampton Court which exerted a wide influence —William III spent some £83,000 by 1696 on his gardens there and at Kensington.

Though formal gardens proliferated in the late seventeenth and early eighteenth centuries a strong counter-movement developed from about 1710. At heart the reaction stressed the superiority of the natural over the man-made. Pope, an ardent advocate of the new approach, commanded 'First follow NATURE, and your Judgment frame . . . At once the *Source*, and *End*, and *Test* of *Art*.'[63] This standard was put forward with elegance and vigour in the pages of both the *Guardian* and the *Spectator*—indeed, the link between gardening and literature was a practical one for Pope established a famous garden at Twickenham. Addison was sure that '*Art*' was 'very defective' in comparison to '*Nature*', that 'There is something more bold and masterly in the rough careless Strokes of Nature, than in the nice Touches and Embellishments of Art', and that in his mind's eye 'my Compositions in Gardening are altogether after the *Pindarick* manner, and run into the beautiful Wildness of Nature'.[64] Addison's reference to the Greek lyrical poet Pindar nicely points up the classical context for this line of thinking about the landscape. In particular the publication of Dryden's translation of Virgil's *Georgics* in 1697 had done much to champion the pastoral and natural ideals—though the importance of the garden of Eden to Christianity is also worth recalling. Consequently, enthusiasm for the simplicity of the natural landscape could have political connotations, implicitly criticizing the formality and corruption of a socially regimented court.

---

[62] George London, d. 1714; Henry Wise, 1653–1738, served William and Mary, Queen Anne, and George I. Some of their most important work was at the palaces of Hampton Court, Kensington, and Blenheim.

[63] A. Pope, 'An Essay on Criticism' (1711), ll. 68 and 73, in *The Poems of Alexander Pope*, ed. J. Butt (1996), p. 146.

[64] *The Spectator*, ed. D. F. Bond, 5 vols. (Oxford, 1965), vol. 3, pp. 548–9; vol. 4, pp. 190–1.

In practical terms, an enthusiasm for nature meant making gardens more like a natural landscape and placing few barriers between a house and garden (hence the term 'landscape garden'). There was still to be artifice by means of digging, hiding, and planting (61 new species of trees and 91 new species of shrubs were introduced into England between 1700 and 1751), but all with a view to creating a natural effect. So called 'ha-ha's', a term first used in 1712, were essential to this. They were sunken fences or walls invisible from view at short distance, allowing the landscape, particularly one grazed, to appear to be brought right up to the house. Grottoes, mock ruins, and classical temples might dot the landscape to evoke a mood of quiet contemplation and contentment, if one touched by an elegiac quest for perfectibility in a fallen world.

Pope's small garden, just a part of a mere five-acre estate, had a disproportionate influence upon the taste for landscape gardening as it developed in the 1720s. Even so, in practical terms no less influential were gardeners such as Charles Bridgeman and, from the end of our period, William Kent.[65] Among Bridgeman's best-known work was the remodelling of Wimpole Hall in Cambridgeshire, Houghton in Norfolk, and Boughton in Northamptonshire. Most famously, he was employed at Stowe in Buckinghamshire from 1714. In many ways Stowe encapsulates all that was distinctive about eighteenth-century English landscape gardening. It was brought into being by Sir Richard Temple, 1675–1749, who rose from the ranks of the middling gentry to become a leading peer. He served with Marlborough in the War of the Spanish Succession, made a financially astute marriage to the daughter of a Suffolk brewer, was raised to the peerage in 1714, became a Privy Councillor in 1716, was made Viscount Cobham in 1718, and led a raid on Vigo Bay in Spain in 1719. But it was at Stowe that he really looked to leave his mark. There Vanbrugh was 'much entertain'd with . . . the Improvements of his House and Gardens, in which he Spends all he has to Spare'.[66] Elysian fields were laid out, lakes dug, and temples planned. Not least the gardens were gradually extended from twenty-four acres in 1724 to over 200 by mid-century. If Stowe lacks the more entrancing elegance and balance of Rousham in Oxfordshire (remodelled by Bridgeman, Kent, and others from the early 1720s) it certainly impressed contemporaries, including Pope, and provided something of a blueprint followed elsewhere. Replacing box hedges and flower-knots with ha-ha's and glades naturally took many decades and, thankfully, bypassed some formal gardens. But the early decades of the eighteenth century had seen a real sea change in aesthetic responses to the landscape. The power and imagination was still there, but it now took a more restrained and more subtle form.

---

[65] Also spelt Bridgman; d. 1738.   [66] *Vanbrugh Works*, vol. 4, p. 112.

THE SOCIAL MOBILITY OF POLITE SOCIETY

Though much political, economic, and social power was held by those families at the head of English society, high social rank did not, of itself, automatically count for much. The law made few concessions to those of high status, indeed equality before the law was a central principle of the English system, and the wealthy in countryside and town had to pay a full share of taxes. No less significantly membership of the elite (or indeed of any broad social group) was not rigidly defined. This had important implications in the context of Gregory King's observations on the close relationship between social status and income.[67] Thus if a family's income rose or fell then its social position might also change. Certainly, theoretically England had an open society, with prospering families able to climb up the pyramid and indebted ones likely to fall down it. But the nature of a family's income mattered, for if new forms of wealth such as financial assets were increasingly important the ownership of broad acres was, at the head of society, still the supreme badge of status. Estate size, patterns of consumption, and social position were therefore tied, if somewhat loosely. When, for example, the great Whig lawyer John Somers was in line for a peerage in 1697 it was reported, perhaps ironically, that 'to induce him to accept of it he hath a grant of lands made him to the value of near 2,000l per annum', and in 1702 Marlborough, contemplating the prospect of a dukedom, noted that 'wee ought not to wish for a greater title till wee have a better estate.'[68] Furthermore, in purely economic terms land was seen as a remarkably stable investment. Not surprisingly, with such powerful social and economical factors operating upon a finite resource land was not only highly prized but increasingly highly priced.

With land so valued few landowners ever wanted to sell unless circumstances forced it, usually to meet debts, rationalize the layout of an estate, or because of a failure in the line of inheritance. The power of the first of these could be very considerable, for social expectations required expenditure on a lifestyle commensurate with status—for the elite this included going to London for the season, taking the waters at Bath, improving home and garden, cutting a figure in local society, and undertaking good works. However, if patterns of conspicuous consumption were critical to reputation and socially unavoidable, when they were combined with inefficient estate management then unbearable debts might accumulate, necessitating the sale of all or part of an estate. By 1708, for example, the Earl of Yarmouth 'hath vast debts, and

---

[67] See above, pp. 69–73.
[68] H. M. C., *Calendar of the Manuscripts of the Marquis of Bath*, vol. 3 (1908), p. 112; *Marlborough–Godolphin Correspondence*, vol. 1, p. 142.

suffers every thing to run to extremity; soe his goods have been all seised . . .
he hath scarce a servant to attend him or an horse to ride abroad upon'.[69] A
second major factor in bringing land onto the market was the disruption of
inheritance—though the inheritance of an estate by a minor often reduced
expenditure significantly and allowed a period of retrenchment and reorganization. If no heir existed, then an estate might be sold off intact; if no direct
heir existed, then it might be broken up, parts given to distant relatives and
other parts sold. No less significant, the practice of primogeniture ensured that
daughters and younger sons of landed families struggled to maintain social
position, with marriage providing the most likely way out of declining fortunes. The marriage market was just that, a place where children were com-
petitively priced to attract partners with similar resources. As such, ultimately
the source of money each brought to the marriage was less important than
its amount, so 'now 'tis common for Gentlemans and Merchants Sons and
Daughters to Intermarry.'[70] Even so, younger sons might have to forsake a life
of ease for one of toil to be able to maintain gentlemanly status, though often
they were well positioned to exploit patronage connections. The State provided an increasing number of openings in this period, as the growth of parliamentary government and the demands of two great wars created more and
more jobs in the nascent civil service or the armed forces. Others turned to the
professions of the Church and the law. And the relatively high status afforded
to commerce, especially overseas trade, provided a potentially lucrative if risky
career. Whether such a path was often taken is debatable. Though it was
claimed that 'The Opinion, that *Merchandizing debases Blood*, is a Folly' it
was also noted that 'it is very rare for Peers to put their younger Sons out
Apprentices . . . As to the Sons of Knights, nothing can be more common.'[71]

If landowners did sell, they were as likely to hive off modest parcels as complete estates, which, in turn, were as likely to be bought by other landed families, great and small, as outsiders to landed society. Indeed, many parcels were
too small to have been economic to anyone but neighbouring landowners looking to consolidate their holdings. Away from the capital many small estates
were often purchased by existing landowners, slowly hauling themselves up
the ladder of provincial society by careful estate management or fortunate
marriage. This was a form of silent social mobility, but it was often of striking

[69] *Letters of Prideaux*, p. 200.

[70] G. Miege, *The New State of England under our Present Monarch K. William III* (4th edn., 1702), p. 156.

[71] W. Bond and A. Hill, *The Plain Dealer, being Select Essays on Several Curious Subjects . . . Publish'd Originally in the Year 1724*, 2 vols. (2nd edn., 1734), vol. 2, p. 237; H. Misson, *Memoirs and Observations in his Travels over England* (1719), p. 190.

local significance. But in the counties surrounding London many purchasers of small estates were men of new wealth, perhaps being less concerned with upward social mobility than prudently diversifying their assets or establishing a bolt hole from summer stinks and winter fevers. Some of the urban well-to-do, however, certainly aspired to gentry status and establishing a landed family, turning their back as quickly as possible on the world of business. Social assimilation, however, usually took a generation or two before it was complete, the children of businessmen finding full integration into and acceptance by landed society much easier than had their parents. Many established landowners accepted new wealth with open arms, but others, hamstrung by arrogance and tradition, were distrustful. Typical of the latent resentment was the view of North who believed that the 'upstart citisen . . . retein their native litleness, even when they aim at, and spend to obtein grandure.'[72]

It needed a catastrophe to befall a family for a large and compact estate to be brought to market. This might be because of a complete failure of inheritance patterns, though distant heirs could usually be found, or because of a disastrous miscalculation, as many made in the South Sea Bubble. When large estates came onto the market they were so expensive that potential purchasers were either already very large landowners or those few who had amassed fortunes in the worlds of finance, law, public service, medicine, trade, industry, and the military. So, for example, by his death in 1711 the Duke of Newcastle had purchased land to the total value of £250,000, which included estates from the earls of Kingston, Bolingbroke, and Radnor. Yet it was purchases by those from outside established landed families which caught the eye of contemporaries. Evelyn, markedly embittered, noted in 1696 that '*Duncumb* not long since, a meane Goldsmith . . . made a purchase of neere 90000 pounds of the late D. of Buckinghams estate'.[73] Henry Hoare, the London banker, spent £37,150 between 1718 and his death in 1725 on estates in Wiltshire, Dorset, and Hampshire. The physician John Radcliffe, a great benefactor to Oxford University, bought an estate at Wolverton in Buckinghamshire in 1713 for £40,000 and in 1714 a large country house at Carshalton for over £7,000. James Brydges as Paymaster of the forces syphoned off £600,000 from the public purse, which he then poured into buying estates in seven counties and building and filling his great house at Cannons near Edgware in Middlesex. Raised to the peerage in 1714 and made Duke of Chandos in 1719 he was renowned (and sometimes mocked) for his patronage of the arts, notably Handel's Chandos anthems.

[72] *Of Building: North's Writings*, p. 9.   [73] *Evelyn's Diary*, vol. 5, p. 246.

England's landed elite was open rather than closed, but it is unclear how representative the likes of Duncombe, Hoare, Radcliffe, and Brydges were.[74] Certainly landed society experienced a high degree of turnover. Family fortunes were much more unsettled and unpredictable than might be first imagined, and few were able to survive for more than three or four decades untroubled and unscathed. Families might die out or merge with another, or their fortunes shrink and disappear. Significant amounts of land did come up for sale and it was the capacity of the elite to mutate that is striking. Ultimately landed society overcame its reluctance to outsiders and accepted the inflow of new sources of wealth. Not least this was because the elite was itself very commercially orientated, well aware that estates were financial assets to be exploited and never just status indicators. Moreover, estates comprised a variety of sources of revenue, from fields to woods, mines, urban property, and docks. Ambitious landowners could not afford to turn their back on the opportunities their estates provided. Consequently, more than any other European country English landed society was plutocratic and pragmatic. And it was no less powerful for that.

COUNTY SOCIETY, COUNTRY PURSUITS

Though contrasts between the values of town and country have long been a commonplace, this was particularly stimulated in England by the great growth of London in the seventeenth century. One strain of thought which gathered in strength through the seventeenth and early eighteenth centuries argued for the superior politeness, manners, taste, and civility of the urban, decrying the rudeness, backwardness, and provincialism of the countryside. Some argued that elegance and sophistication reached its apogee in cities, to an extent epitomized by the *Spectator* loudly championing urban civility and civic virtue. In this spirit Dudley Ryder, very much a Londoner, complained that 'The great difficulty in the country is to find matter of entertainment and how to employ one's self.'[75] Yet if rural society was undeniably distinctive whether it was less polite is highly questionable.

In the first place town and country were interdependent, not separate, distant, or remote. The dichotomy between London and the provinces was becoming less and less significant as more and more gentry families spent time in the capital. When there they enjoyed the distinctive pleasures of the place, but they usually kept in close touch with those they had left behind, from estate stewards to family and friends. In the same way Parliament was an assembly

[74] This point has divided historians. For contrary views, see L. and J. C. F. Stone, *An Open Elite? England, 1540–1880* (Oxford, 1984) and E. and D. Spring, 'The English Landed Élite, 1570–1879: A Review', *Albion*, 17 (1985), pp. 149–66.
[75] *Ryder Diary*, p. 99.

of predominantly provincial interests interacting with central government. MPs well knew the importance of representing and obliging their constituents. Many gentlemen also sought to signal their provincial identity in London by patterns of socializing. The 'Amicable Society of Gentlemen born in the County of Cumberland' was but one of many such associations, existing not only to feast but also to raise money for the county's poor suffering hardship in London.[76] Nor was London the only significant urban locale of provincial society. Bath and other spa towns were of increasing significance. Preston, for example, was described as 'a very pretty town, with abundance of gentry in it'; at Bury St Edmunds 'more Gentry meet, then in any other Country town in England, & for that reason call'd little London'; and at York the 'abundance of good families [who] live here, for the sake of the good company and cheap living; a man converses here with all the world as effectually as at London; the keeping up assemblies among the younger gentry was first set up here'.[77] On a more day-to-day basis many county and cathedral towns, with their assizes, fairs, parliamentary elections, and horse races all played prominent parts in a flourishing county society that was both urban and rural. The comings and goings of circuit judges and bishops were often occasions for the county gentry to congregate for work and play just as fairs were places of trade and assembly. The frequency of parliamentary elections in this era often required the landed gentry to meet, not so much to cast votes as to voice opinions about potential candidates and issues. In 1704, for example, Harley received a report from the peripatetic Defoe on the 'State of Parties in Hertfordshire', noting how 'The Gentlemen of the Royston Club settle all the affairs of the county and carry all before them . . . There is a monthly meeting of the gentlemen of all the neighbourhood'.[78]

Perhaps nothing expressed the interplay between town and country and the vitality of provincial and county society as powerfully as the growth of horse racing. That expansion had begun after the Restoration and continued apace through the early eighteenth century, and is neatly marked by the appearance in 1727 of what was to become an annual publication: the *Historical List of all the Horse Matches Run, and all Plates and Prizes Run for in England and Wales (of the Value of Ten Pounds or Upwards)*. Produced by John Cheney, supported by 660 subscribers, including 15 dukes, it recorded racing at some 112 English towns or cities. Newmarket was especially prominent, Epsom an ostentatious

---

[76] *Post Boy*, 23–26 June 1711, [p. 2]. Henry Purcell, the composer, wrote a song ('Of old when heroes thought it base') for the feast of Yorkshire gentlemen in London.

[77] E. Calamy, *An Historical Account of my Own Life, with Some Reflections on the Times I have Lived in (1671–1731)*, 2 vols. (1829), vol. 2, p. 221; *The English Travels of Sir John Percival and William Byrd II: The Percival Diary of 1701*, ed. M. R. Wenger (Columbia, Missouri, 1989), p. 65; Defoe, *Tour*, p. 520.

[78] H. M. C., *The Manuscripts of his Grace the Duke of Portland*, vol. 4 (1897), pp. 153–4.

social occasion, with 'vast crowds on horseback, both men and females; many of the latter wore men's clothes and feathered hats', and at Nottingham races there was 'such an assembly of gentlemen of quality, that not Bansted Down [i.e. Epsom], or New Market Heath, produces better company, better horses, or shows the horses and master's skill better.'[79] Not only prize money but gambling drove the sport on, but it all depended upon the patronage of the great and the good. Godolphin was a prominent enthusiast, and other land-owners spent heavily on stables and gambling (the ne'er-do-well Duke of Wharton reputedly lost £13,000 at Newmarket in the spring of 1720).

The melding of the rural and the urban was real enough, but both were also singular and distinctive. With regard to provincial landed society this found notable expression in hunting which was limited by the confines of the game laws. Legislation governing hunting had a long heritage in England before 1689, but the most significant development had come in 1671 when the Game Act was passed. For the most part this law limited the hunting of wild game to gentlemen and to those who had freeholds worth at least £100 per annum, or leaseholds worth £150 per annum, financial qualifications that remained in place until the nineteenth century. In theory both the non-landed and the non-propertied were excluded from the right to hunt; it was the exclusive preserve of the landed gentry. The Game laws were, indeed, an important part of the landscape of social identity in rural England, of the superiority of the rich over the poor and of the landed over the monied. As framed, however, the 1671 Act left many loopholes and it says much that Parliament expended considerable effort in trying to fill them, passing thirteen game laws between 1689 and 1727 (there were also six failed attempts at legislation). In 1707, for example, it became an offence for an unqualified person to own a snare or keep a hunting dog, or for any higgler, chapman, carrier, innkeeper, victualler, or alehouse-keeper to sell game. Every effort was made to give the landed gentry an effect-ive monopoly over the hunting of game. In practice, however, hunting was not altogether socially exclusive. Landowners might invite yeomen farmers to hunt, and others turned a blind eye to hunting by the unqualified. Commercial pressures to supply London and other towns with game such as duck, rabbit, and par-tridge also encouraged a good deal of poaching by the labouring poor. Indeed, at times gamekeepers found themselves serving on what seemed to be a front line, waging war against villagers intent on making what they could from wild animals they well knew were ignorant of private property and social prejudices.

As might be expected, the game laws and the hunter attracted much com-ment. In particular, the gamesman and fox hunter became totemic figures in contemporary discourse, symbolizing blustering heartiness, animalistic

[79] *London in 1710: From the Travels of Zacharias Conrad von Uffenbach*, trans. and ed. W. H. Quarrell and M. Mare (1934), p. 106; Defoe, *Tour*, p. 452.

passion, and the battle of man with nature. Addison, for example, used the figure of the fox hunter to symbolize unthinking Toryism, High Church extremism, jingoistic nationalism, and antipathy to London, trade, and industry. From his Whig and urban standpoint he complained of 'The wrong Notions and Prejudices which cleave to many of these Country-Gentlemen', of their vulgarity and coarse habits.[80] Hunting was also a largely male preserve and an important part of the gender distinctions that ran through the heart of landed society. Judith Drake, a keen observer of the inequality of the sexes, mocked the country squire whose 'Entertainment is stale Beer, and the History of his Dogs and Horses' and whose 'grand Business is to make an Assignation for a Horse Race, or a Hunting Match'.[81] From another perspective, however, it was claimed that 'Hunting is a noble Exercise and Recreation, not only commendable for Princes and great Persons, but also for Gentlemen; there is nothing that does more recreate the Mind, strengthen the Limbs, whet the Stomach, and chear up the Spirits'.[82] The enthusiasm for hunting among landed society was real enough. Fishing was of long standing—Isaak Walton's *The Compleat Angler* (1653) had already acquired an extensive readership—and hare coursing and the shooting of duck, pigeons, and other birds were especially common. It was claimed that 'Deer are allow'd by all Sports-Men, to be the most Noble Game we have in *England*', but relatively few could indulge in this.[83] Fox hunting, however, was of growing significance. The keeping of packs of hounds began in earnest in this period, usually taking a lead from a substantial landowner, and the development of the hunting saddle around 1700, which by providing the rider with more support made it easier and safer for horsemen to jump hedges, fences, and ditches. The Cottesmore hunt in Leicestershire was established in the late seventeenth century, and early in the eighteenth century those of Brocklesby in Lincolnshire, Holderness in Yorkshire, Puckeridge in Hertfordshire and Essex, and famously Quorn in Leicestershire. As the social significance of hunting grew so it became an increasingly common artistic theme, notably in the work of John Wootton (1682–1764) and Peter Tillemans (1684–1734) who by the 1720s were painting horses, hounds, hunts, and races.

CONCLUSION

Since at least the early nineteenth century, disquiet over the social costs of urbanization and the pace of change in all walks of life have encouraged romantic celebrations of the world we have lost. From such a view it is easy to imagine

[80] J. Addison, *The Freeholder*, ed. J. Leheny (Oxford, 1979), p. 130.

[81] *An Essay in Defence of the Female Sex* (1696), pp. 32–3.

[82] [J. Worlidge], *Dictionarium Rusticum, Urbanicum & Botanicum: or, a Dictionary of Husbandry, Gardening, Trade, Commerce*, 2 vols. (3rd edn., 1726), vol. 1, q.v. 'Hunting'.

[83] Jacob, *Country Gentleman's Vade Mecum*, p. 24.

rural England before the mechanization of agriculture in this century as essentially timeless. If work was hard it was honest, if life was difficult it had meaning, if few had power they were socially responsible. But the English countryside at the start of the eighteenth century was neither a golden age nor a prelapsarian paradise. It was, indeed, remarkably commercial in spirit, hindered in its aspirations and achievements more by the supremacy of the natural world over available technology than by naked ambition. Agriculture struggled to expand, but expand it slowly did, in the process helping over the longer term to raise standards of living for many. Such an achievement was not peculiar to this period, but part of a process of change in the countryside stretching from at least the sixteenth to the nineteenth centuries.

In so far as agriculture did develop it did so because of the creativity, vitality, and industry of those who worked the fields, managed the farms, and owned the land. Those virtues were socially widely distributed, with England's elite playing its full part. Indeed, the enthusiasm with which it embraced commercial opportunity set it apart from many members of landed society on the Continent. Certainly English landed society rested on the foundations of gross inequality, but criticisms of the vices of the rich, of their propensity to luxury, idleness, and immorality, need to be taken with a large pinch of salt. For every example of the cavalier and the rake may be found the case of the improver and economizer. Indeed, agricultural advance provided the bedrock upon which was built the edifice of the power of landowners that reached such heights in the eighteenth century. Consequently, the Glorious Revolution played little direct part in their fortunes except in the forum of high politics. Indeed, one of the most important consequences of political and social changes after 1688 was the disengagement of many members of the elite from purely local society, of a reconstitution of the social environments of the rich both at the metropolitan and county levels. The symbols of that disengagement may be seen in Palladian mansions, landscaped parks, and the game laws. But by themselves those symbols were something of a mask hiding the fact that at the local level the distance between rich and poor had been growing, leaving increasingly open a middle ground to be occupied by provincial gentry and urban patrician. Filling that middle ground was a challenge that was fully met by eighteenth-century England's 'polite and commercial people'.[84]

---

[84] The phrase comes from W. Blackstone, *Commentaries on the Laws of England*, 4 vols. (1765–9), vol. 3, p. 326, and is the title to the next volume in this series.

CHAPTER 12

The Political World of George I

When Queen Anne died her subjects had little reason to eye their political prospects optimistically. Looking back they saw generations of political discord and gazing forward they easily imagined the terrifying prospect of civil war between Hanoverians and Jacobites. Instability seemed as integral a feature of the political system as ever, with Whigs battling Tories, the Low Church the High Church. Yet within just ten years such instability had largely disappeared, with the last years of King George being the first since 1689 generally to enjoy peace and quiet. Crucially, the waxing and waning between the two parties was ended by the new King enthusiastically embracing the Whigs and rejecting the Tories. No less importantly, for the first time since 1689 the electorate consistently followed the monarch's lead, providing ministers with large majorities in the Commons. Such a distribution of power was encouraged by the surprisingly muted Jacobite rising in 1715. Indeed, one of the most remarkable features of the political landscape after 1715 was the success with which Jacobite threats were contained by George and the Whigs. After 1716 the Pretender became a somewhat pathetic figure on the fringes of European power politics, struggling amidst poverty in Italy to keep up the appearance of a monarch in waiting. If the Protestant succession was secure after 1715, worries that the Church was in danger also began to lessen, in part perhaps because the High Church reaction of Anne's last years singularly failed to reinvigorate the religious basis of civil society. By 1720 the religious settlement of the 1690s was back in place and, for a time at least, was usually off the political agenda.

There was no inevitability about such a political transformation, though in part it rested upon changes that had been underway for several decades, and nor was it as complete as it at first appears. If there were structural developments in the political system after 1688 which encouraged order, particularly relating to the redistribution of power between monarch and Parliament and the institutionalization of political debate, much also depended upon the way particular political interests contested for place and policy after 1714. In fact politically the years from 1714 to 1722 were as eventful as any since the Revolution, not least because George I's pro-Hanover foreign policy divided the Whigs. Nor was it obvious to contemporaries that the political stability achieved by the mid-1720s was to be long lasting. That it was owed much to the lessons ministers, especially Walpole, had learned from the earlier achievements of Godolphin and Harley, and the removal of the disturbances posed by frequent elections and Convocation. Gradually, moreover, George withdrew from day-to-day involvement in politics, lessening a source of tension within the political order, underscoring the longer term development that while monarchs continued to head the government ministers very largely controlled it. In the short term one consequence of one-party rule and monarchical disassociation was the lack of effective opposition. Yet it says much for the political fertility of early eighteenth century England that by 1727 there were already clear signs of how the court Whig hegemony might be challenged in new and forceful ways. Peace and quiet were not to be enjoyed for long.

GEORGE I, HANOVER, AND EUROPE

Though George was in Hanover when Anne died on 1 August 1714 he was immediately and loudly proclaimed, and the plans William III had carefully laid in 1701 were implemented without hesitation or rancour. At the end of the first week there were 'comfortable accounts from all places of peace and quietness; and that there appears not a dog to move his tongue against the Protestant succession.'[1] After a fortnight even Bolingbroke related that 'there never was yet so quiet a transition from one government to another . . . for we are at this moment in as perfect tranquility as ever.'[2] Though the moment Jacobites had long waited for had finally arrived they did not stir, their muttering speaking loudly of their lack of numbers, organization, resources, and commitment. Yet, so little known as he was, George I was initially accepted more as an idea and as a symbol than as a man or a monarch. Moreover, what he was not was almost as important as what he was: he was Protestant not Catholic; an ally of Britain and Holland not France; apparently committed to parliamentary government rather than kingly prerogatives; and bound by the terms of the Act of Settlement and the Bill of Rights rather than an ideology of divine right. Yet despite his rather colourless reputation George was flesh and blood, with passions and interests he pursued even at the cost of alienating some of his new subjects. Indeed, he brought to England and Britain rich experiences and great expectations which decisively influenced political developments in his reign.

---

[1] *The Life and Diary of Lieut. Col. J. Blackader*, ed. A. Crichton (Edinburgh, 1824), p. 449.
[2] *Letters and Correspondence, Public and Private, of the Right Honourable Henry St. John, Lord Viscount Bolingbroke*, ed. G. Parke, 2 vols. (1798), vol. 2, p. 680.

George Ludwig of Brunswick-Lünenburg was born in 1660, the son of Ernst August (1622–98) Duke of Hanover from 1679 and Elector from 1692, and Sophia of the Palatinate (1630–1714). In marked contrast to the Stuarts the Hanoverians were adept at producing legitimate heirs. George's father was one of six children; he had five brothers and one sister; and he fathered two legitimate and probably four illegitimate children (including one when he was only 16). Whereas the childhoods of both William III and Anne had been scenes of loneliness and isolation, chaos and strife, George came from a large and relatively secure family. Moreover, he was taken under the wing of a father intent on territorial expansion and who saw in his son a means to fulfil and develop his ambitions. One manifestation of this was that in 1682 George was married to his 16-year-old cousin Sophia Dorothea, only child of the Duke of Celle whose territories Ernst August looked longingly upon. Though the union soon produced two children—the future George II in 1683 and a sister, who took her mother's name, in 1687—any affection between the couple quickly disappeared. By the early 1690s both had taken lovers. Whatever the morality of the matter in 1694 the rift became an abyss as a tragedy of Shakespearean proportions unfolded. Perhaps by accident, perhaps by design, Sophia's lover, the Swedish Count Philipp Christoph von Königsmarck, was killed by courtiers and his body dumped in a river; Sophia Dorothea was made a virtual prisoner for the rest of her life at Ahlden; and in December George obtained a divorce. Clearly the light of enlightenment shone but faintly here.

The darkness in George's life covered not only the court, but Hanover in general. Like William III he was bred in a world which feared the might of France and the ambitions of Louis XIV. Hanover, like the Dutch Republic, was small and insecure, its Lutheranism like the Republic's Calvinism attracting the Sun King as a moth to a flame. George was bred to face this challenge. He soon learned French, German, and Latin well, and a little Dutch and Italian. In 1680 he had travelled to England, via Holland, for a stay of three months, perhaps with a view to negotiating a marriage to Anne (which came to nought). Thus even before he became King of England he had some experience of diplomacy. Moreover, he was interested in the sword and the saddle as well as the treaty and the map. He had joined his father on campaign when only 15 and also fought France in 1676, 1677, and 1678. He went on further campaigns against the Turks in 1683–5 and briefly saw action against France in the early part of the Nine Years War. Nor was he personally untouched by the carnage of all this, two brothers being killed in battle in 1690 and a third in 1703. By 1714 George well knew the fear of defeat, the capricious hand of fate, and the bloody costs of war. If he lacked William III's evangelical sense of purpose as Protestant Europe's saviour his interest in foreign affairs was just as central to his character. He 'knows all about the affairs of his own country and about those of foreign nations'.[3]

Ernst August had never believed that Hanover need merely be passive or reactive in European affairs and was always looking to strengthen its position through advantageous alliances and expansive borders, a lesson George well learned. In 1660 Hanover was, indeed, still a small land-locked duchy, accounting for just a corner of Lower Saxony. By 1727, however, it had expanded to include Diepholz, Hoya, Celle, Lauenburg, Bremen, and Verden and, of course, it had become joined to Great Britain. George's outlook was, therefore, not only Hanoverian but also 'German' and European. Such a perspective was decisively unlike the insularity and self-absorption that had marked English domestic politics during Anne's last four years and was, of itself, bound to be a source of tension and difficulties for George as King. It was also true, however, that the peace settlements reached in 1713 and 1714 had not effectively established a secure European balance of power. In the south Spain and the Empire were both dissatisfied with what they had gained and lost. Similarly, the death of Louis XIV in 1715 and the establishment of the regency of the Duc d'Orléans also cast considerable doubt upon the future role of France in European affairs. And the Great Northern War, begun in 1700, was still continuing, with Sweden's tenuous hold on Bremen and Verden particularly attracting Hanoverian attention. These were uncertainties Britain, with its new-found significance and interests, could not afford to ignore, irrespective of where its monarch hailed from.

George's dramatic personal life, active career, and European background did not, it must be said, make for an engaging man. Whatever his faults, William's personal bravery, intelligence, and steadfastness could not but command respect. But by the time George reached England he was 54. The years had taken their toll and altered international circumstances meant that he had few opportunities to display his worth so obviously as had William. Nor was he physically impressive, he was 'short of stature and very corpulent . . . his cheeks are pendent, and his eyes are too big; he looks kind and amiable'.[4] But whereas Anne's Englishness had allowed all her physical and intellectual failings to be forgiven, George was faced by many subjects who never forgot or excused his origins. In a sense they could hardly be blamed. His knowledge of English was very rudimentary, forcing him to conduct much business with ministers in French. In religion he was a Lutheran by upbringing and a latitudinarian by disposition, temperamentally hostile to the High Church reaction

[3] *A Foreign View of England in the Reigns of George I and George II. The Letters of Monsieur César de Saussure to his Family*, trans. and ed. Madame van Muyden (1902), p. 45.

[4] *Letters of de Saussure*, p. 45.

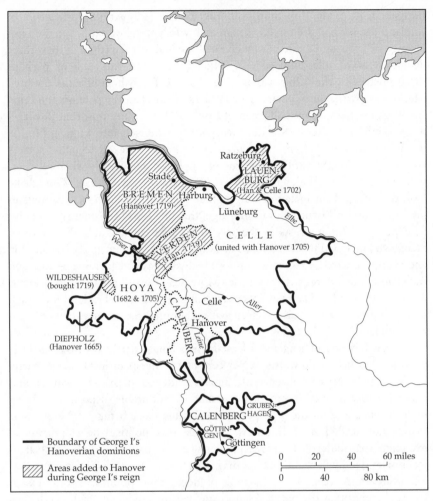

MAP 7. Hanover in 1700
After R. Hatton, *George I: Elector and King* (1978), pp. 378–9.

of Anne's last years. His view of kingship also appears to have followed William in its pragmatism and worldliness—he disliked formality, show, and crowds. And if eventually he came to admire and trust some English ministers in ways William always found impossible, in 1714 he brought with him from Hanover some 90 ministers, courtiers, and servants (including two influential Turkish grooms, Mehemet and Mustapha). Further, he ignored the terms of the Act of Settlement forbidding non-English people from advising the monarch on English matters. In particular, he continued to depend upon Baron von

Bernstorff, Jean de Robethon, and his long-time mistress, Melusine.[5] In England the couple often lived as man and wife, and he raised her to the Irish peerage in 1716, and made her Duchess of Kendal in 1719 (though their three daughters went unacknowledged). Though she was only one of perhaps three mistresses the King had in England few English politicians doubted Melusine's particular importance or influence—in 1720 Walpole quipped that she 'was, in effect, as much Queen of England as ever any was; that [George] did everything by her.'[6] Nor did George throw himself into English life. As in the previous two reigns the court was no longer integral to polite society and the King sought out the company of English notables only when relations with the Prince of Wales broke down between 1717 and 1720. Though he looked to project an image of kingship in England, by such benefactions as professorships at Oxford and Cambridge, this involved little energy, thought, or expense. If his interests in the arts were more considerable than is often recognized he failed to leave a mark as clearly as had William at say Kensington and Hampton Court. George was indeed reclusive for considerable periods and travelled about his realms very little. Moreover, during his thirteen years as King he returned to Hanover six times, being absent from England for a total of 33 months, making it all too clear that his adopted country was certainly not his homeland.

George I is one of England's least-known kings, partly because too little attention has been paid to the 85 per cent of his life spent in Hanover, partly because of the relative absence of English evidence in British archives, and partly because he was unremarkable, a man of 'admirable disposition, willing to doe every thing for the best' perhaps, but more like a benign and grey uncle than a hot-headed son.[7] But it is also true that political developments in his reign, particularly its increasingly oligarchic nature and the revival of Jacobitism, fatally flawed though it may have been, do not readily engage modern sympathies weaned on the milk of democratic politics. Yet it was in George's reign that the political landscape became obviously 'eighteenth century' in complexion and mood, even if this was enabled by prior developments. The Protestant succession was decisively established, religious controversy largely sidelined, party conflict tempered, and parliamentary activity put upon a routine footing. The uncertainties that had plagued the political system since

---

[5] John de Robethon, d. 1722, a Huguenot refugee, employed by William III, entered George's service in 1705, effectively as secretary. Melusine von der Schulenburg, 1667–1743, born Saxony, George's mistress from 1698, lived in retirement at Isleworth after his death.

[6] W. Michael, *England under George I: The Beginnings of the Hanoverian Dynasty* (2nd edn., 1936), p. 82.

[7] 'The Letters of Henry Liddell to William Cotesworth', ed. J. M. Ellis, *Publications of the Surtees Society*, 197 (1987), p. 149.

the 1640s were by the death of George I fast becoming a thing of the past. In that he played no small part.

THE WHIG MOMENT, 1714–1715

George took the death of Anne in his stride, lingering in Hanover before setting out for his new realms. Contrary winds delayed him for a time in the Republic, allowing him to refresh some important connections, and he did not finally arrive at Greenwich until 18 September. Such a languid journey speaks volumes about the security of his position in England and his personal priorities—he well knew that being King would be a burden as well as an opportunity and his tardiness also allowed the enfeebled nature of the Jacobite opposition to become readily apparent. He was fêted on his arrival, even the Jacobite Duke of Berwick acknowledging that he 'was received with every possible demonstration of joy'—by one report his procession into London comprised 260 coaches and took three hours to pass 'streets crowded with innumerable spectators [and] balconies hung with tapestry'.[8] As soon as he arrived he was surrounded by leading peers looking to ingratiate themselves in the hope of finding favour, place, and profit. Not all were welcome. Bolingbroke had already been dismissed from his post and the Earl of Oxford had to suffer the indignity of having the King publicly turn his back upon him.

The slighting of Oxford stung the Tories but their general position was far from hopeless. They had countered some of the Whig position papers George had received and in Parliament (admittedly not then sitting) they were more dominant than ever, having over 360 seats. And there was the hope that like William and Anne the new King would seek to establish mixed ministries, filled by the able rather than the compliant. But George soon sided with the Whigs, seeing the Tory administration's Treaty of Utrecht as a betrayal of the Grand Alliance and Oxford and Bolingbroke's dealings with the Jacobite court as a betrayal of the Protestant succession. Unsurprisingly, the King immediately came under considerable pressure from the Whigs to support only them and by December 1714 the Whig Countess of Cowper claimed that 'The *King* is as we wish upon the Subject of Parties, and keeps my Lord's Manuscript by him, which he has read several Times.'[9] This document, the misnamed 'An impartial history of parties', written for the King by her husband, the Lord Chancellor, was certain that experience since 1679 demonstrated that only the

---

[8] *Memoirs of the Duke of Berwick, Written by Himself*, 2 vols. (1779), vol. 2, p. 194; *The Diary of Ralph Thoresby*, ed. J. Hunter, 2 vols. (1830), vol. 2, p. 260.

[9] *Diary of Mary Countess Cowper, Lady of the Bedchamber to the Princess of Wales, 1714–1720*, ed. C. Spencer Cowper (1864), p. 32. Mary Cowper, 1685–1724, married 1st Earl Cowper 1706, Lady of the Bedchamber to Princess of Wales 1714.

Whigs fully supported the Protestant succession, warning against a mixed ministry. Cowper further stressed that the King had a wider influence, noting that 'the parties are so near an equality, and the generality of the world so much in love with the advantages a King of Great Britain has to bestow . . . that 'tis wholly in your Majesty's power, by showing your favour in due time (before the elections) to one or other of them, to give which of them you please a clear majority in all succeeding parliaments.'[10] This last point was, ultimately, of decisive significance.

George soon embraced the Whigs, but he also left room for some Tories. As one leading Whig noted, though there was 'no room to doubt wch. way ye King intends to steer his course. Yet . . . thô ye changes wch. have been made, are wholly in favr of ye Whigs, the King does not intend to govern so much upon that bottom, as to exclude all others'.[11] The new ministry constructed in September 1714 was indeed very largely Whig. The two key posts of Secretary of State went to Stanhope and Townshend; Halifax was made First Lord of the Treasury; Cowper was Lord Chancellor; Walpole was Paymaster; and Marlborough replaced Ormond as Captain General.[12] But George sought to introduce some Tories. Nottingham was made Lord President and places were offered to, but declined by, Sir Thomas Hanmer and William Bromley (formerly one of the Secretaries of State). The Privy Council was also overwhelmingly Whig. A similar pattern was reflected in the series of peerage promotions in October, when eight men were raised earldoms, one to a viscountcy, and five to baronies, a plenitude of creations going beyond even those Anne had undertaken in 1711/12 to gain the compliance of the House of Lords for her ministry's peace. There could be no question which way the political wind was blowing by the coronation on 20 October. Nor was the isolation of the Tories restricted to the political elite. Stanhope, Townshend, Cowper, and other leading ministers were soon putting friendly faces into central government offices; beyond Westminster there was an extensive remodelling of county lord lieutenancies and shrievalties in favour of the Whigs; and Cowper was soon adding many Whigs to the Commission of the Peace, though removing far fewer Tories. By New Year 1715 the change of scene from a year earlier was truly remarkable. Tories could not but lament and mourn.

> Farewell old year, for Thou to us did bring
> Strange changes in our State, a stranger King;

---

[10] Lord Cowper, in John, Lord Campbell, *The Lives of the Lord Chancellors and Keepers of the Great Seal of England*, 8 vols. (1845–69), vol. 4, pp. 428–9.

[11] G. Davies and M. Tinling, 'Letters from James Brydges, Created Duke of Chandos, to Henry St. John, Created Viscount Bolingbroke', *Huntington Library Bulletin*, 9 (1936), p. 136.

[12] James Stanhope, 1673–1721, educated Eton College and Trinity College, Cambridge, created Viscount Stanhope of Mahon 1717, Earl Stanhope 1718.

> Farewell old year, for thou with Broomstick hard
> Hast drove poor Tory from St. James's Yard;
> Farewell old year, old Monarch, and old Tory,
> Farewell old England, Thou has lost thy glory.[13]

The new year brought no respite for the Tories, for when the writs for a new Parliament were issued on 15 January 1715 Whig control of most of the reins of both central and local government enabled them to exert considerable influence on the electoral process. Their fortunes were given a further fillip by the King's proclamation praising the Protestant succession. Even so, however, some 46 per cent of constituencies went to a poll and the Tories fought hard, warning of a Whig backlash against the achievements of Anne's last four years—Atterbury's *English Advice to the Freeholders of England* was effectively the party's eloquent manifesto. But they were swimming against a strong counter current and the new Commons comprised some 341 Whigs to 217 Tories, a more or less direct reversal of their fortunes in the 1713 election.[14] If the Whig revolution was somewhat incomplete it was, nevertheless, still very extensive, forcing the Tories even from some of their old strongholds in the counties. Few were in much doubt as to the consequences of such a Whig victory: 'there will in all probability be some violent measures set forward'.[15]

George's first Parliament opened on 17 March 1715, over eight months since his accession. The delay had not, however, led to the formulation of new policies. Rather from the outset the Whigs looked to revenge themselves upon their opponents, raking over the ashes of the Oxford administration in general and the Utrecht settlement in particular. The Commons, responding to the speech from the throne, bemoaned 'the reproach brought on the nation by the unsuitable conclusion of a war, which . . . was attended with such unparalleled successes'.[16] There was, of course, no question of remaking the peace so the Whigs looked to bring its authors to account. Papers were seized and a Commons Committee of Secrecy was established on 9 April, providing some of the material for the impeachments launched in June against Oxford, Bolingbroke, and Ormond for treason, and against Strafford for high crimes and misdemeanours.[17] In this outpouring of vindictiveness Stanhope and

[13] 'A farewell to the year 1714', in *Poems on Affairs of State: Augustan Satirical Verse 1660–1714*, vol. 7. *1704–1714*, ed. F. H. Ellis (New Haven, 1975), p. 613.

[14] These figures, which are for the whole House, are from R. Sedgwick (ed.), *The History of Parliament: The House of Commons, 1715–1754*, 2 vols. (1970), vol. 1, p. 79. W. A. Speck has suggested that for England and Wales there were 289 Whigs and 224 Tories: 'The General Election of 1715', *English Historical Review*, 90 (1975), p. 518, note.

[15] Davies and Tinling, 'Brydges Letters', p. 140.

[16] W. Cobbett (ed.), *A Parliamentary History of England*, 36 vols. (1806–20), vol. 7, p. 47.

[17] Thomas Wentworth, 1672–1739, served in both the Nine Years War and the War of the Spanish Succession, he was a leading negotiator for Britain at Utrecht, created Earl of Strafford in 1711.

Walpole played a leading part, encountering no opposition from the King—in direct contrast to William's policy in 1689 of turning his back on the past. So impassioned was the mood of many Whigs that the Tory leaders had real reason to fear not only for their property and reputation but also for their lives. Bolingbroke fled to France on 27 March and Ormond followed in late July, demonstrating to many their guilt and leading to the passing of Bills of Attainder. But Oxford and Strafford stayed and took on their foes, justifying their actions as just and necessary, emphasizing the parts played by Anne's prerogative, collective ministerial responsibility, and, most important, legislative endorsement. Oxford in particular defended his position at length and with great skill, even if it was not enough to save him from the Tower. Bowed but not broken he played a major part in placing considerable limits upon the Whig backlash. Proceedings against him were eventually dropped in 1717.

THE TORIES, THE JACOBITES, AND THE '15

The Tory party had been the dominant political force in England between 1710 and 1714, even if cracks in its façade had been visible since 1713. Clearly its fortunes were dramatically impoverished by the Hanoverian accession, but it was still a potent force in late 1714. It had in Bolingbroke an inspiring leader; it was already making great efforts in the constituencies in preparation for the forthcoming general election; and the decisions of Hanmer and Bromley to decline office could only strengthen a sense of unity and integrity in a party facing a difficult transitional phase. And though the party suffered badly at the polls early in 1715 it was far from being decimated and in the new Commons showed considerable common cause and fighting spirit. It had, moreover, a very clear programme it might pursue, one that not only sought to keep in place what had already been achieved but, no less importantly, one that protected England from the depredations of Hanoverian interests, be it with regard to foreign policy, the Church, dignities, or estates. But Tory fortunes were transformed by the flight of Bolingbroke and Ormond, for the party was quickly and thoroughly tarred by the brush of Jacobitism. Just how many Tories were Jacobites, in the sense of being fundamentally committed to the accession of the Old Pretender as James III, will never be known with any certainty. Some, very probably a small minority, were and had long been so; some, again most probably only a minority, were 'forced' into the arms of Jacobitism in reaction to Whig one-party rule, viewing it as the only positive way forward; but some, probably most, could never forget the Pretender's religion and French ways, deeply committed as they were to the Protestant succession.[18]

---

[18] The case for viewing the Tories after 1714 as predominantly a Jacobite party is put in Sedgwick (ed.), *The House of Commons*, vol. 1, pp. 63–79 and the contrary case in L. Colley, *In Defiance of Oligarchy: The Tory Party, 1714–60* (Cambridge, 1982), especially ch. 2.

What is clear is that by August 1715 the Tories not only lacked an established leadership but were fundamentally riven. In a minority in both the Commons and the Lords, and with only the renegade Nottingham in the ministry, it was not a party which could now successfully oppose Whig one-party rule.

In July 1715 one observer even contended, somewhat wishfully, that 'the spirit of party begins to cool among us, and in a little time there is hopes we may be a quiet and united people.'[19] Just the opposite was the case, for if George's accession provoked remarkably little opposition the growing strength of the Whigs and the threats hurled out at the Tories led to increasing extra-parliamentary disquiet. It is notable that such disquiet was expressed at all levels of society. At first disturbances were few and far between, but on coronation day 'There were strange tumults and disorders . . . at Bristol, and at Chippenham, in Wilts, at Norwich and Birmingham, and divers other places.'[20] Riots took place in at least thirty towns, mainly in southern and western England. The general election was noted for its violence and in 1715 there was a revival of the same sort of political rioting which had marked the Sacheverell affair in 1710—including attacks on Dissenters' meeting houses. Disturbances were widespread by the summer, a sign to some of 'the common Genius and inclination of the Nation to another Revolucion'.[21] In August it was suggested that 'mobs have been raized in many parts of the nation to try the affections of the people and discover the pretenders fire.'[22] The suggestion that such disturbances might have been initiated by leading Jacobites as a litmus test of popular feeling may have some truth in it, but the discontent of ordinary people may also have been more spontaneous and heartfelt, the expression of a real dissatisfaction with the Whig pillorying of the *status quo ante*. The reaction of the Whig ministry in passing the Riot Act and suspending habeas corpus only served to inflame the situation, for they might be viewed as further evidence of ministerial high-handedness.

Tory proscription and effervescent popular discontent naturally caught the attention of the Jacobite court languishing in Lorraine. The Duke of Berwick believed that 'disturbances continued in every part of England; and the people not only exclaimed publicly against the government, but in many places went so far as to speak in favour of the Pretender', wildly guessing that in England

---

[19] *Berkeley and Percival: The Correspondence of George Berkeley Afterwards Bishop of Cloyne and Sir John Percival Afterwards Earl of Egmont*, ed. B. Rand (Cambridge, 1914), p. 139.

[20] E. Calamy, *An Historical Account of my Own Life, with Some Reflections on the Times I have Lived in (1671–1731)*, 2 vols. (1829), vol. 2, p. 301.

[21] *The Diary of Henry Prescott, LL. B, Deputy Registrar of Chester Diocese*, vol. 2, ed. J. Addy and P. McNiven, Record Society of Lancashire and Cheshire, 132 (1994), p. 445.

[22] *The Diary of James Clegg of Chapel en le Frith*, part 1, ed. V. S. Doe, Derbyshire Record Society, 2 (Matlock, 1978), p. 8.

five out of six were for the Pretender.[23] Having missed the boat in 1714 neither the Pretender nor most of his advisers, including by now Bolingbroke as his Secretary of State, wanted to repeat the mistake in 1715. As the Pretender declared 'now more than ever *Now or Never!*'[24] Ormond had, in any case, been at the centre of preparations for a Jacobite rising, especially in western England, before his flight. In Scotland discontent was widespread and had at its head the Earl of Mar, a man sufficiently embittered and ambitious to risk all. Yet circumstances were far from ideal for the Pretender. Since Utrecht France had been unable to give any meaningful support and on 21 August 1715 Louis XIV died. The Regency would not contemplate helping James and neither Spain nor Sweden could be tempted to fill the breach. Without foreign aid an invasion was out of the question and a rising or coup were the only alternatives. A coup had very little chance of success and a rising would have to be carefully co-ordinated and be met with general popular acceptance to make real headway. It was not. Popular hostility to the new regime and popular Jacobitism were two different, if overlapping, positions. Townshend reasonably claimed that 'the discontented people are rather cold to the present government, than dispos'd to venture anything against it.'[25] It did not help matters that Bolingbroke's attempt to widen the Pretender's appeal by putting in his declaration a commitment to the Church of England was excised by James's priests, leaving the movement fatally flawed in the eyes of many in England. Moreover, in England the flight of Ormond not only rid the Jacobites of a prominent and popular leader but also strongly suggested that he was much more isolated among the political elite than the Jacobite court believed. And fundamental divisions within Jacobitism were exposed when Mar raised the Pretender's standard at Braemar on 6 September before the Jacobite community across Britain was ready.[26]

The government in London was caught somewhat unprepared by Mar's action and there is no doubt that the rising was a major challenge to the Hanoverian monarchy. There was a very real prospect that Scotland, embittered by the Union, would quickly and completely become a Jacobite stronghold and the nation's independence re-established. Much more debatable was what the reaction in England would be. If London could cope with

[23] *Memoirs of Berwick*, vol. 2, pp. 198–9.
[24] Lord Mahon, *History of England from the Peace of Utrecht to the Peace of Versailles, 1713–1783*, 7 vols. (3rd edn., 1853–4), vol. 1, Appendix, p. xx.
[25] H. M. C., *The Manuscripts of the Marquess of Townshend* (1887), p. 163. On the other side Berwick believed much the same in 1715, recognizing that support in England for the Pretender was 'not so much on account of his incontestible right, as from hatred to the house of Hanover, and to prevent the total ruin of the church, and the liberties of the kingdom'. *Memoirs of Berwick*, vol. 2, pp. 201–2.
[26] For the Scottish dimension to the '15, see above, pp. 255–6.

passive disobedience it would certainly struggle to counter a mass uprising. However, given the limited men, arms, and horses immediately available to the Jacobite leadership without such an uprising their prospects were very poor indeed. But that leadership in England was in such disarray that it could not foment such an uprising. That disarray arose from two causes: from the fact that there were too few active and committed Jacobites among the political nation to provide sufficient leadership and from the fact that though the Hanoverian regime had been caught out by Scottish developments it had been battening down the hatches in England since July. An effective intelligence network gathered information of Jacobite comings and goings in northern France. The arms and horses of Catholics and non-jurors were seized, the militia called up, troops stationed in important towns, including Bristol, Southampton, Plymouth, and Oxford, and the army expanded. Prominent suspects were arrested, including Lord Lansdowne and Sir William Wyndham, leaving much of English Jacobitism rudderless.[27] And fines were handed out in considerable numbers to those who dared mutter seditious words. Nor was this clamp-down a notably unpopular one. Loyal addresses to the Crown were prepared by both Houses of Parliament, by the Anglican clergy in Convocation, and by many counties and boroughs, Whig and Tory alike willingly expressing their full commitment to the Protestant succession. With justice the Pretender observed in September that 'I must confess my affairs have a very melancholy prospect.'[28] Jacobite self-delusion, however drove the rising on, still reckoning 'themselves sure of all the West, of Wales, of Staffordshire, Worcestershire, Derbyshire, Lancashire.'[29] However, when Ormond sailed for the Devon coast in late October he was not met by a rising of the gentry but rebuffed by the King's customs officers. Nothing could have demonstrated more completely the weakness of English Jacobitism. And nothing demonstrates the Pretender's lack of judgement than his insistence that Ormond set sail and try again—this time a storm forced him back.

English Jacobitism was not wholly ineffectual in 1715. There was a small rising in Northumberland, where the Pretender was proclaimed in 9 October, and some support was forthcoming in Lancashire, both areas where Roman Catholics were relatively numerous. The Northumberland rising was headed by Thomas Forster, MP, a man of no military experience and unable to muster

---

[27] George Granville (or Grenville), 1666–1735, educated Trinity College, Cambridge, MP 1702, Secretary at War 1710, created Baron Lansdowne 1711, Privy Councillor 1712, imprisoned in the Tower 1715–17, also a poet and dramatist. William Wyndham, 1687–1740, educated Eton College and Christ Church, Oxford, MP for Somerset 1710, Chancellor of the Exchequer 1713–14, on close terms with Bolingbroke.

[28] H. M. C., *Calendar of the Stuart Papers Belonging to His Majesty the King*, vol. 1 (1902), p. 425.

[29] H. M. C., *Townshend*, p. 174.

more than a few hundred men at arms.[30] Still if a link could be forged to Mar's rising then Jacobite fortunes would be significantly enhanced. This they did at Kelso on 22 October. But the forces involved were still tiny, only 1,400 foot and 600 horse. The only hope was to attract further support, in search of which they marched towards Lancashire. By the time they reached Preston on 10 November the Jacobite army had grown threefold, but as soon as they met determined if limited resistance from government troops they capitulated, surrendering unconditionally on 13 November. The English phase of the Jacobite rising was at an end. Many Jacobites were given their freedom, but a good number were marched to London where 'The Mob insulted them terribly, carrying a Warming-pan before them, and saying a thousand barbarous Things, which some of the Prisoners returned with Spirit.'[31] In Scotland the indecisive Battle of Sherrifmuir exposed the limitations of the Jacobites and by the middle of December it was noted that 'the rebells strength shortens daily'.[32] Those limitations were dramatically exposed by the Pretender's purposeless sojourn to Scotland just before Christmas that ended with his humiliating return to the Continent on 4 February 1716.

The immediate aftermath of the Jacobite rising in England was retribution. In Lancashire less than two dozen were executed but a good number were transported to America. The estates of nearly 50 English rebels were seized. In London seven peers were tried and six sentenced to death. George I was anxious to see these punishments through and on 24 February Lords Derwentwater and Kenmure were executed on Tower Hill before a huge crowd who were 'as quiet as lambs'.[33] But three of the peers were reprieved and the fourth, Nithisdale, managed to escape from the Tower dressed in his wife's clothing. And though four other rebels were executed in London later in the year, few at the time thought the government acted with undue severity and it is notable that the scale of retribution was a fraction of that which had followed Monmouth's abortive rebellion against James II in 1685. The failing of the rising also threw into dramatic perspective the nature of the Jacobite threat to the newly established Hanoverian dynasty. Like his father, the Pretender had deserted his people in time of great need and would never again be able to inspire many to risk their lives or estates for him—not least because from 1717

[30] Thomas Forster, 1683–1738, MP for Northumberland 1708–16; captured, he escaped from Newgate prison, entering the Pretender's service on the continent.

[31] *Cowper Diary*, p. 62.

[32] *Letter-Books of John Hervey, First Earl of Bristol*, [ed. S. H. A. Hervey], 3 vols. (1894), vol. 2, p. 12.

[33] *The Diary of Dudley Ryder, 1715–1716*, ed. W. Matthews (1939), p. 188. James Radcliffe, Earl of Derwentwater, 1689–1716, was the son of an illegitimate daughter of Charles II, a Roman Catholic, and companion of the Pretender at St Germain. William Gordon, Viscount Kenmure, was a Protestant.

he was a distant figure, living in Rome. Stuart reality had been seen by friend and foe to be very different to Stuart promise. That is not to say that after the '15 there was no Jacobite threat at all—it may even be, as was claimed in 1722, 'That the Number of *Jacobites* has been greatly increased since His Majesty's Accession to the Throne'—rather that with care the government never doubted that it was possible to contain.[34] It is, for example, remarkable how little political capital the Jacobites were able to make from either the serious political divisions of 1717–20 or the catastrophe of the South Sea affair. Thus given Jacobitism's limitations in Britain its future prospects rested heavily upon altered international circumstances and these were distinctly unpropitious. George quickly appreciated that the Pretender was isolated, travelling to Hanover on 17 July 1716 and not returning for five months. For the King to leave his new realms for long and so soon after the '15 puts the Jacobite threat vividly into context.

WHIG HEGEMONY, WHIG DISHARMONY

In English domestic political terms the rebellion enhanced Whig claims to be George's true champions. Though many Tories immediately threw in their lot with the new King in the summer of 1715 the actions of Bolingbroke, Ormond, Forster, Wyndham, and Mar considerably damaged the party's reputation with the King (it mattered little that the Pretender dismissed Bolingbroke in 1716, except in confirming the Pretender's lack of judgement). Tory political marginality was confirmed in February 1716 when Nottingham, the only minister with any Tory credentials, was dismissed by a King tired by his harangues and calls for clemency towards the condemned Jacobite peers. By the spring of 1716 there was nothing to stop the Whigs strengthening their already formidable position.

The Whig party after the failure of the '15 had no clear leader as the old Junto was replaced by men largely of a new generation. Four men stood out: Stanhope, Sunderland, Townshend, and Walpole. In the Commons both Stanhope and Walpole were in the van, the former very much the King's favourite. Born in 1673, Stanhope's education had been truly international, having travelled to France, Italy, and Spain as a young man where he became 'a perfect Master of the Laws, Constitutions, as well as the Languages of those Places.'[35] He was no mere gentleman diplomat, however, having seen considerable military service in the wars of William and Anne's reigns and having endured two years as a prisoner in Spain. None, the King included, ever

---

[34] *Copies of Some Letters from Mr. Hutecheson, to the Late Earl of Sunderland* (2nd edn., 1722), p. 7.
[35] *Memoirs of the Life and Actions of the Right Honourable James Earl Stanhope* (1721), p. 2.

questioned his courage or his commitment to the Protestant succession. If he had a weakness it was that he had 'a vehemency and fervidness of speech, that always hurt his hearers', which is to say that his oratorical and parliamentary skills were limited.[36] Such abilities came much more naturally to Walpole, appointed First Lord of the Treasury in October 1715, so beginning his long struggle with the financial consequences of a generation of intensive war. At this date his Whiggism, like Stanhope's, was pure and unalloyed. Both had played prominent parts in the trial of Dr Sacheverell and in the investigations of 1715 into the Tory ministry that had come to power in 1710. In the House of Lords the 3rd Earl of Sunderland acted as a close ally of Stanhope, being noted for his 'great knowledge of foreign affairs . . . more perhaps than any man of this time', which endeared him to the King, while his 'quickness and dispatch and clearness in all business that he understood' gave him consider-able authority in Parliament.[37] His rival in the Lords was Townshend, Walpole's brother-in-law and neighbouring Norfolk landowner, who if able to win support by manners and mien lost it because 'His diction was . . . inelegant . . . frequently ungrammatical, always vulgar; his cadences false, his voice unharmonious . . . Nobody heard him with patience'.[38]

On the surface the Whigs were a united and powerful force in 1716. Not least they were able to push through the Septennial Bill which was introduced into the Lords on 10 April and passed the Commons on 26 April. But this meas-ure, which extended the life of Parliaments to seven years, and meant that a general election need not now be held until 1722, also provided a major focus for opposition discontent. That discontent came most prominently from the Tories, 147 of whom voted against it in the Commons. But it also threw into doubt Whig integrity, principles, and unity. Frequent and short Parliaments had for decades been seen by the Whigs as a fundamental check upon mon-archical and executive excess, such that to abandon the Triennial Act of 1694 was a clear volte-face for the party, shamelessly aiming to perpetuate their control of government. Even the Speaker was moved to comment that the Bill would 'highly infringe the liberties of the people'.[39] Yet though the Whigs were also able in June to reverse the clauses of the Act of Settlement requiring parlia-mentary authority for the King to leave his kingdom their power was not unre-strained. At the start of that month, for example, the Lords rejected the Select

[36] 'A Manuscript Belonging to the Earl of Onslow', in H. M. C., *Fourteenth Report, Appendix, Part ix* (1895), p. 512.

[37] 'Onslow Manuscript', p. 510.

[38] *The Letters of Philip Dormer Stanhope 4th Earl of Chesterfield*, ed. B. Dobrée, 6 vols. (1932), vol. 4, pp. 1454–5.

[39] Cobbett (ed.), *Parliamentary History*, vol. 7, p. 327.

Vestries Bill, a measure aimed at diminishing the autonomy of parochial government, and the impending departure of George for Hanover opened up worries about the nature of the regency to be conducted in his absence by the Prince of Wales. Father and son were, for a time, at loggerheads. Though a split was avoided this clash was, with hindsight, portentous of more serious divisions that the political elite would soon exploit to the full.

Though measures for the consolidation of the Whig grip on power were an important feature of the political landscape after the failure of the Jacobite rising it was foreign affairs which was the main catalyst for changes in the distribution of places and power within England. Foreign policy was directed by the general considerations of establishing an effective balance of power consequent upon the end of the War of the Spanish Succession and the death of Louis XIV in 1715, and by the more particular considerations of George's Hanoverian interests in the context of the continuing Great Northern War. Thus a new Barrier Treaty with the Dutch was signed in 1715, a further alliance in February 1716, and in the spring the Treaty of Westminster was signed with Austria. The latter Treaty was in considerable measure stimulated by George's desire as Elector to halt Imperial support for Sweden, but it had the consequence of drawing Britain further into the murky waters of squabbling between the Empire and Spain over their territorial losses and gains in the Mediterranean—though it should be noted that Britain also signed commercial treaties with Spain in 1715 and 1716. Already, moreover, ships of the Royal Navy were cruising in the Baltic, mainly to protect shipping from the depredations of Swedish privateers, but also serving to demonstrate the weight of international authority Hanover was now allied to. To many it seemed as if Britain was being drawn into the fringes of the Great Northern War. But the most sensational development was the alliance of Britain and France signed in November 1716, which was expanded into a triple alliance with the inclusion of the Dutch in December. By any standard this was a diplomatic revolution, a decisive rejection of those factors which had for so long produced bile and bloodshed. As might be expected, it was a revolution born of the conjunction of the Hanoverian succession, the Jacobite menace, and the Regency in France. For a time it suited both great powers to be able to take their eye off their traditional enemy—for Britain it ensured that the Pretender would have to leave Avignon, where he had settled in the wake of the '15, for Italy, and it allowed George to simplify his calculations as how best to maximize Hanoverian interests in the Baltic.

From the Whig perspective it could reasonably be claimed at the end of 1716 that 'our enemies are dispirited and the nation begins to feel the blessings of A wise and steady administration of the Government. The nation recovers its reputation abroad'.[40] Not only had a major Jacobite rising been subdued but once again many points of fundamental agreement across the political nation had been powerfully exposed. On the international stage, moreover, Britain was playing an important role in constructing a new order. However, it was just this position of strength which provided the opportunity for the revival of intense debate, even among the Whigs. Townshend in particular was concerned at the course of George's foreign policy, especially at the use of the Royal Navy in the Baltic, where it effectively aided Sweden's enemies without Britain actually being at war. Anxieties that Sweden would turn on Britain were given credence when late in 1716 it was discovered that the Swedish minister in London, Count Gyllenborg, had been plotting with Jacobites, promising 10,000 Swedish troops would invade Britain. In contravention of diplomatic protocol and what then passed for international law the count was arrested, his house searched, and papers seized. Whatever the justice of the methods none could doubt the seriousness of the Swedish plans nor that they were a direct consequence of George's pursuit of Hanoverian interests in the Baltic. Townshend did not hesitate to tell his master of his worries but his voice now carried too little weight. The King was in Hanover, from where he had negotiated the alliance with France, and where he had the constant advice and support of Stanhope. There, the King and Stanhope, encouraged by Sunderland, the Lord Privy Seal and Marlborough's son-in-law, turned decisively against the absent Townshend. They accused him of being a little Englander, indeed of being a Tory, and of obstructing the conclusion of the Treaty with France. Given the primacy of foreign affairs to George's ambitions it was impossible that he could continue with Townshend in office and in December he was dismissed and replaced by Methuen.

When George returned to England in January 1717 he managed to paper over some of the cracks by persuading Townshend to accept the post of Lord Lieutenant of Ireland—with some arrogance Townshend received an assurance that he need not actually go to Ireland. But the tensions were still there, it being noted that 'the division of the Whigs is so great, that . . . nothing but another Rebellion can unite 'em.'[41] Parliament met on 20 February and business soon turned to debating the Swedish plot. Walpole, who could not support with any enthusiasm the proposal to commit significant resources to the Royal Navy for action in the Baltic, effectively encouraged other Whigs to join with the Tories. On one key vote the government majority was reduced to just

[40] *Clegg Diary*, p. 9.
[41] *The Correspondence of Jonathan Swift*, ed. H. Williams, 5 vols. (Oxford, 1963–5), vol. 2, p. 246.

four. Clearly the government was riven, with Stanhope and Sunderland fully supporting the King, Walpole, Townshend, and others only partially. In April Townshend was dismissed once again. But it was less easy to do the same to Walpole, for he had been preparing schemes for the overhaul of public finances, including establishing a sinking fund to begin the repayment of the national debt, and his expertise was vital to guiding such measures through Parliament. However, feeling politically isolated in the ministry he resigned, which the King accepted only very reluctantly. Hardly less significantly some of his followers left their junior posts, showing the depth of divisions, and the ministry was remodelled: Stanhope was made First Lord of the Treasury, with Sunderland and Addison, Mr Spectator, as the Secretaries of State. Not the least consequence of Walpole's resignation, however, was the way it pointed up ministerial rather than monarchical responsibility for government policy, nicely marking constitutional developments which had been in train for some time.

It was bad enough for Stanhope and Sunderland that men of the stature of Townshend, Walpole, and their allies were now out of the government. But those Whig outsiders now set themselves to oppose as effectively as they could most of the measures the government brought forward, in the hope that the King would then be forced to acknowledge their authority and abilities (a hope that was enhanced in April 1718 when Stanhope was elevated to the Lords.) In this they were prepared to seek allies from wherever they could, be they Whig or Tory. It was little wonder that some complained of the way the 'outed Ministry . . . barefacedly join with the King's Enemys in opposing his Majesty's and publick business.'[42] In that way the party divisions which had been so central in the reigns of William and Anne were being significantly blurred. The parliamentary session, which concluded on 15 July, was indeed notably bereft of innovative legislation and by the start of October 1717 Chandos, a major beneficiary of the Hanoverian succession, reported that 'The breach between the Whigs is irreparable'.[43] Moreover, tensions between the King and the Prince of Wales, which had been growing since the discussions for the arrangements for the regency in 1716, gradually led to the emergence of a rival court to St James which provided a further focal point for opposition interests. When his father was in Hanover Prince George, aided by his popular wife Caroline, had made great efforts to provide a focal point for London society, admitting 'everybody of any fashion', showing himself to be much more accessible and likeable than the King, though the Prince was also noted

[42] *The Letters of Thomas Burnet to George Duckett, 1712–1722*, ed. D. N. Smith (Oxford, 1914), p. 131.
[43] Davies and Tinling, 'Brydges Letters', p. 153.

for his impetuosity and temper.[44] No less importantly, at this juncture he was prepared to ignore party distinctions and courted the regard of Whig and Tory alike. Though this stimulated the King to energize his own social life at Hampton Court, and though he made efforts to build bridges to his son, on 2 December he ordered the Prince (but not his children) to leave St James'—hoping thereby to neutralize his son's influence and so diminish the gravity of the Townshend–Walpole opposition. In turn the Prince asserted his independence by setting up house in Leicester Fields which for the next two years this was to be a rival court and the resort of those disaffected politicians prepared to play the long game.

The split within the ranks of the Whigs was to remain in place until 1720. But whatever the strength of the Townshend–Walpole axis it was insufficient to blunt the foreign policy conducted by George and Stanhope. In July 1718 Britain entered a Quadruple alliance with the Empire, France, and Holland which had the particular effect of challenging Spanish claims in the Mediterranean. Though Stanhope worked hard to avoid a breakdown in relations with Madrid (he and George seriously considered returning Gibraltar, though not the more valuable Port Mahon on Minorca) there was a fundamental clash of interests here, not least that Spain had a higher opinion of her own power than the members of the new alliance. Stanhope's quest for peace, which took him on a mission to Spain in the summer of 1718, was at odds with Spain's desire to regain those Italian territories it had lost at Utrecht. It had been active in that area in 1717 and in June 1718 a Spanish force invaded Sicily provoking the Royal Navy to engage and defeat the Spanish fleet off Cape Passaro in August. Though this could be justified by reference to Britain's alliance with the Empire, it was unquestionably a battle fought between two powers formally at peace with one another. Diplomatic niceties were made good on 17 December when Britain and France declared war on Spain. It was, thankfully, so one-sided a contest as to be short and slight, though it did lead to Spanish support for the Jacobite cause. In September 1717 Spanish moves in Italy had stimulated Jacobites to 'pluck up their spirits'.[45] Indeed, Spain sent two invasion forces to England early in 1719, the first of which was turned back by bad weather but the second and smaller of which reached Scotland. But a force of just 300 Spanish soldiers, even when joined to some 1,000 clansmen, was unlikely to make much of an impact and was soon defeated by a regime that even hired Swiss troops to bolster its strength. Britain's contribution to war with Spain was mainly naval, though France sent troops into north-western Spain and Catalonia in 1719. Threats to Spain that it would lose all of its territories

[44] *Ryder Diary*, p. 310. Princess Caroline, 1683–1737, married 1705.
[45] 'The Diary of the Rev. John Thomlison', *Publications of the Surtees Society*, 118 (1910), p. 82.

in Italy unless it joined the alliance system was enough to bring the war to an end in January 1720. With it a balance of power of sorts was established in southern Europe. At much the same time international agreements were also reached in northern Europe where the death of Charles XII of Sweden in December 1718 opened up new possibilities for peace that culminated in the Treaty of Hystad of August 1721. Stanhope and Lord Carteret played a full part in bringing to an end a generation of warfare in the Baltic, stimulated in good measure by a desire to secure Hanover's position. The claim made in the King's speech in November 1719 that 'all Europe, as well as these kingdoms, is upon the point of being delivered from the calamities of war by the influence of British arms and counsels' was not altogether a piece of patriotic bluster.[46]

BACK TOGETHER AGAIN

As George gradually attained his foreign policy objectives so he increasingly came to appreciate British interests and outlooks. By degrees he distanced himself from his Hanoverian ministers in London, to the extent that in November 1719 it was claimed that he had resolved 'not to suffer his Germans to meddle in English affairs, he having forbid them to presume so much as to speak to him about them'.[47] Naturally this removed a fundamental source of tension from the domestic political scene, but it could not end the powerful opposition of Townshend and Walpole to the ministry. In the 1718–19 parliamentary session they had again swallowed their principles and unsuccessfully opposed the repeal of the Occasional Conformity and Schism Acts, and in December 1719 they were at the forefront of the forces ranged against the Peerage Bill. The struggles over those Bills were important lessons to George and the ministry, showing that the Tories were still numerically significant and able to act in concert, and that opposition to controversial measures could be both vociferous and effective. The Peerage Bill was met by a wave of publications that debated the nature of the constitution and the social implications of closing off a channel of personal advancement. Many Whig MPs who had supported the Septennial Act saw the Peerage Bill as a step too far and were unwilling to ignore the weight of public opinion, the vote against it being 269 to 177. The 'great appearance' of victors celebrating at Leicester House on the night of the vote only added 'more Fuel to the Flame' of political divisions between the King and his son and between the court Whigs and the composite opposition.[48]

[46] Cobbett (ed.), *Parliamentary History*, vol. 7, p. 602.

[47] H. M. C., *The Manuscripts of the Earl of Carlisle* (1897), p. 23.

[48] *Tory and Whig: The Parliamentary Papers of Edward Harley, Third Earl of Oxford, and William Hay, MP for Seaford, 1716–1753*, ed. S. Taylor and C. Jones, Parliamentary History Record Series, 1 (1998), p. 225.

This defeat clearly established the political value of Townshend, Walpole, and discontented Whigs, and opened up the prospect that their 'Low'ring Venom' would lead to further defeats for the ministry.[49]

That prospect was soon closed, however, when in April 1720 the King was formally reconciled with his son and the Whig breach was healed. Clearly these were not coincidental developments, but it is less obvious why each occurred. Certainly Walpole increased his value to George dramatically in 1720. First his support for the payment of a debt of £600,000 on the civil list effectively guaranteed its success and naturally endeared him to the Crown. Second, he played a leading (though far from sole) part in reuniting the royal family. In the winter of 1719–20 he 'was every Day . . . once, if not twice, at *Leicester House*', and looked to Caroline as the means of persuading the Prince of Wales to end the breach. He 'engrossed and monopolised the *Princess* to a Degree of making her deaf to Everything that did not come from him', recognizing that relations between her and the King had remained sympathetic despite the breach in 1717 (she had continued to see her children at St James's Palace).[50] The rift was finally ended when the King and the Prince met privately, if very stiffly, on St George's Day. Londoners immediately celebrated. Two days later there was a reconciliation for the leaders of the two sides of the Whig party at Sunderland's house, though what brought this about, or what deals were struck, is unknown. Perhaps Stanhope and Sunderland feared that they were going to lose their monopoly of the King's affections—though that seems unlikely given their successes in foreign policy; possibly they badly needed Walpole's skills of financial management; more likely they just desired an easier time in Parliament, especially the Commons, for the ministry and found that this could be achieved without giving either of their opponents particularly powerful positions. This last point is crucial, for in June 1720 Walpole was made Paymaster-General again and Townshend was appointed Lord President, neither position being in the front rank. Perhaps Townshend and Walpole were themselves weary of opposition, eager for place and profit. Either way the Whig schism had ended, closing a brief period in which the Tories enjoyed some heightened influence. Surely now, with agreement at both home and abroad, with the end of the parliamentary session on 11 June, and with the King in Hanover from 15 June to 10 November, there would be Whig dominance and domestic tranquillity? Instead London was engulfed in the frenzy of the South Sea Bubble.[51]

---

[49] *The Complete Works of Sir John Vanbrugh*, ed. B. Dobrée and G. Webb, 4 vols. (1928), vol. 4, p. 124.

[50] *Cowper Diary*, p. 134.   [51] See above, pp. 334–5.

The absence of Townshend and Walpole from government between 1717 and 1720 meant that they were quite unconnected to the political chicanery and corporate skulduggery which led to the madness of the summer of 1720 (Townshend may have lost a little money in the stock market collapse, Walpole made some). By contrast the Duchess of Kendal, Sunderland, and other ministers had all benefited from gifts of stock from the Company. Moreover, solving the crisis in public finances consequent upon the bursting of the Bubble was beyond the limited and tainted financial abilities of either the Chancellor of the Exchequer, John Aislabie, or the First Lord of the Treasury, Sunderland, whose 'reputation was not very high in matters of the revenue'.[52] Rather, from outside the Cabinet Walpole, following the advice of his banker, Robert Jacombe, devised the means of rescuing the situation by relieving the South Sea Company of some of its obligations and involving the Bank of England and the East India Company in the scheme to manage the national debt. Though this plan was not put into practice for more than a year it had the effect of re-establishing some measure of confidence in the public finances, just as Walpole's presence in the government reassured City interests. In 1721 stock prices slowly began to recover some of the ground they had lost in the second half of 1720. But a subtler change was also at work, for Walpole's success in reordering public finances enhanced his reputation and authority while Townshend's marked time. What had hitherto been an equal partnership was soon to be headed by the socially inferior Walpole.

The financial problems facing the ministry after the hastily-called Parliament met on 8 December paled in comparison to the political problems. So many people had lost such huge sums in the South Sea speculation, including MPs and peers, and the scale of the fraud was so considerable, that the conduct of both the Company and ministry came under intense scrutiny. Outside Parliament a wave of pamphleteers and journalists sought out culprits as well as explanations. Most notably in the *London Journal* John Trenchard and Thomas Gordon's 'Cato's letters', which began on 5 November 1720, explored not only the madness of Exchange Alley but also the failings of a political system which had enabled the catastrophe to occur. Typical was their view that 'Publick corruptions and abuses have grown upon us: Fees in most, if not in all, offices, are immensely increased: Places and employments, which ought not to be sold at all, are sold for treble values . . . salaries have been augmented, and pensions multiplied'.[53] The mood in London could not have been darker,

---

[52] 'Onslow Manuscript', p. 510. John Aislabie, 1670–1742, educated St John's College and Trinity Hall, Cambridge, entered Commons 1695, Privy Councillor 1716–21, and Chancellor of the Exchequer 1718–21.

[53] J. Trenchard and T. Gordon, *Cato's Letters: or, Essays on Liberty, Civil and Religious, and Other Important Subjects*, ed. R. Hamowy (Indianapolis, 1995), vol. 1, pp. 145–6.

breeding such a witchhunt that rational argument, hard evidence, party strength, and personal interest counted for little. 'Let us pursue to disgrace, destruction, and even death, those who have brought this ruin upon us, let them be ever so great, or ever so many'.[54] The Commons established a thirteen-man committee to enquire into the débâcle, five of whom were Hanoverian Tories and six were independent Whigs. Papers were seized, witnesses called, and the directors of the Company forbidden to leave the country. Parliamentary punishments were easily meted out, the estates of all directors were seized, and four who were also MPs—Sir Robert Chaplin, Sir Theodore Janssen, Eyles, and Sawbridge—were expelled from the House and sent to the Tower. Much more controversial was the fate of those politicians who had been embroiled in the affair. Sunderland, Aislabie, and Charles Stanhope, secretary of the Treasury and first cousin to James Stanhope, were all accused of having accepted huge bribes. Aislabie, 'dark, and of a cunning that rendered him suspected and low in all men's opinion', was thrown to the wolves, losing his offices and expelled from the Commons, but in late February and early March 1721 the ministry fought hard and ultimately successfully to save Sunderland and Stanhope.[55] The pressure was too much for some. On 16 March 1721 James Craggs senior, Postmaster General, probably killed himself for fear of what might befall him (the details of his death are hazy).

The first three or four months of 1721 were pivotal to the political history of George's reign as the ministry headed by Stanhope and Sunderland was replaced by one headed by Townshend and Walpole. This began with the death of James Stanhope on 2 February, probably of a stroke, after a bruising encounter in the Lords with the Duke of Wharton—they traded insults by adept reference to the history of ancient Rome. George I was deeply moved by the death of a minister who had never wavered in his support for him but now had to turn to Townshend to fill his boots. Yet this was not a decisive appointment as two weeks later the equally surprising death from smallpox of the other Secretary, James Craggs junior, led to the succession of Lord Carteret who was a follower of Sunderland and a favourite of the King not an ally of Townshend or Walpole.[56] Walpole was, of course, best suited to succeed Aislabie as Chancellor of the Exchequer and by mid-February was inspecting 'all the Treasury business tho' he do's not take the direction of it in form till the end of the Sessions.'[57] He came into the Treasury on 3 April, however, because

[54] Trenchard and Gordon, *Cato's Letters*, vol. 1, p. 122.

[55] 'Onslow Manuscript', p. 510.

[56] John Carteret, 1690–1763, succeeded as Baron Carteret of Hawnes 1695, took seat in House of Lords 1711, envoy to Sweden in 1719, and prominent in the peace negotiations in the Baltic 1719–20, his ability to speak German helped him in relations with George I.

[57] *Vanbrugh Works*, vol. 4, p. 128.

Sunderland as First Lord felt bound to resign for his part in the South Sea fiasco. Sunderland was also valued by the King, but the fact that he had depended on Walpole for his defence and that on 15 March 172 voted him guilty, against 233 for acquittal, left him innocent but also tainted and enfeebled. He soon resigned as First Lord of the Treasury though he retained his post of Groom of the Stole in the King's household, continuing to provide him with some means of influencing the King. He remained temperamentally hostile to Townshend and Walpole and with his supporters in the ministry continued to provide an important alternative view even though his grip on power was now mainly indirect.

Even in June 1721, with the parliamentary session in its last phase, so awful had been the experience of the South Sea Bubble that it was observed that 'People are very angry'.[58] This continuing turmoil was in some measure due to Walpole's skilful defence of those accused of ill-doing. He wore down opposition in Parliament by prolonging proceedings, but at the cost of so increasing antipathy towards him that he became what he forever remained in the minds of opponents, an unprincipled 'skreenmaster general'. So bitter was the memory of the Bubble and so hostile were the reactions to Walpole's subsequent tactics that with a general election due in the following spring there was a very real chance of a significant change in the fortunes of the Whigs. Nor were the Tories a spent force, for if they continued to lack powerful leadership they offered a viable alternative to the Whigs and were in policy terms relatively untainted by the South Sea Bubble. Indeed, Sunderland kept open some channels of communication to them through 1721 and early in 1722—it was even claimed in February 1721 that they were 'offered carteblanche if they would heartily come in to support the present government', presumably in the hope of halting Walpole's rise to eminence.[59] And Jacobites naturally took heart from the government's difficulties in 1720 and 1721. Though the Pretender now lived in some poverty in Italy, though they were bereft of foreign support, they could suppose that more and more people had come to see the damage brought by the Hanoverian succession. Opportunities of sorts were available to opponents of the Whigs, even if with hindsight they look hopeless.

WALPOLE'S MOMENT

The appointment of Walpole as Chancellor of the Exchequer in April 1721 marked the beginning of his political pre-eminence and by the summer of 1722 he had become the dominant force in the political world. A number of factors contributed to this. First, his management of the aftermath of the South Sea

[58] H. M. C., *Carlisle*, p. 34.   [59] Mahon, *History of England*, vol. 2, Appendix, p. xvii.

crisis gave him an importance that none could deny, raising his stature and significance above that of Townshend. As part of this he assiduously attended to the parliamentary session that ran from 19 October 1721 to 7 March 1722, tirelessly attending to business in the Commons, producing an atmosphere of stability where passions cooled. Second, and partly as a consequence, the general election of March 1722 did not lead to a rejection of either the Whigs or of Walpole. Certainly there were many contests, more indeed than in any other general election in this period, but only 170 Tories were returned. The ministry threw everything into getting their way and many were the complaints of 'prodigious Bribery' and 'vile Corruptions', of 'men who prowl about the country to buy boroughs', and 'of a deal of Riotous doings'.[60] Third, Sunderland's death on 19 April of pleurisy, aged only 48, removed at a stroke the major source of opposition to Townshend and Walpole. Finally, an ageing King showed little interest in affairs now that his European schemes were settled—since 1719, more especially since he became reconciled with his son, his ministers had enjoyed considerable freedom of action. Though George never admired Walpole he well knew his political skills and administrative capacities and after Sunderland's death never thought seriously about replacing him—nor was royal favour showered on Townshend, who was later reckoned by George II 'as no more than an honest man . . . and attributed to the warmth of his temper and his scanty genius, the strength of his passions and weakness of his understanding, all the present intricacy, uncertainty, and confusion in the affairs of Europe.'[61]

Walpole was the leading politician, the Prime Minister, from 1722 until 1742. His longevity was in stark contrast to those frequent changes of government which had marked the reigns of both William III and Anne. With the benefit of hindsight explaining his success is not difficult, but contemporaries in the early and mid-1720s had no reason to suppose that he would survive in power any longer than had, say, Godolphin or Harley. They knew, of course, that the Septennial Act meant that he might not have to face the electorate until 1729. But they knew that in 1722 Walpole was personally unpopular—because of his unprincipled actions during the Whig schism, his avarice, and his antics as the 'skreenmaster'—and they supposed that future political crises were inevitable and would soon consume his political career. Surely the King or his son would make demands that Walpole could not meet? Surely France, Spain, Sweden, or Russia would so menace English interests that the army and navy would be mobilized, taxes raised, and public credit exploited? Surely

---

[60] 'Diary of Thomas Smith, Esq., of Shaw House', *Wiltshire Archaeological and Natural History Magazine*, 11 (1869), p. 87; Trenchard and Gordon, *Cato's Letters*, vol. 2, p. 507; *Vanbrugh Works*, vol. 4, p. 141.

[61] *Lord Hervey's Memoirs*, ed. R. Sedgwick (2nd edn., 1952), p. 35.

Dissenters and latitudinarians would press hard for full toleration, perhaps even comprehension? Surely an effective opposition to Walpole would emerge from the ranks of disaffected Whigs and Tories?

Walpole's success was built upon a studious appreciation and, wherever possible, avoidance of the sources of political instability under William and Anne, an admiration and adaptation of the techniques of political management advanced by Godolphin and Harley, and by an iron determination to remain in power. He threw all of his very considerable energy into running and justifying his government. The value of this should not be underestimated for he appreciated more clearly than any of his predecessors, save Harley perhaps, that this meant winning the approval of the Commons. He knew that it was the ability to carry measures there, especially money Bills, which determined whether a ministry was sound or hollow. Whereas Harley and Stanhope had been happy to be elevated to the Lords while they were leading ministers Walpole remained in the Commons until he fell from grace—though partly because the Lords no longer provided the opposition it once had to ministries. He declined a peerage in 1723 (his son accepted one in the same year), though he characteristically revelled in the distinction of being made a knight of the revived Order of Bath in 1725 and of the Order of the Garter in the following year. Yet it was not simply his presence in the Commons which was crucial, but the fact that he took infinite pains to explain questions to MPs. He would layout the government's programme to Whig backbenchers *en masse* before each session, frequently attend sittings, speak powerfully, and critically judge the mood of the House so quickly as to allow tactical retreats to be easily made when needed. Nor was he above taking every effort to load the dice, establishing what contemporary critics referred to as the 'Robinocracy'. He kept a close eye on all levels of government appointments in the hope of forming a phalanx of dependable placemen—by 1727 there were nearly 150 in the Commons. Even the impeachment of the Lord Chancellor Macclesfield on charges of bribery and selling offices in 1725 (for which he was fined £30,000) allowed him to bring in a more loyal follower, Sir Peter King.[62] Later he worked hard at general elections to get his followers returned. In the Lords too he did not take the Whig majority for granted, though he often used the Lords as a convenient means of blocking measures which he preferred not to oppose in the Commons. Indeed, in the Lords Townshend was both an able spokesman

---

[62] Thomas Parker, 1666–1732, educated Trinity College, Cambridge, barrister Inner Temple 1691, MP 1705, knighted 1705, active in prosecuting Sacheverell in 1710, Lord Chief Justice of England 1710, created Baron Macclesfield 1716, Lord Chancellor 1718, created Earl of Macclesfield 1721. Peter King, 1669–1734, barrister Middle Temple 1698, MP 1701, knighted 1708, defended Whiston against charge of heresy in 1713, Chief Justice of Common Pleas 1714, Privy Councillor 1715, created Baron 1725, Lord Chancellor 1725–33.

and a committed ally until his retirement in 1730, just as Gibson, Bishop of London, provided some control of the episcopal bench, earning the sobriquet 'Walpole's pope'—Walpole was also fortunate in directing the appointment of 16 bishops between January 1722 and December 1725.

Close control of the parliamentary arena was just one arm of Walpole's hold on power, the other being the policies he pursued. His agenda was as carefully considered as it was moderate: peace, low taxes, unrestrained exports, and limited toleration for Dissenters were his watchwords. At every turn he sought to avoid controversy, looking to lower the political temperature. On the face of it this was the programme of a Norfolk squire, not of a former champion of metropolitan Whiggism who had railed at Sacheverell in 1710. Doubtless his own bitter experiences in 1710 and 1711 were formative here. Certainly, such a middle way was attractive both to many Whigs and Tories, encouraging some of the latter to change their colours. Yet with the Protestant succession secure, the Pretender in Italy, a new European balance of power established (more especially with both France and Spain weakened), and Dissent in the doldrums the old Whig agenda was no longer as relevant as it had once been. In that sense Walpole's pragmatism merely continued the drift of the Whigs towards the middle ground that had first been visible when the Junto gained the upper hand under William III. What should not be underestimated is Walpole's very considerable skill in composing a set of policies that was attractive to a substantial proportion of the political nation. He constantly sought to cheapen government by making the revenue services more efficient, renegotiating parts of the national debt to take advantage of falling interest rates, and limiting spending upon the military to immediate areas of national security. He also fully appreciated the benefits of economic well-being, encouraging exports of manufactures by removing duties and agriculture by keeping the land tax as low as possible.

Walpole also sought not only to avoid confrontation but also to undermine opposition. The failure to call Convocation after 1717, if not his decision alone, ensured that a once potent source of discontent was silenced. The sting was taken out of the complaints of Dissenters by improving the right of Quakers to affirm rather than swear in 1722, by making a limited commitment to Indemnity Acts that eased the restrictions of the Test and Corporation Acts, and by the small treasury grant to the widows of Dissenters begun in 1722 (the 'regium donum').[63] The City Elections Act of 1725 helped to control London's influential role as a leading voice in the opposition. And, most importantly of

---

[63] The first Indemnity Act was passed in 1714, but they became almost annual from 1727 with 13 George I, c. 29, 'An Act . . . for Indemnifying Such Persons who have Omitted to Qualify Themselves Within the Time Limited for that Purpose'.

all, Walpole sought constantly to isolate the Tories and to have 'everybody to be deemed a Jacobite who was not a professed and known Whig.'[64] The death of Sunderland had closed off the only significant link the Tories had had with the King, indeed just before he died he had been struggling with a 'Tory Scheme' which 'he was endeavouring to work the King to'.[65] More important, the discovery of the Atterbury 'plot' in May 1722 allowed Tory associations with Jacobitism to be kept in the political foreground. Atterbury had been the High Church Bishop of Rochester since 1713 and was prominent in sustaining the Tory party through the wilderness years since 1714. In December 1721 he had so despaired of seeing the party come to power that he committed himself, with Lords North and Grey, Strafford, and Arran, and Sir Henry Goring, a former MP, to an armed Jacobite uprising in England. It completely failed to get off the ground. By the following May the government in London, which got wind of the plot from Paris (where the Regent notified Britain's ambassador and the Earl of Mar was pushed into revealing plans), had opened the posts, arrested the main conspirators in England, and moved its forces in a display of strength that was in dramatic contrast to Jacobite impotence. In truth the plot was no different from many other desperate schemes hatched by the Pretender and his supporters, and was certainly less of a threat than the Assassination plot against William III in 1696 (or arguably of that of Christopher Layer in 1721 and 1722), but Walpole was determined to maximize its political value to him despite the rather scanty information to hand. In October 1722 there were rumours that the Pretender was in Spain and about to sail, causing a minor panic, though one leading Whig noted that 'we seem to have the hearts of the mob . . . there was two or three thousand . . . in [Hyde] Park, huzzaing the whole royal family'.[66] Habeas corpus was suspended, the Commons investigated the plot, and Atterbury was subjected to a parliamentary show trial in the form of a Bill of Attainder (the evidence against him was too flimsy to be risked before a court of law) that led to his banishment. If the punishment was harsh for an aged, recently widowed, and sick man, then at least, unlike Layer, he escaped with his life.

On 18 June 1723 Atterbury sailed away and with him went many of the last hopes of the High Church and the Tories. Walpole assiduously cultivated the public perception that both were virtually synonymous with Jacobitism. That perception was all the easier to sustain with the return from exile of Bolingbroke, the one-time Tory leader and Jacobite, in the same month as Atterbury departed (he had in part obtained a royal pardon through a bribe to the Duchess of Kendal, the King's mistress). Though Bolingbroke was not

[64] 'Onslow Manuscript', p. 465.   [65] *Vanbrugh Works*, vol. 4, p. 143.
[66] *Hervey Letter-Books*, vol. 2, p. 245.

allowed back into the Lords his mere presence served as a general reminder of the Tories' chequered relationship with the Protestant succession. In reality, of course, the threat posed by Jacobites and Tories was now minimal. Walpole purred with contentment that 'we are otherwise in a state of tranquility and satisfaction beyond what I have ever known'.[67] The view from the other side was little different. In November 1723 the Pretender was told that

Those that govern at present are generally despised and abhored, but their power is too great not to be feared . . . they have a large army, well paid, clothed, and well provided for in all respects . . . a large fleet, and the officers of it generally, I believe, devoted to them; the comand of all the public money; and by the fatal corruption that prevails almost over the whole nation, the absolute power in both Houses of Parliament. This is a true state of the strength of your enemies—formidable it is and requires a proportional strength to contend with it . . .[68]

But neither Tories nor Jacobites had anything like enough strength to battle the Whigs and Walpole. If they were still numerous amongst the electorate and in the constituencies, in Parliament they kept a low profile. By 1727 it could be claimed that 'there is not one Tory left in England' and though that was certainly an exaggeration there is no question that the Whig's triumph was complete.[69] For the most part Walpole's opponents could do little more than wage an ideological battle and look forward to the death of George I, hoping that the new King would change the government.

Walpole's political supremacy rested upon his skilful control of an oligarchical political system as much as his ability to satisfy public opinion. Indeed, if he was able to convince many among the political nation that only he could find the holy grail of stability and prosperity, and if it can be plausibly claimed that by the standards of the time he did not so much change the political system as make it work without undue friction, many found his achievements somewhat unsavoury. To a degree unmatched by any other leading minister in this period Walpole suffered numerous and scathing attacks on his character, attacks that in due course coalesced into something approaching an effective opposition. As the very epitome of the selfish Whig oligarch he provided many opportunities for castigation and censure. If politically he was renowned for his care and energy, well earning the reputation as 'one of the best talkers in the kingdom', none doubted by 1720 that his ambition was rarely bridled by principles.[70] His manipulativeness was legendary and no less importantly as a

[67] W. Coxe (ed.), *Memoirs of the Life and Administration of Sir Robert Walpole*, 3 vols. (1798), vol. 2, p. 266.

[68] Mahon, *History of England*, vol. 2, Appendix, p. xx.

[69] *The Complete Letters of Lady Mary Wortley Montagu*, ed. R. Halsband, 3 vols. (Oxford, 1965), vol. 2, p. 81.

[70] *A Foreign View of England*, p. 228.

person he offended many: he was a dressy showman; he wallowed in the fruits of office; his enjoyment of luxury was legendary (he built a grand house at Houghton, filling it with exquisite furniture, fabrics, paintings, and china); and he eschewed the virtues of charity and paternalism. Both in public and in private Walpole enjoyed living life to the full at other people's expense.

THE LAST FOUR YEARS OF GEORGE I

Politically the four years between Atterbury's banishment and the death of George in 1727 were the most uneventful since the Revolution. Whereas the last four years of William III and Anne were full of machinations the last four years of King George were something of a damp squib. It was as if the nation, exhausted as it was, had been sedated into conformity and compliance. For the most part Parliament became a matter of routine, bereft of meaningful controversy. Except for the usual round of legislation to perpetuate taxes and the military, little major legislation was initiated. Constitutional questions were avoided and such important statutes as were passed were often specific- ally focused. Consequently, legislation such as 'An Act for Encouraging the Greenland fishery' or 'An Act for to Prevent Unlawful Combinations of Workmen Employed in the Woollen Manufactures' may have been profoundly important to particular interests but they did not provoke general debate.[71] There appears to have been a real dropping away of controversy on the floor of the Commons. Looking at the sessions 1694–5, 1708–9, and 1724–5, for ex- ample, the number of petitions relating to general Bills sent into Parliament shrank from sixteen, to fourteen, and three respectively, and the number of divisions on all legislation in those sessions from thirty-six, to thirty-three, and twenty-three respectively. And whereas in the 1690s it had still been common for Parliament to reject over a half of all legislative proposals put before it, by the end of George I's reign this proportion had shrunk to only about a quarter. Increasingly business was so well organized that Parliament did not need to sit on Saturdays and it says much that the House of Commons had but one Speaker, Spencer Compton, from March 1715 to January 1728.[72]

In so far as there were unpredictable elements which might break the somnolence that enveloped England's political world from 1723 they were largely in the area of foreign policy. Even here the uncertainties were limited in number and scale. After the death of Charles XII Sweden posed little threat, except in its vulnerability to Russian expansionism, and the French and Russian

---

[71] 10 George I, c. 16 and 12 George I, c. 34.

[72] Spencer Compton, 1673?–1743, created Earl of Wilmington 1730, MP 1698–1710, 1713–27, Speaker 1715–28, Paymaster General 1722–30, Lord Privy Seal and Lord President of the Council 1730, First Lord of the Treasury 1742.

ships of state were for a time left rudderless with the deaths of the Regent in November 1723 and of Peter the Great in 1725. In southern Europe, however, stability was overturned by the forging of an alliance of convenience between Austria and Spain in 1725, provoked in part by France's rejection of the Infanta as a match for the 15-year-old Louis XV. Townshend viewed this as a grave threat to the European balance of power (not least because it was conceivable that one man might inherit France, Spain, and Austria), to the security of the Protestant dual alliance, and to British commercial interests in the Mediterranean. He quickly cobbled together the Alliance of Hanover between Britain, France, and Prussia, signed in September 1725. But in November Russia joined Austria and Spain and two great powerblocks faced one another in an atmosphere of considerable mistrust. By May 1726 'Wars and rumours of Wars make all the conversation at present' and the nation was put on a defensive footing, to pay for which the land tax was raised.[73] Though war was formally avoided there were skirmishes at sea and for much of 1727 Spain besieged Gibraltar, only moving back in the following year after the Convention of the Pardo.

Such developments gave the ministry's opponents some issues they could look to exploit, though with the Tories isolated and divided such opposition was hard to find. Within the ministry some remnants of Sunderland's adherents, notably Lord Carteret, Secretary of State, remained in 1723 to provide something of a counterweight to Walpole. An able diplomat, a German speaker, and respected by the King, he was also intent on a degree of independence and ambition for Britain which filled Walpole with anxiety, reluctant as he was to see Britain abandon the Quadruple Alliance or take on new commitments. But by degrees Walpole and Townshend managed to edge their rival out of the King's affections and in 1724 he was replaced by Thomas Pelham-Holles, the Duke of Newcastle, a man of immense wealth and significant electoral influence.[74] However, this promotion stimulated a second serious source of opposition from within the ranks of discontented Whigs. William Pulteney had followed Walpole into opposition in 1717 but had been rewarded with only minor if lucrative office after 1720.[75] For a man of great ambition, certain of his abilities, he was particularly angry at the promotion of Newcastle who was honest and loyal but lacked political insight, imagination, and decisiveness. By 1725 Pulteney opposed Walpole actively. This he did by his power of oratory,

[73] *Montagu Letters*, vol. 2, p. 65.

[74] Thomas Pelham-Holles, 1693–1768, educated Westminster School and Clare Hall, Cambridge, created Earl of Clare 1714 and Duke of Newcastle 1715, held high office for over forty years.

[75] William Pulteney, 1684–1764, educated Westminster School and Christ Church, Oxford, MP for Hedon 1705–34 then Middlesex 1734–42, created Earl of Bath 1742.

often confronting Walpole head on in questions of public finance and, in the aftermath of the Macclesfield scandal, by joining with Bolingbroke in a paper campaign carried on in the pages of the *Craftsman*. This first appeared in December 1726 and elegantly explored alternative definitions of the public good as well as outlining the dangers of executive corruption. Central to this view was the definition of the true 'Patriot', to the extent that by the early 1730s this had become a label attached to the opposition. For ten years the *Craftsman* would keep up a remorseless attack on Walpole, by the early 1730s having a circulation of perhaps 10,000.

In part the Patriot opposition drew some of its inspiration from the campaign waged in *Cato's Letters*, the last of which was published in November 1723, and which, in turn, had links back to the radical Whig and Country programmes of the 1690s and 1700s—in 1724 some could still refer to the existence of a 'country party'.[76] Moreover, that opposition was part of a wider and powerful journalistic assault on Walpole's ministry which by 1727 was of much greater significance than anything the Tories or Jacobites could then muster. The literary opposition to Walpole took several overlapping forms: the neo-Country *Craftsman*; the radical tradition of the 'True Whigs'; the Jacobitism of *Mist's Weekly Journal*; and the Tory Wits, notably Pope, Gay, and Swift. The last of these, the 'Scriblerians', has left a particularly powerful impression. Swift's *Gulliver's Travels*, published in October 1726, immediately became celebrated as a commentary on human affairs and the moral poverty of the contemporary political world. 'From the highest to the lowest it is universally read, from the Cabinet-council to the Nursery.'[77] Yet the very breadth of the literary attacks on Walpole also meant that they were inchoate. Moreover, if some ideological positions were considered and incisive others were curious and quizzical. The Duke of Wharton, godson of William III, used his paper the *True Briton* sometimes to attack the government in 1723–4 before joining the Pretender's cause abroad and converting to Roman Catholicism, all the while proclaiming his Whig credentials.[78] Nor was Walpole prepared to turn a blind eye to attacks on him and his government, indeed as a political pugilist he never pulled his punches. By libel accusations he used the courts to try to silence his critics and also put much time and money into waging a massive counter campaign that in quantitative terms dwarfed the ministerial propaganda of the previous two reigns. Newspapers such as the *London Journal*, *Free Briton*, *Daily*

---

[76] *The Parliamentary Diary of Sir Edward Knatchbull, 1722–1730*, ed. A. N. Newman, Camden Society, 3rd Series, 94 (1963), p. 31.

[77] *The Letters of John Gay*, ed. C. F. Burgess (Oxford, 1966), p. 60.

[78] Son of the Junto lord, Thomas Marquis of Wharton. Born 1698, created Duke in 1718, he opposed the South Sea scheme and Atterbury's attainder. He served with Spanish forces against Gibraltar in 1727 and died in poverty in 1731.

Courant, *Corn-Cutter's Journal*, and *Daily Gazetteer* were begun or bought up and made to toe the party line, and hired hacks advertised the regime's achievements. If this campaign lacked the literary genius of the opposition—its most prominent voices were William Arnall, Thomas Gordon, Benjamin Hoadly, and John Hervey—it was not without effect. In May 1727 Swift was apoplectic at Walpole's willingness to hire 'Scoundrels . . . Beasts and Blockheads for his Pen-men, whom he pays in ready Guineas very liberally.'[79] Slowly a 'Court Whig' ideology, justifying the middle way, was constructed and propagated.

Though the paper war between Walpole and his opponents was a war over what was done at Westminster and who was responsible for it, it was in a very real sense also extra-parliamentary, spreading political debate and gossip across the nation. Papers and pamphlets were read widely, and not just by the electorate. Indeed, they were particularly attractive to those with some education, some financial security, and few if any opportunities to vote. Economic advances and urban growth were gradually creating a class of artisans, shop-keepers, and merchants who were eager to imbibe the likes of the *Craftsman* and the *Free Briton* in coffee-houses and inns—not to mention those Dissenters who continued to scowl at their legal inferiority. In time this developing political consciousness would powerfully challenge the assumptions that had created the dead hand of oligarchical politics. Bristol, Newcastle, Norwich, Birmingham, Manchester, and other centres would become important voices of an alternative political vision that was often industrial, commercial, and imperial and which complained that the balance of the constitution had been weighted in favour of aristocracy at the expense of democracy. But if by 1727 that voice had only effectively been raised in London its potential was clear, partly provoking Walpole to pass the City Elections Act. Indeed, Walpole found it much easier to calm Westminster than the sites of local politics. Even after 1722 the vestry and the corporation often continued to be a battleground between Tory and Whig, between Jacobite and Hanoverian, and between High Church and Low Church.

CONCLUSION

On 15 May 1727 Parliament was prorogued and at the start of June the King set out for Hanover where he was to spend the summer and early autumn. He never made it, for on 11 June he unexpectedly died, aged 67, at Osnabrück. Townshend, who had been travelling with the royal party, soon returned to London, while George's body was taken to Hanover for burial. In London both Whigs and Tories immediately submitted themselves to George II at Leicester

---

[79] *Swift Correspondence*, vol. 3, p. 207.

House. In the spirit of the last four years of George I there was a palpable sense of a non-event. Some mourned the loss of the King, to some he was 'great and good', but to many he was simply unmissed.[80] He had not led the nation in feats of war, or presided over impressive artistic endeavours. And undeniably his contribution to the greatest political achievement of his reign, the supremacy of the Whigs and Walpole, was relatively modest. Had he meant more then his death might have provoked more changes. It did not. Rather, Walpole was able to ingratiate himself with George II with unexpected ease by using his close friendship with the Queen and offering to find funds for a larger civil list than any monarch had previously enjoyed. There was, in any case, no credible alternative that George II could turn to. An attempt to frame a new distribution of power under the leadership of Spencer Compton quickly collapsed. Even before the end of June it was noted how 'The political world rolls on just as it did.'[81]

Politically, therefore, the period ended very calmly. The corridors of power echoed with the heavy shoes of continuity. Yet that was only possible because there had been such profound changes—the creation of one-party rule, the heightening of Walpole's political conservatism, septennial elections, the passage of the Riot Act, the collapse of Jacobitism, a largely effective European balance of power, a cultural drawing together of the political elite, and a significant reduction in the political significance of religious questions. Consequently, in the 1720s many among the propertied showed less and less interest in political issues. Parliament became increasingly a matter of routine, increasingly an arena not of fractious debate but of a consensus that often went unspoken. It still had the teeth which Charles II and James II had feared, but for a time at least it had little to chew upon. And aside from brief flurries that was not really to change for a generation.

[80] *Clegg Diary*, p. 24.
[81] Earl of Ilchester (ed.), *Lord Hervey and his Friends, 1726–38* (1950), p. 21.

CHAPTER 13

Urban and Urbane

The dramatic urbanization of English society in the seventeenth century rested fairly and squarely on the explosive growth of London. But though the capital's growth continued in the eighteenth century collectively the expansion of hundreds of small and large towns scattered across the nation was now of greater significance. The economic causes and consequences of this have already been explored—towns were important sites of processing and manufacturing, fulcrums for rural domestic industry, conduits for marketing goods and raw materials from both home and abroad, and lures to internal migrants.[1] But towns also played wider and increasingly significant social and political roles: as opinion formers, as places of resort and pleasure, and as the nodal points in the government of the nation. In a very real sense towns linked English society: centre with regions, patricians with plebs, buyers with sellers, minds with ideas.

More and more people were coming into contact with towns, permanently or fleetingly, remoulding English society in the process. If this was felt most immediately by those who became town dwellers, it had a wider impact through the ways in which new urban functions, tastes, and habits spread out into the country more generally. One of the most important aspects of this was the role towns played in changes in the pursuit of leisure in this period, of establishing the empire of 'the Taste of the Town'.[2] Increasingly towns offered the attractions of spas, horse-racing, balls, assemblies, clubs, plays, concerts, bookshops, printsellers, and art dealers. Such lures were important in satisfying the needs of both social conviviality and what Addison memorably called the 'Pleasures of the Imagination or Fancy'.[3] He argued that such pleasures —visual, literary, and aural—occupied an important middle ground between mere sensual enjoyments on the one hand and a philosophically robust

---

[1] See particularly, Chapter 3.

[2] *A Comparison Between the French and Italian Musick and Opera's. Translated from the French; with Some Remarks. To which is Added A Critical Discourse upon Opera's in England, and a Means Proposed for their Improvement* (1709), p. 85.

[3] *The Spectator*, ed. D. F. Bond, 5 vols. (Oxford, 1965), vol. 3, p. 536.

aestheticism on the other. Even so, Addison's argument was avowedly elitist, 'A Man of a Polite Imagination, is let into a great many Pleasures that the Vulgar are not capable of receiving.'[4] If there was no place here to celebrate the popular world of the alehouse and cockpit, or of the ballad singer, juggler, contortionist, or magician, Addison was identifying and also helping to champion an important new dynamic in the cultural world, the conspicuous and self-conscious consumption of leisure and pleasure by the middling and upper sorts. That dynamic was of crucial significance both in stimulating artistic endeavour and in helping to reshape notions of politeness and civility that, through a renewed censoriousness, affected the lives and social identities of the poor as well as the rich.

THE URBAN SCENE

In 1700 about one in four or five English people were urban dwellers, though a much larger proportion would have come into regular contact with the 800 or so towns and cities scattered across the nation. Indeed, town and countryside were mutually dependent partners, not different worlds, with the growth or decay of one necessarily affecting the fortunes of the other. On the urban side generally there was growth, the proportion of the national population living in centres with at least 5,000 people rising from perhaps 8 per cent in 1600 to 17 per cent in 1700 and 21 per cent in 1750. But such figures, even allowing for their speculative nature, are something of an oversimplification. In the first place contemporaries defined towns not with reference to a quantitative threshold but as an amalgam of population concentration and function, which is to say that they knew a town when they saw one. To them towns could be very small places indeed, perhaps with no more than several hundred people and differentiated from villages only by the range and scale of facilities available. If they well knew the significance of London, or a large regional centre such as Norwich, they also called 'towns' those hundreds of small centres which today would be seen as little more than villages with markets. Put another way, there were 31 towns or cities with populations above 5,000, 37 with populations between 2,500 and 5,000, and about 700 with less than 2,500. So prevalent were these small towns that it has been estimated that some 54 per cent of urban dwellers in the early eighteenth century lived in centres of less than 5,000 people.[5]

[4] *The Spectator*, vol. 3, p. 538.

[5] All these estimates are tentative. See P. J. Corfield, *The Impact of English Towns, 1700–1800* (Oxford, 1982), ch. 1; P. Clark, 'Small Towns in England 1550–1850: National and Regional Population Trends', in P. Clark (ed.), *Small Towns in Early Modern Europe* (Cambridge, 1995), pp. 90–120.

TABLE 17. *Towns with a population of at least 10,000*

c.1670		c.1750	
Town	Population	Town	Population
London	475,000	London	675,000
Norwich	20,000	Bristol	50,000
Bristol	20,000	Norwich	36,000
York	12,000	Newcastle	29,000
Newcastle	12,000	Birmingham	24,000
		Liverpool	22,000
		Manchester	18,000
		Leeds	16,000
		Exeter	16,000
		Plymouth	15,000
		Chester	13,000
		Coventry	13,000
		Nottingham	12,000
		Sheffield	12,000
		York	11,000
		Chatham	10,000
		Great Yarmouth	10,000
		Portsmouth	10,000
		Sunderland	10,000
		Worcester	10,000

Source: E. A. Wrigley, *People, Cities and Wealth: The Transformation of Traditional Society* (Oxford, 1987), p. 160.

England's urban hierarchy was dominated by London, which was more than twenty times the size of the next largest city, Norwich. The capital's population had grown rapidly in the seventeenth century, from some 200,000 to about 490,000, thereby doubling its share of the national population from about 5 to 10 per cent. However, though in absolute terms London continued to grow rapidly in the eighteenth century (by 1720 its population was about 600,000 and by 1800 very nearly one million), in relative terms its share of national population hardly changed. Such relative stagnation should not be overemphasized, not least because London's absolute growth took place from a very large base. Nevertheless, the fact that England was increasingly urbanized after 1700 was due to new sources of dynamism within the urban hierarchy, a sense of which can be gained by comparing the number and size of larger towns in 1670 and 1750 (see Table 17). There were just five such large towns or cities in 1670, but twenty by the middle of the eighteenth century—a rate of expansion wholly distinctive in European terms where the proportion of people living in large towns hardly changed over the period. Most of these 'new' large towns were either ports or manufacturing centres, or both. They fed into and drew strength from the slow but evident expansion in England's industrial base and commercial world. Thus, for example, by the 1720s Liverpool was already 'the Third Town in *England* for Trade, especially to the Plantations' and at Birmingham "'tis incredible the Number of People maintained by those Iron and Bath-Metal Works, and the great Perfection they have brought it to; furnishing all *Europe* with their Toys, as Sword-Hilts, Screws, Buttons, Buckles, and innumerable other Works.'[6] But many large towns also served as important regional centres, as focal points for an agrarian economy which, as has been seen, was also enjoying some expansion. Indeed, the regional realignment which was such an important part of agricultural change was only possible because of the facilitating role played by towns—as markets, both for purchase and sale, as co-ordinating points in transportation networks, as information gateways, as repositories of professional expertise, as centres of law and government, and as concentrations of capital and credit. Finally, Britain's developing State stimulated the growth of some towns. Royal dockyards were the lifeblood of Chatham and Portsmouth—'the two great arsenals of England'—but many towns and cities served as major sites of local government, as boroughs sending MPs to Parliament, as staging posts for assize judges on their circuits, or as local centres for the customs and excise services.[7]

The forces stimulating the growth of England's larger towns also played upon those hundreds of smaller towns scattered across the countryside, many of which grew substantially. Such small towns thrived especially in the West Midlands, South Yorkshire, the Thames valley, to the north of London, and on the south coast. But the forces which stimulated their growth might work against other towns. Difficulties in the East Anglian and Devon textile industries led to a degree of urban decay, and if developments in transportation, financial services, and interregional trade helped some towns this was sometimes at the expense of near neighbours. As some towns began to enjoy economies of scale so others found themselves increasingly uncompetitive, leading to a thinning out of England's market towns in this period. That is to say, there existed an urban hierarchy and interdependence which was being reformed under competitive pressures. Of course the influence of economic forces was not simply consequent upon industrial, commercial, or agricultural developments. Small towns might retain their local government functions even as their trade declined; despite increasing religious heterodoxy the function of cathedral cities was undiminished; and since the Restoration other towns

---

[6] [J. Macky], *A Journey Through England*, 2 vols. (2nd edn., 1722), vol. 2, pp. 151, 170.
[7] D. Defoe, *A Tour Through the Whole Island of Great Britain*, ed. P. Rogers (Harmondsworth, 1978), p. 152.

had developed as social centres serving a wide hinterland. The last of these was especially and increasingly important in this period. Changes in the taste of the gentry, particularly their increasing resort to towns for an active social life, was a major general factor at work. At Beverley, for example, Sir John Perceval noted the 'great resort of Gentry upon account of its pleasant Scituation for game, nearness to York, and goodness of the town, the Streets are broad, & well pav'd, the houses, new, large, & handsome & the Churches very bewtyfull.'[8] Such changes of taste of polite society was most obvious with the growing fashion for taking the waters at spas such as Bath, Epsom, and Tunbridge Wells. For example, if Tunbridge had been a spa since 1606 it was still little more than a hamlet in 1680 when it began to grow quickly. The patronage of Princess Anne in the 1690s enhanced its popularity significantly, such that by 1703 it was even the subject of a London play, Thomas Baker's *Tunbridge Walks, or, the Yeomen of Kent*. Celia Fiennes was probably a typical visitor, drinking the water at Tunbridge for 'many years with great advantage', but also relishing the wider gentry society there, not to mention the 'shopps full of all sorts of toys, silver, china, milliners, and all sorts of curious ware . . . besides . . . two large Coffee houses for Tea Chocolate etc., and two roomes for the Lottery and Hazard board'.[9]

The development of Beverley and Tunbridge Wells were a part of what has been labelled an 'English urban renaissance', of a growth and cultural re-formation of many towns.[10] Not the least part of this was the changing physical environment within towns: the growing use of brick, tile, and sash windows (and hence the declining incidence of devastating town fires); a willingness architecturally to employ classical references or allusions; a greater attention to ordering streets, most notably in the laying out of squares; and the erection of public buildings, be they town halls, customs-houses, assembly rooms, or theatres. Towns as diverse as Ludlow, Warwick, and King's Lynn were involved in this trend—Warwick, for example, had been largely destroyed by fire in 1694 but it was soon 'rebuilt in so noble and so beautiful a manner, that few towns in England make so fine an appearance.'[11] Much of this effort at urban

---

[8] *The English Travels of Sir John Percival and William Byrd II: The Percival Diary of 1701*, ed. M. R. Wenger (Columbia, Missouri, 1989), p. 104. Sir John's family name is more usually spelt 'Perceval'.

[9] *The Journeys of Celia Fiennes*, ed. J. Hillaby (1983), pp. 152–3. Fiennes, 1662–1742, was the granddaughter of William Fiennes, 8th Baron and 1st Viscount Saye and Sele. Defoe, *Tour*, p. 166, believed that different spas attracted particular visitors: 'the nobility and gentry go to Tunbridge, the merchants and rich citizens to Epsome; so the common people go chiefly to Dullwich and Streatham'.

[10] P. Borsay, *The English Urban Renaissance: Culture and Society in the Provincial Town, 1660–1760* (Oxford, 1989).

[11] Defoe, *Tour*, p. 405.

renewal and regeneration was private, the cumulative outcome of thousands of disconnected decisions, as land and homeowners looked to keep in touch with current taste. That is to say there was a quest for fashion, an enthusiastic embracing of what for them was contemporary and new and which, in the process, began to create what is loosely described as 'Georgian'. But occasionally this atomised approach was circumvented, with large landowners pursuing a broad urban plan, using their wealth in pursuit of income and cultural advantage. This was markedly the case at Whitehaven where the presiding influence was Sir John Lowther, a man whose fortune rested upon coal, agriculture, and trade. One visitor noted,

This town is very well built the Streets being broad and regular and the houses very large and even. Within 40 years ago there were not 40 houses now by their own industry & Sr: John Louthers help there have 6 or 700. Sr: John has a Seat just without it built A Church and free School and owns most part of the town. The Harbour will hold neer a 100 Shipps . . . who fetch great quantitys of tobacko from Virginia, and transport to Ireland much coal & Iron Oar.[12]

Lowther was certainly not unique, many other landowners, such as the Grevilles at Warwick, were similarly influential, but local government provided a more pervasive influence upon the urban landscape by increasingly attempting to regulate and stimulate towns by reference to best practice and taste. Liverpool's local council, for example, obtained an Act of Parliament allowing it to build England's first commercial wet dock (opened in 1715) with which it quickly established a significant presence in the burgeoning world of Atlantic commerce. Other towns sought economic advantage by drawing in the well-to-do, most famously at Bath and most generally through encouraging or undertaking the building of assembly rooms for the consort of local polite society.

The early Georgian townscape was distinctive, with an identity setting it apart from what had come before. Of course the extent of building and rebuilding by 1727 was limited, with much of the urban scene still old, but a new trajectory had been set which proved highly durable—here at least 'Georgian' has proved more durable than 'Stuart'. But towns were also becoming different because of who was to be found there, especially of the prospering middling sort and provincial gentry. Some sense of this has been gained by the observations cited of Fiennes and Perceval. But much is summed up by the increasing significance of the professions in towns—especially of doctors and lawyers, but also of bankers, surveyors, clerics, and military men. From about 1680 doctors gradually established professional status, eating into the territory previously divided between apothecaries and surgeons. In part this was because they

---

[12] *English Travels of Percival and Byrd*, pp. 128–9.

purported to have access to a controlled and verified body of knowledge available only at university and overseen by the Royal College of Physicians. Many had been educated at Leiden, though Scotland was also 'really fruitful of Surgeons' who came south 'like flocks of Vultures' in pursuit of prosperity and pleasure.[13] Numerically more significant than doctors were the 5,000 or so attorneys in England and Wales by the end of the period. They too were distinguished by the body of knowledge they claimed to utilize, but some were as important for their functions as financial intermediaries as lawyers. Because they were so heavily involved in drawing up land contracts and wills they were well sited to provide a bridge between those with and those in need of investible funds and in the eighteenth century played a pivotal role in the operation of local capital markets that helped to fund the first industrial revolution.

Growing numbers of doctors and attorneys, along with other emerging professions, helped to strengthen the place of the middling sort in towns as well as serving the world of the propertied more generally. Certainly it is easy to assume that the spirit of early Georgian town is encapsulated by such men and their families inhabiting the 'new worlds of squares, walks, and coffee-houses. But order and politeness was but a part of the urban scene. As ever urban growth posed problems of the provision of basic amenities which were often addressed only once they had become acute; housing the large labour force needed to make towns work was subject to economic pressures which gave little opportunity for producing neatly framed squares or uniform streets; successful towns attracted poor as well as rich, increasing the burdens upon labour markets, poor law provision, and charitable impulse alike; and as focal points in the pursuit of pleasure towns became a bloody battleground between different visions of taste and decency. Bristol provides a case in point, a city which flourished through its involvement in the trade of slaves, sugar, tobacco, and Midlands hardware—its population rose from 20,000 to 36,000 between 1670 and 1750 and its transatlantic trade by 53 per cent over the first three decades of the eighteenth century. Certainly this encouraged the upgrading of the urban landscape—three squares, a new council house, and two theatres were built in our period—and polite diversions flourished, from a music society to winter assemblies. But such prosperity attracted migrants from near and far, leading at times to unemployment and destitution. With rising poor rates the city established a workhouse to which it might send 'Rogues Vagrants Sturdy Beggars and idle and disorderly persons', but even so complaints continued of the city being 'pestered and filled with Vagabonds Vagrants and Wandring

---

[13] *James Thomson (1700–1748) Letters and Documents*, ed. A. D. McKillop (Lawrence, 1958), pp. 12–13.

poor'.[14] In 1698 there was a concerted attempt to return many of the poor to their home parishes and 'The Ballad-singers . . . received a strict charge to appear no more'.[15] And alongside complaints of idleness went those of loose living, the local Society for the Reformation of Manners cajoling and nagging the city authorities to halt 'all manner . . . disorderly practices that may further prophaness and debauchery'.[16] Nor should the wider disruptive effects of Bristol's success be underestimated. If its merchants and businessmen stimulated trade up and down the Severn, and later invested in the burgeoning industries of South Wales, from another perspective the city could be seen as sucking the vitals out of local communities. At Worcester market in 1693, for example, corn factors from Bristol were perceived as raising local prices, which 'occasioned a mutiny'.[17]

LONDON LIFE

In 1700 London was over twice the size of such major cities as Madrid and Venice, and was just then overtaking Paris as the largest city in Western Europe. It was indeed 'the chief City of the *British* Empire . . . one of the biggest and richest Cities of the World'.[18] In England's urban hierarchy it was a giant among dwarfs, altogether different and distinct. Yet if it was an extraordinary city, it was also an equivocal one. It could on the one hand be reckoned 'the greatest City in Europe' and 'the most Spatious, Populous, Rich, Beautiful, Renowned and Noble [city] that we know of at this day in the World: 'Tis the Seat of the *British* Empire, the Exchange of *Great Britain* and *Ireland*; the Compendium of the Kingdom, the Vitals of the Common-wealth, and the Principal Town of Traffic'.[19] But to others it was 'monstrous', or 'being one tenth of the People of England, it is too numerous in Proportion to the rest of the Kingdom'.[20] Certainly there was no question about its great size and enormous variety. One guide book reckoned it had 844 streets and lanes, 2,152

[14] *Bristol Corporation of the Poor: Selected Records, 1696–1834*, ed. E. E. Butcher, Bristol Record Society, 3 (1932), pp. 51 and 62.

[15] *Post Boy*, 19–22 February 1698, [p. 1].

[16] *Reformation and Revival in Eighteenth-Century Bristol*, ed. J. Barry and K. Morgan, Bristol Record Society, 45 (1994), p. 22.

[17] N. Luttrell, *A Brief Historical Relation of State Affairs from September 1678 to April 1714*, 6 vols. (1857), vol. 3, p. 29, see also p. 32.

[18] [T. Cox], *Magna Britannia et Hibernia, Antiqua & Nova. Or, a New Survey of Great Britain*, 6 vols. (1720–31), vol. 3, p. 69.

[19] B.-L. de Muralt, *Letters Describing the Character and Customs of the English and French Nations* (2nd edn., 1726), p. 75; *A New View of London; or, an Ample Account of that City*, 2 vols. (1708), vol. 1, p. i.

[20] *Diary and Correspondence of John Evelyn*, ed. W. Bray, 4 vols. (1850–2), vol. 3, p. 356; A. R. Fry, *John Bellers, 1654–1725: Quaker, Economist and Social Reformer* (1935), p. 61.

lesser lanes and alleys, 20 squares 'mostly very large and pleasant', 20 markets, 2 cathedrals, 122 Anglican churches and chapels, 4 colleges, 24 free schools (and at least 600 private ones), 28 courts of law, 40 livery company halls, 70 incorporated companies and societies, and 700 Hackney coachmen.[21]

Not the least significant aspect of London's history in this period was its demographic expansion. It was not simply that it grew rapidly, but that its growth impacted upon much of the rest of Britain, largely because it took place despite deaths significantly exceeding births in the capital. Death was omnipresent in London in this period, giving its social world a particularly bitter flavour. About a half of deaths in the capital were of children under the age of 10, one-third under the age of 1. 'Consumption' (varieties of tuberculosis and other respiratory diseases) and smallpox were common killers, but the causes of death were very various. Because of such high levels of mortality London was something of a demographic black hole, sucking in migrants from near and far to feed its appetite for expansion. Between 1690 and 1730 there were something like 710,000 baptisms in London, but over 901,000 burials. This imbalance, averaging 4,775 per annum, was a major structural feature of England's demographic system, in place through much of the seventeenth and eighteenth centuries, though particularly marked in the second quarter of the eighteenth century. To make up this shortfall and to fuel growth of about 2,750 persons per annum meant that London was attracting about 7,500 migrants each year in our period. Integrating so many newcomers into the markets for accommodation and jobs, as well as into new ways of life, was inevitably stressful and chaotic producing a society of extraordinary extremes and novelties.

People literally risked their lives in moving to London, though of course the risks were much greater for the poor and the very young than the rich and the adult. But they did so because the vibrancy of the capital provided opportunities on a scale and range unavailable elsewhere. London was much more than simply the nation's political capital, it was a centre of commerce (domestic and foreign), manufacturing, law, the arts, and many professions. Consequently occupationally it was formidably diverse, 'the mighty *Rendezvous* of *Nobility*, *Gentry*, *Courtiers*, *Divines*, *Lawyers*, *Physitians*, *Merchants*, *Seamen*, and all kinds of Excellent *Artificers*, of the most Refined Wits, and most Excellent Beauties'.[22] Making some sense of this variety and dynamism is not easy, but crudely speaking the sources of growth can be characterized as either those operating upon the old City (the square mile) or in the rapidly developing West End.

For the City much rested upon its role as the nation's premier port, though it was an exaggeration to claim that 'the City of London owes its whole being

---

[21] *New View of London*, pp. i–v.

[22] T. de Laune, *Angliæ Metropolis: or, the Present State of London* (1690), p. 298.

to the Thames'.[23] Nevertheless, the quays, wharfs, dockyards, and warehouses that ran from London bridge and the Tower east were integral to the fortunes and character of the capital. Huge amounts of capital and labour were caught up in this vast trade, and merchants and distributors were the princes of the City's business world. London was indeed a great clearing-house, for the manufactures of provincial England, for its own large industrial sector, and for imports from Europe, the Americas, and Asia. Looking downstream from London bridge all one saw was 'a continued Forest of Ships of all Nations'.[24] Thousands of jobs, often highly insecure, depended upon that forest. Such insecurity was largely caused by trading to distant and unpredictable markets: the seasons, storms, wars, and pirates all took a heavy toll. More than any other town or city London was embroiled in international affairs, its health dependent upon channels of trade that were becoming more and more distant. Hardly less important, however, were the financial aspects of the City's prosperity, of the development of insurance and banking, partly arising from the growth of overseas trade but partly from the establishment of the national debt and changing attitudes towards insurance provision. The success in this period of the Bank of England and of Lloyds hints at these transformations. Two revolutions, the 'commercial' and the 'financial', profoundly influenced the growth of London, the first generally since the Restoration, the second almost exclusively since the wars following William's invasion in 1688. The financial revolution did not merely expand the scale and scope of London's economic base, it also began to transform its political functions, for financiers increasingly had a powerful voice at Westminster, providing something of a bridge, but also a potential source of tension, between the East and the West Ends.

In the middle of the seventeenth century 'London' was almost two separate cities, of Westminster in the west and the City of London in the east, joined only by the umbilical chord of the Strand. There had been little development north of Covent Garden, west of Charing Cross, or, because there was only one bridge across the Thames, south of the river, though Southwark was already being described as a '*Suburb*'.[25] But the West End rapidly developed from the late seventeenth century, extending it 'to Hide Park Corner in the Brentford Road, and almost to Maribone in the Acton Road, and how much farther it may spread, who knows? New squares, and new streets rising up every day'.[26] Such developments, largely accommodating middling sorts of people, drew their initial stimulus from the growth of parliamentary government, both because of the regular influx of MPs and peers and their families and the permanent

[23] J. Beeverell, *The Pleasures of London*, trans. W. H. Quarrell (1940), p. 19.
[24] [Macky], *Journey*, vol. 1, p. 78.   [25] [Macky], *Journey*, vol. 1, p. 291.
[26] Defoe, *Tour*, p. 286.

presence of the clerks and officers of the wider State, and of the development of the London season. That season, running through much of the winter and spring, had its origins in the early seventeenth century, but in this period gained a new impetus from the absolute and relative increase in a more consumer orient-ated pursuit of fashion and pleasure. As will be seen, this was the world of the coffee-house, club, lodge, opera, and masquerade. It was a world of enjoyment, display, association, and competition—as at St James's park with its 'hand-some Walks of Lime-trees and Elms' where 'Society comes to walk . . . Some . . . to see, some to be seen, and others to seek their fortunes', among them 'many priestesses of Venus'.[27] As in provincial urban England the increasing presence in London of landowners provided fertile conditions for the growth of the service and leisure sector, not only maintaining but heightening London's role as the heart of England's emerging professions and polite pleasures.

So powerful was the draw of London that labour was rarely in short supply there. Indeed, people struggled to find sufficient well-paid work to allow them to enjoy a reasonable living standard in a city already renowned for exorbitant prices. For good and ill the decline of the regulatory efficiency of the guilds, not least because of the growth of London outside the old City, left an increas-ing proportion of workers open to the unimpeded force of the market mechan-ism. Seasonality was an integral part of the capital's economy, arising from the rhythms of Parliament, the law courts, the weather, and the trade winds. Visitors were frequently struck by the numbers of men and women who existed on the margins, of the beggars, pickpockets, and prostitutes. Indeed in 1716 a committee investigating the poor rates in London concluded that there had been a marked 'Increase of strange Beggars, Cripples, lusty Men and Women, Vagbonds, Blind People, pretended and real Mad Folks'.[28] Marcellus Laroon's engravings of the dozens of criers and hawkers of London, published in 1687 and going through six editions by the early eighteenth century, gives another sense of the ingenuity of people in selling either goods or themselves to make ends meet. Women particularly struggled to find good jobs. Many spinsters, perhaps 60 per cent, worked in domestic service, though such work was usu-ally closed to married women. Among women over the age of 24 the needle trades, charring, laundry work, nursing, and hawking provided many jobs, but these were often very poorly paid indeed. In such an environment the connec-tion between poverty on the one hand and prostitution and alcohol misuse on the other (the 'gin age' began in the 1720s) seems clear enough, though few contemporaries made it.

---

[27] T. Fairchild, *The City Gardener* (1722), p. 11; *A Foreign View of England in the Reigns of George I and George II. The Letters of Monsieur César de Saussure to his Family*, trans. and ed. Madame van Muyden (1902), p. 48.

[28] *Weekly Journal, or British Gazetteer*, 17 March 1716, p. 360.

London suffered from its own problems and, frequently, of those of the nation as a whole in concentrated form. Not least, nowhere showed up better the paradox of poverty amidst plenty. Contemporaries were not blind to this. '*London*, every Body knows, is a City extreamly rich . . . and yet the Town is crouded with Beggars.'[29] Such a paradox posed huge problems of order and challenged polite notions of decency, calling forth attempts to reform the criminal justice system and poor law provision while stimulating others to extend the scale and scope of charity. Moreover, the urban fabric was also badly disordered in places. If the townscape of the West End was regular, the street lighting generally good, and the shops impressive, the streets were famously muddy in the wet, forcing women 'to raise themselves upon Pattins, or Galoshoes of Iron to keep themselves out of the Dirt and Wet.'[30] If clean water was generally available the Thames was fast becoming a common sewer and the winter air was already thick with coal smoke. Crucially London lacked a unitary political authority to attempt a concerted solution to such problems. Much was left to individual parishes, which often lacked the resources to act, while the Corporation's efforts were limited by its restricted jurisdiction, myopic vision, and lack of political will.

London was in certain senses two cities: of Westminster and the City; of the West and the East Ends; and of the court and the port. If it was not actually schizophrenic it was certainly frenetic, a boom city that was at times out of control. Little wonder then that with its size this led some to stigmatize it as destructive and parasitic. Certainly it drew in not only people but food, fuel, raw materials, and manufactured products from near and far. Defoe was worried that 'London . . . sucks the vitals of trade in this island to itself', particularly noting how East Anglian ports were losing out from 'the immense indraft of trade to the city of London'.[31] It was, of course, easy enough to note how many routes led to London and to imagine that the flow of benefits was entirely centripetal. But it was possible to argue a different case. Houghton was sure that the size of London invigorated the rest of the country, promoting 'great designs', wanting to hear nothing of those 'petty objections of the heads being too big for the body'.[32] From this perspective London's vast market heightened productivity in provincial agriculture, trade, and industry by supporting a more extensive division of labour and specialization of function. Moreover, it supplied the rest of the country with many goods, services, and ideas in return, and its absorption of much labour presumably alleviated poverty elsewhere. More than that, however, London was at the forefront of those developments

---

[29] H. Misson, *Memoirs and Observations in his Travels over England* (1719), p. 221.

[30] Misson, *Memoirs and Observations*, pp. 214–15.   [31] Defoe, *Tour*, p. 68.

[32] J. Houghton, *A Collection for the Improvement of Husbandry and Trade*, 4 vols. (1727–8), vol. 1, p. 443.

which were eventually to produce long-term economic growth. It was a modern and socially diverse city where tradition had less play. In so far as people chose to embrace it, as both gentry and poor seemed to, they were on balance happy with that sense of novelty. It was a place of prosperity, promise, and pleasure, as well as of poverty.

THE PURSUIT OF PLEASURE

In a sense there were two types of urbanization occurring in the seventeenth and eighteenth centuries, a growth of permanent town dwellers as well as of a significant minority of more or less temporary visitors. Among this second group were poor people on the move in search of work, business people (from hawkers to merchants) in search of trade, governors in search of authority, and everyone in search of amusement, leisure, and companionship. The last of these, the pursuit of pleasure, had emerged as a particularly distinctive feature of English society after the Restoration to became a powerful motor of change around 1700. Though the pleasures sought looked to gratify mind and body with bewildering variety—from the politeness of Addison and Steele's *Spectator* to the sexual license of a masquerade, or from tea to gin drinking—common threads ran through the social form these took, for pleasure was often pursued not individually and narcissistically but collectively and socially.

Nowhere shows up the social world of pleasure better than the development of Bath, which grew rapidly from the late seventeenth century to become the pre-eminent 'Georgian' city, both then and now. Initially the waters attracted visitors, the Roman antiquity of which only served to underscore their supposedly efficacious properties. They were 'hot, of a blueish Colour, strong scent, and send forth thin Vapours; and as, without question, they have strengthened many weak and feeble Limbs, so they do cure divers Diseases', 'especially Impotency Sterrility &c'.[33] Certainly most visitors took a dip in the baths, but relatively few were ill and Bath attracted most as a playground of the well-to-do, albeit only on a seasonal basis—'five Months in the Year 'tis as Populous as *London*, the other seven as desolate as a Wilderness'.[34] Vital to establishing such a function were visits by Queen Anne and the Prince of Denmark in 1702 and 1703, royal patronage that was vigorously exploited by the corporation, who not only built a new road to the town for the royal party but welcomed them with a keen sense of kitsch. By one report they were met by a 'fine Company of Citizens, all clad like Grenadiers', and by '200 Virgins richly attired,

---

[33] J. Brome, *Travels over England, Scotland and Wales* (2nd edn., 1707), p. 42; *Britannia Depicta or Ogilby Improv'd* (1720), p. 85.
[34] [E. Ward], *A Step to the Bath: with the Character of the Place* (1700), p. 16.

many of them like *Amazons*, with Bows and Arrows' with 'a Set of Dancers, who danc'd by the Sides of her Majesty's Coach'.[35]

If such taste is curious, the corporation had a deep insight into the town's potential as a leisure resort and pursued such an ambition with real imagination and commendable commitment. In the first place it was actively involved in building some of the facilities which were to be vital to Bath's fortunes—a playhouse was opened in 1705, the first Pump room in 1706, the first Assembly rooms in 1708, and a Ballroom in 1720. No less critical, in about 1705 it appointed Beau Nash as Master of Ceremonies.[36] He became the guiding life of society at Bath, directing many events and defining standards of decorum that served it through much of the eighteenth century. By 1716 it was reported that 'Gnash is the man here that is the life and soul of all their diversions. Without him there is no play nor assembly nor ball and everybody seems not to know what to do if he is absent. He has the privilege of saying what he pleases and talking to the ladies as his fancy leads him and no affront is to be taken'.[37]

But Bath was no paradise of politeness undisturbed by more down to earth considerations. Sexual licence was a notable feature, beginning at the baths where one could view 'Celebrated Beauties, Panting Breasts, and Curious Shapes, almost Expos'd to Publick View'.[38] No less important there was often a keen sense of social competitiveness among the visitors. In part this was because Bath attracted company as diverse as dukes, minor gentry, clerics, and prosperous businessmen, which in a world wedded to distinctions of rank and degree set up clear enough tensions. No less important was Bath's function as a clearing-house for marriage partners among the gentry and urban middling sort. Gossip of eligibility was vital, but more significant was ranking the eligible according to their actual or prospective fortunes. Little wonder then that 'There is a sort of Civil War here among the Quality, who run into Parties in all their Diversions, occasioned by the private Balls carry'd on one against the other, insomuch, that when they meet at the Publick Balls, those, of different Sides, will sooner speak to Plebians, than to one another'.[39]

Bath provides the most significant example of a type of polite sociability increasingly to be found in many towns in early eighteenth-century England.

---

[35] A. Boyer, *The History of the Reign of Queen Anne, Digested into Annals*, 10 vols. (1703–13), vol. 1, p. 78.

[36] Richard 'Beau' Nash, 1674–1762, born in Swansea, educated Jesus College, Oxford, briefly tried the army in 1692 and the law in 1693 before settling on gambling as a source of income. First visited Bath in 1705, drew up a code of conduct in 1742, though his star quickly waned, given pension by Bath Corporation 1758.

[37] *The Diary of Dudley Ryder, 1715–1716*, ed. W. Matthews (1939), p. 240.

[38] [Ward], *A Step to the Bath*, p. 13.   [39] *Mist's Weekly Journal*, 9 October 1725, [p. 2].

Such urban sociability might, however, be seasonal and relatively ephemeral, determined more than anything by the rhythms of Parliament, the court, and the assize circuits. More permanent resorts of pleasure were provided in towns by coffee-houses (including chocolate houses), taverns, and clubs. The first coffee-house had been opened in Oxford in 1650, with London following in 1652. Soon they proliferated everywhere, a town such as Ipswich having at least eight open in our period. But they were especially numerous in the capital, which Macky guessed at 8,000 in 1722 though the true number is likely to have been about 500 or 600.[40] Often charging admission of a penny, serving coffee, chocolate, and other drinks, making available newspapers, periodicals, and pamphlets, they were arenas for the dissemination of news and rumour, places of conversation and opinion, meeting rooms for buyers and sellers, and dens of friends and acquaintances. 'They smoak, game, and read the *Gazettes*, and sometimes make them too. Here they treat of Matters of State, the Interests of Princes, and the Honour of Husbands, &c. In a Word, 'tis here the *English* discourse freely of every Thing, and where they may be known in a little Time'.[41] Though in one sense generally available, in practice they were exclusive, most notably as male bastions, but also because of their emphasis upon literacy and expense (coffee was still relatively expensive and admission charges, modest though they were, kept out many). Instead 'The common people and low populace have their taverns, or rather spirit shops', but among skilled artisans, shopkeepers, tradesmen, and successful businessmen coffee-houses were vital places of resort.[42]

More than anything coffee-houses were stores of news and factories of opinion. Conversation played upon fact, rumour, and fiction to produce ideas of society. Given their popularity the importance of this in defining public opinion should not be underestimated. Many men would go to coffee-houses daily, often having one or two favourites—in his diary the law student Dudley Ryder mentioned twenty-four he went to in a period of eighteen months. Few doubted the wider significance of this, Addison complaining of 'The Dictators in Coffee-Houses' and Swift that 'It is the Folly of too many, to mistake the Eccho of a London Coffee-house for the Voice of the Kingdom.'[43] In practice, especially in London, coffee-houses often specialized as meeting places. They could, of course, be small or large, formal or not. Notably, some became the

---

[40] A number of historians have cited a figure of 2,000, perhaps because of the 2,034 listed in B. Littlewhite, *London Coffee Houses: A Reference Book of Coffee Houses of the Seventeenth, Eighteenth and Nineteenth Centuries* (1963), though as the title hints many of these were not operating in our period.

[41] Muralt, *Letters*, p. 82.   [42] *A Foreign View of de Saussure*, p. 165.

[43] J. Addison, *The Freeholder*, ed. J. Leheny (Oxford, 1979), p. 266; J. Swift, 'Conduct of the Allies', in *Political Tracts, 1711–1713*, ed. H. Davis (Oxford, 1973), p. 53.

focal points of particular interests. For example, stockjobbers mainly operated out of Jonathan's and Garraway's, the marine insurance market began life in Edward Lloyd's coffee-house in the 1680s, and the Cocoa Tree chocolate house established about 1698 became a haunt of Tories. Steele mocked such specialization, that 'All accounts of Gallantry, Pleasure, and Entertainment, shall be under the Article of *White's Chocolate-house*; Poetry, under that of *Will's Coffee-house*; Learning, under the title of *Grecian*; Foreign and Domestic News, you will have from the *St. James's Coffee-house*', though when Addison, his friend and colleague, set up the *Guardian* as a new periodical in 1713 its famous lion's head letterbox was put in Button's coffee-house.[44]

As Steele's observation suggests in some cases the lives of clubs and societies, formal or not, intermingled with coffee-houses. Like coffee-houses, clubs had emerged in the Restoration era, but attained major prominence after 1689. Such prominence was due to two main reasons. First, the increasing use of clubs for political debate and organization outside the corridors of power. This had its origins in the 1640s and 1650s and had been further encouraged in the Exclusion crisis, but now, in an era of continuous, heightened but structured political factionalism, became a major link between parliamentary and extra-parliamentary politics. On one side were the likes of the Whig Mughouse club, on the other the Tory Calves Head or October clubs. Second, but far from separately, there was a close relationship between clubs and the expansion of literary life under William III and Anne—in one guise coffee-houses acted as quasi-subscription libraries. Dryden had shown the way in the 1670s and 1680s at Will's coffee house, but it was to be carried to new heights at the Whig Kit Cat club, formed in 1696 and effectively defunct by 1717, 'the best Club, that ever met' in Vanbrugh's view.[45] Though the Kit Cat had at its heart such political heavyweights as Somers, Wharton, and Walpole, it also included among its members Addison, the dramatist Congreve, and the publisher Jacob Tonson. Its memory has been vividly perpetuated because between 1702 and 1717 Kneller, another member, produced his famous 42 'Kit Cat portraits', many of which now hang in the National Portrait Gallery. That it had no effective competitor on the Tory side only served to emphasize its prominence, though attempts were made with the smaller coteries of the St John's Brothers club in 1711 and

---

[44] R. Steele, *The Tatler*, ed. D. F. Bond, 3 vols. (Oxford, 1987), vol. 1, p. 16. Richard Steele, 1672–1729, born Dublin, educated Charterhouse, London, some military experience, for a time ran the *London Gazette*, much involved with journalism and literary life, entered House of Commons 1713, confirmed Whig, expelled for seditious libel 1714, returned 1715, knighted 1715. Joseph Addison, 1672–1719, also educated at Charterhouse, and at Queen's College, Oxford, Fellow of Magdalen College, Oxford, 1698–1711, combined a career in literature with one in government service as a Whig.

[45] *The Complete Works of Sir John Vanbrugh*, ed. B. Dobrée and G. Webb, 4 vols. (1928), vol. 4, p. 167.

the Scriblerus club of Pope, Swift, Arbuthnot, Gay, and Parnell briefly established in 1713 and 1714.

Clubs existed in all shapes and sizes, and if their motives might be laudable, as often as not they were devoted to excess. Ward mocked the pretence for 'Humane Conversation', satirizing clubs as 'Suck-Bottle Assemblies' given over to 'inebrious Health-Drinking and impertinent Tittle Tattle'.[46] The very name of the Beefsteak club, founded in 1705, gives some credence to the view that clubs might be dens of gluttony. Most notoriously, the pleasures of the flesh were championed in the nascent Hell Fire clubs which emerged about 1720, prompting a royal proclamation in April 1721. In 1721 one visitor to London from Wiltshire was so shocked by their 'blasphemous Impieties' that quite what they got up to were 'not fit to be committed to paper', though he did note that they involved 'Several Persons of high Rank and of both Sexes'.[47] Three years later Lady Mary Wortley Montagu reported with characteristic directness that '20 very pritty fellows (the duke of Wharton being President and cheif director) . . . meet regularly 3 times a week to consult on Galant Schemes for . . . Whoring.'[48] Contemporaries were indeed so struck by the links between clubbability and libertinism that they almost certainly exaggerated its potency.

If there was a halfway house between clubs that were polite and those that were licentious they are perhaps best summed up by the development of freemasonry in this period. In London the craft guild of masons had a charter dating back to 1410, and elsewhere masons had been long established as skilled workers with a clear collective identity and authority over particular skills. But most guilds had begun to lose their regulatory functions in the seventeenth century. What set the masons apart is that their guild took on a new direction and sense of purpose, becoming not a collection of operatives but a society dedicated to a particular moral and convivial order, all enjoyed secretly amidst a wash of ritual. Because of the quest for secrecy it is not easy to delineate the development of what is known as 'speculative' masonry. There is evidence of lodges at Chichester in 1696, Scarborough in 1705, and York in 1712, and in London a grand lodge, meeting at the Stationer's Hall, was established in 1717. Indeed, the establishment of the grand lodge, along with the grand mastership of the Duke of Montagu in 1721, and publication of the Revd James Anderson's *The Constitutions of Masons* (1723) are all evidence of the growing

---

[46] [E. Ward], *The Secret History of Clubs: Particularly the Kit-Cat, Beef-Stake, Vertuosos, Quacks, Knights of the Golden-Fleece, Florists, Beaus* (1709), pp. 1–2.

[47] 'Diary of Thomas Smith, Esq., of Shaw House', *Wiltshire Archaeological and Natural History Magazine*, 11 (1869), p. 91.

[48] *The Complete Letters of Lady Mary Wortley Montagu*, ed. R. Halsband, 3 vols. (Oxford, 1965), vol. 2, p. 38.

institutionalization of these associations.[49] Initially four London lodges were regularly represented at the grand lodge, but by 1724 this had risen to 31, and it is likely that the total number of formal lodges in England at that date was between 50 and 60 (10 of which survived into this century).

Most freemasons were men of property and orthodoxy, providing something of a buttress to the Whig regime after 1714 (Walpole was a mason), even though some lodges appear to have had freethinkers as members. In 1723 one pamphleteer noted their enthusiasm for drinking the health of 'the Royal Family; the Church as by law established; Prosperity to old *England* under the present Administration; and Love, Liberty, and Science'.[50] In point of fact the link with science was fairly substantial, in London there being a significant number of Fellows of Royal Society who were also masons—one, Desaguliers, was a leading light among masons after 1717.[51] Indeed, masons celebrated the 'Seven *Liberal Sciences*, of . . . *Grammar, Rhetorick, Logick, Arithmetick, Geometry, Musick*, and *Astronomy*', perhaps reflecting the architectural and mathematical skills of their forebearers among operative masons.[52]

The world of masons, clubs, and coffee-houses was one with little or no place for women, giving a largely new institutionalized form to some older aspects of the separate social worlds of men and women. But in many other ways women were integral to the pursuit of pleasure, both within and outside of the home— of the concert room, stage, assembly, and library. And their role as consumers, at least among families living in some comfort, was probably particularly important because of their control over household expenditure. Such an imprint was certainly greatest in towns, which were vital to developing new patterns of consumer behaviour, not only by simply increasing expenditure but also through a greater emphasis upon fashion and social emulation. Because cities and towns were large places with a high population turnover and degree of anonymity, how one looked or spoke, and where one consumed goods and diversions, were vital social indicators. Towns also acted as agents in the dissemination of new products and taste, with London being especially important. New products and designs spread out from London through the urban hierarchy into the surrounding countryside, a pattern fictionalized in the *Spectator* report of a lawyer's journey from London into western England. At Staines,

---

[49] James Anderson, 1680?–1739, a Scot, educated at Aberdeen, he was a Presbyterian minister in London.

[50] *Early Masonic Pamphlets*, ed. D. Knoop, G. P. Jones, and D. Hamer (Manchester, 1945), p. 109.

[51] John Theophilus Desaguliers, 1683–1744, a Huguenot refugee from La Rochelle, educated Christ Church, Oxford, Fellow of the Royal Society 1714, presented to the living of Whitchurch Middlesex in the same year; invented the planetarium, published in a number of areas of natural philosophy.

[52] *Early Masonic Pamphlets*, p. 113.

less than 20 miles from the metropolis, the lawyer encountered 'One of the most fashionable Women I met with . . . my landlady', but at Salisbury a socially superior 'Justice of Peace's Lady . . . was at least ten Years behind in her Dress', and still further away 'we fancied our selves in King *Charles* the Second's Reign, the People having made very little Variations in their Dress since that time.'[53] Such a pattern, if overdrawn, shows some aspects of the influence of towns, though of course it was also part of the developing ideology of sophisticated urbanity that rubbished rural backwardness and rusticity.

PRODUCING AND POLICING PLEASURE

So far little attention has been directed towards the content of pleasure and leisure. There is no question that there were dramatic developments in the literary, performing, and visual arts. But such developments did not simply happen, they had to be produced—which involved important changes not only in consumer wants, but in the role of patronage, businesses, and taste. Nor was this uncontentious, for if many devoured the new world of pleasure, others were so shocked by those aspects they judged immoral that they both practised and counselled abstemiousness, complaining long and hard about the evils of luxury, licentiousness, and libertinism.

A key feature of English cultural history in these years was the often muted lead provided by the court, leaving to one side the crucial development of the increasing willingness of ministers to employ writers to put the government's case. Of course, William and Mary did plough much money and thought into their homes and gardens—employing the likes of Wren and Gibbons—and George I often attended the theatre. But there was little that was systematic, energetic, or innovative about such patronage. Similarly, though titles or pensions were conferred on deserving luminaries, and the Crown had some notable positions at its disposal, they were also often gifted to the second rate. So if, for example, Kneller held the position of Principal Painter with distinction from 1688 to 1723, the Poet Laureateship rarely went to those of exceptional literary distinction after Dryden's removal in 1689 if the court odes which by 1714 were traditionally produced for New Year's Day and the monarch's birthday are any evidence (just as the Historiographer Royal, sometimes held jointly with the Laureateship, appears to have involved undemanding and unspectacular work). So whereas the court had been a vital part of the artistic endeavours of the Restoration period, after the Revolution it became more peripheral, in part because the reluctance of all the monarchs in this period to promote the court as a vital and constant part of aristocratic society, forcing that society to look elsewhere for company and diversions—to horse-racing,

[53] *The Spectator*, vol. 2, pp. 13–14.

clubs, assemblies, opera, and spas. William, Mary, Anne, and George were for different reasons—birth, temperament, health, faith, and interests—unwilling actively to involve themselves in an increasingly vibrant polite society.

If monarchs were rarely artistic patrons, the rich more often were. Because patronage often involved a degree of personal self-advertisement it was usually done on an individual basis, though collective support from among the peerage underpinned the Royal Academy of Music founded in 1719 to produce opera in London. Many of the rich never acted as patrons, but there were the likes of the Duke of Chandos who supported Handel, Somers who helped Addison, Steele, Garth, and Swift, Halifax who aided Congreve, Prior, and others, and the Earl of Burlington who kept open house for the likes of John Gay and Alexander Pope. Quite how effective such patronage was is debatable, however, Gay complaining to Swift that though resident at Burlington house and gaining the esteem of 'many great men' this had produced 'few real benefits. They wonder at each other for not providing for me, and I wonder at 'em all.'[54] Much patronage involved, therefore, not direct financial support, but a certain recognition and esteem which enhanced an artist's chances of selling his work (if women were often patronized they rarely benefited from patronage). It might be supposed that such a relationship was usually initiated by the patron, but in publishing at least authors frequently took the lead by dedicating their work to some lofty figure in the hope of gaining credibility. Not all were impressed by such fawning, Pope adopting a posture of independence, declaring dedications a 'Prostitution of Praise', and Swift notably putting a dedication to only one of his works, *A Tale of a Tub*.[55] A growing form of patronage that was effective was subscription publishing, whereby an author and/or publisher printed the subscribers's names at the front of a work in return for a guaranteed sale. This was particularly useful in allowing greater publishing risks to be run, as in large and complex works, such as major translations, or those with a number of expensive plates, and began to become common in this period though its peak was reached later in the eighteenth century. But again such patronage was not innocent or disinterested, for a subscriber was also putting down a social marker, such as the patriotism of the 2,180 who supported Thomas Brodrick's *Complete History of . . . War in the Netherlands* (1713), the High Church credentials of the 1,417 subscribers to John Walker's *Sufferings of the Clergy* (1714), and the Whiggism and politeness of the 1,064 subscribers to Joseph Addison's posthumous *Works* (1721).[56]

[54] *The Letters of John Gay*, ed. C. F. Burgess (Oxford, 1966), p. 41.

[55] *The Guardian*, ed. J. C. Stephens (Lexington, Kentucky, 1982), p. 50.

[56] Most books published via subscription attracted far fewer supporters. The evidence here is taken from P. J. Wallis, *The Social Index: A New Technique for Measuring Social Trends* (Newcastle, 1978), pp. 49–50; see also P. J. Wallis and R. Wallis, *Book Subscription Lists Extended to Supplement the Revised Guide* (Newcastle, 1996).

If both court and private patronage played only a modest part in the expansion of the world of pleasure from the late seventeenth century, then for the most part that growth must have rested upon market forces. Consequently, not only did the creators of culture need to attend to what the public wanted, but they had to find efficient ways of reaching them. The business side of the world of culture in this period was, indeed, notably energetic and adventurous, from the book and printsellers crowded around St Paul's to theatrical entrepreneurs such as Thomas Betterton and John Rich. Indeed, rich rewards were reaped by some. In publishing, Jacob Tonson (1656?–1736) handled works by Addison, Congreve, Oldmixon, Prior, Rowe, Vanbrugh, and Wycherley, and frequently went to book markets on the Continent, before retiring in 1720 with a fortune of perhaps £50,000 to set himself up as a country gentleman at Ledbury in Herefordshire. In the theatrical world the Swiss-born and famously ugly 'Count' Heidegger (1659?–1749), who became manager of the Haymarket theatre in 1713, appreciated better than most contemporaries that the market for 'high' art was limited, but that for pantomimes, masquerades, and the like near insatiable.

In the market for culture some consumers will have much money to spend, others far less, and others none at all. A seamless hierarchy of disposable income precludes robust distinctions between the worlds of high and low art, or polite and popular culture, though a division of sorts existed between those who purchased their pleasure and those who through poverty had to make it themselves. Such seamlessness did not appeal to all, particularly those guardians of public taste who worried that market pressures were forcing the production of culture that was sensationalist, lowbrow, irreligious, and lewd. Indeed, a significant stream of criticism was produced, reminiscent of hostility to be found in the Interregnum and the 1590s, linked in part to the worries that provoked the Societies for the Reformation of Manners.[57] Coffee-houses might be condemned as nurseries 'of Indolence, and Sloth. The *Forge* of Lies.'[58] Famously, in 1698 Collier published his attack on the theatre, arguing that 'the *Present English Stage* is superlatively Scandalous. It exceeds the Liberties of all Times and Countries'. He catalogued their faults, 'Their *Smuttiness* of *Expression*; Their *Swearing, Profainness*, and *Lewd Application of Scripture*; Their *Abuse* of the *Clergy*; Their *making* their *Top Characters Libertines*, and giving them *Success* in their *Debauchery'*, and singled out such notable plays as Vanbrugh's *Provoked Wife* and Congreve's *Double Dealer* for censure.[59] In a

---

[57] See above, pp. 238–9.

[58] C. R., *The Danger of Masquerades and Raree-Shows, or the Complaints of the Stage* (1718), p. 28.

[59] J. Collier, *A Short View of the Immorality, and Profaneness of the English Stage* (1698), pp. 54 and 2. Collier, 1650–1726, educated Ipswich and Caius College, Cambridge, an active nonjuring divine, he absolved on the scaffold two to be executed for involvement in the 1696 Assassination plot which led to him being outlawed.

similar vein later there were attacks on masquerades and pantomimes as undermining serious theatre, true 'wit', and elegant thought, as well as encouraging
illicit sexual adventures. And the blame for this was often laid at the door of
the '*Managers* of our *Stage*' whose 'Excuse for this, is, their Business is to get
Money'.[60] Gambling, gin drinking, and prostitution were similarly censured,
as other pleasures were defined as luxurious and, therefore, liable to charges of
extravagance, wastefulness, effeminacy, and foreignness.

It is important to emphasis that all levels of society were subject to arguments against the unbridled pursuit of pleasure. Rich and poor alike were chas-
tised for their love of drink, proclivity to gamble, luxurious living, and sexual
promiscuity. Distinctions were naturally drawn by reference to the different
venues of and means by which 'vices' were consumed, but perhaps more
significant was the line of thought which excoriated the rich for failing to set a
proper example for the poor. In particular, many worried that young gentlemen were especially prone to fail and fall, calling them 'rakes', 'blades', 'fops',
'beaus', 'sparks', or 'gallants' because of their supposed love of ostentatious
display, frivolous fashions, drunken violence, and sexual excess (heterosexual
and homosexual). Such was the power of those fears that in 1712 it generated
something close to a moral panic, when young men allegedly ran 'out at 12 a
clock from Taverns and beat Watchmen, slit fellows noses and cut women's
arms, stop coaches or chairs, and offer violence to Ladys even of Quality'.[61]
Called 'Mohocks' because their barbarity was likened to that alleged of
American Indians, the panic was sufficient to inspire a royal proclamation,
even though hard evidence of organized or sustained violence was and is hard
to find.

Attacks on licentiousness, libertinism, and luxury were sustained and serious, demonstrating a fundamental ambivalence surrounding the production
and consumption of pleasure. And if attacks by the likes of Collier met
thoughtful and concerted opposition Dryden had in 1693 already nicely
pointed up the difficulties of defending the stage when it mocked contemporary manners. He reported how Congreve's *The Double Dealer* 'is much
censured by the greater part of the Town: and is defended only by the best
Judges, who, you know, are commonly the fewest . . . The women thinke he has
exposed their Bitchery too much; and the Gentlemen, are offended with him;
for the discovery of their follyes'.[62] But Dryden was also pointing to the
eternal tension between the expansive and adventurous tastes of some artists

[60] *A Letter to my Lord ******* on the Present Diversions of the Town. With the True Reason of the Decay of our Present Dramatic Intertainments* (1725), pp. 13–15.
[61] *The Letters of Thomas Burnet to George Duckett, 1712–1722*, ed. D. N. Smith (Oxford, 1914), p. 2.
[62] W. Congreve, *Letters and Documents*, ed. J. C. Hodges (1964), p. 95.

and the more traditional sensibilities of many consumers and critics, a tension that aesthetic theories were only slowly addressing and which would provide one line of defence against the censorious. Still, major developments did take place, notably in the *Spectator's* famous essays on the 'pleasures of the imagination and fancy', and which in the context of Shaftesbury's ideas of beauty, virtuosity, and politeness were brought to something of a pitch by Richardson's *An Argument in Behalf of the Science of the Connoisseur* (1719). There he powerfully and to an extent innovatively linked connoisseurship to gentlemanly conduct, the former requiring 'Beautiful Ideas! Clearly Conceiv'd, Strongly Retain'd, and Artfully Manag'd! What a Solid, and Unbiass'd Judgment! What a Fund of Historical, Poetical, and Theological Science'.[63] Such an argument did not offer luxury a moral *carte blanche*, of course, but that which was in good 'taste', a malleable standard of increasing significance in the early eighteenth century, could now be positively and publicly condoned.

Whatever the moralists or aesthetes might say there is no question that the pursuit of pleasure in towns not only increased in this period, but did so significantly. More and more ways of gratifying body and mind were explored, both for selfish and social reasons. Drinking, eating, dressing up, gambling, and being seen were all part of this. But if the pursuits of such pleasures had been developing through the Restoration period, after the Glorious Revolution pursuing the 'pleasures of the imagination' not only grew dramatically but took significant changes of direction. Even amidst the chaos of the years of war, political uncertainty, and religious tension the worlds of literature, drama, music, and art developed in new directions and were vigorously championed. A new confidence was developed both in producing and enjoying such pleasures, such that by the time the *Spectator* had run its course in 1714 urbanity had been dramatically extended and redefined.

THE WORLD OF READING AND THE ART OF WRITING

The efflorescence of print culture was one of the most notable developments in England in this period.[64] Enabled by the ending of licensing of the press in 1695 and partly consequent upon the intensity of political debate, it was also due to a growing thirst for literature among a wide public. It is clear that this craving for fact and fiction, poetry and prose was experienced among men and women, young and old, rich and poor. Higher disposable incomes, more leisure time for some, and an increasingly efficient publishing industry were all parts

---

[63] J. Richardson, *Two Discourses. I An Essay on the Whole Art of Criticism as it Relates to Painting . . . II An Argument in Behalf of the Science of a Connoisseur* (2 vols. in 1, 1719), vol. 2, p. 219. Richardson, 1665–1745, was a leading portrait painter of the period.

[64] For some estimates of the growth of output of published works, see above, p. 178.

of this process. It is important to emphasize that in two vital senses there existed no clear division between 'two cultures', either between science and the arts or between a literate written culture and an illiterate oral one. In a world in which music was innocently declared to be a science, and where a gentleman was expected to be acquainted equally with the classical world and contemporary astronomy the first point is obvious enough. But the second was no less important. Even those unable to read might hear the latest ballads sung, or listen to reports from newspapers read out at alehouses. Oral and literary cultures were overlapping and not separate worlds.

For the most part the growth of the printed word reflected consumer demand—most literature was written for commercial as well as artistic reasons, with many authors hoping, because of their sense of the market, to earn a living from their writing. Thus a man such as Defoe, multi-talented as he was, poured out some 318 works by the latest count because, recovered bankrupt that he was, he saw it as a good source of income.[65] He wrote not only novels but political pamphlets, social commentaries, economic analyses, a periodical, history, didactic literature, satire, and a travel account. The market for words, as has been seen, was developing and changing significantly after 1688. In crude terms there was an increase of scale, as works of all sorts proliferated, from sermons to instructional literature, learned tomes to ephemera, the salacious to the serious, and much more besides. But this growth is particularly vividly evidenced by the emergence of London's 'Grub Street' as the home of hundreds of hacks who could only survive by knowing their market. They produced not the likes of the *Spectator*, *Robinson Crusoe*, or *Gulliver's Travels* but work that was invariably ephemeral, slight, yet in its way highly significant.

Characterizing the output of Grub Street is hard, but the Pepys collection of 1,671 ballads left when he died in 1703 provides a deep insight into this world of small books, pamphlets, and broadsheets. Instructively he catalogued these under ten heads:

Devotion & Morality	History True & Fabulous
Tragedy viz. Murdrs, Execut[ions], Judgements of God & c	State & Times
Love Pleasant	Love Unfortunate
Marriage, Cuckoldry &c	Sea Lore, Gallantry, & Actions
Drinking & Good Fellowshipp	Humour, Frollicks &c mixt[66]

---

[65] Many of Defoe's works were published anonymously and there is considerable uncertainty as to what he wrote. See P. N. Furbanks and W. R. Owens, *Defoe De-Attributions: A Critique of J. R. Moore's Checklist* (1994) and M. E. Novak, 'The Defoe Canon: Attributions and De-Attributions', *Huntington Library Quarterly*, 59 (1998), pp. 83–104. More ascribed 570 titles to Defoe.

[66] *The Pepys Ballads*, ed. W. G. Day, 5 vols. (Cambridge, 1987), vol. 1, unpaginated.

Such was the popular taste of those who could afford the few pennies these works cost, and which were readily available from the chapmen, hawkers, and peddlers who carried them about the country for the small group of publishers who dominated ballad production in London. Readers rarely seemed able to get enough of them, though to the authorities the culture of ballads sometimes seemed to encourage disorderliness, the pious Arthur Bedford complaining of 'those *scandalous Songs* and *Ballads*, which swarm in *Town* and *Country*, and by the Cheapness of the Price seem wholly intended to debauch the poor, as well as the rich.'[67]

If one important element of the market for literature was its social diversity, another was that the market comprised both men and women, such that if many works appealed to both some were consciously directed only at one or the other. Many men read or heard the printed word in the tavern, coffee-house, and club—where there was probably a heavy emphasis upon news in some form or other. For women the setting was usually more or less domestic. What was read there is less clear, though Mary Astell complained of those male presumptions that 'Poetry, Plays, and Romances' were best suited to the female mind.[68] Certainly some periodicals were begun specifically for women and many often addressed what were thought to be 'feminine' questions; and the great expansion of literature involved working out and setting down representations of men and women in ways comprehensible and engaging to readers and which, therefore, often made play of their supposed or actual differences. But it was also true that in a period usually celebrated for its male authors a significant minority of published writers were women—among them Delarivière Manley, the Countess of Winchelsea, and Susanna Centlivre.[69] Quite how numerous they were is impossible to say, not least because many hid their sex behind a veil of anonymity or masculine pseudonymity, but in one large database of published English poetry men appear to have outnumbered women authors by 10:1 between 1660 and 1700 and by 18:1 between 1700 and 1750.[70]

[67] *The Great Abuse of Musick* (1711), p. 65.

[68] [M. Astell], *The Christian Religion, as Profess'd by a Daughter of the Church of England* (1717), p. 206.

[69] [Mary] Delarivière Manley, 1663–1724, author of novels, plays, poetry, and political tracts; for a time she edited the *Examiner*. Anne Finch, Countess of Winchelsea, 1661–1720, wrote poems, plays, and fables, and also translated works from French and Italian. Susanna Centlivre, 16??–1723, playwright, possibly born in Holbeach, Lincolnshire; Whig by disposition, author of sixteen full-length plays, many highly successful.

[70] Taken from Chadwyck Healey's *English Poetry 600–1900* database, which contains 7,434 poems for the first period (8.7 per cent by women) and 16,769 for the second (5.4 per cent by women). In the same company's less comprehensive *English Drama (1280–1915)* database women were authors for 6.3 per cent of titles 1660–1700 and 8.9 per cent 1700–50. These full-text databases are available online at http://lion.chadwyck.co.uk; both were searched in May 1999.

A thirst for romances, adventures, fables (especially animal), and the fantastic provided a general context out of which emerged two particularly important literary developments in this period, novels and periodicals. Largely for definitional reasons the first is much harder to pin down than the second. To argue that this period saw the 'rise of the novel' requires giving a different label and status to earlier fictional works which existed in considerable numbers. The grounds for doing so are insecure, though interestingly Congreve did distinguish 'romances' from 'novels'. Romances were 'generally composed of the Constant Loves and invincible Courages of Hero's, Heroins, Kings and Queens . . . and so forth; where lofty Language, miraculous Contingencies and impossible Performances, elevate and surprize the Reader into a giddy Delight'. On the other hand, he thought, 'Novels are of a more familiar nature; Come near to us, and represent to us Intrigues in practice, delight us with Accidents and odd Events, but not such as are wholly unusual or unpresidented . . . which . . . bring also the pleasure nearer to us.'[71] Such an emphasis upon the social and psychological realism of novels, and of their effect in encouraging a certain sensibility through a high degree of reflectiveness, is important, but it is impossible to assert that this began at any given date. Rather it was a development spread over many decades, beginning well before the 1690s and taking place while ballads, romances, and the like proliferated. That is not to underestimate the achievements of Defoe and other leading authors, rather to stress that his novels were part of a vibrant literary scene that had been evolving for many years.

A literary development that was much more decisively a product of the 1690s and 1700s was the emergence of the periodical—usually at least monthly, often more frequently. Such frequency was common to newspapers and periodicals, but the latter were distinguished not by avoiding news, though they sometimes did, but often by fictionalizing it to a degree and particularly by reflecting upon its exemplary nature, moral universe, and economic, social, and cultural import. Periodicals were discursive, newspapers were not, though both were increasingly being distributed throughout the kingdom. In so far as one periodical led the way it was John Dunton's *Athenian Mercury*, but it was followed by many others, with at least 74 being published between 1691 and 1697 (the most prominent in this period are listed in Table 18).[72]

At one extreme some periodicals were highly political, while at the other some eschewed politics altogether. It is of some significance that the most

---

[71] Congreve, *Letters and Documents*, pp. 158–9.

[72] Dunton, 1659–1733, spent some time in New England before becoming a bookseller in London. The *Athenian Mercury* began as the *Athenian Gazette* and in 1696–7 he published in seven monthly parts *The Night-Walker: or, Evening Rambles in Search of Lewd Women* which also proved popular.

TABLE 18. *Select list of periodicals published*

Athenian Mercury	1691–7
Gentleman's Journal	1692–4
A Collection for Improvement of Husbandry and Trade	1692–1703
Ladies Mercury	1694
Whig Observator	1702–12
[Defoe's] *Review of the Affairs of France*	1704–13
British Apollo	1708–11
Tatler	1709–11
Female Tatler	1709–10
Examiner	1710–14
Spectator	1711–12, 1714
Guardian	1713
Plain Dealer	1724–5

important, the *Spectator*, classed itself, not altogether convincingly, in the second category. More than that, however, it asserted that it avoided personalizing its pages.

As, on the one Side, my Paper has not in it a single Word of News, a Reflection in Politicks, nor a Stroke of Party; so, on the other, there are no fashionable Touches of Infidelity, no obscene Ideas, no Satyrs upon Priesthood, Marriage, and the like popular Topicks of Ridicule; no private Scandal, nor any thing that may tend to the Defamation of particular Persons, Families, or Societies.[73]

Such an approach, even if overdrawn (at the very least it was Whiggish in its sympathies), might suggest that the *Spectator* was insipid and anodyne. Yet it was probably the most important literary production of the period, becoming required reading for gentlemen and gentlewomen across the English-speaking world through the eighteenth and into the nineteenth centuries. At its peak 3,000 copies of an issue were sold, and read in clubs, coffee-houses, and drawing-rooms by thousands more, with collected editions frequently reprinted after its demise. Its appeal lay in the power of its prose and the quality of its judgement when considering the worlds of human emotions, social mores, and artistic taste.

The *Spectator* was published in 635 issues, frequently appearing six times a week, and was very much the work of Addison and Steele, though other authors also occasionally leant a hand. They invented and adopted the persona of Mr Spectator, a man who though born in the country relished London life, passing judgement on it and much else besides, often in the company of a small stock of fictional characters—Sir Roger de Coverley, a Worcestershire baronet of Tory views; the young lawyer studying at the Inner Temple; the eminent London merchant Sir Andrew Freeport of Whig sympathies; Captain Sentry,

[73] *The Spectator*, vol. 2, p. 517.

an army officer; Will Honeycomb, a gallant, 'very ready at that Sort of Discourse with which Men usually entertain Women', and an expert on finery and foppery; and the faintly sketched clergyman.[74] By placing an event or question before one or more of this 'club' conclusions were reached which helped vividly to develop and articulate notions of politeness, morality, civility, taste, wit, and selfless sociability in a changing world. Certainly it championed the benefits to society at large of the worlds of commerce, business, and finance, but it also argued for the cultured urbanity of city life, though it also often looked to build bridges between town and countryside—it is worth recalling that Gay's analysis of the periodical press in 1711 was entitled *The Present State of Wit, in a Letter to a Friend in the Country*.[75]

If periodicals and, to a lesser extent, novels were new voices in this period, satire and its bedfellows burlesque and lampoon were revived to devastating effect. All of the most famous authors of the period employed it—Defoe, Addison, Steele, Swift, and Pope—and it became a commonplace among engravers and printmakers. Satire attacked human follies both personal and public, and did so in essays, books, songs, and, especially, poems. One stimulus was that 'The end of Satyr is reformation' another, in an age frequently preoccupied with ancient Greece and Rome, its antiquity.[76] Addison was sure that at looking at the classical world 'there are none who instruct us more openly in the Manners of their respective Times in which they lived, than those who have employed themselves in Satyr'.[77] The *éminence grise* of these satirists was Dryden, who abandoned the mode in the 1690s so that he could live quietly with his literary reputation intact despite his Roman Catholicism and close associations with the James II.[78] In the early eighteenth century satire reached a highpoint in Pope's 'Dunciad' (composed between about 1719 and 1728) which commented bitterly on the Grub Street world, and Swift's *Gulliver's Travels*, published in 1726—making 'a very good diversion to all the town' it soon sold out.[79] The popularity of Swift's book was due to many factors, its

[74] *The Spectator*, vol. 1, p. 12.

[75] J. Gay, *Poetry and Prose*, ed. V. A. Dearing, 2 vols. (Oxford, 1974), vol. 2, pp. 449–56.

[76] D. Defoe, *The True-Born Englishman and Other Writings*, ed. P. N. Furbank and W. R. Owens (1997), p. 24.

[77] *The Spectator*, vol. 2, p. 318.

[78] John Dryden, 1631–1700, educated Westminster School and Trinity College, Cambridge, playwright and poet, Poet Laureat 1670–89, converted to Roman Catholicism 1686, in his last years he translated Juvenal, Persius, and Virgil, was buried in Poet's corner, Westminster Abbey, at the expense of the Kit Cat club.

[79] Alexander Pope, 1688–1744, the leading poet of his age, a Roman Catholic. H. M. C., *Calendar of the Manuscripts of the Marquis of Bath*, vol. 1 (1904), p. 252; *Letters of Gay*, p. 60. Not everyone was impressed, Voltaire complaining that the 'continued series of new fangled follies, of fairy tales, of wild inventions, palls at last upon our taste.' *Voltaire's Correspondence*, ed. T. Besterman, 107 vols. (Geneva, 1953–65), vol. 2, p. 48.

fantasy, its lack of explicit personal targets, and its questioning of wider political and social values. It is noticeable that this preoccupation with and uncertainty about social values was something that was also shared with many of the
most popular periodicals, hinting at a certain nervous disposition towards, or
insecure appreciation of, the political, religious, economic, and social trans-
itions at work. That such feelings were in part worked out by exercising the
pleasures of the imagination marks in fact an important step away from the
turmoils of the seventeenth century.

PLEASURABLE PERFORMANCES

In the late seventeenth century many leading authors, notably Dryden, wrote
not only for the printed page but also for the stage, not least because the
theatre was a better paymaster. Indeed, the loosely-termed 'Restoration
theatre', which in practice ran from about 1660 to 1700, was markedly successful
in both commercial and literary terms—in those years London saw about 440
new plays performed and 120 revivals. The inventiveness of playwrights down
to the first decade of the eighteenth century was indeed remarkable, including the work not only of Dryden but of Wycherley, Farquhar, Congreve, and
Vanbrugh.[80] As sometimes happens these authors often sparked off one
another and, in a bid for mutual esteem, produced major works of satire and
comedy, especially the 'comedy of manners'. But such creativity was also a
response to the wider social energy poured into theatre-going at the time. In
London and other major cities attending the theatre was a major form of entertainment that encompassed a reasonably wide social circle (though tickets were
too expensive for many).

Theatre life was most vibrant in London, despite the existence of a monopoly of theatrical enterprises, usually in two patent companies. In January 1726,
for example, thirty-six plays could be seen in the capital:[81]

[80] William Wycherley, 1641–1715, educated partly in France, the Inner Temple, and Queen's
College, Oxford, saw military service, among his most famous plays are *The Country Wife* (1675)
and *The Plain Dealer* (1676). George Farquhar, 1678–1707, born Ulster, educated Trinity
College, Dublin, his best known plays include *The Recruiting Officer* (1706) and *The Beaux'
Stratagem* (1707), though he died in poverty. William Congreve, 1670–1729, born in Yorkshire,
but partly raised in Ireland, and educated at Kilkenny and Trinity College, Dublin, at both a
contemporary of Jonathan Swift. His first play was *The Old Bachelor* (1693), his best known *The
Way of the World* (1700).

[81] Because this is a list of those productions for which evidence survives many minor productions will have been lost from view. Taken from E. L. Avery (ed.), *The London Stage 1660–1800:
A Calendar of Plays, Entertainments and Afterpieces*, Part 2. *1700–1729*, 2 vols. (Carbondale, 1960),
vol. 2, pp. 848–52.

Hamlet, Prince of Denmark
The Squire of Alsatia
Rodelinda (4 Performances)
The Conscious Lovers
The Emperor of the Moon
The Distrest Mother
The Confederacy (2)
Volpone
King Henry IV, Part 1 (2)
The Tempest
The Royal Merchant (2)
The Mourning Bride
The Female Fortune Tellers (7)
The Careless Husband
Amphitryon
The Provok'd Wife (7)
Aesop
The Merry Wives of Windsor (2)

Elisa (5)
The Drummer
The Fair Penitent
Measure for Measure
The Twin Rivals
The Recruiting Officer
Theodosius
The Lady's Last Stake
The Country Wife
The Amorous Widow
The Way of the World
Julius Caesar
The Busie Body
The Double Gallant
The Cheats of Scapin
Rule a Wife and have a Wife
A Woman's Revenge
The Man of Mode

Many of these were performed by established companies at substantial venues. Prominent were those at Lincoln's Inn Fields (1661–1708 and from 1714), Dorset Gardens (1671–1709), Drury Lane from 1674, Vanbrugh's Queen's (King's) in the Haymarket, opened in 1705, and Greenwich (1709–12). Moreover, plays were often performed at Bartholomew, Southwark, and May fairs. Everywhere productions might be put on in the backrooms of taverns or clubs, in Norwich a company was active at the White Swan by the 1720s, and many towns were visited by 'strolling companies' which often followed the circuits of assize judges, fairs, or race meetings. Slowly, moreover, theatres were beginning to appear in provincial towns and cities as well, at Bath in 1705, Bristol in 1706, and Richmond in Surrey in 1718.

One of the most important features of the history of the stage in this period is that it was effectively abandoned by Dryden in the 1690s and Vanbrugh and Congreve in mid-career in the 1700s—Vanbrugh's last finished play being *The Confederacy* (1705) and Congreve's being *The Way of the World* (1700). One explanation is that the political and moral climate forced them out, and others into evasiveness or conformity. Certainly plays were seen as potentially dangerous by the authorities and were formally subject to censorship by the Master of Revels and Lord Chamberlain. Politically, for example, it says much that Dryden's early anti-Catholic *The Spanish Friar* (1681) was performed at Queen Mary's command a month after her coronation, as well as in the aftermath of the Jacobite risings of 1715 and 1745, but that his new *Cleomenes* was briefly banned in 1692 for reflecting ill on the government. Similarly, Rowe's *Tamerlane* (1701) was initially fêted as a positive allegory of William III, but in the Tory-dominated last four years of Queen Anne was not performed. The stage also had to work within significant religious restrictions, with productions prohibited on Sundays, on Wednesdays and Fridays in Lent, and over Passion week. Despite such factors concern with the morality of the stage reached new heights in the 1690s, with the Lord Chamberlain issuing orders in 1697 against the 'Prophaneness and Immorality of the Stage', followed a year later by Collier's outburst. This was sustained into the following decade by the Reformation of Manners movement—who characterized Vanbrugh's plays as 'more remarkable for Irreligion than for Wit and Humour'—and in 1705 by the lower house of Convocation.[82] In 1700 one actor was fined £10 for jesting profanity about God on stage and further legal attacks on other actors followed. Such a climate must have given pause for thought. Vanbrugh, whose talents were widely spread, soon came to exercise them as a theatre promoter and architect, while Congreve took up a series of relatively minor government posts, culminating in 1714 as Secretary for Jamaica.

If from 1700 the 'comedy of manners' stagnated—it was kept alive if not developed by other writers—theatre as a whole developed in three main alternative ways: by an increasing interest in Shakespeare; the commercial success of masquerades, and song and dance shows; and a developing interest in opera. In 1660 Shakespeare (1564–1616) was relatively rarely performed on the English stage, but over the next century he became more and more popular, increasingly marvelled at for his dramatic merit and held up for patriotic admiration. Astell thought no one 'has given us Nobler, or juster Pictures of Nature than Mr. *Shakespear*', a modern edition of his works was first produced in 1709, edited by Rowe and published by Tonson, and he was celebrated in an essay by Dennis in 1712.[83] Yet it was a particular kind of Shakespeare that made it to the stage in this period. As with most productions the name of the playwright was not attached to stagings, and his texts and titles were frequently substantially altered—there was nothing sacred about his writing, he was revered as a storyteller. So, if his plays were performed 680 times in London between 1700 and 1720 nearly two-thirds of these were adaptations—among them 96 of Davenant's *Macbeth* and 76 of an operatic *Timon of Athens*. Only eight of Shakespeare's plays were performed in an unaltered form, in those years the most popular being *Hamlet, Henry IV part 1, Julius Caesar*, and *Othello*. In the following decade, however, a vogue for performing *The Merry*

---

[82] Congreve, *Letters and Documents*, p. 102, note; *A Letter from Several Members of the Society for Reformation of Manners. To . . . Lord Arch-bishop of Canterbury* [1704], p. 1.

[83] [M. Astell], *An Essay in Defence of the Female Sex* (1696), p. 48.

Wives of Windsor and *Measure for Measure* in the original meant that adaptations accounted for only four in ten productions. Even so it was not until the 1730s that the shift from viewing Shakespeare as popular entertainment to great literature passed mid-point.

Bowdlerizations of Shakespeare provide an important insight into the nature of the stage in this period. It had an unreverential and undogmatic approach to the literary efforts of its authors. Frequently an evening's entertainment would comprise several works, with the main production sandwiched between songs, displays, and comic afterwords. There was, moreover, in practice little distinction between those works now accorded a place in the canon of high art and those which were explicitly populist and present-minded. Indeed, an important dynamic element on the stage was the increasing popularity of pantomimes, songs, jugglers, harlequins, and exhibitionists of all shapes and sizes, what collectively were often called 'drolls'. This worried many, Dennis complaining that because 'Operas, and Entertainments of Singing and Dancing' were flourishing 'Dramatick Poems' were losing pride of place, a loss with the awful precedent that 'The Declension of Poetry in *Greece* and antient *Rome*, was soon follow'd by that of Liberty and Empire.'[84] Similarly there were a number of attempts in the period to put a stop to the drolls performed at London's main fairs. If most of these were unsuccessful a proclamation against May fair in 1709 did have a significant effect. An associated development to pantomimes and the like was the emergence and growing popularity of masquerades, effectively commercialized masked balls offering food, music, and dancing, 'not vastly different . . . from a Venetian or Roman Carnaval, a merry open Festival'.[85] Heidegger was instrumental in promoting the rage for masquerades, his events at the Haymarket in the 1710s and 1720s sometimes attracting up to 1,000 people a week. That so many attended despite the great costs (both of entrance and costume) reflects on how many well-to-do enjoyed using disguise to escape normal social conventions and constraints, an escape which inevitably led to masquerades being censured as stews of lewdness and 'the Undoers of Beauty, Honour, and Innocence'.[86]

The third major development on the stage in this period was the popularity of Italian opera. Combining music and drama had an established popularity in England by 1700. For example, Henry Purcell, without question the leading English composer at work in this period, provided the music for D'Urfey's *The Comical History of Don Quixote* (1694–5), and other plays as well as

---

[84] *The Critical Works of John Dennis*, ed. E. N. Hooker, 2 vols. (Baltimore, 1939 and 1943), vol. 1, pp. 385 and 390.

[85] E. Ward, *The Amorous Bugbears: or, the Humours of a Masquerade* (1725), p. 2.

[86] W. Bond and A. Hill, *The Plain Dealer: being Select Essays on Several Curious Subjects . . . Publish'd Originally in the Year 1724*, 2 vols. (1734), vol. 1, p. 7.

writing semi-operatic works of his own such as *Dido and Aeneas* (1689) and *King Arthur* (1691).[87] Though these might be expensive to produce (*The Fairy Queen* (1692) reputedly cost £3,000), their popularity usually made them profitable. However, from 1705 there was a significant turn towards Italian operas in London after the Italianate pastiche *Arsinoe* was staged. In 1707 it was reported that 'New operas we have often, all Italian' and fifty-four were performed by the 1710–11 season at the Queen's theatre.[88] Handel, who first visited London in 1710 and returned permanently in 1712, became the leading resident composer of Italian operas (he had been in Italy from 1706 to 1710), producing the likes of *Radamisto* (1720) and *Giulio Cesare* (1724). However, the history of Italian opera in this period was chequered. For financial and political reasons they disappeared in 1717, returning only with the foundation in 1719 of a Royal Academy of Music to promote Italian opera seria. Yet even though the Academy had some seventy wealthy subscribers putting up over £17,000, was supported by the King, and often put on more than fifty performances in a season, it collapsed insolvent in 1728. Simply put the costs of performance exceeded income from ticket sales, largely because opera lacked a sufficiently broad social basis of support. With ticket prices about twice the level of the theatre it was indeed very much a plaything of the rich—as one cleric observed in 1726 operas were 'the continued and cardinal entertainments of our Princes, our Nobles, and the chief of our *Israel*.'[89] Indeed a fierce competitiveness seized this form of conspicuous consumption, with foreign composers, musicians, and singers engaged at great expense in a quest for beauty and authenticity. Among the leading singers something approaching a star system was created, with the most favoured getting as much as £1,500 a season. By 1727, with 'Opera feuds . . . hotter than ever', the bottom of the well had run dry.[90]

Whatever their musical or dramatic merits Italian operas of the early eighteenth century were assuredly inaccessible to most and unattractive to some. Cost kept many out of the theatres, and those that did get inside faced the intimidating spectacle of long performances sung in a foreign tongue—Sir Isaac Newton, his patience exhausted, fled in the third act of the only opera he ever attended. Steele mocked the castrati for being 'every way impotent to please' and the *Tatler* and *Spectator* were not alone in launching broadsides at the opera vogue.[91] It was argued that Italian operas made an 'Audience . . . Foreigners in their own Country', encouraged the aping of foreign vices, and

---

[87] Henry Purcell, 1658?–1695, chorister Chapel Royal, 1664, organist Westminster Abbey 1680, wrote instrumental and vocal music, including that for the funeral of Queen Mary in 1694.

[88] H. M. C., *Report on the Manuscripts of the Earl of Egmont*, vol. 2 (Dublin, 1909), p. 216.

[89] T. Bisse, *Musick the Delight of the Sons of Men: a Sermon Preached at the Cathedral Church of Hereford, at the Anniversary Meeting of the Three Choirs* (1726), p. 23.

[90] Earl of Ilchester (ed.), *Lord Hervey and his Friends, 1726–38* (1950), p. 18.

[91] *The Correspondence of Richard Steele*, ed. R. Blanchard (Oxford, 1941), p. 25.

produced a situation where '*English* Musick is quite rooted out'.[92] Certainly music composed by foreigners was an increasingly important part of the musical life of early eighteenth-century England. Handel had been born in Halle and was not naturalized until 1727, while both Corelli (1653–1713) and Vivaldi (1678–1741) were also popular (J. S. Bach (1685–1750) was largely unknown). Given the lack of contemporary composers of unquestioned excellence this meant that a patriotic celebration of English music had to point to its powerful heritage, though religious, academic, and social factors also helped to establish a 'classical' canon about this time. Purcell, who died in 1695, was widely acknowledged as a composer of genius, but he was also placed in a tradition encompassing Tallis, Byrd, Gibbons, Child, and Blow. Encouraging the celebration of that heritage was given a great boost through the annual musical festivals of the Sons of the Clergy charity begun about 1678 (and held at St Paul's cathedral from 1697), and with the foundation of the Academy of Ancient Music in 1726 (originally called the Academy of Vocal Music).

If many developments in music-making in this period took place in London, music certainly played an important part in provincial life, especially in the towns and often in a religious context. Most notably the annual Three Choirs Festival (of Gloucester, Worcester, and Hereford) was established about 1713, attracting county society to a celebration of both secular and spiritual music. A fashion for celebrating St Cecilia's Day (as patron saint of music) with a sermon and music had recently sprung up in many towns, and occasional concerts, small clubs, or informal gatherings of skilled amateurs and semi-professionals were becoming more common. Subscription concerts were advertised at Bury St Edmunds in 1721, and societies that performed music were apparently operating in Bristol, Norwich, Oxford, Salisbury, Spalding, Wells, Worcester, and York by the end of our period. That at Wells was an enthusiastic and energetic society, frequently playing contemporary or near contemporary music by Albinoni, Handel, Purcell, Scarlatti, and Vivaldi. Claver Morris, the physician whose diary provides us with the evidence of this society, clearly thoroughly enjoyed this music-making. For him the pleasure was pure and unalloyed, giving no cause for concern. And such innocent pleasure was, in the end, more pervasive and probably more important than the world of the London masquerade and opera, despite the noise they have left in the records.

THE ART OF SEEING

An increasingly active art market developed in England in this period, with consumer demand running strongly. In purely quantitative terms that market was dominated not by paintings but, because of their relative cheapness, by

[92] *The Spectator*, vol. 1, pp. 79 and 82.

prints bought largely for decorative purposes. Such prints ranged from cheap woodcuts, costing a penny or two, through satires, to the elaborate and expensive engravings of great buildings or notable paintings. Moreover, if much art was produced in England, a huge amount was also imported from abroad. Evidence from customs duties paid at the end of the period suggests that something of the order of 650 paintings and 11,200 prints were being imported each year, mostly from Italy, France, and Holland. Certainly for prints, and probably for paintings, imports dominated the middle and upper reaches of the art market, a market that was actually in a state of some flux. Attempts by the Painter-Stainers' Company to regulate the trade in London were proving less and less successful and ended completely in 1708, unable to resist the specialist dealers who were coming into the business. A nice indicator of this is provided by the increasing use of art auctions, which had only been introduced as recently as 1676.

Gaining some sense of the types of art that people bought is very difficult. Among prints the most popular were copies of maps, buildings, paintings (particularly of politicians and leading public figures such as the Duke of Marlborough or Henry Sacheverell), and, especially, satires. Satiric prints frequently addressed newsworthy issues such as political, religious, or military events, as well as chiding the world of manners. Among painting it is clear that much domestically produced art was portraiture. For the most part these were of individuals, though the early 1720s saw the emergence of the 'conversation piece', usually rather stilted compositions of families in domestic settings, as an important genre. The demand for portraiture and the development of conversation pieces reflects of course the social values of the rich, of the force of patriarchy, the sanctity of the family, and the value of dynasticism. Obviously imported paintings were much more rarely portraits, with landscapes and 'history' paintings highly prized—the latter depicting the past, be it real, biblical, or mythical. But other types of painting were frequently purchased. One analysis of sales of 3,739 Dutch paintings in England between 1689 and 1692 shows that just over 50 per cent were social and religious satires, with the next largest category, physical, sexual, and scatological, accounting for just 7 per cent. That is to say, the market for art must not be conceived in overly serious or supremely aesthetic terms. Many people desired paintings that were humorous as well as attractive.

One of the most prominent features of the English art scene in this period was the significance of foreign art and artists. As has been seen, much of the art which made it to the market was imported rather than domestically produced. Moreover, foreign-born artists were responsible for much of the best work undertaken in England. In portrait painting, Kneller, born in Lübeck and trained in Amsterdam, was a dominant figure. He arrived in England in 1675

and soon became the most successful painter at work, a position he held down
to his death in 1723 and buttressed by the formal title of 'Principal painter'
from 1689, a knighthood in 1691, and a baronetcy in 1715. Certainly he and his
highly efficient studio—many 'Kneller's' are more the work of his assistants
than of him—were both highly fashionable and extraordinarily productive,
painting most of the leading political, religious, and social figures of the day.
Importantly, his most serious rivals were also foreign-born, Michael Dahl from
Sweden and John Closterman from Osnabrück, though the English Jonathan
Richardson also completed some important commissions. Leading painters in
other fields were also often foreign-born, such as Leonard Knyff in landscapes
and Peter Tillemans and Jan Wyck in sporting art. The influence of foreign-
born artists was just as great in the numerically much more significant market
for prints. London had few engravers in 1689 and was heavily dependent
upon importing not only prints but engravers, notably Johannes Kip in 1686,
Michael van der Gucht in 1690, Louis du Guernier in 1708, Nicholas Dorigny
in 1711, and Claude du Bosc about 1717.

One reason for the success of foreign-born artists in England was the
absence of a well-developed domestic art scene. At the top end of the market
purchasers had long preferred Continental art, perhaps inclined to view
English painters and engravers as craftsmen rather than artists, in a way mir-
roring the elite's taste for Italian opera, and was another example of how conspicuous consumption could act as a powerful social marker, a large collection
of foreign paintings supposedly providing proof positive of great wealth and
exquisite taste. Perhaps another explanation is that there was, as Steele suggested, a sort of international division of labour at work: '*Italy* may have the
Preference of all other Nations for History-Painting; *Holland* for Drolls, and a
neat finished manner of Working; *France*, for Gay, Janty, Fluttering Pictures;
and *England* for Portraits'.[93] If from an English perspective there was such
specialization it was, in practice, likely to reflect purchasing habits first and
foremost. However, as with the opera, such tastes were questioned, most
powerfully by Richardson. He noticed 'a thing as yet unheard of . . . the
English School of Painting', complaining how poorly developed was an appreciation of art, even though the country abounded with 'Gentlemen of a Just,
and Delicate Taste, in Musick, Poetry, and all kinds of Literature'.[94] In this
argument because English gentlemen were too poorly educated to judge painting they followed the herd and bought conservatively abroad, lacking the
confidence to act as patrons. He argued that painting was the supreme art, able
to communicate ideas beyond even those of history, poetry, and sculpture and
was a powerful champion of a vigorous domestic art scene.

[93] *The Spectator*, vol. 4, p. 496.   [94] Richardson, *Two Discourses*, vol. 2, pp. 51 and 3.

Steele was right to point out the strength of portraiture in England, but he underestimated the breadth of artistic skill available of whatever nationality. In important ways the world of art did not follow that of opera. It was socially more broadly based, there was far less dependency upon a handful of foreign stars, and many who came from abroad to practise their skills became permanent residents, integrating themselves fully within the wider society of artists. A good indicator of the vitality of the artistic community is provided by the various art clubs and societies that came into existence in London for the first time in the period. The first of these, the Virtuoso of St Luke, was established in 1689 and survived until 1743. Among its members were the likes of Closterman, Dahl, Tillemans, Mercier, and Sir James Thornhill. About 1705 a convivial club was begun on Saturday nights at the Rose and Crown, which had 85 members at its peak and helped to develop a sense of professional collective identity, if not especially a collective programme for promoting the profession (though some projects were undertaken). That was attempted by the Gt Queen St Academy, founded in 1711 of which Kneller was Governor. Just to call it an 'academy' underscored the professionalization, and the independence, of artists in this period. That it was selective in its membership enhanced this, the 70 or so being 'most of them the Eminent Artists & Lovers of Art in this Nation'.[95] But that process was not yet institutionally secure. The academy split in 1720 and was re-established in St Martin's Lane, but collapsed in 1724 when one of its leading lights, John Vanderbank, fled to France to escape his creditors. In its place Sir James Thornhill set up a drawing school with much more modest aims.

Despite the failure of the St Martin's Lane Academy, by 1724 foreign- and English-born artists in London were thoroughly integrated and increasingly professionalized. Indeed, that integration, along with the improving skills of home-grown artists was helping to produce an 'English school'. Vertue thought that by 1722 that 'Engraveing has much improv'd & makes a tolerable figure' in England, while the death of Kneller in 1723 briefly left Thornhill, 'the most Excellent Native history painter', the leading active artist.[96] Largely famed for his decorative painting—at Greenwich, St Paul's Cathedral, Hampton Court, and numerous country and town houses of the aristocracy— in 1720 he became Sergeant Painter to the King and was knighted, the first English-born artist to be so. Though he left off painting in the 1720s he had shown a way forward that was to be seized by his future son-in-law, William Hogarth. Born in London in 1697 Hogarth began his career as an engraver, soon finding his satirical feet. In 1721 he produced a print assaulting the folly

[95] G. Vertue, 'Vertue Note Books', *Walpole Society* [Publications], 22 (1934), p. 7.
[96] Vertue, 'Note Books', pp. 8 and 38.

of the South Sea year and in 1724 *The Lottery* (both drawing inspiration from contemporary Dutch satirical prints). But his *Bad Taste of the Town* (1724), also known as *Masquerades and Operas*, was of more decisive significance, and not only because it was a foretaste of the modern moral subjects later perfected in such famous series as *A Harlot's Progress* and *Industry and Idleness*. There he first presented his xenophobic side, assaulting as un-English Heidegger's operas and masquerades as well as Burlington's Palladian architecture. Hogarth explicitly set himself up as a champion of English values and taste, not only in art but in London society more generally. Such were his abilities and sense of certainty, such was the vibrancy of the market that he served, that he helped to fertilize the soil in which Gainsborough (born in 1727), Reynolds (born 1723), and the Royal Academy later flourished. By 1727 a distinctive and distinguished era in English art was slowly but surely dawning.

CONCLUSION

One of the most important distinguishing features of modern English society is that it is predominantly urban. Yet if it was only in the mid-nineteenth century that over half the population become town dwellers the process of significant urbanization had been under way for over two centuries. In the late seventeenth century, however, that process took an important new direction as London's dynamism was adopted and adapted by many other towns. If the raw demographics of this newly-burgeoning urban system are impressive, no less significant were the wider social implications. The positive aspects of that are easily seen in the coffee-house and club, in the bookshop or on the stage, and in the squares and walks. Indeed, when all the qualifications are made Addison and Steele were emblematic of such developments, distinctively contributing to a novel cultural expansionism which, if focused upon London, was experienced throughout urban England at a time, moreover, when the interplay of town and countryside was also heightening.

Yet the din caused by the confident enjoyment of new worlds of pleasure could not swamp the frequent shrill jeremiads. Just as changes in the political and religious order provoked furious debate, so the growth of towns in general and of the press, stage, club, fairground booth, and assembly room in particular stimulated vigorous criticism. Undeniably, dark alleys surrounded light squares, prosperity masked terrible poverty, and politeness rubbed shoulders with incivility. Central to all this was the fear of many that society was becoming more and not less disordered. To them society was viewed less as an organism, naturally able to repair a bruise or a gash, than as a highly complex web of obligations and duties that might completely unravel if a single strand were broken—it is interesting to note here the declining use of the metaphor of the 'body politic' in the late seventeenth century. From such a perspective, if the anonymity afforded by town life enabled those social responsibilities to be avoided, the unbridled pursuit of pleasure appeared to prove that such opportunities were often seized with relish. In itself that was bad enough to those in authority, but their fears were magnified by a keen sense of just how limited were the means by which signs of disorder could be contained. Anarchy and chaos were always there, lurking in the shadows, ready to assault Mr Spectator.

CHAPTER 14

An Ordered Society?

To its supporters the Glorious Revolution rid England of many sources of disorder. Local government was purged of Catholics and the judicial bench of enthusiasts for Stuart absolutism. The beginnings of an effective relationship between the centre and the localities, forged through a reinvigorated Parliament, promised a closer identity of interests across the political nation. And France provided a sufficiently potent external threat to allow many internal divisions to be pushed into the background. Seemingly the public good had been effectively defined and power handed to those who could be depended upon assiduously to pursue it. But in practice the Glorious Revolution replaced not chaos by order but one sort of disorder by another. Not least, by definition it created the potential for Jacobite rebellion, the Toleration Act strained traditional ties of religion and morality, and the two major wars against France caused enormous disruption, especially economic. Moreover, such dislocation was long-lived, with the era between the Treaty of Utrecht and the establishment of Walpole's premiership widely viewed as being particularly lawless —smuggling, highway robbery, poaching, and piracy were all supposedly at fever pitch.

Despite the constant hope of the authorities that they might be able to create an earthly paradise by modifying the rule of law, and despite the rhetoric that those laws were 'generous, mild, and gentle; built on equal *Foundations of Justice* and *Mercy* . . . such, as every *Freeman* wou'd *wish* to be govern'd by', it is clear that attempts to extinguish disorder fuelled as well as doused the flames.[1] Initiatives to clamp down on crimes were markedly ad hoc and unsystematic; passive opposition from those actually operating the law was sometimes encountered; overlaps and conflicts between the jurisdictions of those different bodies concerned with law and order only aided inefficiency; and governors never resolved the paradox that while they wished to exercise greater control over people they would never countenance the introduction of any sort of police force. Order was kept by a power that was notably fragmented, in

---

[1] W. Bond and A. Hill, *The Plain Dealer: being Select Essays on Several Curious Subjects . . . Publish'd Originally in the Year 1724*, 2 vols. (1734), vol. i, p. 83.

certain respects riven, and significantly limited. Ultimately, therefore, much depended upon establishing a consensual view of a good society. If many ascribed to this only reluctantly, both rich and poor generally embraced the spirit of the public good, even to the extent of occasionally compromising their interests. Thus the rule of law shines a powerful light upon social arrangements and of the interaction between religious mores, social ideals, political authority, and economic power, providing therefore an effective way of seeing how many of the period's main features were linked one to another.

Order was sought by a 'system' that was disordered. But because of its considerable flexibility, and freedom from an overpowering dogma of social exclusiveness, its failure was partial not complete. Nor, despite its dependence upon corporal and capital punishment, was it unbearable to most. Not least, in a world where liberty was as potent a totem as property, 'the two Darlings of an *English* Subject', the power employed by the authorities was conditional and limited.[2] Indeed the poor employed such rhetoric to make their voice powerfully heard when they saw their fundamental interests threatened. They, like their rulers, desired the peaceful enjoyment of their lives, liberties, and property, and by and large both did so.

IDEAS OF THE LAW

Among England's governors in this period it was a commonplace that a constant battle had to be waged to keep society in good order, to protect lives, liberties, and property. Private passions and public feuds forever threatened chaos and anarchy. At the most general level such a fear took its origins from the biblical certainty of mankind's fallen state—as one Justice put it 'I am not to judge for man but for the Lord'.[3] The devil was always seeking to lure people into the abyss of evil. Nor was this merely a concern with individuals, for the elite vividly recalled the triumph of republicanism and anti-clericalism in the 1650s as evidence of the ease with which the social fabric could unravel when caught on the briars of excess and interest. And once society had been ripped asunder stitching it back together again was a prolonged and painful process. James II's reign had been a clear enough demonstration of that, to the extent that the Glorious Revolution was in many respects fundamentally conservative. To many William's arrival provided 'an opportunity to declare for the defence of . . . the Laws, Liberties & and Protestant Religion'.[4]

[2] *Authentic Memoirs of the Life and Surprising Adventures of John Sheppard* (2nd edn., 1724), p. 52.

[3] 'A Brief Memoir of Mr Justice Rokeby, Comprising his Religious Journal and Correspondence', *Publications of the Surtees Society*, 37 (1861), p. 35.

[4] *Norfolk Lieutenancy Journal, 1676–1701*, ed. B. Cozens-Hardy, Norfolk Record Society, 30 (1961), p. 95.

If both individually and collectively mankind was viewed as fundamentally weak it was not surprising that most governors were certain that order could only be maintained by the exercise of power, subtle at times, blatant and brutal at others. Such power might be utilized in many ways, not least economically and politically, but took its most important form in the rule of law. Many of society's ultimate limits and its most important characteristics were set by saying what was and what was not within the law, a role only underscored by its supposed universality, applying to all without fear or favour. By common repute justice was blind, weighing dispassionately and disinterestedly facts and fictions, rights and wrongs. In this rhetoric 'The Law is deservedly accounted a Man's best Birth-right' because it protected one and all alike.[5] Moreover, though the rule of law was absolutely integral to the maintenance of social inequalities, because it was exercised almost exclusively by resort to unpaid amateurs—there was, for example, no police force and military might was rarely used—and rested for the most part upon private prosecutions, to work it had to be, or seem to be, acceptable to a goodly majority of rulers and ruled alike. If often contested, at heart the rule of law depended upon a high degree of consensus.

If the governors were certain that the rule of law was right and proper its justness could not be silently assumed. Consensus had to be forged. Much of this took place casually, within the day-to-day workings of the law and local government, from debates in the vestry to the deliberations of jurors. Yet if this was haphazard, by involving a significant spectrum of society it had strength in breadth. As an explicit ideology, however, it was employed in a variety of settings. Most generally the rule of law was seen as a distinguishing mark of England's constitution, with Parliament both a guarantor of fundamental rights embodied in the likes of Magna Charta, trial by jury, and habeas corpus, and the forum for the reasoned adaptation of laws to suit altered circumstances. For many, of course, this had immediate relevance in the perceived threat of absolutism at home and abroad from James II and Louis XIV: 'In *France* . . . the meer Will of the Prince is *Law*, his Word takes off any Man's Head, imposeth Taxes, or seizes any Man's Estate . . . But in *England* the Law is both the *Measure and the Bond* of every Subject's Duty and Alleigiance, each Man having a fixed Fundamental Right born with him, as to *Freedom of his Person, and Property in his Estate*'.[6] As such, at the most general level ideas of law were highly politicized in this era, prey to a significant degree of factionalism. But ideologies were also formed and used on a more day-to-day basis,

---

[5] *Observations on the Dilatory and Expensive Proceedings in the Court of Chancery, in Relation to the Bill now Depending in the House of Commons for Lessening the Number of Attorneys and Solicitors* (1701), p. 3.

[6] [H. Care], *English Liberties: or, the Free-Born Subject's Inheritance* (1691), pp. 1–2.

notably in the 'charges' presented by Justices to juries, occasional addresses
sent by Grand Juries to Crown or Parliament, and the numerous sermons
preached at the beginning of assizes (the courts which tried the most serious
crimes). Though discussion of the rule of law took place very widely, in these
instances the audience was limited to people of some property. Charges were
meant to enlighten jurors as to various aspects of the law, and if they were often
cursory and preoccupied with pressing concerns, sometimes they were more
reflective and general in approach. Variants of the latter often began by considering the distribution of power in general before moving on to consider particular categories of crimes and laws. In this period the first of these was far
from innocent or straightforward. Thus, for example, the Earl of Stamford's
charge to the general quarter sessions for Leicestershire in Michaelmas 1690
began by establishing William and Mary as 'our Rightful and Lawful King and
Queen' with reference to many historical examples, before briefly defining
types of crime, from treason to murder, robbery, and those associated with
'loose and idle Living'. He concluded by urging those working within the legal
machinery to the conscientious exercise of their office, but warning that 'the
Law is so careful to prevent men in Office from oppressing the People, that
there can be no Oppression it does not take notice of to punish.'[7] Assize sermons were another important source for over-arching ideologies of the rule
of law and it says much that at least 300 were printed in this period (out of
perhaps some 3,000 that were delivered). There the rightness of the current
distribution of power was again justified, frequently in terms such as that
'Government it self is the Institution and Ordinance of God', and the supposed
justness of justice celebrated.[8] One cleric, for example, was certain that 'the
Laws of Men are necessary and useful to secure every man's Property', that
private property was sacrosanct, and that 'God only know how many are kept
from doing, or suffering injuries at all thro' the sense and power of the Law'.
Yet like the Earl of Stamford he stressed social equality before the law, that 'the
men of Wealth and Power have no Protection by Law against the just complaints of the Poor . . . *the Law is open*'.[9]

The potency of charges to jurors and assize sermons was considerable. As
functional set pieces they were a vital means by which the wider purposes of
the law were formally articulated and understood amongst the propertied. Yet

[7] *Charges to the Grand Jury 1689–1803*, ed. G. Lamoine, Camden Society, 4th Series, 43 (1992),
pp. 37–40.
[8] D. Trimnell, *The Great End and Usefulness of Government. In a Sermon Preach'd at the Assizes
held at Aylesbury . . . 2d of March . . . 1714* (1715), p. 9.
[9] H. Downes, *The Necessity and Usefulness of Laws and the Excellency of our Own. A Sermon
Preach'd at Northampton before Mr. Justice Powell and Mr. Baron Lovel, at the Assizes held there,
July the 13th, 1708* (1708), pp. 7, 13, and 11.

such words should not be analysed without reference to the social and cere-monial aspects of the rule of law, contexts which in fact undermined claims to the law's universality. If the law was meant to be accessible to all it was also in certain fundamental respects distant and imposing—it was indeed meant to put people in awe. The majesty of the law was expressed both within and without the courts. Bewigged figures still employing bastardized Latin and French in some of their written (though not spoken) proceedings occupied a territory beyond the comprehension of most accused. That the exercise of justice was part of elite society, helping indeed to define the county community, only emphasized the point. Assize judges, sent out from the central courts at Westminster, were usually met at county boundaries by mounted guards of honour drawn from resident local gentry, entertained by local dignitaries at an assize ball, and, as has been seen, comforted by sermons certain of the divine ordination of their mission. And if to be tried by one's peers was alleged to be a happy birthright of the English—'Tryals by Juries are a distinguishing Mark of our Freedom'—grand and perhaps assize juries were gradually becoming socially more and more exclusive.[10] Indeed, as will be seen, the theory of equal access to the law was often hard to translate into practice. So, if the law was meant to be universal, not only symbolically but also in reality it was often remote.

Yet to suggest that the ideology of the law constructed and consumed by the elite was no more than socially self-serving is a gross oversimplification. Not least it underestimates the extent of debate within the elite about the rule of law. Again much of that was implicitly expressed by the way the law was variously exercised in practice, but it also included discussions of the alleged inadequacies of the rule of law. A number of complaints, few of them new, were frequently voiced, especially against the civil law: that the law was a 'monstrous Hydra', too vast to be generally understood; that its complexity and extent allowed it to be controlled for huge personal benefit by a burgeoning popula-tion of lawyers; that it was in the interests of lawyers and those living off fees income in the courts to avoid the determination of cases for as long as possible; that consequently 'the Laws of *England* are cobweb Laws, that catch small flies, and let the great ones run through'; and that, with crime appearing to pro-liferate, the 'system' simply was not working.[11] If some of these points were fiercely debated, none doubted that the extent of law had and was growing, partly through the proliferation of statutes, partly through the ever-growing

---

[10] [C. Tancred], *An Essay for the General Regulation of the Law, and the More Easy and Speedy Advancement of Justice* (1727), p. 54.

[11] *The Locusts: or, Chancery Painted to the Life, and the Laws of England Try'd in Forma Pauperis. A Poem* (1704), p. 1; A. Grey, *Debates of the House of Commons, from the Year 1667 to the Year 1694*, 10 vols. (1763), vol. 9, p. 282.

body of case law. The consequences of this were highly significant, making the law at least appear vast, unsystematic, and poorly structured, even at times contradictory, '*our Laws are now so Ambiguous, that they may be eternally disputed and never reconciled.*'[12] Nor were such consequences insignificant, for if parts of the law might be interpreted for personal interest that could only be at the cost of its supposed universal legitimacy.

Publicly debated complaints about the law sometimes concentrated upon more specific objectives than its monstrous proportions, concerns which frequently had their roots in the quest for law reform that had flourished in the interregnum. Three stood out. First, some expressed concern about the laws covering insolvent debtors, especially of the power of creditors to imprison them. Many a debtor (guesses ranged from Defoe's 5,000 to Baston's 60,000) languished in gaol because they might only be released either by payment of the debt—which would be impossible for an insolvent without family or friends to call upon—or by occasional but unpredictable parliamentary amnesties (6,000 were released in the wake of one Act in 1722). Some contemporaries, well aware that 'gaol fever' (typhus) was rife, were deeply disquieted by this scope for personal tyranny, seeing it as a 'great Scandal to the Constitution'.[13] Second, several observers, disturbed by levels of civil litigation, called for land or deed registries to be established to clarify the ownership of property. Though a few local registries were created in this period, more ambitious attempts ran into stiff opposition. In 1696 Evelyn complained 'Will ever those swarms of *locusts*, lawyers and attornies, who fill so many seats [in the Commons], vote for a public *Register*, by which men may be secured of their titles and possessions, and an infinity of suits and frauds prevented?'[14] That society was prey to such a swarm constituted in fact the third main specific complaint about the law in this period, even leading in March 1701 to the Commons considering but not passing a Bill to reduce the number of attorneys and solicitors. To some the growing scale and complexity of the law was the product of its self-interested practitioners and that to restrict their numbers would render the law once again compact, cogent, and accessible.

Such discussions of the rule of law were, for the most part, written by and for the governing classes. But for many, ideas of the rule of law were expressed unsystematically and emblematically. In particular, crime and the judicial process were seized upon by a growing Grub Street world desperate for copy. Newspapers carried notices of heinous crimes, trials, and punishments from near to far and far to near; an increasing number of short 'criminal lives' found

---

[12] [T. Baston], *Thoughts on Trade, and a Publick Spirit* (1716), p. 85.
[13] [Tancred], *Essay*, p. 24.
[14] *Diary and Correspondence of John Evelyn*, ed. W. Bray, 4 vols. (1850–2), vol. 3, p. 357.

their way into print (sometimes in ballad form); accounts of trials, especially of those in London, proliferated; and more and more 'last dying speeches' of the condemned were being published—those issued by the Ordinary (i.e. chaplain) of Newgate became especially regularized and semi-official in the early eighteenth century. The market for such materials was undoubtedly growing, both for cheaper and more substantial productions. Stories of murder, rape, sodomy, and, especially, robbery were the stock-in-trade. If the wider consequences of particular crimes were sometimes stressed in such stories, frequently their emphasis was upon how criminals were made—of the long slippery slope from an initial failing to the gallows, and of the links between crime, drunkenness, gambling, Sabbath-breaking, and sexual promiscuity. This was a world where servants and apprentices were led astray in alehouses by prostitutes and pawnbrokers. It was not one, however, that often raised questions about the rule of law, being preoccupied with the causes and form of criminality. Even then the terms of analysis were frequently restricted to the role of mischance and of how the smallest character flaw might lead inexorably to dire consequences. Only spectacular criminals seemed to encourage more general reflections and then but rarely.

Sensationalist depictions of the lives and deaths of criminals were by no means aimed only at the lower end of the market. A four-volume work such as *A Complete Collection of Remarkable Tryals of the Most Notorious Malefactors, at the Sessions-House in the Old Baily, for near Fifty Years Past* (1718–21) would, of course, have been bought only by the better off. Nor was there a clear line between factual and fictional accounts. If the status of Defoe's *Moll Flanders* (1722), a highly-charged tale of a descent into a life of crime, was clear others were more ambiguous. Captain Alexander Smith's popular *The History of the Lives of the Most Noted Highway-Men, Foot-Pads, House-Breakers, Shop-Lifters and Cheats* . . . , 2 vols. (1714) was a medley of truth and literary licence that every reader would have struggled to separate. If crime and the law was an attractive subject for the literary world, writers and publishers desperate for sales presented it in particular and exaggerated ways. Consequently, across the social spectrum many viewed crime and the law through a muddied and distorted lens, and such distortion could have done little to aid the reasoned pursuit of order.

For most in England in this period what was and what was not a crime was generally understood and taken for granted. What was less clear was whether the rule of law worked effectively and fairly. Even then there was surprisingly little discussion of processes which made great play of brutal punishments, in which the accused was rarely allowed to mount a defence or employ counsel, and where the resources of victims often decisively influenced whether crimes were brought before the authorities at all. Yet the absence of marked public debate over these distinctive features should not be taken as a sign that the judicial machinery was simply experienced and endured. Far from it. As will be shown, it was subject to a high degree of discretion as to how it was implemented in practice and was also significantly remodelled both in theory and practice in this period. The law was not static and unyielding, but a tool that could be exploited with great skill and flexibility across a surprisingly wide part of society.

GOVERNING BODIES

Responsibility for the maintenance of order across society via the law was divided among a variety of institutions in this period, from central government to parochial and manorial bodies—though other bodies such as the Church, armed forces, revenue services, guilds, universities, and Inns of Court also kept a regulatory watch upon their own particular areas. What many of these had in common was that they were manned—women were universally excluded—by the unpaid, the untrained, and the largely unsupervised. That alone produced a 'system' subject to a good deal of local colouring, but it was also true that the form of certain institutions varied from place to place. If England was notionally subject to one law and one government in practice it was experienced in subtly different ways according to local circumstance and personnel. Furthermore, the 'system' was as striking for the absence of certain agencies as its variegated nature. Suspicion of the executive, most evident in the anti-standing army arguments of the late 1690s, meant that no police force existed (though some policing was undertaken by local officials), that the militia was very largely concerned with civil defence, and that troops were rarely called out to buttress the rule of law. (It also meant that torture was prohibited, treason trials made reasonably impartial, and the severity of the Riot Act (1715) kept in the hands of JPs.) Related to this, it is striking that after the Revolution worries about the misuse of the law by the government diminished. Such depoliticization, partial rather than complete, took place at the same time as the Church's direct authority over people's lives waned. Not least the ecclesiastical courts, which had regulated swearing, Sabbath-breaking, and the like, were gradually falling into disuse, though again this was more marked in some places than others. Still the decline could be considerable, the consistory court at Chester, for example, which had been considering over 100 cases annually before the Civil Wars was by 1730 dealing with only 20 or so.

At bottom the government of England was based upon the ecclesiastical unit of the parish. Through the vestry, the poor, highways, and, in towns, sewers, watch, and light were administered. Rates were levied upon the better off members of the parish to pay for some of these, though statutory labour to maintain roads (traditionally six days annually) fell heaviest upon the poor. In the parishes the 'chief inhabitants' drawn from the middling sort filled the offices of overseers of the poor, surveyor of the highways, and parish constable, exercising a significant degree of authority over day-to-day life. Not all were happy to undertake these responsibilities, even at the cost of fines. It was not just that they took time but that the vestry was also a place where power was contested. The trouble involved could be significant if rival visions of parochial order existed—for example of the care of orphans or the mentally ill, building new cottages on the edge of the commons, and road maintenance. Not only policies but personalities might clash. Moreover, if central government rarely intruded into this world, local Justices of the Peace did. Parish officers were sandwiched uneasily between the labouring poor and those with substantial amounts of property. Of course parishes varied significantly in size, obligation, and resources. A small poor parish in London put quite different burdens upon the vestry than a prosperous rural parish with a stagnant population. In turn, if many vestries were 'open', and positions in them available to all ratepayers, others were 'closed' or 'select', no more than self-perpetuating oligarchies which 'stagnate and stink in the Nostrils of their Fellow Citizens.'[15] Select vestries were common in London, Bristol, and in some northern counties.

The authority of the parish stood alongside and overlapped with a number of other local jurisdictions. Though of dwindling significance manorial control was still exercised in places, the affairs of the manor being settled through a court. More generally, towns and cities usually had some form of borough government and local court—Newcastle, admittedly commercially highly developed, had a sheriff's court, a mayor's court, and a new court of conscience for the recovery of small debts. The supra-parochial authority of these gave them considerable significance, a point only heightened when they coincided with parliamentary constituencies, ensuring that they were highly politicized through much of this period. Indeed, control of local government provided the sort of direct influence that many members of the middling sort did not or could not aspire to at the national level—Anglicans particularly complained at the influence Dissenters exercised within boroughs. No less significant, many of the perceptions of disorder in England in this period were framed in towns. It was there that begging, prostitution, robbery, and irreligion were felt most keenly and the shortcomings of the existing methods of control became most evident. In particular there was concern that crime and disorder were growing beyond the capacity of the constables, watch, and Justices to control. London

---

[15] A. Moreton (i.e. D. Defoe), *Parochial Tyranny: or, the House-Keeper's Complaint against the Insupportable Exactions, and Partial Assessments of Select Vestries* (n.d., 1727?), p. 10.

was the *locus classicus* of such concerns and the limitations of the watch in particular were legendary, 'The City Watches are defective, and many of the Watchmen are corrupted'.[16] Defoe calculated that in London watchmen 'have a Beat of four or five Hundred Houses, and many of those in Courts and Alleys; so that while he is at one Part of his Rounds, many Robberies may be easily committed at the other'—though likely this only applied to large parishes.[17]

Above the parish and the borough stood the county, at whose pinnacle were the Lord Lieutenant, his Deputies, and the Sheriff. Though such offices now carried few formal obligations and were largely held for reasons of status the Lord Lieutenant still provided an important link between central and local government, especially by recommending who might serve as Justices of the Peace. (Indeed, their importance is nicely suggested by the fact that thirty-two out of forty-two in England were replaced by William in 1689.) The hard work of county government had for some decades increasingly been borne by Justices of the Peace, who also provided a vital link between the county on one side and the parish and the borough on the other. They exercised a good deal of the law, commanding a high degree of discretion in the process. Trivial matters might be dealt with summarily with a colleague in 'petty sessions'; at the county quarter sessions an oversight was provided of much of the administrative apparatus of local government, the regulation of wages and prices was still sometimes attempted, and more serious crimes brought to trial before a jury; many JPs served as grand jurors that were integral to the trial of serious offences at the assize courts; and some JPs were also MPs. To be a member of the Commission of the Peace was, indeed, a position of some status and importance to one's reputation among gentry society, such that to be removed might be a matter of distress and dishonour, indeed 'the honour of being in, is not so great as the disgrace of being turn'd out'.[18] Furthermore, it says much that in an era of such intense party strife the Commission was frequently remodelled by the Lord Chancellor on political grounds—from 1700 to 1704 some 656 were removed from a total of about 3,700. Even so, as successive governments sought to buy support, it is notable that the size of the Commission grew in this period—in the West Riding of Yorkshire, for example, from 76 in 1688 to 254 in 1727, though this seems to have been particularly quick. However, such a growth was somewhat illusory. It certainly did not mean that England was being more carefully governed by Justices. Many new appointees looked upon the office as purely honorific and were never active, which because much

---

[16] [C. Hitchin], *The Regulator: or a Discovery of the Thieves, Thief-Takers, and Locks, Alias Receivers of Stolen Goods in and about the City of London* (1718), p. 16.

[17] Moreton, *Parochial Tyranny*, p. 13.

[18] Quoted in L. K. J. Glassey, *Politics and the Appointment of Justices of the Peace, 1675–1720* (Oxford, 1979), p. 7.

depended upon where suitable men of property lived meant that some areas were poorly served—the proportion who were active in Norfolk fell from a half in the period 1660–1675 to a quarter between 1710–18. In 1711 Harley received a report that in Cornwall there were two hundreds 'that have no justice of the peace who will act' as well as 'a great many' in Devon 'and indeed all over England'.[19] Nearly a third of the Justices in the West Riding in 1727 were inactive and in the East Riding the figure may have been nearly a half.

The lack of active Justices led to the appointment of less prosperous men to undertake the donkey work of ordering and regulating local society. In parts of London this took particular form with the emergence of so-called 'trading Justices', who sought to make a living by administering justice, though who also filled a gap left in a machinery essentially constructed with a view to serving rural England. Even in rural England the urgent need for active Justices prompted the appointment of some clerics to the bench, though only later in the eighteenth century did the parson-squire alliance become a common feature (nationally there were just 51 clerical JPs in 1702 but 932 by 1761). Such developments led to complaints that some Justices lacked the requisite stature for the office—being of 'meane qualitys, none being of the degree of a gentleman'.[20] Indeed, between 1689 and 1727 there were six attempts in Parliament to attach a property qualification to appointment as a Justice, that in 1711 settling on the figure of £300 per annum (in the 1690s Gregory King put the average annual income of gentlemen at £280). All failed, and the Act passed in 1732 set the fairly low limit of £200.

Certainly to be an active Justice was no small undertaking. Edmund Bohun listed nine main requisites, from natural abilities to a religious disposition and an abhorrence of perjury. He was, moreover, certain that 'The Justice of the Peace enters upon an imployment that will occasion him much loss of Time, some Expence, and many Enemies, and after all will afford him little or nothing towards the bearing these inconveniences, but a little unprofitable Honour attended with much Envy'.[21] Few had received any formal legal training, though some finished their education by a spell at one of the Inns of Court. For most, what legal knowledge they had was acquired casually or, perhaps, by recourse to one of the increasing number of published guides to the law—Dalton's *The Country Justice*, first published in 1619 was still popular in new editions, and was joined in this period by works such as Blackerby's *The Justice of the Peace, his Companion*, and the anonymous *The Justice of the Peace's Vade Mecum*. It was never imagined that Justices would commit to memory an ever-growing statute book or master the intricacies of extensive case law, for

[19] H. M. C., *The Manuscripts of his Grace the Duke of Portland*, vol. 5 (1899), p. 72.
[20] H. M. C., *The Manuscripts of Lord Kenyon* (1894), p. 377.
[21] E. Bohun, *The Justice of the Peace: his Calling and Qualifications* (1693), p. 14.

they were gentlemen not professionals, whose primary obligation was to be judicious—balanced, disinterested, and honest—rather than knowledgeable. Few saw a problem here. As one author reflected 'The Law of *England*, is not, *in it self*, such a Difficulty for Persons, of common Understandings, to attain a tolerable Knowledge of . . . But 'tis the *Perplexity*, and the *Multiplicity* of our Laws, that renders the Knowledge of them Difficult.'[22]

The authority of JPs was extensive, but their lack of expertise placed limits on what they could do. Most importantly serious crimes tried outside London, especially those liable to the death penalty, were dealt with by the peripatetic assize courts. Twice a year, usually in February–March and July–August, pairs of judges left the central courts on six circuits (Home, Midland, Norfolk, Oxford, North, and the West) stopping off at major towns to try cases. Such circuits varied in length (Oxford being the longest and usually lasting nearly 30 days, the Home circuit being the shortest) and the towns visited might change a little from year to year—39 were visited in the summer of 1720. Assize judges were at the peak of the legal profession, sitting in the central courts and often being called upon by the House of Lords to vet proposed legislation—Lord Chief Justice Holt was the most eminent of these in this period.[23] Though senior judges were increasingly sensitive on questions of independence and incorruptibility by the early eighteenth century the fact remains that they were appointed by the Crown because of their loyalty as well as abilities. Indeed, though the Revolution established the principle that they might be removed only for misbehaving not at the whim of the current regime (a principle given statutory force in Act of Settlement of 1701), and executive interference in judicial matters did decline significantly after 1688, the Crown continued to see judicial appointments as integral to its prerogative and patronage, maintaining other ways of influencing the judiciary (such as pensions and promotions). Moreover, there was some scope for overt politicization of judges through the orders issued to them by the government before setting out on their circuits. In 1691 and 1692, for example, they were told to prosecute those not sub-scribing to the oaths of supremacy and allegiance. Indeed, the assize circuits were a vital means by which the centre might influence the localities and seek to communicate and impose its view of order, not only through the formal business of the courts but also through the social and ceremonial aspects of the circuits. But this influence was complicated by two factors. First, the declining role of the Crown and the Privy Council left the assizes increasingly under the

---

[22] *An Essay on the Amendment, and Reduction, of the Laws of England* (1724), p. 33.

[23] John Holt, 1642–1710, educated at Winchester College, Oriel College, Oxford, and Gray's Inn, knighted 1686, Lord Chief Justice King's Bench 1689. A powerful advocate, he was noted for his impartiality, discouraged prosecutions for witchcraft, and was lenient on matters of church attendance.

Legend:
① Home
② Oxford
③ Western
④ Midland
⑤ Norfolk
⑥ Northern

Newcastle-upon-Tyne
Carlisle
Durham
⑥
Appleby
Lancaster
York
Lincoln
Nottingham
Derby
④
Oakham
Norwich
Stafford
Shrewsbury
Leicester
Coventry
Huntington
⑤ Bury St Edmunds
Warwick
Worcester
Northampton
Cambridge
Hereford
Bedford
Gloucester
Aylesbury
Monmouth ②
Oxford
Hertford
Chelmsford
Bristol
Reading
Kingston-upon-
Thames
Maidstone
Wells
Salisbury
①
Sherborne
Winchester
Horsham
③
Exeter
Launceston

0   50 miles
0   50   100 km

MAP 8. The assize circuits in August and September 1690

gaze of the Lord Chancellor who was appointed for professional as well as political reasons. Second, the influence might flow from the localities through the assizes to the centre as well as vice versa. In 1693, for example, the whiggish Justice Rokeby was taken aback when at Dorchester the preacher of the assize sermon complained that the Toleration Act allowed 'every man liberty to spit in ye face of ye Church, & had taken away all ye means of correcting strife & envyings in ye Church'.[24] If assize judges could pontificate to the grand jury on the state of the nation, they were just as likely to have their ear bent at the assize ball by the local gentry. Indeed, the reciprocity of the relationship was vital to its effective functioning.

Central to the operation of both quarter sessions and the assizes were juries. For many trial by one's peers, twelve good men and true, was a pillar of English liberty, an ultimate guarantee against enslavement. Whatever the rhetoric, property qualifications aimed to exclude the bulk of the population from serving. But the rich were often reluctant to act (except on assize grand juries which were becoming more exclusive), and the reduction of the property qualification in 1692 simply underscored the fact that most jurors were drawn from fairly restricted social groups, especially the middling sections of society such as farmers, businessmen, and skilled craftsmen. Many such jurors acted on more than one occasion, picking up a degree of experience of the law in the process, and most appear to have been independent and reasonably conscientious. Doubtless many were hard on the poor, but they were local men who had to live not only with but often amidst the consequences of their decisions. Nor did jurors necessarily mimic the ideals of gentlemen, especially in the realm of the civil law. One author complained of 'Another thing for which the Country seems to call for Relief, is the miscarriages of Jurors, who being for the most part of the Yeomanry, Mercenary and Ignorant, and having no Good-liking of the Gentry, who are their Betters, are very Incompetent Judges of Differences wherein a Gentleman is concern'd'.[25]

If most of the rule of law was experienced locally within the county context, sometimes the centre was important. Royal proclamations were still significant in prompting action and instigating initiatives (they were indeed especially important after 1714); royal pardons were vital in regulating capital punishments; many people continued to petition the Privy Council for the resolution of disputes; the House of Lords was the final court of appeal and heard impeachments; Parliament was more and more the great law-maker; the legal

[24] *The Diary of Mr Justice Rokeby* (1888), p. 33. Thomas Rokeby, *c.*1631–99, educated at Catharine Hall, Cambridge, barrister Gray's Inn, Puisne Judge in Common Pleas 1689 then King's Bench 1695, knighted 1689.

[25] T. Nourse, *Campania Foelix: or, a Discourse of the Benefits and Improvements of Husbandry* (1700), p. 289.

profession was organized through London's Inns of Court; and at Westminster the courts of Chancery, King's Bench, and Common Pleas were crucial to dealing with bitterly contested civil cases. On this last point, it would be a mistake to think that the maintenance of order through the rule of law was merely a question of dealing with crime. Numerous interpersonal disputes also had to be dealt with, from contests over debts, to disputed contracts, and uncertain inheritances.

HANGING NOT PUNISHMENT ENOUGH?

In the generation after the Glorious Revolution few contemporaries doubted that crime and disorder were not only increasing but rampant. In particular they saw towns and cities as sinks of vice, stores of disrespect, and dens of thieving. For the most part they were just as certain that dramatic and at times drastic initiatives were necessary to stem this tide. Most obviously this might be by more rigorously implementing the laws and systems of control already to hand as, for example, in the efforts of the Societies for the Reformation of Manners who prosecuted the disorderly and chided constables to do their duty. But the period also saw significant developments in the letter of the law and, to a lesser extent, its processes. Loopholes were closed, crimes more carefully defined, harsher penalties extended, and new punishments instituted.

Undoubtedly, the most dramatic aspect of the redrawing of the rule of law was the extension of the death penalty to dozens of offences, the creation of what came to be called the 'bloody code'. This was done in two ways. First, by removing 'benefit of clergy' from a number of capital felonies. Benefit of clergy, which had its origins in medieval England, had mutated from its original purpose of ensuring that clerics were tried by their peers to become a way the laity might escape the hangman's noose when found guilty of certain capital felonies. Those claiming 'clergy' were required to prove it by reading the start of Psalm 51 (in medieval England literacy was largely confined to the clergy), which if successfully accomplished would be followed by a branding on the thumb to ensure that it was not claimed again. Increasing literacy, and the ability of the illiterate to commit to memory the crucial words, had gradually undermined the credibility of the test and by the late seventeenth century benefit of clergy had become a full-blown legal fiction. Often the test was administered in the most cursory fashion and between 1692 and 1706 women were not legally required to take it at all, a concession extended to men in 1706. Earlier extensions of benefit of clergy took place because judges allowed it, presumably viewing capital punishment as ill-fitting the crime, and the statutory change of 1706 also showed that the wider governing class felt that even as a fiction it needed to be placed on a more reasoned footing. That some felt the process was being abused is clear enough. From 1699 to 1706 those claiming clergy were branded on the left cheek to stigmatize them more obviously. More importantly, after the Revolution, very largely between 1689 and 1713, clergy was removed from specific capital felonies, so anyone found guilty of such crimes would be sentenced to death, with the only escape being a subsequent pardon. In particular a series of Acts of Parliament removed clergy from certain larcenies according to the value of the goods involved and the circumstances of the theft, including: theft of goods from a house when the owner was at home and put in fear; breaking into and stealing goods to the value of five shillings or more from houses, shops, and warehouses; shoplifting goods worth at least five shillings; thefts from stables and warehouses of at least five shillings; and simple theft (i.e. without breaking in or putting the owner in fear (say by servants)) to the value of forty shillings from a house or outhouse.

The second strand to the establishment of the 'bloody code' was by attaching capital punishment to certain crimes for the first time. Sometimes this was done to protect new forms of property which had come into existence, as in the 1697 statute which made it a non-clergyable felony to forge or counterfeit the seal of the Bank of England. But often old forms of property were so protected, undoubtedly the most remarkable of which was 9 George I, c. 22, 'An Act for the More Effectual Punishing Wicked and Evil-Disposed Persons Going Armed in Disguise, and Doing Injuries and Violences to the Persons and Properties of his Majesty's Subjects, and for the More Speedy Bringing the Offenders to Justice', better known as the 'Black Act'. This statute created about fifty capital offences—because of its roughly framed clauses it is impossible to be precise—which had a national jurisdiction even though it was apparently prompted by the activities of the Blacks, that is people disguising themselves by blacking their faces, of Waltham in Hampshire, Farnham in Surrey, and Windsor forest in Berkshire. Among the offences now made capital were cattle maiming, destroying young trees, breaking the heads of fishponds, extortion, and blackmail. As with so much of the capital legislation of this period it was passed in Parliament without much comment, but appears to have been seen as the only means of ensuring that particular crimes, even when only threatening in particular places, did not spiral out of control.

The causes and consequences of the Black Act shine a powerful light on the governors' perceptions of crime and their desire to see off fresh threats by enhancing their authority. The problem of the Blacks first appeared in the late 1710s. In June 1718 a royal proclamation was issued for catching armed men who had broken into the Bishop of Winchester's park at Farnham in Surrey, and in the following January another proclamation offered a reward of £100 for the capture of those who had stolen 100 deer there. In February 1719 a newspaper reported that the bishop's park had suffered heavily from poaching for three years, which had then coalesced into organized crime: 'Twenty Persons or More, armed and disguised, did in an outrageous Manner with Guns, kill, wound, and carry away several Brace of Deer.'[26] The new reward failed to halt this and events took a decisive turn for the worse in 1721 when one of the bishop's keepers was shot. By one report attempts to suppress this 'Gang of *Banditti*' only forced them to Waltham where 'they render'd themselves terrible to all the adjacent County', not only poaching but sending threatening letters and destroying trees.[27] At the same time, and probably only faintly connected, Blacks began operating in Windsor forest. There the violence was more marked, not least because the forest was subject to closer, royal, government: two keepers were killed, several injured, property attacked, and game taken. Even so, to create fifty new capital offences was a drastic and draconian step, and suggests that the authorities felt that the Blacks were part of a wider problem of attacks on property as well as being part of a particular emergency. Certainly it is important to stress that organized attacks on parks were far from new and the Blacks may have been seen as part of the increasing menace of organized poaching (perhaps to supply the illicit market in London). In 1697, for example, the Lords Justices in Council complained of the attacks by 40 horsemen with dogs (and thus men of some substance) on the park of Sir John Banks at Aylesford in Kent, and amongst other things 'killed and carried away several Deer, broke up and threw down great part of the park pales.'[28] Similarly, in Buckinghamshire deer stealing was a serious problem at just the same time as in Berkshire, Surrey, and Hampshire. In fact in many ways the Black Act betrayed the weakness rather than the strength of the elite, not least that the Blacks were often able to hide behind the sympathies of the local communities they operated from, cocking a snook at the rule of law. The threat was heightened, moreover, by the development in the late 1710s and early 1720s of a general sense of intense lawlessness, fed most conspicuously by the wave of highway robberies of the period, a surge of smuggling to and from France, the corruption of thieftakers and gaolers, and renewed Jacobitism. On this last point, it was significant that the Black Act came soon after the Atterbury plot (when habeas corpus was suspended and fines on Roman Catholics increased), for there were fears that the Blacks might be recruited to do the dirty work of Jacobite gentlemen—though the Waltham Blacks explicitly professed their loyalty to the Hanoverian succession.

Contemporary governors stressed the supposed deterrent effects of the death penalty. With the detection of crime unprofessional and occasional, and

[26] *Post Boy*, 3–5 February 1719, [p. 1].

[27] *The History of the Blacks of Waltham in Hampshire; and those Under Like Denomination in Berkshire* (1723), pp. 3 and 6.

[28] *By the Lords Justices a Proclamation, 17 September 1697*.

with private prosecution ensuring there was no certainty that suspected criminals would be brought to justice, some argued that to hang some would hopefully persuade others to keep to the straight and narrow. Certainly, the dozens of gibbets across the country constantly reminded all of the terror of the law and many people will have witnessed hangings, though few with the scientific detachment of a doctor at Wells who 'Saw out of my Garret Window Cox hangd at Stookley Hill with my little Telliscope.'[29] Publication of 'last dying speeches' helped to bring the lesson home. Yet it was far from clear that hanging was having the desired effect. Conspicuously, offences within the scope of the Black Act continued to haunt the authorities after 1723, with attacks within forests and parks on game, trees, fish, and keepers unabated. To some the 'bloody code' was not inspiring fear, even that 'The lower classes do not consider it a great disgrace to be simply hanged'.[30] In London it was noted how the procession of the condemned to Tyburn too often degenerated into a drink-sodden carnival—'All the Way, from *Newgate* to *Tyburn*, is one continued Fair, for Whores and Rogues of the meaner Sort'—and in popular parlance execution day was called 'Paddington fair'.[31] Some thought this could only be tackled by aggravating capital punishments: 'they who shew no mercy should find none; and if Hanging will not restrain them, Hanging them in Chains, and Starving them, or (if Murtherers and Robbers at the same time, or Night-incendiaries) breaking them on the Wheel, or Whipping them to Death, a *Roman* Punishment should.'[32] Some bodies were indeed left to rot on the gibbet, as others were denied a decent burial and handed over to medics for dissection, occasionally provoking 'a Squabble between the Surgeons and the Mob'.[33]

BEYOND THE 'BLOODY CODE'

The extension and enhancement of the 'bloody code'—the most important parts of which had actually been put in place in the sixteenth century—must not detract from the significance of other changes in the law and its operation in this period, nor from the fact that these often significantly modified or contradicted its intentions. Not least, there is good evidence, as will be seen, that

[29] *The Diary of a West Country Physician, A.D. 1684–1726*, ed. E. Hobhouse (1934), p. 51.

[30] *A Foreign View of England in the Reigns of George I and George II. The Letters of Monsieur César de Saussure to his Family*, trans. and ed. Madame van Muyden (1902), pp. 126–7.

[31] B. Mandeville, *An Enquiry into the Causes of the Frequent Executions at Tyburn* (1725), p. 20; *The Thieves New Canting Dictionary of Words, Proverbs, Terms, and Phrases Used in the Modern Language of the Thieves, Augmented by Captain Alexander Smith* (1719), s.v.

[32] *Hanging not Punishment Enough, for Murtherers, High-Way Men, and Home Breakers* (1701), p. 3.

[33] Mandeville, *Enquiry into Executions at Tyburn*, p. 26.

many of those central to the criminal justice 'system'—victims, juries, Justices, and judges—believed that the scope of capital punishment was too extensive. Many held implicitly to a view that crimes and punishments should be proportionate to one another, silently endorsing the expansion of benefit of clergy and agonizing about extensions of the 'bloody code'. Moreover, those extensions were made still more unsettling by efforts to encourage private prosecution of serious crimes. In 1693 an Act of Parliament introduced a reward of £40 to anyone who caught and successfully prosecuted a highwayman, a reward extended in 1706 to burglary. The reward was made more valuable when in 1699 a certificate, the 'Tyburn ticket', excusing a man from holding parish office was issued with the payment. Through the period, especially after 1714, the Crown and Privy Council frequently offered rewards in reaction to particular crimes. If such rewards did help many poorer victims mount a prosecution, they were also soon exploited for private gain, notably by 'thief-takers'. The potential consequences of this should not be underrated, for one effect was to increase the likelihood that very large numbers of people might be hanged. Given that the administration of criminal justice depended heavily upon consensus and amateur volunteers, the potential challenge excessive punishments posed to sensibilities might be considerable. If many embraced capital punishment, many also believed that it should be used sparingly and selectively.

What many victims and prosecutors longed for was an available and reasonable punishment between whipping and hanging. As so many criminals were poor heavy fining was not an option. Branding clergied felons on the cheek rather than the thumb was one response, but was soon found to make the person unemployable and desperate. Thus when branding was returned to the thumb in 1706 judges were given discretion to sentence the person to hard labour in a house of correction or workhouse. This did lead to the imprisonment of some felons—in Devon nearly a quarter of those accused of felony before the assizes in the period 1707–17. That hitherto imprisonment had been little used marked the 1706 legislation as a new departure, not least that the criminal might be reformed. But gaols were too expensive for many contemporaries, and because prisoners' labour rarely raised significant income houses of correction provided only a limited solution to the problem of finding a serious punishment beneath the death penalty. Indeed gaols were never seen by the authorities as something worth investing public money in, even at the expense of a lack of regulation, criminal opportunism on the part of keepers and warders, and notorious scandals. It was in this environment that transportation emerged as the most significant secondary punishment in this era. Some convicts, pardoned capital felons, had been shipped to the American colonies since the early seventeenth century, but never in any great numbers. In 1702 a Bill to put transportation on a statutory basis failed, but another was passed in 1718, based as the Act's preamble stated on the belief that the 'bloody code' was not working effectively. The perceived virtue of transportation was that it rid society of malefactors, was liable to a degree of proportionality by varying the length of banishment (usually either seven or fourteen years), provided the underpopulated colonies with labour, and was not very costly (initially the shipping charge was £3 a head but this rose to £5 by 1727). Soon considerable numbers of convicts were being sent to the colonies, a London merchant with experience in the slave trade, Jonathan Forward, being contracted to carry convicts from the Home Counties—they were sold into servitude in the colonies. Resistance by colonial governments to this onslaught was swiftly dismissed by London, and before halted by the onset of the American War of Independence in 1775 over 36,000 English convicts had been shipped across the Atlantic. Such numbers are clear enough evidence that the benefits of this forced migration were seen to be considerable, more than offsetting the cost, colonial resistance, and the complaints of families left fatherless (over four out of five convicts were men).

It is clear that the development of the 'bloody code' was but part of a wider reformulation of ways of tackling serious crime. Though some of those changes had begun before the Revolution, they became much more concerted from 1689. Interestingly this was not because of central government initiatives, for most of the relevant statutes appear to have emanated from the efforts of particular interests. In so far as one predominated it was London, both through its governing bodies and its commercial interests such as guilds, chartered companies, and financial institutions. In that rapidly urbanizing environment not only were traditional modes of control often ineffective, but the opportunities for crime, especially theft, were very much greater. It was not just that there were more pockets to pick, shops to rifle, and coaches to prey upon, or that disposing of goods was much easier, not least through pawnbrokers, but that the cramped urban environment offered a degree of anonymity and escape impossible in the hamlets and villages of rural England. Such features, however, were hardly new, even if they were ever growing. But their profile was now much greater because the proliferating press assiduously publicized crime and because the governing classes were now visiting London more frequently and for longer periods. Not the least cause of the latter development, the growth of parliamentary government, was also integral to the statutory changes in the criminal law after 1689. Parliament's enhanced presence now made possible the passage of a significantly greater volume of legislation.[34] Yet it must be stressed that it was no mere rubber stamp, uncritically extending the 'bloody code' or secondary punishments. There was debate, outside lobbying, and kite

---

[34] See Chapter 2.

flying, and Bills were rejected, especially in the 1690s. Indeed, rejection of such measures was common—under William and Anne only 36 per cent of attempts at Westminster to enact legislation that might be classed as 'law and order' succeeded, whereas for other types of legislation 53 per cent passed.

A sense of the legislative patterns of changes in the law in this period introduces an important sense of scale. Not least it points up how much more extensive were changes in the rule of law than those suggested by concentrating on the 'bloody code' alone. There were in fact nearly 1,100 Acts passed in this period which might be counted as general, and if many of these dealt with matters such as public finance and the armed forces, many others dealt with regulating everyday lives. It is difficult to draw out any pattern in this growth of the law, but two might be cited. The first were those associated with the expanding State through the growth of the army and navy and of the financial mechanisms to pay for it. Increasing duties and the growth of the customs and excise services to collect them necessarily created the potential for smuggling and enhanced its threat to the State. New ways of proceeding, such as the use of particular weights and measures, were required of merchants and manufacturers. A second important change affected the world of contracts, of attempts to make the processes of exchange of property smoother and less liable to litigation. For example, in the commercial world, the legal status of bills of exchange and promissory notes was enhanced in 1704; the law of bankruptcy was overhauled in 1706 to encourage reasonable risk-taking and honesty on the part of the failed business person (fraudulent conveying goods by a person aware of their insolvency was made a capital crime); courts for the cheap and easy resolution of small debts were instituted in a few cities; and debtors' sanctuaries, popularly held to be beyond the law's jurisdiction, were outlawed in 1697. The world of landownership saw significant developments with the introduction of county registers of deeds for Middlesex in 1709, and for the West Riding of Yorkshire in 1704 and the East Riding in 1709 (and the North Riding in 1736).[35]

Significant extensions of the rule of law made it at once more brutal in places, rational elsewhere, and confused over all. That was because there was no grand plan being followed, rather the interplay of some common assumptions, conflicting interests, and a newly available legislative process. The government had no department with particular oversight of law and order issues —the Lord Chancellor, Attorney-General, and Solicitor-General were principally concerned with matters of administration and personnel. And if many initiatives emanated from the backbenches or outside Parliament they often ran into opposition that was sometimes successful, sometimes not. Thus if land

---

[35] These developments need placing in the context of other changes in economic policy in the period. See above, pp. 339–43.

registries or small debt courts were established in some places they were denied to others. Attempts at more general reform were few and far between—Somers attempted some overhaul of systems—and attracted not only principled opposition but the ire of vested interests. A further source of confusion was that through poor draughtsmanship it was 'so hard to find the true meaning of some Acts of Parliament'.[36] Thus, just as those responsible for maintaining law and order varied from place to place, so the legal framework within which they worked pulled in a number of directions.

CRIMES AND PUNISHMENTS

It is impossible to know how much crime and disorder there was in England in this period. Neither contemporary laments nor Hogarth's engravings can be taken at face value, and court records reveal only those cases brought before the judiciary—much crime, the so-called 'dark figure', will have gone unrecorded. Nor was that figure likely to be small, for dependence upon private prosecutions ensured that many were afraid to involve themselves in a process they knew little of and which might cost them dearly in time and money and perhaps even in reputation. Still, legal records can fruitfully suggest some patterns and vividly show how the law was variously used by victims and authorities to maintain order.

According to contemporary newspapers England after the Glorious Revolution was awash with theft and violence, of daring robberies, despicable rapes, and dastardly murders. Yet in purely quantitative terms the law most people encountered was civil not criminal and petty not serious. Litigation involved a surprisingly high proportion of society at the time, embroiled as they were in disputes over contracts, exchanges, agreements, property rights, payments, and debts. The mutual responsibilities of tenant and landlord, purchaser and seller, provided plentiful opportunities for dispute, even among neighbours. Disputes also often concerned slander or alleged negligence, not least because the maintenance of reputation, to be 'creditable', was of considerable social and economic significance. A good deal of court time was given over to defamation cases. Such civil cases emphasize contemporary use of the law as a regulatory mechanism. It was used not merely to punish, but to direct—for example, encroachments onto the commons, highway maintenance, and poor law eligibility especially still preoccupied the vestry and the quarter session. But the old apparatus of control was on the wane as, somewhat silently and unconsciously, the benefits of a great economic liberalism were embraced, especially with regard to apprenticeship, wages, prices, and markets.

[36] [Baston], *Thoughts on Trade*, p. 80.

Most crime in this period, and accounting for an overwhelming number of the cases considered by the judicial process, were petty crimes. Many such misdemeanors were concerned with order in some way—of assault, riot, defamation, disorderly alehouses—many others with getting local government officers to do their jobs. Orderliness and regulation were the watchwords. 'Excessive' behaviour—from boisterousness to minor acts of violence, from drunkenness to promiscuity—among private citizens was to be contained, dutiful behaviour among public officers ensured. Such crimes might be dealt with informally by Justices acting alone or in pairs, or relatively quietly at the quarter sessions, and were collectively of considerable significance, involving thousands of people in legal processes. In Middlesex in this period two-thirds of those accused of such crimes pleaded guilty and escaped with a small fine. Of course, many of those could not afford to pay more than a small fine, and levels of fines were varied according to ability to pay. Rarely were offenders punished in other ways, though some were whipped, consigned to a stint in the pillory, and in places scolds might still suffer the ducking stool: 'The *Stocks* are used for Vagabonds . . . The *Pillory* is used for Cheats, Perjurers, Libellers, and Blasphemers . . . *Whipping* is properly inflicted for Petty Larceny'.[37] Such punishments were designed to be painful to body and reputation, though the pilloried might be fêted as well as abused.

A short spell in a house of correction (or 'bridewell') was also often seen as an appropriate means of dealing with idleness and loose living. Vagrants, the unemployed, prostitutes, bastard bearers, and pilferers, might be sent to such houses for a few days, rarely for more than two weeks, making them indeed 'prisons for the poor'.[38] Such institutions had their origins in the sixteenth century, but a wave of about thirty new ones was established between 1690 and 1720, partly in response to new patterns of poverty, partly to the moral reform agenda that also gave rise to the Reformation of Manners societies (much of whose work was, of course, given over to prosecuting varieties of disorderliness) and the workhouse movement.[39] To the authorities houses of corrections took potential troublemakers off the street and by a dose of hard labour or the lash hopefully transformed them into good citizens. That this could be done summarily by Justices acting alone or with a colleague only made them more attractive. They were especially popular in towns, most notably in the capital. In the 1690s some 900 to 1,000 people were being committed annually to houses of correction in London and Middlesex, a figure that had risen to 1,300 by the

[37] G. Miege, *The New State of England Under our Present Monarch K. William III* (4th edn., 1702), part 3, p. 71.

[38] J. Innes, 'Prisons for the Poor: English Bridewells, 1555–1800', in F. Snyder and D. Hay (eds.), *Labour, Law and Crime: An Historical Perspective* (1987), pp. 42–122.

[39] See above, pp. 238–9.

1720s. That in and around the capital fully two-thirds of those committed were women, many for prostitution, neatly shows the ways houses of correction were being used to control symptoms of poverty (in Suffolk in this period more or less equal numbers of men and women were committed).

More serious crimes, felonies, included most thefts and violent attacks on persons and property, from murder to rape and arson. Crimes of violence were very much in the minority among felonies. At the Devon assizes between 1700 and 1709 76 per cent of cases concerned property offences, homicide and infanticide 15 per cent, arson 3 per cent, and coining 2 per cent, figures that appear to have been similar to the experience elsewhere. Similarly, in Surrey in the late seventeenth century 84 per cent of felons executed had been found guilty of property offences. In crude quantitative terms, therefore, when dealing with serious crimes the authorities mainly tackled various types of theft. Crimes against property not the person predominated and that much theft was defined as a felony speaks volumes about contemporary priorities. Private property was sacrosanct, with even thefts of minor items occasionally being severely dealt with. A distinction was drawn between petty and grand larceny according to whether the value of the good stolen was more or less than one shilling, with petty larcenies punished mainly by whipping, though sometimes after 1718 by transportation to the American colonies.

Though property was hedged by an increasingly extensive 'bloody code' in practice the use of execution was far from increasingly frequent and merciless. Indeed, from abroad the rule of law seemed unexceptional: 'the Laws of this Country are far from being rigorous; but if any of them happen to be more severe than ordinary, they are but faintly executed.'[40] Contemporaries were, in fact, often loath to follow the letter of the law and a surprisingly small proportion of those tried for committing a capital felony were actually executed—in Cheshire in 1700–9 about 10 per cent, and in Devon 1700–50 about 8 per cent, largely because of the actions of juries and the judiciary. Grand juries might decide that the evidence against an accused was insufficient to warrant a trial, and trial juries might either find the accused innocent or guilty of a lesser crime. The former course might be taken even in the face of directions from the bench. At Norwich assizes in April 1696, for example, seven were sentenced to death but 'Others as guilty were discharged, contrary to the directions of ye judge, by an over-kind jury'.[41] The latter course, reaching 'partial verdicts', was often used to reduce the value of goods stolen to take the accused

[40] B.-L. de Muralt, *Letters Describing the Character and Customs of the English and French Nations* (2nd edn., 1726), p. 73.

[41] *Letters of Humphrey Prideaux Sometime Dean of Norwich to John Ellis Sometime Under-Secretary of State 1674–1722*, ed. E. M. Thompson, Camden Society, New Series, 15 (1875), p. 168.

outside the scope of capital punishment. Interestingly they were much more likely to do that in relation to those crimes from which benefit of clergy had been removed after 1689. In Surrey between 1660 and 1800 trial juries reached partial verdicts in only 17 per cent of 'old' pre-1689 capital offences but in 49 per cent of 'new' post-1688 capital offences. All such partial verdicts were manipulations. Richard Gough recounted the case of a man accused of stealing two dozen chickens: 'The Judge, seeing him a silly man, told the Jury that the matter of fact was soe fully proved that they must finde the prisoner guilty, but they would doe well to consider of the value, and thereupon the Jury found him guilty of fellony to the value of eleven pence, at which the judge laught heartily and said he was glad to heare that cocks and henns were soe cheap in this country.'[42] But the joke had a deeply serious side, for the jurors were very consciously and publicly turning their backs on inflexible interpretations of the 'bloody code'. Having to live amidst the consequences of their decision they bore the wider social ramifications of capital punishment—the reactions of family, friends, neighbours, and colleagues—in a way legislators were unlikely to.

Gough's story neatly points to the role judges might play in mitigating the severity of the law. In fact, in addition to directing juries they could also make recommendations that those sentenced to death receive a royal pardon. Such pardoning was common, and was greatly encouraged by the advent of organized transportation, probably amounting to about a half of those sentenced to death. The grounds for pardons though not formally specified were generally understood. Those most likely to be pardoned were women, those with many dependants, the criminally inexperienced, the non-violent, and those said to be of good character by local worthies. There was nothing exact about this, and in particular cases contradictory perceptions might do battle, producing more or less random outcomes. So, for example, when Justice Eyre reported on two horsestealers found guilty before him he reprieved one 'in compassion to his wife & nine small Children' but not the other who was 'represented to me, by several Gentlemen & Justices of the Peace, to be a man of Ill fame, & dangerous to the country'. Yet later the local Undersheriff, 'a very Honest Man', declared that both men 'are two very notorious Rogues, have behaved themselves very rudely, and have attempted to break the Gaol . . . the Country would be very well pleas'd to have them Both executed'.[43]

It is an important curiosity of the adminstration of criminal justice in this period that just as it dramatically extended the scope of the death penalty so fewer and fewer people were actually hanged—in the late sixteenth century about one in four of those tried at assizes for a capital felony were executed, but

[42] R. Gough, *The History of Myddle*, ed. D. Hey (Harmondsworth, 1981), pp. 145–6.
[43] P. R. O., SP35/1/12, 9 August 1714.

by the early eighteenth century the proportion had fallen to about one in ten. The rigours of the law were circumvented by the use of acquittals, partial verdicts, pardons, and transportation. Yet if such means were used to make punishments better fit the crime this was done only in the most loosely structured of ways. Inconsistency necessarily resulted, with some of those condemned of essentially trivial offences being hanged, but others not. This could and did cause public disquiet, though it was expressed only occasionally and in muted form, as in a report from York of two executed as being 'much pitied and lamented . . . in regard, that what they took, was only Three Half-pence'.[44] Equally, the accused had little certainty before trial how they would be dealt with. Nor could they have much confidence in a trial procedure that gave little or no scope for an active defence—the accused were rarely represented in court. Trials were essentially cursory affairs, conducted with a constant eye on the clock. On the summer circuit of the Western assize in 1693, for example, Justices Rokeby and Atkyns tried 268 cases in seven or so towns over about a month. If some cases might hear a number of witnesses, many trials, even in capital cases, lasted little more than half an hour. To the accused the criminal justice 'system' could easily look cursory and devoid of transparency, accountability, and consistency.

THE FALL AND RISE OF CRIME

A striking feature of this period is the apparent contradiction between the commonly held contemporary view that in general crime was increasing and the evidence from the courts that it was probably decreasing. At one extreme, for example, homicide rates in Kent fell from an estimated 5.3 to 1.7 per 100,000 per annum between the end of the sixteenth century and the final decade of our period (in 1985 the national rate was 1.1), with a particularly marked drop between 1680 and 1720. In Cheshire a similar fall appears to have taken place, and between 1660–79 and 1720–39 the rate fell from 2.6 to 1.1 in Sussex and from 8.1 to 2.8 in those parts of Surrey near London. Various explanations for this might be advanced, including a growing abhorrence of violence, a decline in weapon carrying, and improved medical provision. However, it would also appear that a similar fall took place with regard to property offences. In Cheshire indictments for property felonies rose to a peak of nearly 500 in the decade 1620–9 but by the first decade of the eighteenth century had fallen to well under a hundred, and in Essex, Sussex, and rural Surrey comparable declines were experienced. A further piece of evidence can be set alongside this, that there was a significant decline in the volume of civil litigation from

[44] *Weekly Journal, or British Gazetteer*, 15 September 1716, p. 518.

the mid-seventeenth to the mid-eighteenth centuries. On the Oxford assize circuit the number of civil cases fell from 564 in 1661 to 334 in 1697, and on the Home circuit from 411 in 1673 to 122 in 1713. In London at the central courts of King's Bench and Common Pleas the number of cases fell by 40 per cent between 1670 and 1700 and even more sharply in the next twenty years, though in Chancery the decline does not appear to have begun until after 1700.

By most available measures English courts were generally less and less busy over the late seventeenth and early eighteeth centuries and this was experienced across most areas of the law. Explaining it is far from easy, not least because the coincidental effect of several causes may well have been at work differentially upon particular parts of the rule of law. Schematically it might result from a growing unwillingness to use the rule of law, or a decline in the incidence of crime. In turn, a heightened unwillingness to use the law may have resulted from wider social changes or from developments within the rule of law. As to the first it is notable that it was in the 1620s and 1630s that great resort was made to the courts, decades of great political, religious, and economic uncertainty. It is possible that greater social stability after the Restoration in general, and the Glorious Revolution in particular, meant that social relations became less fraught, producing an attitudinal shift towards less litigiousness in the civil law. Perhaps slow expansion of the economy also helped, taking the tension out of many exchanges, and perhaps changes in the laws surrounding credit and debt reduced the scope for litigiousness. Similarly, in the area of the criminal law it is possible that changes made it less attractive. Not only were harsher punishments frequently unacceptable, but the degree of randomness inherent to the judicial process may well have made it less desirable to use. Equally, complaints about 'the excessive Delay and Expences in the Administration of Justice' appear to have had some foundation, especially with regard to the central courts, though contemporaries seem to have grabbed the wrong end of the stick by putting this down to increasing numbers of attorneys.[45]

At the time no one imagined that the flow of business into the courts was falling, if anything quite the opposite. Three factors were crucial to that misperception: the role of the expanding press in publicizing crime; the particular problems in the rapidly expanding metropolis and an increasing knowledge of them because of the growth of parliamentary government and the London season; and the impact of crime waves. The first two of these have already been touched upon but the last had a particular importance, both because it is clear that the volume of crime did vary over the short term and because contemporaries were inclined to react to a heightening of the perceived causes of crime by

---

[45] [Tancred], *Essay*, p. 2.

pursuing prosecutions more vigorously, further 'inflating' levels of crime. Two perceived causes were especially important here, variations in the standard of living associated with the state of harvests, business, and trade, and the impact of war through mobilization and demobilization.

The relationship between poverty and crime was well attested by 1700, hardship driving people to disorder as well as theft: 'People are never so irreconcileably *angry* and *quarrelsome*, as when they are hungry . . . It fills a Land with a *Rabble* of Mendicants, Malecontents, and Rebels'.[46] Such commonplaces helped to frame reactions to individual acts of desperation (frequently the theft of food) as well as the collective energies of the food riot, though many distinguished between understanding and excusing poverty-induced crime. It meant, however, that crime was frequently comprehended in relation not only to patterns of employment and prices, but also to the operation of the poor law, such that it is easy to see why it was recommended 'The *Justice of the Peace* his principal Care is to provide for the Poor'.[47] It was similarly widely understood that the coming of peace would lead to the dumping of tens of thousands of generally young soldiers and sailors in major towns to wend their way homewards. With little cash to pay their way some turned to crime to make ends meet. After the Nine Years War it was complained that 'We need not go far for Reasons of the great Numbers and increase of these vermin [highwaymen and robbers] . . . after so many Thousands of Soldiers disbanded, and Mariners discharged, many of them are driven upon necessity, and having been used to an idle way of living, care not to work . . . Besides, the Poor are exceedingly numerous'.[48] If anything the problem was the more acute after the Treaty of Utrecht in 1713.

There were two significant crime waves noted in this period, in the 1690s and in the decade following the end of the War of the Spanish Succession, but it is impossible to judge the extent to which these were 'real' and the extent to which they were 'imagined'. Common to both was the reputed proliferation of criminal gangs in and around London, especially of highway robbers. Concern with highway robbers—both mounted and 'footpads'—had increased after 1660 as the growing traffic of people and goods into and out of the capital provided enormous opportunities for theft. After the Glorious Revolution increased flows of taxes from provincial England to London brought the problem into stark relief and made it a matter of urgent concern to the government. In December 1691 the Worcester wagon was robbed of £2,500 of taxes destined for the Treasury. By November 1692, in the aftermath of an audacious and violent robbery of £15,000 of taxes being carried to London, it was being

---

[46] O. Dykes, *English Proverbs, with Moral Reflexions* (3rd edn., 1713), p. 221.
[47] Bohun, *The Justice of the Peace*, p. 44.   [48] *Hanging not Punishment Enough*, p. 21.

complained that 'The highway men do as much infest the roads as pirates do the sea', an environment which provoked putting onto a permanent statutory footing what had been occasional Royal proclamations offering rewards for the apprehension and successful prosecution of highwaymen.[49] Further attempts to legislate against them in the 1690s all failed, despite continued complaints, especially after the end of the war, that 'The Highway-men and Footpads continue to infest the Roads leading to this City, more than ever', echoed in Evelyn's lament about 'Horrible roberys, high-way men, & murders'.[50] The 1700s, by contrast, were relatively quiet and if prosecutions mounted after 1713, it was not until the late 1710s that the problem was tackled with renewed vigour, particularly when in 1719 the Privy Council added a reward of £100 to the £40 already on offer. This did not immediately turn the tide for early in 1720 it was claimed that 'The Insolence of the Highwaymen, and other Robbers, is come to a greater height than ever was known; for they even rob now in the high Streets'.[51] In part this surge was caused by the endeavours of a small number of criminal gangs. Boastfully, one claimed that 'One Morning we robb'd the *Cirencester*, the *Worcester*, the *Glocester*, the *Oxford*, and *Bristol* Stage-Coaches, all together; the next Morning the *Ipswich* and *Colchester . . .* Our Evening Exercises were generally between *Hampstead*, *Hackney*, *Bow*, *Richmond*, and *London*'.[52]

Such depredations were soon contained by vigorously prosecuting high-waymen, with a peak being reached in 1721 and 1722, aided by a £200 reward for the prosecution of those who had robbed the mails. Significant numbers were hanged, still more transported. All this was undeniably important, but to contemporaries the real end to the crime wave came with the executions of Jack Sheppard in November 1724 and, more especially, Jonathan Wild in May 1725. Sheppard, a Londoner born in 1702, had been consigned to a spell in a work-house as a boy, and in 1723 broke his apprenticeship and turned to a life of crime. He was eventually captured and executed, but he also captivated the public imagination by his pathological disregard for the rule of law—not only did he dramatically escape from chains, cells, guards, and prisons, but having done so he gorged himself on a rich diet of robbery, seeming to invite further capture. Yet Sheppard's story was essentially a particular one whose general resonances were muted. Wild, on the other hand, symbolized the collapse of

[49] H. M. C., *The Manuscripts of his Grace the Duke of Portland*, vol. 3 (1894), p. 507.

[50] *Post Boy*, 29–31 August 1699, [p. 2]; *The Diary of John Evelyn*, ed. E. S. de Beer, 6 vols. (Oxford, 1955), vol. 5, p. 366.

[51] [Applebee's] *The Original Weekly Journal*, 23 January 1720, p. 1646.

[52] R. Wilson, *A Full Account of all the Robberies Committed by John Hawkins, George Sympson, (Lately Executed for Robbing the Bristol Mails) and their Companions* (3rd edn., n.d. [1722?]), pp. 17–18.

integral parts of law enforcement in the capital, especially the use of rewards to encourage private prosecution, and appeared to provide plentiful evidence of the existence of a vicious criminal class. He had arrived in London in 1709, was briefly imprisoned for debt, and around the time of the end of the War of the Spanish Succession established himself as a thieftaker, that is a form of private detective looking to live off the proceeds of rewards or the commissions of clients. He established his Lost Property Office near the Old Bailey and at his peak had agents operating in several major towns and cities. From an early date, however, Wild's activities had been corrupt, for he acted as a receiver of stolen goods and commissioned thieves to steal to order, in both cases apparently miraculously reuniting goods with their true owners for a fee. By satisfying both thieves and the thieved he satisfied all. He also legitimated his activities by occasionally offering up rival criminals to the authorities, in so doing further organizing and disciplining significant parts of London's underworld. Because he traced so much stolen property and caught many criminals he was initially celebrated, with even the Privy Council courting his advice. Yet he was soon identified not as a solution but as a principal cause of the crime wave. In 1718 corrupt thieftakers in general—Wild was neither an innovator nor one of a kind—and Wild in particular were singled out: 'The *Thief-Taker* is a *Thief-Maker*'.[53] Such an attack, so serious as it was and coming from a tainted source, was initially hardly credited. Yet gradually the truth of Wild's activities became apparent and his fall became increasingly dramatic. Huge crowds gathered to see him executed, 'Never was there seen so prodigious a Concourse of People before, upon any Occasion', and Grub Street exploited the story to the full before it was further refined to provide a fable of the general corruption of English government in Gay's highly popular *Beggar's Opera* (1728) and Henry Fielding's *Jonathan Wild* (1743).[54] As Gay put it, 'I cannot indeed wonder that the Talents requisite for a great Statesman are so scarce in the world since so many of those who possess them are every month cut off in the prime of their Age at the Old-Baily.'[55]

A CUSTOMARY ORDER

Clearly the letter of the law was not the unwavering practice of the law in England in this period. If in good measure that was because the elite was itself not fully sure of what needed to be done, the different ideas of order which existed in society at large were hardly less significant. Alternative conventions and priorities, expressed individually and collectively, passively and actively,

[53] [Hitchin], *The Regulator*, p. 16.   [54] *Mist's Weekly Journal*, 29 May 1725.
[55] *The Letters of John Gay*, ed. C. F. Burgess (Oxford, 1966), p. 45.

challenged those beloved by the governors. But whatever form they took their significance to a law so dependent upon voluntary participation was no less great than those ideologies handed down by such means as the grand jury charge or assize sermon. The voice of those with little or no property mattered, though if conflict pinpointed different ideas of order the consensus at the heart of the rule of law could only be built on the back of compromise and reciprocity.

Most generally such challenges took the form of particular lifestyles, from the rowdiness of the alehouse to the deliberate disrespect of Sabbath breaking, blasphemy, and seditious utterances. It is notable that these tensions particularly involved contests over the proper ways to spend leisure time. Here popular culture—such as gambling, drinking, and football—was consciously articulated as distinct and different, quite alien to the mannered politeness of those in power. To the elite such a culture contained the potential for wider disorder. So, for example, one hostile report of the custom of 'bull running' at Stamford, held annually six weeks before Christmas, not only complained of 'the greatest Cruelty to the poor Bull', but 'that till this heathenish Custom, and idolatrous Practice be restrain'd by a Law, the ordinary sort of People in this Town will continue a turbulent, violent, headstrong People, inclinable to join in all Riots and Tumults, and delighting in Violence and Oppression'.[56] In practice, however, because such customs were integral to local social identities they were too important and protean to be easily suppressed from above. Moreover, if the polite constantly lamented such revelry, the power they commanded to contain it was fractured and confined. Not only could constables and Justices do only so much, not least because they were members of the communities they sought to regulate, but the ecclesiastical courts and the Reformation of Manners societies made only limited headway. Indeed, arguably the identification between culture, customs, and social solidarity required that 'challenges' from within as well as above be met. This might take highly ceremonial form, especially when shaming or humiliating those held to have challenged popular social conventions, particularly surrounding patriarchy and marriage. One foreigner noted, for example, that

I have sometimes met in the streets of *London* a Woman carrying a Figure of Straw representing a Man, crown'd with very ample Horns, preceded by a Drum, and follow'd by a Mob, making a most grating Noise with Tongs, Grid-Irons, Frying-pans, and Sauce-pans: I ask'd what was the Meaning of all this; they told me, that a Woman had given her Husband a sound beating, for accusing her of making him a Cuckold, and that upon such Occasions some kind Neighbour of the *poor innocent injur'd Creature* generally perform'd this Ceremony.[57]

[56] *Weekly Journal, or British Gazetteer*, 26 January 1717, p. 636.
[57] H. Misson, *Memoirs and Observations in his Travels over England* (1719), p. 129.

Such 'ridings' and 'rough music' attempted to impose norms using a grammar similar to those of the stocks and pillory, albeit with a particularly exuberant dialect. Threats, ostracization, and malicious violence were also used to attain the same ends and if the extent and influence of such informal power is difficult to judge it appears to have been considerable, at least in terms of its potential.

More direct and serious challenges to the elite's definition of order involved collective action in support of customary rights judged to be under attack from above. Most frequently such battlegrounds were economic and took especially prominent form in rioting, particularly in food riots where the play of unfettered market forces was contested by popular notions of local self-sufficiency and the just price.[58] Such collective bargaining by riot was also occasionally more obviously a form of trade unionism. London was well used to the efforts of the Spitalfields weavers to improve their lot, and in 1721 the first Act limiting trade unionism was passed with reference to London tailors. Textile workers appear to have had a particularly well-developed sense of collective identity and of how they might be able to use that to improve their lot. At the very end of the period, in the midst of a trade depression and in the wake of the recent 'Act to prevent unlawful Combinations of Workmen employed in the Woollen Manufactures, and for better Payment of their Wages', weavers in the West country struck for better wages and were contained only by the use of military force.[59] But such trade unionism also occasionally articulated a direct challenge to the social distribution of power. Among weavers at Melksham in Wiltshire in 1727 'Some odd heterodox Notions began to be started among them, like those of Wat Tyler and Jack Straw, of rebellious memory . . . viz. That all Laws were illegal, That Papers and Parchments scrawled over with Ink in any Sort of Characters, were the Operations of Tyranny and Witchcraft, and ought to be burnt, That Adam made no Will when he died, and therefore all the Goods he left behind him should be equally distributed among his Children.'[60] Even if such an ideology was self-serving, and judging how popular it was is very hard to uncover, eschewing private property challenged the very heart of English society, evoking memories of the Levellers of the Interregnum. That was a challenge the authorities could not afford to let pass unnoticed.

Extension of the dominion of private property had since at least the sixteenth century been an occasional source of conflict between communities and those in power. Though this involved disputes over the game laws, customary perquisites, as well as ownership of wrecks cast ashore, it was access to and

---

[58] See above, p. 84.   [59] 12 George I, c. 34.
[60] *Mist's Weekly Journal*, 14 January 1727, [p. 2].

ownership of land and its produce that created particularly bitter confrontations, most obviously in relation to enclosure, and most spectacularly when associated with land drainage. Transforming common wetlands into fertile fields under individual proprietors might have raised agricultural output and productivity but it also ended the ability of villagers to build their own living from reed-cutting, fowling, rough grazing, and the like. Such a change was not merely economic, for the nature of the community, of its extent and relationships, was also changed. Little wonder that popular traditionalism sometimes boiled over. In January 1699, for example, major rioting broke out in the Lincoln-shire fens. Some 500 rioters, 'some with Guns, some with Halberts, some with great Hodding-Spoades, Forks, Shod-rudders and Haffock-knives . . . went on with Fury and Resolution', cutting drainage banks, sluices, and locks, thereby flooding 30,000 acres of fenland, 40 houses, and 15 drainage 'Engines'.[61] In March there were still threats that 'The Inhabitants of the Levells threaten still to break down more Banks, and let in the Water', though the spread of the disorder onto the Cambridgeshire fens was halted by the govern-ment ordering the Deputy Lieutenants and JPs into preemptive action.[62] Nor was this an isolated incident. A quarter of a century later, for example, at Stokesby in Norfolk 'a great many poor People, both Men and Women, in a Tumultuous Manner, threw down a new Mill, and divers Gates and Fences upon the Marsh'.[63]

Concerted collective opposition to the rule of law mainly concerned prop-erty, its 'ownership' and 'cost'. But such opposition might take the form of challenging the authority of the law more directly. For example, the crowd deriding the Tyburn procession undermined its terror. Such a disavowal of the rule of law could, moreover, take pointed form, as when weavers from Trowbridge in Wiltshire broke into workshops and destroyed cloths, appar-ently mocking the Black Act by appearing with 'their Faces sooted'.[64] Contempt for the law was vividly expressed when the authorities attempted to suppress those several debtors' sanctuaries existing in London. Such places were held to offer debtors immunity from attempts by creditors to use the law to imprison them. Quite how many people took solace there is unclear, Defoe improbably put their number at 20,000, but it is clear that the shelterers were certain of the legitimacy of their extra-legal status. Creditors who ventured inside to extricate a debtor were liable to be attacked, including tarring and feathering, and attempts to close off a part of the Whitefriars sanctuary in 1691 provoked a riot. Moreover, though it was claimed that the 1697 Act to suppress sanctuaries led to an exodus of those inside, new sanctuaries sprang up first in

[61] *Post Boy*, 24–26 January 1699, [p. 2].   [62] *Post Boy*, 16–18 March 1699, [p. 2].
[63] *Mist's Weekly Journal*, 24 July 1725, [p. 2].   [64] *Mist's Weekly Journal*, 3 June 1727, [p. 2].

Southwark, then in Wapping. By 1706 Defoe was chastising the Mint sanctuary in Southwark, 'where Insolent debttors *raise War* against the Laws, *Bully* the Magistrates, *Defie* the Parliament, stand Battle with the *Posse*, *Drench* the Officers, *Debauch* their own Principles, and Damn their *Creditors*'.[65] By another description it was a 'little Republick' with 'a very regular Government, executed by their Senators'.[66] Only slowly and after many battles between bailiffs and debtors were these new sanctuaries suppressed by new Acts in 1723 and 1725.

Popular opposition to the rule of law was extensive but patchy and episodic, not least because collective action required 'communities' to be defined as well as mobilized. That was far from easy in thinly populated rural areas with highly-variegated interests. Solidarity was most easily achieved in places with particular economic identities—such as in weaving towns, fenland villages, and mining communities—when faced by an obvious intruder. It is notable, for example, that the spirit of debtors's sanctuaries was restricted only to highly specific locales and did not spread more generally through the capital. It was also important that the governing classes sometimes saw the benefits of heeding disagreement. Concession and conciliation might attain objectives more easily, completely, and permanently than could conflict. So, for example, many Justices fully sympathized with the complaints of food rioters, embracing the view that '*Forestallers*, *Regrators* and *Ingrossers* . . . are now spread all over the Kingdom . . . and all these in Conjunction do now oppress the Poor in the most arbitrary manner'.[67] Similarly, the clergy often played an intermediary role between the rulers and the ruled and the poor law was an important mechanism regulating some of the fundamental tensions within a profoundly unequal society. Moreover, if in the last resort the elite's idea of order might be imposed by brute force in practice this was done relatively rarely: the spirit of rebellion was ultimately restricted and aversion to potential agencies of absolutism too general. Conspicuously, if in the wake of the '15 the Highlands were contained by being militarized England was not.

CONCLUSION

Early eighteenth-century England was, ultimately, a civil society that managed to reconcile many different ideas of order. Far from everyone was happy with the compromise, but for a 'system' built on the cheap it was surprisingly

---

[65] *Defoe's Review*, facsimile edn., 22 vols. (New York, 1938), vol. 3, p. 69.

[66] [Baston], *Thoughts on trade*, p. 111.

[67] *An Essay to Prove, that Regrators, Engrossers, Forestallers, Hawkers and Jobbers of Corn, Cattle, and other Marketable Goods, Provisions and Merchanidizes, are Destructive of Trade, Oppressive to the Poor, and a Common Nuisance to the Kingdom in General* (1718), p. 11.

effective—there was justice, and crime was contained. The power of that 'system', moreover, increased because of the impact of increased numbers of JPs, the widespread use of rewards, the rationalization of benefit of clergy, and the introduction of transportation. But such developments did not make the authorities sleep more easily. If they celebrated the rule of law as guaranteeing England's supreme constitution their anxieties about maintaining order remained as strong as ever. In part that was because many of the most profound causes of crime remained or had, indeed, changed, and the rapidly expanding press was reporting crime to an unprecedented extent. In part, however, it was because the rule of law was a jumble, at times even a shambles.

The rule of law was not a 'system' but a flexible patchwork that dealt with crime and disorder variably. This of course allowed it to tailor processes to circumstances, both individual and social, a merit which impressed many. And there were powerful checks on the misuse of the law. But the lack of rationality was soon to grate. If Locke observed that '*where there is no Law, there is no Freedom*' he also noted that such liberty could only be enjoyed 'within the Allowance of those Laws under which he is; and therein not to be subjected to the arbitrary Will of another, but freely follow his own'.[68] The Glorious Revolution did substantially remove one source of arbitrary will, but just as an enhanced Parliament was occasionally capricious so the day-to-day operation of the rule of law still afforded opportunities for the local dictator. Not until the rapid growth of population, towns, industry, and trade in the age of the American and French revolutions was the application of Lockean reason to that rule vigorously championed. Only then was it widely felt to be impossible to muddle through with the muddle that till then had served surprisingly well as the rule of law.

[68] J. Locke, *Two Treatises of Government*, ed. P. Laslett (Cambridge, 1991), p. 306.

Epilogue

When George I died the Pretender rode fast across Europe to Lorraine, hoping beyond hope that his moment had arrived at long last. He could have saved his horses and his pride so completely was he disregarded in England. Nothing sums up better the nature of political changes between 1685 and 1727 than that wasted journey. At the first date James II was acclaimed as King and generously provided for by a compliant Parliament, but at the second his only son was ignored by the vast majority in England. In turn, Handel's powerful 'Zadok the priest' anthem, performed at every coronation from George II to the present, symbolizes the relative security of the Hanoverian regime. It says much that in 1727 England was happy enough with a German King and his German composer.

The irrelevance of the Pretender in 1727 was not the only change that had taken place in this period, for if William's reign had only been possible because of a mighty invasion, that of George II was based very largely on consent. Dramatic alterations in both domestic and international circumstances brought this about. Questions over the Protestant succession and French aggrandizement, which were so crucial in the Glorious Revolution, had been rendered largely irrelevant by the time George I died. This did not happen spontaneously, fortuitously, or with any degree of certainty. Different options were bitterly debated and if there were winners there were also losers. So England had made a choice of sorts in 1689, which was reconfirmed in 1701, and willingly agreed to by most in 1714. She had, moreover, played a very full part in the two great wars against France that had achieved all of their defensive and many of their offensive aims. Not least, because of these wars Britain had entered the mainstream of European affairs and attained great power status. There is no question that what made these developments possible was the extensive and intensive use of parliamentary government to gain consent, money, and men. If there were fractious battles between monarch, ministers, and Parliament until the early 1720s none seriously doubted the supremacy of statutory authority in defining the public good. Yet at the moment when that authority became a commonplace so Parliament's capacity for independence appears to have weakened. Surely the rise of oligarchical politics—of infrequent elections and mutated debate—rendered Parliament a mere tool, prey to the whims of Whig grandees? Such a paradox is largely illusory. Though Walpole was adept at controlling both Commons and Lords they too controlled him, to the degree that the hothead who had waged a violent ideological duel at Sacheverell's trial had become not just weary and wary of European commitments but also, as the skreenmaster, a scourge of Whig traditionalists.

Thus not only circumstances but also political ideologies changed between the accession of William and Mary and the death of the first Hanoverian. In the process the meaning of Whig and Tory, which had been so clear in the 1690s, had become muddled and confused. If it is true that the supremacy of the Whigs was extraordinarily secure in the 1720s it must be remembered that the meaning of 'Whig' had changed in a generation and that politics was in a sense multi- rather than bi-polar. This was not immediately apparent, for whereas the Glorious Revolution had been akin to a torrent, sweeping away much of the old, subsequent political developments were less obvious and brutal. Yet if they were not so singular or spectacular they were not without force or effect. In time the political developments that began in earnest in the 1720s, particularly with regard to the multi-faceted nature of oppositional politics, would underpin the Wilkite challenge of the 1760s, contribute to the support for American resistance in the 1770s, and encourage the radicalism of the 1790s. In that sense the Glorious Revolution and its aftermath brought one political era to an end and the reign of George I initiated another.

Such a chronology applies less well to the growth of the State, the decisive period of which was the 1690s under the stimuli of the Glorious Revolution, war, the financial revolution, and the expansion of legislative action. The first ultimately caused England to exert heightened control over Ireland and Union with Scotland—the State was simply enlarged. It also involved Britain deeply in European affairs and, despite considerable fears about standing armies, required a hugely expanded military. Central to the financial revolution was the creation of institutions to pay for this, such as the Bank of England and a permanent national debt. Such developments were certainly not merely bureaucratic, for they very directly changed the lives of people through an expanded and intrusive administration and heightened taxation. Thus, a nation which in 1688 had turned its back on one form of 'slavery' had by the time of the Treaty of Ryswick in 1697 reluctantly built a more powerful and present State than ever.

Such reluctance was overcome for two main reasons. First, one of the most remarkable features of the State after 1688 was the way in which the propertied, individually or collectively, often utilized it when pursuing their own specific interests. Statutory authority, of course, provided not only power but also legitimacy and was, therefore, crucial in tying the political nation together and formalizing the most profound social inequalities. Second, an enhanced State was seen as a price worth paying to secure the Protestant succession. Central to the political instability of the 1680s had been anxieties about the religion of James both as heir and then as King. The complexity of those anxieties is nicely illustrated by the willingness of Archbishop Sancroft to be tried in 1688 for standing against James's religious policy yet less than a year later being quite unable to embrace the new regime. Moreover, Toleration and the renewed challenge of freethinkers initially increased such complexity. Yet by the 1720s heterodoxy posed far fewer immediate problems and the harmony of Church and State was confirmed by Bishop Gibson's role as 'Walpole's Pope'. Such a relationship, of the primacy of the secular over the spiritual arm of government, speaks volumes however. And if the Church of England was still a vital force politically and socially, its significance had subtly altered. It was slightly less widely respected and its place in people's lives less dominant than it had been. The SPCK, the SPG, and Queen Anne's Bounty were, after all, reactive rather than proactive initiatives attempting to stem the tide of religious indifference among the English.

Not the least of the challenges that the Church faced was of scepticism expressed through a liberated press. If such challenges were often thinly spread, indirect, or even denied they could be real enough and intellectually religious orthodoxy was by the 1720s less dominant than it had been a generation earlier. But arguably more characteristic of intellectual developments in this period were the efforts of those such as King and Davenant in political arithmetic, Newton in optics, Halley and Flamsteed in astronomy, Locke in philosophy, Ray in biology, Burlington in architecture, Kent in gardening, and Defoe, Swift, Pope, Congreve, Addison, and Steele in literature. It is the enormous enriching of the life of the mind from all directions in this period which stands out, of new discoveries, information, categories, and values.

It was not, of course, just that such ideas were being produced in greater abundance than ever, but that they found people eager to encounter and embrace them. Undeniably the consumption of culture grew strongly in these years, especially in towns. If London was the focal point for this, and one whose significance was only heightened by the expansion of parliamentary government, the growth of provincial towns and cities such as York, Exeter, and Bury St Edmunds was a particularly powerful social development. Rural isolationism was thereby eroded and new habits, wants, and expectations formed nationally, be they to do with goods, leisure, self-identity, or social responsibility. Such urbanization was only possible, however, because the wider economy was growing, especially due to greater regional specialization and international expansion. The infrastructural changes necessary to allow this visibly tied the nation together more closely than before, even if roads might still be wretched and the posts irregular.

It is easy to see, therefore, how different was England in 1727 than in 1689. It was a period of remarkable developments. It is less immediately obvious how it was the same. Yet continuity was there in abundance. Certainly inequality in all its forms, social ideologies, demographic dynamics, village life, the incidence and treatment of poverty, and patterns of work were largely unchanged. Popular beliefs, from ideas of a customary order to folklore, also remained largely intact, even if the cultural gap between rich and poor widened. Good health was still a very precious commodity and sickness ever-threatening. The effects of the weather and the rhythms of the seasons were still too strong to be controlled. Local weights and measures were everywhere, the Julian calendar universally used. Wind, water, and muscle continued to power everyday endeavours.

When all is said and done, like any period this one cannot be neatly summarized by weighing continuity and change in the balance or by counting the winners and losers. Rather, the period is best understood as one full of anxiety and prospects, each feeding off the other. People, often provoked by changes they disliked, usually sought stability and order, clamouring for an earthly paradise. But their anxieties appear to have diminished in the 1710s and 1720s, or at least have become less public and more private, and prospects were certainly increasing then. In 1727, however, it was very unclear where such prospects might lead. Then as now foresight was frail and the long view was usually backwards and not forwards. Thus in 1727 George II provoked little respect or ardour, the Whig monopoly excluded many, the horrors of the gin age were dawning, the gallows still groaned, and Hogarth was about to launch his print broadsides against the manners and morals of the times. England may have left many of its troubles behind by 1727, but where it might go now was very unclear.

Chronology

People and Projects	Intellectual and Cultural Life	Date
John Bunyan, religious enthusiast, dies Alexander Pope, author, born		1688
Aphra Behn, author, dies Mary Wortley Montagu, writer, born Samuel Richardson, author and printer, born	Thomas Shadwell succeeds John Dryden as Poet Laureate and Historiographer Royal Godfrey Kneller, Principal Painter to Crown Kensington Palace remodelled by Christopher Wren, to 1696 John Locke, *Two Treatises on Government* (dated 1690) John Dryden, *Don Sebastian* Virtuoso of St Luke, artists club	1689
	John Dunton, *Athenian Gazette/ Mercury*, to 1697 John Locke, *An Essay Concerning Human Understanding* William Petty (died 1687), *Political Arithmetic* John Dryden, *Amphitryon* William Temple, *Essay upon Ancient and Modern Learning*	1690
First Society for the Reformation of Manners Richard Baxter, divine, dies Robert Boyle, scientist, dies George Fox, Quaker, dies Boyle lectures founded	John Ray, *The Wisdom of God Manifested in the Works of the Creation* Dudley North, *Discourses upon Trade* Henry Purcell, *King Arthur*	1691
Witch trials at Salem, Massachusetts, to 1693 Thomas Shadwell, author, dies John Houghton, *Collection for the Improvement of Husbandry and Trade*, to 1703	Nathan Tate, Poet Laureate Thomas Rymer, Historiographer Royal Roger L'Estrange, *Fables of Aesop and other Mythologists* Henry Purcell, *The Fairy Queen* Thomas Shadwell, *The Volunteers*	1692

Date	Politics and Religion	State and War
1693	William vetoes Triennial Parliaments Bill	Destruction of Anglo-Dutch Smyrna convoy
		Battle of Neerwinder/Landen, allied defeat
		French capture Charleroi
		Land tax made permanent
		Long-term national debt begun
		Financial rewards for prosecution of certain felons initiated
1694	William vetoes Place Bill	Bank of England established
	Tenison Archbishop of Canterbury	Construction of Greenwich Hospital begins
	Triennial Act	
	Death of Mary II	
	Whig Junto dominant in ministry	
1695	Speaker of House of Commons, Sir John Trevor, dismissed for corruption	Allied forces successfully besiege Namur
	General election	Death of Duke of Luxembourg, leading French general
	Royal Bounty for relief of Huguenot refugees	
	John Locke, *The Reasonableness of Christianity*	
1696	Jacobite Assassination Plot	Recoinage
	Trial of Treasons Act	Failed attempt to establish the Land bank
	John Toland, *Christianity not Mysterious*	Board of Trade established
		Inspector General of Customs established
		Register of Shipping established
		Treaty of Turin between Savoy and France
1697	Standing army controversy begins	Treaties of Ryswick end Nine Years War
	Francis Atterbury, *Letter to a Convocation Man*	
	Philadelphian Society	
1698	General election	First Partition Treaty concluded by Louis XIV and William III
	Society for the Promotion of Christian Knowledge (SPCK) founded	William Molyneux, *Case of Ireland's being Bound by Acts of Parliament in England*
		Civil List Act
1699	Parliament challenges William's disposal of forfeited Irish estates	Shoplifting made a capital offence
		Irish Woollen Act

People and Projects	Intellectual and Cultural Life	Date
	John Locke, *Some Thoughts Concerning Education*	1693
	John Dennis, *The Impartial Critic*	
	William Congreve, *The Double Dealer*	
Warwick badly damaged by fire	William Wotton, *Reflections upon Ancient and Modern Learning*	1694
	Robert Molesworth, *An Account of Denmark*	
	John Dryden's last play *Love Triumphant*	
	Thomas D'Urfey, *The Comical History of Don Quixote*	
First of 'Seven ill years' in Scotland	William Congreve, *Love for Love*	1695
Press Licensing Act lapses	Gregory King's 'social table'	
Marquis of Halifax, politician and pamphleteer, dies		
Henry Purcell, composer, dies		
Bristol Corporation of the Poor established	William Whiston, *A New Theory of the Earth*	1696
Kit Cat club founded	James Tyrrell, *The General History of England*, to 1704	
Recipients of poor relief badged	John Dryden's translation of Virgil's *Georgics*	1697
Stockjobbers Act		
John Castaign's *Course of the Exchange* begins	William Dampier, *A New Voyage Round the World*	
John Aubrey, polymath, dies	Daniel Defoe, *An Essay upon Projects*	
Thomas Firmin, philanthropist, dies	John Vanbrugh, *The Relapse* and *The Provok'd Wife*	
William Hogarth, artist, born		
Tsar Peter the Great visits England	Edward Ward, *The London Spy*, to 1700	1698
Royal Africa Company monopoly ended	Aphra Behn, *The Histories and Novels*	
New East India Company chartered	Jeremy Collier, *Short View of the Immorality and Profaneness of the English Stage*	
Thomas Savery develops steam engine	Algernon Sidney (died 1683), *Discourses Concerning Government*	
Sir William Temple, statesman and author, dies	Castle Howard, designed by John Vanbrugh, begun	1699

Date	Politics and Religion	State and War
1700	Duke of Gloucester dies	Second Partition Treaty
		Death of Charles II of Spain
		Great Northern War, to 1721
1701	General election	French troops move into Spanish Netherlands
	James II dies	Marlborough restored to royal favour
	Convocation meets	Treaty of 'Grand Alliance' between England,
	Portland, Somers, Orford, and Halifax	Holland, and Austria
	unsuccessfully impeached	
	Kentish petition	
	Act of Settlement	
	Commons blocks Bill to reunite	
	American colonies under the Crown	
	General election	
	Society for the Propagation of the	
	Gospel (SPG) founded	
1702	Abjuration Act	War of the Spanish Succession, to 1713
	Death of William III, accession of Anne	Marlborough made Captain General
	Godolphin made Lord Treasurer	Spanish treasure fleet destroyed at Vigo Bay
	General election	
	Daniel Defoe, *Shortest Way with*	
	Dissenters	
1703	First Occasional Conformity Bill fails	Anglo-Portuguese 'Metheun' Treaty
	English and Scottish Union	
	Commissioners fail	
	Anne vetoes Scottish Act of Security	
	Second Occasional Conformity Bill fails	
1704	Queen Anne's Bounty established	Scottish Act of Security
	Third Occasional Conformity Bill fails	Battle of Blenheim, allied victory
		Anglo-Dutch forces take Gibraltar
		Naval Battle of Málaga, inconclusive
1705	Climax of 'Aylesbury men' case	Alien Act
	General election	Barcelona taken by allied forces
	House of Lords declare Church not in	
	danger	
1706	Regency Act	Battle of Ramillies, allied victory
	Treaty of Union between England and	Antwerp, Dunkirk, Dendermonde, and Ath fall
	Scotland	to allies
		Battle of Turin, allied victory

People and Projects	Intellectual and Cultural Life	Date
Collapse of Scotland's Darien scheme John Dryden, author, dies James Thomson, author, born First wet dock opened at Rotherhithe	John Dryden, *Fables Ancient and Modern* James Harrinton (died 1677), *Works* William Congreve, *The Way of the World*	1700
Captain Kidd, pirate, executed Yale College, Connecticut, founded	Daniel Defoe, *The True-Born Englishman* Nicholas Rowe, *Tamerlane* *Norwich Post*, first provincial newspaper	1701
	Earl of Clarendon (died 1674), *History of the Great Rebellion*, to 1704 *Daily Courant*, to 1735, first daily newspaper Edmond Halley, *Chart of the Whole World Shewing Variations of the Compass*	1702
The Great Storm Robert Hooke, scientist, dies Samuel Pepys, diarist and navy administrator, dies John Wesley, Methodist, born		1703
John Locke, political theorist, dies	Isaac Newton, *Opticks* Thomas Rymer and others, *Foedera*, to 1735 Jonathan Swift, *Tale of a Tub, Battle of the Books* *Ladies' Diary*, to 1840 Daniel Defoe's *Review*, to 1713	1704
John Ray, naturalist, dies Stephen Duck, poet, born	Blenheim Palace begun, designed by John Vanbrugh and Nicholas Hawksmoor John Vanbrugh opens Haymarket opera house Edmond Halley, *Astronomiae Cometicae Synopsis*	1705
Bankruptcy Act John Evelyn, polymath and diarist, dies Benjamin Franklin, politician, born	White Kennett and others, *Complete History of England* *London Gazette* under Richard Steele's editorship, to 1709 John Dennis, *Operas after the Italian Manner* George Farquhar, *The Recruiting Officer*	1706

Date	Politics and Religion	State and War
1707	Isaac Watts, *Hymns*	Battle of Almanza, allied defeat Failure of Touloun expedition Somers' 'No peace without Spain' motion adopted Union of England and Scotland
1708	Harley and followers resign from government General election Anne's husband, Prince George, dies	Failed Franco-Jacobite landing in Scotland Scottish Privy Council abolished Battle of Oudenard, allied victory Minorca seized by British forces Lille falls to allies
1709	Naturalization Act Sacheverell preaches against 'false brethren' in St Paul's Cathedral	Failure of peace negotiations Battle of Malplaquet, allied victory but at great cost Act establishes diplomatic immunity Anglo-Dutch Barrier Treaty
1710	Marlborough threatens resignation over Abigail Masham's influence Split between Queen and Duchess of Marlborough Trial of Sacheverell Godolphin dismissed, Tory administration formed under Harley's lead General election	Battle of Brihuega, Spain, allied defeat Nova Scotia captured by British
1711	Duchess of Marlborough dismissed from offices by Anne Act for Fifty New Churches in London Property Qualification Act Attempt to assassinate Harley Act against Occasional Conformity Harley made Earl of Oxford and Lord Treasurer	Allies take the '*Ne Plus Ultra*' lines Jonathan Swift, *Conduct of the Allies* France and Britain sign peace preliminaries Marlborough dismissed
1712	12 new peers created to secure government majority in House of Lords (Dec. 1711–Jan. 1712) Walpole sent to Tower Repeal of Naturalization Act Last trial of a witch in England	Ormonde now Commander-in-Chief Peace negotiations at Utrecht Death of two main heirs to French throne Ormonde receives 'restraining orders'

People and Projects	Intellectual and Cultural Life	Date
George Farquhar, dramatist, dies	Edward Lhwyd, *Archaeologia Britannica*	1707
Henry Fielding, writer and Justice of the Peace, born	Laurence Echard, *History of England*, to 1718	
	Johnannes Kip and Leonard Knyff, *Britannia Illustrata*	
	George Farquhar, *Beaux's Stratagem*	
	Society of Antiquaries founded	
John Blow, composer, dies	John Oldmixon, *British Empire in America*, to 1741	1708
1708–9 very cold winter	George Berkeley, *New Theory of Vision*	1709
Old and New East India Companies unite	Daniel Defoe, *History of the Union of Great Britain*	
'Poor Palatines' arrive		
Abraham Darby first smelts iron with coke	Richard Steele, *Tatler*, to 1711	
Samuel Johnson, writer, born		
Sun Fire Office established	Copyright Act	1710
Lord Chief Justice John Holt dies	*The Examiner*, to 1711	
	George Berkeley, *Principles of Human Knowledge*	
South Sea Company formed	*The Spectator*, to 1714	1711
David Hume, philosopher and historian, born	Alexander Pope, *Essay on Criticism*	
	Earl of Shaftesbury, *Characteristics*	
	Great Queen Street Academy for artists founded	
	Georg Handel, *Rinaldo*	
Georg Friedrich Handel settles in England	Stamp Act taxes print	1712
Mohock scare in London	Alexander Pope, *Rape of the Lock*	
Thomas Newcomen improves steam engine	John Arbuthnot, *History of John Bull*	
Sidney, Earl of Godolphin, politician, dies		
Gregory King, political arithmetician, dies		
Thomas Danby, Duke of Leeds, politician, dies		
Richard Cromwell, Lord Protector 1658–9, dies		

Date	Politics and Religion	State and War
1713	Crisis over the Union Anglo–French Commerce Bill fails General election Anne seriously ill	Anglo–Dutch Barrier Treaty Treaty of Utrecht ends war Theft by servants made capital offence
1714	Richard Steele's *The Crisis* leads to his expulsion from House of Commons Schism Act Oxford dismissed Death of Anne, accession of George I Whig ministry formed First Indemnity Act	Death of Sophia, Electress of Hanover
1715	General election Impeachment of former ministers, Bolingbroke and Ormonde flee to France, Oxford in Tower Riot Act Suspension of habeas corpus Wake Archbishop of Canterbury	Louis XIV dies Jacobite rising Old Pretender briefly in Scotland Barrier Treaty
1716	Execution of two Jacobite lords Septennial Act Failure of Select Vestries Bill Political supremacy of Stanhope and Sunderland Whig schism follows Townshend's dismissal as Secretary of State	Anglo–French alliance Treaty of Westminster with Emperor
1717	Last significant meeting of Convocation in century Walpole and followers resign office Bangorian controversy Rift between King and Prince of Wales Collapse of Oxford's impeachment	Triple alliance of Britain, France, and Dutch Republic Swedish Jacobite plot uncovered Old Pretender moves to Rome 'Sinking Fund' established
1718		War of the Quadruple Alliance (Britain, France, Dutch Republic, and the Empire) against Spain Transportation Act

People and Projects	Intellectual and Cultural Life	Date
Swift Dean of St Patrick's Cathedral, Dublin	*The Guardian*, to 1714	1713
Earl of Shaftesbury, philosopher, dies	Joseph Addison, *Cato*	
Henry Compton, Bishop of London, dies	Scriblerus club formed	
Laurence Sterne, writer, born	John Gay, *Rural Sports*	
	Alexander Pope, *Windsor Forest*	
	Sir Matthew Hale (died 1676), *History of the Common Law*	
	William Derham, *Physico-Theology*	
	Richard Bentley, *Remarks upon a Discourse of Freethinking*	
	Three Choirs Festival established	
Riots accompany and follow coronation	St Mary-le-Strand begun, James Gibbs architect	1714
Usury law reduces legal interest rates to 5 per cent	Thomas Maddox, Historiographer Royal	
Parliament establishes reward for measuring longitude accurately		
John Radcliffe, physician and benefactor, dies		
George London, formal gardener, dies		
Charles Davenant, economist and public servant, dies		
Cattle disease rife in southern England	Solar eclipse accurately predicted by Edmond Halley	1715
Gilbert Burnet, Bishop of Salisbury, dies	Nicholas Rowe, Poet Laureate	
Marquis of Wharton, politician, dies	Colen Campbell, *Vitruvius Britannicus*, to 1725	
	Andrea Palladio (died 1580), *Four Books of Architecture*, ed. Leoni, to 1719	
	Joseph Addison, *The Freeholder*, to 1716	
	Alexander Pope translation of Homer's *Iliad*, to 1720	
William Wycherley, playwright, dies	Nichoals Hawksmoor's designs for All Souls College, Oxford begun	1716
John, Lord Somers, lawyer and politician, dies	Lady Mary Wortley Montagu, *Town Eclogues*	
Thomas Gray, poet, born		
Grand Lodge of Freemasons in London	Georg Handel's first Chandos anthem	1717
David Garrick, actor, born	Georg Handel, *Water Music*	
Horace Walpole, connoisseur, born		
William Penn, Quaker, dies	Laurence Eusden, Poet Laureate	1718
Thomas Lombe builds silk-throwing mill at Derby	Society of Antiquaries refounded	
	Abraham de Moivre, *Doctrine of Chances*	

Date	Politics and Religion	State and War
1719	Occasional Conformity and Schism Acts repealed	Attempted Spanish-Jacobite landing in Scotland
	Peerage Bill defeated	
	University Bill defeated	
	Dissenters split over Trinity	
1720	Walpole and Townshend return to office, ending Whig schism	Declaratory Act
	King and Prince of Wales reconciled	End of war with Spain
		Anglo-Swedish alliance
		Charles Edward Stuart, the 'Young Pretender', born
1721	House of Commons investigates South Sea affair	
	Sunderland resigns	
	Death of Stanhope	
	Walpole First Lord of the Treasury and Chancellor of the Exchequer	
1722	General election	Case of Wood's half-pence begins in Ireland
	Jacobite Atterbury plot	
	Habeas corpus suspended	
	Penal taxes levied on Roman Catholics	
	Regium Donum – state aid to some poor Dissenters	
1723	Atterbury banished	Black Act
	Bolingbroke pardoned	
1724		Jonathan Swift, *Drapier's Letters*

People and Projects	Intellectual and Cultural Life	Date
Joseph Addison, writer and statesman, dies	Daniel Defoe, *Robinson Crusoe*	1719
John Flamsteed, Astronomer Royal, dies	Eliza Heywood, *Love in Excess*	
	Royal Academy of Music	
	Nicholas Dorigny, engravings of Raphael Cartoons at Hampton Court	
Bubble Act and South Sea Bubble	John Trenchard and Thomas Gordon, *Cato's Letters*, to 1723	1720
Quarantine to stop spread of plague from Marseilles	Mereworth Castle, Kent, designed by Colen Campbell	
Royal Exchange Assurance established	James Thornhill, Sergeant Painter to King	
London Assurance established		
Hell Fire clubs reported		
Anne Finch, Countess of Winchelsea, author, dies		
Gilbert White, naturalist, born		
Samuel Foote, dramatist, born		
Statutory ban on importation of Indian calicoes	Edmond Halley, Astronomer Royal	1721
First use of smallpox inoculation in England		
Grinling Gibbons, wood carver, dies		
Matthew Prior, poet and diplomat, dies		
Tobias Smollett, author, born		
Earl of Sunderland, politician, dies	St Martin-in-the-Fields begun, designed by James Gibbs	1722
Duke of Marlborough, soldier, dies	Houghton Hall begun, designed by Colen Campbell and James Gibbs	
John Toland, political theorist, dies	Daniel Defoe, *Moll Flanders*	
	Daniel Defoe, *Journal of the Plague Year*	
Workhouse Test Act	Bernard Mandeville, *Fable of the Bees*, 2nd edition	1723
Sir Christopher Wren, architect, dies		
Sir Godfrey Kneller, painter, dies		
Susanna Centlivre, playwright, dies		
Thomas D'Urfey, dramatist, poet, and song writer, dies		
Joshua Reynolds, painter, born		
Adam Smith, social scientist, born		
William Blackstone, jurist, born		
Robert Harley, Earl of Oxford, politician and collector, dies	Gilbert Burnet (died 1715), *History of my Own Time*, to 1734	1724
Thomas Guy, bookseller and philanthropist, dies	Daniel Defoe, *Roxana*	
Delrivière Manley, author, dies	Daniel Defoe, *Tour Through Great Britain*, to 1726	
Jack Sheppard, criminal and escapologist, executed	Georg Handel, *Giulio Cesare*	
	George I establishes regius professors of History and Languages at Cambridge and Oxford	

Date	Politics and Religion	State and War
1725	Lord Chancellor Macclesfield found guilty of corruption, resigns City Election Act Order of the Bath revived	Treaty of Hanover between Britain, France, and Prussia Peter the Great dies Wood's patent annulled First of Wade's roads in Highlands
1726		
1727	Indemnity Acts now usually annual Death of George I, accession of George II	Hostilities between Britain and Spain

People and Projects	Intellectual and Cultural Life	Date
Jonathan Wild, corrupt thief-taker, executed	Chiswick House, designed by Earl of Burlington	1725
Robert Bakewell, agriculturalist, born	Alexander Pope translation of Homer's *Odyssey*, to 1726	
	Francis Hutcheson, *Original of our Ideas of Beauty and Virtue*	
	John Flamsteed (died 1719), *Historia Coelestis Britannica*	
Middlesex JPs report on gin drinking	Jonathan Swift, *Gulliver's Travels*	1726
Voltaire in England, to 1729	Viscount Bolingbroke and others, *The Craftsman*, to 1747	
'Rabbit woman' case (Mary Toft)	James Thomson, *Winter*	
Sir John Vanbrugh, architect and playwright, dies	Academy of Vocal Music formed, later renamed Academy of Ancient Musick	
Charles Burney, musician and author, born		
Sir Isaac Newton, scientist, dies	*Designs of Inigo Jones*, ed. William Kent	1727
Edward Lloyd, marine insurer, dies	John Gay, *Fables*, vol. 1	
John Wilkes, 'radical' politician, born	James Thomson, *Summer*	
Thomas Gainsborough, artist, born		

Bibliography

The past may remain the same, but history always changes—both because research accumulates and because the interests and perspectives of historians constantly evolve. Certainly a very large and rapidly growing body of literature on England's history in this period is available, most obviously of secondary works but also of new editions of primary sources. Indeed, so substantial is this material that it is easy to feel overwhelmed by it. Consequently, this bibliography is just a personal and selective view of what is most useful and interesting, frequently inclining to more recently published titles. Much good work is therefore not listed below and, for reasons of space, titles are usually cited only once even if they might be placed under other headings. It is also worth remembering that the period covered by this book rarely corresponds precisely to that addressed by other historians, and that especially in the fields of social and economic history the long view is the norm. Unless otherwise stated place of publication is London.

Great changes are afoot in the world of words. Not least microfilms and new electronic resources are proliferating rapidly. Second, much of the best new research is to be found not in books but in articles in learned journals and unpublished doctoral theses. Third, local libraries are finding it increasingly difficult to maintain substantial history sections, even of more popular-style works. Consequently, many of the works listed below will take some effort to find, though it is worth remembering that in Britain at least most titles should be available through the inter-library loan system.

BIBLIOGRAPHIC AND REFERENCE WORKS

Unquestionably, the best general bibliography of secondary literature is *The Royal Historical Society Bibliography on CD-ROM: The History of Britain, Ireland, and of the British Overseas* (Oxford, 1998)—a rich resource that allows specifically tailored searches to be undertaken on 250,000 titles published before 1993. Although new editions to keep it reasonably current are envisioned, more recent publications can be followed up immediately in the same Society's *Annual Bibliography of British and Irish History* and via annual surveys in the *Economic History Review*, *English Historical Review*, and *History*. Among selective bibliographies of secondary literature G. Davies and M. F. Keeler (eds.), *Bibliography of British History: Stuart Period, 1603–1714* (Oxford, 1970) and S. Pargellis and D. J. Medley (eds.), *Bibliography of British History: The Eighteenth Century, 1714–1789* (Oxford, 1951) are both extensive but dated. More up-to-date and compact are J. S. Morrill, *Seventeenth-Century Britain, 1603–1714* (Folkestone, 1980) and R. C. Richardson and W. H. Chaloner (eds.), *British Economic and Social History: A Bibliographical Guide* (3rd edn., Manchester, 1996). Lists of theses completed and in preparation, along with much other useful information, can be found on the website of the Institute of Historical Research at http://www.ihr.sas.ac.uk.

Contemporary publications are best searched for by the *English Short Title Catalogue*, available on CD or online, for details of which see http://www.bl.uk/services/bsds/ nbs/blaise. At heart it is a union catalogue of extant works published in the English language before 1801. Because it may be searched by author, title significant word, and place and date of publication, its appearance is transforming the study of early modern England. Good printed bibliographies of contemporary works include: G. Watson (ed.), *The New Cambridge Bibliography of English Literature*, vol. 2 (Cambridge, 1971) and L. W. Hanson, *Contemporary Printed Sources for British and Irish Economic History, 1700–1750* (Cambridge, 1963). The National Register of Archives provides listings of many manuscript sources and can now be easily contacted via the internet at http://www.hmc.gov.uk.

Many reference works might be cited. General in scope is C. Cook and J. Stevenson (eds.), *British Historical Facts, 1688–1760* (1988). Etymology can, of course, be traced in the *Oxford English Dictionary*, 20 vols. (2nd edn., Oxford, 1989). The *Dictionary of National Biography*, ed. L. Stephen and S. Lee, 63 vols. (1885–1901) is a wonderfully rich source for pursuing famous and not so famous lives. A new edition, due for publication in about 2005, is currently in preparation. Both the *OED* and the *DNB* are currently available in CD versions. Much useful information about the history of politics, religion, and the elite is to be found in E. B. Fryde, D. E. Greenway, S. Porter, and I. Roy, *Handbook of British Chronology* (3rd edn., 1986). A good introduction to the economic statistics available for the period is B. R. Mitchell, *British Historical Statistics* (Cambridge, 1988).

PRINTED SOURCES

A very wide range of manuscript sources are now available in print, offering a direct and stimulating way of seeing the past, though only those published since 1800 are listed here. A. Browning (ed.), *English Historical Documents*, vol. 8. *1660–1714* (1966) and D. B. Horn and M. Ransome (eds.), *English Historical Documents*, vol. 10. *1714–1783* (1969) are wide-ranging selections, if traditionally conceived. J. P. Kenyon (ed.), *The Stuart Constitution, 1603–1688* (2nd edn., Cambridge, 1986) and E. N. Williams (ed.), *The Eighteenth-Century Constitution, 1688–1815* (Cambridge, 1960) are excellent within their specific field, as are G. S. Holmes and W. A. Speck (eds.), *The Divided Society: Parties and Politics in England, 1694–1716* (1967), B. P. Lenman and J. S. Gibson (eds.), *The Jacobite Threat—England, Ireland, Scotland, France: A Source Book* (Edinburgh, 1990), F. Madden with D. Fieldhouse (eds.), *Select Documents on the Constitutional History of the British Empire and Commonwealth*, vol. 2. *The Classical Period of the First British Empire, 1689–1783. The Foundations of a Colonial System of Government* (Westport, New York, and London, 1985), and J. Thirsk and J. P. Cooper (eds.), *Seventeenth-Century Economic Documents* (Oxford, 1972) which actually contains documents down to 1714. Parliamentary debates were not routinely or accurately reported at the time. For a selection of what is available, with some relevant pamphlets, see W. Cobbett (ed.), *The Parliamentary History of England*, 36 vols. (1806–20)—vols. 5–8 cover this period.

The Historical Manuscripts Commission has reprinted the papers of many leading political families from the period, often in abbreviated form, notably *Report on the Manuscripts of the Late Allan George Finch, Esq.*, vols. 2 and 3 (1922 and 1957), *The Manuscripts of his Grace the Duke of Portland*, vols. 3–5 (1894–99), *Calendar of the Manuscripts of the Marquis of Bath*, 3 vols. (1904–8), *The Manuscripts of Lord Kenyon* (1894), *Report on the Manuscripts of the Earl of Mar and Kellie* (1904), *The Manuscripts of the Marquess of Townshend* (1887), and *Calendar of the Stuart Papers Belonging to His Majesty the King*, vol. 1 (1902). Among other political correspondence also available is *Letters Illustrative of the Reign of William III. From 1696 to 1708. Addressed to the Duke of Shrewsbury by James Vernon, Esq. Secretary of State*, ed. G. P. R. James, 3 vols. (1841), *Letters of William III and Louis XIV, and of their Ministers*, ed. P. Grimblot, 2 vols. (1848), *The Marlborough–Godolphin Correspondence*, ed. H. L. Snyder, 3 vols. (Oxford, 1975)—a magnificent edition, *Private Correspondence of Sarah, Duchess of Marlborough*, 2 vols. (1838), *The Letters and Diplomatic Instructions of Queen Anne*, ed. B. C. Brown (1968), *The Letters of Daniel Defoe*, ed. G. H. Healey (Oxford, 1955), *The Letters of Joseph Addison*, ed. W. Graham (Oxford, 1941), *The Wentworth Papers, 1705–1739. Selected from the Private and Family Correspondence of Thomas Wentworth, Lord Raby, Created in 1711 Earl of Strafford*, ed. J. J. Cartwright (1883), G. Davies and M. Tinling, 'Letters from James Brydges, Created Duke of Chandos, to Henry St. John, Created Viscount Bolingbroke', *Huntington Library Bulletin*, 9 (1936), pp. 119–66, and *Letter-Books of John Hervey, First Earl of Bristol*, [ed. S. H. A. Hervey], 3 vols. (1894).

Political memoirs and diaries are usually more reflective, making them at once more readable and self-justificatory. Particularly useful are *Memoirs of Mary Queen of England (1689–1693)*, ed. R. Doebner (1886), *Memoirs of Thomas, Earl of Ailesbury, Written by Himself*, 2 vols. (1890), *The Parliamentary Diary of Narcissus Luttrell, 1691–1693*, ed. H. Horwitz (Oxford, 1972), G. Burnet, *History of his Own Time*, 6 vols. (Oxford, 1823), *The London Diaries of William Nicolson, Bishop of Carlisle, 1702–1718*, ed. C. Jones and G. Holmes (Oxford, 1985), *The Diary of Sir David Hamilton, 1709–1714*, ed. P. Roberts (Oxford, 1975), *Memoirs of Sarah Duchess of Marlborough, Together with her 'Characters of her Contemporaries' and her 'Opinions'*, ed. W. H. King (1930), and *Diary of Mary Countess Cowper, Lady of the Bedchamber to the Princess of Wales, 1714–1720*, ed. C. Spencer Cowper (1865).

Record societies have published many documents arising from local government that demonstrate the particular nature of authority and inequality within society. For a cross-section, see *Norfolk Lieutenancy Journal, 1676–1701*, ed. B. Cozens-Hardy, Norfolk Record Society, 30 (1961), 'A Brief Memoir of Mr Justice Rokeby, Comprising his Religious Journal and Correspondence', *Publications of the Surtees Society*, 37 (1860), *Charges to the Grand Jury, 1689–1803*, ed. G. Lamoine, Camden Society, 4th series, 43 (1992), *Hertford County Records*. I and II *Notes and Extracts from the Session Rolls*, ed. W. Le Hardy (Hertford, 1905), the *Shropshire County Records: Orders of the Shropshire Quarter Sessions*, have been edited for 1638–1708 by R. Lloyd Kenyon and for 1709–26 by O. Wakeman, both volumes lacking a publication date, and *Liverpool Vestry Books, 1681–1834*, ed. S. H. Peet, 2 vols. (Liverpool, 1912).

Material relating to public figures in the arts and sciences is also widely available. For the former, see W. Congreve, *Letters and Documents*, ed. J. C. Hodges (1964), *The Letters of John Dryden*, ed. C. E. Ward (Durham, North Carolina, 1942), *The Complete Works of Sir John Vanbrugh*, vol. 4. *The Letters*, ed. G. Webb (1928), *The Correspondence of Richard Steele*, ed. R. Blanchard (Oxford, 1941), *The Letters of John Gay*, ed. C. F. Burgess (Oxford, 1966), *The Correspondence of Jonathan Swift*, ed. H. Williams, 5 vols. (Oxford, 1963–5), *The Correspondence of Alexander Pope*, ed. G. Sherburn, 5 vols. (Oxford, 1956), and *The Complete Letters of Lady Mary Wortley Montagu*, ed. R. Halsband, 3 vols. (Oxford, 1965). For the latter both *The Correspondence of Isaac Newton*, ed. H. W. Turnbull, J. F. Scott, A. R. Hall, and L. Tilling, 7 vols. (Cambridge, 1959–77) and *The Correspondence of John Locke*, ed. E. S. de Beer, 8 vols. (Oxford, 1976–89) are monumental. Shorter, and no less illuminating, are R. T. Gunther (ed.), *Life and Letters of Edward Lhwyd*, Early Science in Oxford, 14 (Oxford, 1945), 'The Diary of Abraham de la Pryme, the Yorkshire Antiquary', *Publications of the Surtees Society*, 54 (1870), *The Life and Times of Anthony Wood, Antiquary, of Oxford, 1632–1695*, vol. 3, ed. A. Clark, Oxford Historical Society, 26 (Oxford, 1894), and 'The Family Memoirs of the Rev. William Stukeley, M. D.', *Publications of the Surtees Society*, 73 (1880).

Diaries, letters, and memoirs provide excellent ways of exploring private perceptions. Among diaries *The Diary of John Evelyn*, ed. E. S. de Beer, 6 vols. (Oxford, 1955—vols. 4–6 cover this period) is supreme. Also useful is that of the young law student in London, *The Diary of Dudley Ryder, 1715–1716*, ed. W. Matthews (1939). The provincial perspective is nicely observed in *An Astrological Diary of the Seventeenth Century: Samuel Jeake of Rye, 1652–1699*, ed. M. Hunter and A. Gregory (Oxford, 1988), R. Gough, *The History of Myddle*, ed. D. Hey (Harmondsworth, 1981), and *The Autobiography of William Stout of Lancaster, 1665–1752*, ed. J. D. Marshall (Manchester, 1967). Rather less rich though still enlightening are *The Diary of a West Country Physician, A. D. 1684–1726*, ed. E. Hobhouse (1934), *Two East Anglian Diaries, 1641–1729: Isaac Archer and William Coe*, ed. M. Storey, Suffolk Records Society, 36 (1994), *The Diary of James Clegg of Chapel en le Frith*, part 1, ed. V. S. Doe, Derbyshire Record Society, 2 (Matlock, 1978), *The Rector's Book, Clayworth Notts.*, ed. H. Gill and E. L. Guilford (Nottingham, 1910), and *The Diary of Henry Prescott, LL. B, Deputy Registrar of Chester Diocese*, ed. J. Addy and P. McNiven, Record Society of Lancashire and Cheshire, 127 and 132, 2 vols. (1987 and 1994). For private correspondence, see *Verney Letters of the Eighteenth Century from the Mss. at Claydon House*, ed. M. M. Verney, 2 vols. (1930), *The Flemings in Oxford Being Documents Selected from the Rydal Papers in Illustration of the Lives and Ways of Oxford Men*, ed. J. R. Magrath, Oxford Historical Society, 44, 62, and 79, 3 vols. (1904–24); *Letters of Humphrey Prideaux Sometime Dean of Norwich to John Ellis Sometime Under-Secretary of State, 1674–1722*, ed. E. M. Thompson, Camden Society, New Series, 15 (1875), *Private Correspondence and Miscellaneous Papers of Samuel Pepys, 1679–1703*, ed. J. R. Tanner, 2 vols. (1926), *The Portledge Papers Being Extracts from the Letters of Richard Lapthorne*,

Gent, of Hatton Garden London, to Richard Coffin Esq. of Portledge, Bideford, Devon, from December 10ᵗʰ 1687–August 7ᵗʰ 1697, ed. R. J. Kerr and I. C. Duncan (1928), and *Atlantic Merchant-Apothecary: Letters of Joseph Cruttenden, 1710–1717*, ed. I. K. Steele (Toronto, 1977).

Travel accounts shed considerable light on England in this period. Best known is D. Defoe, *A Tour Through the Whole Island of Great Britain*, first published in the 1720s and readily accessible in an edition by P. Rogers (Harmondsworth, 1978). Also excellent are *The English Travels of Sir John Percival and William Byrd II: The Percival Diary of 1701*, ed. M. R. Wenger (Columbia, Missouri, 1989) and *The Journeys of Celia Fiennes*, ed. C. Morris (1947). Foreign accounts of England are often especially perceptive: pre-eminent is Voltaire, *Letters on England*, ed. L. Tancock (Harmondsworth, 1980) though just as illuminating is *A Foreign View of England in the Reigns of George I and George II. The Letters of Monsieur César de Saussure to his Family*, trans. and ed. Madame van Muyden (1902). Also useful are *London in 1710: From the Travels of Zacharias Conrad von Uffenbach*, trans. and ed. W. H. Quarrell and M. Mare (1934) and *Ludvig Holberg's Memoirs: An Eighteenth Century Danish Contribution to International Understanding*, ed. S. E. Fraser (Leiden, 1970).

I   ENGLAND AFTER THE GLORIOUS REVOLUTION

This period is not well served with general surveys, partly because many either begin or end in 1714, partly because of the now dated tradition of treating 'general' and 'political' as synonyms.

Though originally published from 1849–65, though only taking the story down to 1702, though very long, and though polemical in character T. B. Macaulay, *The History of England from the Accession of James II*, ed. C. H. Firth, 6 vols. (1913–15) is undeniably one of the great studies of any period of England's history. W. Prest, *Albion Ascendant: English History, 1660–1815* (Oxford, 1998) is the best recent truly general survey, while G. Holmes, *The Making of a Great Power: Late Stuart and Early Georgian Britain, 1660–1722* (Harlow, 1993) and G. Holmes and D. Szechi, *The Age of Oligarchy: Pre-Industrial Britain, 1722–1783* (Harlow, 1993) have plenty of well-ordered information. W. A. Speck, *Stability and Strife: England, 1714–1760* (1977) adopts a broad approach, but its companion volume, J. R. Jones, *Country and Court: England, 1658–1714* (1978), is largely concerned with political history. G. N. Clark, *The Later Stuarts, 1660–1714* (2ⁿᵈ edn., Oxford, 1956), a volume from the original Oxford history of England series, is still valuable—crisp, sensible, wide-ranging. G. Holmes (ed.), *Britain after the Glorious Revolution, 1689–1714* (1969) is good on political and constitutional themes. J. H. Plumb, *The Growth of Political Stability in England, 1675–1725* (1967) provides an exciting general analysis that attempts to integrate various aspects of the period's history.

General works on economic and social history tend to treat the period either as at the end of a 'Pre-Industrial' era or as the start of 'industrialization'. Such teleology means that too little is taken on its own terms. E. Lipson, *An Introduction to the Economic History of England*, 3 vols. (1915–31) is innocent on that count, but it is a somewhat dated heavyweight. However, D. C. Coleman, *The Economy of England, 1450–1750* (Oxford, 1977) is a model of lithe structural analysis which can be fleshed out with C. Wilson, *England's Apprenticeship, 1603–1760* (2nd edn., 1984). M. J. Daunton, *Progress and Poverty: An Economic and Social History of Britain, 1700–1850* (Oxford, 1995) is a very good recent survey, though its centre of gravity is the industrial revolution, as is R. Floud and D. McCloskey (eds.), *The Economic History of Britain Since 1700*, vol. 1. *1700–1860* (2nd edn., Cambridge 1994), a good introduction to quantitative approaches. Social history is not yet well served, though P. Laslett, *The World We Have Lost, Further Explored* (1983) is important. J. A. Sharpe, *Early Modern England: A Social History, 1550–1760* (2nd edn., 1997) is mainly concerned with pre-1689 and D. Hay and N. Rogers, *Eighteenth-Century English Society: Shuttles and Swords* (Oxford, 1997) post-1727. R. Porter, *English Society in the Eighteenth Century* (Harmondsworth, 1982) is lively but, despite its relative youth, has not worn well.

2 THE GLORIOUS REVOLUTION AND THE REVOLUTION CONSTITUTION

The background to the Dutch invasion can be seen via J. Miller, *Popery and Politics in England, 1660–88* (Cambridge, 1973), the same author's *James II: A Study in Kingship* (revised edn., 1989), and J. R. Western, *Monarchy and Revolution: The English State in the 1680s* (1972). For its clarity, insights, and economy G. M. Trevelyan's *The English Revolution, 1688–1689* (Oxford, 1938) is still the best introduction to the remarkable events of 1688–9, though W. A. Speck, *Reluctant Revolutionaries: Englishmen and the Revolution of 1688* (Oxford, 1988) provides an effective modern view. L. G. Schwoerer, *The Declaration of Rights, 1689* (Baltimore, 1981) explores a central aspect of the Glorious Revolution. The tercentenary of the Glorious Revolution spawned many volumes of essays, addressing various themes, of which J. Israel (ed.), *The Anglo-Dutch Moment: Essays on the Glorious Revolution and its World Impact* (Cambridge, 1991) is the best. Other useful volumes include R. Beddard (ed.), *The Revolutions of 1688* (Oxford, 1991), W. A. Maguire (ed.), *Kings in Conflict: The Revolutionary War in Ireland and its Aftermath, 1689–1750* (Belfast, 1990), L. G. Schwoerer (ed.), *The Revolution of 1688–1689: Changing Perspectives* (Cambridge, 1992), and J. R. Jones (ed.), *Liberty Secured? Britain before and after 1688* (Stanford, 1992). A good collection of source material relating to the political crises of late 1688 is to be found in R. Beddard (ed.), *A Kingdom Without a King: The Journal of the Provisional Government in the Revolution of 1688* (Oxford, 1988) and the vital parliamentary debates of early 1689 are reprinted in D. L. Jones (ed.), *A Parliamentary History of the Glorious Revolution* (1988).

The question of the Protestant succession is central to this period. For a broad consideration, see H. Nenner, *The Right to be King: The Succession to the Crown of England, 1603–1714* (Basingstoke, 1995). Except in the realm of the history of ideas, for which see below, curiously little work has been done on the continued devotion by most in England to the Protestant succession. A good survey of Jacobitism is D. Szechi, *The Jacobites: Britain and Europe, 1688–1788* (Manchester, 1994) and P. K. Monod, *Jacobitism and the English People, 1688–1788* (Cambridge, 1989) is the most thorough discussion of modes of attachment to the Stuarts in exile. E. Cruickshanks (ed.), *Ideology and Conspiracy: Aspects of Jacobitism, 1689–1759* (Edinburgh, 1982) and E. Cruickshanks and J. Black (eds.), *The Jacobite Challenge* (Edinburgh, 1988) have some useful essays but some that are overstrained.

Constitutional history is currently unfashionable and little good modern work exists. Outstanding, however, is P. Langford, *Public Life and the Propertied Englishman, 1689–1798* (Oxford, 1991); a dense and rich book, it is primarily concerned with the exercise of authority amongst society as a whole rather than its religious basis or relations between the executive, legislative, and judicial branches of government. A good introduction to such relations is provided by M. A. Thomson, *A Constitutional History of England, 1642 to 1801* (1938), and if B. Kemp, *King and Commons, 1660–1832* (1957) is a little tired J. P. Greene, *Peripheries and Center: Constitutional Development in the Extended Polities of the British Empire and the United States, 1607–1788* (Athens, Georgia, 1986) provides an interesting broad view. Contemporary debates about the nature of the constitution are well explored in J. P. Kenyon, *Revolution Principles: The Politics of Party, 1689–1720* (Cambridge, 1977), J. W. Gough, *Fundamental Law in English Constitutional History* (Oxford, 1955), J. G. A. Pocock, *The Ancient Constitution and the Feudal Law: A Study of English Historical Thought in the Seventeenth Century: A Reissue with a Retrospect* (Cambridge, 1987), and H. T. Dickinson, *Liberty and Property: Political Ideology in Eighteenth-Century Britain* (1977).

Many parts of the State are underexplored. A good general account, synthesizing effectively the secondary literature, is the introduction to L. Davison, T. Hitchcock, T. Keirn, and R. B. Shoemaker (eds.), *Stilling the Grumbling Hive: The Response to Social and Economic Problems in England, 1689–1750* (Stroud, 1992). General interpretations have also been advanced by a succession of distinguished political scientists and sociologists, often employing a comparative perspective. For a recent interpretation which also introduces earlier views, see T. Ertman, *Birth of the Leviathan: Building States and Regimes in Medieval and Early Modern Europe* (Cambridge, 1997). The official history of the Commons is in progress, with the section covering 1690–1715 nearing completion. It promises to be a decisive contribution to the parliamentary and political history of the period, as was B. D. Henning (ed.), *The History of Parliament: The House of Commons, 1660–1690*, 3 vols. (1983), though R. Sedgwick (ed.), *The History of Parliament: The House of Commons, 1715–1754*, 2 vols. (1970) is often inadequate. There is no good general study of the House of Lords in this period, but see two dated works by A. S. Turberville, *The House of Lords in the Reign of William III* (Oxford, 1913) and *The House of Lords in the Eighteenth Century* (Oxford, 1927). On one major aspect of the growth of parliamentary government, see J. Hoppit, 'Patterns of Parliamentary Legislation, 1660–1800', *Historical Journal*, 39 (1996), pp. 109–31 and J. Hoppit and J. Innes, 'Introduction' to J. Hoppit (ed.), *Failed Legislation, 1660–1800: Extracted from the Commons and Lords Journals* (1997), pp. 1–40. Little general work has been done on the nature of executive or judicial government in the period—there are, for example, no good general studies of the operation of the Privy Council, royal proclamations, the central courts, or the appellate jurisdiction of the House of Lords. But see C. Roberts, *The Growth of Responsible Government in Stuart England* (Cambridge,

1966) which occasionally pushes the argument too far but is full of interest, and also J. H. Plumb, 'The Organization of the Cabinet in the reign of Queen Anne', *Transactions of the Royal Historical Society*, 5th series, 7 (1957), pp. 137–57. Rather antiquated now is E. R. Turner, *The Privy Council of England in the Seventeenth and Eighteenth Centuries, 1603–1784*, 2 vols. (Baltimore, 1927–8). On law and government, see W. Holdsworth, *A History of English Law*, 17 vols. (1922–72), especially vol. 11. Relations between Church and State are surveyed by N. Sykes, *Church and State in England in the Eighteenth Century* (Cambridge, 1934). For the crucial area of local government fundamental, if sprawling, is S. and B. Webb, *English Local Government from the Revolution to the Municipal Corporations Act*, 9 vols. (1906–29)—for a brief introduction see G. C. F. Forster, 'Government in Provincial England under the Later Stuarts', *Transactions of the Royal Historical Society*, 5th series, 33 (1983), pp. 29–48.

3   THE FACTS OF LIFE

Over the past generation work by the Cambridge Group for the History of Population and Social Structure has transformed our understanding of pre-census England. Their two fundamental, long, and technical works are E. A. Wrigley and R. S. Schofield, *The Population History of England, 1541–1871: A Reconstruction* (1981) and E. A. Wrigley, R. S. Davies, J. E. Oeppen, and R. S. Schofield, *English Population History from Family Reconstitution, 1580–1837* (Cambridge, 1997). Some pathbreaking essays are reprinted in E. A. Wrigley, *People, Cities, and Wealth: The Transformation of Traditional Society* (Oxford, 1987). Much of this work is valuably synthesized in R. A. Houston, *The Population History of Britain and Ireland, 1500–1750* (Basingstoke, 1992).

For mortality, see L. A. Clarkson, *Death, Disease and Famine in Pre-Industrial England* (Dublin, 1975) as an introduction, R. Houlbrooke, *Death, Religion, and the Family in England, 1480–1750* (Oxford, 1998) has a wealth of information, and C. J. Gittings, *Death, Burial, and the Individual in Early Modern England* (1984) explores contemporary attitudes. M. J. Dobson, *Contours of Death and Disease in Early Modern England* (Cambridge, 1997) is demographic and innovative in approach, as well as long and complex. For crisis mortality, see R. S. Schofield, 'The Impact of Scarcity and Plenty on Population Change in England, 1541–1871', *Journal of Interdisciplinary History*, 14 (1983), pp. 265–91, J. Walter and R. Schofield (eds.), *Famine, Disease, and the Social Order in Early Modern Society* (Cambridge, 1989), A. Appleby, 'Epidemics and Famine in the Little Ice Age', *Journal of Interdisciplinary History*, 10 (1980), pp. 643–63, and P. Slack, *The Impact of the Plague in Tudor and Stuart England* (1985).

For healthcare a brisk overview is provided by R. Porter, *Disease, Medicine, and Society in England, 1550–1860* (2nd edn., Basingstoke, 1993) while somewhat fuller is R. Porter and D. Porter, *In Sickness and in Health: The British Experience, 1650–1850* (1988). On important changes underway prior to 1689, see R. K. French and A. Wear (eds.), *The Medical Revolution of the Seventeenth Century* (Cambridge, 1989). On mental healthcare, R. Porter, *Mind Forg'd Manacles: A History of Madness from the Restoration to the Regency* (1987).

On fertility, see R. A. Houlbrooke, *The English Family, 1450–1750* (1984) and J. R. Gillis, *For Better, for Worse: British Marriages 1600 to the Present* (Oxford, 1985) for introductions; A. McLaren, *Reproductive Rituals: The Perception of Fertility in England from the Sixteenth to the Nineteenth Century* (1984) is full of interest, if a little rushed. L. Stone, *The Family, Sex, and Marriage in England, 1500–1800* (1977) is lively but, resting as it does on narrow foundations, has not stood up well to criticism, notably by A. Macfarlane, *Marriage and Love in England: Modes of Reproduction, 1300–1840* (Oxford, 1986). The economic context of marriage, a crucial theme, is explored in D. Levine, *Family Formation in an Age of Nascent Capitalism* (New York, 1977). For irregular marriages, see B. Outhwaite, *Clandestine Marriage in England, 1500–1850* (1995) and L. Stone, *Uncertain Unions: Marriage in England, 1660–1753* (Oxford, 1992). Illegitimacy is explored in depth in R. Adair, *Courtship, Illegitimacy and Marriage in Early Modern England* (Manchester, 1996) and the cognate issue of infanticide in P. C. Hoffer and N. E. H. Hull, *Murdering Mothers: Infanticide in England and New England, 1558–1803* (New York, 1981). For divorce and separation, see L. Stone, *Road to Divorce: England, 1530–1987* (Oxford, 1990). The history of the social conventions of sexuality is rapidly unfolding, and good syntheses are as yet few and far between, but see T. Hitchcock, *English Sexualities, 1700–1800* (Basingstoke, 1997) and R. Norton, *Mother Clap's Molly House: The Gay Subculture in England, 1700–1830* (1992). K. Thomas, 'The Double Standard', *Journal of the History of Ideas*, 20 (1959), pp. 195–216 is still unsurpassed.

Geographical mobility is explored in the important study by P. Clark, 'Migration in England during the Late Seventeenth and Early Eighteenth Centuries', *Past and Present*, no. 83 (1979), pp. 57–90, which is reprinted along with other important essays in P. Clark and D. C. Souden (eds.), *Migration and Society in Early Modern England* (1987). For emigration, see D. Cressy, *Coming Over: Migration and Communication between England and New England in the Seventeenth Century* (Cambridge, 1987) and H. A. Gemery, 'Emigration from the British Isles to the New World, 1630–1700: Inferences from Colonial Populations', *Research in Economic History*, 5 (1980), pp. 179–231. Immigration is surveyed in D. Statt, *Foreigners and Englishmen: The Controversy Over Immigration and Population, 1660–1760* (Newark, Delaware, 1995), though attention is largely directed at contemporary attitudes.

Discussions of social structure must attend to Gregory King's account. His social table is dissected in G. Holmes, 'Gregory King and the Social Structure of Pre-Industrial England', *Transactions of the Royal Historical Society*, 5th series, 27 (1977), pp. 41–68. Two excellent discussions of contemporary languages of organizing society are in P. J. Corfield (ed.), *Language, History, and Class* (Oxford, 1991), one by K. Wrightson, 'Estates, Degrees, and Sorts: Changing Perceptions of Society in Tudor and Stuart England', the other by the editor, 'Class by Name and Number in Eighteenth-Century Britain'. E. P. Thompson, *Customs in Common* (1991) is a brilliant view of 'history from below', if occasionally partial and self-indulgent and M. Rediker, *Between the Devil and the Deep Blue Sea: Merchant Seamen, Pirates, and the Anglo-American Maritime World, 1700–1750* (Cambridge, 1987) adopts a similar approach. For 'history from above', J. V. Beckett, *The Aristocracy in England, 1660–1914* (Oxford, 1986) is solid; J. Cannon, *Aristocratic Century: The Peerage in Eighteenth-Century*

England (Cambridge, 1984) crisp but too narrowly conceived to convince completely; and J. C. D. Clark, *English Society 1688–1832: Ideology, Social Structure, and Political Practice during the Ancien Regime* (Cambridge, 1985) raises important questions but too often tilts at windmills. For 'history from the middle', see J. Barry and C. Brooks (eds.), *The Middling Sort of People: Culture, Society, and Politics in England, 1550–1800* (Basingstoke, 1994) and the stimulating M. Hunt, *The Middling Sort: Commerce, Gender, and the Family in England, 1680–1780* (Berkeley and Los Angeles, 1996). The view from the middle must also be linked to the question of professionalization, for which see W. Prest (ed.), *The Professions in Early Modern England* (1987), G. Holmes, *Augustan England: Professions, State, and Society, 1680–1730* (1982), and P. J. Corfield, *Power and the Professions in Britain, 1700–1850* (1995).

The identities and communities people belonged to need to be considered in relation to a number of interlocking and overlapping areas. On the self and social responsibility, M. Mascuch, *Origins of the Individualist Self: Autobiography and Self-Identity in England, 1591–1791* (Cambridge, 1997) and F. Heal, *Hospitality in Early Modern England* (Oxford, 1990) are both interesting—most historians are now unsympathetic to general accounts such as R. H. Tawney, *Religion and the Rise of Capitalism: A Historical Study* (1926) and A. Macfarlane, *The Origins of English Individualism: The Family, Property, and Social Transition* (Oxford, 1978), though both are very thought provoking. On gender, R. B. Shoemaker, *Gender in English Society, 1650–1850: The Emergence of Separate Spheres?* (Harlow, 1998) is a useful survey, S. D. Amussen, *An Ordered Society: Gender and Class in Early Modern England* (New York, 1988) is based on local studies, A. Vickery, 'Golden Age to Separate Spheres? A Review of the Categories and Chronology of English Women's History', *Historical Journal*, 36 (1993), pp. 383–414 raises crucial questions, and A. Fletcher, *Gender, Sex, and Subordination in England, 1500–1800* (New Haven, 1995) is best on the pre-1700 period. Little work has been done on issues surrounding life-cycle identities in this period, but see K. Thomas, 'Age and Authority in Early Modern England', *Proceedings of the British Academy*, 62 (1976), pp. 205–48 and the questions raised in H. Cunningham, 'The Employment and Unemployment of Children in England, c.1680–1851', *Past and Present*, no. 126 (1990), pp. 115–50. The historiography of national, regional, and local identities is in a state of flux, with the meanings of 'Britishness' being much more fully explored than other collective politico-cultural identities. On the complex relationship between Englishness and Britishness, K. Thomas, 'The United Kingdom', in R. Grew (ed.), *Crises of Political Development in Europe and the United States* (Princeton, 1978), pp. 41–97, D. Cressy, *Bonfires and Bells: National Memory and the Protestant Calendar in Elizabethan and Stuart England* (1989), and L. Colley, *Britons: Forging the Nation, 1707–1837* (New Haven, 1992) are all important in rather different ways. On regional and local identities, C. Phythian-Adams, *Re-Thinking English Local History* (Leicester, 1987) is a broad brief review, an excellent example of a local study is K. Wrightson and D. Levine, *Poverty and Piety in an English Village: Terling, 1525–1700* (New York, 1979), the final part of R. Hutton, *The Rise and Fall of Merry England: The Ritual Year, 1400–1700* (Oxford, 1994) is a useful introduction to local society viewed through folk-lore, antiquarianism, and the calendar, and N. E. Key, 'The Localism of the County

Feast in Late Stuart Political Culture', *Huntington Library Quarterly*, 58 (1996), pp. 211–37 opens up interesting and important issues. Much local history can be explored in detail through the eternally on-going *Victoria History of the Counties of England* series.

The fundamental fact of economic uncertainty is discussed in the classic study by T. S. Ashton, *Economic Fluctuations in England, 1700–1800* (Oxford, 1959), which may be supplemented by W. G. Hoskins, 'Harvest Fluctuations and English Economic History, 1620–1759', *Agricultural History Review*, 16 (1968), pp. 15–31. A pathbreaking attempt to quantify the course of standards of living is E. Phelps Brown and S. V. Hopkins, *A Perspective of Wages and Prices* (1981). A valuable study stressing varieties of experiences is D. Woodward, *Men at Work: Labourers and Building Craftsmen in the Towns of Northern England, 1450–1750* (Cambridge, 1995) though see also E. W. Gilboy, *Wages in Eighteenth-Century England* (Cambridge, Massachusetts, 1934). D. C. Coleman, 'Labour in the English Economy of the Seventeenth Century', *Economic History Review*, 8 (1955–6), pp. 280–95 explores the important question of underemployment. On the experience of poverty: T. Arkell, 'The Incidence of Poverty in England in the Late Seventeenth Century', *Social History*, 12 (1987), pp. 23–47 is a useful introduction but the best studies for this period are in two unpublished doctoral theses (available through inter-library loan): T. V. Hitchcock, 'The English Workhouse: A Study in Institutional Poor Relief in Selected Counties, 1696–1750', D.Phil. thesis (University of Oxford, 1985) and S. Macfarlane, 'Studies in Poverty and Poor Relief in London at the End of the Seventeenth Century', D.Phil. thesis (University of Oxford, 1983). Also useful are K. D. M. Snell, *Annals of the Labouring Poor: Social Change and Agrarian England, 1660–1900* (Cambridge, 1985), which is stimulating but somewhat overdrawn, and T. Wales, 'Poverty, Poor Relief, and the Life-Cycle: Some Evidence from Seventeenth-Century Norfolk', in R. M. Smith (ed.), *Land, Kinship, and Life Cycle* (Cambridge, 1985) which is of wide import.

Because the makeshift economy of the poor drew on so many different sources of income, often only faintly glimpsed in the records, historians struggle to put the pieces together and tend to explore aspects such as work, recycling, customary rights, pawning, and neighbourliness separately. However, works such as A. Clark, *The Working Life of Women in the Seventeenth Century* (1919), B. Hill, *Women, Work, and Sexual Politics in Eighteenth-Century England* (Oxford, 1989), and A. Kussmaul, *Servants in Husbandry in Early Modern England* (Cambridge, 1981) do address a number of themes in an integrative way. There is, however, an extensive and first-rate literature on poor relief. An excellent account is P. Slack, *Poverty and Policy in Tudor and Stuart England* (1988), while the same author's *From Reformation to Improvement: Public Welfare in Early Modern England* (Oxford, 1999) is more synoptic. Good studies of charity are D. Owen, *English Philanthropy, 1660–1960* (Cambridge, Massachusetts, 1965) and D. T. Andrew, *Philanthropy and Police: London Charity in the Eighteenth Century* (Princeton, 1989). W. A. Bewes, *Church Briefs or Royal Warrants for Collections for Charitable Objects* (1896) is an important study that would repay reworking (though see T. L. Auffenberg, 'Organized English Benevolence: Charity Briefs 1625–1725', Ph.D. thesis (Vanderbilt University, 1973)).

4 A BLOODY PROGRESS

Britain's place in this era of European warfare is brilliantly surveyed by a collection of leading authorities in J. S. Bromley (ed.), *New Cambridge Modern History*, vol. 6. *The Rise of Great Britain and Russia, 1688–1715/25* (Cambridge, 1970). Numerous studies of diplomatic and balance of power questions exist, but for introductions, see D. McKay and H. M. Scott, *The Rise of the Great Powers, 1648–1815* (1983), R. M. Hatton (ed.), *Louis XIV and Europe* (1976), R. M. Hatton and J. S. Bromley (eds.), *William III and Louis XIV: Essays 1680–1720 by and for M. A. Thomson* (Liverpool, 1968), and J. Black, *The Rise of the European Powers, 1679–1793* (1990). A close conceptual interpretation of the Utrecht settlement is provided in A. Osiander, *The States System of Europe, 1640–1990: Peacemaking and Conditions of International Security* (Oxford, 1994). The conduct of British foreign policy is surveyed in J. Black, *A System of Ambition? British Foreign Policy 1660–1793* (Harlow, 1991) and P. Langford, *The Eighteenth Century, 1688–1815* (1976). For the personnel of diplomacy, see M. A. Thomson, *The Secretaries of State, 1681–1782* (Oxford, 1932) and D. B. Horn, *The British Diplomatic Service, 1689–1789* (Oxford, 1961). Particular aspects of British foreign policy are discussed in D. Coombs, *The Conduct of the Dutch: British Opinion and the Dutch Alliance during the War of the Spanish Succession* (The Hague, 1958), R. Geikie and I. A. Montgomery, *The Dutch Barrier, 1705–1719* (Cambridge, 1930), J. B. Hattendorf, *England in the War of the Spanish Succession: A Study of the English View and Conduct of Grand Strategy, 1701–1712* (New York, 1987), A. D. Francis, *The Methuens and Portugal, 1691–1708* (Cambridge, 1966), G. C. Gibbs, 'Parliament and Foreign Policy in the Age of Stanhope and Walpole', *English Historical Review*, 77 (1962), pp. 18–37, R. Hatton, *Diplomatic Relations between Great Britain and the Dutch Republic, 1714–1721* (1950), and R. Hatton, *The Anglo-Hanoverian Connection, 1714–1760* (1982).

Two good general histories of warfare in this era are D. Chandler, *The Art of Warfare in the Age of Marlborough* (2nd edn., Tunbridge Wells, 1990) and M. S. Anderson, *War and Society in Europe of the Old Regime, 1618–1789* (1988), which might usefully be related to G. Parker, *The Military Revolution: Military Innovation and the Rise of the West, 1500–1800* (Cambridge, 1988). Important aspects of military strategy are also discussed in C. Duffy, *The Fortress in the Age of Vauban and Frederick the Great, 1660–1789* (1985), D. French, *The British Way in Warfare, 1688–2000* (1990), D. A. Baugh, 'Great Britain's "Blue-Water" Policy, 1689–1815', *International History Review*, 10 (1988), pp. 33–58, and the crucial associated issue of logistics in G. Perjés, 'Army Provisioning, Logistics, and Strategy in the Second Half of the Seventeenth Century', *Acta Historica Academiae Scientiarum Hungaricae*, 16 (1970), pp. 1–52. The Royal Navy, privateers, and convoys are explored in G. N. Clark, *The Dutch Alliance and the War against French Trade, 1688–1697* (Manchester, 1923), J. Ehrman, *The Navy in the War of William III: Its State and Direction* (Cambridge, 1953), J. H. Owen, *War at Sea under Queen Anne, 1702–1708* (Cambridge, 1938), G. Symcox, *The Crisis of French Sea Power, 1688–1697* (The Hague, 1974), D. J. Starkey, *British Privateering Enterprise in the Eighteenth Century* (Exeter, 1990), and P. Crowhurst, *The Defence of*

British Trade, 1689–1815 (Folkestone, 1977). General histories of the army include the old war horse of Sir John Fortescue, *A History of the British Army*, vol. 1 (1899) and more recently J. Childs, *Armies and Warfare in Europe, 1648–1789* (Manchester, 1982), J. Childs, *The British Army of William III, 1689–1702* (Manchester, 1987), J. Childs, *The Nine Years' War and the British Army, 1688–1697: The Operations in the Low Countries* (Manchester, 1991), R. E. Scouller, *The Armies of Queen Anne* (Oxford, 1966), and A. J. Guy, *Œconomy and Discipline: Officership and Administration in the British Army, 1714–1763* (Manchester, 1985).

Histories of particular campaigns are best explored either through the histories just listed or via accounts of leading military figures, at the forefront of which are studies of Marlborough, on whom millions of words have been showered. His descendant, W. S. Churchill, has written the standard life, *Marlborough: His Life and Times*, 4 vols. (1933–8), which is full of information, wonderfully realized, if understandably occasionally partisan. Shorter studies include D. Chandler, *Marlborough as Military Commander* (2nd edn., 1979), C. Barnett, *Marlborough* (1974), and J. R. Jones, *Marlborough* (Cambridge, 1993). Marlborough's great military associate is the subject of N. Henderson, *Prince Eugen of Savoy* (1964). Studies of admirals in this period are thin on the ground. Military biographies can be supplemented by G. N. Clark, 'The Character of the Nine Years War, 1688–97', *Cambridge Historical Journal*, 11 (1954), pp. 168–82, J. G. Simms, *Jacobite Ireland, 1685–91* (1969), W. R. Meyer, 'English Privateering in the War of 1688 to 1697', *Mariner's Mirror*, 67 (1981), pp. 259–72, W. R. Meyer, 'English Privateering in the War of the Spanish Succession, 1702–1713', *Mariner's Mirror*, 69 (1983), pp. 435–46, D. W. Hayton and G. O'Brien (eds.), *War and Politics in Ireland, 1649–1730* (1986), H. H. Peckham, *The Colonial Wars, 1689–1762* (Chicago, 1964), H. Kamen, *The War of Succession in Spain, 1700–1715* (1969), and D. Francis, *The First Peninsular War, 1702–1713* (1975).

The means of paying for war are expertly summarized in H. Roseveare, *The Financial Revolution, 1660–1760* (1991) and P. K. O'Brien, 'The Political Economy of British Taxation, 1688–1815', *Economic History Review*, 41 (1988), pp. 1–32. The pathbreaking work of P. G. M. Dickson, *The Financial Revolution in England: A Study in the Development of Public Credit, 1688–1756* (1967) stresses the establishment of the national debt, the key institution of which is the subject of J. H. Clapham's uncharacteristically flat *The Bank of England: A History*, 2 vols. (Cambridge, 1944). J. Brewer, *The Sinews of Power: War, Money, and the English State, 1688–1783* (1989) is a marvellous synthesis, emphasizing taxation's role, for which also see M. J. Braddick, *The Nerves of State: Taxation and the Financing of the English State, 1558–1714* (Manchester, 1996) and C. Brooks, 'Public Finance and Political Stability: The Administration of the Land Tax, 1688–1720', *Historical Journal*, 17 (1974), pp. 281–300. Particular aspects of the State are explored in S. B. Baxter, *The Development of the Treasury, 1660–1702* (1957), E. E. Hoon, *The Organization of the English Customs System, 1696–1786* (New York, 1938), E. Hughes, *Studies in Administration and Finance, 1558–1825* (Manchester, 1934), R. G. Albion, *Forests and Sea Power: The Timber Problem of the Royal Navy, 1652–1862* (Cambridge, Massachusetts, 1926), and D. A. Baugh, *British Naval Administration in the Age of Walpole* (Princeton, 1965).

A good survey of the domestic consequences of war is H. V. Bowen, *War and British Society, 1688–1815* (1998); the essays in L. Stone (ed.), *An Imperial State at War: Britain from 1689 to 1815* (1994) explore a wide range of similar themes; while the economic stresses of coping with the burdens of intense warfare are well brought out in D. W. Jones, *War and Economy in the Age of William III and Marlborough* (Oxford, 1988) and M.-H. Li, *The Great Recoinage of 1696 to 1699* (1963). But the social consequences of war need much more study.

5   THE POLITICAL WORLD OF WILLIAM III

The standard life of William is S. B. Baxter, *William III* (1966). Mary II is still a rather shadowy figure, but see H. W. Chapman, *Mary II, Queen of England* (Bath, 1972). Biographies of many of the leading politicians of the period are available. J. P. Kenyon, *Robert Spencer, Earl of Sunderland, 1641–1702* (1958), A. Browning, *Thomas Osborne, Earl of Danby and Duke of Leeds, 1632–1712*, 3 vols. (Glasgow, 1951), H. Horwitz, *Revolution Politicks: The Career of Daniel Finch, Second Earl of Nottingham* (Cambridge, 1968), and W. L. Sachse, *Lord Somers: A Political Portrait* (Manchester, 1975) are all authoritative. Unfortunately, no historian seems yet to have captured Robert Harley well, but see A. McInnes, *Robert Harley: Puritan Politician* (1970) and B. W. Hill, *Robert Harley: Speaker, Secretary of State, and Premier Minister* (New Haven, 1988).

The best general political history of the period is now C. Rose, *England in the 1690s: Revolution, Religion, and War* (Oxford, 1999). An effective survey of party politics in this period is T. Harris, *Politics under the Later Stuarts: Party Conflict in a Divided Society, 1660–1715* (Harlow, 1993), and to carry the story on B. W. Hill, *The Growth of Parliamentary Parties, 1689–1742* (1976). The best detailed narrative of the complex parliamentary politics is provided by H. Horwitz, *Parliament, Policy and Politics in the Reign of William III* (Manchester, 1977). The standard work on the Tory party is still K. Feiling, *A History of the Tory Party, 1640–1714* (Oxford, 1924), though no comparable work exists for the Whigs. Among more detailed studies of party politics, G. S. de Krey, *A Fractured Society: The Politics of London in the First Age of Party, 1688–1715* (Oxford, 1985) is excellent. The complicated question of the relationship between court–country and Whig–Tory divides is explored unconvincingly in D. Rubini, *Court and Country, 1688–1702* (1967). Less ambitious but more persuasive accounts are provided in C. Brooks, 'The Country Persuasion and Political Responsibility in England in the 1690s', *Parliaments, Estates and Representation*, 4 (1984), pp. 135–46, J. A. Downie, 'The Commission of Public Accounts and the Formation of the Country Party', *English Historical Review*, 91 (1976), pp. 33–51, D. Hayton, 'Moral Reform and Country Politics in the Late Seventeenth-Century House of Commons' *Past and Present*, no. 128 (1990), pp. 48–91, and D. Hayton, 'The "Country" Interest and the Party System, 1689–c.1720', in C. Jones (ed.), *Party and Management in Parliament, 1660–1784* (Leicester, 1984), pp. 37–85.

The ideological dimensions to party politics was central in this period, for which, in addition to the works by Kenyon and Dickinson listed earlier in section 2, see

M. Goldie, 'The Roots of True Whiggism, 1688–1694', *History of Political Thought*, 1 (1980), 195–236, M. Goldie, 'The Revolution of 1689 and the Structure of Political Argument: An Essay and an Annotated Bibliography of Pamphlets on the Allegiance Controversy', *Bulletin of Research in the Humanities*, 83 (1980), pp. 473–564, C. Robbins, *The Eighteenth-Century Commonwealthman* (Cambridge, Massachusetts, 1959), and J. G. A. Pocock, *The Machiavellian Moment: Florentine Political Thought and the Atlantic Republican Tradition* (Princeton, 1975).

For discussions of key areas in domestic affairs, see: E. A. Reitan, 'From Revenue to Civil List, 1689–1702: The Revolution Settlement and the "Mixed and Balanced" Constitution', *Historical Journal*, 13 (1970), pp. 571–88 on the vital issue of Parliament's control of Crown finances; on William's ecclesiastical policy, see J. Israel, 'William III and Toleration', in O. P. Grell, N. Tyacke, and J. Israel (eds.), *From Persecution to Toleration: The Glorious Revolution in England* (Oxford, 1991), pp. 129–70 and G. V. Bennett, 'King William III and the Episcopate', in G. V. Bennett and J. D. Walsh (eds.), *Essays in Modern English Church History in Memory of Norman Sykes* (1966), pp. 104–32; William's attempts to project an image to his subjects is imaginatively explored in T. Claydon, *William III and the Godly Reformation* (Cambridge, 1996); J. Garrett, *The Triumphs of Providence: The Assassination Plot, 1696* (Cambridge, 1980) explores a pivotal moment in William's reign; L. G. Schwoerer, *'No Standing Armies!': The Anti-Army Ideology in Seventeenth-Century England* (Baltimore, 1974) on the battle over the army after the end of the Nine Years War; J. G. Simms, *The Williamite Confiscation in Ireland, 1690–1703* (1956) on opposition to William's patronage; and L. K. J. Glassey, *Politics and the Appointment of Justices of the Peace, 1675–1720* (Oxford, 1979) for the relationship between party politics and the personnel of local government.

6   WARS OF WORDS AND THE BATTLE OF THE BOOKS

For discussions of literacy, see D. Cressy, *Literacy and the Social Order: Reading and Writing in Tudor and Stuart England* (Cambridge, 1980) and T. Laqueur, 'The Cultural Origins of Popular Literacy in England, 1500–1850', *Oxford Review of Education*, 2 (1976), pp. 255–75, and for the neglected theme of numeracy K. Thomas, 'Numeracy in Early Modern England', *Transactions of the Royal Historical Society*, 5th series, 36 (1987), pp. 103–32. How literacy and numeracy were acquired may be followed up through works on schooling such as R. O' Day, *Education and Society, 1500–1800: The Social Foundations of Education in Early Modern Britain* (1982), N. Hans, *New Trends in Education in the Eighteenth Century* (1951), W. A. L. Vincent, *The Grammar Schools: Their Continuing Tradition, 1660–1714* (1969), V. E. Neuberg, *Popular Education in Eighteenth Century England* (1971), and R. S. Tompson, *Classics or Charity? The Dilemma of the Eighteenth Century Grammar School* (Manchester, 1971). Two important educational developments in this period can be explored through M. G. Jones, *The Charity School Movement: A Study of Eighteenth-Century Puritanism in Action* (Cambridge, 1938) and J. W. A. Smith, *The Birth of Modern Education: The Contribution of the Dissenting Academies, 1660–1800* (1954).

There is now a solid body of research on the two universities, more particularly on Oxford, for which, see N. Tyacke (ed.), *The History of the University of Oxford*, vol. 4. *The Seventeenth Century* (Oxford, 1997) and L. S. Sutherland and L. G. Mitchell (eds.), *The History of the University of Oxford*, vol. 5. *The Eighteenth Century* (Oxford, 1986)—which may usefully be supplemented by L. Stone, 'The Size and Composition of the Oxford Student Body, 1580–1910', in L. Stone (ed.), *The University in Society*, 2 vols. (Princeton, 1975), vol. 1, pp. 3–110. J. Gasgoigne, *Cambridge in the Age of the Enlightenment: Science, Religion and Politics from the Restoration to the French Revolution* (Cambridge, 1989) is a stimulating study. Useful insights into the university world are provided by histories of libraries, for which, see J. Harrison, *The Library of Isaac Newton* (Cambridge, 1978), J. Harrison and P. Laslett, *The Library of John Locke* (Oxford, 1971), and D. McKitterick, *Cambridge University Library: A History*, vol. 2. *The Eighteenth and Nineteenth Centuries* (Cambridge, 1986).

'Gentlemanly' education can be explored in general terms through J. Locke, *Some Thoughts Concerning Education*, ed. J. W. and J. S. Yolton (Oxford, 1989), G. C. Brauer, *The Education of a Gentleman: Theories of Gentlemanly Education in England, 1660–1775* (New York, 1959), A. Goldgar, *Impolite Learning: Conduct and Community in the Republic of Letters, 1680–1750* (New Haven, 1995), S. Shapin, *A Social History of Truth: Civility and Science in Seventeenth-Century England* (Chicago, 1994), and S. de Ricci, *English Collectors of Books and Manuscripts (1530–1930)* (Cambridge, 1930). Consideration also has to be given here to the inns of court, for which, see the excellent D. Lemmings, *Gentlemen and Barristers: The Inns of Court and the English Bar, 1680–1730* (Oxford, 1990), and the grand tour, an introduction to which is provided by J. Black, *The British Abroad: The Grand Tour in the Eighteenth Century* (Stroud, 1992). Far less work has been done on the educational world of gentlewomen, but see R. Perry, *The Celebrated Mary Astell: An Early English Feminist* (Chicago, 1986), M. Reynolds, *The Learned Lady in England, 1650–1760* (Boston, Massachusetts, 1920), and P. McDowell, *The Women of Grub Street: Press, Politics, and Gender in the London Literary Marketplace, 1678–1730* (Oxford, 1998).

Good discussions of the popular world of the print culture are provided by B. Capp, *Astrology and the Popular Press: English Almanacs, 1500–1800* (1979), P. Curry, *Prophecy and Power: Astrology in Early Modern England* (Cambridge, 1989), and M. Spufford, *Small Books and Pleasant Histories: Popular Fiction and its Readership in Seventeenth Century England* (1981). The crucial development of newspapers is discussed in J. Sutherland, *The Restoration Newspaper and its Development* (Cambridge, 1986), J. Black, *The English Press in the Eighteenth Century* (1987), M. Harris, *London Newspapers in the Age of Walpole: A Study of the Origins of the Modern English Press* (1987), R. M. Wiles, *Freshest Advices: Early Provincial Newspapers in England* (Ohio, 1965), and G. A. Cranfield, *The Development of the Provincial Newspaper, 1700–1760* (Oxford, 1962). The history of the book (and of readership) is currently much studied. See, for example, A. Johns, *The Nature of the Book: Print and Knowledge in the Making* (Chicago, 1999) which raises important doubts, if in a somewhat convoluted way. The question of the freeing of the press is addressed in L. Hanson, *Government and the Press, 1695–1763* (Oxford, 1936) and C. R. Gillett, *Burned Books: Neglected Chapters in*

British History and Literature, 2 vols. (New York, 1932), while for key legal developments, see R. Astbury, 'The Renewal of the Licensing Act in 1693 and its Lapse in
1695', *The Library*, 5th series, 33 (1978), pp. 296–322, J. Feather, 'The Book Trade
in Politics: The Making of the Copyright Act of 1710', *Publishing History*, 8 (1980),
pp. 19–44, and P. B. J. Hyland, 'Liberty and Libel: Government and the Press during
the Succession Crisis in Britain, 1712–1716', *English Historical Review*, 101 (1986),
pp. 863–88.

Perceptions of a rapidly expanding natural world were in a considerable state of flux.
The English experience is charted in K. Thomas, *Man and the Natural World:
Changing Attitudes in England, 1500–1800* (1983) and D. E. Allen, *The Naturalist in
Britain: A Social History* (1976). For further afield P. J. Marshall and G. Williams, *The
Great Map of Mankind: British Perceptions of the World in the Age of Enlightenment*
(1982) is wonderfully rich, and Douglas Chambers, *The Reinvention of the World:
English Writing, 1650–1750* (1996) makes some additional points. The fictionality
of foreign 'facts' needs to be kept constantly in view, for which, see P. G. Adams,
Travelers and Travel Liars, 1660–1800 (Berkeley and Los Angeles, 1962). Specific
encounters with other peoples are explored in R. H. Pearce, *The Savages of America: A
Study of the Indian and the Idea of Civilization* (Baltimore, 1953), L. E. Huddleston,
Origins of the American Indians: European Concepts, 1492–1729 (Austin, 1967),
R. F. Berkhofer, jnr., *The White Man's Indian: Images of the American Indian from
Columbus to the Present* (New York, 1978), and A. J. Barker, *The African Link: British
Attitudes to the Negro in the Era of the Atlantic Slave Trade, 1550–1807* (1978).

The literature on the Scientific Revolution is enormous and any selection seems
particularly invidious. Among general accounts H. Butterfield, *The Origins of
Modern Science, 1300–1800* (1949) and A. R. Hall, *The Revolution in Science, 1500–
1750* (revised edn., Harlow, 1983) are somewhat traditional but still valuable, while
newer approaches, often emphasizing social contexts, may be found in S. Shapin, *The
Scientific Revolution* (Chicago, 1996)—which has an excellent annotated bibliography,
R. Porter and M. Teich (eds.), *The Scientific Revolution in National Context*
(Cambridge, 1992), J. G. Burke (ed.), *The Uses of Science in the Age of Newton* (Berkeley
and Los Angeles, 1983), and D. C. Lindberg and R. S. Westman (eds.), *Reappraisals of
the Scientific Revolution* (Cambridge, 1990). Excellent detailed research is provided by
M. Hunter, *Science and Society in Restoration England* (Cambridge, 1981). Newton was,
of course, the commanding figure of the scientific world in England in this period and
I. B. Cohen, *The Newtonian Revolution* (Cambridge, 1980), R. S. Westfall, *Never at
Rest: A Biography of Isaac Newton* (Cambridge, 1980), and F. E. Manuel, *Portrait of
Isaac Newton* (Cambridge, Massachusetts, 1968) are all rich and illuminating. Newton's
wider impact is considered in M. C. Jacob, *The Newtonians and the English Revolu-
tion, 1689–1720* (Hassocks, 1976) and L. Stewart, *The Rise of Public Science: Rhetoric,
Technology, and Natural Philosophy in Newtonian Britain, 1660–1750* (Cambridge,
1992). Studies of other leading scientists include A. Cook, *Edmond Halley: Charting the
Heavens and the Seas* (Oxford, 1998), R. E. W. Maddison, *The Life of the Honourable
Robert Boyle F. R. S.* (1969), M. Hunter and S. Schaffer (eds.), *Robert Hooke: New
Studies* (Woodbridge, 1989), F. Wilmoth (ed.), *Flamsteed's Stars: New Perspectives on*

the Life and Work of the First Astronomer Royal (1646–1719) (Woodbridge, 1997), G. R. de Beer, *Sir Hans Sloane and the British Museum* (1953), E. St John Brooks, *Sir Hans Sloane: The Great Collector and his Circle* (1954), and C. E. Raven, *John Ray, Naturalist: His Life and Works* (2nd edn., Cambridge, 1950).

At the time economics was not a separate area of intellectual enquiry and the history of economic ideas has been seriously distorted by relating developments to the 'birth' of modern economics in Adam Smith's writings (especially his *Wealth of Nations* (1776)) and by some authors using the anachronistic and variously defined concept of 'mercantilism'. J. A. Schumpeter, *History of Economic Analysis* (Oxford, 1954) is a brilliant account, largely avoiding both malignities—and though T. Hutchinson, *Before Adam Smith: The Emergence of Political Economy, 1662–1776* (Oxford, 1988) and W. Letwin, *The Origins of Scientific Economics: English Economic Thought, 1660–1776* (1963) do not, both are useful. Economic ideas certainly had a practical import at the time, for which G. N. Clark, *Science and Social Welfare in the Age of Newton* (2nd edn., Oxford, 1949) and L. Daston, *Classical Probability in the Enlightenment* (Princeton, 1988) are exceptional. Clearly the growth of the state after 1688 and its increasing demand for money influenced its perception of the economy, for which D. C. Coleman (ed.), *Revisions in Mercantilism* (1969) is the pre-eminent introduction and D. C. Coleman, 'Mercantilism Revisited', *Historical Journal*, 23 (1980), pp. 773–91 a further refinement provoked by J. O. Appleby, *Economic Thought and Ideology in Seventeenth-Century England* (Princeton, 1978).

An overview of the world of ideas in this period is provided in the still valuable L. Stephen, *History of English Thought in the Eighteenth Century*, 2 vols. (1876). The history of political thought is effectively surveyed in J. G. A. Pocock (ed.), *The Varieties of British Political Thought, 1500–1800* (Cambridge, 1993), S. Burtt, *Virtue Transformed: Political Argument in England, 1688–1740* (Cambridge, 1992), and A. Pagden (ed.), *The Languages of Political Theory in Early-Modern Europe* (Cambridge, 1987)—though also see the works by Kenyon and Dickinson cited earlier in section 2. The legacy of Hobbes is discussed in S. I. Mintz, *The Hunting of Leviathan: Seventeenth-Century Reactions to the Materialism and Moral Philosophy of Thomas Hobbes* (Cambridge, 1962) and of Filmer in J. Daly, *Sir Robert Filmer and English Political Thought* (Toronto, 1979) and G. Schochet, *Patriarchalism in Political Thought: The Authoritarian Family and Political Speculation and Attitudes Especially in the Seventeenth Century* (Oxford, 1975). As with Newton a huge literature surrounds the commanding figure of John Locke. His works are, for the most part, relatively approachable and good modern editions of two of his key works are J. Locke, *Two Treatises of Government*, ed. P. Laslett (2nd edn., Cambridge, 1991) and J. Locke, *An Essay Concerning Human Understanding*, ed. P. H. Nidditch (Oxford, 1979). For introductions to his ideas V. Chappell (ed.), *The Cambridge Companion to Locke* (Cambridge, 1994) and J. Dunn, *Locke* (Oxford, 1984) are effective. Valuable detailed works include J. W. Yolton, *Locke and the Compass of Human Understanding* (Cambridge, 1970), M. Cranston, *John Locke: A Biography* (1957), J. Marshall, *John Locke: Resistance, Religion and Responsibility* (Cambridge, 1994), J. Dunn, *The Political Thought of John Locke* (Cambridge, 1969), and R. Ashcraft, *Revolutionary Politics and Locke's Two Treatises of Government* (Princeton, 1986). C. B. Macpherson, *The Political Theory of Possessive Individualism: Hobbes to Locke* (Oxford, 1962) is not now thought to be persuasive.

A good deal of attention has been paid to developing ideas of virtue and politeness in the altered circumstances of the post-1688 world. In the vanguard are J. G. A. Pocock, *Virtue, Commerce, and History* (Cambridge, 1985), D. D. Raphael (ed.), *British Moralists, 1650–1800*, 2 vols. (Oxford, 1969), M. M. Goldsmith, *Private Vices, Public Benefits: Bernard Mandeville's Social and Political Thought* (Cambridge, 1985), T. A. Horne, *The Social Thought of Bernard Mandeville: Virtue and Commerce in Early Eighteenth-Century England* (1978), I. Kramnick, *Bolingbroke and his Circle: The Politics of Nostalgia in the Age of Walpole* (Cambridge, Massachusetts, 1968), and L. E. Klein, *Shaftesbury and the Culture of Politeness: Moral Discourse and Cultural Politics in Early Eighteenth-Century England* (Cambridge, 1994). A sense of ancient Greece and Rome was integral to conceptualization of the contemporary social and political world. Both J. W. Johnson, *The Formation of English Neo-Classical Thought* (Princeton, 1967) and P. Ayres, *Classical Culture and the Idea of Rome in Eighteenth-Century England* (1997) are good introductions to general influences, while M. L. Clarke, *Greek Studies in England, 1700–1830* (Cambridge, 1945) looks at the more educational and scholarly aspects. The contest between the ancients and the moderns is expertly discussed in J. M. Levine, *The Battle of the Books: History and Literature in the Augustan Age* (Ithaca, 1991).

An excellent introduction to the writing of history is provided by D. C. Douglas, *English Scholars, 1660–1730* (2nd edn., 1951). More recent studies of note include J. M. Levine, *Humanism and History: Origins of Modern English Historiography* (Ithaca, 1987), J. M. Levine, *Dr Woodward's Shield: History, Science and Satire in Augustan England* (Berkeley, 1977), and P. Hicks, *Neoclassical History and English Culture: From Clarendon to Hume* (Basingstoke, 1996). Overviews of antiquarianism are provided by S. A. E. Mendyk, *'Speculum Britanniae': Regional Study, Antiquarianism, and Science in Britain to 1700* (Toronto, 1989) and G. Parry, *The Trophies of Time: English Antiquarians of the Seventeenth Century* (Oxford, 1995), though the topic can also usefully be approached through S. Piggott, *William Stukeley: An Eighteenth Century Antiquary* (2nd edn., 1985).

7   FAITH AND FERVOUR

An excellent introduction to the religious history of the period is available in J. Walsh, C. Haydon, and S. Taylor (eds.), *The Church of England, c.1689–c.1833: From Toleration to Tractarianism* (Cambridge, 1993), which has many valuable essays and an introduction which cogently reviews the historiography. A very general survey of religious history—and some sense of developments since the Reformation is an essential foundation stone for understanding this period—is provided by S. Gilley and W. J. Shiels (eds.), *A History of Religion in Britain: Practice and Belief from Pre-Roman Times to the Present* (Oxford, 1994). Less expansive yet still summary is D. Hempton, *Religion and Political Culture in Britain and Ireland: From the Glorious Revolution to the Decline of Empire* (Cambridge, 1996). It says much that among general works neither

N. Sykes, *From Sheldon to Secker: Aspects of English Church History, 1660–1768* (Cambridge, 1959) nor G. R. Cragg, *From Puritanism to the Age of Reason: A Study of Changes in Religious Thought within the Church of England, 1660 to 1700* (Cambridge, 1950) have been supplanted by E. G. Rupp, *Religion in England, 1688–1791* (Oxford, 1986).

The nature of the Church of England in the late seventeenth and early eighteenth centuries is a somewhat neglected theme. There is, for example, no good general study of Convocation, diocesan organization, or of the episcopal bench in the House of Lords. One valuable approach is via biographies of leading clerics, such as N. Sykes, *Edmund Gibson, Bishop of London, 1669–1748: A Study of Politics and Religion in the Eighteenth Century* (1926), E. F. Carpenter, *The Protestant Bishop: Being the Life of Henry Compton, 1632–1713 Bishop of London* (1956), A. T. Hart, *The Life and Times of John Sharp, Archbishop of York* (1949), G. V. Bennett, *White Kennett, 1660–1728: Bishop of Peterborough* (1957), and A. T. Hart, *William Lloyd, 1627–1717: Bishop, Politician, Author, and Prophet* (1952). Given the inseparability of politics and religion in this period many works on wider constitutional developments and the day-to-day political manoeuvering (as in the battles over occasional conformity for example) listed elsewhere in this bibliography will be important. However, the important issue of patronage is discussed by D. R. Hirschberg, 'The Government and Church Patronage in England, 1660–1760', *Journal of British Studies*, 20 (1980), pp. 109–39.

Local religious practice is ably surveyed in W. M. Jacob, *Lay People and Religion in the Early Eighteenth Century* (Cambridge, 1996) and in the older but still useful J. H. Overton, *Life in the English Church, 1660–1714* (1885). More detailed studies are provided in R. O'Day and F. Heal (eds.), *Princes and Paupers in the English Church 1500–1800* (Leicester, 1981), J. H. Pruett, *The Parish Clergy under the Later Stuarts: The Leicestershire Experience* (Urbana, 1978), A. Warne, *Church and Society in Eighteenth-Century Devon* (Newton Abbot, 1969), S. J. Wright (ed.), *Parish, Church and People: Local Studies in Lay Religion, 1350–1750* (1988), while F. C. Mather, 'Georgian Churchmanship Reconsidered: Some Variations in Anglican Public Worship, 1714–1830', *Journal of Ecclesiastical History*, 36 (1985), pp. 255–83 attempts a synoptic view. Popular religious practice needs to be placed within wider systems of belief. A classic, if far from uncontested account, is K. Thomas, *Religion and the Decline of Magic: Studies in Popular Beliefs in Sixteenth- and Seventeenth-Century England* (1971), some of whose themes are further explored and developed in I. Bostridge, *Witchcraft and its Transformations, c.1650–c.1750* (Oxford, 1997). D. P. Walker, *The Decline of Hell: Seventeenth-Century Discussions of Eternal Torment* (1964) addresses an important topic, but it is given greater social reality through works such as M. MacDonald and T. R. Murphy, *Sleepless Souls: Suicide in Early Modern England* (Oxford, 1990), a compelling study of wide significance.

There is a rich literature discussing those outside the established Church. However, the best study of the non-juring schism remains an unpublished work, J. C. Findon, 'The Non-Jurors and the Church of England, 1689–1716', D.Phil. thesis (University of Oxford, 1979). An excellent general discussion of Nonconformity is provided by M. Watts, *The Dissenters: From the Reformation to the French Revolution* (Oxford, 1978), while M. Spufford (ed.), *The World of Rural Dissenters, 1520–1725* (Cambridge, 1995) presents the results of detailed local research. H. Schwartz, *The French Prophets: The History of a Millenarian Group in Eighteenth-Century England* (Berkeley and Los Angeles, 1980) is a good study of the continued occasional significance of millenarian movements. Good general accounts of Roman Catholicism are E. Norman, *Roman Catholicism in England from the Elizabethan Settlement to the Second Vatican Council* (1985) and J. Bossy, *The English Catholic Community, 1570–1850* (1975). C. Haydon, *Anti-Catholicism in Eighteenth-Century England, c.1714–80: A Political and Social Study* (Manchester, 1993) is the leading study of a vital force within English life.

Debates over theological questions and biblical authority are generally discussed in P. Harrison, *'Religion' and the Religions of the English Enlightenment* (Cambridge, 1990), G. Reedy, *The Bible and Reason: Anglicans and Scripture in Late Seventeenth-Century England* (Philadelphia, 1985), I. Rivers, *Reason, Grace, and Sentiment: A Study of the Language of Religion and Ethics in England, 1660–1780*, vol. 1. *Whichcote to Wesley* (Cambridge, 1991), R. N. Stromberg, *Religious Liberalism in Eighteenth-Century England* (Oxford, 1954), and J. A. I. Champion, *The Pillars of Priestcraft Shaken: The Church of England and its Enemies, 1660–1730* (Cambridge, 1992). Good studies of key intellectuals in this debate are A. Fox, *John Mill and Richard Bentley: A Study of the Textual Criticism of the New Testament, 1675–1729* (Oxford, 1954), J. E. Force, *William Whiston: Honest Newtonian* (Cambridge, 1985), and R. E. Sullivan, *John Toland and the Deist Controversy* (Cambridge, Massachusetts, 1982).

The vitality of the Church of England in the post-toleration order is explored with great insight by G. V. Bennett, *The Tory Crisis in Church and State, 1688–1730: The Career of Francis Atterbury, Bishop of Rochester* (Oxford, 1975) and with crisp efficiency in G. Every, *The High Church Party, 1688–1718* (1956)—R. D. Cornwall, *Visible and Apostolic: The Constitution of the Church in High Church Anglican and Non-Juror Thought* (Newark, Delaware, 1993) is less successful. A leading High Churchman is brilliantly explored in G. Holmes, *The Trial of Dr Sacheverell* (1973). Practical initiatives pursued within the Church are discussed in A. Savidge, *The Foundation and Early Years of Queen Anne's Bounty* (1955), E. H. Pearce, *The Sons of the Clergy, 1655–1904* (1904), and N. Cox, *Bridging the Gap: A History of the Corporation of the Sons of the Clergy over 300 Years* (Oxford, 1978). Much work has been done on the religious societies which flourished in this period. An old but still very valuable study is G. V. Portus, *Caritas Anglicana: or, an Historical Inquiry into those Religious and Philanthropic Societies that Flourished in England between the Years 1678 and 1740* (1912), with more modern perspectives provided by W. K. L. Clarke, *A History of the SPCK* (1959), W. A. and P. W. Bultmann, 'The Roots of Anglican Humanitarianism: A Study of the Membership of the S. P. C. K. and the S. P. G., 1699–1720', *Historical Magazine of the Protestant Episcopal Church*, 33 (1964), pp. 3–48, E. Duffy, 'Primitive Christianity Revived: Religious Renewal in Augustan England', *Studies in Church History*, 14 (1977), pp. 287–300, and T. Isaacs, 'The Anglican Hierarchy and the Reformation of Manners 1688–1738', *Journal of Ecclesiastical History*, 33 (1982), pp. 391–411. H. P. Thompson, *Thomas Bray* (1954) is the best if rather limited life of a key figure.

8   ENGLAND, BRITAIN, EMPIRE

Unquestionably the best introductions to the English and British empires in this period
are the first two volumes in the Oxford history of the British empire, N. Canny (ed.),
The Origins of Empire: British Overseas Enterprise to the Close of the Seventeenth Century
(Oxford, 1998) and P. J. Marshall (ed.), *The Eighteenth Century* (Oxford, 1998), though
the view of J. Holland Rose, A. P. Newton and E. A. Benians (eds.), *The Old Empire
from the Beginnings to 1783* (Cambridge, 1929) retains some value. The empire's
cultural dimensions, broadly defined, are skilfully considered in B. Bailyn and
P. D. Morgan (eds.), *Strangers Within the Realm: Cultural Margins of the First British
Empire* (Chapel Hill, 1991) and the ideological dimensions in A. Pagden, *Lords of all the
World: Ideologies of Empire in Spain, Britain and France, c.1500 to c.1800* (New Haven,
1995). The political web of empire is explored widely in J. P. Greene, *Peripheries and
Center: Constitutional Development in the Extended Polities of the British Empire and the
United States, 1607–1788* (Athens, Georgia, 1986) and a particularly important aspect
of it in I. K. Steele, *Politics of Colonial Policy: The Board of Trade in Colonial Administration, 1696–1720* (Oxford, 1968).

General considerations of the relationships between the polities and peoples of the
British Isles include S. J. Connolly, R. A. Houston, and R. J. Morris (eds.), *Conflict,
Identity and Economic Development: Ireland and Scotland, 1600–1939* (Preston, 1995),
M. Hechter, *Internal Colonialism: The Celtic Fringe in British National Development,
1536–1766* (1975), and S. G. Ellis and S. Barber (eds.), *Conquest and Union: Fashioning
a British State, 1485–1725* (1995). A useful study of one aspect of Anglicization is
V. E. Durkacz, *The Decline of the Celtic Languages: A Study of Linguistic and Cultural
Conflict in Scotland, Wales and Ireland from the Reformation to the Twentieth Century*
(Edinburgh, 1983). There is no good study of Anglo-Welsh relations in this period,
though G. H. Jenkins, *The Foundation of Modern Wales: Wales, 1642–1780* (Oxford,
1987) and P. Jenkins, *The Making of a Ruling Class: The Glamorgan Gentry, 1640–1790*
(Cambridge, 1983) make many useful points.

There is a tendency to see Anglo-Scottish relations in this period exclusively in relation to the Union and Jacobitism. W. Ferguson, *Scotland's Relations with England: A
Survey to 1707* (Edinburgh, 1977) manages to adopt a broader perspective, often very
productively, as does N. T. Phillipson and R. Mitchison (eds.), *Scotland in the Age of
Improvement: Essays in Scottish History in the Eighteenth Century* (Edinburgh, 1970),
especially the essay by Mitchison. A very detailed study of resistance to the new regime
and the Glencoe massacre is P. Hopkins, *Glencoe and the End of the Highland War*
(Edinburgh, 1986). Much has been written on the Union. Both T. I. Rae (ed.), *The
Union of 1707: Its Impact on Scotland* (Glasgow, 1974) and J. Robertson (ed.), *A Union
for Empire: Political Thought and the British Union of 1707* (Cambridge, 1995) are good
introductions, and for the important economic background, see T. C. Smout, *Scottish
Trade on the Eve of Union 1660–1707* (Edinburgh, 1963). The government of Scotland
after the Union is considered in P. W. J. Riley, *The English Ministers and Scotland,
1707–1727* (1964) and J. S. Shaw, *The Management of Scottish Society, 1707–1764:
Power, Nobles, Lawyers, Edinburgh Agents and English Influences* (Edinburgh, 1983).

The wider consequences of Union are explored in different ways by C. Kidd, *Subverting Scotland's Past: Scottish Whig Historians and the Creation of an Anglo-British Identity, 1689–c.1830* (Cambridge, 1993), C. W. J. Withers, *Gaelic Scotland: The Transformation of a Culture Region* (1988), and of Jacobitism in B. Lenman, *The Jacobite Risings in Britain, 1689–1746* (2nd edn., Aberdeen, 1995) and A. I. Macinnes, *Clanship, Commerce and the House of Stuart, 1603–1788* (East Linton, 1996).

Good general histories of Ireland in this period and which, perforce, consider the English impact are T. W. Moody and W. E. Vaughan (eds.), *A New History of Ireland*, vol. 4. *Eighteenth-Century, 1691–1800* (Oxford, 1986) and T. Bartlett and D. Hayton (eds.), *Penal Era and Golden Age: Essays in Irish History, 1690–1800* (Belfast, 1979). An important, generally conceived, reinterpretation of the period is S. J. Connolly, *Religion, Law and Power: The Making of Protestant Ireland, 1660–1760* (Oxford, 1992). D. Hayton, 'From Barbarian to Burlesque: English Images of the Irish, c.1660–1750', *Irish Economic and Social History*, 15 (1988), pp. 5–31 provides an important backdrop for consideration of particular aspects of Ireland's experience of England, notably T. Bartlett, *The Fall and Rise of the Irish Nation: The Catholic Question, 1690–1830* (Dublin, 1992), L. M. Cullen, *Anglo-Irish Trade, 1660–1800* (Manchester, 1968), P. Kelly, 'The Irish Woollen Export Prohibition Act of 1699: Kearney Re-Visited', *Irish Economic and Social History*, 7 (1980), pp. 22–41, I. Victory, 'The Making of the 1720 Declaratory Act', in G. O'Brien (ed.), *Parliament, Politics and People: Essays in Eighteenth-Century Irish History* (1989), pp. 9–29, F. G. James, 'The Irish Lobby in the Early Eighteenth Century', *English Historical Review*, 81 (1966), pp. 543–57, and A. Goodwin, 'Wood's Halfpence', *English Historical Review*, 51 (1936), pp. 647–74.

The economic framework of the empire of trade is discussed by H. V. Bowen, *Elites, Enterprise, and the Making of the British Overseas Empire, 1688–1775* (1996) and P. J. Cain and A. G. Hopkins, 'Gentlemanly Capitalism and British Expansion Overseas, I: The Old Colonial System, 1688–1850', *Economic History Review*, 39 (1986), pp. 501–25. Works dealing with patterns of overseas trade are listed below for section 10, but J. J. McCusker and R. R. Menard, *The Economy of British America, 1607–1789* (Chapel Hill, 1985) and T. H. Breen, 'An Empire of Goods: The Anglicization of Colonial America, 1690–1776', *Journal of British Studies*, 25 (1986), pp. 467–99 are of general significance here. An excellent study of the physical infrastructure of empire is I. K. Steele, *The English Atlantic, 1675–1740: An Exploration of Communication and Community* (Oxford, 1986), which may be supplemented with K. G. Davies, *The North Atlantic World in the Seventeenth Century* (Minneapolis, 1974).

A huge literature now exists on the rise of the plantation economies of the West Indies and of the place of slavery and the slave trade within them. General discussions of the development of the economies of the Caribbean include D. Watts, *The West Indies: Patterns of Development, Culture and Environmental Change since 1492* (Cambridge, 1987) and R. S. Dunn, *Sugar and Slaves: The Rise of the Planter Class in the English West Indies, 1624–1713* (1973). Statistics of the slave trade are provided in D. Richardson, 'The Eighteenth-Century British Slave Trade: Estimates of its Volume and Coastal Distribution in Africa', *Research in Economic History*, 12 (1989), pp. 151–95 and D. Richardson, 'Slave Exports from West and West-Central Africa, 1700–1810: New Estimates of Volume and Distribution', *Journal of African History*, 30 (1989), pp. 1–22. K. G. Davies, *The Royal African Company* (1957) is the standard history of the major institution involved in the early slave trade and J. Thornton, *Africa and Africans in the Making of the Atlantic World, 1400–1800* (2nd edn., Cambridge, 1998) provides a context that has often been ignored. A scathing analysis of slavery is R. Blackburn, *The Making of New World Slavery: From the Baroque to the Modern 1492–1800* (1997), a more muted one H. Thomas, *The Slave Trade: The History of the Atlantic Slave Trade, 1440–1870* (1997). For the impact of West Indian experiences in England, see F. Shyllon, *Black People in Britain, 1555–1833* (1977) and J. Walvin, *Fruits of Empire: Exotic Produce and British Trade, 1660–1800* (Basingstoke, 1997). For piracy, not just in the Caribbean, see R. C. Ritchie's rich, *Captain Kidd and the War Against the Pirates* (Cambridge, Massachusetts, 1986).

There is an even larger literature surrounding colonial North America. For introductions, see W. F. Craven, *The Colonies in Transition, 1660–1713* (New York, 1968) and J. P. Greene and J. R. Pole (eds.), *Colonial British America: Essays in the New History of the Early Modern Era* (Baltimore, 1984), while J. Axtell, *The European and the Indian: Essays in the Ethnohistory of Colonial North America* (New York, 1981) and I. K. Steele, *Warpaths: Invasions of North America* (New York, 1994) provide introductions to the impact of colonists upon indigenous peoples. Particular connections across the Atlantic are discussed in D. H. Fischer, *Albion's Seed: Four British Folkways in America* (New York, 1989), L. W. Labaree, *Royal Government in America: A Study of the British Colonial System* (New Haven, 1930), A. G. Olson, *Making the Empire Work: London and American Interest Groups, 1690–1790* (Cambridge, Massachusetts, 1992), R. R. Johnson, *Adjustment to Empire: The New England Colonies, 1675–1715* (New Brunswick, NJ, 1981), C. Bridenbaugh, *Mitre and Sceptre: Transatlantic Faiths, Ideas, Personalities, and Politics, 1689–1775* (New York, 1962), and J. J. Malone, *Pine Trees and Politics: The Naval Stores and Forest Policy in Colonial New England, 1691–1775* (1964).

The spread of English and British interests between the capes of Good Hope and Horn is considered comparatively in H. Furber, *Rival Empires of Trade in the Orient, 1600–1800* (Minneapolis, 1976). P. Lawson, *The East India Company: A History* (Harlow, 1993) is a crisp introduction to the main agency in this expansion, but the definitive study is K. N. Chaudhuri, *The Trading World of Asia and the English East India Company, 1660–1760* (Cambridge, 1978)—L. S. Sutherland, *The East India Company in Eighteenth-Century Politics* (Oxford, 1952) is mainly concerned with the mid- and late eighteenth century. P. J. Thomas, *Mercantilism and the East India Trade* (1926) explores reactions to the growing trade and H. Horwitz, 'The East India Trade, the Politicians and the Constitution, 1689–1702', *Journal of British Studies*, 17 (1978), pp. 1–18 the political wrangles. G. Williams, *The Great South Seas: English Voyages and Encounters 1570–1750* (New Haven, 1997) is a rich exploration of an obsession.

9   THE POLITICAL WORLD OF QUEEN ANNE

The work of Geoffrey Holmes dominates the historiography of the politics of Queen Anne's reign. His *British Politics in the Age of Anne* (revised edn., 1987) is the single most important work on this period, his *The Trial of Dr Sacheverell* (1973) definitively explores the pivotal events of 1710, and his important essays have been collected together in *Politics, Religion and Society in England, 1679–1742* (1986). In its day G. M. Trevelyan, *England under Queen Anne*, 3 vols. (1930–4) enjoyed a similar stature, and for a compelling narrative it is still hard to beat.

W. A. Speck, *The Birth of Britain: A New Nation, 1700–1710* (Oxford, 1994) provides a recent review of the period, though its year-by-year arrangement is sometimes awkward and inelegant. A considerable literature on party politics is available—for general works, see those listed under section 5 above. R. Walcott, *English Politics in the Early Eighteenth Century* (Oxford, 1956) attempted to apply a 'Namierite' analysis to the period, but has convinced few scholars. Holmes explicitly refuted Walcott, but see also H. L. Snyder, 'Party Configurations in the Early Eighteenth-Century House of Commons', *Bulletin of the Institute of Historical Research*, 45 (1972), pp. 38–72, J. O. Richards, *Party Propaganda under Queen Anne: The General Elections of 1702–13* (Athens, Georgia, 1972), and W. A. Speck, *Tory and Whig: The Struggle in the Constituencies, 1701–1715* (1970), though much of this will soon be superseded by publication of the History of Parliament's 1690–1715 section on the House of Commons. Good essays may be found in C. Jones (ed.), *Britain in the First Age of Party, 1680–1750: Essays Presented to Geoffrey Holmes* (1987). Central to the conduct of politics in this period was its increasing scope and intensity. The growing role of the press in this is very successfully explored in J. A. Downie, *Robert Harley and the Press: Propaganda and Public Opinion in the Age of Swift and Defoe* (Cambridge, 1979) and W. A. Speck, 'Political Propaganda in Augustan England', *Transactions of the Royal Historical Society*, 5th series, 22 (1972), pp. 17–32, though see also M. Schonhorn, *Defoe's Politics: Parliament, Power, Kingship, and Robinson Crusoe* (Cambridge, 1991) and I. Higgins, *Swift's Politics: A Study in Disaffection* (Cambridge, 1994) for particular literary interventions. R. O. Bucholz, *The Augustan Court: Queen Anne and the Decline of Court Culture* (Stanford, 1993) shows in convincing detail the declining significance of the court.

Political manoeuvering may also be approached through biographies of the leading figures. E. Gregg, *Queen Anne* (1980) is wonderfully crafted, the best biography of a monarch in this period, and just as good is F. Harris, *A Passion for Government: The Life of Sarah Duchess of Marlborough* (Oxford, 1991), a study of her confidante. Godolphin has not yet been successfully brought to life by biographers, though best is R. A. Sundstrom, *Sidney Godolphin: Servant of the State* (Newark, Delaware, 1992). For the Duke of Marlborough and Harley, see sections 4 and 5 above and H. L. Snyder, 'Godolphin and Harley: A Study of their Partnership in Politics', *Huntington Library Quarterly*, 30 (1966–7), pp. 241–71. Bolingbroke's colourful life is well observed by H. T. Dickinson, *Bolingbroke* (1970). Also useful is H. Horwitz, *Revolution Politicks: The Career of Daniel Finch, Second Earl of Nottingham, 1647–1730* (Cambridge, 1968).

Key specific issues are discussed in J. Flaningham, 'The Occasional Conformity Controversy: Ideology and Party Politics, 1697–1711', *Journal of British Studies*, 17 (1977), pp. 38–62, H. T. Dickinson, 'The Poor Palatines and the Parties', *English Historical Review*, 82 (1967), pp. 464–85, B. W. Hill, 'The Change of Government and the "Loss of the City", 1710–1711', *Economic History Review*, 24 (1971), pp. 395–413, and D. C. Coleman, 'Politics and Economics in the Age of Anne: The Case of the Anglo-French Trade Treaty of 1713', in D. C. Coleman and A. H. John (eds.), *Trade, Government and Economy in Pre-Industrial England: Essays Presented to F. J. Fisher* (1976), pp. 187–211. The crucial last four years of Queen Anne, and the machinations over a Hanoverian succession or Jacobite restoration, are well explored in G. V. Bennett, 'English Jacobitism, 1710–1715: Myth and Reality', *Transactions of the Royal Historical Society*, 5th series, 32 (1982), pp. 137–51, D. Szechi, *Jacobitism and Tory Politics, 1710–1714* (Edinburgh, 1984), and E. Gregg, 'Was Queen Anne a Jacobite?', *History*, 57 (1972), pp. 358–75.

10   PROFITS, PROGRESS, AND PROJECTS

Only since about 1970 have historians paid much attention to patterns of consumption in this period. J. Thirsk, *Economic Policy and Projects: The Development of a Consumer Society in Early Modern England* (Oxford, 1978) was an early and successful foray, while L. Weatherill, *Consumer Behaviour and Material Culture in Britain 1660–1760* (2nd edn., 1996), C. Shammas, *The Pre-Industrial Consumer in England and America* (Oxford, 1990), and P. J. Bowden, 'Agricultural Prices, Wages, Farm Profits, and Rents', in J. Thirsk (ed.), *The Agrarian History of England and Wales*, vol. 5. *1640–1750*, pt. 2, *Agrarian Change* (Cambridge, 1985), 1–118 provide masses of information. J. Brewer and R. Porter (eds.), *Consumption and the World of Goods* (1993) has many stimulating essays.

Broad patterns of overseas trade have been expertly set out by R. Davis in 'English Foreign Trade, 1660–1700', *Economic History Review*, 7 (1954), pp. 150–66 and 'English Foreign Trade, 1700–1774', *Economic History Review*, 15 (1962), pp. 285–303—though see also J. J. McCusker, 'The Current Value of English Exports, 1697 to 1800', *William and Mary Quarterly*, 3rd series, 28 (1971), pp. 607–28. Davis's essays, and others, have been usefully brought together in W. E. Minchinton (ed.), *The Growth of English Overseas Trade in the Seventeenth and Eighteenth Centuries* (1969). R. Davis, *The Rise of the English Shipping Industry in the Seventeenth and Eighteenth Centuries* (1962) is the standard work, while good explorations of the nature of overseas enterprise include K. Morgan, *Bristol and the Atlantic Trade in the Eighteenth Century* (Cambridge, 1993), J. M. Price and P. G. E. Clemens, 'A Revolution of Scale in Overseas Trade: British Firms in the Chesapeake Trade, 1675–1775', *Journal of Economic History*, 47 (1987), pp. 1–43, and J. M. Price, 'What Did Merchants Do? Reflections on British Overseas Trade, 1660–1790', *Journal of Economic History*, 49 (1989), pp. 267–84.

A number of leading industries have their specific histories, including J. de L. Mann, *The Cloth Industry in the West of England from 1640 to 1880* (Oxford, 1971), A. P. Wadsworth and J. de L. Mann, *The Cotton Trade and Industrial Lancashire, 1600–1780* (Manchester, 1965), J. Hatcher, *The History of the British Coal Industry*, vol. 1. *Before 1700: Towards the Age of Coal* (Oxford, 1993), M. W. Flinn, *The History of the British Coal Industry*, vol. 2. *1700–1830: The Industrial Revolution* (Oxford, 1984),

C. K. Hyde, *Technological Change and the British Iron Industry, 1700–1870* (Princeton, 1977), and P. Mathias, *The Brewing Industry in England, 1700–1830* (Cambridge, 1959). All are definitive.

Attempts to explain the patterns of industrial growth and decay in this period have concentrated on the dynamics of the rural domestic system. Older but still highly valuable accounts are D. C. Coleman, *The Domestic System in Industry* (1960) and J. Thirsk, 'Industries in the Countryside', in F. J. Fisher (ed.), *Essays in the Economic and Social History of Tudor and Stuart England in Honour of R. H. Tawney* (Cambridge, 1961), pp. 70–88. More recently industrial change has been explored within the conceptual framework of 'proto-industrialization'. This literature is well surveyed in L. A. Clarkson, *Proto-Industrialization: The First Phase of Industrialization?* (Basingstoke, 1985) and placed in a wider context in S. C. Ogilvie and M. Cerman, *European Proto-Industrialization* (Cambridge, 1996). Proto-industrialization has emphasized the regional nature of economic dynamics, good case studies of which include J. D. Chambers, 'The Vale of Trent, 1670–1800: A Regional Study of Economic Change', *Economic History Review Supplement*, 3 (1957), D. G. Hey, 'A Dual Economy in South Yorkshire', *Agricultural History Review*, 17 (1969), pp. 108–19, W. H. B. Court, *The Rise of the Midland Industries* (Oxford, 1953), and M. B. Rowlands, *Masters and Men in the West Midland Metalware Trades before the Industrial Revolution* (Manchester, 1975).

The nature of business enterprise in this period has been addressed in a rather fragmented way. There is some useful material in P. Earle, *The Making of the English Middle Class: Business, Society and Family Life in London, 1660–1730* (1989) and masses of it in R. Grassby, *The Business Community of Seventeenth-Century England* (Cambridge, 1995). For a study of the problems faced, see J. Hoppit, *Risk and Failure in English Business, 1700–1800* (Cambridge, 1987). The mania for projecting is explored in a number of works. Good introductions are K. G. Davies, 'Joint-Stock Investment in the Later Seventeenth Century', *Economic History Review*, 4 (1952), pp. 283–301 and C. MacLeod, 'The 1690s Patent Boom: Invention or Stock-Jobbing?', *Economic History Review*, 39 (1986), pp. 549–71. More detailed studies include, pre-eminently and exhaustingly, W. R. Scott, *The Constitution and Finance of English, Scottish and Irish Joint-Stock Companies to 1720*, 3 vols. (Cambridge, 1910–12) and statistically L. Neal, *The Rise of Financial Capitalism: International Capital Markets in the Age of Reason* (Cambridge, 1990). Inventing activity is expertly studied in C. MacLeod, *Inventing the Industrial Revolution: The English Patent System, 1660–1800* (Cambridge, 1988). The standard account of the mania of 1720 is J. Carswell, *The South Sea Bubble* (revised edn., Stroud, 1993), though also valuable is J. G. Sperling, *The South Sea Company: An Historical Essay and Bibliographical Finding List* (Boston, Massachusetts, 1962).

Projecting needs to be set in the context of the nature of contemporary financial markets. Historians have increasingly come to appreciate the ubiquity and wider significance of locally organized credit. B. A. Holderness, 'Credit in English Rural Society before the Nineteenth Century, with Special Reference to the Period, 1650–1720', *Agricultural History Review*, 24 (1976), pp. 97–109 was an important study, but best is C. Muldrew, *The Economy of Obligation: The Culture of Credit and Social Relations in Early Modern England* (Basingstoke, 1998), a book of very wide significance. The rise of financial services is explored in A. H. John, 'The London Assurance Company and the Marine Insurance Market of the Eighteenth Century', *Economica*, 25 (1958), 126–41 and B. Supple, *The Royal Exchange Assurance: A History of British Insurance, 1720–1970* (Cambridge, 1970).

The fabric of the internal service economy is ably surveyed in J. A. Chartres, *Internal Trade in England, 1500–1700* (1977). Important detailed studies of distribution include R. B. Westerfield, *Middlemen in English Business Particularly between 1660 and 1760* (New Haven, 1915) and J. A. Chartres, 'The Marketing of Agriculture Produce', in J. Thirsk (ed.), *The Agrarian History of England and Wales*, vol. 5. *1640–1750*, pt. 2. *Agrarian Change* (Cambridge, 1985), pp. 406–502. Infrastructural arrangements can be approached through T. Barker and D. Gerhold, *The Rise and Rise of Road Transport, 1700–1990* (Basingstoke, 1993), D. Hey, *Packmen, Carriers and Packhorse Roads: Trade and Communications in North Derbyshire and South Yorkshire* (Leicester, 1980), E. Pawson, *Transport and Economy: The Turnpike Roads of Eighteenth Century Britain* (1977), W. Albert, *The Turnpike Road System in England, 1663–1840* (Cambridge, 1972), D. Gerhold, 'The Growth of the London Carrying Trade, 1681–1838', *Economic History Review*, 41 (1988), pp. 392–410, D. Gerhold, 'Packhorses and Wheeled Vehicles in England, 1550–1800', *Journal of Transport History*, 14 (1993), pp. 1–26, T. S. Willan, *The English Coasting Trade, 1600–1750* (Manchester, 1938), T. S. Willan, *River Navigation in England, 1600–1750* (Oxford, 1936), and D. Swann, 'The Pace and Progress of Port Investment in England, 1660–1830', *Yorkshire Bulletin of Economic and Social Research*, 12 (1960), pp. 32–44. The flow of information is discussed in J. J. McCusker, 'The Business Press in England before 1775', *The Library*, 8 (1986), pp. 205–31, F. Staff, *The Penny Post, 1680–1918* (1964), B. Austen, *English Provincial Posts, 1633–1840: A Study Based on Kent Examples* (Chichester, 1978), and K. Ellis, *The Post Office in the Eighteenth Century: A Study in Administrative History* (Oxford, 1958).

The impact of the State on the economy has most frequently been addressed by relation to the anachronistic concept of 'mercantilism'—for which see section 6 above. Detailed aspects are considered in L. Harper, *The English Navigation Laws: A Seventeenth Century Experiment in Social Engineering* (New York, 1939), E. S. Furniss, *The Position of the Laborer in a System of Nationalism* (Boston, Massachusetts, 1920), and R. Davis, 'The Rise of Protection in England, 1689–1786', *Economic History Review*, 19 (1966), pp. 306–17. L. Davison, T. Hitchcock, T. Keirn, and R. B. Shoemaker (eds.), *Stilling the Grumbling Hive: The Response to Social and Economic Problems in England, 1689–1750* (Stroud, 1992) has some important essays and S. Handley, 'Local Legislative Initiatives for Economic and Social Development in Lancashire, 1689–1731', *Parliamentary History*, 9 (1990), pp. 14–37 is a good close study.

II THE WEALTH OF THE COUNTRY

Rural England is expertly, extendedly, and somewhat minutely surveyed in J. Thirsk (ed.), *The Agrarian History of England and Wales*, vol. 5. *1640–1750* (2 parts, Cambridge, 1984–5). The pace of agricultural change is estimated in R. V. Jackson, 'Growth and Deceleration in English Agriculture, 1660–1790' *Economic History Review*, 38 (1985), pp. 333–51 and important essays are brought together in J. Thirsk, *The Rural Economy of England: Collected Essays* (1984), E. L. Jones (ed.), *Agriculture and Economic Growth in England, 1650–1815* (1967), and E. L. Jones, *Agriculture and the Industrial Revolution* (Oxford, 1974). A more recent general account is provided by M. Overton, *Agricultural Revolution in England: The Transformation of the Agrarian Economy, 1500–1850* (Cambridge, 1996), which though reasonably brief is dense. R. A. Dodgshon and R. A. Butlin (eds.), *An Historical Geography of England and Wales* (2nd edn., 1990) is an easier introduction. An inventive if technical work, adopting a bird's eye view, is A. Kussmaul, *A General View of the Rural Economy of England, 1538–1840* (Cambridge, 1990). An important attempt to delineate the chronology of enclosure is J. R. Wordie, 'The Chronology of English Enclosure, 1500–1914', *Economic History Review*, 36 (1983), pp. 483–505 and good explanations of patterns of enclosure include J. A. Yelling, *Common Field and Enclosure in England, 1450–1850* (1977), R. C. Allen, *Enclosure and the Yeoman: The Agricultural Development of the South Midlands, 1450–1850* (Oxford, 1992), and J. M. Neeson, *Commoners: Common Right, Enclosure and Social Change in England, 1700–1820* (Cambridge, 1993).

For landed society in general, J. V. Beckett, *The Aristocracy in England, 1660–1914* (Oxford, 1987) and G. E. Mingay, *English Landed Society in the Eighteenth Century* (1963) explore the upper reaches conventionally and effectively, while J. M. Rosenheim, *The Emergence of a Ruling Order: English Landed Society, 1650–1750* (Harlow, 1998) adopts thought-provoking new perspectives. J. Habakkuk, *Marriage, Debt, and the Estates System: English Landownership, 1650–1950* (Oxford, 1994) is a monument to a lifetime of thinking, research, and writing about landownership, though it is not for the faint-hearted. L. Bonfield, *Marriage Settlements, 1601–1740: The Adoption of the Strict Settlement* (Cambridge, 1983) considers an earlier thesis advanced by Habakkuk, while other issues are reviewed in J. V. Beckett, 'English Landownership in the Later Seventeenth and Eighteenth Centuries: The Debate and the Problems', *Economic History Review*, 30 (1977), pp. 567–81. Estate management is considered in D. R. Hainsworth, *Stewards, Lords and People: The Estate Steward and his World in Later Stuart England* (Cambridge, 1992). Good case studies of landowners include R. A. C. Parker, *Coke of Norfolk: A Financial and Agricultural Study, 1707–1842* (Oxford, 1975), J. M. Rosenheim, *The Townshends of Raynham: Nobility in Transition in Restoration and Early Hanoverian England* (Middletown, 1989), O. R. F. Davies, 'The Wealth and Influence of John Holles, Duke of Newcastle 1694–1711', *Renaissance and Modern Studies*, 9 (1965), pp. 22–46, and J. V. Beckett, *Coal and Tobacco: The Lowthers and the Economic Development of West Cumberland, 1660–1760* (Cambridge, 1981).

Considerable ink has been spilt on the question of the extent of mobility into the elite (very much less on exiting). L. and J. C. F. Stone, *An Open Elite? England, 1540–1880* (Oxford, 1984) is important, impressive, but far from convincing. It might usefully be placed alongside the careful regional analysis of P. Roebuck, *Yorkshire Baronets, 1640–1750: Families, Estates and Fortunes* (Hull, 1980). An excellent study of one example of upward social mobility is provided in C. G. A. Clay, 'Henry Hoare, Banker, his Family, and the Stourhead Estate', in F. M. L. Thompson (ed.), *Landowners,*

Capitalists, and Entrepreneurs: Essays for Sir John Habakkuk (Oxford, 1994), pp. 113–38, a more detailed one in C. H. C. and M. I. Baker, *The Life and Circumstances of James Brydges, First Duke of Chandos* (Oxford, 1949).

Little work has been done upon the precise nature of the 'landed interest', but both J. M. Rosenheim, 'Country Governance and Elite Withdrawal in Norfolk, 1660–1720', in A. L. Beier, D. Cannadine, and J. M. Rosenheim (eds.), *The First Modern Society: Essays in English History in Honour of Lawrence Stone* (Cambridge, 1989) and E. A. Wasson, 'The House of Commons, 1660–1945: Parliamentary Families and the Political Elite', *English Historical Review*, 106 (1991), pp. 635–51 are highly suggestive. The political economy of agriculture may be approached through D. G. Barnes, *A History of the English Corn Laws from 1660–1846* (1930), D. Ormrod, *English Grain Exports and the Structure of Agrarian Capitalism, 1700–1760* (Hull, 1985), and A. H. John, 'English Agricultural Improvement and Grain Exports, 1660–1765', in D. C. Coleman and A. H. John (eds.), *Trade, Government, and Economy in Pre-Industrial England: Essays Presented to F. J. Fisher* (1976), pp. 45–67.

There is a huge literature on the homes and gardens of England's elite. A good brief introduction to the former is provided by J. Summerson, *Architecture in Britain, 1530–1830* (8th edn., Harmondsworth, 1991), which has been partly overtaken by G. Worsley, *Classical Architecture in Britain: The Heroic Age* (New Haven, 1995). A not totally convincing attempt to chart the chronology of house building is provided in R. Machin, 'The Great Rebuilding: A Reassessment', *Past and Present*, no. 77 (1977), pp. 33–56. A brilliant exploration of one great creation is C. S. Smith, *The Building of Castle Howard* (1990). The definitive reference work for architects is H. M. Colvin, *A Biographical Dictionary of British Architects, 1600–1840* (3rd edn., New Haven, 1995) and good studies of particular architects include K. Downes, *The Architecture of Wren* (1982), J. Summerson, *Sir Christopher Wren* (1953), K. Downes, *Sir John Vanbrugh: A Biography* (1987), and M. I. Wilson, *William Kent: Architect, Designer, Painter, Gardener, 1685–1748* (1984). Standard accounts of baroque architecture are K. Downes, *English Baroque Architecture* (1966) and J. Lees-Milne, *English Country Houses: Baroque, 1685–1715* (1970), and of the rise of Palladianism J. Harris, *The Palladian Revival: Lord Burlington, his Villa and Garden at Chiswick* (New Haven, 1994) and R. Wittkower, *Palladio and English Palladianism* (1974). E. Harris, *British Architectural Books and Writers, 1556–1785* (Cambridge, 1990) discusses an important aspect of the spread of architectural ideas. The decorative arts can be explored via G. Beard, *The Work of Grinling Gibbons* (1989), E. Croft-Murray, *Decorative Painting in England, 1537–1837*, 2 vols. (1962–70), and C. S. Smith, *Eighteenth-Century Decoration: Design and Domestic Interior in England* (1993).

H. Prince, *Parks in England* (Newport, Isle of Wight, 1967) provides a context within which to explore changes in gardening. J. Dixon Hunt and P. Willis, *The Genius of the Place: The English Landscape Garden, 1620–1820* (1975) collects together many interesting contemporary views of gardening, showing the evolution of tastes. Good assessments of more formal gardens include D. Jacques and A. J. van der Horst (eds.), *The Gardens of William and Mary* (1988) and D. Green, *Gardener to Queen Anne: Henry Wise, 1653–1738 and the Formal Garden* (1956). The development of landscape gardening is considered in T. Williamson, *Polite Landscapes: Gardens and Society in Eighteenth-Century England* (Baltimore, 1995), C. Hussey, *English Gardens and Landscapes, 1700–1750* (1967), D. Chambers, *The Planters of the English Landscape Garden: Botany, Trees, and the Georgics* (New Haven, 1993), P. Martin, *Pursuing Innocent Pleasures: The Gardening World of Alexander Pope* (Hamden, 1984), P. Willis, *Charles Bridgeman and the English Landscape Garden* (1977), J. Dixon Hunt, *William Kent Landscape Garden Designer: An Assessment and Catalogue of his Designs* (1987), and J. Dixon Hunt, *Garden and Grove: The Italian Renaissance Garden in the English Imagination, 1600–1750* (1986).

Rural sociability is put in a general context in D. Brailsford, *Sport and Society: Elizabeth to Anne* (1969). There is no good modern history of the rise of horseracing, so see J. C. Whyte, *History of the British Turf, from the Earliest Period to the Present Day*, 2 vols. (1840). The game laws and hunting, on the other hand, have been well studied, especially in P. B. Munsche, *Gentlemen and Poachers: The English Game Laws, 1671–1831* (Cambridge, 1981). S. Deuchar, *Sporting Art in Eighteenth-Century England: A Social and Political History* (New Haven, 1988) successfully looks at the ways the elite came to have its sporting endeavours visually rendered.

12 THE POLITICAL WORLD OF GEORGE I

The political world of George I has attracted relatively little attention from historians and traditional interpretations frequently still hold the high ground. Pre-eminent among general accounts are the two volumes by W. Michael, *England under George I: The Beginnings of the Hanoverian Dynasty* (2nd edn., 1936) and *England under George I: The Quadruple Alliance* (1939), though much brisker is J. H. Plumb, *The Growth of Political Stability in England, 1675–1725* (1967). J. Cannon (ed.), *The Whig Ascendancy: Colloquies on Hanoverian England* (1981) lacks a cutting edge, but J. C. D. Clark, 'A General Theory of Party, Opposition and Government, 1688–1832', *Historical Journal*, 23 (1980), pp. 295–325 is much sharper.

The standard life of the King is R. Hatton, *George I: Elector and King* (1978), though even it struggles to bring his time in England to life. J. Beattie, *The English Court in the Reign of George I* (Cambridge, 1967) is an important study. A major consequence of the Hanoverian succession is explored in W. A. Speck, 'The General Election of 1715', *English Historical Review*, 90 (1975), pp. 507–22 and for the Jacobite rising (in addition to works already cited in sections 2 and 8), see N. Rogers, 'Popular Protest in Early Hanoverian London', *Past and Present*, no. 79 (1978), pp. 70–100, C. Petrie, *The Jacobite Movement* (3rd edn., 1959), A. N. Tayler and H. Tayler, *1715: The Story of the Rising* (London and Edinburgh, 1936), G. H. Jones, *The Mainstream of Jacobitism* (Cambridge, Massachusetts, 1954), J. Baynes, *The Jacobite Rising of 1715* (1970), and P. Fritz, *The English Ministers and Jacobitism between the Rebellions of 1715 and 1745* (Toronto, 1975). There is no good modern life of the Old Pretender.

The fortunes of the Whigs are often best approached through studies of their leaders. For George's favourite, see B. Williams, *Stanhope: A Study in Eighteenth-Century War and Diplomacy* (Oxford, 1932). There is no good printed life of the 3rd Earl of

Sunderland, so see the unpublished G. M. Townend, 'The Political Career of Charles Spencer, Third Earl of Sunderland, 1695–1722', Ph.D. thesis (University of Edinburgh, 1985). The major biography of Walpole is by J. H. Plumb, *Sir Robert Walpole: The Making of a Statesman* (1956) and *Sir Robert Walpole: The King's Minister* (1960), though for a succinct and balanced introduction, see H. T. Dickinson, *Walpole and the Whig Supremacy* (1973). See also B. Williams, *Carteret and Newcastle: A Contrast in Contemporaries* (Cambridge, 1943) for other leading Whigs. For particular aspects of the Whig split of 1717–20, see J. J. Murray, *George I, the Baltic and the Whig Split of 1717* (Chicago and London, 1969), C. Jones, ' "Venice Preserv'd; or a Plot Discovered": The Political and Social Context of the Peerage Bill of 1719', in C. Jones (ed.), *A Pillar of the Constitution: The House of Lords in British Politics, 1640–1784* (1989), pp. 79–112, and J. F. Naylor (ed.), *The British Aristocracy and the Peerage Bill of 1719* (New York, 1968).

Walpole's premiership can be explored through the biographies listed above. A very good brief analysis of his career is S. J. C. Taylor, 'Robert Walpole, First Earl of Orford', in R. Eccleshall and G. Walker (eds.), *Biographical Dictionary of British Prime Ministers* (1998), pp. 1–14. Walpole's use of the Jacobite card is discussed in G. V. Bennett, 'Jacobitism and the Rise of Walpole', in N. McKendrick (ed.), *Historical Perspectives: Studies in English Thought and Society* (1974), pp. 70–92. J. Black (ed.), *Britain in the Age of Walpole* (Basingstoke, 1984) has its moments, but some of the essays skate on the surface of the issues. N. Rogers, 'The City Elections Act (1725) Reconsidered', *English Historical Review*, 100 (1985), pp. 604–17 looks at an important attempt to increase Whig control over a potentially serious source of opposition. The ideological case of the Whig oligarchy is examined in R. Browning, *Political and Constitutional Ideas of the Court Whigs* (Baton Rouge, 1982) and T. Horne, 'Politics in a Corrupt Society: William Arnall's Defense of Robert Walpole', *Journal of the History of Ideas*, 41 (1980), pp. 601–14.

Opposition to the Whig supremacy needs first to consider the fortunes of the Tories, for which L. Colley, *In Defiance of Oligarchy: The Tory Party, 1714–1760* (Cambridge, 1982) is now the standard account, though it has not gone unchallenged, not least by E. Cruickshanks' reassertion of the case she helped to assemble in the so-called 'official history' of R. Sedgwick (ed.), *The History of Parliament: The House of Commons, 1715–1754*, 2 vols. (1970). G. V. Bennett, *The Tory Crisis in Church and State: The Career of Francis Atterbury, Bishop of Rochester* (Oxford, 1975) is a wonderful study of a leading Tory. General discussions of opposition to the Whigs include A. S. Foord, *His Majesty's Opposition, 1714–1830* (Oxford, 1964), C. B. Realey, *The Early Opposition to Sir Robert Walpole, 1720–1727* (Lawrence, 1931), W. T. Laprade, *Public Opinion and Politics in Eighteenth Century England to the Fall of Walpole* (New York, 1936), A. J. Henderson, *London and the National Government, 1721–1742: A Study of City Politics and the Walpole Administration* (Durham, North Carolina, 1945), and N. C. Hunt, *Two Early Political Associations: The Quakers and the Dissenting Deputies in the Age of Sir Robert Walpole* (Oxford, 1961). Much can be discerned by exploring the career of Bolingbroke, for which, see H. T. Dickinson, *Bolingbroke* (1970), Q. Skinner, 'The Principles and Practice of Opposition: The Case of Bolingbroke vs. Walpole', in

N. McKendrick (ed.), *Historical Perspectives: Studies in English Thought and Society in Honour of J. H. Plumb* (1974), pp. 93–128, and I. Kramnick, *Bolingbroke and his Circle: The Politics of Nostalgia in the Age of Walpole* (Cambridge, Massachusetts, 1968). Attacks from the world of letters are considered in B. A. Goldgar, *Walpole and the Wits: The Relation of Politics to Literature, 1722–1742* (Lincoln, Nebraska and London, 1976).

The significance of extra-parliamentary opposition is considered in general terms in H. Horwitz, 'Party in a Civic Context: London from the Exclusion Crisis to the Fall of Walpole', in C. Jones (ed.), *Britain in the First Age of Party 1680–1750: Essays Presented to Geoffrey Holmes* (1987), pp. 173–94. The best detailed work has been undertaken by N. Rogers, especially in his books *Whigs and Cities: Popular Politics in the Age of Walpole and Pitt* (Oxford, 1989) and *Crowds, Culture, and Politics in Georgian Britain* (Oxford, 1998). Some additional points are made in K. Wilson, *The Sense of the People: Politics, Culture and Imperialism in England, 1715–1785* (Cambridge, 1995), though its interests largely lie after 1730.

13   URBAN AND URBANE

An excellent introduction to the urban scene in this period is P. J. Corfield, *The Impact of English Towns, 1700–1800* (Oxford, 1982), though with regard to small settlements it should be supplemented with P. Clark, 'Small Towns in England, 1550–1850: National and Regional Population Trends', in P. Clark (ed.), *Small Towns in Early Modern Europe* (Cambridge, 1995), pp. 90–120—and for the wider European context see J. de Vries, *European Urbanization, 1500–1800* (1984). A very important interpretation of urban social and cultural developments is P. Borsay, *The English Urban Renaissance: Culture and Society in the Provincial Town, 1660–1770* (Oxford, 1989). Some important essays are brought together in P. Clark (ed.), *The Transformation of English Provincial Towns, 1600–1800* (1984) and P. Borsay (ed.), *The Eighteenth Century Town: A Reader in English Urban History, 1688–1820* (Harlow, 1990). R. S. Neale, *Bath: A Social History, 1680–1850* (1981) investigates an especially significant case of urban growth.

The standard work on the capital is still M. D. George, *London Life in the Eighteenth Century* (1925), though it is very much concerned with social experiences amongst the poorer sections. The contrast with another classic, J. Summerson, *Georgian London* (1945), preoccupied as it is with architectural matters, is marked. The important question of London's demography is minutely considered in J. Landers, *Death and the Metropolis: Studies in the Demographic History of London, 1670–1830* (Cambridge, 1993). Working patterns are assessed in P. Earle, *A City Full of People: Men and Women of London, 1650–1750* (1994). Some important essays on all these themes may be found in A. L. Beier and R. Finlay (eds.), *London, 1500–1700: The Making of the Metropolis* (Harlow, 1986). Contemporary responses to the energy and chaos of London are examined in M. Byrd, *London Transformed: Images of the City in the Eighteenth Century* (New Haven, 1978). For browsing through a mass of information there is nothing to beat a few minutes here and there with B. Weinreb and C. Hibbert (eds.), *The London Encyclopaedia* (1983). A stimulating attempt to provide a framework within which to consider London's importance is E. A. Wrigley, 'A Simple Model of London's Importance in Changing English Society and Economy, 1650–1750', *Past and Present*, no. 37 (1965), pp. 44–70.

The changing world of male urban sociability can be approached through R. J. Allen, *The Clubs of Augustan London* (Cambridge, Massachusetts, 1933), A. Ellis, *The Penny Universities: A History of the Coffee-Houses* (1956), D. Knoop and G. P. Jones, *The Genesis of Freemasonry: An Account of the Rise and Development of Freemasonry in its Operative, Accepted, and Early Speculative Phases* (Manchester, 1947), M. C. Jacob, *The Radical Enlightenment: Pantheists, Freemasons and Republicans* (1981), and C. Kerby-Miller (ed.), *Memoirs of the Extraordinary Life, Works, and Discoveries of Martinus Scriblerus* (New Haven, 1950). An aspect of the rakish extreme of such developments is uncovered in D. Statt, 'The Case of the Mohocks: Rake Violence in Augustan London', *Social History*, 20 (1995), pp. 179–99.

The continuing significance of patronage to the arts is generally explored in M. Foss, *The Age of Patronage: The Arts in Society, 1660–1750* (1971), while specific aspects are discussed in D. Griffin, *Literary Patronage in England, 1650–1800* (Cambridge, 1996), R. McGuiness, *English Court Odes, 1660–1820* (Oxford, 1971), L. D. Mitchell, 'Command Performances during the Reign of George I', *Eighteenth Century Studies*, 7 (1974), pp. 343–9, and E. Kemper Broadus, *The Laureateship: A Study of the Office of Poet Laureate in England with Some Account of the Poets* (Oxford, 1921). The growing force of a widening consumption of pleasure are considered with characteristic insight, if a little flabbily, in J. Brewer, *The Pleasures of the Imagination: English Culture in the Eighteenth Century* (1997). Many important essays can be found in J. Brewer and A. Bermingham (eds.), *The Consumption of Culture, 1600–1800: Image, Object, Text* (1995), though R. Porter and M. Mulvey Roberts (eds.), *Pleasure in the Eighteenth Century* (Basingstoke, 1996) is much more modest. For an excellent brief discussion of the philosophical and aesthetic environment surrounding the pleasures of the imagination, see J. Sambrook, *The Eighteenth Century: The Intellectual and Cultural Context of English Literature, 1700–1789* (Harlow, 1986)—Pat Rogers, *The Augustan Vision* (1974) is also useful.

Mountains of words have been heaped upon English literature in this period, only a few prominent landmarks of which can be given here. Standard surveys are provided by J. Sutherland, *English Literature of the Late Seventeenth Century* (Oxford, 1969), B. Dobrée, *English Literature in the Early Eighteenth Century, 1700–1740* (Oxford, 1959), and S. N. Zwicker (ed.), *The Cambridge Companion to English Literature, 1650–1740* (Cambridge, 1998), though many of the lines of discussion were established by A. Beljame, *Men of Letters and the English Public in the Eighteenth Century: 1660–1714, Dryden, Addison, and Pope*, ed. B. Dobrée, trans. E. O. Lorimer (1948). The world of Mr Spectator is set out in E. A. and L. D. Bloom, *Joseph Addison's Sociable Animal: In the Market Place, on the Hustings, in the Pulpit* (Providence, 1971), of fables in J. E. Lewis, *The English Fable: Aesop and Literary Culture, 1651–1740* (Cambridge, 1996), of satire in P. K. Elkin, *The Augustan Defence of Satire* (Oxford, 1973), and of narratives in J. J. Richetti, *Popular Fiction before Richardson: Narrative Patterns, 1700–1739*

(2nd edn., Oxford, 1992) and Pat Rogers, *Literature and Popular Culture in Eighteenth Century England* (Brighton, 1985).

Authorial output needs, of course, to be related to rapid changes afoot in the world of publishing (see above, section 6). For the era after the Glorious Revolution a wonderfully researched and realized study is P. Rogers, *Grub Street: Studies in a Sub-culture* (1972), while H. M. Geduld, *Prince of Publishers: A Study of the Work and Career of Jacob Tonson* (Bloomington, 1969) provides an effective study of the leading publisher of the period. Recently much attention has been devoted to the prominent part women played as readers and writers in this period. A selection of the best works includes C. Barash, *English Women's Poetry, 1649–1714: Politics, Community, and Linguistic Authority* (Oxford, 1996), J. Todd, *The Sign of Angellica: Women, Writing, and Fiction, 1660–1800* (1989), J. Todd (ed.), *A Dictionary of British and American Women Writers, 1660–1800* (1984), K. Shevelow, *Women and Print Culture: The Construction of Femininity in the Early Periodical* (1989), and C. Turner, *Living by the Pen: Women Writers in the Eighteenth Century* (1992).

The major literary figures have been well served by biographers. Standard (if often bulky) works are P. Smithers, *The Life of Joseph Addison* (2nd edn., Oxford, 1968), L. M. Beattie, *John Arbuthnot, Mathematician and Satirist* (Cambridge, Massachusetts, 1935), J. C. Hodges, *William Congreve, the Man* (New York, 1942), P. R. Backscheider, *Daniel Defoe: His Life* (Baltimore, 1989), A. J. Murphy, *John Dennis* (Boston, Massachusetts, 1984), J. A. Winn, *John Dryden and his World* (New Haven, 1987), E. Rothstein, *George Farquahar* (1967), D. Nokes, *John Gay: A Profession of Friendship* (Oxford, 1995), I. Grundy, *Lady Mary Wortley Montagu: Comet of the Enlightenment* (Oxford, 1999), M. Mack, *Alexander Pope: A Life* (New Haven, 1985), C. K. Eves, *Matthew Prior, Poet and Diplomatist* (New York, 1939), G. A. Aitken, *The Life of Richard Steele*, 2 vols. (1889), I. Ehrenpreis, *Swift: The Man, his Works and the Age*, 3 vols. (1962–83), and D. Nokes, *Jonathan Swift: A Hypocrite Reversed* (Oxford, 1985).

The stage must be approached from several directions, not simply from that of high culture. An excellent discussion of a major development is T. Castle, *Masquerade and Civilization: The Carnivalesque in Eighteenth-Century English Culture and Fiction* (1986), while C. L. Day (ed.), *The Songs of Thomas D'Urfey* (Cambridge, Massachusetts, 1933) looks at one of the most popular producers for the stage. S. Rosenfeld, *The Theatre of the London Fairs in the Eighteenth Century* (Cambridge, 1960) shows the ways in which the stage was occasionally part of the street culture of the time. Good general works on the theatre include J. Loftis, *The Politics of Drama in Augustan England* (Oxford, 1963), J. Loftis, *Comedy and Society from Congreve to Fielding* (Stanford, 1959), R. D. Hume, *The Development of English Drama in the Late Seventeenth Century* (Oxford, 1976), and S. Rosenfeld, *Strolling Players and Drama in the Provinces 1660–1765* (Cambridge, 1939). The canonization of Shakespeare is discussed in M. Dobson, *The Making of the National Poet, Shakespeare, Adaptation, and Authorship, 1660–1769* (Oxford, 1992) and T. D. Hume, 'Before the Bard: "Shakespeare" in Early Eighteenth-Century London', *ELH*, 64 (1997), pp. 41–76. What was actually performed can be explored through the wonderfully rich, if still not entirely comprehensive, *The London Stage, 1660–1800: A calendar of Plays, Entertainments and Afterpieces* (5 parts, Carbondale, 1960–8), part 1

1660–1700, ed. W. van Lennep (1965), part 2 1700–1729, ed. E. L. Avery (2 vols. 1960). A good study of a particular theatre is J. Milhous, *Thomas Betterton and the Management of Lincoln's Inn Fields, 1695–1708* (Carbondale, 1979).

Much of the history of music in this period has concentrated upon studies of either eminent composers or the craze for opera. For the former, see M. Burden, *Purcell Remembered* (1995), F. B. Zimmerman, *Henry Purcell, 1659–1695: His Life and Times* (2nd edn., Philadelphia, 1983), O. E. Deutsch, *Handel: A Documentary Biography* (1955), W. Dean and J. M. Knapp, *Handel's Operas, 1704–1726* (revised edn., Oxford, 1995), and D. Burrows (ed.), *The Cambridge Companion to Handel* (Cambridge, 1997). For opera, E. W. White, *The Rise of English Opera* (1951) is a general account and E. Gibson, *The Royal Academy of Music, 1719–1728: The Institution and its Directors* (New York and London, 1989), R. D. Hume, 'The Sponsorship of Opera in London, 1704–1720', *Modern Philology*, 85 (1988), pp. 420–32, and J. Milhous, 'Opera Finances in London, 1674–1738', *Journal of the American Musicological Society*, 37 (1984), pp. 567–92 important particular studies. Good studies setting music in a wider social setting are W. Weber, *The Rise of Musical Classics in Eighteenth-Century England: A Study in Canon, Ritual, and Ideology* (Oxford, 1992), J. Harley, *Music in Purcell's London: The Social Background* (1968), and R. Leppert, *Music and Image: Domesticity, Ideology and Socio-Cultural Formation in Eighteenth-Century England* (1988), while H. Knif, *Gentlemen and Spectators: Studies in Journals, Opera and the Social Scene in Late Stuart London* (Helsinki, 1995) fruitfully considers the relationship between the growth of the literary periodical and opera. Most attention has been devoted to London, but a sense of provincial developments is gained through W. Shaw, *The Three Choirs Festival: The Official History of the Meetings of the Three Choirs of Gloucester, Hereford and Worcester, c.1713–1953* (Worcester and London, 1954), which also underscores the neglected themes of church music and music in churches.

A good general account of the importance of prints is provided by T. Clayton, *The English Print 1688–1802* (New Haven, 1997) and for painting by E. Waterhouse, *Painting in Britain, 1530 to 1790* (4th edn., Harmondsworth, 1978). The significance of portraits is considered in J. D. Stewart, *Sir Godfrey Kneller and the English Baroque Portrait* (Oxford, 1983), R. Wendorf, *The Elements of Life: Biography and Portrait-Painting in Stuart and Georgian England* (Oxford, 1990), and *The British Portrait, 1660–1960* (Woodbridge, 1991). Two excellent works on developments in the art market are L. Lippincott, *Selling Art in Georgian London: The Rise of Arthur Pond* (New Haven, 1983) and I. Pears, *The Discovery of Painting: The Growth of Interest in the Arts in England, 1680–1768* (New Haven, 1988). The growth in organized training for artists is considered in I. Bignamini, 'George Vertue, Art Historian and Art Institutions in London, 1689–1768: A Study of Clubs and Academies', *Walpole Society*, 54 (1988), pp. 1–148.

14 AN ORDERED SOCIETY?

A general introduction to the rule of law is provided in J. A. Sharpe, *Crime in Early Modern England, 1550–1750* (1984) but the field is dominated by the exceptional

J. M. Beattie, *Crime and the Courts in England, 1660–1800* (Oxford, 1986). The essays in D. Hay, P. Linebaugh, E. P. Thompson, and C. Winslow, *Albion's Fatal Tree: Crime and Society in Eighteenth-Century England* (1975) are all important and challenging and other good collections include J. S. Cockburn (ed.), *Crime in England, 1550–1800* (1977) and J. Brewer and J. Styles (eds.), *An Ungovernable People: The English and their Law in the Seventeenth and Eighteenth Centuries* (1980). An exceptional historiographical review is J. Innes and J. Styles, 'The Crime Wave: Recent Writings on Crime and Criminal Justice in Eighteenth-Century England', in A. Wilson (ed.), *Rethinking Social History: English Society 1570–1920 and its Interpretation* (Manchester, 1993), pp. 201–65.

Good overviews of the nature of the law are H. Horwitz, 'Liberty, Law, and Property, 1689–1776', in J. R. Jones (ed.), *Liberty Secured? Britain Before and After 1688* (Stanford, 1992), pp. 265–98 and J. H. Baker, *An Introduction to English Legal History* (3rd edn., 1990). The culture and wider ideology of the law are discussed from very different perspectives in J. G. A. Pocock, *The Ancient Constitution and the Feudal Law: A Study of English Historical Thought in the Seventeenth Century: A Reissue with a Retrospect* (Cambridge, 1987), W. Prest, 'Judicial Corruption in Early Modern England', *Past and Present*, no. 133 (1991), pp. 67–95, B. J. Shapiro, 'Law Reform in Seventeenth-Century England', *American Journal of Legal History*, 19 (1975), pp. 280–311, D. Lemmings, 'The Independence of the Judiciary in Eighteenth-Century England', in P. Birks (ed.), *The Life of the Law: Proceedings of the Tenth Legal History Conference, Oxford 1991* (1993), pp. 125–49, and L. B. Faller, *Turned to Account: The Forms and Functions of Criminal Biography in Late Seventeenth- and Early Eighteenth-Century England* (Cambridge, 1987). See also the works on the constitution in section 2 above.

The major histories of the institutions of the rule of law are S. and B. Webb, *English Local Government from the Revolution to the Municipal Corporations Act: The Parish and the County* (1906) and S. and B. Webb, *English Local Government from the Revolution to the Municipal Corporations Act: The Manor and the Borough* (1908). Up-to-date surveys are A. Fletcher, *Reform in the Provinces: The Government of Stuart England* (New Haven, 1986) and J. R. Kent, 'The Centre and the Localities: State Formation and Parish Government in England, circa 1640–1740', *Historical Journal*, 38 (1995), pp. 363–404. Counties provided the context for the organization of much governance, with the major figures of JPs thoroughly explored in N. Landau, *The Justices of the Peace, 1679–1760* (Berkeley, 1984) and of their superiors less fully in V. L. Stater, *Noble Government: The Stuart Lord Lieutenancy and the Transformation of English Politics* (Athens, Georgia, 1994). The major study of the practice of power is P. Langford, *Public Life and the Propertied Englishman, 1689–1798* (Oxford, 1991). The work of the peripatetic judges of the central courts is discussed in J. S. Cockburn, *A History of English Assizes, 1558–1714* (Cambridge, 1972).

The nature of law in this period is surveyed in three great works. Older, but still worth dipping in to is J. F. Stephen, *A History of the Criminal Law of England*, 3 vols. (1883). L. Radzinowicz, *A History of English Criminal Law and its Administration from 1750*, 4 vols. (1948–68) is especially valuable for its discussion of the 'bloody code' in vol. 1. And W. Holdsworth, *A History of English Law*, 17 vols. (1922–72) is very wide ranging, though not always well organized. In the past generation much attention has been devoted to the 'bloody code', prompted particularly by E. P. Thompson, *Whigs and Hunters: The Origin of the Black Act* (1975), a deeply thought, imaginatively researched, brilliantly crafted, passionately committed, and occasionally infuriating book. P. Linebaugh, *The London Hanged: Crime and Civil Society in the Eighteenth Century* (1991) develops some associated points. Counter positions are well advanced in J. Langbein, 'Albion's Fatal Flaws', *Past and Present*, no. 98 (1983), pp. 96–120, J. Broad, 'Whigs and Deer-Stealers in Other Guises: A Return to the Origins of the Black Act', *Past and Present*, no. 119 (1988), pp. 56–72, and J. Beattie, 'London Crime and the Making of the "Bloody Code", 1689–1718', in L. Davison, T. Hitchcock, T. Keirn, and R. B. Shoemaker (eds.), *Stilling the Grumbling Hive: The Response to Social and Economic Problems in England, 1689–1750* (Stroud, 1992), pp. 49–76.

Patterns of crimes and punishments are best detailed in Beattie's *Crime and the Courts* (see above), but other important work on the nature of crime includes D. Hay, 'War, Dearth and Theft in the Eighteenth Century: The Record of the English Courts', *Past and Present*, no. 95 (1982), pp. 117–60, R. B. Shoemaker, *Prosecution and Punishment: Petty Crime and the Law in London and Rural Middlesex, c.1660–1725* (Cambridge, 1991), J. S. Cockburn, 'Patterns of Violence in English Society: Homicide in Kent, 1560–1985', *Past and Present*, no. 130 (1991), pp. 70–106, and J. A. Sharpe, *Crime in Seventeenth-Century England: A County Study* (Cambridge, 1983). Developments in prosecution and punishment are studied in A. R. Ekirch, *Bound for America: The Transportation of British Convicts to the Colonies, 1718–1775* (Oxford, 1987), J. Innes, 'Prisons for the Poor: English Bridewells, 1555–1800', in F. Snyder and D. Hay (eds.), *Labour, Law and Crime: An Historical Perspective* (1987), pp. 42–122, and G. Howson, *Thief-Taker General: The Rise and Fall of Jonathan Wild* (1970). The operation of the civil law is only now being closely studied and much still remains to be done. A pathbreaking exploration was C. W. Brooks, 'Interpersonal Conflict and Social Tension: Civil Litigation in England, 1640–1830', in A. L. Beier, D. Cannadine, and J. M. Rosenheim (eds.), *The First Modern Society: Essays in English History in Honour of Lawrence Stone* (Cambridge, 1989), pp. 357–99 and a major survey of a central court is H. Horwitz and P. Polden, 'Continuity or Change in the Court of Chancery in the Seventeenth and Eighteenth Centuries', *Journal of British Studies*, 35 (1996), pp. 24–57.

Social challenges to the rule of law are surveyed in J. Stevenson, *Popular Disturbance in England, 1700–1870* (2nd edn., 1992) and B. Bushaway, *By Rite: Custom, Ceremony, and Community in England, 1700–1800* (1982). Undoubtedly the efforts of E. P. Thompson have been the most stimulating here, and his best essays are brought together in *Customs in Common* (1991). Some of Thompson's themes have been taken further in A. Randall and A. Charlesworth (eds.), *Markets, Market Culture and Popular Protest in Eighteenth-Century Britain and Ireland* (Liverpool, 1996).

Index

Note: Titled persons are normally cited by the styles most commonly used, with cross-references where appropriate. Biographical summaries in footnotes are indicated by page references in bold.